Appraising
Real Property

Appraising Real Property

Byrl N. Boyce
William N. Kinnard, Jr.
Center for Real Estate and
Urban Economic Studies
The University of Connecticut

Published for the Society of Real
Estate Appraisers

LexingtonBooks
D.C. Heath and Company
Lexington, Massachusetts
Toronto

Library of Congress Cataloging in Publication Data

Boyce, Byrl N.
    Appraising real property.

    Published for the Society of Real Estate Appraisers.
    Includes index.
    1. Real property—Valuation—United States.
I. Kinnard, William N.   II. Society of Real Estate
Appraisers.   III. Title.
HD1387.B68   1984   333.33′2   73–11688
ISBN 0–669–83097–6

Copyright © 1984 by The Society of Real Estate Appraisers

Sixth printing, February 1986

Published simultaneously in Canada

Printed in the United States of America on acid-free paper

International Standard Book Number: 0–669–83097–6

Library of Congress Catalog Card Number: 73–11688

*To Bill, Janet,
Brian, Brendan,
and my parents*

—B.N.B.

Contents

Chapter 3   The Nature of Value   47

Chapter 4   Financing Single-Family Residences   73

Chapter 7   The Direct Sales Comparison Approach   167

Chapter 8   Site Valuation   203

Chapter 11   Estimation of Accrued Depreciation (Diminished Utility)

Chapter 15 Appraisal Reporting; Professional Ethics and Standards of Practice   391

Chapter 16 Alternatives to Single-Family Detached Residences   407

Figures and Tables

Tables

Preface and Acknowledgments

In 1968, the Society of Real Estate Appraisers (SREA), in response to the changing and expanding educational needs of the real estate appraisal profession, introduced a new course: "An Introduction to Appraising Real Property." Dr. William N. Kinnard, Jr., SREA, MAI, CRE, had the signal responsibility for that initial step in what became a major restructuring of the Society's educational program. Since that initial offering, the Course Reference has been revised twice (1975 and 1978) and has been brought up to date to reflect new developments, new thinking, and new tools of analysis in real property appraising. Dr. Byrl N. Boyce, SREA, CRE, and Dr. Kinnard produced those revisions jointly.

The materials covered in those earlier publications of SREA are fundamental to all appraisal practice and serve as the base from which this text was developed. The philosophy as well as much of the content of those early materials, has been retained (albeit revised and reordered) in this text. That the bulk of the materials has survived periodic revision and this current change of direction (from Course Reference to textbook) is a credit to the original sole author, Dr. Kinnard. He has a penchant for expressing concepts so well the first time that very little else needs to be done to his material.

Purpose and Scope

These materials provide a first exposure to the principles and techniques of real property valuation, with special emphasis on residential (amenity) properties. As presented, the materials presume that the reader has little, if any, background in real estate and thus little, if any, prior formal training in real property valuation. Further, it is neither intended nor expected that careful study of these materials will make one an appraiser. After exposure to this text, however, the student should have a good working knowledge of the basic principles of value and of valuation, as well as the ability to recognize and use accepted appraisal terminology. In addition, the student should develop a facility with the tools of amenity property appraisal, plus a familiarity with and sensitivity to the rules and standards of professional behavior and practice.

Beyond a working knowledge of the "rules and tools" of amenity property valuation, the text is intended to provide the student with an appreciation of the fact that the field of appraising is dynamic and constantly changing. Therefore, it is intended to provide the incentive to pursue further study so as to keep current with new developments in appraisal theory and practice. It is also intended to whet the appetite of those who wish to expand their knowledge beyond amenity properties to the valuation of income-producing property and to the analysis and/ or appraisal of special property types and components. The principles, methodology, and techniques presented here provide the basis for application of analytical tools, plus interpretation of the results, in evaluating investment alternatives.

Organization and Content

The text is divided into 17 chapters and 3 appendixes. The outline and the content of the Society's Course 101 manual ("An Introduction to Appraising Real Property") served as the base for the current work. Substantial and substantive revision and reordering of materials were necessary, however. Most significant was the telescoping of five initial sessions (in the SREA Course 101 manual) to the first three chapters in the text. Chapter 4 is, for the most part, entirely new and exposes the reader to analytical tools for financial analysis and adjustments.

Chapters 5 and 6 cover area, neighborhood, and property analysis, while Chapters 7 through 11 present the traditional methodology utilized in the valuation of real property. Chapters 12 and 13 represent a reordering and expansion of statistical and quantitative materials from the SREA Course 101 manual. The reordering of these two chapters had as a conscious objective a change in the emphasis of statistical analysis from direct application in appraisal methodology and procedure to measurement of market description, growth, and change.

Chapters 14 and 15 have been carried over from the SREA Course 101 manual with only modest updating and revision. Chapter 16, which is new, covers valuation of amenity-property alternatives to the detached single-family residence. Finally, in the revision of Chapter 17, an example of the application of income capitalization methodology and procedure to value a 20-unit apartment complex has been included. The revision of Chapter 17 is intended to provide a more substantive bridge between the valuation of amenity properties and that of income-producing property.

Each chapter begins with a list of key terms and ends with a summary statement. The reader is advised to use these two features to good advantage. In addition, there is extensive reliance on *Real Estate Appraisal Terminology,* edited by Byrl N. Boyce, throughout this text as well as an extensive, but selective, list of references at the end of each chapter. A complete index is provided for ease in using these materials as a reference.

Acknowledgments

At the beginning of this preface, special mention was made of Dr. William N. Kinnard, Jr., for his unique and continuing contributions to these materials. His involvement in this project cannot be overstated. His insight, widsom, and guidance over the years have been and continue to be an inspiration to those of us who have had the good fortune to work with him.

This project, for a variety of reasons, has required the forbearance of both officers and staff of the Society of Real Estate Appraisers. Foremost among those to be singled out are H. Grady Stebbins, Jr., SREA, MAI, President of SREA; Richard E. Nichols, SREA, MAI, Sector Vice-President for Education Standards; and E. Roger Everett, SREA, MAI, Chairman of the Education Committee and Member of the Executive Committee. In addition, two SREA staff members handled difficult problems of contract negotiations and coordination of review, publication and marketing of the book: Karen S. Trisko, Staff Vice-President for Professional Development, and Donna Johnson, Manager of the Education Department.

The following members of SREA reviewed the draft manuscript:

William L. Christensen, SRPA, MAI
Vice-President, Christensen, Willey, Snell & Ivie, Inc.
Salt Lake City, Utah

Joseph S. Durrer, Jr., SRPA, MAI
Durrer Appraisal and Consulting Services
Roanoke, Virginia

E. Roger Everett, SREA, MAI
Vice-President, Manufacturers Hanover Mortgage Company
Southfield, Michigan

Donald C. Hambleton, SREA, MAI
Hambleton Real Estate Consultants
Columbus, Ohio

James H. Hubert, SRA
Washington Credit Union League
Bellevue, Washington

James W. Klopfenstein, SRPA
President, Morton Community Service Corporation
Morton, Illinois

Richard E. Nichols, SREA, MAI
President, Richard E. Nichols Associates, Inc.
Indianapolis, Indiana

A penultimate review was conducted by the Society's education consultants: Dr. Dan L. Swango, SREA, MAI, CRE and Dr. William N. Kinnard, Jr., SREA, MAI, CRE.

While the contributions of those who are listed above, and others too numerous to mention, are highly regarded and greatly appreciated, four staff members of the Center for Real Estate and Urban Economic Studies (CREUES) at the University of Connecticut deserve very special consideration and recognition. In their inimitable but reliable manner, they have assumed primary responsibility for the production of this book and the completion of this project. Whatever success this book achieves, much of the credit goes to these delightful people:

Judith B. Paesani, Assistant Director;
Fran Jaffe, Administrative Assistant;
Nancy J. Easton, Production Specialist; and
Sandra J. Mazzola, Production Specialist.

In addition to the staff members singled out for individual thanks, CREUES itself deserves special mention. The facilities and personnel of the Center combine to provide an atmosphere that makes an undertaking of this magnitude doable and almost enjoyable. Throughout its 18 years of existence, CREUES has served as the setting for a broad range of industry-oriented research projects and monographs, texts, and seminar materials. This text represents yet another item in the Center's extensive contributions to the real estate industry in general, and to the valuation profession in particular.

With all the talent I have had to assist me on this project, I cannot conceive even the possibility of error in any form. If any flaws do remain, however, I assume full responsibility.

Storrs, Connecticut   *Byrl N. Boyce*
January, 1984

Appraising
Real Property

1

Introduction to Appraisal and Appraising

Key Terms

Amenities Agreeable or pleasant qualities; attractiveness; pleasant satisfactions typically received in non-monetary form.

Appraisal A supportable and defensible estimate or opinion of value.

Fee simple estate The highest form of ownership rights.

Market price An amount actually paid for a property in a particular transaction; an historic fact; may be forecast as most probable selling price.

Market value The most probable price in terms of money which a property should bring in a competitive and open market under all conditions requisite to a fair sale, the buyer and seller each acting prudently and knowledgeably, and assuming the price is not affected by undue stimulus.

Personalty Movable physical assets.

Real estate The physical asset; the business; the field of study.

Real property Rights in realty.

Realty The physical asset: land and all improvements on and to the land. *is a solution to clients problem.*

An *appraisal* is a supportable or defensible estimate of value.[1] It is important to emphasize that an appraisal is an estimate, not a prediction. An appraisal is derived from forecasts of the future, however, since real estate is a long-term asset capable of producing benefits (amenities or income) over a prolonged period of time.

An appraisal is made because someone (client or employer) has a decision to make or a question to answer and believes that an estimate of real property value will help in making that decision or answering that question. A potential purchaser may need advice on how much to pay for a property or on whether it is fairly priced by the seller. A mortgage lender may need to know how much the property is worth to decide how large a mortgage loan to advance. A court may need an indication of value to help decide how much just compensation should be paid in a public taking under eminent domain.

This chapter discusses the nature of appraisals and the nature of real estate. Further, it considers the characteristics of real property

1

valuation and the role of appraisals and appraisers. Finally, it includes a limited discussion of professional appraisal practice, which will be expanded in a subsequent chapter.

The Nature of Appraisals

Although the emphasis in this book is on residential (amenity) properties for illustrative and discussion purposes, the principles and techniques presented throughout are applicable to the appraisal of all types of real estate. A residential property is a single-family residence designed or intended for owner-occupancy. The benefits received by the owner-occupant are nonmonetary benefits, or *amenities*.[2] The presumed motivation of the purchaser or owner is to enjoy the amenities of ownership, rather than net investment income.

As noted earlier, an appraisal is an estimate or an opinion of value. It is value, not price or cost, that is estimated. Value can only be approximated as a point of tendency under specified market conditions. Because value is man-made, the appraiser must identify, forecast, and measure the appropriate market or environment in terms of which the value estimate is to be made. Value changes as market conditions change, whether through economic, political, social, or legal influences. Therefore, an appraisal is always made as of a given date. This identifies the market environment within which the value estimate is valid. The "as of date" is commonly the date of the last property inspection by the appraiser, unless otherwise specified in the appraisal assignment.

Anyone can estimate value. The professional appraiser's estimate is significant and useful because the appraiser marshals facts and data from the pertinent market, and then applies rigorous and logical analysis to them in a systematic framework to derive the value estimate. An appraisal is not a personal opinion. It is the appraiser's professional conclusion, based upon market data, logical analysis, and judgment. The appraiser measures value from market data and trends, coupled with property information; the forces of the market determine value.

Although an oral statement may occasionally be given, the results of an appraisal are usually, and preferably, presented in a written report. This report sets forth the appraiser's findings and conclusion, together with data and analysis to support and justify the conclusion. An appraisal report should be convincing (through data and logic rather than the appraiser's powers of persuasion) to the client or to any other reader legitimately in possession of the report. It should lead the reader inevitably to the same conclusion(s) reached by the appraiser, given the same facts and data.

Whatever form the appraisal report takes, the same underlying appraisal process should be followed by the appraiser. The definition of value to be estimated in the appraisal dictates the form the appraisal report should take. The requirements of professional appraisal reporting are presented and discussed in detail in Chapter 15. In essence, every appraisal is a research problem. The first step is to identify the question(s) to be answered. Then the type of data needed and the approaches or techniques to be used become apparent.

The Nature of Real Estate

The terms *real estate, realty,* and *real property* must be defined carefully and used precisely because they have been improperly utilized synonymously and because individually they can have different meanings.

Real Estate

The ambiguity of the term *real estate* stems from its multiple meanings. It refers not only to the physical asset but also to the business and the field of study. Reference to the physical thing is the most common meaning; it consists of all land and all improvements on and to the land.

Land refers to the surface of the earth, including water, subsurface area (e.g., mineral deposits), and suprasurface area (e.g., aboveground space occupied by a residence). Land is provided by nature, although sites can be and are created by man. Land does not depreciate; it does not lose utility or value systematically with the passage of time.

Improvements, on the other hand, are man made. They depreciate or lose utility somewhat systematically with the passage of time. Improvements on the land include buildings and fixtures. The manner, permanency, and intent of attachment determines what is a fixture. Improvements to the land include grading, drainage, utilities, fertilizer, landscaping, and the like.

The real estate business incorporates a wide range of activities and services of market intermediaries dealing with the production, financing, and marketing of the physical asset (or, preferably, rights in that asset). These activities would include brokerage, management, counseling, leasing, financing, investment, development, and appraising. Although the emphasis in this text is on appraising, the appraiser needs to have an understanding of the functions of the other market intermediaries, for among other reasons, any information and data that may be of value in the performance of the appraiser's function.

As noted above, real estate also refers to the field of study. In essence, the field of study addresses the improvement of decision making about the use and allocation of real estate resources. This involves continuing efforts to improve the efficiency of allocation and use of real estate resources. The appraisal provides information to the client or employer by which decisions are made to buy, sell, lease, finance, develop, abandon, or hold real estate resources.

Realty

LEASE
a lease is personalty

Realty is the historical, technical, legal term for the physical asset: land and all improvements on and to the land. It is therefore synonymous with real estate. It is specific to the physical asset, however, and as such is used to distinguish real estate from personalty. *Personalty* refers to movable physical assets. Thus, anything that is not realty is personalty. Personalty permanently attached to realty becomes a fixture; it becomes part of the real estate or realty.

Real Property

Although in some jurisdictions real estate and real property are used synonymously, there is an important practical and operational distinction between the two. *Real property* consists of rights in realty. These rights are claims or interests enforceable at law (in the courts). These rights are both divisible and separable. This means that more than one party can have a portion of any given right. A right of way or easement, for example, gives the holder part of the right to use the real estate within the limits prescribed by the right of way or easement, while the fee owner retains the rest of the right of use. Additionally, in leasing a residence, the owner-landlord gives up the right of use and most of the right of exclusion; if no subletting is permitted, the landlord retains the full right of disposition.

The full set of private ownership rights is termed a *bundle* (bundle of rights theory of real property ownership). This is because the rights are separable and divisible, as parts of a bundle. Although terminology for ownership rights varies from one authority to another, the basic right of private ownership of real property includes possession, control, enjoyment, and disposition. Obviously, owners also have the right *not*

exclusion is keeping anyone out or off property

to exercise any of the basic rights of private ownership, subject to limitations imposed by law.

Rights in real property are transferable; realty (real estate) is not transferable and cannot be. Thus, it is real property that is transferred and valued on the market, not real estate. This means that in every appraisal, it is necessary to identify what rights or what parts of the total bundle are being valued. The most common, of course, is the *fee simple estate,* which contains the full bundle.

Characteristics of Real Estate Appraising (Real Property Valuation)

A real estate appraisal is a supportable and defensible estimate of the value of specified property rights as of a given valuation date. Every real estate appraisal and appraisal report must state clearly the rights appraised and the valuation date. Therefore, while the objective of any appraisal is to estimate value, the particular value to be estimated must be specified. Although there are many different types or concepts of value that might be estimated, by far the most common and usual objective of a real estate appraisal is to estimate market value. To avoid any possible misunderstanding, the definition of value being sought needs to be provided whether it be market value or any of the different types of value often required in appraisal reports. The type of value to be estimated in any appraisal dictates the data to be gathered and used in the appraisal, as well as the analytical valuation techniques to be employed.

There is an almost limitless list of different types of value that might be used in particular circumstances by real estate appraisers. In practice, however, only a few are used with any degree of regularity. There are also some value titles or labels that are logically meaningless but are nevertheless used (more by public agencies or legislatures than by professional appraisers). Except for market value, the titles of other types of value tend to describe their uses in appraising.

Market Value

Market value is the value most often sought in residential, indeed all, appraisals. It is the price (value in exchange) that would tend to prevail or occur as a result of the interaction of the forces of supply and demand, under market conditions in existence as of a stipulated date. Market value as used in real estate appraisal is defined as follows:

The most probable price in terms of money which a property should bring in a competitive and open market under all conditions requisite to a fair sale, the buyer and seller each acting prudently and knowledgeably, and assuming the price is not affected by undue stimulus.

Implicit in this definition is the consummation of a sale as of a specified date and the passing of title from seller to buyer under conditions whereby:

1. buyer and seller are typically motivated.
2. both parties are well informed or well advised, and both are acting in what they consider to be their own best interest.
3. a reasonable time is allowed for exposure in the open market.
4. payment is made in cash or its equivalent.
5. financing, if any, is on terms generally available in the community at the specified date and typical for the property type in its locale.
6. the price represents a normal consideration for the property sold unaffected by special financing amounts and/or terms, services, fees, costs, or credits incurred in the transaction.[3]

The six foregoing items are modifiers to the definition of market value; they add some clarification to the components of the definition and presume that certain conditions must exist to ensure that the parameters of the definition are met. It is presumed, for example, that market conditions are competitive so that supply and demand have an opportunity to interact freely. The condition of an informed buyer and seller includes the presumption that there is an awareness of the alternatives that are available to each (i.e., that buyers and sellers have reasonable or normal market information, rather than absolute knowledge). The requirement of no undue pressure on either party often is not met in actual market conditions. This is one important reason why the appraiser must investigate the conditions of sale for each comparable sale property utilized in direct sales comparison analysis, as well as in gross rent multiplier analysis.

Rational or prudent economic behavior by both buyers and sellers presumes that the parties in the transaction each act in their own enlightened self-interest in buying or selling. Further, a quick or forced sale is not presumed, as evidenced by the reference to a reasonable turnover period. Moreover, sellers often may receive their asking price if they are willing to wait an unduly long time to find a buyer. Neither of these cases meets the condition of market value. The appraiser must ascertain the normal or typical turnover period for properties of the type being appraised, in the market in question, as of the date of the appraisal.

Payment is presumed to be consistent with the standards of behavior in the market. This is almost always interpreted as cash to the seller. This modifier (i.e., payment made in cash or its equivalent) along with the fifth and sixth modifiers in the foregoing list are sources of potential difficulty or conflict because of the cash equivalent concept and the terms *generally available* and *typical* as they apply to financing, as contrasted to the use of the term *special financing amounts*. A partial resolution of this problem is to consider any form of subsidized financing (below market or creative financing) as being atypical, even though it may be generally available in the market.

Market value, therefore, looks at the transaction from the point of view of the buyer. It is the maximum price that an informed purchaser would pay under the stipulated conditions. It is the price that would tend to prevail under typical (nonsubsidized) competitive open market conditions.

Market Value versus Market Price. *Market price* is defined as

> "The amount actually paid, or to be paid, for a property in a particular transaction. [Market price] Differs from market value in that it is an accomplished or historic fact, whereas market value is and remains an estimate. . . . Market price involves no assumption of prudent conduct by the parties, of absence of undue stimulus or of any other condition basic to the market value concept."[4]

As noted in the definition, the concept of market price is normally viewed as being historical. It is reportorial, whereas market value is normative. Market price reports what is or was; market value indicates what would be or should be under assumed market conditions. Market price may be greater than, less than, or possibly equal to market value in any given transaction.

In an actual sales transaction, the parties involved are not necessarily informed, nor do they act rationally, free from pressure, or at arm's length (independently). Market price does not have to be justified, as does market value. Financing or other terms of sale may be unique or may vary widely from typical market practice. The entire transaction does not have to be typical.

Market price may also be future oriented. Once market value has been estimated, it is possible to forecast most probable selling price under alternative (subsidized) financial packages. This point is particularly relevant because the cash equivalent adjustment (or financing differential adjustment) is often viewed as being exclusively a discount from market price. This is the case when sales prices of comparable properties are adjusted to cash equivalent estimates in the sales comparison approach. Market price, however, can be future oriented when a premium is added to a market value estimate to reflect favorable financing terms necessary to sell the property in the market.

Historically, *most probable selling price* has been considered virtually synonymous with *market value*. It represents what is most likely to occur, given available market data on market conditions and market sales. Since it emphasizes the influence of the market in determining transaction prices, most probable selling price was useful primarily as an antidote to the highly legalistic and artificial definitions of market value used in the past, especially by the courts. In less stable times, when there is substantial deviation from nonsubsidized financing, divergence exists between the concepts of market value and most probable selling price. The suggestion is that under such circumstances, most probable selling price becomes a forecast market price. That market price reflects a premium most generally added to market value as a payment made in the market for favorable financing.

Market Value versus Cost. Cost does not create value; cost is not value. Under given conditions, however, cost may be an appropriate measure of value. As used in appraisal, cost is the outlay of capital (including financing and selling expenses) for supervision, land, materials, and labor sufficient to bring an improvement into existence. The amount of capital required depends upon economic conditions at the time. The important point is that cost as used in appraising is the cost of production.

Price is the cost of acquisition to the buyer. This is not the sense in which cost is used in appraisal analysis.

Other Types of Value

Almost limitless types of value may be estimated by an appraiser, depending upon the objective or purpose of the appraisal. The following are illustrative of the kinds of value that might be estimated in a real estate appraisal and the reasons for their use. The list is by no means comprehensive, but the items included are all used in practice. As noted previously, the labels or titles of these types of values tend to indicate the uses to which they are put.

Investment Value. This is the value of a property to a particular investor, based on the investor's standards of investment acceptability rather than on objective market standards.[5] This concept has little applicability in residential appraisal. An example would be an investor who is willing to accept a lower rate of return on an income property than the going rate on the market. For this reason, the investment value to that investor would be greater than the market value.

Mortgage Value or Loan Value. These terms are misnomers.[6] A property being considered for a mortgage loan should be, and usually is, evaluated as loan security in terms of its market value. It does not have a different value simply because it is security for a mortgage loan. The amount of loan to grant on the property is an underwriting decision, not a value decision. Appraisers should avoid these terms.

Assessed Value. This is the amount of value assigned to a property for property tax assessment purposes.[7] In most taxing jurisdictions, it is supposed to be a stipulated percentage of market value. Thus, a residence with a market value of $100,000 in a jurisdiction with a 70 percent assessment ratio has an assessed value of $70,000. The property tax rate is multiplied by the $70,000 assessed value to derive the annual property tax bill or levy. As an indicator of market value, however, assessed value may be invalid.

Insurable Value. This is a fire and casualty insurance term that indicates the base used to calculate the dollar amount of insurance that may be or should be carried on the destructible portions of the realty in order to indemnify the owner in the event of loss.[8] Typically, it is calculated in terms of cost new less physical deterioration and insurance exclusions, without reference to obsolescence. For purposes of indemnification, the nonappraisal concepts of actual cash value and replacement value are also used. A homeowner might have insurable value estimated to make sure there is adequate insurance coverage on the residence.

Book Value. This is an accounting term.[9] It is the dollar amount at which real estate and other assets are carried on the books of account of a business or individual. Book value is based on original acquisition cost less accounting depreciation and is used as a basis for calculating income tax profit or loss as well as rate of return on investment. It is rarely used for residential properties.

Rental Value. This is virtually synonymous with market rental.[10] It is the reasonable rental that a property should be worth on the competitive open market. Homeowners planning to rent their residences could use a rental value estimate to establish the rental the house should command.

Use Value. This is the value of property that is designed to fit the particular requirements or needs of a specific owner or user.[11] In non-residential real estate, it is the contribution the real estate makes to the value of the business. A custom-designed residence may have great value to the particular owner, but little marketability and hence a lower market value. Because residential use value is highly subjective to the particular owner or user, it cannot be measured by an appraiser, nor has it any applicability in appraisal practice.

Warranted Price (Value); Reasonable Value. This is the amount that a purchaser would be justified in paying for a particular property under current market conditions.[12] This concept differs little from market value and has little justification for separate classification. It is used, however, by the Veterans Administration (VA) and the Federal Housing Administration (FHA). Residential appraisers should be aware of the terms, especially if they are making FHA or VA appraisals. These terms are being supplanted by *market value* on Federal National Mortgage Association (FNMA) and Federal Home Loan Mortgage Corporation (FHLMC) forms.

Liquidation Price (Value). This is the amount for which a property is likely to sell at forced sale.[13] A residence on which the mortgage has been foreclosed or property being sold for unpaid property taxes would most probably not sell at its market value, because the requisite market conditions for a fair sale will likely not be met (see earlier definition of market value). An estimate of liquidation value might be made to inform the lender or the taxing authority whether the amount owed is likely to be realized at forced sale.

Salvage Value. This is the amount obtainable for all or some parts of a building for removal from the site, usually for use or assembly elsewhere.[14] This could be an issue in setting damages in a condemnation or a residential property under eminent domain. If the building is removable to a nearby site, the condemning authority might well choose to let the condemnee move it or sell it rather than having it demolished. The salvage value could then affect the final determination of damages and of just compensation.

Scrap Value. This is the estimated price obtainable for materials in a dismantled structure to be sold for scrap.[15] It implies removal from the premises of the basic materials themselves for reclamation of their value (e.g., the copper of the piping), not for continued use of the components as building components elsewhere. This could be a consideration in establishing the price of an existing residence scheduled to be acquired and demolished to produce a vacant site, as in the case of an urban renewal project.

Alternative Approaches to Market Value Estimation

The concept and definition of market value presume that informed purchasers will consider all of the alternatives that are available to them. Aside from purchasing the property being appraised, potential purchasers may consider three or four available alternative courses of action. Three of the four alternative courses of action represent the conceptual foundation for the basic three approaches to value estimation that are potentially available to the appraiser in any appraisal assignment.

1. Purchasers may acquire an existing substitute property with the same utility or desirability as the subject property. This is the basis for direct sales comparison analysis and for gross rent multiplier analysis (frequently termed the income approach in residential appraisal). If purchasers are acting prudently, they should pay no more for the subject property than the cost of acquiring an existing competitive substitute property with the same utility. This course of action requires the appraiser to analyze the market in terms of comparability and competitiveness of similar properties that have recently sold in the open market. It also requires the appraiser to identify carefully and precisely the market in which the property being appraised is actually located.

2. Purchasers may acquire a property or investment producing the same income with the same risk as that forecast for the subject property (an alternative investment). The anticipated flow of benefits (dollar income or amenities) to be derived from ownership of the property, together with the reversion at the end of some specified holding period, constitutes the basis for the income approach to value estimation. This approach is much more widely applied in income-producing properties. It has little applicability in appraising residential or amenity properties, although gross rent multiplier analysis is used.

3. The purchaser may have a property produced with the same utility as that of the subject property. Although cost does not create value or necessarily equal value, cost may be a reasonable measure of value in given circumstances. This is the basis for cost analysis in value estimation. If purchasers are acting prudently, they will pay no more for the subject property than the cost of having a competitive substitute property produced, assuming no unusual delay.

4. A final alternative available to purchasers, which is of little consequence to appraisers or appraisal analysis, is to do nothing. There is

no way to measure the value of this course of action, but it is an alternative available to purchasers and must be considered.

A great deal has been written in appraisal literature about the applicability and validity (or lack thereof) of the three approaches to market value estimation. Such argument is essentially sterile. The important point is that, from the viewpoint of the typically informed prudent purchaser, there are different ways of examining and analyzing the property being appraised. These are useful tools if they are based on good, verified market data. They can be used effectively in residential real estate appraisal. Although it is required that a professional appraiser consider the applicability of these alternative types of analysis in every appraisal assignment, it is not required that the appraiser use them.

Role of Appraisals and Appraisers

Appraisals are made because a client or employer has a decision to make, a question to answer, a choice to make, or a course of action to choose. The client or employer believes that an estimate of value (as defined) would help in reaching the decision, making the choice, or answering the question.

An appraisal does not recommend or tell the client what to do. It merely provides the client with a supportable and defensible opinion of value. The client must use that estimate as information to help in making a decision. Appraisers should not advise or participate in the decision in their role as appraisers. The nature of the question or decision determines what value is to be estimated and, therefore, the objective of the appraisal.

Appraisals can be helpful in decisions about whether to buy or not to buy, to sell or not to sell, to buy or to lease, to sell or to lease, to lend or not to lend, to hold or to sell a mortgage, to accept an offer or to reject it and go to condemnation, to buy or to build. Appraisals and appraisal reports are intended for use by others (not by the appraiser) as a basis for decisions about whether or not to act. Other kinds of studies and reports can also be helpful to clients and often are performed by appraisers. An appraisal is an estimate of value—which is supportable and defensible, but it is still only an estimate of value (as defined).

Appraisers measure value; the market creates or determines value. The actions of buyers and sellers, landlords and tenants, borrowers and lenders make the market and thereby determine value.

An appraisal is an objective, dispassionate report of market facts.

The appraiser's personal opinions or prejudices should never appear. Conclusions are based on professional judgment only. The appraisal report should be a complete, self-contained document that can stand alone on its own merits. Appraisals influence decisions involving substantial sums of money. Each appraisal, therefore, is a research project requiring care and professional skill.

Professional Appraisal Practice

This topic is introduced here simply to suggest the standards that appraisers should adhere to in developing value estimates using the materials, tools, and techniques presented in this text. Professional appraisal practice is discussed in greater detail in Chapter 15.

Professional Standards. Professional standards require that the appraiser make a total effort on every appraisal assignment, regardless of the form of the report or the fee. The appraisal framework and the analysis involved are the same whatever form the report takes. The conditions and assumptions should always be spelled out carefully, as should the value to be estimated and the valuation date.

Competence. Appraisers have a responsibility to keep current with new developments in appraisal theory, techniques, and practice. This involves continuing study and formal training. Appraisers should not accept assignments on property types or problems with which they are not familiar, except with the assistance of experienced colleagues. The client should always be informed when this is done.

Ethics. The confidential nature of appraisals should be scrupulously observed by the appraiser. Findings should not be revealed without the client's prior written consent. Fees contingent upon value conclusions, competitive bidding, and active solicitation of business (including nonprofessional advertising) are considered unprofessional and unethical. Fees should be based upon professional services rendered (contract, per diem, and so forth), but not as a commission. Derogation of colleagues or competitors is unethical; however, the appraiser has a responsibility to help police unethical or unprofessional actions.

Professional Appraisal Organizations. Improvement of the profession is achieved through formal training and educational courses, refresher conferences, seminars and clinics, publications, research (including sponsorship), and certification or professional designation. Experience is essential and is made more meaningful through prior formal training programs. Education and training in more than appraisal techniques are essential.

There are several major professional appraisal or appraisal-related organizations. Those considered to be the major professional appraisal organizations, in addition to the Society of Real Estate Appraisers (SREA) include the American Institute of Real Estate Appraisers, the American Society of Appraisers, the Appraisal Institute of Canada, and the International Association of Assessing Officers.

Summary

An appraisal is a supportable and defensible estimate of value; it estimates the value of specified real property rights as of a given date. An appraisal is a conclusion based on objective market analysis rather than personal opinion. The objective of the appraisal must be known by the appraiser, as it indicates the value to be estimated. Appraisals are made for different purposes, with different types of value to be estimated; they are sought to assist in making business, investment, or legal decisions. The uses of appraisals vary widely, but the particular objective determines the data and techniques to be used. Appraisals should always be made in conformity with standards of professional appraisal practice and conduct.

Notes

1. For a more detailed definition of appraisal, see Boyce, Byrl N., ed., *Real Estate Appraisal Terminology,* rev. ed. (Cambridge, Mass.: Ballinger [joint publication of the American Institute of Real Estate Appraisers and Society of Real Estate Appraisers], 1981), p. 14.

2. Amenities are defined as "the pleasant satisfactions that are received through using rights in real property but that are not necessarily received in the form of money. The tangible and intangible benefits generated by a property"; Ibid., p. 11.

3. Ibid., pp. 160–161.

4. Ibid., p. 160.

5. Ibid., p. 140.

6. Ibid., p. 169.

7. Ibid., p. 19.

8. Ibid., p. 136.

9. Ibid., p. 32.

10. Ibid., p. 204.
11. Ibid., p. 250.
12. Ibid., p. 255.
13. Ibid., p. 153.
14. Ibid., p. 213.
15. Ibid., p. 215.

Suggested Readings

American Institute of Real Estate Appraisers. *The Appraisal of Real Estate,* 8th ed. Chicago: American Institute of Real Estate Appraisers, 1983, chapters 1 and 2.

Bloom, George F., and Harrison, Henry S. *Appraising the Single Family Residence.* Chicago: American Institute of Real Estate Appraisers, 1978, chapters 1 and 2.

Boyce, Byrl N., ed. *Real Estate Appraisal Terminology,* rev. ed. Cambridge, Mass.: Ballinger (Joint publication of the American Institute of Real Estate Appraisers and Society of Real Estate Appraisers), 1981.

Friedman, Edith J., ed. *Encyclopedia of Real Estate Appraising,* 3rd ed. Englewood Cliffs, N.J.: Prentice-Hall, 1978.

Kahn, Sanders A., and Case, Frederick E. *Real Estate Appraisal and Investment,* 2nd ed. New York: Ronald Press, 1977, chapter 2.

Kinnard, William N., Jr. *Income Property Valuation.* Lexington, Mass.: Lexington Books, D.C. Heath, 1971, chapter 2.

Smith, Halbert C. *Real Estate Appraisal.* Columbus, Ohio: Grid, 1976, chapter 1.

Society of Real Estate Appraisers. "Standards of Professional Practice and Conduct." Chicago: Society of Real Estate Appraisers, 1979.

2 Real Estate Principles and Markets

Key Terms

Allodial system   A system of private land tenure in which land is held in absolute independence.

Chattels   Any property other than a fee estate in land (e.g., leasehold, easement, lien).

Cloud (on title)   An encumbrance that may affect marketability.

Feudal system   A system of land tenure in which the majority of rights in the land are held by the sovereign.

Freehold estate   An estate that continues for an indefinite period and may be inherited.

Natural increase   A demographic term relating to change in population resulting from an excess of births over deaths.

Net in-migration   The balance of migration; the difference (in this case presumed positive) between in- and out-migration.

Nonfreehold estates   Personal property; a possessory estate (e.g., leasehold).

The basic characteristics of real estate, realty, real property, personalty, and personal property were discussed briefly in Chapter 1, along with the nature of the bundle of rights that constitutes real estate ownership. In this chapter, the physical, legal, and economic aspects of real estate and real property are considered in greater depth and detail.

The Study of Real Estate

There are many important reasons for studying the basic characteristics of real estate. A discussion of the physical characteristics of real estate is necessary so that the beginning appraiser can appreciate how these physical characteristics (especially those that distinguish and separate real estate from other assets) influence the legal system that has evolved to accommodate the ownership, use, and transfer of rights in real estate. Since every appraisal assignment stems from a client's decision about the ownership, use, or transfer of rights in real estate, the appraiser must first understand the framework within which these activities take place.

The physical characteristics of real estate also largely determine its behavior as an economic good or asset and the way in which real estate markets are structured and function. Those physical characteristics are basic to the economic characteristics of real estate. Since value is an economic-market phenomenon and the fundamental function of appraisers is to estimate value from market data, it is essential to understand how real estate behaves on the market as an economic good.

The legal framework within which rights in real estate or realty are owned, exercised, and transferred is cumbersome and complex. The brief exposure presented in this chapter cannot make one an expert in real estate law. It is important, however, for the appraiser to know what rights are involved in the assignment; what limits there are to the free exercise of those rights; how the real estate may or may not be used; when and in what form comparable sales or rental transactions occurred; and what kinds of documents are involved, what they can reveal to the appraiser to help in the investigations, and where and why they are recorded. These and related issues are considered in this chapter.

Physical Considerations

The physical point of view is a descriptive approach concerned with real estate as a physical thing. In this context, real estate consists of all land and all improvements on and to the land. Buildings are examples of improvements *on* land, while sewer or drainage facilities are examples of improvements *to* land. Land is provided by nature; improvements are man made.

The distinguishing physical characteristics of land include immobility, indestructibility, and nonhomogeneity or heterogeneity. Real estate is fixed in location; it cannot be moved. It provides services or income at a fixed location. Because of this, real estate cannot be physically transferred from one owner to another or from one user to another. That is why the legal system of property rights developed. Rights can be and are transferred, whereas the real estate itself cannot be transferred.

Land is effectively indestructible. Sites, however, can be created and destroyed. Buildings are man's longest-lived asset. A common cliché expressed in real estate courses and texts is that more buildings are torn down than fall down. The point is that real estate is a long-term, durable asset.

No two parcels of real estate are alike (i.e., real estate parcels are highly differentiated). Every parcel is unique, at least with respect to location, because of its immobility. Different parcels can be similar, but they are never identical. Even two parcels with identical physical characteristics are still differentiated by location.

Property Description. Property description provides unequivocal identification of the real estate being described. It locates the site beyond question. Effective property description is required by appraisers and their clients. Appraisers must know and report precisely where the property is located and the dimensions or size of the land. This information is also useful for cross-reference purposes, such as location of the property on a zoning map.

Real estate may be described in several ways:

1. *Street or mail address.* This is easy to obtain, but it is least satisfactory because it is least precise. It can be useful, however, in a community where a formal and official street-numbering system has been established.
2. *Map and lot number.* This is legally or technically precise, but it is often difficult to translate to clear identification in the field, especially in undeveloped or rural areas. It may be based on subdivision plats, tax maps, zoning maps, and the like. In some areas, such as Puerto Rico, an official mapping and coding system has been established, which makes parcel indentification clear and easy.
3. *Monuments.* This is description by reference to natural or manmade objects in the field. If the monuments are permanently fixed and unequivocally identifiable, description by monuments is satisfactory. It is used primarily in rural areas of the 13 original states. Mere stones or corner markers are frequently used in cities as well.
4. *Metes and bounds.* This is identification by direction (bounds) and distance (metes) from a permanently fixed official marker. It requires a professional land survey. It can be quite accurate, but translation from a map or plot plan to field identification is difficult for a layman. (See figure 2-1).
5. *U.S. Government Survey.* This describes land most precisely and accurately in terms of a standardized system of benchmarks, parallels, and meridians. It applies in all areas of the United States outside the original 13 states. (See figure 2-2.)[1]

Land Surveying. Land surveying involves location and indentification of a parcel of land in the field by a professional surveyor or engineer. It is employed in property description by metes and bounds and by

Said real estate is described as follows:

A certain tract or parcel of land with the buildings and improvements thereon situated on the southerly side of the State Highway leading from Ellmont towards Ashland, known as State Highway Route #78, and being within the Town of Ellmont, County of Wayne and State of Confusion, and more particularly bounded and described as follows:

Beginning at an iron, near a corner of wall, set in the southerly line of said highway at the northwesterly corner hereof and the northeasterly corner of land formerly of Jonathan E. Mason, more recently of Patrick and Charlene Flanery. Thence, S. 9°-30' W. 218.9 feet along a wall to an iron set at the southerly end thereof; thence S. 67°-06' E. 150.0 feet to an iron and continuing the same course 7.0 feet to a drill-hole in the top of a concrete wall, and still continuing the same course to the westerly shore of said lake to a point at the rear of westerly side of the masonry wall situated on the westerly side of the spillway from said lake at the dam. (The air-line distance from said drill-hole to said spillway wall is about 183 feet, more or less.) Thence northerly, northeasterly and easterly along the rear side of said masonry wall to an iron set at the end thereof and in the line of a former wall or fence. Thence N. 18°-18' W. 33.2 feet along the line of said former wall or fence to an iron set in the line of a wall to the said southerly line of said highway. The last three courses adjoin said Ellmont Lake or land used in connection therewith, being property of the Town of Ellmont. Thence from said iron S. 72°-10' W. partly along a wall 81.44 feet to a State Highway Department Bound stone. Thence S. 88°-16' W. 164.45 feet partly along a wall to an iron to the point of beginning.

The last two courses are along the southerly side of said highway.

Containing 1.12 acres, more or less, and being the same and all of the same land however otherwise it may have been or ought to have been described as is contained in a certain Warranty Deed from Andrew P. Stone to Elise Stone, dated August 18, 1955 and recorded in the Ellmont Land Records in Volume 30 at Page 588.

Excepting herefrom, the crossing right as reserved in said deed, if such right still exists.

The premises as above described are shown on a certain map which is filed with the Town Clerk of said Town entitled "Map Showing Property of Andrew P. Stone situated on Ellmont Lake, Town of Ellmont, Confusion. Surveyed August 24, 1955, Thurman L. Bitters—Engineer."

Figure 2–1. Land Described by Metes and Bounds: Legal Description

government survey. It is sometimes used in description by monuments as well. Benchmarks or monuments are essential as a starting point. A plot plan is then prepared, based upon the survey.

The legal description and a survey will establish the boundaries and dimensions of a parcel. The size or area, however, is not always provided. This is an important consideration to the appraiser, since size

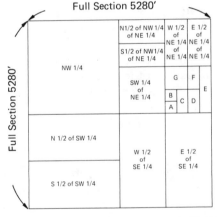

6	5	4	3	2	1
7	8	9	10	11	12
18	17	16	15	14	13
19	20	21	22	23	24
30	29	28	27	26	25
31	32	33	34	35	36

Township 1 North
Range 1 West

Base Line   TWP. 1 N.

TWP. 1 S.   6 Miles

RG. 1 W.   RG. 1 E.

Township 1 South
Range 1 West

Township 1 South
Range 1 East

Meridian

6 Miles

Full Section 5280'

Full Section 5280'

NW 1/4

N1/2 of NW 1/4 of NE 1/4

S1/2 of NW1/4 of NE 1/4

W 1/2 of NE 1/4 of NE 1/4

E 1/2 of NE 1/4 of NE 1/4

SW 1/4 of NE 1/4

G   F

B
    C   D
A

E

N 1/2 of SW 1/4

S 1/2 of SW 1/4

W 1/2 of SE 1/4

E 1/2 of SE 1/4

DESCRIPTIONS

A is SW 1/4 of SW 1/4 of
      SE 1/4 of NE 1/4 = 2.5 AC.
B is NW 1/4 of SW 1/4 of
      SE 1/4 of NE 1/4 = 2.5 AC.
C is E 1/2 of SW 1/4 of
      SE 1/4 of NE 1/4 = 5 AC.
D is W 1/2 of SE 1/4 of
      SE 1/4 of NE 1/4 = 5 AC.
E is E 1/2 of E 1/2 of
      SE 1/4 of NE 1/4 = 10 AC.
F is W 1/2 of NE 1/4 of
      SE 1/4 of NE 1/4 = 5 AC.
G is NW 1/4 of SE 1/4
      of NE 1/4   = 10 AC.

1 SECTION = 1 SQUARE MILE = 640 ACRES

Selected Measures

NW 1/4   = 160 Acres
SW 1/4 of NE 1/4 =   40 Acres
N 1/2 of SW 1/4 =   80 Acres
W 1/2 of SE 1/4 =   80 Acres

Source: Byrl N. Boyce, ed., *Real Estate Appraisal Terminology*, rev. ed. (Cambridge, Mass.: Ballinger [Joint Publication of the American Institute of Real Estate Appraisers and the Society of Real Estate Appraisers], 1981), p. 294. Reprinted with permission.

Figure 2–2. U.S. Government Survey Diagram of Four Townships

or number of units is an important determinant of the final value estimate. The calculation of area requires application of the techniques of basic trigonometry, especially for irregularly shaped parcels.[2]

All linear measures and area or surface measures in the United States are on the English system: inches, feet, yards, square feet, acres, and other measures. Currently, however, there is some movement toward using the international metric system.[3] (Note that the land codification system used in Puerto Rico is referred to as a *cadastral program*. This is a complete inventory of land in an area by ownership, descriptions or maps, and values. It also uses the international metric system.)

Legal Considerations

The legal point of view identifies and describes property rights in and to the real estate. Rights in realty are called real property. Legal rights in real estate typically require documentation to be enforceable. Property consists of enforceable rights in an asset. The private property system protects ownership rights under law.

The private property system in the United States is derived from the *allodial system,* under which there is individual ownership with the right of inheritance or transfer without approval of the sovereign. This is distinguished from the *feudal system,* under which all land ownership and control ultimately rested with the sovereign.

Private ownership of real estate is never complete or unrestricted. There are always public limitations (statutory and common law) to the exercise of private property rights. There may also be private limitations (contractual or involuntary) as well. The appraiser must be aware of these limitations to be able to identify precisely what rights are being appraised.

Public Limitations. There are four basic public limitations on the private ownership of real estate: taxation, eminent domain, police power, and escheat.

Property taxes represent a lien on real estate until the taxes are paid. Typically, a property tax lien is superior to all other liens, both those recorded before and those recorded after the date on which the tax lien attaches to the land. Tax liens are enforceable through the forced sale of the real estate to satisfy the claim.

Through eminent domain, public bodies (and some private organizations, such as utilities) may acquire rights in privately owned real estate, provided it is for public use or a public purpose, and provided further that just compensation is paid. Part or all of the private owner's bundle of rights may be acquired. Transfer of rights may be forced through the process of condemnation (sometimes called expropriation).

Government may limit the exercise of private rights in real estate through the police power. Rights may be limited without compensation, provided the limitation is not specific to one parcel. The limitation must serve the interests of public health, public safety, public morals, and the general welfare. Zoning, environmental protection, and building codes are examples of land use controls based on the police power.

If an owner of real estate dies without a will and has no heirs, title to the property reverts to the state. This is referred to as the doctrine of escheat, the fourth public limitation on the exercise of private property rights.

Private Voluntary. These are contractual limitations placed in favor of others. So long as they are enforced, they pass with the land. Transfer of ownership does not extinguish private voluntary limitations.

Deed restrictions are limitations that pass with the land regardless of owner; they most commonly limit the type of use or intensity of use of the real estate. Easements provide others the right to cross or use part of the land. These include rights of way, in which the owner's rights are limited. Leases are contracts that transfer all or part of the rights of use, exclusion, and disposition from the owner to the tenant in exchange for a promise to pay rent.

Mortgages or deeds of trust are liens against the real estate in consideration of a loan with the real estate as collateral. Mortgages are usually enforceable through foreclosure and forced sale of the real estate to satisfy the claim.

Private Involuntary. Private involuntary limitations are limitations placed by others, usually because of some action or inaction by the owner that damages the other parties. These limitations also go with the land so long as they are enforced.

Liens are a form of private involuntary limitations that represent claims for payment of debt under which the forced sale of the real estate may be used to satisfy the claim. Encroachments are also private involuntary limitations that represent unauthorized use of an owner's property. Though not usually enforceable rights at law, encroachments may become clouds on the owner's title. Finally, prescriptive easements represent open, continuous but unauthorized use of an owner's property. Under adverse possession, for example, limitations may be placed on an owner's title. Prescriptive easements are usually difficult to enforce, but they can be an economic nuisance and a potential cloud on the owner's title.

Estates and Chattel Interests. Estates are ownership interests in real estate. They can represent all or part of the full bundle of rights. They are generally marketable if they are transferable. Therefore, they can have value. It is important for the appraiser to know what estate is involved in the property being appraised, because it identifies what rights are being valued.   *tenants interest*

Chattel interests, on the other hand, are nonownership rights in real estate. They include leaseholds, easements, and liens; the latter two are nonpossessory interests. Leaseholds are generally marketable unless specifically made nontransferable by contract.

Estates can be classified in a number of ways. These classifications are helpful to the appraiser primarily to help identify when legal advice or assistance is necessary. Fee simple or fee simple absolute is the fullest type of private ownership possible. It is still subject to all the public limitations (both operative and potential) noted earlier, and may be subject to some private encumbrances as well (e.g., mortgages). Fee simple is termed the highest estate of private ownership. In most instances, the residential appraisal will involve valuation of the fee simple interest. If other estates are encountered, legal advice should be sought.

Estates may also be classified by quantity of interest or duration, time of enjoyment, and number of owners. For quantity of interest or duration, there are two further subclassifications: freehold estates and nonfreehold estates. *Freehold estates* represent ownership interests (that is the usual intent) and are usually of indeterminate length or duration. *Nonfreehold estates,* on the other hand, may contain some ownership interests, but they are always of determinate or finite length. Nonfreehold estates are usually treated as personal property (e.g., a leasehold estate) but are still enforceable at law. They are frequently called tenancies because they are possessory interests. They pass with a transfer of ownership as limitations on the fee estate.

An interest in realty may be exercised or enjoyed immediately or at some time in the future. Immediate enjoyment of rights would include freehold estates and leasehold estates. Interests to be enjoyed at some time in the future occur under life estates, leases (the lessor's interest or reversion), and conditional estates. These interests are frequently assignable and marketable, and hence can have value.

Ownership interest in real estate may reside in one owner or in multiple concurrent owners. The type of tenancy is usually clearly stated in the deed. There are four common types of tenancy by number of owners. Ownership interest in real estate residing in one owner is referred to as *tenancy in severalty.* Ownership by two or more owners with unseparated ownership interests of the same degree, usually with the right of survivorship, is referred to as *joint tenancy.* This type is widely used for ownership by husband and wife, especially in states that do not provide for community property. One joint tenant cannot sell his or her interest separately. The survivor usually obtains full ownership (tenancy in severalty). Similar relationships exist under *tenancy by entireties* and *community property*.

Ownership by two or more owners, each with an undivided fractional interest in the real estate, is referred to as *tenancy in common*. Each owner may sell or devise its interest separately, without consent of the others, unless limited by contract. The tenants in common do not have survivorship rights in one another's interests.

Fee ownership of individual units in multi-unit property (residential, commercial, or industrial) represents a *condominium ownership* interest. Individual estates can be transferred without consent of other unit owners in a condominium development. There may be other restrictive language, however.

Leases. A lease is a contract for the use of specified premises in exchange for the payment of rent. The occupant (called tenant or lessee) has limited rights of use or possession, exclusion, and disposition during the term of the lease. The lease is an encumbrance on the owner's title that goes with the land; the owner or landlord is the lessor. The lessor's (owner's) interest is the leased fee. The lessee's (tenant's) interest is the leasehold. State laws usually provide for the type of lease contract, if the rights are to be enforceable at law. Typically, a lease for a term of more than one year must be in writing to be enforceable. It may also be recorded. A lease for a term of less than one year may be in writing and may be recorded to enhance its enforceability. A lease for a term of less than one year may also be oral and still be enforceable, but oral leases are more difficult to enforce because of potentially conflicting testimony.

The term of a lease can range from at will to 99 years or more. Some states have set limits on lease terms. A lease may be terminated for several reasons. Transfer of ownership of the real estate, however, does not terminate the lease.

Real Estate Contracts. Contracts are used to commit two or more parties to a transfer of property rights in exchange for some payment (usually money). Real estate contracts must usually be in writing to be enforceable. They may be recorded. They are useful in establishing the date of a transaction as well as its terms (some or all) and the parties involved. A lease, for example, is a contract between a landlord and tenant for the use and occupancy of leased premises in exchange for the payment of rents. Several other forms of contracts are discussed briefly in the following paragraphs.

 Listing contracts are written agreements between an owner and a broker, employing the broker to sell the owner's real estate. Types of listing agreements include open listings, exclusive agency listings, exclusive right to sell listings, and multiple listings.

In some states, a *land contract* is used for an installment sale of real estate. Periodic payments are made by the buyer until a specified portion of the purchase price has been paid. Only then does title transfer from seller to buyer. This is really a financing instrument, and extreme care should be exercised in using land contract transactions as comparable sales.

A *sales contract* (contract for deed or bond for deed) is the basic, written document signed by buyer and seller, agreeing to the transfer of ownership interest in real estate. It must be in writing to be enforceable. It may be recorded. Time is required to verify the seller's title and to compare documents for the passage of title. The sales contract binds both parties to the terms of the agreement, provided all conditions of the contract are met. The date of the sales contract, if the transaction is completed, is the effective date of the sale. A sales contract can be used as evidence of a sale until the deed passes. The contents of a real estate sales contract that can be useful to an appraiser include identification of the parties (seller or grantor and buyer or grantee); date of contract; legal, unequivocal description of the property; and any statements about price, payment terms, and/or financing.

An *option agreement* is a specific form of sales contract. The purchaser pays a fixed sum for the right to purchase the property at a stipulated price within a specified period of time. If the transaction is not completed, the option payment usually remains with the seller. This cannot be used as evidence of a sale.

Deeds. A deed is a document to transfer title to real estate. Since deeds are typically recorded, whereas sales contracts need not be, they are an important source of market data to the appraiser. Some types of deeds do not necessarily transfer full title, and indeed some do not represent bona fide transactions. The types of deeds that typically represent bona fide sales and transfers of fee estates are warranty (warrantee), grant, and executor's or administrator's deeds. Types of deeds that do not necessarily represent unequivocal transfers of fee estates or actual sales are quitclaim, tax, sheriff's, and bargain and sale deeds.

In some jurisdictions, a mortgage deed or deed of trust technically transfers title or mortgaged property to the mortgagee or a trustee. The transfer is null and void if the loan is satisfied in accordance with the terms of the note.

Normally, the deed will (or may) contain information useful to the appraiser in gathering market data. The identification of the parties involved and the description of the property conveyed represent information that is similar to that in the real estate sales contract. In addition, when provided, the statement of the consideration can be very helpful. Tax stamps also may be included; this information must be used with caution, however. Further, a statement of interest conveyed together with limitations, if any, may also be helpful, as well as the date of signing and recording the deed.

Title, Title Transfer, and Records. Title represents evidence of ownership (i.e., enforceable ownership claims or rights). This is typically in writing. Title passes when a deed is accepted by the grantee. Recording is required in many states and is permitted in all others. The record (in the Hall of Records, Recorder's Office, Town Clerk's Office) represents public notice of a formal claim or rights. This is called *constructive notice.*

Title transfer may be accomplished by private grant (from a private owner on a voluntary basis); by public grant; from nature (by accretion, such as shifting of a river bed); by civil or political action (eminent domain, escheat, confiscation, forfeiture); and by public policy (adverse possession, prescription).

All claims may also be recorded; many must be. This includes liens and limitations as well as deeds and contracts. Land records are a basic and important source of market data for the appraiser. The purpose of recording instruments is to preserve evidence of all items affecting title so that their contents and conditions may be examined and evaluated. In addition, recording provides notice of the existence and content of a claim.

Claim records are recorded at the office of the County Recorder of Deeds, Town Clerk (in New England), or Probate Court. Recording of title is not compulsory, but it is necessary for the enforcement of claims in approximately 20 states. Since claims are paid in order of recording priority, recording dates are important to the appraiser. The priority of claims generally follows the pattern of tax lien, labor lien, mechanics lien, and then chronological order of recording.

Title Search. A title search is an attempt to discover recorded liens, claims, or flaws in the chain of title. It provides a basis for judgment of whether the title is good and merchantable. The title examiner (possibly but not necessarily an attorney) goes back through the chain of title approximately 60 years and produces a report. The exact procedure varies with local law and custom.

The *abstract of title* represents a summary history based on the title search, prepared by the title searcher. An *opinion of title,* on the other hand, is a certificate from an attorney, which can be the basis for a title insurance policy or a mortgage loan. It lists recorded encumbrances subject to which the purchaser may take title and recorded encumbrances to be removed (if any) before the purchaser should accept a deed. In an opinion or certificate of title, protection to the buyer is based primarily on an attorney's or searcher's competence and ability to back up the opinion. Title insurance offers both indemnification and defense in the event of a claim based on an undiscovered defect (real or imagined). Title insurance is often required by lenders before a mortgage loan is granted.

Economic Considerations

The economic approach is a descriptive and analytical concern with real estate as an asset or economic good that is capable of satisfying human wants and desires. It considers the organization and functioning of real estate markets, real estate investment decisions, real estate financing, and the income and benefits derived from the ownership or use of real estate. While appraisers must be aware of and understand the physical and legal characteristics of real estate, their interests center primarily on real estate as an economic good.

Economic Characteristics of Real Estate. Economic characteristics stem from both the physical and the legal characteristics of real estate, and they influence, in turn, the structure and functioning of real estate markets. Because of its immobility, realty cannot move to better markets. It must be used or exploited where it is. This is why market and neighborhood analysis are important in any appraisal. In addition, because of the physical characteristic of nonhomogeneity, comparison requires analysis and judgment. This is why there are appraisers.

Each valuation problem is a separate research study requiring specific analysis. This is the basis for the adjustment process in sales comparison analysis. Because of its characteristic immobility, real estate is particularly sensitive to its immediate environment. This is an important influence on value.

Further, real estate is a very long-term asset. Decisions involve long-term commitments of resources, and annual income is relatively low compared with value or price. As a result, real estate is a high-priced asset, based on long-term income (money or amenity) expectations. Further, debt financing is usually employed, is frequently necessary, and is nearly always desirable. Real estate is used and transferred in large economic units; large monetary sums are involved. This is a market-limiting factor, a market imperfection. Specialized financial institutions are required to assemble both debt and equity funds.

Fundamentals of Urban Land Economics. Economics is the study of the allocation of scarce resources among competing and relatively unlimited desires in such a way as to maximize human satisfactions. These satisfactions usually may be expressed and measured in dollar terms. Urban land economics concentrates on the allocation of scarce urban space among alternative uses.

Price is the basic device by which allocation of resources occurs in the competitive market of economic theory. In that market, *price* and *value* are synonymous terms. Both are tendencies under assumed market conditions. Price/value is always a market phenomenon. It is determined by the interaction of supply and demand factors. Equilibrium price, the intersection of supply and demand, is just sufficient to clear the market; that is, the quantity of the good or service (i.e., urban space) offered for sale at the equilibrium price just equals the quantity demanded at that price.

A basic assumption in all urban land economics analysis is that all market participants act rationally. This means that they act independently, on the basis of the information available to them, to maximize their own satisfactions. This action usually is expressed in terms of maximizing money income or wealth, whenever satisfactions or amenities can be measured in dollars.

Price and market analysis is concerned with economic goods. Both tangible, physical assets and intangible services are goods. An economic good must possess three characteristics: it must have the capacity to satisfy human desires or needs (utility); the available supply must be limited relative to the desire for the good (scarcity); and ownership must be capable of being passed from one individual to another (transferability).

The basic decision in urban land economics analysis is the use to which the land or urban space is to be put. The fundamental principle in terms of which use allocations are made is the principle of highest and best use (or most profitable use). Simply stated, urban space tends in the long run to be put to its most productive, most profitable (or highest and best) use. This is the use at which maximum value or present worth is developed.

Use decisions must be made at two levels: type of use (e.g., residential, commercial, industrial, public) and intensity of use (e.g., density of land use, height of buildings, land/building ratios, capital investment per unit of land area). Productivity is a direct function of use. The productivity of urban space determines the net value of its services.

In allocating urban space among competing alternative uses, one important issue to be resolved is the question of whose standards or criteria are to be applied. In most instances involving appraisals, a private market environment is assumed, and private, individual standards prevail. This means that the most productive use from the point of view of the private purchaser becomes the highest and best use. Public or community standards of the priority or order of uses are often superimposed on private standards, however, so that zoning regulations or environmental protection standards, for example, take precedence over private desires and aspirations. Thus, private decisions must always be considered in the framework of public constraints and limitations. Public bodies also frequently make land-use decisions, such as decisions about highway locations, public building locations, redevelopment projects, or parks. The benefits of or restrictions from such uses are often not measurable in money terms.

Different levels of use decisions must be distinguished in urban land economics analysis:

1. *Legal use:* Is it permissible at all and therefore legally possible?
2. *Possible use:* Is it physically possible on the site or in the building in terms of size, shape, and the like?
3. *Appropriate use:* Are the necessary supporting facilities (utilities, access, linked uses, and so on) available for the proposed use, regardless of whether it makes economic or financial sense to inaugurate the use?
4. *Feasible use:* Will it pay? Does it appear to meet the minimum standards of acceptability of the decision maker?
5. *Highest and best use:* Which is the most profitable use among the competing alternatives at the time the decision is made? It must be legal, physically possible, appropriate, and feasible before it can even be considered in highest and best use analysis.

Concept of Location. It is important to recall that urban real estate produces services (amenities, income) at a fixed location. The uses that are appropriate, feasible, and most profitable are thus a direct function of *location*. Because urban real estate is dependent on its environment for the uses to which it may appropriately and profitably be put, the services that urban real estate can produce are subject to continuous (occasionally dramatic) change as that environment changes. Thus, stability of the environment is a major factor to be analyzed in evaluating the location. Use and productivity are basic value determinants, and location largely determines use and productivity.

Location is an economic concept, even though it can be described in physical and legal terms. The services of the real estate must be produced and enjoyed at a particular spot or not at all. This has already been noted, together with the fact that its immobility makes urban real estate especially sensitive to the market forces of its immediate surroundings.

Cities and neighborhoods are under constant pressure to change because of the dynamics of urban growth and development. The characteristics of a location are thus in a continuing state of flux. This factor emphasizes the importance of background and area analysis in evaluating a location for appraisal purposes. It also underscores the critical necessity to forecast market conditions in making any appraisal.

A location must be adequately served by man-made facilities that are appropriate for the use or uses proposed. Use depends on the availability and proper size of utilities, public services, and roads. Road and other transportation access is especially important to a good location. The free market creates the demand for particular types of locations, but the supply of proper locations depends on the willingness and ability of both public officials and private investors (or developers) to act.

Supporting facilities and related uses on which a particular use depends are termed *linkages*. Linkages are defined as the costs of overcoming friction in the urban real estate market. They involve the proximity of necessary and desirable supporting facilities. Time and distance, for example, are frictions of space. A location that is far removed from a major employment center may be more desirable and appropriate for residential development if convenient and quick access is provided to a modern, high-speed highway or to a public transit system to that center of employment. The nearby transportation facility is then a part of the necessary linkage system for the site in question, because it overcomes or reduces travel time (a space friction). Supporting facilities must be both conveniently located and appropriate. A freight rail line may be an important linkage for industrial use in a given location, but it would be a deterrent to residential use.

The spatial distribution of the basic elements of location actively influences value. The influence may be positive or negative. Site characteristics that influence value (but still involve location) are those that can be enjoyed without leaving the site itself. These might include a view (which depends upon the spatial relationship with a nearby lake and the absence of intervening structures), the prevailing breeze, favorable exposure, or the absence of highway noise.

Convenience is related to the proximity or access to desired or required supporting facilities. Convenience elements are measured by the disutilities of moving people or goods from the site in question to other points to which such movement is either necessary or desirable. The disutilities to be overcome are time, cost, and aggravation. The greater the convenience and linkages, the lower the disutilities are— and thus the higher the value, all other factors being the same.

The degree of exposure to offensive or deterring influences that detract from the utility of the site (and hence its value) for the intended use is the final element of location to be considered. This exposure includes, but is not limited to, such items as unsightly and incompatible uses near a residential development; intruding noise and unpleasant odors, including smog; and, perhaps, heavy through traffic on a residential street.

Location decisions involve a balancing of desires, advantages, and costs. To choose a location or embark on location analysis without the site, use, environment, and time clearly and unequivocally specified is meaningless. Location decisions include a balancing of cost-reducing factors, benefit-generating factors, and personal or noneconomic factors. Thus, every location choice requires some compromise with the ideal. It is important to ascertain which desired factors are critical and necessary and which are simply nice to have.

In evaluating access, it is important to specify access to what. The "what" of access analysis varies considerably from one type of use to another and among different types of users. Locations that afford the maximum economy of movement to and from related activities and places tend to draw urban activities. Each location tends to be occupied by the use and the improvements for which it is best suited. This is the result of the operation of the principle of highest and best use.

In evaluating a location as part of the appraisal process, an appraiser must make a thorough study of the location in terms of specific use, environment, time, and anticipated pattern of change. The linkages (utilities, roads) that are necessary or essential for the specific use must be identified. This is an early step in highest and best use analysis. A judgment must be made about the relative importance of the various linkages desired and those that are actually available. The required linkages must be located in reference to the specific site. The costs of providing necessary linkages that are missing must be identified and measured.

Trends in the direction and magnitude of probable market changes must be estimated. The appraiser must develop a sensitivity to possibilities for change in technology, social standards, legal standards, and transportation channels (both methods and directions). This is a part of area and neighborhood analysis.

An estimate must be made of the exposure to both favorable and unfavorable environmental factors. Once again, a forecast must be made of the probable changes and trends. This should include an estimate of the strength of the forces of change, as well as of the protections against change.

Market Identification and Market Forces

Before proceeding to an analysis of market trends and influences on value, in general, and on that of the subject property in particular, it is important for the appraiser to have some understanding of what markets are and how they function. It has already been noted that the basic decision in urban land economics is the allocation of urban space among alternative competing uses. The allocation decision, in the private sector at least, is based on the conclusion or indication of highest and best use or most profitable use. Use is a fundamental determinant of value, and market value tends to be measured in terms of highest and best use.

The determination of what uses are legal and feasible results, to a large extent, from the interaction of market forces external to the property itself or the decision maker. These market forces are what determine value. They do so, in part, by determining use. The appraiser measures or estimates value, in part, by estimating the character and impact of these market forces.

As the materials in this chapter indicate, there is no single market for real estate or rights in realty. One of the tasks of the appraiser is to identify and specify in which of many markets the property being appraised is to be found and is competing. This determination may specify geographic area, type of use, type of improvement, price range, and so forth. Identification of the appropriate market then helps specify which data are to be used in the appraisal and which data sources are to be used. An understanding of the nature, structure, and functioning of real estate markets in turn helps the appraiser make this identification.

The particular real estate markets of interest to the appraiser are sales and rental markets, plus mortgage markets. Their structure, the functions they perform, and their specific characteristics should be understood so that the appraiser can proceed to apply market (area and neighborhood) analysis in every appraisal assignment. Then, behavior of buyers and sellers, of landlords and tenants, or of borrowers and lenders can be identified and translated into market data.

The Nature of a Market

A market is defined as a set of arrangements for bringing buyers and sellers together through the price mechanism.[4] A market may be a specific geographic location or place, but it need not be. In either case, it is the total set of activity in which a particular economic good or service is exchanged. The New York Stock Exchange is a specific place where securities are exchanged; so is the Commodity Exchange. The over-the-counter market is a network of brokers representing securities buyers and sellers scattered throughout the nation and linked by telephone and computer. It is everywhere and nowhere. Buyer and seller may never meet or know each other's identities.

Tangible goods, services, rights, and money may be exchanged. Any economic good or service that is transferable and which has value can and usually does have a market. Markets for different goods and services are separate and distinct from one another. They are interrelated, however, because they tend to be subject to the same general economic forces. What happens in the market for petroleum, for example, can influence the market for houses in resort developments. Similarly, the market for rental housing is influenced by what happens in markets for construction materials (lumber, structural steel, window glass).

The analysis of markets and the price mechanism in economic theory is based on the assumption of a given set of market characteristics and structure. For the market and especially the price mechanism to work efficiently and effectively, these market conditions must be met. Otherwise, the market is said to be imperfect in varying degrees. The major implication or result is that price is indeterminate and not an effective or efficient allocative device. In economic theory, the ideal is perfect competition, with monopolistic competition a close approximation. These terms and their associated requirements and characteristics are not used here because they are too abstract and unrealistic.

However, the conditions and requisites of an open, competitive (free) market considered here in contrast to real estate markets are close to those of the competitive market of economic theory.

The Competitive Market of Economic Theory

In the competitive market of economic theory, the units of the good or service being exchanged are nearly perfect substitutes for one another. This means that it is a matter of indifference to buyers which items are purchased, and it is also a matter of indifference to the seller which items are sold. The purchaser of General Motors common stock, for example, does not really care which 100 shares are bought, since they are all the same. The holder of 500 shares does not care which 100 shares are sold.

It is also a matter of indifference to the buyer whose units are bought, and it is a matter of indifference to the seller to whom the units are sold. In most securities transactions, for example, the buyer and seller do not know each other's identities. There are no effective qualitative differences among the units of the good or service. Goods can be bought from samples, because all units are essentially the same.

Another feature of the competitive market of economic theory is large numbers of buyers and sellers. This means that no one buyer or seller has a large enough share of the market to have a direct and measurable influence on price. As an important corollary, no buyer or seller behaves as though the action could have a direct and measurable influence on market price. This means that negotiation on price between buyers and sellers does not occur. The market itself takes the place of negotiation in setting market price.

Further, all market participants (buyers and sellers) are presumed to be informed and therefore to have the requisite information about market conditions, behavior of others, past market activity, and product quality and substitutability. Buyers and sellers also are presumed to act rationally on the basis of the good information they possess. Rational behavior consists of acting to maximize the market participants' economic well-being as measured by profit and/or wealth.

Price is the sole consideration in purchase or sale decisions, since the quality of the good or service is the same (perfect substitutability). there is no product differentiation. Demand and supply interactions are always expressed in terms of money (price). There is an organized market mechanism to bring buyers and sellers together.

Finally, there is open and free competition among market participants (buyers and sellers, buyers and buyers, sellers and sellers). There is also open and free competition among units of the good or service being exchanged, and competition is the regulative force. The market always tends to move toward balance (or equilibrium) through the effects of competition. The market price is the balancing mechanism. There is little or no government restriction or restraint on the free functioning of the market.

Real Estate Markets

A real estate market is "A commercial activity designed to facilitate the exchange of rights in realty, set prices for mutually advantageous exchanges, allocate space among competing alternative uses, determine the pattern of space and land use, and adjust supply to demand."[5]
   A real estate market deals in rights in realty. These rights constitute what is exchanged, bought, and sold. A real estate market may be defined geographically, or it may extend among properties competing with one another over a widespread area with no precise definition. The market for residences in a given neighborhood area, for example, may be defined by and limited to the boundaries of that neighborhood, or it may include one or more other neighborhoods in which similar residences are competing for buyers with those in the neighborhood in question. On the other hand, the market for nuclear power plants may be spread over a large region and may include those specific sites within the region that meet the requirements for such a development. Finally, the market for secondary mortgage money may be spread over an entire nation or even beyond, just as the over-the-counter securities market.
   General types of real estate markets include sales markets, where properties are bought and sold; rental markets; and mortgage markets. Although different types of rights are exchanged in each, they are at the same time interrelated. In addition, real estate markets may be classified by type of real estate or space involved; by the use to which the space is put or is intended to be put; or by the price level or range of the properties. In brief, a real estate market is a market in which rights in realty are exchanged and which is competitive in the minds of potential buyers.

Characteristics of Real Estate Markets. Although there are many different markets for the exchange of rights in realty, there are certain similarities among all real estate markets that stem primarily from the characteristics of real estate. Because of its immobility and spatial characteristics, real estate is a unique good. No two parcels or units of space are exactly alike. They are not and cannot be perfect substitutes for one another. It does make a difference to the buyer which property is acquired, and often the identity of the buyer or seller does make a difference to the other party.

Different rights or estates in similar, competitive properties can exist and are exchanged. There is a difference between a fee simple encumbered with easements and one that is unencumbered. There is a difference between a fee simple and a leased fee or a leasehold. There are differences in the marketability of titles. Legal complexities exist for even the simplest real estate transaction. The special legal circumstances surrounding each transaction make each one a special case. This also has the operational effect of making real estate transactions prolonged and time-consuming affairs.

The norm in real estate markets is few buyers and sellers for each transaction or market segment. Buyers and sellers, landlords and tenants, borrowers and lenders all believe they can influence price or rental terms or loan terms. Therefore, negotiation between parties is the rule, and price tends to be indeterminate. Price and transaction terms are strongly influenced by the subjective perceptions and desires of individual participants. The relative bargaining strength and pressure, or lack of it, on individual participants to a transaction can and does influence transaction price. A seller who is under pressure and anxious to sell will generally accept less favorable terms than one who is not. A borrower who is desperate for loan funds will generally accept less favorable loan terms than one who is not.

Because of the distinctiveness of different properties and the rights in them, the competitiveness of other properties is also a subjective determination for each individual market participant. Competitiveness of other properties can be measured only approximately by measuring buyer behavior after the fact.

Much market information is difficult if not impossible to obtain. Sales prices are not publicly and widely reported, as sales prices on stock exchanges are. The terms of individual mortgage loan and lease agreements are rarely made public and may be treated as confidential. In addition, market participants are often in the market without the knowledge of market behavior and trends that comes from continuous participation. This is especially true in residential real estate markets. Buyers and sellers respond to specific pressures on them to buy and sell; they tend to act on the basis of subjective judgments. Moreover, it is not always true or determinable by the market analyst, however, that they act so as to maximize their economic well-being, wealth, or profit. Seemingly unreasonable prices are often paid or accepted in residential markets.

As noted earlier, there are many submarkets in the real estate market. Each is identified and characterized by the competitive properties that potential buyers and sellers perceive to exist in the area of the property being analyzed. Because real estate is fixed in location and immobile, the applicable market area for a particular property or type of property tends to be restricted to a relatively small geographic area, determined by its locational and access characteristics. For residential properties, the area within which alternative properties are effectively competitive with one another is determined by such considerations as commuting time to jobs, access to shopping and recreational facilities, the reputation of the school district, and living amenities characterized by the reputation of the area.

Demand for residential real estate is uneven, stratified, and volatile. This demand, in particular, is a function of population, employment, and income. The demographics of number and size of households, net in-migration, social and economic characteristics, age distribution, and the like, can change unpredictably in local areas, primarily as a result of factors unrelated to the real estate or residences themselves. Further, purchasing power makes demand effective on the market.

The supply side of the real estate market equation is considered to be relatively sluggish or unresponsive (i.e., inelastic), at least in the short run. Supply is not particularly price-responsive. The available quantity of both properties and property services changes slowly. They tend to be insensitive to short-run changes in demand or price. Construction, including conversion, is time-consuming. There are physical, legal, and financial deterrents to speed. Moreover, new construction is but a small percentage of the total existing stock at any given time. Probably no area of activity is more regulated and influenced by government than is real estate activity. Government controls of land use (especially zoning, environmental protection, and building regulations) are widespread. Historically, lenders and loan terms have been directly influenced by government regulation, and indirectly influenced through parallel governmental programs and policies.

Real estate markets are not free markets. Real estate is a creature of its surroundings. It cannot be moved to a more favorable market environment; therefore, it is much more sensitive to and influenced by non-real estate market forces. For all these reasons, a real estate market is not a competitive, open, and free market.

Functions of Real Estate Markets. The functions of real estate markets are basically those of any market. Real estate markets facilitate exchanges of rights in realty between buyers and sellers, landlords and tenants, borrowers and lenders. They further set price for mutually advantageous exchanges. The real estate market does not set value, but it does set market price. Price, of which value is an approximation or tendency, is still the basic allocative mechanism.

Real estate markets allocate urban space among competing alternative uses. Individually, this involves decisions in terms of highest and best use. Collectively, rational decisions in terms of highest and best use should lead to maximum values and maximum satisfactions. The desired combination of uses is a function of the consensus of individual market decisions, subject to private or community influence or limitations through zoning, environmental protection regulations, and other governmental standards and controls.

In real estate markets, demand is volatile and is essentially the result of forces external to the market (exogeneous forces). Supply is more clearly dependent on demand. One function of the market is to provide the proper economic, financial, and legal environment for supply to respond effectively to changes in demand. Technical, legal, and financial considerations generally make this adjustment process a slow one. Construction and conversion take time and large amounts of money. In the short run, price, including rents, is more likely to change in direct response to a change in demand; with changing prices influencing profitability, physical activity eventually responds in the longer run.

Categories of Real Estate Markets. Real estate markets can be classified for analytical and operational purposes into several different categories according to type of use, type of tenancy, objective of occupancy or ownership, locality or geographic area, price or rental level, and rights or estate involved. In operation, all of these categories are important. It is usually necessary, for example, to specify the fee simple interest in a single-family, owner-occupied residential property in a given locality in the $70,000 to $80,000 price range in order to identify which properties are competitive with it and which therefore constitute the market to be identified and analyzed.

Determinants of Demand. The appraiser should investigate, identify, and measure the quantity of the determining elements of demand for real estate of the type being appraised. This should be concentrated in the particular market in which it is most likely to sell. The emphasis here is on demand for residential space.

The number of persons within households is the basic determinant of the quantity of demand in any residential market area. Detailed and specific study are required to identify the segment of the population particularly involved with the type of housing being appraised. In addition, past trends and expected future changes in population are essential to appreciate the impact of population on current market conditions. The current numbers and rates of change of total population to be housed need to be identified. Further, the origin of population change in terms of *natural increase* (births over deaths) or *net in-migration* must also be identified and analyzed. Natural increase may mean that fewer additional units are desired, but they may be different with changed family structure (e.g., larger units to house larger families). Net in-migration usually means that more units are required immediately. The type of units required will depend on economic status (income price level, rent versus ownership) and family size.

The basic unit to be housed is the household. A market area with large numbers of single individuals seeking independent housing will have quite a different demand from one in which childless couples predominate (either young or elderly). That demand will also be different from that of a market area in which families with resident children represent the greatest segment of the population. A population composed of relatively young couples will more likely require smaller units, often rental units, than those required by a population composed largely of families with heads of households in the 35-to-44 age bracket. Increasing numbers of elderly couples create still different requirements in terms of types of units desired and their location.

A highly mobile population is more likely to be interested in rental units and more likely to create sudden changes in neighborhood acceptance than is a relatively immobile population. Los Angeles and New York are examples of the former, while New England and Midwestern cities and towns illustrate the latter. Architectural styles can easily go out of fashion. The relative desire for homeownership as opposed to renting will decidedly influence the character of demand for housing units. This type of information is usually obtainable only through interviewing or continuing personal experience.

Population levels and trends will create needs and desires for housing and will indicate the types of units wanted. Unless there is purchasing power in the form of income (and, in the case of home purchase, savings), however, these needs and desires do not constitute demand—in the private sector of the housing market, at least. A study of current and expected future trends and income levels will help clarify whether the means exist to support housing desires in the market in question. In particular, the stability of income sources is extremely important in judging whether current market conditions warrant long-term commitments in ownership housing.

It is important to know how many and what types of households have incomes in different brackets. To measure demand in any particular submarket, it is necessary to discover the income status, age composition, household size, and mobility of the particular income group. Rates of employment and unemployment are important guides to the probable stability of incomes over time and to the character of demand in the market in question. Even these averages can be misleading, however; therefore, it is also necessary to consider the sources of employment and their stability. Highly volatile defense industries, for example (such as airframe manufacturers and aircraft assemblers in Southern California), have led to major disruptions in housing markets during periods of declining activity.

A study of family cash savings and debt structures is necessary to indicate the probable demand for rental housing as opposed to ownership housing. It also influences the price levels at which effective demand for housing (rental or ownership) will be experienced, given the lending capabilities and policies of financial institutions operating in the area. A market area with relatively young couples earning high incomes, for example, will be quite different in character from one in which the same levels of income are earned by older families with a backlog of savings. Even in analysis of asset holdings, it is not sufficient to study cash and quick assets only. The debt burden of the households should be considered so that the ability to carry the responsibility of homeownership, including mortgage obligations, can be estimated.

Demand is not isolated from cost, price, or rental. Demand represents the quantity of housing of a particular type that will be taken off the market at a given price level. Prices of existing housing (sales or rental) influence how the available incomes and savings can and will be utilized. In particular, expectations of price changes in the near future influence decisions made currently. The distribution of prices by location, age of housing, architectural style, and price range will also influence the final matching of needs and incomes, on the one hand, with the available supply, on the other.

Because most real estate sales transactions require (or at least utilize) debt financing, the availability and cost of mortgage money will determine, in part, how effective demand will be in a given submarket. Construction costs will influence the type of housing demanded. A relative rise in construction costs will tend to make existing housing more attractive until price adjustments occur.

Legal restrictions often inhibit new construction techniques and materials (e.g., building codes, fire codes, union rules). Legal restrictions also influence the number and type of housing units that can be provided within a market area through zoning (e.g., two-acre minimum

lot sizes and only one-family use in many Connecticut zoning ordi-
nances). Environmental protection regulations have the same impact.
Legal restrictions also influence new housing costs through subdivision
regulations that require public facilities in new developments—costs
paid for by the developer and typically passed on to the purchaser.

The policies and regulations of financial institutions also frequently
inhibit the range of housing alternatives. Many smaller institutions re-
strict their lending areas, will not participate in multifamily housing or
development loans, and have limits on the size and terms of loans they
make.

Components of Supply. The analysis of supply in a particular submarket
requires indentification and measurement (to the extent possible) of
both the current status and the trends in the several elements that
combine to make up supply. The prices at which competing units are
available on the market, and the quantity in which they are available,
will influence the asking prices of those attempting to sell or rent.

Only the segment of existing stock of housing that is likely to be
placed on the market in a given period constitutes effective supply, but
some idea of the character of the entire standing stock is useful. This
requires a detailed analysis by type, size, age, condition, location, style,
price level, and the like. Current offerings represent the most probable
portion of effective supply and should be studied in at least the same
detail as the standing stock. Multiple listing services and newspaper
advertisements are good sources of this information.

The number, type of unit, location, and price (or rent) level of new
construction is a major guide to how effectively and how rapidly demand
is being met. The rate of new construction is particularly useful information, especially if it is broken down in sufficient detail by type of
unit. Construction costs are important determinants of how many and
what kinds of units are likely to be made available through new construction in the near term. Trends and expectations about construction
costs will indicate whether new construction appears to pay in the face
of current and anticipated demand.

Doubling, undoubling, and conversions represent changes within
the standing stock. They are particularly important for analysis of a
given submarket. They can influence considerably the attractiveness of
new construction activity. Vacancies and turnovers are indicators of
the strength of market activity and of the apparent need for new units.
They are also part of the competitive picture considered here.

The availability of mortgage money and construction financing is
a factor in effective supply as well as in effective demand. It is important
to study the size of the mortgage pool in the market area and to discover

the probable availability of funds in the particular submarket in question. In addition, supply may be affected by the requirement that sellers take back purchase-money mortgages in part payment for their properties. In certain money market conditions, this becomes necessary in order to transfer any real property.

The Real Estate Business and Real Estate Markets

The organized real estate business has developed primarily to overcome the imperfections of real estate and mortgage markets. The intent is for these markets to perform better their function of facilitating exchanges and adjusting supply to demand. Except for the development-construction aspect of the real estate business, most activities provide informed and skilled specialists who serve as intermediaries between buyers and sellers, landlords and tenants, or borrowers and lenders to reduce the uninformed character of real estate markets. A corollary result is better quality decisions about the allocation of use of urban space.

The real estate business is organized generally by type of activity, which includes agency, investment, operations, building construction, and government services and influence. Agency activity involves acting on behalf of another for a fee or commission and includes brokerage, management, appraising, counseling, and the like. Investment refers to the placement or commitment of funds in real estate for a profit. It includes equity investment, mortgage financing (since lending is a form of investment), and leasehold positions. Operations activity involves managing investments to generate maximum long-run returns, consistent with maintaining safety of investment and marketability of real estate. Profits are made on trading. Operations activity includes management of investments in land, buildings, or improved properties, mortgages, and leaseholds. Building construction incorporates a wide range of activities, including development, pioneering or speculation, contract construction, and alteration or conversion.

Government service to and influence on real estate markets are achieved through property taxation and assessment; income taxation; acquisition, sale, and management of public property; land use regulations and controls; financing; and conservation and development.

Summary

Real estate may be analyzed in terms of its physical, legal, and/or economic characteristics. Realty or real estate consists of land and all

improvements on and to the land. The distinguishing physical characteristics of realty are its immobility or fixity of location, extreme du-
rability (long life), and heterogeneity (diversity). Each parcel of real
estate is a unique entity, different from all others.

Legally, real property consists of enforceable rights in realty. Interests in realty are called estates. Estates may contain all or some of
the bundle of rights. Rights are both divisible and separable. Estates
in realty may be classified by quantity of interest or duration, by time
of enjoyment, and by number of owners.

Real estate contracts are evidences of a meeting of minds between
buyer and seller or landlord and tenant. Deeds are documents that
transfer title to realty. They all represent transactions useful to the
appraiser as market data. The real estate appraiser should be familiar
with the physical and legal characteristics of real estate in order to
understand what is being appraised.

The four basic public or governmental limitations on the free exercise of private property rights in real estate are taxation, police power,
eminent domain, and escheat. Title to real estate consists of ownership
of enforceable rights in realty. Title passes with the acceptance of a
properly executed deed. Claims to rights in real estate are recorded to
give constructive notice. Real estate records are an important source
of market data for the appraiser.

The economic characteristics of real estate are conditioned by its
physical characteristics. Real estate provides services or income at a
fixed location. The value of urban space stems directly from its use.
Location is a prime determinant of the use and value of urban space.
Because its location is fixed, the use and value of urban space are
strongly influenced by the market forces of its surrounding environment. Urban space is allocated in terms of the principle of highest and
best use. Use decisions involve both type of use and intensity of use.
Use determines productivity or income, whereas productivity determines value. To be a competitor for highest and best use, a proposed
use must be legal, possible, appropriate, and feasible.

Location analysis is economic in character and emphasis. It recognizes the impact of a changing external market and physical environment on immobile urban space. Location decisions may be influenced
by three sets of factors: cost-reducing, benefit-creating, and personal.
Personal factors are particularly important in residential location decisions. Residential location analysis involves a study of specific use,
environment, time, and anticipated pattern of change.

Real estate markets are localized, specialized, stratified, uninformed, and generally unresponsive to price changes, especially in the
short run. Land and space are allocated in accordance with economic

considerations, especially the principle of highest and best use. The real estate market is the area within which land and space allocation decisions are made among competing alternative uses.

The structure of the real estate business and real estate markets is influenced by the physical, legal, and economic characteristics of real estate. Real estate markets serve to facilitate exchange of rights in realty (real estate), to set price for exchanges, to allocate urban space among alternative competing uses, to determine the pattern of urban land and space use, and to adjust supply to demand. Real estate markets are imperfect because of institutional limitations, imperfect knowledge, limitations on entry and exit, and differentiated (heterogeneous) product. As a result, they perform their functions imperfectly.

The real estate business exists to help overcome market imperfections and to facilitate exchanges. Real estate market demand is relatively volatile and income-responsive. Supply is relatively unresponsive to price (inelastic). Supply usually adjusts to demand. Effective demand is desire or need reinforced by purchasing power (income, savings).

The determinants of demand include population, income, and costs of acquiring housing. Effective supply is the amount of housing of a particular type that will be made available at given price levels. The determinants of housing supply include competition; standing stock; current offerings; new construction; costs; doubling; undoubling; and conversions; vacancies and turnovers; and availability of financing.

Real estate values stem from the market. Market analysis enables the appraiser to draw conclusions regarding the defined value of the specified rights in certain described real estate.

Notes

1. See also, Boyce, Byrl N., ed., *Real Estate Appraisal Terminology,* rev. ed. (Cambridge, Mass.: Ballinger [Joint publication of the American Institute of Real Estate Appraisers and Society of Real Estate Appraisers], 1981), pp. 119 and 294.
2. For an illustration of the calculation of areas, see Ibid., p. 268.
3. For an illustration of the metric-English equivalence and conversion factors, see Ibid., pp. 271–277.
4. Ibid., p. 159.
5. Ibid., p. 200.

Suggested Readings

American Institute of Real Estate Appraisers. *The Appraisal of Real Estate,* 8th ed. Chicago: American Institute of Real Estate Appraisers, 1983, chapters 2 and 4.

Bergfield, Philip B. *Principles of Real Estate Law*. New York: McGraw-Hill, 1979.

Bloom, George F., and Harrison, Henry S. *Appraising the Single Family Residence*. Chicago: American Institute of Real Estate Appraisers, 1978, chapter 2.

Bloom, George F.; Weimer, Arthur M.; and Fisher, Jeffrey D. *Real Estate,* 8th ed. New York: John Wiley & Sons, 1982, chapters 2, 3, and 4.

Boyce, Byrl N., ed. *Real Estate Appraisal Terminology,* rev. ed. Cambridge, Mass.: Ballinger, (Joint publication of the American Institute of Real Estate Appraisers and Society of Real Estate Appraisers), 1981.

French, William B., and Lusk, Harold F. *Law of the Real Estate Business*. Homewood, Ill.: Richard D. Irwin, 1979.

Jacobus, Charles J. *Real Estate Law*. Reston, Va.: Reston, 1980.

Jaffe, Austin J., and Sirmans, C.F. *Real Estate Investment Decision-Making*. Englewood Cliffs, N.J.: Prentice-Hall, 1982, chapters 5, 6, and 7.

Smith, Halbert C.; Tschappat, Carl J.; and Racster, Ronald L. *Real Estate and Urban Development,* 3rd ed. Homewood, Ill.: Richard D. Irwin, 1981, chapters 8, 9, 10, and 11.

3 The Nature of Value

Key Terms

Anticipation   The valuation principle which states that value is a function of anticipated future benefits.

Appraisal process (framework)   A systematic analysis of factors that bear upon the value of real estate.

Change   The valuation principle which states that trends in economic, physical, governmental, and social forces brought about by change in those forces may affect property and property values.

Forecasting   Estimating a future happening or condition, based upon past trends and analytical judgment.

Gross rent multiplier (GRM)   A ratio between the sales price of a property and its monthly unfurnished rental.

Highest and best use   The reasonable and probable use that supports the highest present value.

Marginal productivity (contribution)   A valuation principle which states that value of a component part of a property depends upon its contribution to the value of the whole.

Market analysis   The projection and analysis of the components of demand.

Objective (purpose) of appraisal   The type of value sought (e.g., market value).

Substitution   The valuation principle which states that a purchaser would pay no more for real property than the cost of acquiring an equally desirable substitute.

Value in exchange   A value concept based upon a relative comparison of available alternatives from which a potential purchaser may make a choice.

Value in use   A value concept based upon the productivity of a property to its owner-user.

Variable proportions (increasing and decreasing returns)   The valuation principle which states that successive increments of one or more factors of production added to fixed amounts of other factors enhance income to a point of maximum return.

An appraisal is a supportable and defensible estimate of value. The specific type of value to be estimated in any appraisal assignment is defined by the objective or purpose of the appraisal. For the appraiser to approach appraisal assignments with full understanding of what is to be done and why, it is necessary to have a good working knowledge of value. Moreover, the appraiser must be able to identify and apply the working of the principles by which value is determined by the market and measured by the appraiser. Value should be considered both as a general economic concept and as a measure in real estate analysis and appraisal. The principles of real estate valuation also influence the ways in which real property value estimation is approached.

The Concept of Value

Value is a relationship between a thing desired and a potential purchaser. Value is the desirability or worth of a thing. The most frequently and widely used definition of value identifies its role as *value in exchange:* i.e., "The quantity of one thing which can be obtained in exchange for another."[1]

Value exists in the mind of man. It is not inherent in the thing (e.g., real property) itself. Value exists because one or more persons want something (e.g., a house) and are willing to give up something in exchange to acquire and possess it. Value varies from person to person and from time to time, largely as a reflection of changing individual desires.

In the perfectly competitive market of economic theory, value and price are identical and synonymous. In imperfect markets, such as those for real estate, value and price are neither identical nor synonymous. Thus, value is a price that would tend to prevail under specified market conditions. This is why specification of the date of a value estimate is critically important; it identifies the market conditions in terms of which value is estimated.

Money is the yardstick or standard by which value is measured. The value of money itself varies with market conditions. This reinforces the necessity to specify the date of the value estimate, so that the purchasing power of the dollar is clearly identified.

Value in exchange is market-determined. It is primarily the result of the interactions of the forces of supply and demand on the market. This is why an identification and analysis of the market conditions prevailing on the date of the value estimate are necessary. Value is also the result of productivity, which in turn is determined by use. This is the basis for the concept of value in use. It also helps explain why highest and best use analysis is necessary in every appraisal. Appraisers measure value by measuring the impact of market forces. Appraisers do not determine value.

To have value, a good must have the characteristics of an economic good: utility, scarcity, and effective demand (desire backed by purchasing power). In addition, for these elements to be manifested in market value, the good must be transferable. Since rights in realty are typically transferable or marketable, they can and do have value.

A good such as real property cannot have value unless it has utility. Utility is "the capacity of an economic good to satisfy human desires or needs."[2] This emphasizes the fact that value is not inherent in the thing but exists in the minds of those who desire it. Homesites do not possess value unless someone wants to buy them. A desired or needed good must be scarce to have value. If the good is available in virtually unlimited quantities and is obtainable without any effort or cost to the user, then it cannot have value no matter how desirable or necessary it is.

For a good to have value, there must also be ability to pay or purchasing power in the hands of potential users. It is not enough that families or households need housing and that housing is scarce. If the income to support purchase prices or rentals required to make that housing available on the market is not present, there is no market and no value. A good must also be transferable. It must be capable of being exchanged for money or for other goods measured in money. If it is not, then it cannot have value on the market, although it may still have value in use. A property with clouds on the title that keep it from being marketable, for example, can have no market value.

All value is subjective in the sense that value exists only in the minds of potential buyers, sellers, owners, and users. There is considerable discussion in appraisal and valuation literature, however, about the distinction between subjective and objective value. In reality, this is a false distinction. More properly, it should be made on the basis of whether or not value is measurable.

Personal or individual feelings, attitudes, and desires are not readily or directly measurable. If they are not translated to market behavior (which is measurable objectively) by buyers and sellers, they are little help in estimating values. This is true even though the analyst knows they exist. Such feelings, attitudes, and desires are the basis for value in use, amenity value, or capricious value, which cannot be measured with a high degree of confidence or support. When personal or individual feelings, attitudes, and desires are reflected in market behavior through the actions of many buyers and sellers, then the market conditions created by these actions can be measured. These market conditions result in prices. This is the basis for market value, which is estimated objectively, and for investment value.

Value in Real Estate Analysis

As previously indicated, value can have different meanings. The applicable meaning depends on the identity or character of the individual in whose mind value exists. This individual can be a potential purchaser, in which case value in exchange is the applicable value to be estimated; the user, in which case value in use may apply; or the potential seller, in which case value in exchange, cost or value in use may be appropriate.

Value is a price that would tend to prevail under specified market conditions. Moreover, price is the basic allocative or rationing mechanism in real estate markets. The task of the appraiser is to measure or estimate value from market and property data. Except in very special circumstances, therefore, value in use is not estimated, even though it is a valid concept in real estate decision making. In identifying what category of value is applicable and therefore to be estimated, it is necessary to answer the basic question: value to whom?

The value to be estimated is defined by the objective or purpose of the appraisal. Appraisers are continually answering different questions. The estimated value, as defined, is the answer in each assignment.

Value in Exchange. Value in exchange is "the amount of goods and services or purchasing power which an informed purchaser would offer in exchange for an economic good under given market conditions."[3] It is relative. There must be comparison with another economic good or goods. There must also be alternatives from which a potential purchaser may make a choice.

Rights in realty are transferable and have the requisite characteristics of utility and scarcity. When there is purchasing power to back up desire or need, those rights can therefore have value. This is because there can be and is a price that would tend to prevail under specified market conditions resulting from the interplay of supply and demand factors under those market conditions. It is what an informed purchaser would pay to acquire the property being appraised or one with similar utility.

If comparisons with other rights in realty are made and there are alternatives available to the purchaser, the requisite conditions of value in exchange are met. This is true of virtually all residential real estate.

Value in exchange is represented by market value in real estate appraisal. Value in exchange is the conceptual basis for direct sales comparison analysis in estimating real property value.

Value in Use. Value in use is "based upon the productivity of an economic good to its owner-user. Value in use may be a valid substitute for market value when the current use is so specialized that it has no demonstrable market and when the use is economic and likely to continue."[4] Since real estate is a long-term capital asset capable of producing money or amenity income over an extended period of years, its value can also be regarded as the present worth of anticipated future benefits.

The present worth of those benefits to a specific purchaser or investor is investment value, which can be measured by the appraiser. The use generating forecast income may be of the highest and best use or the actual use. The present worth to a specific owner or user is value in use, which can rarely be measured by the appraiser for amenity property. The use generating forecast income to the current user is always the present use, whether or not it represents highest and best use.

Value in use or investment value frequently will be different from value in exchange or market value. Usually, it will be greater than market value. Otherwise, the owner-user would logically and rationally sell. Value in use is approached from the viewpoint of the owner-user. It is the amount of money the owners of rights in realty must be offered or paid to persuade them to give up those rights. Market value and investment value, on the other hand, are viewed from the position of the potential buyer. Value in use or investment value, which is derived from the forecast productivity of real estate in a specified use pattern, provides the rationale for income capitalization analysis in estimating real property value.

Cost of Production. Cost of production is the expenditure of resources or money required to bring an economic good into being. This concept of value approaches valuation from the viewpoint of the potential seller, who wishes to cover the cost associated with the four factors of production: land, labor, capital, and entrepreneurship.

Compensation to all four factors of production is required at the competitive market rate, at least. Otherwise, the factors will be put to alternative use or withheld from the market. These costs are opportunity costs (i.e., what is given up from other alternatives by putting the factor of production to use in the particular project or undertaking in question). The compensation to land is rent. The compensation to labor is wages. The compensation to capital is interest, which means a competitive or required rate of return on the investment. The compensation to entrepreneurship (essentially the risk-taking function of putting together and managing the enterprise) is profits. A competitive or required rate of return for risk taking and entrepreneurship is a cost. Cost of production is the conceptual basis for estimating real property value through cost and accrued depreciation analysis.

What Is To Be Valued. Appraisal consists of estimating the value, as defined, of a specified set of rights in realty. Real estate may be analyzed as an asset in at least three ways. It is necessary for the appraiser to understand each of these bases of analysis and to identify which components are meaningful in the appraisal assignment. A value estimate cannot be defensible or supportable if the object of that estimate is not carefully and precisely identified.

As noted previously, realty consists of land (or site) and improvements on and to the land. The quantity and quality of the real estate must be identified and analyzed carefully if a physical approach to value estimation is to be taken. This analysis includes the location of the realty; the dimensions and characteristics of the site; and the dimensions, components, quality, and condition of the structure or structures on the site.

Ownership of real estate consists of possession of certain rights in realty. In actuality, it is not the physical real estate that is valued but rather the particular rights that a typical purchaser might acquire. Normally, this will be the unencumbered fee simple estate, subject only to the four basic public limitations on the free exercise of those rights. Even then, it is essential to know precisely what those limitations are in the case in question and what the implications are for the uses to which the realty may be put. Zoning restrictions, for example, may preclude a use that is supportable in the market but simply is not legal because of the restrictions. An excessive tax burden may detract from the benefits of ownership of a particular piece of realty and thereby reduce its value. The threat of an impending public taking under eminent domain (as, for example, a proposed highway or an urban renewal project) will often have a dampening effect on the properties to be affected either by the taking or by the proposed new public use.

The rights being appraised may also be subject to private restrictions or limitations. These restrictions may very well detract from value (e.g., a right of way across a portion of the land that precludes construction of any type on the right of way). On the other hand, an easement across adjoining land, which goes with the realty being appraised, may very well enhance its value. A property subject to a lease may be adversely or favorably affected, depending upon the relationship of the rental and other terms of the lease to going market rentals and lease terms at the time of the appraisal. The appraiser must therefore identify which segments of the bundle of rights the typical purchaser of the realty in question would receive, and then must proceed to base the value estimate on the present worth of those particular segments.

Since the purchase and ownership of real estate typically involve a substantial amount of debt financing, the terms and conditions under which financing is available in the present market are of considerable importance to the appraiser. The typical purchaser is acquiring an equity interest in realty, subject to limitations imposed by the mortgage lender. The amount and terms of financing available as of the date of the appraisal, as well as existing financing arrangements (if the typical purchaser would acquire the property subject to a mortgage or assume the existing mortgage), will also influence the marketability and price (not value) of the property in question.

Date of Value Estimate. Value is always estimated as of a given date. The date of the appraisal specifies the market and environmental conditions in which the value estimate is made. Any value estimate takes into account certain market conditions, regardless of the nature of the value being estimated. Market value will be a direct function, for example, of supply and demand conditions prevailing on the market at the time of the appraisal. Because the forces that make up supply and demand on the market are subject to constant change, value itself changes with these market conditions.

Utility can vary with changing tastes and standards. What is regarded as modern and acceptable at one time can be outmoded by a change of tastes. In many parts of the country, for example, the one-story ranch house has superseded the two-story (bungalow, Cape Cod) house in acceptance. In many income brackets, a residence with a one-car garage is regarded as inadequate. In some parts of the country, a house set well back from the street with a large front lawn is less desirable than one set relatively close to the street with a considerably larger rear yard for privacy and family recreation.

Utility can also vary with changing technology. New materials, new equipment, and new methods that do the job well and efficiently make existing housing appear outmoded. In many parts of the country, for example, centralized heating and cooling systems will render obsolete otherwise modern houses that have separate heating and cooling facilities.

Purchasing power is a direct function of incomes and employment in an area. Purchasing power is the ability of the potential buying public to make its desires and wishes felt. A sudden and sharp curtailment of employment in a given market area can reduce significantly the demand for ownership housing and can affect values markedly. Sharp rises in mortgage rates can have an impact on housing demand, prices, and values.

The volume of construction can affect the availability of housing substantially. The availability of alternatives has a direct influence on the value of real estate in a given market area. Moreover, varying tastes and standards can affect the availability of certain features in residences. In a university town, for example, the typical house might well have an extra room to be used as a study or den, at the expense of one bay of a two-car garage for houses in the same general price range. These market standards will affect the availability of houses with two-car garages and will influence their value in that market.

The reputation of an area or neighborhood can have an important influence on the value of properties in that area. If it is regarded as a desirable area in which to live, values will be enhanced. If it loses this reputation over time, this will have a decidedly detrimental impact on residential values in the area.

Value Estimation as a Forecast. Because value is the present worth of anticipated future benefits or income, the appraiser's task is to forecast the benefits and amenities that will be produced by the realty being appraised over its remaining economic life. Then the appraiser must forecast the manner in which the typical, informed purchaser will react to these anticipated future benefits. Real estate appraisal is always forward-looking from the date as of which the value estimate is made, whenever that may be.

Forecasting involves making an estimate of a future happening or condition. It consists of estimating what will most probably happen in the future, based in part on trends in the recent past, but tempered with analytical judgment. The appraiser making an estimate of value is, in fact, making a forecast of what will probably occur under stipulated market conditions. Prediction involves foretelling the future with an applied degree of accuracy or precision that is beyond the capacity of the appraiser. An estimate of value is simply that—an estimate. The appraiser has no mystic or occult powers to foresee the future with certainty.

Projection is a mechanical process of extrapolation or extending the experience of the past into the future via a mechanical formula. This may be simple straight-line projection or it may be based on a more complex formula. In either event, it is based on the presumption that the same conditions and rates of change that have prevailed in the past will continue in precisely the same way in the future. In market analysis, an appraiser may begin with projections of past trends as a basis for an estimate of the future. These must be tempered, however, with judgment based on an appreciation of the forces making for different market conditions in the future.

Whatever type of real estate is being appraised, including residential real estate, there are two elements of future benefits or amenities that must be forecast by the appraiser in estimating value. The first element is the flow of benefits, whether in dollar income or amenities (or both), which are expected to be received from the real estate throughout its remaining economic life. The second element (called the reversion) occurs at the end of the economic life of the real estate, when something of value still remains. At the least, the land will have value for an alternative and new use. It is rarely valid to assume that the remainder or reversion will have the same value at the end of the economic life of the improvements as it has on the date of the appraisal.

Principles of Real Property Valuation

The valuation of real property (appraisal of real estate) proceeds in accordance with a set of general economic principles whose application is conditioned by the characteristics of real estate as an asset and is tempered by the characteristics of real estate markets. These principles are operative continuously in the determination of real property value, and they apply to every type of real estate and every type of value to be estimated. They influence what an appraiser does (or should do) in every appraisal assignment. Their peculiar applicability in residential appraisal is emphasized here.

Supply and Demand. Market value is determined by the interaction of the forces of supply and demand in the appropriate market as of the date of the appraisal. The appropriate market forces must therefore be analyzed and evaluated carefully in terms of their impact on the value of the property in question. A sudden influx of new workers into a market area, for example, will increase the demand and thus result in an increase in both market prices and market values for the type of housing the workers are seeking. A sharp increase in mortgage interest rates will increase housing costs and will tend to lessen demand and hence values in the market area.

(most profitable use)

Highest and Best Use. Real estate is valued in terms of its highest and best use. The highest and best use of the land (or site), if vacant and available for use, may be different from the highest and best use of the improved property. This will be true when the improvement is not an appropriate use and some contribution to total property value in excess of the value of the site has to be made.

Highest and best use (highest and most profitable use, optimum use) is that reasonable and probable use that will support the highest present value, as defined, as of the effective date of the appraisal.[5] Alternatively, it is the most profitable likely use to which a property can be put. It may be measured in terms of the present worth of the highest net return that the property can be expected to produce over a stipulated long-run period.

The principle of highest and best use is that urban space (land or improved properties) tends to be put to its highest and best use in a competitive market over the long run. This is the basis for decision making about the allocation of urban space among alternative competing uses. Since the owner, user, or potential buyer is presumed to plan to put real estate to its highest and best use, it is the basis for valuation. So long as the buildings on an improved property contribute something to total property value in excess of the value of the vacant site, it would pay the owner to continue it in that use. That use is its highest and best use.

Substitution (Opportunity Cost). The upper limit of value of real estate tends to be set by the cost of the acquisition of an equally desirable substitute, provided there are no costly delays in affecting the substitution. A prudent purchaser would pay no more than the cost of acquiring such a substitute on the open market.[6]

The application of the principle of substitution presumes that the purchaser will consider available alternatives and will act rationally or prudently on the basis of available information about those alternatives. Time or speed of acquisition is not a factor. Acquiring an equally desirable substitute means obtaining one of equal utility. Considering the alternatives involves application of the concept of opportunity cost.

Marginal Productivity (Contribution). The value of an agent of production or of a component part of a property depends on either how much it contributes to the value of the whole or how much its absence detracts from the value of the whole.[7] This is a measure of its marginal productivity (i.e., how much it adds to the total productivity of the property).

This principle is the basis for estimating accrued depreciation because of deficiencies or superadequacies in cost analysis. In addition, it is the basis for the measurement of differences between the subject property and comparable properties in the adjustment process of direct sales comparison analysis. It is also the basis for the valuation of component parts of the real estate in the residual techniques of income capitalization analysis.

Variable Proportions (Increasing and Decreasing Returns; Diminishing Returns). When successive increments of one or more factors of production are added to fixed amounts of the other factors, income (in dollars, benefits, or amenities) first increases at an increasing rate, then increases at a decreasing rate, and finally decreases absolutely.[8] This is an important principle in comparing alternative use patterns and intensities of use to reach a conclusion about highest and best use. In such analysis, the amount of land is typically the fixed factor, and alternative improvement programs represent the variable factors. A house, for example, may be an overimprovement or an underimprovement of its site.

The point of maximum productivity, and hence of maximum value, is achieved when all factors of production are in balance with one another.[9] This principle applies to a development program for a parcel of land. It also applies to maximizing the amenities of a neighborhood. The point of maximum productivity or balance is known in economic analysis as the point of diminishing returns. Beyond this point, successive increments of the variable factors of production result in a less than proportionate increase in productivity and hence in value. This could apply to putting more and more improvements on a single site.

Because of its fixity of location, land cannot be moved to more profitable areas of use or more active markets. The income attributable to land (or site) is said to be residual in character. After all other factors of production (labor, capital, management) have been paid a competitive market return, the remaining income is available to the land. For all but marginal land for any use, the residual income will be in excess of the amount necessary to keep it in production or in the use in question.[10] This surplus income is termed economic rent in economic analysis. This is why the term *market rent* is preferred to *economic rent* in referring to the rental that a property would demand on the open market.[11]

Change. Because of the dynamics of the marketplace, which depend on the forces of supply and demand, continuous change is a basic characteristic of the real estate market. Value itself is therefore subject to change as market conditions change.[12] This is why every value estimate must be made as of a given date. This is also why an appraiser must forecast market conditions and the reactions of the typical purchaser to expected future market conditions. The appraiser needs to observe and estimate, for example, the current stage in the life cycle of the neighborhood in which the property being appraised is located.

Anticipation. Value is a function of the anticipated benefits to be derived from ownership in the realty.[13] The expectations of buyers or owners can have a direct effect on market value. If a highway is proposed to be built through a given area, there is normally a dampening effect on property values in the path of the highway right of way, as well as a significant lessening of market activity because of the expected public taking. At the same time, properties that will remain in the vicinity of an interchange are often bid up speculatively in anticipation of changed use patterns and increased demand.

Market Value Estimation Requires Market Analysis

An appraisal, which is an estimate of market value, is valid only in terms of a given set of market conditions. The evaluation of the impact of these market conditions on market value requires an analysis of the factors of supply and demand. In making this evaluation, the appraiser actually engages in applied economic analysis and applies the principles and methodology of urban land economics to the specific problem of estimating market value. The techniques of this application to appraisal analysis are discussed in greater detail in Chapter 5.

The definition of market value calls for a careful examination and analysis of the market in which the property being appraised is found. The property is supposed to be exposed on the open market. The transaction is also assumed to take place as an open-market, arm's-length transfer. Both buyer and seller are presumed to be informed about the market. The property is assumed to sell within a normal turnover period for properties of this type on the market in question, as of the date of the appraisal.

Four major sets of forces are at work throughout the economy, continually exerting influence on the values of real estate. They include physical, legal-political, social, and economic forces. These forces operate to create, destroy, or modify value on the market. In particular, the economic, social, and political-legal influences operating in the market as of the appraisal date will influence the alternative uses to which the property can be put, and hence its highest and best use.

Value is estimated in terms of highest and best use as of the date of the appraisal.

All these ingredients in the definition of market value require an awareness of market conditions that influence the value of residential real estate in general and the value of the subject property in particular. The appraiser, therefore, must approach the estimation of value of the subject property in a systematic, analytical way to be sure that the requirements of the concept of market value are met. This involves an identification of the major elements to be analyzed.

What is the market or submarket within which the subject property is located? What kinds of properties are competitive with and comparable to the subject property? Where are those properties located? What is the appropriate geographic range of properties that can compete effectively with the subject? In the minds of typically informed buyers, what are the important characteristics of a property that will make it a reasonable alternative to the subject property? In other words, how far afield does one go in establishing substitutability? It is in these terms that the character and geographic area of the market in which the subject is located can be identified.

In addition, the subject property is located within the political boundaries of a community. Finally, the neighborhood exerts direct influence on the value of the subject property. These factors must be carefully identified because it is within this framework that both substitute properties and the pertinent forces at work on the subject property must be found.

The market, the forces of the market, and market value are all considered through the eyes of the typically informed purchaser in that market as of the date of the appraisal. Therefore, it is necessary to identify who and what the particular purchaser most probably will be. What are the purchaser's desires and tastes? What are the income level, employment status, and family status of the purchaser? In other words, to what kind of individual will this property most probably appeal? What are the purchaser's economic, social, and demographic characteristics? These factors must be ascertained before the appraiser can begin to estimate the market value of the subject property.

Among the many factors of market demand, which ones are really important to the appraisal problem? The character of the market and of the typical purchaser must be identified to provide the appraiser with the best clues to answer this question. Both demand and supply factors must be identified and analyzed in order to reach an estimate of market value. The appraiser's job, once again, is to identify those particular supply and demand factors that are pertinent and essential to the solution of the appraisal problem. The appraiser then proceeds to analyze them.

Steps in the Appraisal Framework:
The Appraisal Process

The appraisal framework is a logical, systematic framework that includes all the necessary ingredients to provide appraisers with an appropriate guide to action in their appraisal work. A graphic representation of this process appears in figure 3–1.

Define the Problem

It may appear self-evident, but appraisers must first ascertain what they are to do, and why, before they can begin to gather and analyze data. A guiding rule in appraisal work should be to make haste slowly. Precipitate action in pulling together materials for analysis before careful delineation of the problem is made can lead to wasted time and effort and, quite possibly, inappropriate results. The appraiser must ascertain what decision is to be made. This means first identifying the client's objectives, which in turn establish the appraiser's objectives. Appraisers may have to return to the definition of the problem several times during the completion of the appraisal problem, as in the conclusion of highest and best use, to make sure that the analysis is pertinent to solving the appraisal problem.

The definition of the problem includes the following elements:

1. Identify the realty.
2. Identify the property rights or interests being appraised.
3. Establish the objective or purpose of the appraisal.
4. Establish the effective date of the appraisal.
5. Reach agreement with the client.

Identifying the realty includes a precise and unequivocal indication of the location of the property, the amount of land that is included, the general character and type of improvements on the land, the address of the property, and the legal description. The legal description is

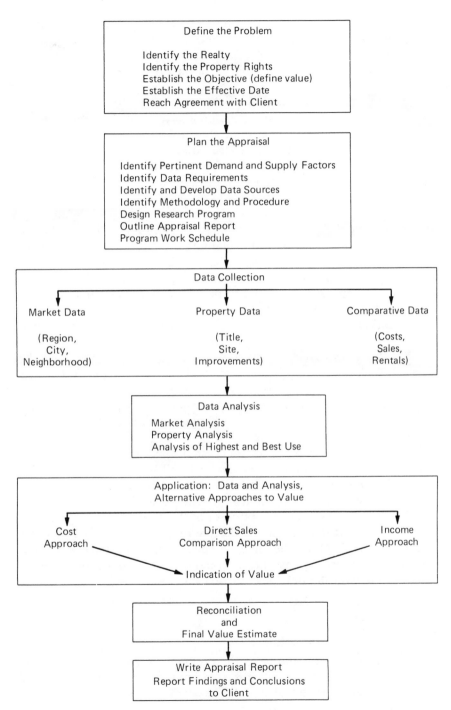

Figure 3–1. The Appraisal Process (Appraisal Framework)

particularly important, because it provides an identification of the realty that is universally accepted and understood. Appraisers must know where to go to obtain this legal description, and they should understand the various methods of property description employed in this identification.

Identification of the property rights or interests to be appraised in essence refers to the segment of the bundle of rights to be appraised. The appraiser should never assume that it will be the unencumbered fee simple estate. This should be cleared carefully with the client. An unequivocal identification is required so that there can be no mistake, such as appraising the wrong estate or interests.

The ojective of any appraisal is to estimate value. Establishing the nature of the specific appraisal problem involves identifying what value is to be estimated. This information must come from the client, although the appraiser can be helpful in explaining the alternatives in terms of what the client wants. The definition of the particular value to be estimated, its component parts, and its requirements will serve as a guide to the approaches that are to be taken. It will also help identify the data that will be required in order to estimate the defined value. Since market value is most commonly sought, the appraiser should have the definition of market value well in mind.

The effective date of the appraisal also usually comes from the client. It is an important fact to obtain early in the assignment, because it establishes the market conditions in terms of which the value estimate is to be made. This, in turn, indicates what types of information are necessary for an effective estimate of value and where they should be sought.

Once the problem to be solved is established, the appraiser should indicate to the client approximately what will be involved in carrying out the assignment to estimate the value. An indication of the probable time required to complete the assignment, as well as the fee, can be provided by the experienced appraiser at this time. A final agreement as to the fee and timing may be deferred until the appraisal plan has been developed. Once the time of delivery and fee have been set, however, the appraiser has a professional and ethical obligation to meet the deadline with the best possible skills and analysis.

Plan the Appraisal

This is sometimes referred to as the preliminary survey and appraisal plan. The most efficient and effective approach to value estimation involves a systematic plan of action. The development of comprehensive checklists and data forms is a valuable adjunct to systematic appraisal analysis. In this way, appraisers will be able to economize on their time and effort. They must make decisions about the data needed and their sources, the personnel and other resources necessary to complete the assignment, the time schedule and work-flow chart, and the final fee.

These decisions are based on preliminary inspection of the subject property and competitive properties in its neighborhood, discussions with the client and other market participants, and a preliminary review of pertinent market data in the appraiser's files.

The components of an appraisal plan and the steps involved are:

1. Identify pertinent demand and supply factors.
2. Identify data requirements.
3. Identify and develop data sources.
4. Identify the appropriate methods and approaches to be employed.
5. Design the research program.
6. Outline the appraisal report.
7. Program the work schedule.

Both the nature of the value being sought (the objective of the appraisal) and the effective date of the appraisal (market conditions) will provide guidance to which demand and supply factors are important in the particular assignment. These factors will also be a function of the character of the property being appraised, the property rights being appraised, and the character of the market in which the property is located.

The identification of data requirements involves both background or market data, including money market information for analyzing terms of financing, and property data. The property data will include information about both the subject property and properties that are deemed to be comparable to it for purposes of analysis. The specific data required will depend on the value being sought, the appraisal date, the property rights being appraised, the character of the realty being appraised, and the nature of the market.

Simply knowing what information will be required for the appraisal analysis is not enough. The appraiser must identify the most reliable data sources in the market area and exploit them as fully as possible. Such procedure will also help economize on the appraiser's time and effort. All data used in the analysis must be correct, accurate, and verified. The most sophisticated analysis is meaningless unless it is based on accurate, reliable data. If secondary data are used, they must come from a thoroughly reliable source.

Data must also be available in sufficient quantity to meet reliability standards of the analytical tools employed. Small numbers (two, three, or four) of comparable sales, rentals, or costs are inadequate for most tools and procedures of appraisal analysis. One of the appraiser's continuing responsibilities is to maintain currency in the office data bank files. This means continual checking with data sources, even when no current assignment requires such information.

When the type of value to be estimated, the character of the property, and the character of the market are given, the appraiser can identify which approach or approaches to value estimation are logical in the particular assignment. With a thorough understanding of the characteristics of each of these approaches, appraisers can reinforce the preliminary estimate of data requirements. They will also be able to save time and effort when the character of the problem and of the property being appraised precludes the use of one or more appraisal methods. Logic, judgment, and experience must all come into play in making this determination.

Designing the research program involves setting out the details of the steps that are to be followed. Here, the use of critical path analysis or some other systematic planning technique can provide considerable savings of time and effort for the appraiser. Such a detailed research design will indicate the sequence in which data are to be gathered and analyzed. It will indicate what facts or quantities are needed before certain steps in the appraisal analysis can be undertaken. It will further indicate to appraisers what parts of the work can be delegated to subordinates and what information they must attempt to obtain from others. This process involves, in effect, a work plan, which should be adhered to as closely as possible, on the assumption that the proper sequence of activities has been identified in the plan.

Appraisers should also prepare an outline of the sequence in which the information will be presented to the client. This does not mean that the appraisers should prejudge or develop their conclusions in advance. Rather, the outline simply sets out the format for presentation of the data, the analysis, the findings, and the conclusions that are to be provided to the client.

Based upon the foregoing planning steps, the appraiser can now assign probable times to the sequence of steps to be followed. At this stage, appraisers can also assign priorities to the various steps, so that there will be an orderly flow of effort and data with minimal expenditure of time and effort.

Gather the Data

Once the data required to carry out the assignment and the sources of those data have been identified, appraisers and their staff must then gather the information in accordance with the detailed plan of procedure. Here, the existence of a programmed work schedule, possibly coupled with a work-flow or critical path chart, can enhance efficiency.

The sequence of data gathering should be in the order in which the data are required for analysis in the appraisal framework. The sequence will also be dictated by the probable sources of the best information. Back-up sources should be available, in the event that anticipated information is not available from the primary sources. A particularly important aspect of the data-gathering process is the verification of the data as they are gathered. Both professional standards of practice and public authorities (especially the courts) require that knowledge of market information be firsthand. Hearsay information is neither acceptable in court nor professionally defensible. The appraiser should verify information with one or more of the principals involved. This is especially true of market sales and market rental information. The source of information should be recorded in every instance, for inclusion in the appraisal report where appropriate and for future reference.

Through experience, appraisers will learn which sources of information are most likely to be fruitful for them and will be able to economize on sources of information. These should be the first priority sources to which they will go for data. In most instances, it will not be necessary to exploit every potential source.

Analyze the Data

After appropriate data have been gathered (not necessarily the end of the entire data-gathering process), the appraiser must subject the data to careful analysis in order to develop both findings and conclusions. Although the final objective of any appraisal analysis is to estimate defined value, a large number of intermediate findings and conclusions must be reached during the process. The analytical approach and techniques utilized in reaching these intermediate findings and conclusions are critical to an appropriate final estimate of value.

The appraiser should not assume, however, that any mathematical formula can be applied without the exercise of logic and judgment. There is no substitute for careful analysis tempered with the good judgment that comes from experience. Formal training and education in research design, market analysis, and appraisal techniques provide the appropriate foundation on which the appraiser can build a meaningful pattern of such experience. With a good educational foundation, appraisers can understand, benefit from, and apply their experience much more meaningfully to specific problems.

As noted previously, the sequence of the analysis should be related to the appraisal framework and the need for subsequent steps in the process. Based upon the characteristics of the property and the legal and economic environment in which the property is located, the appraiser must reach a conclusion of the highest and best use of the site. The site is valued as if it were vacant and available to be put to its highest and best use. The appraiser must also reach a conclusion about the highest and best use of the improved property. Unless a change of use is called for as a result of market and feasibility analysis, the existing improvement program will represent the highest and best use of the improved property. The appraiser must be prepared to justify both highest and best use conclusions. This process may require the appraiser to reevaluate the definition of the problem and review the client's objectives with the client in light of the conclusion(s) of highest and best use.

Following the identification of the pertinent factors of supply and demand at work in the current market and the gathering of appropriate data to analyze these factors effectively, the appraiser must reach conclusions about the influence of these factors and market forces on the value of the real estate in the competitive market area, on the value of residential properties in the neighborhood, and on the value of the subject property. Because all approaches to value estimation involve comparisons of other properties (termed *comparables*) with the subject property, it is necessary for the appraiser to identify carefully those salient, pertinent characteristics and features of the subject property which are most important in determining its value. Comparisons should be made in terms of these characteristics. Regression analysis may be helpful in making these determinations, in addition to the appraiser's experience with similar properties.

Combining the evaluation of area and neighborhood influences with the salient features of the subject property, the appraiser must then analyze data on comparable sales, comparable costs, and comparable rentals. This analysis provides a basis for the application of all appropriate approaches to value estimation. Each approach requires comparative analysis with alternative properties. The background analysis and property analysis together provide the basis for identifying what constitutes comparability in other properties for appraisal purposes.

Apply the Data and the Analysis

Three approaches to value estimation are potentially available to the appraiser in every appraisal assignment: the direct sales comparison approach (based on opportunity cost, the principle of substitution, and the principle of contribution); the cost approach (based on the principle of substitution, the principle of contribution, and the cost of production); and the gross rent multiplier or income capitalization approach (based on the principle of substitution, the principle of contribution or productivity, and anticipation).

The appraiser should consider each of these approaches in every residential appraisal, even though subsequent analysis may reveal that one or more of these approaches is inapplicable. Each approach offers insights into the forces affecting property value that the typical buyer may not appreciate. Each approach serves as a check on the others to aid in identifying and pinpointing any erroneous assumptions. The applicability of any approach in a given appraisal problem depends on the character of the problem, the type of property involved, the nature of the market, and the availability of required data of appropriate quality in sufficient quantity. (The approaches are discussed in greater detail in subsequent chapters.)

Direct Sales Comparison Approach. This approach is often referred to as the market data approach or the sales comparison approach. It is especially applicable to amenity properties, such as owner-occupied residences, when there is an active market with a substantial volume of good, reliable data. The steps in the direct sales comparison approach are:

1. Identify the pertinent value-determining characteristics of the subject property.
2. Find comparable, competitive properties, with similar characteristics, that have sold recently on the local market.
3. Ascertain the sales price, date of sale, and terms and conditions of sale for each property. All such data must be verified.
4. Compare the comparables with the subject property in terms of the pertinent or salient characteristics of the subject property.
5. Measure the market difference for each characteristic on which the comparable properties differ from the subject property. Adjust the comparable sales to the subject property.
6. Estimate the adjusted sales price for each comparable property. This is the estimated price at which the comparable property would have sold if it had possessed the identical characteristics as the subject property at the time of sale.
7. Reconcile the adjusted sales prices of the comparable properties to an indication of the market value of the subject property via this direct sales comparison approach.

Gross Rent Multiplier (GRM) Analysis. This form of analysis is based on the productivity of the property. It is especially applicable to income-producing properties, but is also appropriate in an active rental market for residential properties. The residential gross rent multiplier is the ratio between sales price and monthly unfurnished rental for comparable properties. Gross rent multiplier analysis is applicable when there are sufficient numbers of comparable properties rented on the current market and when an adequate volume of reliable, verified data is available for comparable rental properties that have recently sold on the local market. The steps in GRM analysis are:

1. Find comparable rental properties in the same market that sold recently and, preferably, were rented at the time of sale.
2. Calculate the gross rent multiplier for each comparable sales property by dividing monthly unfurnished rental into sales price.
3. Reconcile the gross rent multipliers obtained for the comparable properties into an indicated gross rent multiplier for the subject market and, hence, the subject property.
4. Find current monthly unfurnished rentals of property similar to the subject property in the same market area.
5. Reconcile the comparable rentals (via adjustment analysis) to indicate the monthly market unfurnished rental of the subject property. Multiple the monthly market unfurnished rental for the subject property by the monthly gross rent multiplier for the subject property to obtain an indicated market value of the subject property via this gross rent multiplier analysis.

Cost Approach. This approach is based upon cost of production. It is especially applicable for new or proposed construction that represents the highest and best use of the site. It is also frequently applicable in estimating the market value of unique or special-purpose properties, especially when there is little or no sales information in an inactive market. The steps in the cost approach are:

1. Estimate the site value as if the site were vacant and available to be put to its highest and best use. This is usually done through direct sales comparison analysis.
2. Estimate the reproduction cost new of major buildings.
3. Estimate accrued depreciation or diminished utility experienced by the major buildings as of the valuation date.
4. Deduct accrued depreciation (diminished utility) from reproduction cost new in order to estimate the present worth (remaining utility or contribution) of major buildings.

5.   Estimate depreciated reproduction cost new of accessory buildings and site improvements.
6.   Add estimated depreciated reproduction cost new of accessory buildings and site improvements to estimated depreciated reproduction cost new of major buildings in order to estimate present worth (contribution) of all improvements.
7.   Add estimated depreciated reproduction cost new of all improvements to estimated site value to reach an indication of the market value of the subject property via the cost approach.

Final Value Estimate

The data program, data analysis, and application of the appropriate approaches to value estimation should all be reviewed by the appraiser. The estimates of market value from the several approaches applied are then reconciled into one final value estimate. Most appraisal assignments require the appraiser to indicate a single (most probable) market value figure. This is achieved by combining an evaluation of the applicability of the alternative approaches to the problem and to the property at hand with an evaluation of the quality and reliability of the data available and used. In some instances, it is also appropriate for the appraiser to indicate the range within which market value most probably falls.

The estimate of market value should be rounded to an appropriate level, because an unrounded figure indicates a degree of accuracy or precision that simply is not present in an estimate. The final value estimate is never developed by averaging the value indications derived from each of the approaches utilized. Reconciliation and final value estimation are considered in greater detail in Chapter 14.

*Write the Appraisal Report (Report Findings
and Conclusions to the Client)*

The written appraisal report is the culmination of the appraiser's art and skill. It should communicate effectively and convincingly the procedures used by the appraiser in reaching the final estimate of value. It should lead the reader inevitably to the same conclusion reached by the appraiser, given the data and the analysis provided in the report. The appraisal report should be capable of standing alone as a convincing, logical document.

Summary

Value is a price that would tend to prevail under stipulated market conditions. Value and price are synonymous in urban land economic analysis, but they are different in appraisal analysis. Value in use is based on productivity (anticipated future benefits). Value in exchange is based on the capacity of an economic good to command other goods in exchange. Market value is an example of value in exchange.

Value is a relative concept, requiring comparison with alternatives that are available to the potential purchaser on the open market. The estimation of value involves forecasting future benefits from the ownership of the real estate and the reactions of the market to those anticipated future benefits. Real estate valuation requires consideration of real estate as a physical asset, a legal entity (property rights), and a financial investment. Because of the variability of market forces, the date as of which a value estimate applies is a critical consideration in any value estimate.

Market value estimation involves the application of market analysis. To carry out this market analysis effectively, the appraiser must identify the submarket in which the property is operative, the characteristics of the typical purchaser, and pertinent supply and demand factors affecting the value of the subject property. The process of value estimation moves from general market or background analysis to more specific property analysis. The development of good, reliable, verified data from appropriate data sources is crucial to good appraisal analysis.

The appraisal framework or process is a systematic, logical program of steps for the appraiser to follow in order to achieve a defensible conclusion of market value. Every appraisal or valuation problem is essentially a research project. It should be planned and carried out accordingly. The steps in the appraisal framework are:

1. Define the problem.
2. Plan the appraisal.
3. Gather required and necessary market and property data.
4. Analyze the data.
5. Apply the data and analysis to develop preliminary indications of value via appropriate and applicable approaches.
6. Develop a final value estimate via reconciliation of value indications.
7. Write the appraisal report; report findings and conclusions to the client.

Appraisers must understand the rationale underlying each of the three alternative approaches potentially available to them. Each has its uses and applications as well as its limitations. Income capitalization is readily applicable to the valuation of residential amenity property.

Notes

1. Boyce, Byrl N., ed., *Real Estate Appraisal Terminology,* rev. ed. (Cambridge, Mass.: Ballinger [Joint publication of the American Institute of Real Estate Appraisers and Society of Real Estate Appraisers], 1981), p. 251.

2. Ibid., p. 250.

3. Ibid., p. 252.

4. Ibid.

5. Ibid., pp. 126–127.

6. Ibid., p. 234.

7. Ibid., p. 59.

8. Ibid., p. 133.

9. See Ibid., p. 23, for a definition of the principle of balance.

10. See Ibid., p. 236, for a definition of this concept of surplus productivity.

11. See Ibid., pp. 87 and 160, for definitions of economic rent and market rent.

12. Ibid., pp. 44–45.

13. Ibid., p. 14.

Suggested Readings

American Institute of Real Estate Appraisers. *The Appraisal of Real Estate,* 8th ed. Chicago: American Institute of Real Estate Appraisers, 1983, chapters 2, and 3.

Bloom, George F., and Harrison, Henry S. *Appraising the Single Family Residence.* Chicago: American Institute of Real Estate Appraisers, 1978, chapters 2 and 3.

Bloom, George F.; Weimer, Arthur M.; and Fisher, Jeffrey D. *Real Estate,* 8th ed. New York: John Wiley & Sons, 1982, chapters 11 and 12.

Boyce, Byrl N., ed. *Real Estate Appraisal Terminology,* rev. ed. Cambridge, Mass.: Ballinger (Joint publication of the American Institute of Real Estate Appraisers and Society of Real Estate Appraisers), 1981.

Everett, E. Roger, and Kinnard, William N., Jr. *A Guide to Appraising*

Apartments, 5th ed. Chicago: Society of Real Estate Appraisers, 1979, chapters 2 and 3.

Kinnard, William N., Jr. *Income Property Valuation.* Lexington, Mass.: Lexington Books, D.C. Heath, 1971, chapters 2 and 3.

Ratcliff, Richard U. *Valuation for Real Estate Decisions.* Santa Cruz, Calif.: Democrat Press, 1972, chapters 1–4.

Smith, Halbert C. *Real Estate Appraisal.* Columbus, Ohio: Grid, 1976, chapter 1.

Smith, Halbert C.; Tschappat, Carl J.; and Racster, Ronald L. *Real Estate and Urban Development,* 3rd ed. Homewood, Ill.: Richard D. Irwin, 1981, chapter 3.

Wendt, Paul F. *Real Estate Appraisal: Review and Outlook.* Athens: University of Georgia Press, 1974, chapters 1, 2, and 9.

4 Financing Single-Family Residences

Key Terms

ADS (annual debt service)   Periodic mortgage payments that have been annualized.

b Symbol for balance outstanding on the mortgage note.

Buydown   A reduction in the interest rate on the mortgage, typically paid by the seller/developer/builder but often passed on to the buyer in whole or in part via an increase in sales price.

Cash equivalency   The market value of notes or other securities that cannot be sold at their face amount.

Discount point   A charge of $1 per $100 of mortgage funds extended.

ITAO (installment to amortize one)   A compound discount factor used to identify the periodic level payment required to amortize a given mortgage amount at a specified interest rate over a specified period of time.

Lien   A claim against a property when the property serves as security for payment of a debt.

m Symbol for loan-to-value ratio; V_m/V_o.

Mortgage   A legal document representing the pledge of property as security for the repayment of debt under specified terms and conditions.

Mortgagee   The lender.

Mortgagor   The borrower.

R_m Symbol for the mortgage constant; ADS $\div V_m$ or ITAO (monthly) $\times$ 12.

V_m Symbol for value of a mortgage; the principal amount of a mortgage.

V_o Symbol for value of the total property.

Y_m Symbol for interest rate on a mortgage, typically expressed as an annual rate.

Yield   The effective return on investment, typically expressed as an annual rate (e.g., the interest rate on a mortgage, the equity yield rate on an equity investment, and/or the discount rate on total property investment).

Most real estate transactions involve the use of borrowed funds. This occurs either because the purchaser rarely has sufficient cash available to pay the full purchase price, or because the purchaser has alternative uses for some of the available cash that are expected to be more profitable than the cost of paying for borrowed money. This latter consideration represents the concept of leverage, which is discussed later in this chapter. Borrowed funds cost the borrower a price. This price is called interest, which is rent for the use of money.[1] As the price of money (interest) varies, the relative attractiveness of borrowing to help pay for real estate purchases also varies. Both cost and the availability of borrowed funds have a direct and measurable impact on the prices paid for real estate on the market, because borrowing costs add to purchase price and to the cost of retaining the benefits or amenities of ownership.

Since market prices are important indicators of value, the costs of borrowing money and the availability of loan funds are also important influences on value. The appraiser must therefore have a good working knowledge of mortgage markets and of the broader money and capital markets, of which mortgage markets constitute one part. The operations of money and capital markets, and of mortgage markets, influence real estate prices, the volume of real estate activity, and ultimately real estate values. They do so primarily by determining the costs and availability of borrowed funds, especially for residential real estate.

Money and Capital Markets

Money or accumulated wealth is an economic good. It is exchanged for other goods or for future claims to money on markets in exactly the same way another good is exchanged. It has a price, and that price fluctuates with the forces of supply and demand. Money is "any generally accepted medium of exchange and unit of account."[2] Its primary function is to serve as a medium of exchange or yardstick in terms of which values of all other goods and services are measured. It is also termed stored-up purchasing power, because the owner of money has claims on goods and services in the future. Money has complete liquidity: the ability to convert an asset into cash or money promptly and at face value. Liquidity gives the owner of money the ability to acquire other assets quickly.

In the United States, money or the money supply consists of currency (coins and bills), demand deposits, NOW accounts or checking accounts, and certain short-term government bills and notes. "Near money" includes savings and time deposits and certain short-term government notes. Currency is actually only a small portion of the total money supply. Thus, paying cash usually consists of writing a check.

Money has two prices. The first is its purchasing power in terms of other goods and services (as indicated, for example, by the consumer price index) or, in international trade, its purchasing power in terms of other national currencies or gold. This price is the result of broad national and international market forces and affects prices sought by owner-sellers of real estate. The second price of money is the interest rate or loan rates charged for borrowing money. By lending money, a lender gives up the opportunity to put the money to other uses now (liquidity preference), as well as the opportunity to hold the money to take advantage of future opportunities (time preference). Interest is a charge levied by the lender to overcome liquidity preference and time preference.

Interest rates are determined, just as any other price, by the interaction of the forces of supply and demand on the market. They are also determined by expectations of future changes in purchasing power. When inflation is forecast, for example, interest rates will rise (especially on long-term loans that will not be repaid until well into the future). There is a general pattern of interest rates whereby more liquid loan instruments tend to command lower interest rates. Shorter-term loans also carry lower interest rates. Since commitments in real estate are both illiquid and long term because of the basic nature of real estate itself, interest rates on real estate loans (mortgages) tend to be relatively high. There is competition in money and capital markets for money to be put to almost an endless variety of uses. Real estate purchase and ownership is only one such use. Therefore, demand for mortgage loan funds is competing with alternative loan outlets, as well as equity investment outlets, on money markets.

The money supply can be increased by the activities of commercial banks, the Federal Reserve System, and monetary and fiscal operations of the U.S. Treasury. Such increases occur because commercial bank demand deposits constitute the largest component of the money supply. The commercial banking system needs to keep only a portion of its demand deposit liabilities on reserve. This is called the fractional reserve system. Commercial banks can expand their total demand deposits to a multiple of their reserves, subject to limitations and changes established by Federal Reserve and Treasury rules and policy actions. How much money is available for real estate lending at any time and at what price (interest rate) depends on the supply of loanable funds available and on the competition for long-term loan funds from other alternative uses.

Mortgage Markets

Mortgage markets are money or capital markets in which the price of loan funds for real estate is established, borrowers and lenders are brought together, and loan funds are allocated among alternative competing prospective borrowers. Price is set by the interactions of demand and supply for long-term loan funds, with real estate as security or collateral. The basic instrument for pledging the real estate as collateral is the mortgage or, in some jurisdictions, the deed of trust.

Characteristics of Mortgages (Deeds of Trust)

A *mortgage* is "a legal document pledging a described property for the performance of the repayment of the loan under certain terms and conditions."[3] A mortgage (or deed of trust) is thus the pledge of collateral (real estate) for the mortgage loan. The lender is the *mortgagee;* the borrower is the *mortgagor.* All of the requiements of legal documents must be met for the mortgage to be enforceable against the real estate. A mortgage loan is a financing instrument. An alternative to the mortgage loan is the land contract or installment sales contract.

Mortgages may be classified, by priority of claims or liens, as first mortgages or junior mortgages. The mortgage with first priority over all other mortgage claims is a first mortgage. All others are junior mortgages, with priority of claim usually indicated by a label, such as second mortgage, third mortgage, and so forth. In event of default and foreclosure, the first mortgage claim is satisfied entirely before the second mortgage claim receives anything, and so on.

The principal of the mortgage loan may be insured by the Federal Housing Administration (FHA) or a private mortgage insurer, or it may be guaranteed by the Veterans Administration (VA). Loss of principal by the lender is protected up to a specified limit. The net result is that lenders are willing to make loans on terms more favorable to borrowers, or sometimes are willing to make loans at all, because the risk of loss of principal is substantially reduced. Any loan that is not insured or guaranteed by a government agency is called a conventional mortgage loan, although conventional mortgage loans may be insured by a private mortgage insurer.

Historically, most mortgage loans in the United States were straight-term loans, with only interest payable over the term of the loan and the entire principal due and payable at the end. Since 1934, nearly all residential and most nonresidential mortgage loans are amortized; that is, a portion of principal is repaid by contract periodically over the term of the loan. If the entire principal is repaid along with interest on the outstanding balance over the contract term, the loan is said to be fully amortized. If only part of the principal is repaid, it is a partially amortized loan, with a remaining balloon payment to be made at the end.

When a seller takes back a mortgage as part payment for the property in lieu of cash, this mortgage is called a purchase-money mortgage. Credit is extended by the seller, but no money is exchanged to the extent of the purchase-money mortgage loan. This differs from a loan made by a third-party lender, in which the seller receives the amount of the purchase price in cash.

Other types of mortgages are usually classified by type of collateral. *Construction or building loans* are short-term loans to finance construction, with or without a take-out commitment for permanent financing. *Blanket mortgages* encompass several properties under one mortgage. This type of mortgage is common in subdivisions. Usually, individual properties are released as they are sold and as a corresponding portion of the loan is paid off. *Open-end mortgages* are those in which the loan amount may be increased, on specified terms, for improvement of the securing property. *Package mortgages* cover equipment and appliances as well as the realty. In a *participation mortgage,* more than one lender (mortgagee) is at risk on the same loan. If a purchaser buys a property and assumes the responsibility of the guarantor of the unpaid balance of the mortgage, such a buyer is said to have *assumed* the existing mortgage. If the original mortgagor remains liable on the note, then the purchaser is said to buy the property subject to an existing mortgage loan (sometimes referred to as a *simple assumption*).

A loan under which the amount actually advanced by the lender is less than the contract amount the borrower agrees to repay (and debt service payments are contracted to be paid) is said to have been *discounted.* The discount is expressed as a percentage of the nominal or contract amount, measured in terms of points. A *point* is 1 (one) percent of the nominal principal. The calculation and analysis of points charged on loans is illustrated in detail later in this chapter.

Mortgage Loan Terms (Terms of Lending)

Mortgage loans are long-term contractual obligations to repay a specified principal amount by the end of a specified period of time, plus interest on the outstanding balance at the beginning of each interest-paying period. Whereas the mortgage interest rate is an obvious cost to the borrower, other terms of lending also determine the cost of financing and the cost or burden of carrying the debt. The pattern or package of mortgage loan terms determines the feasibility of any financing proposal. This is because the periodic payments to be made by the borrower must be supportable by the borrower's income (in the case of residential or amenity properties) or by the net income produced by the real estate (in the case of income-producing real estate).

The *mortgage interest rate* is the most obvious cost of borrowing. The higher the interest rate, all other things being equal, the higher the total cost of borrowing to the mortgagor, and vice versa. Mortgage interest rates represent the lender's judgment and evaluation of the risks of mortgage lending, taking into account the mortgagor's income or property income, the present and probable future value of the property, the forecast future changes in purchasing power of the dollar, and alternative outlets for the lender's funds (opportunity costs). Mortgage interest rates, as any type of interest rate, are determined competitively on the market and include compensation to the lender for time preference, liquidity preference, management, and risk.

The *contract rate* or *coupon rate* is the nominal rate on the mortgage loan. The *effective rate* is the rate that is actually paid on the amount actually loaned. A 20-year mortgage loan (monthly payments), for example, with a nominal interest rate of 12 percent discounted six points (94 percent of loan funds advanced) has an effective interest rate of 13 percent if the loan is held to maturity. If the note is paid off sooner, the effective rate is higher.

The ratio of the mortgage loan to the (value of security pledged) is the *loan-to-value ratio*.[4] This translates for the borrower to the down payment requirement as a percentage or dollar amount. Generally, buyers try to purchase as much real estate as their cash equity or down payment will permit. The higher the loan-to-value ratio, the less the purchaser must put down as equity, and therefore the more real estate the equity will buy (assuming there is sufficient income to carry the loan). An $80,000 residence with a 70 percent loan requires a $24,000 down payment; with an 80 percent loan-to-value ratio, the down payment is only $16,000. The higher the loan-to-value ratio, however, the greater the periodic payment (debt service) will be.

Maturity on a loan is the time period over which the loan is outstanding and by the end of which the loan must be repaid in full. The longer the maturity, the less the periodic payments (debt service) to carry the loan are, but the more the total amount repaid will be. An $80,000 20-year-level-monthly-payment loan at 12 percent, for example, has monthly payments of $880.87. Over 20 years, the borrower will pay a total of $211,408.80 to repay the loan in full. If the contract maturity is extended to 30 years, monthly payments are reduced to $822.88, but the total amount repaid becomes $296,236.80.

Amortization is "the process of retiring debt or recovering a capital investment through scheduled, systematic repayments of principal."[5] In essence, this refers to the manner in which the principal amount of the loan is repaid. Loans may be nonamortized, fully amortized, or partially amortized. Nonamortized (term) loans call for payment of interest only over the loan maturity, with principal repayable in one lump sum at the end. Debt service is usually lowest under this arrangement, but this form of amortization is rarely used in residential financing.

Fully amortized loans call for periodic payments of both principal and interest on the outstanding balance at the beginning of each period over the entire maturity of the loan. The loan is fully repaid at maturity. The periodic payments can be monthly, quarterly, semiannually, or annually. Monthly payments are most common for residential loans. *Level payment loans* call for equal periodic payments of principal and interest, with the amount of interest declining each period and the amount of principal repaid increasing each period (total amount per period remains constant). This type of loan is most commonly used for residential mortgage loans. Another form of a fully amortized loan is the *constant principal repayment loan*. In the constant principal repayment loan, the same amount of principal is amortized each period. Interest payments decline, so that each periodic payment is smaller. This type of loan is used mostly for financing land or agricultural purchases.

Partially amortized loans call for less amortization per period than do fully amortized loans, with the result that a lump sum (balloon) payment is due at maturity. Suppose, for example, that an $80,000 level-monthly-payment loan at 12 percent interest has a contract maturity of 20 years but that payments are based upon 30-year amortization. Monthly payments would be $822.88, but the balloon payment at the end of 20 years would be $57,355.54.

In some instances, the underlying rationale of certain types of loans, such as the graduated payment loan, is modified to create specifically and consciously a situation in which the periodic payment is insufficient to cover even the interest payments. The differential is added (at compound interest) to the amount of the loan. At some time in the future, the larger amount of loan is due and payable. Frequently, the time period over which such negative amortization is permitted is relatively brief or the amount of negative amortization is limited to some percentage of the original principal amount. This type of loan does allow for lower debt service to the buyer-borrower, but it also increases the investment risk(s) of the lender.

Debt service is the periodic payment of interest and principal required to amortize a mortgage loan. In residential mortgage financing, it is also called the *carrying charge* (usually monthly). Annual debt service (ADS) is used in the analysis and appraisal of income-producing properties. The mortgage constant is annual debt service expressed as a percentage of the original principal amount. An $80,000, 30-year, level monthly payment mortgage loan at 12 percent, for example, has monthly payments of $822.88. Annual debt service is $9,874.56. The mortgage constant is $9,874.56 divided by $80,000, which equals .1234, or 12.34 percent $(R_m = \text{ADS} \div V_m)$.

Sources of Mortgage Funds

Most mortgage loans are made by institutional lenders. Until recently, individuals and government were only minor sources of mortgage funds. Individuals (mostly sellers) have increased in importance as lenders in the sale of their property by taking back a note from the buyer as partial payment for the property. That note is secured by a *lien* on the property; in many jurisdictions it is referred to as a *purchase-money mortgage*. The rationale for such loans is that sellers get their price, borrowers are able to support the debt service associated with the financing, and sellers receive a rate of interest that, while below the institutional lender's market level, is nevertheless as high or possibly higher than rates that the seller-lender could obtain by investing the funds elsewhere. Such seller financing is frequently a junior lien, to supplement either an assumption of existing financing or new financing from an institution. This and other issues are discussed later in this chapter. Still, most mortgage loans are made by institutional lenders. There is a difference between the volume of originations by type of lender and mortgage holdings by type of lender, because mortgage bankers and mortgage companies originate loans to be sold in groups to institutional lenders or quasi-governmental agencies (FNMA, GNMA, FHLMC) in what is called the secondary mortgage market.

The major sources of residential loan funds are savings and loan associations (also sometimes called cooperative banks), mutual savings banks, commercial banks, mortgage bankers and mortgage companies, and life insurance companies. Other sources include individuals, government agencies, corporations, trusts (including Real Estate Investment Trusts), credit unions, endowment funds, and pension funds.

Characteristics and Functions of Mortgage Markets

Loan originations occur on the *primary mortgage market*. The *secondary mortgage market* refers to exchanges (sales or purchases) of existing mortgage loans. There is considerable federal government influence in the secondary market for residential mortgages through the market support of FHA-insured and VA-guaranteed loans by the Federal National Mortgage Association (FNMA), the Government National Mortgage Association (GNMA), and the Federal Home Loan Mortgage Corporation (FHLMC).

Mortgage markets are not highly organized or physically concentrated. They are highly stratified by geographic area or location, by property type, by borrower type (and risk rating), and by size of loan. Demand comes from the purchase and/or refinancing of real estate; supply is determined primarily by the volume of institutional savings and the attractiveness of available competitive outlets for long-term loan funds.

The functions of mortgage markets are the same as those of any market: to facilitate exchanges of mortgage loan funds; to set prices (interest rates) for mortgage loan funds; to allocate mortgage loan funds among competing alternative outlets (borrowers) on the basis of price (yield to lenders); and to adjust supply to demand. Mortgage markets generally do a better job of carrying out their function than real estate markets do, despite the problems of scarcity when competing investment outlets are relatively attractive. This is partly because there are fewer, better informed, more rational market participants, and partly because mortgage notes tend to be more readily transferable and less illiquid than the real estate underlying them.

Although the federal government does not participate directly as a lender to any significant extent, its actions and policies influence mortgage market activities in significant ways. General monetary and interest rate policy helps determine the availability and cost of funds in the economy. FHA insurance and VA guarantees, and the terms on which they are available, help influence the flow and terms of residential mortgage loan funds.

Support of FNMA, GNMA, and FHLMC secondary mortgage market activities influences the availability of terms and loan funds for institutional lenders, especially thrifts and commercial banks. Government at all levels provides direct competition for mortgage funds on mortgage markets when it runs a deficit and must borrow. Government regulation of the policies of financial institutions also influences the availability of mortgage loan funds.

*Relationship of Mortgage Market Activities
to Real Estate Prices and Values*

Since nearly all real estate transactions use borrowed mortgage loan funds and most require it, the availability of mortgage funds for lending has two determining influences on real estate transactions. First, transactions either may not occur or may take place more slowly at reduced prices if adequate mortgage loan funds are not available. Second, the cost of financing reflected in debt service will influence the price paid.

When money is both readily available and inexpensive, this is reflected in an active sales market. Prices tend to be firm but not increasing, at least for financing reasons. When money is relatively tight and expensive, sales activity declines and residential prices soften. Some prices are higher for income-producing properties. When money is relatively plentiful but expensive, prices tend to be higher. These tendencies are conditioned by consensus views about how brief or prolonged current mortgage market conditions are expected to be.

Properties with existing mortgages that can be assumed and that carry terms more favorable than current market loan terms may tend to sell at a premium because debt service is proportionally lower. Market price is an indicator as well as a reflection of value. A financial package that is at variance with market terms of lending can and does influence market price directly. In the development of a market value estimate for a subject property, an adjustment for *cash equivalency* may be required in the market price of comparable properties to account for this financing phenomenon. The financial package associated with the subject property is of no consequence, however, in the estimation of market value, although it has a potentially significant impact on market price.

Leverage is "the use of fixed cost funds [borrowed funds] to acquire an income-producing asset in the expectation of a higher rate of return on the equity investment as a result."[6] The application of this concept occurs primarily in the valuation and analysis of income-producing real estate. Residential property produces amenity benefits to the owner-occupant, so that the equity down payment is not usually approached or evaluated as an investment. Nevertheless, a simple example will illustrate the operation of leverage or trading on the equity.

Suppose that an income property is purchased for $100,000. It is producing, and is forecast to continue to produce, a net return on the investment of $15,000 per year. This is a 15 percent rate of return on the investment. If purchasers pay $100,000 cash equity for the property, the rate of return on the equity investment is also 15 percent. Now, if purchasers can borrow $75,000 (75 percent) at 12 percent interest, they contract to pay $9,000 interest per year, assuming a straight loan for simple illustration purposes. The leverage ratio (total investment divided by equity investment) is 4:1; that is, purchasers have $4 (total) invested and working to earn 15 percent for every $1 of equity invested. The equity earnings are then $6,000 on an equity investment of $25,000, or 24 percent.

So long as the rate earned on borrowed funds is higher than the rate paid for the borrowed funds, leverage or trading on equity is successful. Suppose, however, that the property income on the investment drops to $10,000. Contract interest is still $9,000, so that the return on the $25,000 equity is now $1,000, or 4 percent. This is less than the 10 percent the property is earning, since 75 percent of the property investment requires 12 percent payment by contract (mortgage note). Thus, the use of leverage does carry risks, which are borne entirely by the equity investor.

Analysis of Financing Terms

Most appraisal or valuation assignments call for an estimate of market value. Many others call for an estimate of most probable selling price as well as market value. In a normal market in equilibrium, there should be no difference between these two estimates, either as concepts or as quantities. In markets in which credit availability is in disequilibrium and loan terms vary significantly (seller financing, buydowns, assumption of below market loans, wraparounds, and other subsidized financing terms), these two measures can and do differ.

More basic to the problem of market value estimation is the distinction to be made between price (in addition to market price) and value. Cash equivalent price, time-adjusted sales price, and adjusted sales price (indicating value of the subject) are all price concepts that are applicable to and derived from market price of comparable sales as a result of a series of adjustments that lead to an estimate of market value. Moreover, most probable selling price in markets in disequilibrium can represent an adjustment from the benchmark (market value), generally reflecting some form of subsidized (nonmarket) financing whose benefits are most often reflected by a premium added to a market value estimate.

Adjustments to market price for financing differences in estimating market value and adjustments to market value in the estimation of most probable selling price may be extracted from the market; however, an understanding of the discounting process is also necessary for analyzing and further understanding these market-extracted adjustments. In instances where market-extracted adjustments are unavailable, unclear, or inconsistent, the discounting process can be especially helpful. It may be the only tool available to the appraiser in developing the various scenarios that represent appropriate adjustment for cash equivalency or for the movement from the estimated market value to forecast market price (most probable selling price under given financing terms), as well as in calculating the effective rate associated with subsidized financing that is extracted from the market. *Discounting* is defined as follows:

> A concept of time preference which holds that future income or benefits are worth less than the same income or benefits now, and that they decrease in value systematically as the time for their receipt is further deferred into the future. In appraisal analysis, discounting is the arithmetic procedure of applying a specific rate (usually) derived from the market to the anticipated future income stream in order to develop a present worth estimate.[7]

There are two basic sets of compound interest/compound discount factors. The first set (compound interest or future worth factors) is used to derive a future sum or value from the present. The second set (compound discount or present worth factors) is used to derive a present worth estimate from future cash flows and/or lump sum payments (reversions). The following presentations concentrate on only one compound discount factor—the installment to amortize one (ITAO). There are several ways in which this factor can be utilized to analyze the impact of subsidized financing. It should also be noted that the other five compound interest/compound discount functions may be easily derived from the installment to amortize one.

Installment to Amortize One (ITAO)
and the Mortgage Constant (R_m)

The installment to amortize one (ITAO) identifies the periodic payment necessary to amortize fully a specified loan amount over a finite time period, given the return (interest) requirement of the lender. This factor is applied to the principal amount loaned via multiplication to arrive at the period payment. Appendix B contains a set of tables of installments to amortize one (monthly ITAO) for 1 to 30, 35, and 40 years. The tables also represent a range of rates from 5 percent to 20 percent in half-percent increments. Also derived from the ITAO and incorporated within the same tables is the mortgage constant (R_m).

The *mortgage constant* is "the total annual payments of principal and interest (annual debt service) on a mortgage with a level-payment amortization schedule, expressed as a percentage of the initial principal amount of the loan."[8] The mortgage constant may also be derived directly from compound interest/compound discount tables by annualizing the ITAO (i.e., assuming monthly amortization, one would simply multiply the monthly ITAO by 12). Quarterly or semiannual installments to amortize one may also be converted to mortgage constants by annualizing them. The constant for quarterly payments, for example, would be the quarterly ITAO times four, and the constant for semiannual payments would be the ITAO times two. As noted in the definition of a mortgage constant, this same relationship (ratio) may be established by dividing the annual debt service (ADS) on the mortgage by the initial amount of the loan (V_m).

The foregoing suggests three basic models that may be used in analyzing a variety of loan terms, whether they be subsidized or nonsubsidized:

$$\text{Periodic (monthly) payment} = V_m \times \text{ITAO} \qquad (4.1)$$

$$\text{ITAO} \times 12 = R_m \qquad (4.2)$$

$$V_m = \text{ADS} \div R_m \qquad (4.3)$$

As a continuing example, assume an $80,000 loan at 12 percent interest, to be payable over 30 years in monthly payments. Referring to the tables in Appendix B (12 percent, 30 years), the ITAO of 0.010286 is obtained. Utilizing equation 4.1, the periodic payment, $822.88 ($80,000 × 0.010286) is determined. The mortgage constant (R_m) is obtainable from the same table or from equation 4.2. Utilizing equation 4.2, a mortgage constant (R_m) of 0.123432 (0.010286 × 12) is obtained. Still another method of obtaining the mortgage constant would be to annualize the monthly payment ($822.88 × 12), providing an annual debt service of $9,874.56. A slight rearrangement of equation 4.3 provides the means to calculate R_m via dividing the annual debt service by the value of the mortgage ($9,874.56 ÷ $80,000), resulting again in a constant of 0.123432.

For discussion purposes, refer to the installments to amortize one in table 4–1, which have been extracted from the tables in Appendix B. When interest rates are in the range of 10 percent or less, extending amortization terms can have a significant and measurable impact on debt service, frequently reducing it to levels that are supportable by the new buyer and acceptable to the lender. With rates in excess of 15 percent, however, and even in the 12 to 13 percent range, extending the loan term has little or no impact on debt service. This is illustrated vividly in table 4–1. As discussed later in this chapter, in the section on underwriting, increasing interest rates provide gaps between the amount the lender is willing to lend and the amount the borrower wishes to borrow (or is qualified to borrow). These gaps give rise to a variety of alternative forms of financing in order to effectuate property transfers. Also to be noted in table 4–1 is the fact that all installments to amortize one can be easily converted to mortgage constants (R_m) simply by multiplying each ITAO by 12. Either the ITAO or the R_m, or both, may be used (1) to determine the balance outstanding on a loan at any point in time over the term; (2) to determine the effect of changing interest rates on market value (versus book value) of the loan; or (3) to establish new debt service on variable rate mortgages after the imposition of a rate change.[9] Further, either the ITAO or the R_m may also be used to develop cash flow and reversion projections for discounted cash flow analysis and yield calculations.

Balance Outstanding (b)

Either the constant (R_m) or the installment to amortize one (ITAO) may be utilized to determine balance outstanding or balloon on any mortgage at any point in time during the life of that mortgage. The procedure is simply one of capitalizing periodic payments by the ITAO

Table 4–1
Installments to Amortize One (ITAO) at 10 Percent to 16 Percent Rates (in One-Point Increments) and 20-, 25-, and 30-Year Maturities

Interest Rate (Y_m)	ITAO at Maturity		
	20 Years	25 Years	30 Years
10%	0.009650	0.009087	0.008776
11%	0.010322	0.009801	0.009523
12%	0.011011	0.010532	0.010286
13%	0.011716	0.011278	0.011062
14%	0.012435	0.012038	0.011849
15%	0.013168	0.012808	0.012644
16%	0.013913	0.013589	0.013448

for the remaining term or annual debt service by the effective constant (i.e., the constant for the remaining term). Utilizing the continuing example, suppose that the $80,000, 12 percent loan written for 30 years is to balloon in 20 years. As noted above, monthly payments were $822.88 and annual debt service was calculated at $9,874.56.

Balance outstanding (b) at the end of 20 years would be determined by capitalizing the monthly payment at the ITAO for the remaining term ($822.88 ÷ 0.014347, the ITAO for 10 years at 12 percent). Alternatively, the annual debt service would be divided by the effective mortgage constant [$9,874.56 ÷ 0.172164 ($R_m$) for 10 years at 12 percent]. Both calculations result in the same balance outstanding (b)— $57,355.54. To calculate balance outstanding at any point in time, the first requirement is to determine periodic debt service according to the terms of the loan. The second step is to determine the ITAO at the same interest rate on the loan but for the remaining term. The final step in the process is to capitalize the periodic debt service by the ITAO for the remaining term.[10] Obviously, the same results will be obtained with multiples of the periodic debt service and of the installment to amortize one [i.e., annual debt service (ADS) and the mortgage constant (R_m)].

Book Value versus Market Value

As noted above, book value of a mortgage loan may be determined at any point in time according to the terms of the contract by capitalizing periodic debt service by the installment to amortize one for the remaining term. Because market interest rates may vary from the contract (nominal) rates on mortgage loans, market value at any point in time may be above or below book value, depending upon the relationship between market rates and contract rates. For the continuing example, assume that, 3 years into the loan, market rates have increased to 16 percent. To analyze the relationship between book value and market value, the first step would be to determine balance outstanding on the mortgage at the end of 3 years under the terms of the contract. That would be accomplished simply by dividing the $822.88 periodic debt service by the ITAO for 27 years at 12 percent (0.010414). The result is $79,016.71. Determining the market value of the loan at that point in time follows the same procedure, except that the periodic debt service is capitalized at the ITAO for 27 years at market rates. Thus, $822.88 capitalized at 0.013518 (ITAO at 16 percent for 27 years) results in a market value of $60,872.91. The discount from book value to market value in this instance is $18,143.80 ($79,016.71 − $60,872.91). In effect, the results of these calculations suggest that lenders can invest the market value of the loan at market rates and generate precisely the same income stream as that generated by the contract terms of the mortgage loan. Another way of looking at the calculation is that it indicates the amount of discount that lenders would have to accept if they were to sell the loan to yield 16 percent on the secondary market. Finally, the calculation also represents the range within which borrowers and lender might negotiate to retire the loan.

Discount Points/Buydowns

To accommodate the gap represented by the difference between what a borrower can qualify for and what is desired as a loan amount, the loan may be discounted or the interest rate may be bought down. Essentially, the calculation of either discount points or buydowns involves the same or a similar technique. Using the continuing example and assuming that current market rates are 14 percent, determining the amount of discount or the cost of the buydown is a matter of discounting periodic debt service at the ITAO at 14 percent for 30 years. The calculation would be $822.88 divided by 0.011849 (ITAO at 14 percent for 30 years), resulting in a market value of the loan of $69,447.21. The discount or buydown cost represented by this calculation is $10,552.79 ($80,000 − $69,447.21). Alternatively, the differential in payments ($125.04) on the mortgage note at market ($947.92) and those at contract ($822.88) capitalized at the ITAO for 14 percent over 30 years (0.011849) also results in an amount of $10,552.79. By either method, the calculations result in 13.2 discount points ($10,552.79 ÷ $80,000) or a buydown cost of $10,552.79.

Normally, discount points are expressed as a part of the loan terms, generally without the benefit of the foregoing calculation. In addition, the effective yield, given the discount points, is normally calculated as if it were spread over the entire maturity of the loan. In other words, the calculation represents a yield to maturity calculation. Obviously, if the loan is paid off prior to maturity, then the yield to the lender is enhanced. This calculation is considered later, in the section on analysis of yield.

Although examples of buydowns over the entire term of the loan do exist, they do not represent the norm. Buydowns are usually extended over a 1- to 5-year time frame, with 3 years as the most common interval. The calculation of such a buydown is no more complicated, however, than the calculation presented earlier. It does require calculating the differential payment between market and contract rates, and capitalizing that differential at the ITAO representing the market rate and the term of the buydown. Again utilizing the continuing example, the differential between payments at market and payments at contract is $125.04. The rate at which that differential is to be capitalized is the ITAO for 3 years at 14 percent (0.034178). The resulting cost of the buydown for this particular calculation, then, is $3,658.49.

Alternative Mortgage Terms

Lenders seek to shift market risks from themselves to their borrowers by calling for adjustable or variable interest rates in their residential real estate loan contracts. The variation in rates may be contractually specified or may be related to some market index. Usually, payments vary as rates change; sometimes, loan balances or amortization terms are adjusted. The specifics vary, but the intent in all cases is the same: to protect lenders from the combined eroding effects of declining purchasing power of the dollar and increasing market interest rates obtainable on alternative investments.

Although their motivations may be different, seller-lenders have also adopted variable mortgage loan terms in seller-financed property sales. The variable terms are often more subtle (i.e., renegotiable at some point in time in the future, such as 3 to 5 years) when the note balloons. These terms are often more favorable than alternative forms of financing at the outset. The potential for renegotiating terms under seller financing must always be considered in light of the possibility of refinancing the property under more traditional conditions (instruments and institutions). In any event, the methodology employed to determine the impact of new terms is essentially the same (i.e., determination of balance outstanding at some point in time and payments based upon that balance outstanding, determination of change in interest rate, and determination of the remaining contract term over which payments are to be made).

A significant point to remember in the analysis of variable or alternative mortgage terms is that those terms are fixed within some specified time frame. That means that analyzing them entails a series of calculations to be performed on short terms at fixed rates—essentially the same calculations already encountered on long-term, fixed-rate instruments. The analysis simply involves more calculations. Three alternative mortgage instruments have been selected for analysis here because they are representative of the broad range of instruments that are now available. Other existing mortgage instruments represent variations on a theme of each of those analyzed here, which, in turn, are all extensions of the long-term, fixed-rate instrument. The instruments analyzed here are the variable (adjustable) rate mortgage (VRM/ARM), the graduated payment mortgage (GPM), and the growing equity mortgage (GEM). Obviously, seller financing can also incorporate some of these same features.

Variable (Adjustable) Rate Mortgage (VRM/ARM)

With the proliferation of alternative mortgage instruments (AMIs) in recent years, there has been considerable confusion regarding differing terminology among seemingly similar financial packages. The generic term *adjustable rate mortgage* (ARM) has been adopted to encompass other mortgage loan forms that include such terms as *variable, rollover, renewable, reviewable,* and *renegotiable.* The ARM also encompasses other features, such as the method and frequency of rate changes, demand features on the note, assumability, and the like. For the following discussion, only the rate is varied to emphasize the necessary calculations for changes in periodic payment and balances outstanding, without consideration of those other features, which would only complicate the calculations unnecessarily.

Assume, for the sake of exposition, that the changes in interest rates (annually) over the next 4 years and the resulting changes in balance outstanding and periodic (monthly) payments on the continuing mortgage example, are as shown in table 4–2.

Graduated Payment Mortgage (GPM)

It is frequently anticipated that buyers will have increasing incomes with the passage of time. As a result, various forms of real estate debt arrangements are made to allow for relatively low monthly payments in the early years of the loan, with subsequent increases either on a contractual schedule or based upon market fluctuations in interest rates. This approach produces higher debt service payments in the future, when the purchaser-borrower is presumably better able to support those higher payments.

In some instances, the underlying rationale of the graduated payment mortgage (GPM) loan is modified to create specifically and consciously a situation in which debt service is insufficient to cover even interest payments (negative amortization). The differential is com-

Table 4–2
Variable (Adjustable) Rate Mortgage

Year	Principal Amount ($)[a]	Interest Rate and Term	Monthly Payment ($)	Balance Outstanding ($)[b]
1	80,000.00	12%, 30 yrs.	822.88	79,705.54
2	79,705.54	14%, 29 yrs.	946.58	79,491.10
3	79,491.10	17%, 28 yrs.	1,136.17	79,358.10
4	79,358.10	15%, 27 yrs.	1,009.99	79,121.82
5	79,121.82	12%, 26 yrs.	828.40	78,655,53

Calculations for monthly payment and balance outstanding:

Year	Monthly Payment	Calculation	Balance Outstanding (b)	Calculation
1	$822.88	$80,000 × .010286 (ITAO @ 12%, 30 yrs.)	$79,705.54	822.88 ÷ .010324 (ITAO) @ 12%, 29 yrs.)
2	$946.58	$79,705.54 × .011876 (ITAO @ 14%, 29 yrs.)	$79,491.10	946.58 ÷ .011908 (ITAO @ 14%, 28 yrs.)
3	$1,136.17	$79,491.10 × .014293 (ITAO @ 17%, 28 yrs.)	$79,358.10	1,136.17 ÷ .014317 (ITAO @ 17%, 27 yrs.)
4	$1,009.99	$79,358.10 × .012727 (ITAO @ 15%, 27 yrs.)	$79,121.82	1,009.99 ÷ .012765 (ITAO @ 15%, 26 yrs.)
5	$828.40	$79,121.82 × .010470 (ITAO @ 12%, 26 yrs.)	$78,655.53	828.40 ÷ .010532 (ITAO @ 12%, 25 yrs.)

[a]Principal amount is for beginning of year (BOY).
[b]Balance outstanding is for end of year (EOY).

pounded forward at market rates and is added to the amount of the loan. At some time in the future, the larger amount of loan is due and payable. Frequently, the time period over which negative amortization is permitted is relatively brief (3 to 5 years). Although negative amortization allows for lower debt service (typically, according to the buyer-borrower's ability to qualify) in the early years of the loan, it increases the investment risk(s) of the lender.

Assume, in the continuing example, that the borrower can qualify to pay only $700 per month but wishes to obtain an $80,000 mortgage loan at 12 percent interest with a 30-year maturity. Obviously, with required payments of $822.88 per month at the outset, the borrower is unable to meet even interest costs in the first year. The GPM can be utilized to accommodate the buyer-borrower by adding the difference (appropriately compounded forward) to the balance outstanding at the end of each period. The difference narrows over time as the borrower's payments are increased periodically by some specified contractual amount or rate of increase. This will continue until the contract payment meets or exceeds the payment required to amortize the note fully over the remaining term. For purposes of the following example, assume an annual 6 percent increase in payments. The contract payment schedule, required payments, amortization, and addition of the differential (negative amortization) are indicated in table 4–3.

In Table 4–3, the contract payments start at a base of $700 and increase annually by 6 percent. So long as the contract payment

Table 4–3
Graduated Payment Mortgage (GPM)

Year	Contract Payment	Required Payment[a]	Differential	b at Market Rates[b]	Future Worth Differential at Market Rates[c]	Adjusted b (b plus FW Differential)
1	$700.00	$822.88	$122.88	$79,705.54	$1,558.43	$81,263.97
2	742.00	838.97	96.97	80,934.79	1,229.82	82,164.61
3	786.52	851.72	65.20	81,786.06	826.90	82,612.96
4	833.71	860.33	26.62	82,170.96	337.61	82,508.57
5	883.73	863.86	—	—	—	—

[a]The required payment is a function of the adjusted balance outstanding (b) at the beginning of the year (BOY) times the ITAO at market for the remaining term:

Year	b (BOY)	ITAO @ 12%	Required Payment
1	$80,000.00	0.010286 (30 years)	$822.88
2	81,263.97	0.010324 (29 years)	838.97
3	82,164.61	0.010366 (28 years)	851.72
4	82,612.96	0.010414 (27 years)	860.33
5	82,508.57	0.010470 (26 years)	863.86

[b]The balance outstanding (b) at market rates at the end of the year (EOY) is a function of the required payment capitalized at the ITAO for the remaining term:

Year	Required Payment	ITAO @ 12%	b (EOY)
1	$822.88	0.010324 (29 years)	$79,705.54
2	838.97	0.010366 (28 years)	80,934.79
3	851.72	0.010414 (27 years)	81,786.06
4	860.33	0.010470 (26 years)	82,170.96
5	863.86		

[c]The future worth (FW) of the differential (negative amortization) that is added to the balance outstanding (b) to arrive at the adjusted balance outstanding is a function of the differential times the future worth of one per period factor (FW1/Per) at 12% for one year (12.682503):

Year	Differential	FW1/Per Factor	FW Differential at Market Rates
1	$122.88	12.682503	$1,558.43
2	96.97	12.682503	1,229.82
3	65.20	12.682503	826.90
4	26.62	12.682503	337.61

is below the required interest rate, there is negative amortization (i.e., the differential between payments is carried forward at compound interest and added to the balance outstanding on the loan). It is interesting to note that in year 4, some amortization does take place via the contract payment. In other words, the $833.71 payment in year 4 covers the interest requirement and makes some contribution to the amortization (reduction) of the outstanding debt.

It should also be noted that in year 5, the contract payment exceeds the required payment. Normally, the contract payment would be reduced to the required payment and the loan would be fully amortized over the remaining term. If the contract payment of $883.73 continues, then the instrument takes on the characteristic of a growing equity mortgage (GEM), discussed later (i.e., the remaining term will be reduced from 26 years to slightly more than 22 years because of the additional payments being made to reduce principal—approximately $20 per month). A further complication, which is not considered here but about which the reader should be aware, is the possibility of introducing variable market interest rates to this instrument—making it a graduated payment adjustable mortgage (GPAM).

Growing Equity Mortgage (GEM)

The growing equity mortgage (GEM) in its simplest form can be analyzed directly from ITAO tables (i.e., the reduced term can be determined directly or approximated by interpolation from the tables). In the continuing example, assume that the borrower can qualify for and wishes to pay $960.13 per month, rather than the $822.88 required to amortize the $80,000 loan over 30 years at 12 percent. In other words, the borrower wishes to apply an additional $137.25 to principal each month. Since the loan amount and interest remain constant and the periodic payment is increased, the term must be reduced. The amount of reduction in term can be determined from ITAO tables (in this instance, at 12 percent) by calculating the effective ITAO (i.e., the payment of $960.13 divided by $80,000—the original principal amount—or 0.012002). Thus, the increased payment of $137.25 monthly has reduced the loan balance so that it is paid in 15 years rather than in 30 years.

Obviously, there are many variations to this form of alternative mortgage instrument. The calculations are not as easily accomplished, however, although the concepts are essentially the same as those of the VRM and GPM. Again, for the sake of exposition, assume that payments on the standard loan package are to increase by 5 percent annually. Table 4–4 shows monthly payments, balance outstanding, and remaining term resulting from adjustment in the monthly payment.

The foregoing calculations are more cumbersome than difficult and are best handled with a financial calculator (preferably one that is programmable) or a properly programmed computer. In any event, they show that by applying the annual increase in monthly payments to principal reduction (5 percent), the maturity of the loan is reduced from 30 years to less than 13 (approximately 12 years, 7 months). The last column in Table 4–4 indicates the remaining term if the borrower should opt for continued payments at the same level as in effect for that year (i.e., no further increases in the periodic payment). If the borrower wishes the increase to be applicable for only the first 5 years (monthly payment of $1,000.21 to continue to maturity), for example, then the total term of the loan would be 187+ months (60 months + 127+ months) in this case and would be fully amortized in year 16.

Analysis of Yield

It is often helpful and sometimes required that yield calculations be made in real estate transactions. The yield calculation could be made for the entire property investment or for any of the many components (physical, legal, or financial) that make up that investment, but yield is most generally computed for the debt and equity components. Since

Table 4–4
Growing Equity Mortgage (GEM) Amortization Schedule

Year	Loan Amount, BOY ($)	Monthly Payment ($)	Balance Outstanding, EOY	Remaining Term (months)
1	80,000.00	822.88	$79,705.54	348
2	79,705.54	864.02	78,856.26	245+
3	78,856.26	907.22	77,351.39	192+
4	77,351.39	952.58	75,080.38	155+
5	75,080.38	1,000.21	71,917.29	127+
6	71,917.29	1,050.22	67,718.78	104+
7	67,718.78	1,102.73	62,321.84	83+
8	62,321.84	1,157.87	55,541.12	65+
9	55,541.12	1,215.76	47,166.25	49+
10	47,166.25	1,276.55	36,958.26	34+
11	36,958.26	1,340.38	24,646.12	20+
12	24,646.12	1,407.40	9,922.50	7+
13	9,922.50	1,477.77[a]	—	—

[a]With a payment of $1,477.77 per month, the loan would be fully amortized in the seventh month of the year 13.

the focus of this chapter is on financing, effective yield (interest) on debt will be emphasized. It is to be noted, however, that the following data are required for any yield calculation:

1. The initial amount of the investment.
2. The amount of net cash flows to the investment (both periodic flows and reversion, if any).
3. The timing of those cash flows.
4. The income projection period (investment holding period).

In the absence of discount points, origination fees, or other adjustments to the initial amount of the loan, the nominal rate is the yield. Even though the payments were adjusted on both the GPM and GEM in the foregoing examples, the yield in both instances is 12 percent (the nominal rate). Had discount points been charged on these two loan packages (which is likely), then the yield would have been enhanced (i.e., greater than the 12 percent nominal rate). Often, the yield calculation is a yield to maturity (YTM) calculation, although it need not be. The YTM calculation produces the lowest yield among a whole range of possible yield calculations. This is because the discount is spread, in effect, over the longest potential term of the mortgage. Should the mortgage be paid off earlier, the yield would be higher; the highest yields would be associated with the earliest payoffs. As an example, discount points on the GEM mortgage would automatically produce a higher yield than the YTM calculation because of the reduced term.

The yield on the VRM/ARM mortgage example lies somewhere between the low (12 percent) and high (17 percent) rates for the time period covered. Had discount points been charged on this loan, the yield for the time period covered would move away from the lower rate (12 percent) and toward the higher rate (17 percent). Because of the variable income flow and the reversion (balance outstanding), the yield calculation in this instance is moderately complicated and requires the use of a financial calculator. The following example shows the use of the ITAO in yield calculations.

Assume that the 12 percent, 30 year, $80,000 mortgage has been discounted seven points. The monthly payment based on the face amount of the loan is $822.88, as calculated previously. With the discount, however, the effective amount of the loan has been reduced by $5,600 to $74,400. The yield to maturity calculation, in this instance, is accomplished by first calculating the effective ITAO ($822.88 ÷ $74,400) of 0.011060 and then searching the tables for the rate to accommodate that effective ITAO. A search of the tables indicates the YTM to be 13 percent.

If the yield calculation were made under the assumption that the loan would be paid off at the end of the first year, the yield would be much higher. The data used for this yield calculation are as follows:

1. $74,400 (the initial effective amount of the investment).
2. $822.88 (per month periodic payment) and $9,874.56 (annual debt service).
3. $79,705.54 (balance outstanding—the amount of net cash flows to the investment).
4. 12 months (investment holding period).

The yield calculation in this example can be bracketed with two rather simple calculations. The first calculation is the effective constant ($9,874.56 ÷ $74,400) of 0.1327 or 13.27 percent. The second calculation involves adding the $9,874.56 annual debt service to the excess of the balance outstanding (reversion) over the effective investment, or $5,305.54 ($79,705.54 − $74,400), and dividing by the effective investment. This calculation provides the upper limit to the yield calculation: 20.4 percent ($15,180.10 ÷ $74,400). The actual calculated yield rate is 19.78 percent (via preprogrammed financial calculator). Intuition and logic would suggest to anyone bracketing the yield that, because of the short maturity (1 year), the actual yield would most likely be at the upper end of the established range of 13 percent to 20 percent.

Underwriting the Loan

Lenders, like all other investors, have two prime concerns when making an investment (lending money): maintaining capital investment intact (return of investment) and earning a rate of return on investment. In most instances, the former is accomplished (for the lender) by amortization of the loan and the latter through either the nominal or effective interest rate. To meet these two prime objectives, lenders look to borrower income as their first line of defense. The first concern, therefore, is the borrower's ability to repay the loan, to maintain other carrying costs associated with the home purchase (especially, taxes, insurance, and utilities), and to maintain a reasonable level of other liabilities (other debt). As general guides to the borrower's ability to qualify for a loan, lenders, often as a matter of policy, have established ratios of borrower debt to borrower gross income for underwriting purposes.

Most common among these underwriting ratios is the ratio of principal, interest, real estate taxes, and insurance to the gross income of the borrower (known as the PITI ratio). With the substantial rise in utilities costs over the past few years, that expense item, too, is often included in the calculation of the ratio (known, then, as the PITUI ratio). The PITI or PITUI ratio for underwriting purposes and for a wide range of lending institutions is often in the range of 25 to 30 percent; that is, if the borrower has gross income of a magnitude such that 25 to 30 percent can be allocated to and cover those items included within the ratio, then that borrower will qualify for a loan (as yet of an undetermined amount). From the lender's point of view, one additional item of input is required to determine the amount of loan extended. That item is the mortgage constant (R_m), which reflects the terms on which the lender is willing to lend. Capitalizing the income allocable to principal and interest payments (the annual debt service, or ADS) at the mortgage constant (R_m) provides the estimate of the amount of loan available (V_m); that is, $V_m = ADS/R_m$.

In periods of rising rates, the problem of accommodating both buyers and sellers, as well as keeping within the underwriting rules of the lending institution, becomes quite prominent. Often a gap develops between what a borrower wishes to borrow and what a lender is willing to lend. How that gap is handled in the market by buyers, sellers, and lenders is of substantial interest to appraisers in the performance of their function. If the transaction that takes place in the market is used in appraisal analysis (as a comparable), and if some form of subsidized financing was used to resolve the gap problem, then there is a potential for a financial (cash equivalency) adjustment.

As an example of the use of this underwriting tool and the potential gap that can develop in periods of rising rates, consider the following data:

Borrower gross income (GI):$40,000

Principal and interest ratio (PI):25%

Amount of GI allocable to PI: $10,000 ($40,000 × 25%)

Mortgage amount required: $80,000

Implied (borrower) constant: 0.125 ($10,000 ÷ $80,000)

Lender constant: a function of the current market

Consider, also, the following mortgage constants at 12 percent to 17 percent rates (in one-point increments) for 25 years:

Interest Rate (Y_m)	Mortgage Constant (R_m)
12%	0.126384
13%	0.135336
14%	0.144456
15%	0.153696
16%	0.163068
17%	0.172536

The amount of debt that can be supported as rates increase is a function of the amount of borrower income allocable to principal and interest (ADS) and the lending terms available as expressed by the mortgage constant (R_m).

Interest Rate (Y_m)	Mortgage Amount (V_m)	Gap (Amount Required − Amount Obtainable)
12%	$79,124	$ 876
13%	73,890	6,110
14%	69,225	10,775
15%	65,064	14,936
16%	61,324	18,676
17%	57,959	22,041

The mortgage amount (V_m), as noted previously, represents the amount allocable to annual debt service ($10,000) capitalized at the appropriate constant (R_m). The gap is the difference between the amount the borrower wishes to borrow ($80,000) and the amount the lender is willing to lend. At 12 percent, the gap is manageable in several ways: increasing the down payment; reducing the sales price; increasing the maturity on the note; obtaining a second mortgage from the seller or a third-party lender; or amortizing the difference within the existing package (i.e., slightly bending the underwriting rule of 25 percent and increasing debt service—$80,000 × 0.126384 = $10,110.72).

Obviously, the gap problem becomes larger as rates increase, and therein lies a potential problem for the appraiser, as well as the lender, the borrower, and possibly the seller. How the larger gaps are handled in the market gives rise to the potential for financing adjustments; therefore, the appraiser needs to be aware of the potential problem and needs to have the tools required to measure this phenomenon and its resultant effect on market price.

Summary

Mortgage markets serve to facilitate the flow of mortgage loan funds, set the price (interest rate and other loan terms) of mortgage loan funds, and allocate loan funds among competing alternative outlets. Debt financing is essential to most real estate transactions. The terms of lending, the availability of loan funds, and the required debt service all influence real estate market prices.

Mortgage loan terms (interest rates, down payment, maturity, and amortization provisions) are a function of lender underwriting provisions. To qualify for those loan terms and obtain the amount of loan desired, borrowers must meet certain income requirements currently or must have high prospects of doing so in the relatively near future. To the extent that a gap develops between that which is obtainable and that which is desired, other forms of financing often appear to bridge that gap.

Much of the analysis of loan terms can be accomplished through the use of the installment to amortize one (ITAO) and/or the mortgage constant (R_m). Either factor is applied to periodic debt service or to differentials between debt service at market rates and debt service at contract rates to determine the amount of discount and/or the cost of buydowns. These rates and ratios may also be utilized in calculating the adjustment in the debt service that is necessary to meet changing market interest rate requirements, the amount of negative amortization that is required in certain circumstances, the maturity on growing equity mortgages, an analysis of yield on variable rate or variable term mortgages, and a number of other pertinent calculations that are relevant to the mortgage contract.

Notes

1. For a more detailed definition of interest, see Boyce, Byrl N., ed., *Real Estate Appraisal Terminology,* rev. ed. (Cambridge, Mass.: Ballinger [Joint publication of the American Institute of Real Estate Appraisers and Society of Real Estate Appraisers], 1981), p. 137.

2. Ibid., p. 167.

3. Ibid., p. 168.

4. Ibid., p. 154.

5. Ibid., p. 11.

6. Ibid., p. 151.

7. Ibid., p. 80.

8. Ibid., p. 169.

9. Additional mortgage calculations can be found in this chapter in the section on alternative mortgage terms.

10. See further calculations in the section on alternative mortgage terms.

Suggested Readings

Bloom, George F., and Harrison, Henry S. *Appraising the Single Family Residence.* Chicago: American Institute of Real Estate Appraisers, 1978, chapter 14.

Bloom, George F.; Weimer, Arthur M.; and Fisher, Jeffrey D. *Real Estate,* 8th ed. New York: John Wiley & Sons, 1982, chapters 9 and 10.

Boyce, Byrl N., ed. *Real Estate Appraisal Terminology,* rev. ed. Cambridge, Mass.: Ballinger (Joint publication of the American Institute of Real Estate Appraisers and Society of Real Estate Appraisers), 1981.

Boyce, Byrl N., and Kinnard, William N., Jr. "Adjusting for Financing Differences in Residential Properties (with Specific Reference to FNMA/FHLMC Form 1004/70)." Storrs, Conn.: Real Estate Counseling Group of Connecticut, 1982.

Brueggeman, William B., and Stone, Leo D. *Real Estate Finance,* 7th ed. Homewood, Ill.: Richard D. Irwin, 1981, parts I, II, and V.

Epley, Donald R., and Millar, James A. *Basic Real Estate Finance and Investments.* New York: John Wiley & Sons, 1980, chapters 10 and 11.

Jaffe, Austin J., and Sirmans, C.F. *Real Estate Investment Decision Making.* Englewood Cliffs, N.J.: Prentice-Hall, 1982, chapters 8, 10, and 11.

Messner, Stephen D., et al. *Marketing Investment Real Estate: Finance, Taxation, Techniques,* 2nd ed. Chicago: Realtors National Marketing Institute of the National Association of Realtors, 1982, chapters 3 and 4.

Smith, Halbert C.; Tschappat, Carl J.; and Racster, Ronald L. *Real Estate and Urban Development,* 3rd ed. Homewood, Ill.: Richard D. Irwin, 1981, chapters 16 and 17.

Vidger, Leonard P. *Borrowing and Lending on Residential Property.* Lexington, Mass.: Lexington Books, D.C. Heath, 1981, chapters 1–5, 8, and 11.

5 Area and Neighborhood Analysis

Key Terms

Access   A means of entry into or upon a property.

Conformity   A valuation principle stating that value is maximized by the presence of a reasonable degree of homogeneity.

Economic base   That activity of an area by which it attracts income from outside specifically delineated borders.

Economic base analysis   One of the major tools available for analysis and evaluation of the structure and trends in a local market area.

Encroachment   Displacement (partial or gradual) of an existing use by another use.

Location quotient (LQ)   An index expressing a relationship between the proportion of local employment in a particular industry (to total local employment) and the proportion of national employment in that industry (to total national employment).

Market delineation   Identification of specific boundaries of a market area, expressed in geographic, political, or competitive terms.

Multipliers (economic base)   Indicators of the relationship between the total economic activity of an area and the basic activities of that area.

Neighborhood analysis   The objective analysis of factors relating to urban growth, structure, and change and their effect on property values.

Neighborhood life cycle   The stages of development and growth, stability, transition, and decline in the life of a neighborhood.

Supersession   A transition of use in real property.

Because real estate is fixed in location, its value is largely determined by the impact of interacting external market forces, especially those of demand and supply. The task of the real estate appraiser is to identify the forces at work in the pertinent real estate market segments, to measure their operation in that market, and to evaluate their present and anticipated future impact on the value of the property being appraised. This is the essence of the step in the appraisal framework (or appraisal process) called market analysis.

It is important to note that both analysis and evaluation of the impact of external market forces on property values are required. Market analysis is much more than a mere recital of facts and figures about the pertinent market area or segments. The emphasis must be placed on arriving at a conclusion about why and how much these market factors influence the value of the subject property. This is important both in the appraisal framework, as a step toward reaching a value conclusion, and in the presentation of findings and conclusions about external market influences. These conclusions are included in the area and neighborhood analysis sections of the appraisal report.

The Nature of Market Analysis

At whatever level it is undertaken, market analysis involves identifying the pertinent market area, examining that market, and then drawing conclusions from it about the defined value of specified rights in certain described real estate. Because a wide variety of market forces are at work at all times, it is important to know which market (or markets) is pertinent to the subject property. The appraiser must identify in which market or markets the subject property is competing. The basis for *market identification* or *delineation* is the competitiveness or substitutability of properties for one another, especially the subject property. Two nearly identical properties located side by side, for example, may be in different markets if one is for sale for owner-occupancy and the other is available for rental only.

In addition to identifying or delineating the pertinent market, the appraiser must also learn what current market conditions are. This involves measurement and identification of the components of demand and supply. In addition, the appraiser needs to discover what happened in the specific market in the past that led to current market conditions. This involves the measurement of trends in significant market supply and demand factors.

Once trends have been identified and measured, the appraiser must then forecast or project them into the future to establish the effect of anticipated market conditions (and factors) as they affect the defined value of the subject property today. The objective is a concise, finite dollar conclusion drawn by the appraiser about the impact of the market on the value of the subject property. Finally, the appraiser must provide market data and forecasts for all approaches to estimating market value. All approaches and procedures require and utilize market data. These market data and forecasts are considered in many steps of the appraisal framework (e.g., interest rates, remaining economic life, vacancy ratio).

Market analysis is always oriented toward evaluating the impact of market forces on the value of the subject property as of the valuation date. The analysis of past trends identifies and measures how current market conditions have evolved. It also shows changes in the relationships of market factors over time. The analysis of current conditions shows the relationship of market factors and their quantities prevailing as of the valuation date. Forecasts of future trends and conditions identify what is likely to have an influence on current values by influencing the decisions and actions of buyers and sellers on the current market in response to those future expectations.

Levels of Market and Environmental Influence

The market setting or the environment of forces that influence or determine real estate values and the value of the subject property operates at several different levels simultaneously—the international, national, regional, community, and neighborhood market levels.

The farther removed from the subject property the market level is, the less direct and immediate will be the effect of any change on the subject property and its value. Thus, international market forces (such as oil prices or the price of gold) or national market factors (such as the prime rate of interest or the purchasing power of the dollar) create general market conditions within which real estate values and prices are set and fluctuate along with other prices or values. Regional market forces (such as area employment and construction volume) have a closer, more nearly direct, more nearly immediate impact on the value of the subject property and of properties that are competitive with it. Local or community market forces (e.g., local population, employment, incomes, and competition) are even closer to the subject property and influence its value even more directly. Closest of all is the neighborhood level, where any change tends to have a direct and immediate impact on the value of the subject property.

The preferred approach in market analysis is to start at the more general level, where the market forces have the broadest and most pervasive influence, and work down systematically to the more particular levels. International and national forces have a basic role in the character of regional, local, and even neighborhood forces, which, in turn, are also influenced by peculiar local circumstances. All these factors are part of the location of the subject property.

International and National Forces

International gold flows and balance of payments problems influence price levels and interest rates in the national economy. Resource demands (e.g., plywood for military facilities construction) influence the cost of construction materials and their availability domestically. Tariffs, or the lack of them, influence competition with local industries and hence local employment, income, and housing demand.

Federal Reserve System and U.S. Treasury monetary policies influence rates in the national economy. FHA standards influence construction quality and quantity. Money market competition influences mortgage loan rates. Federal laws and regulations influence the ability of savings institutions to attract savings deposits by affecting the interest rate that may be paid on deposits. National levels of employment and income influence demand for housing and price levels. Federal budgetary policies influence inflationary pressures, which, in turn, affect housing and construction prices.

Regional Forces

Economic and population forces are particularly important at the regional level. Employment, or unemployment, and income trends directly influence demand for housing. The demand comes from local residents (new or existing). Whereas national forces influence this demand, regional-local forces actually determine it. Local trends can run counter to national forces because of such conditions as dependence on declining industries or defense industries, especially good or bad labor relations, population growth rates that differ from the national average, or especially plentiful or scarce savings in local lending institutions. Regional conditions are tempered by national and international trends, but specific identification of local market forces—their direction, their strength, and their estimated future trends—is required.

Local Community Forces

In addition to basic economic influences, such as employment, income, prices, and interest rates, more specific influences operate at the local community level. Property tax level differentials and local community services, including utilities, are operative at this level. So is the quality of local government and the reputation of the community as a good or bad place to live.

Neighborhood Forces

The pattern of land use, the characteristics and incomes of inhabitants, land use control and regulations (especially zoning), school district lines and reputation, the availability of utilities and other public services, and other specific factors operate as value determinants at the neighborhood level. They are conditioned by broader market forces, but specific neighborhood factors are major determinants of what is truly competitive with the subject property.

The market area pertinent for any appraisal, and for a residential appraisal in particular, is that geographic political area within which alternative similar properties are effectively competitive with the subject property in the mind of the most probable potential purchaser of the subject property. The market area always includes one local community and may involve several communities in a region. It also includes one or more neighborhoods. Behavior of buyers on the local market provides the best (and indeed the only) guide to residential market area delineation.

Community or Local Market Area Analysis

Once the appraiser has identified the international, national, and regional forces and trends generally influencing local real estate values, the major focus in a residential appraisal is on local community analysis and neighborhood analysis. The general background influences set the basic framework within which the local market and neighborhood forces operate directly on the value of the subject property. A local market area already has been defined in terms of competitive properties. It is delineated in terms of political boundaries—a city, a village, a borough, a township, a county, or a group of such districts within which properties are or may be competitive with the subject property. It can also be delineated in terms of a time-distance radius (i.e., all the area within 30 to 45 minutes' driving time or travel distance from the subject property or from some common center of employment, such as a manufacturing plant, the central business district, or a financial-commercial district).

Data are rarely readily available, however, for areas other than political subdivisions, census tracts, or enumeration districts. For residential appraisal work, it seldom pays to conduct a survey to delineate or define the specific boundaries of the market area. Therefore, political boundaries for which data are readily available are typically used.

Factors in Local Market Area Analysis

The major factors in any market analysis are the components of demand and supply, but they can also be categorized for analytical purposes as physical, economic-financial, political-governmental, and sociological factors. All of these factors are major market influences on the value of real estate and the value of the subject property. Some operate at all market levels; others are more restricted in their influence, operating primarily at the local level. These same categories of demand and supply are applicable in both local market area analysis and neighborhood analysis.

The lines of demarcation between these classifications are fuzzy and flexible. Property taxes, for example, may be considered as either an economic or a political-governmental factor. Similarly, the ratio of homeownership to rental occupancy might be considered as either an economic or a sociological factor. It does not really matter where such factors are listed or considered. What is important is that they be considered as and when they are pertinent. The classifications are most useful, therefore, as guides to what should be considered in any analysis of the background market environment. Moreover, not every item noted is applicable in every appraisal problem. The appraiser must learn to be discriminating, through experience and judgment. What matters is to include the basic, pertinent factors in the background analysis. Then the forces influencing the value of the particular property being appraised can be properly evaluated.

Physical Factors. In community analysis, the geographic area may be small enough for physical-locational considerations to enter into the supply and demand forces for residential real estate. These considerations include area, topography, soil and subsoil conditions, and climate. The extent of a community's area can influence demand for and supply of housing. Larger areas may mean longer commuting distances, as well as room for further expansion. This is more likely to be a neighborhood factor than a community factor, however.

Topography is also more important in neighborhood and site analysis, but it can affect the cost of construction, the feasible density of development, and the attractiveness of living in an entire community. Soil and subsoil conditions also operate more at the neighborhood and site analysis levels, but again may influence construction styles and costs in entire communities or regions. The permafrost in much of Alaska, for example, makes houses without basements almost imperative.

Whole regions can be affected positively or adversely by temperatures, precipitation levels, and prevailing winds. Smog in many cities, the sun and warmth of much of Florida and Southern California, the low humidity of the Southwest, and the seasonal pattern of much of the Northeast are cases in point. These climatic factors should be noted and included in the analysis only when they are active attractions or deterrents to housing supply and demand, as indicated by the actions of the market itself.

Economic-Financial Factors. By far the most significant and most numerous factors in local market analysis are those generally labeled economic. They have the most direct influence on the quantity and level of both supply and demand for housing. The important points to bear in mind in considering these factors are twofold. First, only the really pertinent factors should be considered in area analysis. Second, they must be analyzed in sufficient detail to bring them to bear meaningfully on the appraisal problem at hand. They also generally operate at all market levels of influence.

Population could easily be regarded as a sociological-demographic factor, but it is included as an economic factor because it influences directly the number and types of housing units demanded or required in an area. The several ingredients of population to be separated and studied include total population, number and size of households (or families), age distribution of population, education and skill distribution, labor force size and labor force participation rates, rates of population growth by subgroup, rates of natural increase, rates of in-migration or out-migration, and sex distribution of population.

In the area of employment, the appraiser must consider not only the number employed and the rates of unemployment but also the kinds and stability of employment in the area. Employment is a major locational influence on families and, hence, on the demand for housing. The several ingredients of employment (for purposes of analysis) include number employed, rates of employment and unemployment, unfilled job vacancies, skills required, industrial mix of employment, growth rates of employers, stability of employment, stability of employing industries, commitment of employers to local area, and labor relations record. The important issue is whether employment is likely to be sustained, so that incomes, in turn, will be steady enough to support given levels of homeownership and rentals.

Income levels are important because they represent the source through which potential demand is made effective demand. The major factors to consider in analyzing incomes are income levels; wage rates; hours worked; overtime; family income patterns, including second and third wage earners; stability of income; trends in income levels and wage rates; and nonsalary or nonwage income, such as property income, pensions, and the like.

Economic base is particularly important in community (and regional) analysis, since it identifies the sum of all income-producing activities by which a community maintains its economy. All local employment and income stems from this source. The economic base of a community may be oriented in one of several different ways, as discussed later, in the section on economic base analysis. The economic base of a community or region must be analyzed and evaluated in terms of orientations; strength and growth, stability, and sensitivity to outside changes; employment and income potential; competition with other cities or regions; and the sustaining character of retail and wholesale trade.

Consumption expenditure patterns directly influence the demand for housing. What families and households do with their disposable income is a major consideration in measuring how much income is traditionally and effectively available to be spent on housing. This varies by region, family income level, social and ethnic group, and family size.

Taxes at all levels of government are effective dampeners of demand. They represent reductions of effective disposable income. Income taxes operate at the national and state levels and must be considered in converting incomes to disposable incomes for housing expenditure estimates. Sales taxes are levied by both states and localities and also tend to reduce the effectiveness of disposable income that may be translated into housing expenditures. Property taxes are levied by local and county governments. To evaluate property taxes effectively, the appraiser must consider tax rates, tax burden, and tax appeals and adjustment. Tax rates are often expressed in mills per dollar of assessment, or dollars per hundred dollars of assessment.

Although trends in tax rates are important, they represent only one ingredient in the calculation of the tax bill—and hence the tax burden—as one basis for comparison among communities. The tax bill or burden is the assessment times the tax rate. This is the real item of comparison, in conjunction with the services that are provided through the taxes. Unequal treatment of individual taxpayers can be either eliminated or aggravated by appeals and adjustment procedures.

Price levels operate at all market levels to influence both the supply and the demand for housing. Rising prices (inflation) can erode the effectiveness of disposable income as much as income taxes do. Three major types of prices should be considered: consumer prices (cost of living), housing prices and rental levels, and materials prices (construction costs). At the community or local market level, price differentials can influence the competitiveness or relative attractiveness of housing in different communities or of new versus existing housing.

Money market developments at all levels of government influence both housing demand and housing supply. Mortgage rates are part of the entire pattern of money rates and generally tend to move with this pattern. Saving deposit rates affect the ability of mortgage lending institutions to attract savings and thus have funds to lend. Mortgage loan rates affect both demand for housing and new construction. Different mortgage loan rates should be recognized (e.g., conventional, VA, FHA, construction, junior). Appraisers should also recognize that loan maturities, down payment requirements (loan-to-value ratios), and amortization-repayment provisions of mortgage loans can have as much effect on home financing costs as do interest rates. Local patterns can also vary widely.

Labor, materials, and other costs of construction influence the relative attractiveness of new construction as opposed to existing housing. They also influence the volume, type, and location of new residential construction, and thus affect the supply of housing in an area. The number, size, type, and quality of housing units in existence at any time represent the range of potential choices for purchase. The only alternative is to wait for a new unit to be constructed. The volume, type, and location of new housing units constructed in any period is the major element of change in the effective supply in a given area. Other ingredients and changes in the standing stock of housing are conversions and demolitions.

The number and types of vacancies at any given time represent the range of existing alternatives (versus waiting for new construction) that confronts the buyer at that time. The duration and types of vacancies, as well as changes over time, also indicate market acceptance or non-acceptance of housing types, prices, and rentals. Turnover rates of both ownership and rental housing provide further guides to market acceptance of housing types and of price or rent levels.

The owner-tenant mix in any area is also considered to be a sociological factor, but it is largely dependent on the income and employment status of the population. Changes in this mix, particularly when coupled with analysis of vacancies, indicate what is most likely to be demanded (and hence to sell readily) in the market area in question at the time of the appraisal.

Fire insurance rates are a function of municipal services that are political-governmental considerations, but they also have a direct impact on housing occupancy costs, which can affect location choices among purchasers. Locational amenities require good and easy access to and from necessary supporting service facilities (schools, recreation, shopping, employment). Value depends on good location, and therefore transportation (fast, easy, cheap) is an important area influence. Transportation is frequently treated as a physical rather than an economic factor. It is included here, however, because it has direct impact on the cost of living in a given area, and thus has an impact on area housing demand.

Political-Governmental Factors. Some political-governmental factors operate at all levels of government. They represent part of the institutional framework that buyers and sellers (and appraisers) must consider in evaluating the market situation confronting them. Government budgets influence housing demand and supply at all levels. Taxes are a demand depressant, but some expenditures can be stimulants to demand or supply. Federal highways, public housing, utilities, and fire protection may all aid the effective functioning of the residential real estate market. Their impact depends on the efficiency of government expenditures relative to tax burdens.

Monetary and fiscal policy is exercised almost exclusively through the Federal Reserve System and the U.S. Treasury. Major impacts of such policy in the housing field are felt on interest rates, price levels, and lending restraints or encouragement. The FNMA also influences mortgage loan rates, especially on new housing. Federal law, Federal Reserve regulations, and Federal Home Loan Bank Board regulations influence bank (and savings and loan) lending policies and interest rates on savings accounts. They limit how much may be loaned, on what types of properties, on what kinds of terms, and where. FHA and VA regulations tend to set similar kinds of standards. For state-chartered institutions, state banking and insurance laws and regulations also limit lending policies. The enforcement and examination programs of regulatory agencies provide effective checks on credit extension beyond these limits, thereby influencing both supply and demand for housing.

Although many states have programs of assistance and encouragement to improve housing quality, the major effect stems from federal agencies. FHA and VA generally operate to encourage homeownership and to stimulate new housing construction. FNMA and GNMA seek to develop an orderly flow of mortgage funds by offering a secondary market facility for FHA-insured and VA-guaranteed mortgages. Federal public housing is designed to offer at least minimally acceptable housing for those who are unable to obtain it through the private sector of the market. Urban renewal seeks to improve the overall level of housing quality—in part through removing substandard housing; in part through stimulating rehabilitation and conservation of existing standard housing; and in part through constructing new standard housing for displaced families.

Political stability and a reputation for clean, honest, and even efficient government can enhance considerably an area's attractiveness as a place to live. If the reputation of a community and the facts of the case are at odds, the appraiser must discover which is the real market influence in the minds of typically informed buyers.

Government service levels influence the locational amenities of residential real estate. They are particularly important at the local level, and they form a basis of comparison of one community with another. The kinds, quality, and costs of services all enter into the comparison. Local fire and police protection can influence insurance rates, among other housing occupancy costs. Municipal or regional water, sewer, gas, and electric service—or any combination of these—may be provided in a given area. The quality, reliability, availability, and costs of these services are all considerations in evaluating the influence of government on residential property values. Although the transportation network has been discussed as an economic factor (and possibly a physical one as well), the quality, number, and location of municipal streets and roads influence the most important locational feature of real estate—access. Government is responsible for providing and maintaining streets and roads, so their adequacy is one aspect of government services. The frequency and adequacy of trash and garbage collection and disposal influence the attractiveness of living in an area. When these services are not provided by the municipality, they represent an added cost of housing occupancy for the homeowner. Among the most important direct influences on real estate values exerted by government, especially at the local level, is the exercise of the police power to control land and urban space uses in the interest of public health, public safety, public morals, and general welfare. Not only the existence of regulations but their enforcement must be evaluated by the appraiser.

Planning may be exercised on a community or regional basis. It sets the foundation for zoning and subdivision regulations, and it often provides the standards in terms of which proposed developments or changes in community development are evaluated. Planning sets the physical pattern of land uses in a community, and it can effectively influence land values by affecting the compatibility and efficiency of land uses. Zoning regulations may specify the uses to which land and buildings may be put and the intensity or density of those uses. Zoning can affect property values by establishing uses that are legal (or illegal) and by determining how intensively land and buildings can be used. Zoning is thus an important ingredient in the determination of highest and best use. As one action arm of planning, it also provides protection of residential uses against the intrusion of uses that might affect residential property values adversely.

Subdivision regulations are also an adjunct of planning. They specify the improvements that a subdivider-developer must install with new housing. These regulations also indicate the manner in which new developments are to be laid out. Variations in such regulations can seriously affect the cost of housing in an area and can lead to differentials in the attractions of living or buying in alternative communities. Local and state codes affecting building construction and occupancy can further influence construction costs significantly, as well as occupancy costs and insurance rates. The major types of codes, often all found in one community, include building codes, housing codes, fire codes, plumbing codes, and electrical codes.

Environmental protection regulations are established and enforced by all levels of government. They can limit or prohibit the use of land, as well as setting the standards by which land and urban space can be used. They have the same basic effect on housing and occupancy cost as zoning does.

The quality and reputation of educational facilities of an area, especially a public educational system, can be an important ingredient in the demand for housing in the area. Many communities, and even districts within communities, are sought after as places to live because of their schools. This attraction is frequently capitalized into higher demand and higher prices for otherwise comparable houses in such communities.

Although it has exhibited spotty growth or even acceptance since World War II, rent control still offers a potentially strong government influence on housing supply and demand. Rent control tends to alter the relationship between sales prices of rental housing and sales prices of owner-occupied housing. It is particularly significant in its effect on gross rent multiplier analysis.

Sociological Factors. People-oriented amenities of an area are generally considered sociological factors. They are based much more on attitudes and impressions than are the physical, economic, or political-governmental factors. They are no less important as determinants of demand and value, however, simply because they are less susceptible to quantification or measurement. The appraiser's task is to identify the attitudes toward the community and its residents that do affect value, and to ascertain from market behavior how these attitudes work their effect on value. Despite statutory and regulatory admonitions to the contrary, the ethnic and social backgrounds of an area's population often do influence the attitudes and behavior of potential buyers. Nevertheless, economic and social position tends to be a stronger influence than national, ethnic, racial, or religious background. Change—especially the anticipation of change—is often a powerful unsettling force on values.

Intangible though it may be, the reputation of an area (whether deserved or not) tends to work a powerful influence on potential buyers. A good address is a stronger consideration in neighborhood analysis than in area analysis. It must be considered at the area level, however, if it pervades the reputation of the entire community—as a high-tax area, for example. In this situation, as in the case of population characteristics, the appraiser is a reporter of the facts of the market, not a commentator or judge. Coupled with the reputation of a community is its economic, political, demographic, and social stability. An area's reputation for tensions, political wrangling, or unstable employment tends to deter families from moving in. This can seriously affect values in the community or neighborhood.

Living amenities in an area are enhanced considerably when parks, playgrounds, and other recreational facilities are available in adequate numbers and kinds and at convenient locations. Similarly, libraries, concert halls, and theaters all add to the attraction of living in an area. Once again, however, the market dictates how significant these features are in affecting housing values.

Economic Base Analysis

One of the major tools available for analysis and evaluation of the structure and trends in a local market area is economic base analysis. Although it is but one of many tools potentially available for use by the appraiser and market analyst, economic base analysis has several advantages: it is relatively simple, it is relatively easy to understand and use, it can be applied with readily available data, and it works. Economic base analysis is explained in further detail in many of the suggested readings cited at the end of this chapter. The *economic base* of a community is "the economic activity of a community which enables it to attract income from outside its borders."[1] Those activities that are net exporters of goods and services are thus basic industries; that is, they produce and sell more of a good or service than is consumed or purchased locally.

Basic industry is generally measured in terms of its employment, although payroll or sales measures can also be used. An industry is basic if local employment in that industry represents a higher percentage of total local employment than national employment in that industry represents of total national employment. This is expressed as the industry's *location quotient* (LQ):

$$LQ = \frac{LE_i}{LE_t} \div \frac{NE_i}{NE_t}$$

where LQ = the location quotient
      LE = local employment
      NE = national employment
       i = the industry being analyzed
       t = total employment at either the
            local or national level

A basic or export industry (E_b) has a location quotient of greater than one (LQ > 1). A nonbasic or service industry (E_s) is a net importer or is not a net exporter. On net balance, its products or services are consumed locally. A nonbasic industry has a location quotient of one or less (LQ ≤ 1).

Economic base analysis is "a technique of analysis which utilizes the relationship between basic and nonbasic employment as a means of predicting population, income, or other variables having an effect on real estate value or land utilization."[2] The structural market relationships observed between basic employment, nonbasic employment, population, and incomes are assumed to remain constant, or nearly so, over the period of analysis and prediction. Economic base analysis assumes, from past observations, that basic employment is the causative factor in changes in total employment, population, or incomes within the area.

The structural relationships within a given market area are found by the following formulas:

$$E_t = E_b + E_s$$

where E_t is total employment, E_b is basic employment, and E_s is service employment;

$$E_t = E_b \times \frac{E_t}{E_b}$$

$$\frac{E_t}{E_b} = k_e$$

where k_e is a constant—the employment multiplier;

$$P = E_t \times k_p$$

where P is total population and k_p is a constant—the population multiplier; and

$$Y = E_t \times k_y$$

where Y is total income and k_y is a constant—the income multiplier. Population, employment, and income data can be obtained from published sources (such as the U.S. Census) and used readily, provided that they are reasonably recent.

Population, total employment, and incomes can be forecast or projected by using the appropriate multipliers, provided basic employment can be forecast or predicted and the assumption of constant relationships or multipliers over the forecasting period is tenable. Then we have

$$\Delta E_t = \Delta E_b \times k_e$$

$$\Delta P = \Delta E_t \times k_p$$

$$\Delta Y = \Delta E_t \times k_y$$

These formulations will be presented in greater detail later, but before applying the formulations and models, it is appropriate to outline the steps in economic base analysis. First, one must identify and delineate the market area, usually in terms of political subdivisions. This delineation indicates the area for which required data are to be gathered. The second step is to classify and identify local basic industries within the market area, generally using employment location quotients. Such identification need not be very detailed, provided the categories of basic industry are clear. Basic industry (export activities) may be manufacturing, wholesale trade for a distribution center, retail trade for a trading center, government services for a state capital, education services for a town with a university, financial or insurance services, health services, or agricultural products. It all depends on what products or services, if any, the community exports. Third, one must measure the relationships of basic employment to total employment, population, incomes, and the like. This requires quantification and calculation of multipliers. Finally, population, total employment, and income levels are estimated by application of multiplier (ratio) analysis. This can be done for current market conditions, or for projections (forecast).

As an example, suppose a community with a population of 100,000 has total employment of 48,000. Basic employment is 20,000. Nationally, the employment in the industries that are basic locally is 12 percent. It is announced that basic industries in this community will increase employment by 3,000 jobs in the next 3 years. What will be the probable ultimate impact on total local employment and population? The first step in the process would be to test for basic employment via the location quotient:

$$LQ = \frac{LE_b}{LE_t} \div \frac{NE_b}{NE_t} = \frac{20,000}{48,000} \div 0.12 = 3.47$$

Next, the appropriate multipliers are calculated:

$$k_e = \frac{E_t}{E_b} = \frac{48,000}{20,000} = 2.40$$

$$k_p = \frac{P}{E_t} = \frac{100,000}{48,000} = 2.08$$

Finally, population and total employment are forecast for 3 years hence:

$$\Delta E_b = 3,000$$

$$\Delta E_t = \Delta E_b \times k_e = 3,000 \times 2.40 = 7,200$$

$$E_t \text{ (3 years hence)} = 48,000 + 7,200 = 55,200$$

$$\Delta P = \Delta E_t \times k_p = 7,200 \times 2.08 = 14,976$$

$$P \text{ (3 years hence)} = 100,000 + 14,976 = 114,976$$

Economic base analysis is thus a simple and direct method for analyzing local market structures and forecasting important determinants of real estate housing demand—population, employment, incomes. It uses readily available data. It enables appraisers to use the studies of others, provided that appraisers learn how to interpret the results. Economic base analysis stands or falls on the assumption that constant ratios or multipliers will remain constant over the period of analysis and that basic employment is the cause of growth. The analysis also requires careful identification of what basic industry is locally and of what basic employment is.

Economic base analysis is not a substitute for the appraiser's judgment. The appraiser must still make clear and definitive conclusions about the impact of the present and projected economic base on the value of the rights being appraised. Economic base analysis does not deal directly with physical, political-governmental, or sociological factors in real estate markets, except to the extent that they are reflected in fundamental economic variables.

Models: Static and Dynamic

Analysis of a market area or neighborhood as of a specific point in time is called *static analysis*. It deals with the relationships of value-determining and value-influencing factors as part of the structure of the market. It is useful in identifying what forces currently make up supply and demand and in determining their quantitative impact. Economic base analysis can be used as a static structure model to show the relationships among basic employment, total employment, population, and incomes. The adjustment process in direct sales comparison analysis is another form of static model. Because they reflect only current market relationships and structure, static models have limited (yet fundamental) usefulness in real estate market and neighborhood analysis.

Analyses or forecasts of changes in a market area or neighborhood over time constitute *dynamic analysis*. Time is a specific variable, often taken as a proxy for changing market conditions or even for changing market relationships. Dynamic models are used for forecasting or projection. Economic base analysis can be used as a dynamic model when multipliers are applied to changes in basic employment. The limitation is that the same structural relationships must be assumed to exist over time.

Trend analysis can also be used to forecast changes in market forces over time. This is illustrated in a subsequent chapter via regression analysis, with time as a variable, as well as in several of the books cited at the end of this chapter. A *trend* is "an arrangement of statistical data in accordance with its time of occurrence. A series of related changes which may be identified and projected into a probable future pattern."[3] Dynamic analysis measures and forecasts growth. In particular, real estate market analysis attempts to measure and forecast economic growth, which is an increase in per capita real income in constant dollars. (Technically, growth is change and can be either positive or negative.) Dynamic market analysis seeks to identify and measure economic growth in a market area, so that the demand and supply factors influencing real estate values in that market can also be measured.

Neighborhood Analysis

Although it is part of the external market for the subject property, the neighborhood has special significance because it is the immediate environment of the subject property. What occurs in the neighborhood has direct and immediate impact on the value of the subject property. Many of the same factors operative at the local market area level are also important considerations in neighborhood analysis, but the neighborhood emphasis is more localized. A *neighborhood* is "a portion of a larger community, or an entire community, in which there is a homogeneous grouping of inhabitants, buildings, or business enterprises. Inhabitants of a neighborhood usually have a more than casual community of interest."[4] The inhabitants typically also share a similar economic level or cultural background. It is important to note that the similarity or relative homogeneity of the residential neighborhood exists in the minds of its residents and of others who are considering living in the neighborhood. The elements of cohesiveness or similarity include similar style of houses; houses of similar utility; similar age and size of houses; similar quality of houses; similar price range of houses; resident's income in the same general bracket; residents of similar cultural, educational, ethnic, and social backgrounds; and similar land uses.

Appraisers must delineate the neighborhood for purposes of analysis. Operationally, it is that area within which any change has an immediate and direct influence on the value of the subject property. Appraisers should understand the reasons for their selection of neighborhood boundaries and should be prepared to explain them in their appraisal reports. Neighborhood boundaries are often established by natural barriers, political boundaries, and/or man-made obstacles.

Because real estate is immobile, its value is a direct function of the forces at work in its immediate environment. The neighborhood is this immediate environment. Favorable factors leading to increased prices in the neighborhood generally have a positive impact on the value of the subject property; negative forces generally have the opposite effect. The appraiser is still seeking the pertinent factors of supply and demand on the market. In neighborhood analysis, the pertinent market area is geographically restricted.

It is necessary for the appraiser to analyze and evaluate the impact of trends in neighborhood factors on the value of the subject property. Mere listing of factors and their amount and direction of movement is not sufficient. The pertinent factors must be identified and analyzed. Two basic questions—Why? and So what?—must be answered before any factor is included in the neighborhood analysis. Neighborhood analysis must be undertaken from the point of view of the typically informed purchaser—not the point of view of the appraiser.

Elements of Neighborhood Analysis

The analysis of a neighborhood follows much the same pattern as analysis of the market area, with the exception that the geographic area is considerably smaller. Many different factors enter into this analysis. For purposes of identification and data gathering, checklists may be used that classify the factors under the same four major headings used in market area analysis: physical, economic-financial, political-governmental, and sociological. As in market area analysis, this classification is not rigid, and factors may appear under more than one heading. What matters is not so much where any item is included but, rather, whether it is included.

Appraisers may find that a checklist of factors is extremely useful in their investigation of the neighborhood. The purpose of a checklist is simply to make sure that no significant factor is overlooked. It does not mean that every factor must be included in every neighborhood analysis in every appraisal. The FNMA/FHLMC Residential Appraisal Report Form 1004/70 shows the kinds of neighborhood factors these two organizations require the appraiser to report and evaluate; it may be used as a form of checklist (see figure 5–1.)

Amenities. In neighborhood analysis, as distinguished from market area analysis, amenities of living are considered and emphasized in each section of the analysis. Amenities are the attractions, benefits, and advantages of living in a particular location.[5] They represent satisfactions and utility of homeownership, but they also may accrue to tenants insofar as neighborhood influences are concerned.

Physical Factors. The physical characteristics of the neighborhood exert an influence on the neighborhood's attractiveness, or lack of attractiveness, as a place to live. The physical setting within which the subject property is fixed must be evaluated. It is a factor in determining the attractiveness of living in the subject property, whether as owner or tenant. The physical factors of area, topography, soil and subsoil conditions, and climate were discussed previously under community or local market area analysis. As indicated, all of these factors operate much more strongly at the neighborhood level. Other physical factors that are to be considered include barriers, drainage, street patterns, conformity of houses, appearance, percent built up, proximity of supporting facilities, and nuisances and hazards.

The physical plan of the neighborhood is influenced by its street pattern. The attractiveness of individual settings depends on how much advantage is taken of topography and climatic factors in laying out the subdivision or neighborhood. The street pattern can also influence the flow of traffic. Ease and convenience of traffic flow to serve the neighborhood must be counterbalanced against the hazards and nuisances of heavy traffic on through arteries at grade level. Ease and convenience

RESIDENTIAL APPRAISAL REPORT

File No. _____

To be completed by Lender

Borrower	Census Tract	Map Reference

Property Address

City	County	State	Zip Code

Legal Description

Sale Price $ _____ | Date of Sale _____ | Loan Term _____ yrs | Property Rights Appraised ☐ Fee ☐ Leasehold ☐ DeMinimis PUD

Actual Real Estate Taxes $ _____ | (yr) Loan charges to be paid by seller $ _____ | Other sales concessions

Lender/Client _____ | Address _____

Occupant _____ | Appraiser _____ | Instructions to Appraiser _____

NEIGHBORHOOD

Location   ☐ Urban   ☐ Suburban   ☐ Rural

Built Up   ☐ Over 75%   ☐ 25% to 75%   ☐ Under 25%

Growth Rate ☐ Fully Dev.   ☐ Rapid   ☐ Steady   ☐ Slow

Property Values   ☐ Increasing   ☐ Stable   ☐ Declining

Demand/Supply   ☐ Shortage   ☐ In Balance   ☐ Over Supply

Marketing Time   ☐ Under 3 Mos.   ☐ 4–6 Mos.   ☐ Over 6 Mos.

Present Land Use ____% 1 Family ____% 2–4 Family ____% Apts. ____% Condo ____% Commercial

____% Industrial ____% Vacant ____%

Change in Present Land Use   ☐ Not Likely   ☐ Likely (*)   ☐ Taking Place (*)

(*) From _____ To _____

Predominant Occupancy   ☐ Owner   ☐ Tenant   ____% Vacant

Single Family Price Range $ _____ to $ _____ Predominant Value $ _____

Single Family Age _____ yrs to _____ yrs   Predominant Age _____ yrs

Note: FHLMC/FNMA do not consider race or the racial composition of the neighborhood to be reliable appraisal factors.

	Good	Avg	Fair	Poor
Employment Stability	☐	☐	☐	☐
Convenience to Employment	☐	☐	☐	☐
Convenience to Shopping	☐	☐	☐	☐
Convenience to Schools	☐	☐	☐	☐
Adequacy of Public Transportation	☐	☐	☐	☐
Recreational Facilities	☐	☐	☐	☐
Adequacy of Utilities	☐	☐	☐	☐
Property Compatibility	☐	☐	☐	☐
Protection from Detrimental Conditions	☐	☐	☐	☐
Police and Fire Protection	☐	☐	☐	☐
General Appearance of Properties	☐	☐	☐	☐
Appeal to Market	☐	☐	☐	☐

Comments including those factors, favorable or unfavorable, affecting marketability (e.g. public parks, schools, view, noise)

SITE

Dimensions _____ = _____ Sq. Ft. or Acres   ☐ Corner Lot

Zoning classification _____ Present improvements ☐ do ☐ do not conform to zoning regulations

Highest and best use: ☐ Present use   ☐ Other (Describe)

	OFF SITE IMPROVEMENTS		Topo
Public Other (Describe)	Street Access: ☐ Public ☐ Private		Size
Elec. ☐ ☐	Surface _____		Shape
Gas ☐ ☐	Maintenance: ☐ Public ☐ Private		View
Water ☐ ☐	☐ Storm Sewer ☐ Curb/Gutter		Drainage
San.Sewer ☐ ☐	☐ Sidewalk ☐ Street Lights		

☐ Underground Elect. & Tel.

Is the property located in a HUD Identified Special Flood Hazard Area?   ☐ No   ☐ Yes

Comments (favorable or unfavorable including any apparent adverse easements, encroachments or other adverse conditions)

IMPROVEMENTS

☐ Existing ☐ Proposed ☐ Under Constr. | No. Units _____ | Type (det, duplex, semi/det, etc.) | Design (rambler, split level, etc.) | Exterior Walls
Yrs. Age: Actual _____ Effective _____ to _____ | No. Stories _____

Roof Material _____ | Gutters & Downspouts ☐ None | Window (Type): | Insulation ☐ None ☐ Floor
☐ Ceiling ☐ Roof ☐ Walls

☐ Manufactured Housing
Foundation Walls _____ | ☐ % Basement | ☐ Outside Entrance | ☐ Storm Sash ☐ Screens ☐ Combination
☐ Concrete Floor | ☐ Floor Drain ☐ Finished Ceiling
☐ Sump Pump ☐ Finished Walls
☐ Slab on Grade ☐ Crawl Space | ☐ % Finished ☐ Finished Floor
Comments | Evidence of: ☐ Dampness ☐ Termites ☐ Settlement

BSMT

ROOM LIST

Room List	Foyer	Living	Dining	Kitchen	Den	Family Rm.	Rec. Rm.	Bedrooms	No. Baths	Laundry	Other
Basement											
1st Level											
2nd Level											

Finished area above grade contains a total of _____ rooms _____ bedrooms _____ baths. Gross Living Area _____ sq. ft. Bsmt Area _____ sq. ft.

INTERIOR FINISH & EQUIPMENT

Kitchen Equipment: ☐ Refrigerator ☐ Range/Oven ☐ Disposal ☐ Dishwasher ☐ Fan/Hood ☐ Compactor ☐ Washer ☐ Dryer
HEAT: Type _____ Fuel _____ Cond _____ | AIR COND.: ☐ Central ☐ Other

Floors	☐ Hardwood ☐ Carpet Over ☐	
Walls	☐ Drywall ☐ Plaster	
Trim/Finish	☐ Good ☐ Average ☐ Fair ☐ Poor	
Bath Floor	☐ Ceramic	
Bath Wainscot	☐ Ceramic	

Special Features (including energy efficient items) _____

ATTIC: ☐ Yes ☐ No ☐ Stairway ☐ Drop-stair ☐ Scuttle ☐ Floored
Finished (Describe) _____ ☐ Heated

CAR STORAGE: ☐ Garage ☐ Built-in ☐ Attached ☐ Detached ☐ Car Port
No. Cars _____ ☐ Adequate ☐ Inadequate Condition _____

FIREPLACES, PATIOS, POOL, FENCES, etc. (describe) _____

PROPERTY RATING

	Good	Avg	Fair	Poor
Quality of Construction (Materials & Finish)	☐	☐	☐	☐
Condition of Improvements	☐	☐	☐	☐
Room sizes and layout	☐	☐	☐	☐
Closets and Storage	☐	☐	☐	☐
Insulation—adequacy	☐	☐	☐	☐
Plumbing—adequacy and condition	☐	☐	☐	☐
Electrical—adequacy and condition	☐	☐	☐	☐
Kitchen Cabinets—adequacy and condition	☐	☐	☐	☐
Compatibility to Neighborhood	☐	☐	☐	☐
Overall Livability	☐	☐	☐	☐
Appeal and Marketability	☐	☐	☐	☐

Yrs Est Remaining Economic Life _____ to _____ Explain if less than Loan Term

COMMENTS (including functional or physical inadequacies, repairs needed, modernization, etc.) _____

FHLMC Form 70 Rev. 7/79   ATTACH DESCRIPTIVE PHOTOGRAPHS OF SUBJECT PROPERTY AND STREET SCENE   FNMA Form 1004 Rev. 7/79

Figure 5–1. FNMA/FHLMC Residential Appraisal Report Form 1004/70

of travel also affect the proximity of supporting facilities and serve as barriers to nuisances and hazards. In making a neighborhood survey, the appraiser should measure the distance to churches, schools, shopping facilities, recreational facilities, and centers of employment. Convenience and ease of access add to the attractiveness of living in the neighborhood; lack of convenience and ease of access to such facilities represents a deterrent to values in the neighborhood. Both natural and man-made barriers (including street patterns) can be effective protections from the intrusion of incompatible uses and nuisances. Effective barriers to such nuisances as noise, traffic, smoke, or odor can be positive attractions to living in the neighborhood. Also, such barriers often form the boundary of the neighborhood.

The characteristics of a neighborhood are set, in part, by the size, architectural style, type, age, condition, or deterioration of the average house in the neighborhood. These physical considerations also have an important economic impact on the desirability of living in the neighborhood. Maintenance of individual houses and their architectural compatibility influence the general appearance of the neighborhood. This is partly a function of planning and partly a function of the pride and care of occupants. Landscaping, plantings, and open spaces (often the function of government) also influence the physical appearance and hence the attractiveness of the neighborhood. The percent built up within a neighborhood has an economic impact on neighborhood analysis. The appraiser should observe this factor as a physical phenomenon at the outset. It indicates the degree of stability that may be expected, at least in the near term.

Economic-Financial Factors. The economic factors of neighborhood analysis are much more closely related to specifics of individual residences than to the economics of market analysis. The general level of prices in the neighborhood, for example, tends to set the range within which the value of any property is most likely to fall. The level of rents in the neighborhood tends to set the range within which the rental of any one property would most likely fall.

Value is enhanced when the uses within a neighborhood are harmonious and there is balance in the land use pattern. This balance includes the availability of commercial facilities and other supporting activities (churches, schools, and the like) but not their intrusion into the neighborhood in such a way as to interfere with or detract from residential use. A degree of homogeneity in uses, buildings, and occupants in the area is a stabilizing and value-stimulating factor. There should be similarity without the monotony of sameness.

Stability in values is enhanced if the neighborhood is in the path of city growth. Neighborhoods outside the path of city growth may have limited marketability and may be exposed to greater deterioration than neighborhoods that are within it. Strongly defined neighborhood areas and a strong economic base tend to go together. A strong, stable single-family neighborhood can support necessary commercial and other facilities effectively.

The type, stability, and location of employment of residents in the area have a strong impact on the level of values in properties in the neighborhood. The level, source, and stability of family incomes in the neighborhood tend to set the level of property values in the neighborhood as well as the social and economic levels of the residents. These factors indicate the most probable type of purchaser likely to be attracted to the subject property. The number of residents in an area and their household sizes also influence the character of the neighborhood. The neighborhood age distribution tends to set the range of possibilities for attracting new purchasers into the neighborhood. An important consideration regarding property taxes and assessments in neighborhood analysis is the tax treatment of properties in the subject neighborhood in comparison with the tax treatment and tax burdens of similar properties in other neighborhoods in the same taxing jurisdiction. In addition, the likelihood of future special assessments is an important financial consideration for potential buyers. Further, the costs of utilities and fire insurance rates also influence occupancy costs.

The direction and rate of change in the neighborhood directly influence values in the neighborhood. They may reflect growth and development or decline. One of the guides is the extent to which the neighborhood is built up and its rate of development. Another guide, especially for older neighborhoods, is the rate of conversion to other uses.

The ratio of ownership to rental occupancy is an indication of the attractiveness of a single-family neighborhood to purchasers. Some turnover of properties in a neighborhood is usually a healthy market indicator, because it indicates attractiveness to outside purchasers. At the same time, stability and enhancement of values are present when residents seek to remain in the area. The rate of vacancy and the duration of those vacancies are good guides to the attractiveness of properties in the area to potential buyers. The availability of financing and the terms on which financing is available to properties in the neighborhood are strong guides to the neighborhood's relative attractiveness and economic strength.

Political-Governmental Factors. At the neighborhood level, government still exerts an influence. Legal considerations with respect to

individual properties also play an important role, however, in determining the attractiveness of the neighborhood as a place to live. Also,
the availability, frequency, and adequacy of municipal services have an
important bearing on the attractiveness of the neighborhood. These
services include fire and police protection, recreation, schools, and
refuse collection.

The plan of development for the community should include maintenance and protection of the integrity of the neighborhood in question.
It also should provide for the anticipated future uses of all undeveloped
areas in the neighborhood. The extent to which zoning regulations
protect and preserve the existing pattern of residential uses in the neighborhood is extremely important. At least as significant as the regulations
themselves is their enforcement. It is important for the appraiser to
understand how, when, and why exceptions or variances to these zoning
regulations may be permitted and the ease with which such changes
may occur.

Requirements imposed on developers and subdividers will influence
the type and quality of basic services available to homeowners in the
area and will also have a bearing on the housing cost to residents. The
nature of building, housing, fire, electrical, and plumbing codes in the
area will have a distinct impact on the cost of construction and the cost
of occupancy of residences in the neighborhood. Consistent and im-
partial enforcement of these codes throughout the area is as important
as the codes themselves.

Neighborhood decline is no more inevitable or irreversible than
neighborhood growth and improvement. Public programs of renewal
(including redevelopment, rehabilitation, and conservation) can reverse
a downward trend. The existence of adverse neighborhood conditions
alone should not be construed to suggest that there will be no change
from those conditions if change were possible. It could very well be
that the conditions are only tolerated by inhabitants of the neighborhood, not accepted by them. Tolerance and acceptance can be distinguished when the market is presented with an opportunity to make a
choice.

Deed restrictions and private covenants, either for individual properties or for groups of properties, can have as much impact on the use,
utility, and value of individual property as zoning and other public
regulations. Appraisers must investigate these deed restrictions and
private covenants carefully and evaluate them in terms of their impact
on the use of the property. They must also recognize conflicts with
public regulations. In general, if there is no violation of statute, private
agreements may be more restrictive than public regulations. As noted

previously, comparisons of taxes and assessments with those of other neighborhoods are necessary to determine consistency and fairness.

Sociological Factors. At the neighborhood level, the specific characteristics and compatibility of area residents are most important influences on prices, rentals, and values. Change and the direction of such change has a direct bearing on the value of the subject property. The characteristics of the people living in the neighborhood are important determinants of the stability of property values. The existence or introduction of contentious groups, whatever their character, often tends to upset the existing pattern of values. Extreme care must be exercised by the appraiser in evaluating both the direction and the duration of changes before attempting to measure their effects.

Generally, land values tend to increase when population densities increase, but property values do not necessarily follow this trend. The most important ingredients for the enhancement and stabilization of value are similarities in the income level, educational level, and social level of the residents of the neighborhood. The maintenance and condition of properties in the neighborhood are major guides to the concern of residents for the maintenance of property values. A high proportion of owner-occupancy tends to enhance this concern.

The level of activity and participation in civic and community affairs by residents of the neighborhood is a further guide to their concern for maintenance of property values in their neighborhood. The attitudes of outsiders toward the neighborhood, as well as the social attitudes of residents about their own neighborhood, exert a strong influence on the stability of property values. The more a neighborhood is regarded both internally and externally as a good place to live, the greater the enhancement and stability of values.

Access. Although it may be included among physical factors, access, including convenience, is such an important consideration that the appraiser should analyze it separately. Access is measured in terms of time-distance, ease, and cost factors. It is always evaluated in terms of access to and from supporting facilities. A general rule is that a support facility should be close enough to be convenient, but not so close as to become a nuisance or a deterrent to the quiet enjoyment of living amenities.

Factors in a Good Residential Neighborhood

It is important for the appraiser to recognize the characteristics of a good neighborhood. A mere listing of physical, economic, legal-political, and social consideration is not enough. The appraiser needs to know what to look for as clues to desirability and enhancement of property values. All of the more positive characteristics noted in the previous section on elements of neighborhood analysis comprise the characteristics of residential neighborhood strengths.

Appraisers may utilize rating grids, charts, or tables in their evaluation of the neighborhood. The ingredients in representative rating grids are as follows:

1. Protection against inharmonious land uses: zoning; protective covenants; geographical position; character of structures.
2. Physical and social attractiveness: presence or absence of special hazards and nuisances; physical features and landscaping; neighborhood design; architectural appearance of buildings; compatibility among neighborhood occupants.
3. Adequacy of civic, social, and commercial centers: quality and accessibility of schools, shopping centers, churches, and recreation centers.
4. Adequacy of transportation: diversity and cost of available services; quality and frequency of service; time required to destination.
5. Sufficiency of utilities and services: type; capacity; cost.
6. Level of taxes and special assessments: tax burden; special assessments.

The FNMA and FHLMC appraisal forms also contain neighborhood ratings (see figure 5–1 and Appendix C). It is important to note that application of the location rating grid involves not only identification of the individual factors but also a rating of each factor on a numerical or qualitative scale in order to develop a final rating for both the location and the neighborhood.

Trends and Forecasts in Neighborhood Analysis

Neighborhoods are not isolated entities. They are part of the larger market area and are subject to the forces and influences that affect the entire market. Even the boundaries of the neighborhood are flexible: new highways may be built; zoned boundaries may be changed; and use patterns may be altered. Neighborhoods are never static; they are always changing.

All neighborhoods exhibit a life cycle that varies only in the intensity and duration of each phase. The initial phase is development and growth. This is the period during which prices are increasing and the neighborhood is becoming built up. The second stage is stability. This is generally the period of highest value and attractiveness of the neighborhood. The third phase is transition and decline. This occurs as the attractions of the neighborhood are offset by those of new, competitive areas. The properties become functionally obsolescent, as does the pattern of the neighborhood. New uses begin to move in, and this transition frequently results in lower values. The fourth and final phase is renewal and rehabilitation. In some instances, it is possible to renew and revive a neighborhood. Examples may be found in nearly every city (e.g., Old Town in Chicago and Society Hill in Philadelphia).This starts the life cycle all over again.

A new and vigorous neighborhood is generally most attractive and most conducive to high values. An older neighborhood is not necessarily bad, but obsolescence may begin to creep in—the prelude to a decline in attractiveness and in property values. To maintain maximum property values, the neighborhood must be attractive to other potential purchasers, on whom future marketability depends.

The appraiser's job is to identify trends in neighborhood factors that will influence value and to forecast the direction and amount of their movement in the future. Identifying the stage in the life cycle of the neighborhood is one step in this process. The estimated period over which the neighborhood will remain attractive is an important ingredient in estimating the remaining economic life of improvements in that neighborhood. This factor is utilized when the appraiser applies several approaches of value estimation to the appraisal problem. The analysis is usually easier if the neighborhood is already well built up, because the pattern of use and values is set. There is still the problem of estimating the remaining period of stability before decline sets in. One guide to this, though only a guide, is the terms of mortgage loans that lenders are willing to grant on properties in the neighborhood.

Although nearly all neighborhood factors are potential ingredients in estimating the future direction of neighborhood value movements, a few key items are particularly useful. It is most important that the appraiser keep in mind that the neighborhood can improve and exhibit rising values rather than declining. In an older neighborhood, improvement usually requires a conscious application of external forces, either publicly or privately initiated. Stability in use patterns usually indicates stability in values, whereas transition or conversion usually indicates a declining movement. A transition back to the previous patterns, however, may result in improvement through renewal. Much of the stability of use patterns depends on the effectiveness of the protective barriers that exist for the neighborhood. A breakdown in the enforcement of zoning use restrictions usually indicates a decline.

Increasing-use densities generally mean a transition to declining residential values in the neighborhood. A reversal of this trend can indicate an improvement in values. Changes in the social and economic characteristics of the residents of a neighborhood give a strong clue to the probable direction of future movement of values in that neighborhood.

Rapid turnover in the population of a neighborhood usually indicates a trend toward declining values. The greatest stability is usually afforded by families with children in school. A shift from ownership to rental occupancy usually indicates neighborhood decline. The older the residences in a neighborhood, the greater the chance that there will be instability, obsolescence, a transition to other uses, and a decline in values. Prices and rentals, community spirit of owners, and reputation are other factors that need to be considered as guides to future conditions.

Collection and Analysis of Data

The determination of pertinent factors to include in local area neighborhood analysis from among the wide range of possibilities considered earlier also identifies the data the appraiser must obtain in order to understand and evaluate the impact of these background forces on the value of the subject property. The appraiser gathers data from and about the market to provide evidence for a reasonable and defensible forecast of the future state of the market area and neighborhood, because these are the background forces that help determine value.

Depending on which factors appear, from their analysis and judgment, to be important to the appraisal problem, appraisers then must obtain data on many, if not most, of the items discussed previously under area and neighborhood analysis. This collection of data is necessary for an effective analysis of the economic and market environment affecting the subject property. Past trends, present conditions, and future forecasts are required. Appraisers should be thoroughly familiar with the sources of important, basic data—both published and unpublished—for market analysis at all levels. They should also be aware of the sources from which advice and guidance may be obtained for gathering less frequently needed or more elusive data. Appraisers should keep informed of current studies that they can utilize in market area and neighborhood analysis. Finally, appraisers should develop the skills and techniques to gather market data in the field as the occasion demands.

The first and most obvious source to which appraisers should turn for obtaining local, regional, and even national data pertinent to the problem is their own files. Once the data are accumulated and the files are organized systematically, a tremendous saving of time and effort can be effected by keeping them current. In collecting and developing these files in the first place, appraisers should turn to other sources. Moreover, they should have a regular, systematic arrangement for obtaining new information to bring the data in their files up to date.

A great deal of the material that the appraiser requires for market area analysis is available in published form.[6] Other sources of information include public records, private sources (although occasionally this may be regarded as privileged or confidential information), and field interviews. With regard to the latter, the appraiser often must obtain some information directly from participants in real estate transactions. This is particularly true when the appraiser is attempting to develop information about attitudes and about differentials in sales prices resulting from the presence or absence of pertinent area factors.

Uses and Applications of Area and Neighborhood Analysis

The major uses and applications of area and neighborhood analysis are to establish the competitive area for the subject property, to provide a basis for identifying highest and best use of the subject property, and to identify trends in local market and neighborhood forces that affect value. Establishing the competitive area identifies the area within which comparable sales and rentals should be sought for direct sales comparison analysis and gross rent multiplier analysis. Local market and neighborhood analysis establishes the uses that are legal and likely feasible, which are two of the basic criteria for highest and best use. It also indicates the conformity of uses within the use pattern of the competitive market area. Rather than relying on their own estimates of how factors and trends affect residential values in the local market area and the neighborhood, appraisers must ascertain what informed buyers think the future will be and adjust their projections accordingly, however informed and objective they may be. The probable direction, magnitude, and character of future market changes must be estimated, along with their probable impact on the attitudes and behavior of buyers. Appraisers must reach a conclusion about the key or critical market factors in their forecasts on the basis of logic, objective analysis, experience, and the nature of the problem—with assistance from professional economic and market analyses when they are available.

A property can generally do no better than its neighborhood, as the principle of conformity suggests. The limits of value are generally set by price ranges in the neighborhood and by the social and economic status of the residents of the neighborhood. It is highly unlikely that the value of houses in a particular area would be above the highest price for which other houses in that area have recently sold. Selling prices at the other end of the spectrum within a particular area give an indication of minimum values in the neighborhood.

In making their presentations in appraisal reports, appraisers assist both themselves and the readers by utilizing illustrations to summarize and exemplify the points made in the analysis. These illustrations for area analysis would include tables and analysis grids; charts and graphs; maps; and photographs.

Summary

Market analysis identifies the pertinent market area that has an impact on real estate values in general, residential real estate values in the market in which the subject property is located, and the value of the subject property in particular. The appraiser should consider influences at all levels of government, working from the general to the specific (international, national, regional, local, neighborhood). Market analysis helps to identify the pertinent factors in the supply of and demand for residential real estate in the market area, including considerations of physical, economic-financial, political-governmental, and sociological factors. Market factors should be analyzed in terms of their relevance to the appraisal problem at hand, as a basis for identifying the data to be gathered for market area analysis.

The appraiser must develop, maintain, and exploit good sources of data. Market analysis must be objective. It is necessary to analyze the data in terms of their impact on real estate values, especially the value of the subject property. The appraiser does not merely list facts and figures without interpretive analysis. Projections of trends in market influences should be made for the pertinent future. This includes evaluating the reaction of the typical purchaser of residential real estate to anticipated developments and trends. Economic base analysis can be a particularly useful method for local market area analysis and forecasting.

The neighborhood is the immediate economic and physical environment within which the forces of supply and demand have a direct and immediate impact on the value of the subject property. Trends in values in the neighborhood directly affect the value of the subject property. Neighborhood analysis is essential in applying comparative approaches to value estimation. Neighborhood analysis establishes the basis for estimating locational (economic) obsolescence in the valuation of the subject property.

A checklist of market and neighborhood factors is a valuable aid to the appraiser in carrying out the survey and analysis of the neighborhood and local market area. Access to and from supporting community and service facilities is a particularly important ingredient in neighborhood analysis. Convenience and satisfction of residents' needs are the basic criteria for evaluating neighborhood access.

Rating grids are a useful device for establishing comparative ratings of neighborhoods. Neighborhoods are subject to continuous shifting and change. The appraiser must identify the stage of life cycle of the neighborhood and estimate its stability or tendency toward decline. The forecast period of stability or decline is an important ingredient in estimating the remaining economic life of the subject property.

Neighborhood values are subject to the influence of intangible and subjective judgments about the amenities or attractions of living in a particular neighborhood. A well-planned neighborhood with effective protective barriers (physical and legal) will generally maintain values over a longer period of time. The limits of value of the subject property are generally set by price ranges and rental ranges of properties in its neighborhood.

Notes

1. Boyce, Byrl N., ed. *Real Estate Appraisal Terminology,* rev. ed. (Cambridge, Mass.: Ballinger [Joint publication of the American Institute of Real Estate Appraisers and Society of Real Estate Appraisers], 1981), p. 86.

2. Ibid.

3. Ibid., p. 245.

4. Ibid., p. 172.

5. For a more detailed definition of amenities, see Ibid., p. 11.

6. Some of the leading sources of information are listed in Ibid., pp. 355–367.

Suggested Readings

American Institute of Real Estate Appraisers. *The Appraisal of Real Estate,* 8th ed. Chicago: American Institute of Real Estate Appraisers, 1983, chapters 6 and 7.

Barrett, G. Vincent, and Blair, John P. *How to Conduct and Analyze*

Real Estate Market and Feasibility Studies. New York: Van Nostrand Reinhold, 1982, chapter 4.

Bloom, George F., and Harrison, Henry S. *Appraising the Single Family Residence.* Chicago: American Institute of Real Estate Appraisers, 1978, chapter 5.

Bloom, George F.; Weimer, Arthur M.; and Fisher, Jeffrey D. *Real Estate,* 8th ed. New York: John Wiley & Sons, 1982, chapters 13 and 14.

Boyce, Byrl N., ed. *Real Estate Appraisal Terminology,* rev. ed. Cambridge, Mass.: Ballinger (Joint publication of the American Institute of Real Estate Appraisers and Society of Real Estate Appraisers), 1981.

Goetze, Rolf. *Understanding Neighborhood Change.* Cambridge, Mass.: Ballinger, 1979.

Harrison, Henry S. *Harrison's Illustrated Guide: How to Fill Out a Freddie Mac-Fannie Mae Residential Appraisal Form.* New Haven: Collegiate Publishing Company, 1978.

HUD Handbook: Single Family Underwriting Reports and Forms Data, no. 4190.1. Washington, D.C.: U.S. Department of Housing and Urban Development, 1974.

Kinnard, William N., Jr. "An Appraisal Report Primer for Residential Lenders and Underwriters." General Series no. 10. Storrs, Conn.: Center for Real Estate and Urban Economic Studies, The University of Connecticut, 1978.

Kinnard, William N., Jr. *Income Property Valuation.* Lexington, Mass.: Lexington Books, D.C. Heath and Company, 1971, chapter 14.

Messner, Stephen D., et al. *Analyzing Real Estate Opportunities: Market and Feasibility Studies.* Chicago: Realtors National Marketing Institute, 1977, chapter 2.

Public Affairs Counseling. "The Dynamics of Neighborhood Change." Washington, D.C.: U.S. Department of Housing and Urban Development, 1975.

Pyhrr, Stephen A., and Cooper, James R. *Real Estate Investment: Strategy, Analysis, Decisions.* Boston: Warren, Gorham and Lamont, 1982, section II, pp. 69–139.

Smith, Halbert C. *Real Estate Appraisal.* Columbus, Ohio: Grid, 1976, chapter 2.

Smith, Halbert C.; Tschappat, Carl J.; and Racster, Ronald L. *Real Estate and Urban Development,* 3rd ed. Homewood, Ill.: Richard D. Irwin, 1981, chapter 9.

Underwriting Guidelines: Home Mortgages. Washington, D.C.: Federal Home Loan Mortgage Corporation, 1979.

U.S. Department of Commerce, Bureau of the Census. "Housing Data

Resources (Indicators and Sources of Data for Analyzing Housing and Neighborhood Conditions)." Washington, D.C.: U.S. Government Printing Office, 1980.

Wendt, Paul F. *Real Estate Appraisal: Review and Outlook.* Athens: University of Georgia Press, 1974, chapter 3.

6 Property Analysis

Key Terms

Economic life   The time period over which improvements contribute to the value of the total property.

Effective age   The age in years indicated by the condition and utility of a structure.

Floor plan   A schematic of the room layout and traffic flow within a structure.

Functional adequacy   A measure of the standard of performance of a structure, as set by the market, as well as the character of the structure itself and its components.

Functional utility   The ability of a property to perform the function for which it was intended in accordance with current market tastes and standards.

Improvements   Permanent structures or developments located on or attached to land.

Improvements analysis   Analysis of the physical ingredients of a property, their condition and character, and, hence, the market acceptability of the property.

Interim use   An existing but temporary use awaiting transition to highest and best use.

Plot plan   A schematic of the site, showing property lines, building lines, easements, placement of improvements, and site measurements, typically drawn to scale.

Remaining economic life   The number of years over which the structure is expected to continue to contribute to the total value of the property.

Site   An improved parcel of land that is ready for the use or purpose for which it was intended.

Site analysis   Analysis of the utility and marketability of a site.

Site improvements   Additions to land to make the property usable (e.g., curbs, sidewalks, sewers, drains, fills).

Area and neighborhood analyses are important components of the appraisal framework or process. They provide the appraiser with required background information and market trends that identify and

quantify the forces of supply and demand, which are primary determinants of value. Important as area and neighborhood analyses are—
especially in establishing market conditions that prevail as of the valuation date, in terms of which the valuation estimate is made—they
deal only with forces external to the subject property. Before defined
value can be estimated, the characteristics of the subject property also
must be identified and evaluated.

The Rationale of Property Analysis

Improved residential properties are those most commonly appraised.
The subject property to be appraised and analyzed is therefore typically
a residential site with a residential structure on it. This is why property
analysis includes both the site and the improvements. If a vacant residential site should be the subject of the appraisal, the same principles,
techniques, and procedures of site analysis are applied as would be
used for analyzing a site improved with a residence.

Components of Property Analysis

An *improved property* is a residential site with a residential structure
on it. A *site* is a parcel of land that is cleared and graded and has
necessary improvements for drainage, water service, sewer service,
electric service, gas service, access (streets and alleys), and sidewalks
as appropriate. A *residential site* is a parcel or plot of land that has the
necessary improvements to make it immediately usable for residential
purposes, in terms of the standards of the market and neighborhood
in which it is located. Land as such is unimproved by man. A site, on
the other hand, is land that has been improved by man for a specific
use or uses. *Site improvements* are improvements to land that make it
usable for a particular purpose or purposes. These improvements include utility connections or installations, landscaping, grading, sidewalks, driveways, patios, and the like.

Improvements are "broadly, buildings or other more or less permanent structures or developments located upon or attached to land."[1]
They consist of improvements on and to land. Improvements *on* land
are the subject of improvements analysis. They are what make a residential site an improved residential property. Improvements *to* land
are "usually additions to land to make property usable, such as curbs,
sidewalks, street lights, sewers, drains, fills."[2] These are site improvements. Improvements are depreciable; they lose value systematically

with the passage of time. This feature is recognized by depreciation (or cost recovery) allowable under the Internal Revenue Code. Land or site, however, is not depreciable. This does not mean that site value cannot or will not change over time. It means that losses in value are not systematically and predictably associated with the passage of time.

Objectives of Property Analysis

The major determinant of property value that is based upon the characteristics of the subject property itself is its use. Form largely determines function, and function determines use—within the context of market constraints and determinants identified and measured through area and neighborhood analysis. Value is always estimated in terms of highest and best use, which may or may not be either the actual or the intended use. Site value is based on the highest and best use of the site, and property value is based on the highest and best use of the entire improved property. The two uses are not always the same, although they frequently are the same for improved residential, amenity properties. A major objective of property analysis is to identify highest and best use of the subject property as of the valuation date. This is accomplished through careful identification, description, and evaluation of the physical, legal, and economic characteristics of the subject property—all in the context of current or given market conditions.

Other objectives of property analysis include identification of the property being appraised, both physically (including location) and legally, and identification of the salient characteristics of the subject property. Knowledge of the salient characteristics of the subject property is necessary in developing an adequately detailed description of the subject property in the appraisal report. In addition, these characteristics indicate what data need to be collected about other competitive or comparable properties in order to apply the several approaches to value in appraising the subject property. Further, they establish a basis for estimating the effective age and remaining economic life of the improvements. They are also helpful in estimating the reproduction cost new of the subject improvements and in identifying deductions for accrued depreciation from that cost new. Finally, they establish a basis for adjustments in the sales adjustment process in direct sales comparison analysis. In sum, these characteristics provide the bases for evaluation of the subject property.

The steps in property analysis (not necessarily in any prescribed sequence) are:

1. Inspect the property, using a prepared checklist to avoid omitting any needed information.
2. Inspect the pertinent legal and public records on the subject property.
3. Observe and note the age, condition, quality, features, siting, and environment of the subject property.
4. Identify the salient characteristics of the subject property.
5. Evaluate the physical, legal, economic, and amenity characteristics of the subject property in terms of current market standards of acceptability.

Site Analysis

In the application of many techniques of valuation analysis, site is valued separately. Before a site can be valued, its pertinent and significant characteristics must be identified and evaluated for purposes of comparison on the market. The acceptability and marketability of the site depends on the extent to which its characteristics meet the desires and standards of potential buyers. Site is always valued as if vacant and available to be put to its highest and best use. Site analysis involves the identification and analysis of the characteristics that create, enhance, or detract from the utility, desirability, and marketability of a site on the market as of the date of the appraisal. The present worth of its utility and desirability constitutes the value of the site.

Factors in Site Analysis

Appraisers must identify and understand the operation of the market factors that enter into the determination of the value of a site. Appraisers must identify the relative importance of the various features of a site and their pertinence to valuation estimation in the particular market at the time of the appraisal. The importance and pertinence of these factors varies with standards of acceptability and desirability on the part of market participants. A major finding, therefore, must be what these standards are in the market at the time of the appraisal.

Physical Factors. Some of the physical characteristics of a residential site may vary in quantity and therefore are termed variables. Others are attributes, in the sense that the site either possesses them or it does not. The quantity of attributes does not change measurably from site to site. Size is decidedly a variable and has several ingredients, including area, effective area, frontage, width, depth, excess land, and shape.

Area is an important determinant of the possible uses for a site. Accurate area measurement is critical. *Effective area* is the area within which building construction may take place. It is determined by the set-back requirements of zoning regulations, deed restrictions, and such standards of lending as FHA or VA maximum coverage limits.

Frontage is the distance abutting a street or other public way. It is measured in front feet, usually in terms of a standard depth. If the depth of the lot is different from the standard for the particular neighborhood or market, the effective frontage may be different from the actual number of feet fronting along the street. *Width,* usually measured at the front building line, is the distance between the two sidelines of the lot at that point. Average width is the mean of the distance between sidelines at the front and rear of the lot. *Depth* is the distance from the front line to the rear line of the lot. Average depth is the mean of two or more side boundaries, measured perpendicularly from the front line of the lot. Effective depth is expressed as a percentage of the standard depth of a lot in the market in question.

Excess land is the area by which the lot exceeds the size of a readily marketable, standard lot in the market. The extent to which lot area is excess depends upon the standards of the market. Surplus land is excess land which may legally be sold off in one or more lots. *Shape* is determined by the lot dimensions. It influences the uses that are possible and the uses that are permissible under public and private use restrictions. Together with the area, it is a guide to what is physically possible and what is legally permissible on the lot.

Topography is a guide to what uses are possible and feasible on the lot in question. Topography will influence the cost of making the lot usable for the purpose intended. It is one ingredient dictating the size of the foundation, the type of construction, and the location of a building on the lot. *Slope* indicates the extent to which the lot is buildable, the type of construction required, and the need for such site improvements as retaining walls and fill. A completely flat lot may cause problems of inadequate surface drainage and pressure on the foundation. A severely sloping lot may cause problems of washout. Either situation may result in additional costs for making the lot an effectively usable residential site.

Soil and subsoil conditions influence what type of construction is feasible, where construction may occur on the lot, and what types of improvements to the lot are necessary to make a residential use both possible and feasible. Soil conditions influence what can be grown on the lot and whether additional top soil would be needed to allow required landscaping. Drainage capabilities are particularly important for private sewer systems or septic tanks. The percolation characteristics and permeability of the subsoil should be ascertained. These characteristics will determine how much waterproofing of the foundation is necessary and how much improvement of subsoil conditions through fill or other drainage features is required. Bearing qualities may also have to be determined by outside technicians. These qualities indicate the type of construction that can be placed on the land, and where.

Physical improvements on and to the site affect its utility. These improvements include walks and driveways, walls and fencing, and landscaping and existing plantings. In addition, the utilities serving the site affect its attractiveness and marketability. The appraiser must ascertain the size and adequacy of the utilities as well as their reliability. One important point is whether they are publicly provided, part of a community system (privately owned), or individual to the site. The utilities include water, sewage disposal, storm and surface water disposal, electricity, and gas. Streets and related improvements, such as sidewalks, curbs, street lights, and alleys, also affect the utility, attractiveness, and marketability of the site. Finally, the relationship of the site to prevailing winds and sun will affect its utility and the enjoyment of its residential use.

Economic Factors. Most economic factors operate at the neighborhood or market area level. Nevertheless, certain elements definitely related to site analysis may be measured in terms of dollars. Most of these elements are really property analysis considerations. Prices of comparable sites tend to set the range within which the value of the subject site is most likely to be found. The level of assessments, taxes, and special assessments for utilities or streets is an important factor in the cost of owning the site or property. One important consideration is the tax treatment of the subject site in comparison with the treatment of competitive sites in the same area. Also, the method of payment of taxes or special assessments can constitute a burden on the landowner and should be investigated. In addition, utilities costs and service costs (refuse collection, fire protection, and the like) need to be considered in terms of both absolute and comparative levels.

For valuation purposes, sites are often analyzed in terms of standard units rather than as an entire site. The appraiser must discover the appropriate unit or units to be used in the specific appraisal problem, as a result of investigating the standards and behavior of buyers in the local market. The units may be physical or economic units of use. Typical physical units of comparison include front foot, square foot, lot, and acre. For front foot or square foot measurements, the number of effective front feet or square feet should be measured carefully. For the front foot measurement, the standard depth for the area in question must be established before effective frontage can be measured. When the lots are approximately the same size in a given neighborhood or subdivision, minor differences in size may not affect market value, so long as the lot is effectively usable for the residential purpose intended. There may still be differentials in assessment and taxation, however. For these purposes, the appraiser should account for even small differences in size. Larger tracts and estate areas are often valued and sold on a per acre basis.

Economic units of comparison include such measures as rooms or square feet of building area. When different development programs are used for similar lots, the value of a lot may be expressed in terms of sales price or value per room of a residential building developed on the site. This approach is more widely used in multifamily site valuation, however. A site may also be valued in terms of the sales price per square foot of building area constructed on it. This, too, is unusual in single-family residential site valuation, although it is widely used for multifamily residential sites.

Locational Factors. Because of its immobility, the most significant single characteristic of any site is its location. Location is always expressed in terms of the relationship of the site to surrounding and nearby facilities and/or hazards and nuisances. The appraiser must consider the pattern of surrounding land uses, traffic patterns, street patterns, alleys, and the like. These features provide the physical setting for the site. The size, shape, and other physical characteristics of the site should be in general conformity with those of competing nearby sites.

Access is always estimated in terms of the ease and convenience of getting to and from desired facilities, such as shopping, schools, churches, places of employment, and recreation. The ideal residential location is one that is close enough to facilities to permit easy, quick, and inexpensive access without being so close that hazards or nuisances are encountered. For a residential site, the safety of pedestrian and/or vehicular access is also important. The existence of nearby hazards and nuisances (inharmonious land uses, noise, light, odor, traffic) should be noted, as well as their distance from the subject site. This is the basis for estimating how significant any existing nuisances or hazards might be to the occupants of residential facilities on the site. Such hazards as nearby bodies of water, ravines, and the like, should also be noted, and their impact on the subject site should be estimated. Protection against nuisances is considered to be a legal-governmental factor under zoning.

Legal-Governmental Factors. Legal-governmental factors can influence the utility and the utilization of the site being appraised. Information about the title must be specific to the subject site. This information is necessary to identify what rights are being appraised. It is important in the definition of the problem in the appraisal framework. Much of this information can be derived from an examination of deeds and other legal records of the municipality or county in question or from access to a title search. The questions to be answered might include: What rights are actually being appraised? What rights are transferable by the current fee owner of the property? What unsatisfied liens or claims exist against the property? How may they be extinguished? Do they represent clouds on the title, which might affect the marketability or transferability of the fee interest? Is title insurance available on the property?

A brief history of transfers (if any) should be developed and noted, with references to the appropriate volume and page of the deeds in question. Deed restrictions and easements should be carefully identified, and an estimate should be made of their impact on the use of the property. Conflicts with public regulations and restrictions should be noted. Both neighborhood agreements and specific deed covenants should be investigated. Easements across the land of others that go with the site in question should be noted and analyzed. They can have a significant impact on the use and utility of the subject site.

Zoning regulations affect a specific site by limiting the uses to which it can be put and the intensity of those uses. In particular, set-back requirements (front yard, side yard, and rear yard) affect the development of the site as well as the positioning of buildings on the site. Zoning can also be a positive influence on value by protecting the subject property from the adverse effects of nuisances or inharmonious uses. Uses or set-backs that are in violation of zoning regulations should be especially noted. Some estimate must be made about the prospect of their continuance in the future over the time during which the violation or nonconforming use may be continued. In some communities, nonconforming uses are limited in time; in others, they may be continued indefinitely. This makes a major difference in the utility of the site over the long run.

The method of assessing sites and of levying special assessments for streets and utilities has an impact on the utility of a residential site. This factor also must be considered in comparison with the treatment of competitive, comparable sites in the area. Not only the availability of municipal services, but their quality, reliability, and frequency should be ascertained. These factors, too, affect the enjoyment of the site for residential purposes.

Amenities of a site or property are those attractions and benefits that accrue to the owner and are directly associated with ownership. They include such items as pride of ownership, quiet enjoyment, and the satisfaction of being in a particular location. To evaluate amenities effectively, the appraiser must ascertain what the desires, tastes, and standards of typical buyers in the market area are at the time of the appraisal.

Evaluation of Site Characteristics

As in market area analysis and neighborhood analysis, site analysis requires the application of logic and experience to the collected facts about the site that are assembled by the appraiser. Once again, mere identification of factors and listing of characteristics are not sufficient. In addition to the basic and fundamental task of developing an estimate of highest and best use as of the valuation date, the evaluation of site characteristics identified by site analysis includes identification of locational obsolescence and noncontributory costs, and estimation of marketability and acceptability.

In analyzing the site, the appraiser will identify the degree of its conformity with sites that are competing with it on the market. The degree of nonconformity or lack of standard attributes is an indication of locational obsolescence or economic obsolescence.

Physical characteristics, as well as poor access, may require that considerable sums be expended to make the site usable for the intended purpose (presumably, its highest and best use). The fundamental principle that cost does not create value has already been discussed. Unusually large expenditures to ready the site for use will not necessarily be recovered through the sale of the site on the open market. The appraiser must be alert to this particular problem whenever any major deficiencies are noted in the site or in the access to the site.

Costs of ownership and operation also must be considered, including taxes, utilities costs, special assessments, and costs of municipal services. If these costs are excessive or unfair, they can have a serious negative impact on the value of the site.

In completing the analysis of the site, the appraiser must reach a conclusion regarding its marketability and acceptability on the market. In effect, the question to be answered is: what would be the reaction of the typically informed buyer to the subject site in the local market on the valuation date? In attempting to answer this question, the appraiser may utilize tools that have already been discussed. For example, evaluating the site in terms of units that the market considers appropriate, or that the appraiser can demonstrate are useful analytical tools, helps considerably in the comparison process of site value estimation. In addition, the relationship of the site to its competition, as well as its relationship to hazards, nuisances, and/or conveniences, is an important determinant of its marketability and acceptability on the market. Finally, the property tax treatment of the subject site in comparison with treatment of competitive properties is an important guide to its relative attractiveness and, hence, its marketability. Not only the current situation, but trends in tax and assessment treatment must be analyzed.

Improvements Analysis (Building Analysis)

A careful, detailed, and accurate identification of all pertinent features of the structure is necessary in every appraisal. Analysis of site improvements is also required, although this is frequently included under site analysis. Because many site improvements are hidden from view, they cannot be identified and inspected in the same detail. The terms *improvements analysis, structure analysis,* and *building analysis* are used interchangeably here. Building analysis is necessary to identify the physical attributes being valued and to make them unequivocally clear. Similarly, an identification of property rights is necessary to make clear the legal characteristics of the property being appraised.

Rationale of Improvements or Building Analysis

Building analysis and evaluation are fundamental to the application of all three approaches to value estimation. Although inspection and physical description of a residential structure are essential to an appropriate appraisal, the emphasis is not placed entirely on physical characteristics. Instead, the physical ingredients of the property, their condition, and their character combine to serve as a guide to the market acceptability and, hence, the marketability of the property. Marketability is a basic determinant of value.

The market acceptability and marketability of improved residential real estate must be measured in terms of the standards established by the market. In other words, the appraiser must ascertain what is sought and accepted by typical purchasers in the market. These standards vary over time as tastes, customs, and technology change. They also vary from one market segment to another at the same time. Therefore, the appraiser must ascertain the standards of acceptability that are both current and local in order to establish the criteria in terms of which the subject property is evaluated.

The standards of at least three entities must be understood by the appraiser so that the acceptability and marketability of the subject property can be measured effectively. Actual and potential purchasers currently active in the local market provide the first set of standards. They are the market that must be satisfied if the property is to be sold. Lenders, the second entity, are interested in the marketability of property that is collateral for a mortgage loan. They want quick disposition of the property in the event of default or foreclosure. This means that the property should be in good physical condition, so that the potential purchaser will not discount the purchase price substantially to account for repairs and deferred maintenance that should be taken care of immediately. It also means that the property should conform generally both to its neighborhood and to the standards of acceptability of potential purchasers. Unusual or unique properties are generally more difficult to mortgage for this reason. Even when mortgage loans are not to be sold on the secondary market, FNMA/FHLMC and GNMA standards of property acceptability frequently are important determinants of lenders' decisions to make mortgage loans. The FNMA/FHLMC Form 1004/70 analysis of the property is divided into site desirability and rating of the physical property. Other underwriting standards are expressed in terms of room sizes, natural light, ventilation, heating, insulation, storage, access, and privacy. The basic question is how adequately the structure performs the function for which it is designed. This question is answered by asking subsidiary questions: What is in the structure? Where is it? How much is there?

Local regulation provides the third set of standards that must be understood by the appraiser. Building codes, housing codes, and zoning regulations set community standards for type of construction, construction methods, and construction materials. Whether or not other items would be acceptable on a completely free market, local codes and regulations must be recognized by the appraiser as setting the limits within which a structure is legally usable and, hence, marketable on the current local market.

Functional Utility

Having identified the physical characteristics of the structure, the appraiser's next major problem is to estimate the functional utility of the structure. A house has been called a machine for living. The ultimate objective of improvements analysis is to establish a basis for estimating value, through the estimate of highest and best, or most probable, use. In this regard, it should be noted that value is not represented by the quantity of brick, lumber, mortar, or other materials within a structure. Values are determined by the buying habits and social traits of people. The basic issue, then, is how the house functions as a facility for serving the daily needs of the household that lives within it. An alternative issue is how acceptable the house is to prospective purchasers or renters.

Functional utility is "the sum of the attractiveness and usefulness of the property. It is the ability of the property to perform the function for which it is intended, in terms of current market tastes and standards."[3] The test of functional utility is whether the residence provides efficiently the services of supplying shelter and other living amenities that people want. The higher that efficiency, the greater the functional utility of the structure. Low utility restricts marketability. It cannot be offset by the best materials or workmanship. Efficiency is measured in terms of the ability to satisfy the wants and needs of people on the market. It is not an objective mechanical or engineering standard, nor is it the appraiser's standard. The appraiser, therefore, must know tastes and desires on the market and what will be accepted. This requires the appraiser to ascertain the needs and desires of the typical buyer.

The measure of functional utility provides the basis for estimating functional obsolescence in the cost approach to valuation. It is also the basis for comparisons in the other approaches to value estimation. It is required in estimating the contribution of the improvements to the total value of the property. The major principles of value that are applicable in the analysis of functional utility are contribution, conformity, and balance.

The function of a residence is to provide the amenities of living and shelter as efficiently and as economically as possible. In estimating functional utility, the appraiser compares the subject building with competitive buildings of similar age and style on the current local market and with a typical modern building performing the same function. The value of improved property is estimated in terms of its highest and best use, which takes into consideration the existing improvements on the site. That value exists in terms of the maximum functional utility of the existing improvements. The function of the building dictates the use or uses to which it can be put. Highest and best use represents the most profitable (in dollars or amenity benefits) use program consistent with the existing improvements. Function dictates use; the market dictates the feasibility and profitability of function.

Amenities were defined earlier as the peculiar and intangible benefits of homeownership, which include, but are not necessarily limited to, personal pride of ownership and sense of accomplishment, belonging, and responsibility. These satisfactions may arise from architectural excellence and attractiveness, scenic beauty, and/or desirable social environment. Amenities are incapable of direct measurement. They can only be inferred from the actions of buyers and owners on the current local market. Amenities are in part determined by and dependent on functional utility. When the residence adds to the enjoyment of living in it (through its design, architectural style, layout, structural quality, fixtures and equipment, and the like), functional utility enhances the amenities of occupancy and thus the value of the property.

For purposes of analysis, the aspects of functional utility may be divided into five main categories. In each category, the ultimate test of functional utility is whether the element enhances the use and enjoyment of the residence, and whether it adds to or detracts from the marketability of the property. The five categories are as follows:

1. *Architecture:* Architectural style and design should enhance the function of the structure as a living unit. It should create a pleasing appearance, both externally and internally, while relating the structure appropriately to its setting and its site. For maximum functional utility to be derived, the architectural style of the subject structure should be in basic conformity with its neighborhood. This simply means that the structure in question should not clash with its environment.

2. *Design and layout:* The principle of balance comes into play here. The planning and layout of the residence are influenced by local conditions, local codes, and local tastes. Good design utilizes the space within the structure well, with little or no waste. Public acceptance is the key to what constitutes proper design and layout.

3. *Traffic pattern:* This might be included under design and layout, but it is particularly important. For the house to function effectively as a machine for living, the placement of rooms, doorways, and equipment must reflect the necessity to route traffic efficiently. There should be no serious competition for the same space.

4. *Rooms—sizes and types:* This is also an element of design and layout, but it deserves special attention in the inspection by the appraiser. There are standards for minimum acceptable sizes and combinations of rooms if the property is to receive FHA insurance. These standards are widely utilized by lenders and others in the real estate field.

   The basic criterion is that rooms should be large enough to meet at least the minimum requirements of the typical purchaser in the market for the particular price level and market segment at the time of the appraisal. The combination of rooms that is acceptable is also set by standards of the market, as well as by FHA or lenders. In a given market at a particular price level, for example, a three-bedroom house may require two baths to be effectively marketable. In other circumstances, one bath may suffice. Separate dining facilities may be required in one market or for a house of a particular size but may not be necessary for marketability in other circumstances.

5. *Performance standards:* This includes the capacity of the structure to provide services of the type required by the market. It involves an analysis and evaluation of equipment and fixtures as well as insulation, heating, ventilation, and light.

Elements of Acceptability, Marketability, and Adequacy

The standards of the current local market must be applied to the observed condition and character of the subject structure(s). Acceptability is judged in terms of the standards of typical buyers in the current local market, of lenders (and the FHA), and of local communities, as expressed through codes and regulations. In the inspection of the subject property, the appraiser gathers information and reaches conclusions about physical condition, effective age, and functional adequacy.

Most of the elements of physical condition may be ascertained by observation of both structural components and fixtures or equipment. Condition influences the usefulness of the structural component or equipment, as well as its probable remaining economic life. Physical condition also influences marketability. It affects the typical purchaser's judgment of how much will have to be spent to bring the structure into acceptable condition.

In evaluating the condition of the structure, the appraiser will consider the following: deferred maintenance; age and adequacy of equipment; quality and type of repairs already made; leakage, water damage, moisture, settling, and cracks; and cost and quality. Deferred maintenance consists of items in need of immediate repair. The standard is whether the typical purchaser would consider the repair necessary and justified immediately upon purchase. Redecoration, replacement of broken items, and replacement of worn-out items are examples of deferred maintenance. Deferred maintenance is the basis for curable physical deterioration when estimating accrued depreciation or diminished utility.

Equipment and fixtures frequently must be replaced before the end of the economic life of the entire structure. The age and condition of such equipment and fixtures set the basis for an estimate of physical deterioration charges, whether deferred curable or incurable. Water damage offers indications of the wearing out of the structure or damage that may not be economically feasible to correct. Such damage provides the basis for estimating incurable physical deterioration in measuring accrued depreciation or diminished utility. Cost and quality set the range within which comparisons can be made with competing structures in the direct sales comparison and gross rent multiplier approaches to residential valuation. They also help in estimating reproduction cost new of the structure in the cost approach. When the inspection and analysis of the structure is completed, the appraiser should describe the physical condition of the various structural components in enough detail to establish the basis for the valuation analysis.

Economic Life and Effective Age. Although the residential structure is inspected and described as a physical entity, its value results from the operation of economic forces. As indicated earlier, there is a difference between the physical life, useful life, and economic life of improvements. The most important consideration in appraisal is the estimated economic life of the structure, as well as the probable economic life of components, equipment, and fixtures that normally will be replaced before the basic structure has been fully depreciated.

There is also a difference between actual age and effective age of improvements; the latter is more significant in appraisal. *Economic life* is "the period over which improvements to real estate contribute to the value of the property."[4] For residential properties, this means the time period over which these properties will provide the services and amenities of residential occupancy consistent with the competitive costs of occupancy. Based on structural condition and quality, the appraiser must estimate the number of years most likely remaining in the economic life of the structure as of the date of the appraisal. This is in part a function of the attitudes and reactions of typical buyers on the market, and in part a function of the market record of competitive properties. The *remaining economic life* is the time period over which the improvements will be depreciated in the cost approach and capital recovery will be provided in physical residual techniques of income capitalization.

The *effective age* of a structure or structural component is the difference between its normal economic life and the estimated remaining economic life, based on observed condition and utility. Effective age may also be determined by comparison. Depending on the quality of maintenance and the degree of use or abuse by occupants, effective age may be greater than or less than actual age or chronological age.

In appraisal analysis, effective age is used as the measure of the proportion of the structural component that has been used as of the date of the appraisal. This provides the basis for estimating physical deterioration observed in the structure. Economic life and effective age depend partly on tastes, standards, and customs in the local market. They also depend on physical condition, as observed in the inspection of the property.

Functional Adequacy. As noted earlier, the functional utility of a structure or structural component depends on the standards of the current local market. These standards tend to vary over time and from market to market. They also vary with the type, price range, and price level of the property being appraised. Therefore, the market plus the character of the structure and its components together set the standards of performance that indicate the functional adequacy of the structure.

Functional adequacy has a direct effect on marketability. Functional inadequacies may result from deficiencies, defects or superadequacies in the structure. In either case, they provide the basis for estimating and measuring functional obsolescence in the improvements in the cost approach. They tend to reduce marketability and, hence, value. Deficiencies may stem from several sources. Lack of facilities or components currently regarded as desirable or essential on the local market is one form of deficiency. Underimprovement of the site, in comparison with typical improvements in the neighborhood, is another. Defects include outmoded or inadequate equipment and facilities; insufficient capacities, such as electrical service, heating system, water supply, insulation, and closet space; improper layout or traffic pattern; and inadequate room sizes.

Superadequacies are elements that are excessive in quality or capacity for the type of structure, as judged by the character of competing properties on the current local market. They represent an expenditure or cost in excess of that necessary to perform the function for which they are intended in a structure of the type that is competitive with the subject residence. Overimprovement of the site in comparison with typical improvements in the neighborhood is one form of superadequacy. Other forms of superadequacy are excessive cost and capacity in fixtures and equipment, excessive maintenance or operating expenses stemming from too-high ceiling heights, costly equipment, and the like. Excessive quality or size of structural components, such as unnecessarily thick foundations or a slate roof on a Cape Cod bungalow, are also forms of superadequacy.

Building and Structural Components

In making the analysis of improvements (especially structures), appraisers should be aware of the basic ingredients that make up a residential structure. They should know what to look for and how to estimate the structural quality and condition of residences. Elements of residential structures, technical terminology and vocabulary, illustrations of floor plans, residential cross sections, roof types and construction details, as well as construction materials, methods, and quality are discussed in some of the selected references cited at the end of this chapter.[5]

Evaluation of Improvements Characteristics

The ultimate objectives of improvements analysis are to establish the basis for estimating the highest and best use (or most probable use) of the improved property (site and buildings) and to provide the basis for estimating the contribution of the improvements to total property value. To achieve these objectives, the appraiser must reach judgments or conclusions about all of the items discussed earlier (i.e., functional utility of the improvements, market acceptability of the improvements, actual and effective age of improvements, remaining economic life of improvements, and condition of improvements).

Property Inspection and Data Collection
for Property Analysis

Most data for property analysis come from direct field inspection, observation, and measurement of the subject property. The rest come from public records about the subject property. These two sources provide the required information to produce a complete physical and legal description of the subject property and of its attributes and characteristics.

Required Data and Sources

The best guide to what data are required for effective property analysis is provided by narrative or form reporting requirements. The FNMA and FHLMC appraisal report forms indicate clearly what information is expected for form appraisals. The SREA Standards of Professional Practice and Conduct provide data requirements for narrative appraisal reports under appraisal reporting standards.[6]

It is important for the appraiser to know what is needed and where to get it, so that the property data-gathering process can be both complete and efficient. The field inspection will reveal property characteristics, equipment, condition, siting, environment, hazards or nuisances, topography, building layout, and floor plan. Interviews with the occupants will often reveal conditions that are not obvious on visual inspection. Public records will reveal legal information and some physical information that is not easily observed and will also confirm observed features. Deeds should indicate the property rights involved, the legal description of the property, and lot dimensions. Assessor's files should indicate property taxes, lot and building dimensions, actual age of improvements, number and type of rooms, construction type and quality, and (sometimes) restrictions on the property. Zoning maps will indicate the zoning of the property. Building inspectors' or engineers' records should reveal age, type, and dimensions of improvements.

Field Inspection

There are several reasons for carrying out a field inspection. First, there is the need to assemble all required data on the physical characteristics of the subject property. The legal characteristics, and some physical characteristics, are provided from public records. In addition, there is a need to acquire first-hand knowledge of the characteristics and attributes of the subject property. This includes, particularly, information about the condition and functional adequacy of the structure(s), siting, and the relationship of the subject property to its immediate environment. Such information can be obtained only from a field inspection of the property. Finally, the appraiser must be able to certify that the subject property has been personally inspected. This is required under the SREA Standards of Professional Practice and Conduct, as well as by most clients, lenders, insurers, and courts.

Preinspection arrangements should be made carefully, so that the inspection itself proceeds expeditiously and efficiently. Appraisers should make a firm appointment with the occupants, either directly or through the broker, lender, or owner. They also should prepare a detailed checklist of items to look for and note. One example of such a checklist is shown in figure 6–1. Another good checklist is provided in the FNMA and FHLMC appraisal report form. The appraiser can take a blank

CONSULTATION AND INSPECTION REPORT

PROPERTY ADDRESS	TOWN	COUNTY	STATE

APPLICANT	OWNER	INSP. DATE

NEIGHBORHOOD DATA

				NEIGHBORHOOD RATING	Good	Avg	Fair	Poor
Location	☐ Urban	☐ Suburban	☐ Rural	Employment Stability	☐	☐	☐	☐
Built Up	☐ Over 75%	☐ 25% to 75%	☐ Under 25%	Convenience to Employment	☐	☐	☐	☐
Growth Rate ☐ Fully Dev.	☐ Rapid	☐ Steady	☐ Slow	Convenience to Shopping	☐	☐	☐	☐
Property Values	☐ Increasing	☐ Stable	☐ Declining	Convenience to Schools	☐	☐	☐	☐
Demand/Supply	☐ Shortage	☐ In Balance	☐ Over Supply	Adequacy of Public Transportation	☐	☐	☐	☐
Marketing Time	☐ Under 3 Mos.	☐ 4 - 6 Mos.	☐ Over 6 Mos.	Recreational Facilities	☐	☐	☐	☐

Present Land Use ___% 1 Family ___% 2 - 4 Family ___% Apts. ___% Condo ___% Industrial ___% Vacant ___% Commercial ___%

Change in Present Land Use ☐ Not Likely ☐ Likely (*) ☐ Taking Place (*)

(*) From _____ To _____

Predominant Occupancy ☐ Owner ☐ Tenant _____% Vacant

Single Family Age _____yrs to _____yrs Predominant Age _____yrs

Single Family Price Range $_____to $_____ Predominant Value $_____

Neighborhood Rating (right column):
- Adequacy of Utilities ☐ ☐ ☐ ☐
- Property Compatibility ☐ ☐ ☐ ☐
- Protection from Detrimental Conditions ☐ ☐ ☐ ☐
- Police and Fire Protection ☐ ☐ ☐ ☐
- General Appearance of Properties ☐ ☐ ☐ ☐
- Appeal to Market ☐ ☐ ☐ ☐

Comments including those factors, favorable or unfavorable, affecting marketability (e.g. public parks, schools, view, noise) _____

SITE DATA

Dimensions _____ = _____ Sq. Ft. or Acres ☐ Inside Lot ☐ Corner Lot

Zoning classification _____ Present improvements ☐ do ☐ do not conform to zoning regulations

Highest and best use: ☐ Present use ☐ Other (specify) _____

	Public	Other (Describe)		
Elec.	☐	_____	Topo	_____
Gas	☐	_____	Size	_____
Water	☐	_____	Shape	_____
San. Sewer	☐	_____	View	_____
Ungrd. El./Tel.	☐	_____	Drainage	_____

Is the property located in a HUD Identified Special Flood Hazard Area? ☐ No ☐ Yes

Property Rights Appraised ☐ Fee ☐ Leasehold ☐ _____

Driveway ☐ Yes ☐ Macadam ☐ Oil & stone ☐ Stone Slope: ☐ None ☐ Moderate ☐ Steep
☐ No ☐ Concrete ☐ Gravel ☐ Dirt _____

Landscaping ☐ Above Average ☐ Minimum Swim pool: ☐ In ground _____ ☐ Above ground _____
☐ Average ☐ Poor Filter _____ Shape _____

Fences: _____ Div. Brd. _____ Deck _____
_____ Size _____ Heated _____

Walks _____

Comments (easements, encroachments) _____

OFF SITE IMPROVEMENTS

Street Access: ☐ Public ☐ Private
Surface _____
Maintenance: ☐ Public ☐ Private
☐ Storm Sewer ☐ Curb/Gutter
☐ Sidewalk ☐ Street Lights

Source: Leland T. Bookhout, SREA, MAI, L.T. Bookhout, Inc., Hyde Park, N.Y.

Figure 6–1. Consultation and Inspection Report

BUILDING DATA

☐ Existing ☐ Proposed ☐ Under Constr. | No. Units _____ | Type (det, duplex, semi/det., etc.) | Design (rambler, split level, etc.)

Yrs. Age: Actual _____ Effective ____ to ____ | No. Stories _____

Roof-Type: Condition: | Window (Type): _____

   Material: | ☐ Storm Sash   ☐ Screens   ☐ Combination

☐ Manufactured Housing | ☐ Double Glaze   ☐ Triple Glaze   ☐ Storm Doors

Foundation Walls | Exterior Walls: Frame   Cover

          Condition

☐ Slab on Grade ☐ Crawl Space | Gutters & Downspouts ☐ None   Material _____

_____ % Basement ☐ Floor Drain   Finished Ceiling _____

☐ Outside Entrance ☐ Sump Pump   Finished Walls _____

☐ Concrete Floor _____ % Finished   Finished Floor _____

Evidence of: ☐ Dampness ☐ Termites ☐ Settlement   Bsmt. Finished area _____ sq. ft.

Comments _____

Room List	Foyer	Living	Dining	Kitchen	Den	Family Rm.	Rec. Rm.	Bedrooms	No. Baths	Laundry	Other
Basement				·							
1st Level											
2nd Level											

Finished area above grade contains a total of _____ Rooms _____ Bedrooms _____ Baths Porch/Deck _____ sq. ft.

Gross Living Area _____ sq. ft. Finish _____ sq. ft. Unfinished _____ sq. ft. Encl. Porches _____ sq. ft.

Comments _____

INTERIOR/MECHANICALS

Condition Good Avg Fair Poor

Floor   ☐ Hardwood ☐ Carpet Over _____ ☐ _____   ☐ ☐ ☐ ☐ | **Kitchen**   **Cabinets**

Walls   ☐ Drywall ☐ Plaster ☐ _____   ☐ ☐ ☐ ☐ | ☐ Modern   ☐ Wood

Ceiling   ☐ Drywall ☐ Plaster ☐ _____   ☐ ☐ ☐ ☐ | ☐ Semi-Mod.   ☐ Metal

Trim/Finish ☐ Softwood ☐ Hardwood ☐ Complete ☐ Incomplete   ☐ ☐ ☐ ☐ | ☐ Out-of-date   **Countertop**

Bath Floor ☐ Ceramic ☐ _____   ☐ ☐ ☐ ☐ | ☐ Eat-in   ☐ Adequate

Bath Wainscot ☐ Ceramic ☐ _____   ☐ ☐ ☐ ☐ | ☐ Galley   ☐ Inadequate

Special Features _____

Equipment: ☐ Refrigerator ☐ Range/Oven ☐ Disposal

☐ Dishwasher ☐ Fan/Hood ☐ Compactor ☐ Washer

ATTIC: ☐ Yes ☐ No ☐ Stairway ☐ Drop-stair ☐ Scuttle ☐ Floored | ☐ Dryer ☐ Intercom ☐ Microwave ☐ _____

Finished (Describe) _____ ☐ Heated | Plumbing: ☐ Brass ☐ Copper ☐ Iron ☐ Plastic

CAR STORAGE: ☐ Garage ☐ Built-in ☐ Attached ☐ Detached ☐ Heated | Electric: Amps _____ Wire _____

☐ Car Port No. Cars _____ ☐ Adequate ☐ Inadequate Condition _____ | Fireplace: No. _____ ☐ Marble ☐ Brick ☐ Stone

ENERGY FEATURES | Energy Cost/SF/Yr. – $ _____

☐ Heatilator ☐ Insert ☐ Glass door ☐ _____

Insulation ☐ None   ☐ Caulking/Weatherstripping

PROPERTY RATING   Good Avg Fair Poor

Foundation R- _____ | Quality of Construction (Materials & Finish) ☐ ☐ ☐ ☐

Floor R- _____ | Condition of Improvements ☐ ☐ ☐ ☐

Walls R- _____ | Room sizes and layout ☐ ☐ ☐ ☐

Ceiling R- _____ | Closets and Storage ☐ ☐ ☐ ☐

Roof R- _____ | Insulation – adequacy ☐ ☐ ☐ ☐

(MATERIAL)

Heat: ☐ Oil ☐ Gas ☐ Elect. ☐ Wood ☐ Coal ☐ Heat Pump | Plumbing – adequacy and condition ☐ ☐ ☐ ☐

☐ Warm Air ☐ Hot water ☐ Steam _____ zones | Electrical – adequacy and condition ☐ ☐ ☐ ☐

Thermostats: ☐ Standard ☐ Clock ☐ _____ | Kitchen Cabinets – adequacy and condition ☐ ☐ ☐ ☐

☐ Flue Damper ☐ Elec./Mech. Gas Furn. Ignition ☐ oil/flame retention burner | Compatibility to Neighborhood ☐ ☐ ☐ ☐

☐ Passive solar ☐ Active solar ☐ Hydronic ☐ Air Storage _____ | Overall Livability ☐ ☐ ☐ ☐

☐ Backup System ☐ Adequate ☐ Inadequate Type _____ | Appeal and Marketability ☐ ☐ ☐ ☐

☐ Wind Protection ☐ Solar Shading ☐ Solar Orientation | Yrs. Est Remaining Economic Life _____ to _____

Hot water: ☐ Oil ☐ Gas ☐ Elect. ☐ Solar ☐ _____ | ENERGY EFFICIENCY APPEARS:

Air Cond. ☐ Central ☐ _____ ☐ Adeq. ☐ Inadeq. | ☐ High ☐ Adequate ☐ Low

COMMENTS (including functional or physical inadequacies, repairs needed, modernization, etc.) _____

Other Buildings _____

Figure 6–1 *(continued)*

Form 1004/70 and fill in the required property and neighborhood data as the inspection proceeds. The appraiser also needs to assemble required field tools and equipment. While the exact equipment used will vary, the items needed will usually include a 100-foot measuring tape and/or a measuring wheel; a hook, ice pick, or nail; a good pocket knife; a flashlight; a clipboard; a checklist form; a marble; a chisel; and a camera (many appraisers favor a Polaroid camera for immediate developing).

Measurement. Careful measurement is absolutely essential. The size or number of units contained in the subject property helps determine standards of comparability for future analysis. More important, since residential properties are commonly valued on a per unit basis, the number of units accurately measured has a major influence on the final value estimate. Site measurement information is usually provided by maps, surveys, or legal descriptions in deeds. The dimensions, frontage, width, depth, and area of the site are often recited in deeds. Area can be expressed in terms of square feet or acres (or possibly even square meters or hectares).

The appraiser sometimes must calculate area from printed dimensions or a sketch plan. In this case, the rules of plane geometry and trigonometry are applied.[7] In measuring dimensions and calculating areas from a map or a sketch plan, the appraiser should be familiar with the use of engineering scales and the planimeter.

Building area and/or volume must be measured. Although most appraisers and appraisals employ area measurement, cubic content computation is still used as well.[8] For residential structures, the usual standard is the total number of square feet of living area. Although there are local variations, the common approach is to measure the area above the basement (or foundation for basementless houses) on the outside dimensions. This takes into account variations in the thickness of exterior walls, which influence cost.

Total living area is a common measure, which involves multiplying the width times the length of the outside dimensions at the foundation and then multiplying by the number of stories. In some instances, standard two-story or one-and-one-half story buildings are measured by the area of the foundation or land area covered by the foundation. This approach can be effective only when virtually identical structures are being compared. Rooms are measured by interior dimensions, from finished wall surface. Basement rooms are measured by interior dimensions and are added to the total living area estimated. Attic rooms or partially finished upper floor rooms are also measured by interior dimensions and are added to the total living area estimated. Local convention prevails in the measurement of porches; the measurement generally varies according to whether the porch is open, enclosed, or finished and heated (as well as enclosed). Alternatively, porches may be measured and their cost estimated separately.

In many sections of the United States, cubic volume rather than area is used for costing and comparing residences. The general rule is simple: cubic content is equal to area (width times length measured on the outside walls) times effective height. The only problem arises in estimating effective height for structures with other than flat roofs. The basic formula for standard cubage is length times width times height, measured from six inches below the basement floor or the finished surface of the lowest finished floor to the top of the upper ceiling joists. Attic areas or upper stories that are less than full stories must be measured by formula. In all cases, the vertical measurement or height is from the top of the upper ceiling joist of the highest full floor to the tip of the roof.

The international metric system is gradually becoming adopted for measurement. The appraiser should become familiar with this system, especially for linear and area (and cubic volume) measurements.[9] As an example of its application, consider a site with dimensions of 75 feet by 150 feet that contains an area of 11,250 square feet, or 0.2583 acres. The metric equivalents for these dimensions would be 22.86 meters (75 feet divided by the number of feet in one meter, or 3.28083) by 45.72 meters (150 feet divided by 3.28083). The area would be 1,045.1505 square meters (11,250 square feet divided by the number of square feet in one square meter, or 10.764). The same calculation may be performed by multiplying the dimensions in meters directly (i.e., 22.86 meters times 45.72 meters, which equals 1,045.1592 square meters).

Similarly, a house with a foundation area of 15.24 by 10.36 meters has an area of 157.8864 square meters. Dividing the dimensions by 0.3048 or multiplying by 3.28083 gives 50 feet by 34 feet. The area is then 1,700 square feet (157.8864 square meters times 10.764 square feet per meter, which equals 1,699.49 square feet).

Building Inspection, Maps, and Plans. The inspection and rating of the property must be both comprehensive and objective. Appraisers must look at the structure(s) through the eyes of the typically informed purchaser. There is no room for personal prejudice in appraisers' inspections. Appraisers will note the physical appearance and condition of the structure as observed. They should obtain information on recent major repairs and inspect those items particularly carefully. Appraisers will estimate the general deterioration of the structure, as well as any rehabilitation or deferred maintenance required. They will estimate the remaining economic life of replaceable items in particular and of the basic structure in general. They will also note those items that appear to be functionally inadequate or superadequate. In this regard, appraisers will note the presence or absence of fundamental features in the structure, as well as the size, quality, and condition of fixtures and equipment. In examining each element of the structure, appraisers should ask the following questions: Does this enhance the use and enjoyment of the structure? Does it add to the amenities of occupancy and to marketability?

During the field inspection, interviews with the owner and/or occupant, the broker, and neighbors or others can confirm or correct impressions gained from visual inspection. Interviewees can provide information not revealed by visual inspection. Maps, plot plans, and floor plans or blueprints are important aids to the work of the appraiser and provide good illustrations of the physical and legal characteristics of the site. Such documents indicate detail that is difficult to put in narrative form. They show the location and dimensions of improvements, relating all information to a common scale. Maps and plot plans can show graphically the effect of set-back requirements in zoning regulations, deed restrictions, easements, alleys, and the like. These points are exemplified in figures 6–2 and 6–3.

The elements of map reading and interpretation are relatively simple. It is necessary merely to understand the symbols used and to understand the application of a scale. A further requirement is the ability to visualize three-dimensional characteristics on a two-dimensional plot plan. Prior field inspection of the site will aid greatly in this interpretation. In addition to maps and plot plans, photographs of the site, the building (exterior and interior), and the surrounding area are significant aids to the appraiser (as well as to the client) in visualizing the characteristics of the property, its orientation, and its setting. Several photographs are usually required to provide a realistic impression of the physical character and setting of the property.

Highest and Best Use: Analysis and Estimate

One major objective of property analysis is to develop a conclusion about the highest and best, or most probable, use of the site and of the improved property. The information gathered and analyzed is all oriented toward that objective. *Highest and best use* is "that reasonable and probable use that supports the highest present value, as defined, as of the effective date of the appraisal."[10] The highest and best use in the context of market value is the most probable use.[11] Both the site

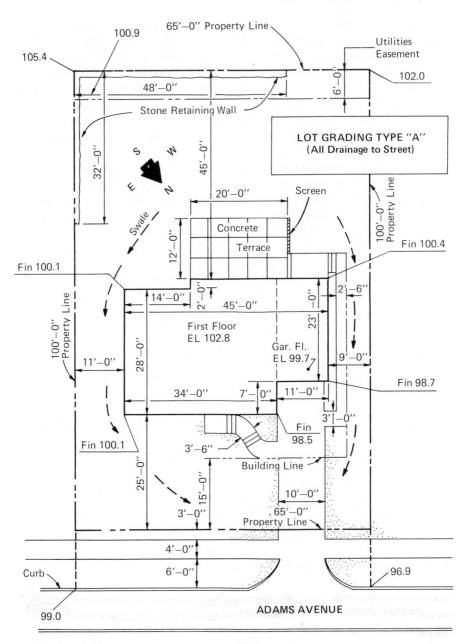

Figure 6–2. Representative Residential Plot Plan

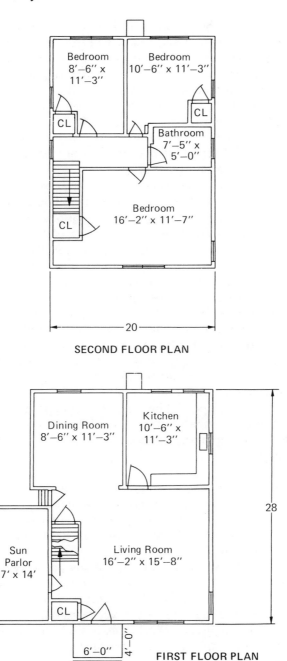

Figure 6–3. Representative Residential Floor Plan

and the improved property have a highest and best use at any given point in time. The highest and best use of the improved property may or may not be the same as the highest and best use of the site.

These definitions imply that ". . . the determination of highest and best use results from the appraiser's judgment and analytical skill, i.e., that the use determined from analysis represents an opinion, not a fact to be found."[12] Highest and best use must be reasonable, probable, and proximate (likely to occur soon, if not immediately). It is not speculative or conjectural. It may or may not be the present use of either the site or the improved property.

Highest and best use can change over time as external market forces change. These forces include effective demand and all its components, public tastes and standards, land use regulations (especially zoning), and competition. In addition, the character of the subject property itself may change, thereby changing its highest and best use. This is why highest and best use is always estimated as of the valuation date. In some instances, highest and best use may anticipate the market, provided the conclusion is reasonable, probable, and proximate.

A property must have utility, reflected through market demand, to have a market function. Function, in turn, determines use, and use is a major determinant of value in the context of existing current market forces. Since market value is always the highest price that an informed and prudent purchaser would pay, the use in terms of which market value is estimated is highest and best use.

In estimating highest and best use following property analysis (site analysis and improvements analysis, as applicable), the appraiser goes through four considerations, which have been referred to earlier but are reiterated here:

1. *Possible use (Physical):* What uses are physically possible on the subject site or in the subject improvements, given the physical characteristics revealed by property analysis?
2. *Permissible use (Legal):* What uses are permitted under existing zoning and other land use regulations and controls, and under existing deed restrictions, for the subject property?
3. *Feasible use (Appropriate Use):* Among legally permitted and physically possible uses for the subject property, which are appropriate, given the characteristics revealed by market, neighborhood, and property analysis? Which uses produce any net return to the owner, or a positive net present value?
4. *Highest and Best Use:* Among appropriate or feasible uses for the subject property, which will produce the highest present value?

Highest and Best Use of the Site

Site is always valued as if vacant and available to be put to its highest and best use, when market value is to be estimated. In the analysis of highest and best use, appraisers must consider not only the suitability of the site for existing or proposed use but also its suitability for alternative uses not specifically mentioned in the appraisal assignment. They must discover that use which is most probable from the point of view of the typically informed buyer on the market. This is the use that will produce the highest present worth of the site.

In the analysis, the appraiser must identify a program of development of the site that will produce the greatest future benefits to the owner. The form that these benefits will take, and the time period over which they can reasonably be anticipated to be received, must also be estimated. In this process, the standard of highest and best use is met by the program that will develop the site to its full potential utility.

Site analysis is necessary before reaching a conclusion about highest and best use of the site. It also provides insight into the desirability of the current use program of the site and whether it should be continued or changed (supersession of uses). This determination is used later in appraisal analysis to ascertain what contribution the improvements are making to the value of the total property. It helps in comparing the highest and best use of the site with the highest and best use of the property. Any difference in value resulting from differences in these two uses is functional obsolescence chargeable to the improvements.

Highest and Best Use of the Property

Highest and best use of the property always takes into consideration existing improvements, as identified and characterized by property analysis (improvements analysis). When there are existing improvements, the highest and best use of the site may be different from that of the improved property. For property valuation purposes, the applicable highest and best use is that of the improved property, which always includes retention and use of existing improvements.

Present use of the property may differ from highest and best use of the site: "The existing use will continue, however, unless and until land value in its highest and best use exceeds the total value of the property in its existing use."[13] Therefore, the present use of an improved property is presumed to be its highest and best use unless it can be demonstrated that change is imminent through the impact of market demand or legal (land use control) forces. If change is demonstrated to be imminent, then the existing buildings must be razed or substantially altered to put the property (and the site) to its new highest and best use. In this case, property value is no more than vacant site value.

To find highest and best use, the appraiser must have knowledge of the subject property and its characteristics; a completed property analysis; knowledge of the community and market forces; area and neighborhood analysis; and knowledge of the principles of land and property utilization.

Special Applications of Property Analysis

In addition to meeting the objectives already itemized and discussed above, especially the objective of providing a basis for estimating highest and best use, property analysis has two other important applications in the appraisal framework: (1) illustrations in appraisal report presentation and (2) property rating. For the former, maps, plot plans, floor plans, and data lists are important information sources for clients and other users of appraisal reports. Such illustrations and exhibits are particularly useful in summarizing and helping the client visualize the detailed characteristics of the subject property.

Using the results of property analysis, it is possible to apply a rating evaluation to the subject property. FHA formerly used a rating grid to assist in the evaluation of residential structure quality. The property quality rating percentage reflects the quality of the subject property in relation to the ideal, 100 percent quality property. It also reflects the relationship of the subject property to nearby properties by an adjustment for nonconformity. Each property is rated by percentage in proportion to the ideal, 100 percent property, which suffers from no physical or functional depreciation. Each property can also be described in such terms as excellent, good, fair, marginal, or poor. Whereas a location rating, discussed in Chapter 5, reflects everything outside the property lines, the property rating reflects everything inside the property lines. Such a property rating grid is illustrated in figure 6–4.

Summary

Property analysis identifies the detailed, salient physical and legal characteristics of the subject property as of the valuation date. A major objective of property analysis is to establish a basis for estimating the highest and best use of the property, and of the site, as of the valuation

	1	2	3	4	5	Rating
Structure	0	10	15	20	25	
Exterior	0	4	6	8	10	
Interior	0	2	3	4	5	
Function	0	8	12	16	20	
Mechanical equipment	0	4	6	8	10	
Light and ventilation	0	4	6	8	10	
Architecture	0	8	12	16	20	
Quality rating (%)	0	40	60	80	100	
Less: Nonconformity	12	9	6	3	0	
Property quality rating (%)						

Figure 6–4. Property Rating Grid

date. Highest and best use of the site and that of the improved property may be different. A site is valued as if it were vacant and available to be put to highest and best use. Improved property is valued in terms of existing improvements on the site, and usually but not necessarily in terms of its present use.

Site analysis requires a combination of physical inspection and a search of public records to ascertain the pertinent characteristics of the subject site. In analyzing a site, the appraiser considers physical, economic, locational, and legal-governmental factors. The standards of market acceptability and marketability provided by buyers on the market at the time of the appraisal provide the basic indication to the appraiser as to what features are in fact pertinent and how important they are. Appraisers rarely measure the site in the field, but they should be familiar with measurement techniques and tools for analyzing plot plans and maps. Appraisers must be able to read and interpret maps and plot plans effectively as part of site analysis.

Building analysis is basic to establishing a standard for comparison and for cost estimation in the appraisal framework. The standards for evaluation of structural quality, adequacy of function, and condition are set by the market. Functional utility is a major ingredient in the evaluation of the contribution of a structure to total property value. Analysis of functional utility involves a consideration of architecture, design, layout, traffic pattern, room sizes and types, and the adequacy of equipment. Structural quality is a major determinant of the functional adequacy of the structure. Both physical condition and functional utility must be identified in building inspection and analysis.

Appraisers must estimate the effective age and remaining economic life of the basic structure, and of all structural components, when conducting the building analysis. Careful and accurate measurement of the structure is necessary to apply the results of building analysis to all approaches to value estimation. In building inspections, a detailed checklist is a particularly helpful aid for identifying both the components of the structure and their condition and functional adequacy.

Notes

1. Boyce, Byrl N., ed., *Real Estate Appraisal Terminology,* rev. ed. (Cambridge, Mass.: Ballinger [Joint publication of the American Institute of Real Estate Appraisers and Society of Real Estate Appraisers], 1981), p. 132.
2. Ibid.
3. Ibid., p. 114.
4. Ibid., p. 87.
5. Most particularly, the reader is referred to Ibid.; *Boeckh Building Valuation Manual* (Milwaukee: Boeckh Publications, periodically updated); and "Minimum Property Standards for One- and Two-Family Dwellings" (Washington, D.C.: U.S. Department of Housing and Urban Development, periodically updated).
6. Further indications are given in *The Official Guide to Appraisal Reporting* (Chicago: Society of Real Estate Appraisers, 1983); and Stebbins, H. Grady, Jr., *A Guide to Appraising Residences* (Chicago: Society of Real Estate Appraisers, 1969).
7. These rules are summarized in Boyce, *Terminology,* pp. 268–269.
8. The techniques for building measurement are summarized in Ibid., pp. 295–297.
9. Metric measurements are noted in Ibid., pp. 272–277.
10. Ibid., p. 126.
11. Ibid., p. 127.
12. Ibid.
13. Ibid.

Suggested Readings

American Institute of Real Estate Appraisers. *The Appraisal of Real Estate,* 8th ed. Chicago: American Institute of Real Estate Appraisers, 1983, chapters 8–11.

Bloom, George F., and Harrison, Henry S. *Appraising the Single Family Residence.* Chicago: American Institute of Real Estate Appraisers, 1978, chapters 7, 8, and 10.

Boeckh Building Valuation Manual, 2d ed. Milwaukee: Boeckh Publications, periodically updated.

Boyce, Byrl N., ed. *Real Estate Appraisal Terminology,* rev. ed. Cambridge, Mass.: Ballinger (Joint publication of the American Institute of Real Estate Appraisers and Society of Real Estate Appraisers), 1981.

Corgel, John B., and Smith, Halbert C. *The Concept and Estimation of Economic Life in the Residential Appraisal Process.* Chicago: Society of Real Estate Appraisers, 1981.

The Official Guide to Appraisal Reporting. Chicago: Society of Real Estate Appraisers, 1983.

Harrison, Henry S. *Houses,* rev. ed. Chicago: Realtors National Marketing Institute of the National Association of Realtors, 1976.

"Minimum Property Standards for One- and Two-Family Dwellings." Washington, D.C.: U.S. Department of Housing and Urban Development, periodically updated.

Stebbins, H. Grady, Jr. *A Guide to Appraising Residences,* 3rd. ed. Chicago: Society of Real Estate Appraisers, 1976.

7

The Direct Sales Comparison Approach

Key Terms

Adjusted sales price   The appraiser's best estimate of what each comparable property would have sold for if it had possessed all of the salient characteristics of the subject property at the time of sale.

Attribute   A characteristic or quality of a property (e.g., good condition, quality of construction, view, design and appeal).

Market conditions adjustment   The initial adjustment (if necessary) in a sequence of adjustments, including conditions of sale and financing differences.

Net adjustment   The sum of all positive and negative adjustments, which is added to or subtracted from the time-adjusted sales price to obtain an adjusted sales price for each comparable property.

Paired sales analysis (market extractions)   A method of estimating the amount of adjustment for the presence or absence of any factor, or for varying quantities of any factor, by pairing the sales prices of otherwise identical properties with and without the factor in question.

Sales adjustment grid   A tabular device to summarize the adjustment process for each comparable sale property.

Time adjustment   An adjustment for the difference (if any) between market conditions at the date of sale of the comparable property and at the date of the appraisal.

Units of comparison   A reduction of properties to some common denominator in order to express sales price on a per unit basis for subsequent comparison analysis and adjustment.

Variable   Quantifiable characteristics of a property that can be measured, compared, and reduced to a unit basis.

The objective of any appraisal is to estimate value as defined. Most commonly, especially in residential appraising, the value to be estimated is market value. The components of the definition of market value indicate the factors to be considered in attempting to judge, from market data on sales of competitive properties, what the subject property is most likely to sell for under specified market conditions (i.e., conditions prevailing for an open market transaction as of the valuation date).

The elements of market value also establish the standards of information that must be obtained about competitive properties that are used as the basis for estimating the market value of the subject property. The appraiser has three alternative approaches or procedures potentially available in every appraisal for estimating the defined value of the specified rights in the subject real estate: direct sales comparison, income capitalization, and cost analyses. Each approach represents a course of action open to the potential typical purchaser as an alternative to purchasing the subject property. Each identifies and measures what it would cost informed purchasers (what they would most probably have to pay) to follow each associated alternative course of action. In addition, each is associated with a different concept of value: value in exchange for direct sales comparison analysis; value in use for income capitalization analysis; and cost of production for cost analysis.

Rationale of the Direct Sales Comparison Approach

The direct sales comparison approach is "that approach in appraisal analysis which is based on the proposition that an informed purchaser would pay no more for a property than the cost of acquiring an existing property with the same utility."[1] Historically, direct sales comparison analysis has been referred to as the market data approach or market comparison approach. Since all approaches to value estimation utilize market data and involve market comparisons, however, especially when market value is to be estimated, the term *direct sales comparison* is preferred as more descriptive of what is actually done.[2]

Valuation Principles Involved

The basic principle underlying the direct sales comparison approach to residential property appraisal is the principle of substitution. In this context, it states that informed purchasers will pay no more for residential property than the cost to them of acquiring satisfactory substitute property, with the same utility as the subject property, on the current market. It will be recalled that market value is always considered from the viewpoint of the typically informed purchaser who acts rationally and prudently on the basis of available information. The key consideration is that comparable sales properties are competitive with the subject property in the minds of potential purchasers.

The market behavior and actions of buyers and sellers reflect their anticipations of the future benefits to be derived from the ownership of competitive properties. The most significant but not the only reflection of anticipations is the price paid. The sales adjustment process, which is at the heart of sales comparison analysis, is based on identification and measurement of the effect that the presence, absence, or amount of some characteristic has on the sales prices of competitive (comparable) sales properties and, hence, on the value of the subject property.

Increasing and decreasing returns (variable proportions), as well as the measurement of the contribution of any property component or factor to total property value, are reflected in the sales adjustment process. Most specifically, that process shows the effect of larger quantities of variable characteristics in comparable sales properties on their sales prices. This concept is also useful in identifying which comparables are truly competitive with the subject property.

Market Standards

Especially since market value is most frequently sought, the direct sales comparison approach is based upon an analysis of the market behavior of purchasers. The standards for comparing sales of competing properties with the subject property are those of the market. The direct sales comparison approach, therefore, requires sufficient quantities of accurate, reliable, and verified market data to be applied properly and effectively.

Market data are analyzed and evaluated as if through the eyes of the typically informed purchaser, who acts prudently in his own self-interest on the basis of the information. The appraiser's personal viewpoint should not intrude into the analysis or the conclusions. The standards utilized in the direct sales comparison approach are those of the local market in which the subject property is located. This market is identified and its characteristics are evaluated through area and neighborhood analysis, which precedes application of the direct sales comparison approach.

Market value is estimated as of the date of the appraisal. The market conditions prevailing on that date are the ones that influence the value of the subject property. Therefore, comparable sales data should be as current as possible for comparative purposes. In the definition of market value, the prudent purchaser acts on the basis of an awareness of the uses to which the property is capable of being put. Rational behavior stipulates that the purchaser plans to utilize the property at its highest and best use. Therefore, the value of improved property is always estimated in terms of its highest and best use. This may or may not be identical with the highest and best use of the site if it were vacant and available for use. It all depends on whether the improvements are most appropriate for the site.

The Process

The essential process of sales comparison analysis is to convert actual, verified sales prices of competitive and comparable properties to a defined value estimate. It involves going to the market to extract indications of defined value from market activities.

Since it is primarily an application of the principle of substitution, the essence of the direct sales comparison approach is to discover the sales prices of competitive properties which sold recently on the local market. Through an appropriate adjustment process, this approach is used to develop indications of what competitive properties would sell for currently if they possessed all of the basic and pertinent physical and economic characteristics of the subject property. Indications of such adjusted sales prices are developed for several comparable sales. These indications are expected to fall into a pattern clustering around one figure, which, when appropriately rounded, provides an indication of the market value of the subject property as of the date of the appraisal.

Data Requirements and Sources

The technique of the direct sales comparison approach involves selecting a number of sales transactions of comparable properties that have transferred recently on the local market. These are then adjusted to provide indications of the market value of the subject property. For comparisons to be made effectively, detailed information must be obtained about each of the comparable sales properties. This requires a systematic data program. The pertinent and salient characteristics of the subject property must be itemized. Then, these same points should be covered for each comparable sales property. Only in this way can any meaningful comparisons and adjustments be made.

Not every residential property that has recently sold on the local market is a comparable sale. Both physical characteristics and market conditions and terms of sale must be investigated. This is where judgment on the part of the appraiser is required. The basic test is whether the property selected as a comparable sale is, in fact, effectively competitive with the subject property in the mind of the typically informed purchaser in the present market.

Sales Comparison

Data on sales comparisons must be obtained to indicate the basic characteristics of both the property and the transaction. This information should be assembled systematically, so that it can be presented in a standard format developed by the appraiser for ease of use and understanding by the client. Basic information about each comparable sales transaction that the appraiser should obtain includes date of sale; volume and page of deed; type of deed; legal description of property; names of grantor (seller) and grantee (buyer); documentary stamps; amount of consideration, if indicated; verified sales price; motivating forces or conditions of sale; terms of financing; and items of personalty included.

The appraiser should also develop information on property data. This usually includes such items as type and style of architecture; size (area, number of rooms); type of rooms and layout; age and condition (effective age); number of baths and bedrooms; special features (fireplaces, built-in equipment, cabinetry, air conditioning, pool); accessory buildings (type, size, age, condition); site (size, topography, and so on); zoning and deed restrictions; location (market and neighborhood influences); taxes and assessment; listing price and length of time on market; and unusual elements of functional or locational obsolescence.

Full Narrative Description and Detail

In making a presentation for comparative analysis in a narrative appraisal report, detailed information about the comparable sales property, with respect to both the property itself and the transaction, should be provided in a systematic format. The reader of the report should be able to visualize the elements of comparability and difference between the comparable sales property and the subject property. All salient and pertinent elements of comparability and difference between the comparable sales property and the subject property should be listed, but only the salient and pertinent features should be listed. Minor elements that have no influence on value or marketability should be omitted to avoid cluttering the presentation. A presentation of data about a comparable sales transaction from a narrative appraisal report is shown in figure 7–1.

Comparable Sale #1

This sale is located at 71 Alexander Lane. It was sold by Sandra J. Mazzola to Byrl N. Boyce on February 14, 1981 for $90,500. It is recorded in Volume 178 on Page 121 in the Deed Records of the Town of Mansfield, Connecticut. The conveyance tax on the deed totals $99.55. This sale is located three miles east of the subject property. It is a two-story, single-family residence built in 1980. It is a seven-room house with three bedrooms and two baths with full basement. Roofing is asphalt shingles, clapboard siding, and the foundation (basement walls and floor) is poured concrete. The house contains 1,713 square feet of livable space. It has hardwood floors throughout. Heating is provided by an oil-fired, hot water furnace. Interior walls consist of dry wall construction. Both bathrooms have asphalt tile floors: one with tub enclosure and the other with shower stall. The kitchen has formica counter tops and stainless steel double sink. Built-in equipment consists of a garbage disposal, dishwasher, and range/oven combination. The floor plan is good and the condition of the property at the time of sale was good. No repairs were deemed necessary. There is a two-car attached garage with concrete floor. The property has an asphalt approach and gravel drive, and a slate walk. Lot size is 2.1 acres. It is level and moderately well landscaped. Extra improvements include a 10' × 10' wood deck off the kitchen/family room area. Financing was considered normal. The property was assessed for ad valorem tax purposes at $21,430: $3,600 for land and $17,830 for improvements. This sale was verified by the grantor, Ms. Mazzola.

Comparable Sale #2

This sale is located at 148 Bark Lane. It was sold by Nancy J. Easton to William N. Kinnard, Jr. on August 15, 1981 for $92,000. It is recorded in Volume 179 on Page 48 in the Deed Records of the Town of Mansfield, Connecticut. The conveyance tax on the deed totals $101.20. This sale is located two miles north of the subject property. It is a two-story, single-family residence built in 1970. It is an eight-room house with three bedrooms and two and one half baths with full basement. Roofing is asphalt shingles, clapboard siding, and the foundation (basement walls and floor) is poured concrete. The house contains 2,112 square feet of livable space. It has hardwood floors throughout. Heating is provided by an oil-fired hot water furnace. Interior walls consist of dry wall construction. Bathrooms have asphalt tile floors. One full bath has a tub enclosure and the other a shower stall. The kitchen has formica counter tops and stainless steel sink. Built-in equipment consists of a garbage disposal and dishwasher. The floor plan is good and the condition of the property at the time of sale was good. No repairs were deemed necessary. There is a two-car attached garage with concrete floor. The property has an asphalt approach and asphalt drive, and a concrete walk. Lot size is one acre (41,000 square feet). It is level and professionally landscaped. Financing was considered normal. The property was assessed for ad valorem tax purposes at $21,850: $2,400 for land and $19,450 for improvements. This sale was verified by the grantor, Ms. Easton.

Comparable Sale #3

This sale is located at 21 Alexander Lane. It was sold by Fran Jaffe to Judith B. Paesani on April 5, 1981 for $87,800. It is recorded in Volume 178 on Page 162 in the Deed Records of the Town of Mansfield, Connecticut. The conveyance tax on the deed totals $96.80. This sale is located three miles east of the subject property. It is a two-story, single-family residence built in 1978. It is a seven-room house with three bedrooms and two and one half baths with full basement. Roofing is asphalt shingles, aluminum siding, and the foundation (basement walls and floors) is poured concrete. The house contains 2,520 square feet of livable space. It has hardwood floors throughout. Heating is provided by an oil-fired hot water furnace. Interior walls consist of dry wall construction. Bathrooms have asphalt tile floors. One full bath has a tub enclosure and the other a shower stall. The kitchen has formica counter tops and stainless steel double sink. Built-in equipment consists of a garbage disposal, dishwasher and range/oven combination. The floor plan is good and the condition of the property at the time of sale was good. No repairs were deemed necessary. There is a two-car attached garage with concrete floor. The property has an asphalt approach and gravel drive, and a slate walk. Lot size is 2.3 acres. It is level but poorly landscaped. Extra improvements include a 12′ × 12′ wood deck off the kitchen/family room area. Financing was considered to be normal. The property was assessed for ad valorem tax purposes at $26,200: $3,600 for land and $22,600 for improvements. This sale was verified by the grantor, Ms. Jaffe.

Figure 7–1. Comparable Sales: Property Description

Verification

All transaction data (especially sales price, date, terms of sale and financing, and motivating forces) should be verified with the buyer or the seller, or with an authorized agent of either. Record data provide indications only. Because heavy reliance is to be placed on the facts of the transaction, the appraiser should verify them personally with a participant in the transaction.

If the motivating force underlying the transaction is not verified with at least one of the major participants, distortions or misrepresentations by the appraiser can result. Common deviations from bona fide, arm's length transactions in residential sales include liquidation for inheritance tax or other pressing reasons; purchase for immediate possession; tax gain or tax considerations in the sale; transactions between related or affiliated parties under nonmarket conditions; and highly superior bargaining power on the part of one party to the transaction. The use of sales transactions affected by such influences should be avoided if at all possible.

Quality of Data

In addition to being verified, transaction data should be as accurate and complete as possible. The appraiser must pay particular attention to the terms of financing and to the conditions of sale (motivating forces) in selecting and analyzing the comparable sales properties. Physical and locational characteristics should be identified and analyzed carefully and accurately, based on appropriate prior property inspection and analysis.

Minimum quality requirements for acceptable comparable sales data include local market transactions; current market transactions; truly comparable properties; and bona fide sales.

Quantity of Data

There is no set number of comparable sales about which information must be obtained by the appraiser in order to carry out appropriate analysis under the direct sales comparison approach. It is generally agreed, however, that the more data there are, the better. Conventional wisdom has long held that three to four good comparable sales transactions are sufficient to do an appropriate job of representing the competitive market. This view has been reinforced by the fact that most appraisal report forms (such as the FNMA and FHLMC forms) require reporting of only three to four comparable sales transactions. There is a major and important distinction, however, between the quantity of data required for analysis to reach a value conclusion and the quantity of data necessary for reporting purposes. The latter quantity can be smaller, provided that the data are truly representative of the sample taken from the market and used in the analysis.

The availability of inexpensive electronic calculating and data storage equipment makes it possible to process larger quantities of data quickly and inexpensively, even if statistical analysis is not applied. For analytical purposes, to provide at least a preliminary indication of value, it is possible and appropriate to use data gathered and verified by others. The appraiser must have confidence in the data source, however. Moreover, the comparable sales data used in the appraisal report must still be verified personally by the appraiser.

Data Sources

Data on comparable sales may be obtained from a variety of sources. The appraiser should exploit these sources effectively and continuously to obtain the necessary data (in terms of both quantity and quality) required for appropriate application of the direct sales comparison approach. Data sources may be generally categorized into two groups: public records and private (non-record) sources.

Public Records. Deed recordings, which indicate transfers of properties, may be found in the office of the recorder of deeds, the county clerk, the town clerk, or some other appropriate local agency. Deeds contain information on the legal description, date of transfer, grantor, grantee, encumbrances, deed restrictions, and indicated consideration via revenue stamps. Together with deeds recorded, collateral note recordings provide an indication of the volume of market activity, and they may show terms of financing. The principal amount, interest rate, and maturity of the loan may be indicated.

Data in the local or county assessor's office usually provide information on transfers of properties in the near vicinity of the subject property. For both the subject property and comparable sales properties, detailed information about the property characteristics is usually available, as well as information about assessments and tax levies. The property data include such information as age, condition, size, rooms, construction details, site size, and outbuildings. In areas in which real estate transfer taxes are levied, a good guide to both transactions and transaction prices can be provided from this source. The office of the local planning and/or zoning commission frequently provides information about the use to which property can be put. This also helps to identify the neighborhood or competitive area from which comparable sales data might be obtained.

Private (Non-record) Sources. Information on sales, listings, offers to buy, and rentals may be obtained from a variety of private sources. Some of these might be regarded as public, but they are not part of the official public or governmental record. Usually, the most important single source of information is the appraiser's own files. If these files are kept current and accurate, they can be an invaluable guide to the appraiser in subsequent assignments. The data should be effectively cross-indexed and catalogued. The staff of the appraisal office should gather information both during appraisal assignments and during any slack periods to make sure that as much coverage of the local market as possible is maintained. Also, it is now feasible for many appraisal offices to store data in some form of computer bank for fast, easy, and systematic access.

In many jurisdictions, local FHA and VA offices provide important data on transactions that have actually occurred. These data are often published by local chapters of the Society of Real Estate Appraisers (SREA) and the American Institute of Real Estate Appraisers (AIREA) or by local Boards of Realtors®. In areas in which the appraiser has access to the data in a Multiple Listing Service (MLS), both listings and actual transactions are reported in detail. Moreover, many MLS and local Boards of Realtors® store data centrally in computer systems.

Information on deed recordings and other transactions is often obtained through local private subscription services. These services offer basic leads to transactions, which the appraiser may then investigate in detail and verify. Other potential private data sources include builders, who can provide information on construction in particular. Banks and other lenders usually regard their information as confidential, but confirmation of sales prices and loan terms may possibly be obtained from them. Also, newspaper stories and advertisements provide leads that can be investigated and verified by the appraiser. Further, investigation of the neighborhood often reveals for-sale and sold signs. These are leads that can be investigated either with a broker or with one of the principals involved.

Several systems operate locally, regionally, or nationally to store area sales transactions data in computer banks for quick, easy, and relatively inexpensive retrieval. Most have the capacity to search for sales transactions with specified characteristics, such as date of sale, terms of lending, locations, size, and so forth. From such data searches, a sample of potentially comparable sales data is provided for analysis and verification. One such system is the SREA Market Data Center, Inc.[3] It provides both a sales data storage and retrieval capability and a multiple regression package. The residential data input form for the SREA Market Data Center is shown in figure 7–2. It indicates the kind of information about the comparable sales transactions that can be stored, searched, and retrieved.

Since all sales and transaction data should be verified, an important source of information is provided by the principals in every transaction investigated or by one of the assisting participants—broker, attorney, or lender. Alert appraisers will develop and cultivate these and other data sources so that they may utilize them continuously and effectively in maintaining a current file of information for their appraisal practice.

Sales Data, Listings, and Offers to Buy

The most desirable information to obtain is data on recent transactions that have actually been completed in the local market. Listings and offers to purchase can also be used, but with care and discretion. Listing prices generally indicate the upper portion of the range of prices or values for properties in an area. Offers to purchase generally indicate the lower segment of that range. With sufficient data and careful analysis, the appraiser can adjust listing prices and offers to buy to compensate for the going difference between them and actual transactions prices. Studies of listings, offers, and actual sales prices can do much to identify how much the adjustments should be.

Tests of Comparability

If the comparable sales data are representative of the market within which both the comparable properties and the subject property are competing, then they are a valid sample from that market. It should thus be possible to subject the data to some simple statistical tests. Suppose, for example, that the subject residence contains 1,248 square feet of living area. Suppose, further, that ten comparable sales properties are considered, with the following areas (in square feet):

980	1,248
1,034	1,316
1,086	1,384
1,160	1,430
1,210	1,820

The arithmetic mean $(\overline{X})$ is 1,267 square feet, and the standard deviation is 243 square feet. The 95 percent confidence interval is 717 to 1,817 feet. Thus all of the observations are in that sense comparable, except the property with 1,820 square feet. Dropping that sale gives a mean of 1,205 square feet, a standard deviation of 155 square feet, and a 95 percent confidence interval of 848 to 1,562 square feet. This illustrates how appraisers can use statistics to test whether their comparables are competitive with the subject property and with one another.

Elements of Comparison

It is possible, but not probable, that the appraiser may find data on sales of properties so current and so comparable with the subject property that direct comparisons can be made with no adjustments. This requires extremely good data, indeed, and is usually restricted to sales in new developments of virtually identical houses. In such cases, when no adjustments are necessary, the process is truly direct sales comparison.

In the normal course of events, however, the appraiser will have to compare the ingredients of the comparable properties on an item-

SREA MARKET DATA CENTER, INC.

SINGLE FAMILY RESIDENTIAL INPUT FORM   REFERENCE NO.

CREATIVE FINANCING DATA (If Applicable)

TYPE FIN. _____ INT. RATE 1st LOAN _____ % TOTAL MO. PYMTS. (Initial Term) $ _____
INIT. TERM MO'S _____ NO MTG'S _____ PTS. BY SELLER _____ TOTAL PTS. PAID _____

AREA CONTROL

(1)

(2) SOURCE OF INPUT

(3) STATE

(4) COUNTY   See Over

(5) GEO CODE. MAP REF OR CITY ABBR.

(6) CENSUS TRACT

PROPERTY ADDRESS OR IDENTIFICATION

(7) Number

(8) Direction

(9) Street Name   St., Av., Bl., Pl., Dr., Etc.

(11) A Conv. B MI C Assum D REO E F Land Cont. Agr. Sale

G Vet H FHA State I VA J SFH K Cash Sale L Cre-ative Sale M Bond Fnce N Verify Assum

(10) APT. OR UNIT NO.

(12) SALES PRICE ($ Only) $

(13) CASH DOWN $

(14) AMT. 1st MORTG. $

(15) 1. ☐ Closed   2. ☐ Committed

(16) DATE OF CONTRACT   Month   Year

(17) L. ☐ LOT SIZE
G. ☐ GROSS AREA
P. ☐ PAD AREA
A. ☐ ACREAGE
C. ☐ CONDO SITE

(18) COMPLETE ONE: SIZE or AREA or ACREAGE

Frontage X Depth   or   Sq. Ft. Area   or   Acreage

(19) ROOM COUNT
(20) Total Rms.
Bedrooms

(21) NO. OF BATHS
(22) Full
(23) No. of ¾ Baths

(23) SQ. FEET LIVING AREA*
(*Include all finished heated areas & heated enclosed porches. Exclude basement area.)

(24) YEAR BUILT   If prior to 1900 enter "XX"

(25) LEASEHOLD   Yes = "L"   If No, leave blank.

(26) OTHER ROOMS
A. ☐ Den
B. ☐ Fam. Rm.
C. ☐ Dining Rm.
D. ☐ Encl. Porch
E. ☐ Bonus Rm.
F. ☐ Lanai
G. ☐ Attic
H. ☐ Florida Rm.
I. ☐ Atrium
J. ☐ Other
K. ☐ Foyer
(Check One or More)

(27) LOT ZONE
R. ☐ Residential
B. ☐ Commercial
I. ☐ Industrial
A. ☐ Apts.
F. ☐ Farms
U. ☐ Rural
T. ☐ Townhouse
C. ☐ Cluster

(28) FLOOD ZONE
Y. ☐ Yes
N. ☐ No

(29) (Frontage) SITE INFLUENCE (Check One Only)
A. ☐ View
B. ☐ Ocean
C. ☐ Bay
D. ☐ Canal
E. ☐ River
F. ☐ Lake
G. ☐ Wooded
H. ☐ Golf
I. ☐ Sound

(30) LOCATIONAL OBSOLESCENCE
Y. ☐ Yes
N. ☐ No

(31) WATER
P. ☐ Public
C. ☐ Comm.
I. ☐ Individ.
K. ☐ CO-OP
M. ☐ M.U.D.

(32) SEWER
P. ☐ Public
S. ☐ Septic
I. ☐ Individ.
C. ☐ Cess Pool

(33) STYLE (Architect.)
A. ☐ Colonial
B. ☐ Bungalow
C. ☐ Cape

(34) TYPE IMPROV.
A. ☐ Detached
B. ☐ Row
C. ☐ End Row

(35) TYPE OWNERSHIP
C. ☐ Condominium
P. ☐ P.U.D.
D. ☐ Di-Minimis

(36) AMENITIES
A. ☐ Security
B. ☐ Club Hse.
C. ☐ Golf

(37) STORIES
A. ☐ 1 Sty.
B. ☐ 1½
C. ☐ 2

(38) TYPE CONSTRUCT.
A. ☐ Frame
B. ☐ Concrete
C. ☐ Masonry
D. ☐ Brick

Single-Family Residential Input Form

D. ☐ Contemp.
E. ☐ Ranch
F. ☐ Tudor
G. ☐ Mediterr.
H. ☐ Georgian
I. ☐ High-Ranch
J. ☐ Victorian

D. ☐ Flat
E. ☐ Townhouse
F. ☐ High-Rise
G. ☐ Garden
H. ☐ Lot Line — or No. of Units 2, 3, or 4
(Check One Only)

P.U.D.
O. ☐ Co-op

D. ☐ Health Club
E. ☐ Tennis
F. ☐ Comm. Pool
G. ☐ Marina
(Check One or More)

D. ☐ 2½
E. ☐ 3
F. ☐ 4
G. ☐ Split Foyer
H. ☐ Bi-Level
I. ☐ Split (3) Level
J. ☐ Split (4) Level
(Check One Only)

E. ☐ Stone
F. ☐ Conc. Block
G. ☐ Manufactured
H. ☐ Metal
I. ☐ Other
J. ☐ Adobe
K. ☐ Dome
L. ☐ Log
(Check One Only)

(39) EXTERIOR WALLS
A. ☐ Wood Siding
B. ☐ Wood Shingle
C. ☐ Asb. Shingle
D. ☐ Stucco
E. ☐ Brick Veneer
F. ☐ Brick or Stone
G. ☐ Block
H. ☐ Metal
I. ☐ Vinyl
J. ☐ Composition
K. ☐ Log
(Check One or More)

(40) TYPE ROOF
A. ☐ Wood Shingle
B. ☐ Wood Shake
C. ☐ Comp. Shingle
D. ☐ Asbestos
E. ☐ Built Up
F. ☐ Tar & Grav.
G. ☐ Slate
H. ☐ Rock
I. ☐ Tile
J. ☐ Other
(Check One Only)

(41) HEATING
A. ☐ Gravity
B. ☐ Forced Air
C. ☐ Fl. Furnace
D. ☐ Wall Furn.
E. ☐ Hot Water
F. ☐ Elec. Basebrd.
G. ☐ Heat Pump
H. ☐ Steam
I. ☐ Radiant
J. ☐ Space
K. ☐ Solar
L. ☐ None
(Check One Only)

(42) FUEL
A. ☐ Gas
B. ☐ Oil
C. ☐ Electric
D. ☐ Coal
E. ☐ Solar
F. ☐ Other
G. ☐ LPG
H. ☐ Wood
(Check One Only)

(43) A/C
C. ☐ Central
L. ☐ Wall
E. ☐ Evap. Cooler
W. ☐ Window
H. ☐ Heat Pump

(44) EQUIPMENT
A. ☐ Range/Oven
B. ☐ Dishwasher
C. ☐ Washer
D. ☐ Washer/Dryer
E. ☐ Disposal
F. ☐ Compactor
G. ☐ Range Hood
H. ☐ Refrigerator
I. ☐ Microwave
J. ☐ Central Vac.
K. ☐ Energy Efficient Items
(Check One or More)

(45) REMODELED
A. ☐ Completely
B. ☐ Kitch. & Bath
C. ☐ Bath
D. ☐ Kitchen
E. ☐ Heat
F. ☐ Addition
G. ☐ Rehabilitated

(46) FLOORING
A. ☐ Carpeting
B. ☐ Carpet & Wood
C. ☐ Hardwood
D. ☐ Softwood
E. ☐ Vinyl
F. ☐ Asphalt Tile
G. ☐ Terrazzo
H. ☐ Cement Tile
I. ☐ Other
(Check One or More)

(47) OTHER IMPROV.
A. ☐ Guest Hse.
B. ☐ Servant's
C. ☐ Covered Patio
D. ☐ Barn
E. ☐ Fence
F. ☐ Laundry Rm.
G. ☐ Shed
H. ☐ Greenhouse
I. ☐ Breezeway
J. ☐ Open Deck
K. ☐ Dock
L. ☐ Tennis Crt.
M. ☐ Sauna
N. ☐ Screened Prch.
(Check One or More)

(48) BASEMENT
☐ % of Sq. Ft. Living Area
F. ☐ Full
S. ☐ Slab
C. ☐ Crawl Space

BEDROOMS (49) ☐
BATHS (50) Full ☐ (51) Half ☐

(52) BASEMENT ☐ % Finish
C. ☐ Completely
U. ☐ Unfinished

(53) QUALITY OF CONST.
P. ☐ Poor
F. ☐ Fair
A. ☐ Average
G. ☐ Good
E. ☐ Excellent

(54) COND. (present)
P. ☐ Poor
F. ☐ Fair
A. ☐ Average
G. ☐ Good
E. ☐ Excellent

(55) FUNCTIONAL FLOOR PLAN
G. ☐ Good
A. ☐ Average
F. ☐ Fair
P. ☐ Poor

(56) POOL
P. ☐ Pool
H. ☐ Heated
E. ☐ Enclosed
I. ☐ Indoor
S. ☐ Spa
C. ☐ Pool/Spa
(Check One Only)

(57) FIREPLACES
☐ Number

(58) PARKING
A. ☐ Attached
B. ☐ Built-In
C. ☐ Carport
D. ☐ Detached
E. ☐ Basement
F. ☐ Off Site
G. ☐ Open
H. ☐ None

(59) NO. OF CARS
☐ 0, 1, 2, 3, etc.

Source: SREA Market Data Center, Inc., 24 West St. Joseph Street, Arcadia, CA 91006-0023. 1981. Reprinted with Permission.

Figure 7-2. Single-Family Residential Input Form

GENERAL INSTRUCTIONS

Submit only *single family residential or condominium purchases of property on this form.*

Please make every effort to fill in this form as completely and accurately as possible. *Please print everything legibly in pen, preferably red ink.*

This form can not be processed if any items with circled numbers are omitted. *Example:* **2** *Source of Input.*

When series of boxes, leave any blanks at end opposite heavy lined box.

Please mail completed input forms to P.O. Box 36A59, Los Angeles, CA. 90036.

2   Use source number assigned to your organization. The source number will not appear in the publication.

3   Place appropriate two letter abbreviation for the state where property is located.

4   Counties are listed below. Find appropriate number and enter.

5   According to the system used in your area, indicate the appropriate map page and grid number in these boxes, such as "22B4", or 13F, or "13001", "15347", etc. For areas outside the map book coverage, use the name of the town (or post office) in these boxes. If the name of the town is more than nine letters, use the first nine letters of the name of the town, *for example: Georgetown = GEOR-GETOW, Fort Lauderdale = FORTLAUDE, San Luis Obispo = SANLUISOB.*

(6)   Indicate census tract in which the property is located, if at all possible.

(8)   Place the letter(s) N, E, S, W, or NE, NW, SE, SW, in these boxes if a direction should be included in the address. Whenever direction follows street-name, enter in street-name field. *Example: 235 N Occidental NW Bl*

(10)   Place number or letter in box if condominium, PUD, etc.

(11)   Put "X" in appropriate box.

(12)   , (13), (14), enter dollars only.

(15)   You are encouraged to submit input forms prior to closing so that we may have the most timely and up-to-date information in your publication. Input forms may be submitted prior to closing of sale, providing that Buyer and Seller have agreed to a transaction and lender has made a firm loan committment. Input forms submitted on this basis should have box No. 2 checked; otherwise, check box No. 1.

(16)   Date of contract should be month and year Buyer and Seller agreed to the transaction. If this date is not accurately known, it is suggested that you use the date of the appraisal. This date should always be entered, regardless of whether the input form is submitted before or after the loan is closed.

(18)   Complete either frontage and depth boxes or square footage or acreage boxes. On all square or rectangular shaped lots show frontage and depth. On all irregular shaped lots show the total square footage of lot. If area is more than 99,999 square feet, calculate acreage to the nearest decimal point and write in the acreage.

(20)   Write total number of bedrooms.

(21)   Write in the total number of full and ¾ baths.

(22)   Write in the total number of ½ and ¼ baths.

(26)   through (47), put "X" in appropriate box or boxes.

(48)   Show what percentage of square feet of living area the basement is or put "X" in appropriate box below. "To calculate the percent of basement area use the actual square footage of living area and basement."

(52)   Show what percentage of basement is finished, or place "X" in appropriate box below.

(50)   through (53), place an "X" in appropriate box.

NOTE: Items omitted are self-explanatory!

Figure 7–2 *(continued)*

by-item basis with those of the subject property and make appropriate adjustments as necessary. Through analysis of the subject property and the current local market and neighborhood, the appraiser will have identified the pertinent and salient features in terms of which comparisons must be made. A similar identification must be undertaken for each comparable sales property. Since one definition of comparability is that the properties possess the same utility, some indication of the relative utility of both the subject property and the comparable properties should be developed. This requires an indication of their market acceptability and functional utility or obsolescence.

Appropriate application of the sales comparison approach requires knowledge of the standards of the local market plus a detailed property inspection and keen observation. The ability to interpret structural quality is necessary, together with knowledge of typical buyer preferences and price reactions in the local market. Finally, the application of sound judgment is required to produce reasonable results. Measurement comes later, when the adjustment process is applied.

In identifying elements of comparability, the appraiser must recognize that defects, deficiencies or superadequacies considered in the cost approach must also be included in the comparative analysis of the direct sales comparison approach. Moreover, the true test of comparability is whether the comparable property is really in the same market with, and therefore competitive with, the subject property. The comparisons must be made in terms of salient characteristics of both the subject property and the comparable sales properties, not in terms of unimportant minutiae.

Direct sales comparison analysis is a process in which the comparable sales property is compared with and to the subject property. The subject property is the standard in terms of which all physical and locational comparisons are made. Thus, the identification of elements of comparison focuses on the differences between the comparable sales properties and the subject property, with respect to the significant or salient property characteristics already identified. The physical and locational differences are measured from the comparable property to the subject property.

The major categories into which elements of comparison fall and in which adjustments for differences must be made—and the sequence of those adjustments—are (1) market conditions (conditions of sale, terms of financing); (2) market to market (time, date of sale); and (3) comparable property to the subject property (locational and physical property characteristics). It should be emphasized that the comparison in the first category is made between comparable properties at the point in time of their sale on the market; the second category involves an adjustment for sales in markets prior to the current market in which the subject property is being appraised; and the third category of adjustments accounts for the locational and physical differences between comparables and the subject property.

Adjustments for Conditions and Terms of Sale

Two potential adjustments can be made at this level: conditions of sale and financing differences (often called "terms of sale"). Conditions of sale are difficult to justify with direct market evidence. Each adjustment requires paired sales of otherwise similar (nearly identical) properties under the same market conditions in order to measure the effects of different conditions of sale. This is often not possible. All things considered, comparable sales transactions requiring adjustments for conditions of sale should be avoided if at all possible. Conditions of sale adjustments, when necessary and possible, must be made between comparable sales properties on the basis of the following elements:

1. Knowledge of market conditions by buyers and sellers.
2. Length of time on the market before sale (typical versus actual).
3. Buyer and seller motivations: no undue pressures on either.
4. Bona fide, arm's length transactions: no close relationship between buyer and seller.

If any deviation from the normal, arm's length, competitive-market conditions of sale postulated in the definition of market value is discovered for a comparable sales transaction, it really should be eliminated from the analysis. If a paucity of data dictates its use, however, then an adjustment is made in the comparable sales price to bring it into line with a typical market transaction, which the sale of other comparable properties is assumed to be.

Financing can be an important influence on differences in residential sales prices in local markets. Terms of financing (as noted previously) include:

1. Down payment requiremnts (loan-to-value ratios).
2. Interest rates (nominal and effective).
3. Loan maturities.
4. Amortization requirements.

Any adjustment for differences between local market terms of financing at the time of the sale of the comparable and those applicable to the comparable sales transaction is made in the comparable sales price.

The appraiser can adjust for terms of financing, but the adjustment usually requires the use of discounting techniques.[4] If otherwise identical (or nearly so) transactions that differ only with respect to terms of financing can be found, the difference in sales prices can be attributed to the difference in terms of financing and can be extracted via *paired sales analysis.*

As an example of this analytical technique, suppose that a residence was sold for $80,000, with the seller taking back a purchase-money mortgage of $60,000 for 30 years at 10 percent interest. The most probable market terms would be a $60,000 loan for 25 years at 15 percent interest. One means of establishing a cash equivalent sales price is found by first calculating the present worth of monthly payments and a balloon at the end of 25 years (current market maturity) on the purchase-money mortgage discounted at 15 percent (current market rate). Those monthly payments amount to $526.56, and the balloon payment at the end of 25 years is $24,782.79. The present worth of the total cash flows at 15 percent is $41,708.36. Adding the $20,000 down payment gives a cash equivalent sales price for the comparable sale of $61,708. This cash equivalent sales price may be used directly as the sales price to be adjusted for time and physical and locational differences. Had the purchase-money mortgage ballooned at the end of 5 years (a balance of $57,946.52), the present worth at 15 percent would have been $49,633.23 and the cash equivalent price would be $69,633. As the foregoing calculations suggest, favorable terms of financing relative to those of the market in which the comparable property sold should be precisely defined for purposes of this adjustment.

Market to Market Adjustments (Time Adjustments)

The date of sale identifies the market conditions under which a comparable sales transaction occurred, just as the date of the appraisal indicates the market conditions in terms of which the subject property is being appraised. Both must be identified so that an appropriate comparison may be made between the conditions prevailing for the comparable sales and those prevailing for the subject property.

Trends and changes in such items as volume of real estate market activity, availability of money for mortgage purposes, employment, and income should be accounted for if there is a difference in market conditions. The point is to identify what the comparable sales property would have sold for if it were offered for sale under current (valuation date) market conditions.

Time adjustments are best extracted from sales and resales of the same property (without major changes). If a property that sold for $61,400 resold for $65,600 14 months later, for example, the time adjustment is plus 6.84 percent for 14 months, or plus 5.86 percent (6 percent) per year.

General trends in price levels may be used, but they are less reliable. The appraiser should avoid relying on conventional wisdom of even informed market participants, unless their views can be justified from market data.

When the appraiser concludes from market evidence that the appropriate time adjustment is, for example, 7 percent per year, it should mean that each year's price level is 7 percent above the previous year's level. This is a compound interest or exponential adjustment, rather than a straight-line adjustment. Thus, if the 7 percent per year adjustment applies over 5 years, the exponential adjustment is + 40.26 percent [$(1.07 \times 1.07 \times 1.07 \times 1.07 \times 1.07) - 1$]. The straight-line adjustment would be + 35 percent (5×0.07).

In the sales adjustment grid included in figure 7–3, time adjustments are at 6 percent per year on a straight-line basis. If compound interest time adjustments were used, the time adjustments would be as follows:

Sale Number	Compound Interest Time Adjustment	Difference
1	+ $3,010	− $ 30
2	+ 1,039	− 21
3	+ 1,886	− 28
4	+ 7,300	+ 160
5	+ 7,345	+ 125
6	+ 7,249	+ 123
7	+ 10,800	+ 700
8	+ 15,802	+ 762

When the rate is low and the time period short, there is virtually no difference between results from the two methods. The longer the time period, the greater the difference is, however. This emphasizes the importance of having recent comparable sales whenever possible.

Comparable Property to Subject Property Adjustments
(Locational and Physical Characteristics)

The neighborhood environment and the zoning or deed restrictions on properties in question are legal and market influences that determine

The following illustrative materials involve the valuation of a single-family, ranch style cement block structure with a stucco exterior finish. The foundation is poured concrete and the basement area is partially developed into a large recreation room. The property contains a total livable area of 1,270 square feet with two bedrooms and one bath. The property is 20 years old and has received average maintenance over the years.

The upper level of the house contains two bedrooms, a study, a dining room, a living room, a kitchen, and a bath. In addition, there is an enclosed porch contiguous to the kitchen area. There are two fireplaces, located in the living room and basement-recreation area. A built-in garage provides access to both the basement and kitchen. There are oak floors throughout the house with asphalt tile in the bath and basement. The enclosed porch and kitchen have indoor/outdoor carpeting.

The following eight comparable sales were analyzed and adjusted to determine the indicated value of the subject property:

Sale #1
Date of Sale: 8 months ago
Age: 19 years   Condition: Similar
Livable Area: 1,109 square feet
Bedrooms: 3
Baths: 1
Sale Price: $76,000
Revenue Stamps: $83.60

Sale #2
Date of Sale: 4 months ago
Age: 22 years   Condition: Similar
Livable Area: 892 square feet
Bedrooms: 2
Baths: 1
Sale Price: $53,000
Revenue Stamps: $58.30

Sale #3
Date of Sale: 6 months ago
Age: 18 years   Condition: Same
Livable Area: 960 square feet
Bedrooms: 2
Baths: 1
Sale Price: $63,800
Revenue Stamps: $70.18

Sale #4
Date of Sale: 1 year 9 months ago
Age: 18 years   Condition: Similar
Livable Area: 1,452 square feet
Bedrooms: 3
Baths: 2
Sale Price: $68,000
Revenue Stamps: $74.80

Sale #5
Date of Sale: 1 year 7 months ago
Age: 18 years   Condition: Similar
Livable Area: 1,460 square feet
Bedrooms: 4
Baths: 2
Sale Price: $76,000
Revenue Stamps: $83.60

Sale #6
Date of Sale: 1 year 7 months ago
Age: 18 years   Condition: Same
Livable Area: 1,452 square feet
Bedrooms: 3
Baths: 1.5
Sale Price: $75,000
Revenue Stamps: $82.50

Sale #7
Date of Sale: 3 years 3 months ago
Age: 18 years   Condition: Similar
Livable Area: 960 square feet
Bedrooms: 2
Baths: 1
Sale Price: $51,800
Revenue Stamps: $56.98

Sale #8
Date of Sale: 2 years 8 months ago
Age: 19 years   Condition: Similar
Livable Area: 2,300 square feet
Bedrooms: 5
Baths: 2.5
Sale Price: $94,000
Revenue Stamps: $103.40

Figure 7–3. The Direct Sales Comparison Approach

Assume for purposes of this illustration that all comparables are from the same neighborhood as the subject. In addition, lot sizes, landscaping, built-ins, fireplaces, garages, and other physical features of both site and improvements are similar. Also the following adjustments are to be made for the remaining physical features, age, and date of sale:

Square Footage: $20 per square foot[a]
Bedrooms: $2,500 per bedroom
Baths: $1,000 full bath; $400 half bath
Age: $750 per year
Date of Sale: 6% per year

[a]This adjustment takes into account the interrelationship between square footage and number of bedrooms and baths. Adjustment is to be applied to the difference in square footage between subject and comparables.

Figure 7–3 *(continued)*

whether properties are truly competitive and comparable. Included in a consideration of neighborhood location would be age and condition of houses in the area; type and size of houses; price range of houses; amenities and facilities in the area; zoning and other use restrictions in the area; income range of residents; and social and economic compatibility of residents. Any adjustment for a difference between the locational influences operating on the subject property and those of the comparable property is made in the comparable sales price.

A comparison of physical characteristics of the comparable sales properties with those of the subject property that are identified as salient in the property analysis is a further step in the process, and it is usually the easiest one. This physical comparison takes into account both *variables* (which can be reduced to a unit basis—area, volume, or number of rooms) and *attributes*. Functional utility is an important ingredient in this comparison, although it is usually inferred rather than measured directly. The elements of physical comparison typically include:

1. An indication of market acceptability and conformity with style and layout.
2. Consideration of size, which would include area or volume, or both.
3. Consideration of the number and types of rooms. Of particular note in residential appraising is the number of bedrooms, the number of baths, the type of basement (if any), and the existence a separate dining room.
4. Age is another important consideration; actual age is usually employed.
5. Condition, including an indication of both effective age and remaining economic life, and needed repairs and maintenance.

Figure 7–3 *(continued)*
Sales Adjustment Grid, Direct Sales Comparison Approach

	Sale Number							
	1	*2*	*3*	*4*	*5*	*6*	*7*	*8*
Sales price	$76,000	$53,000	$63,800	$68,000	$76,000	$75,000	$51,800	$94,000
Time adjustment	+3,040	+1,060	+1,914	+7,140	+7,220	+7,126	+10,100	+15,040
Age	−750	+1,500	−1,500	−1,500	−1,500	−1,500	−1,500	−750
Bedroom	−2,500	0	0	−2,500	−5,000	−2,500	0	−7,500
Bath	0	0	0	−1,000	−1,000	−400	0	−1,400
Square footage	+3,220	+7,560	+6,200	−3,640	−3,800	−3,640	+6,200	−20,600
Net adjustment	+3,010	+10,120	+6,614	−1,500	−4,080	−914	+14,800	−15,210
Adjusted sales price	$79,010	$63,120	$70,414	$66,500	$71,920	$74,086	$66,600	$78,790

Range: $63,120–$79,010

6. Functional adequacy, which must be related to any charges for functional obsolescence included in the cost approach and is based upon the description of the improvements derived from field observation.
7. Site and site improvements, including site size, topography, drainage, and the like, as well as an indication of any site improvements that enter into the value estimate. The legal description is also an important guide to site comparisons.
8. Structural type and quality are derived from field inspection and improvements analysis.
9. Accessory buildings by type, condition, function, size, and age represent an important comparable characteristic.
10. Special features would include such things as built-in equipment; electrical, plumbing, heating, and cooling systems; fireplaces; a pool; and the like.

Units of Comparison

Comparison of comparable sales properties with the subject property, and with one another, is not always feasible or appropriate. For analytical purposes, it is frequently desirable to reduce the properties to some common denominator and express sales price on a per unit basis. Then the adjustment process for other subsequent comparison analysis can be conducted in terms of this common unit of measurement or use.

The important consideration for the appraiser is to select units of comparison that are analytically defensible and that generally reflect the market behavior of buyers and sellers. The units of comparison used in the analysis should reflect the way buyers and sellers act and, preferably, the way they think as well.

Objectives of Using Units of Comparison

Three important purposes can be served by reducing comparable sales properties and the subject property to a common denominator of analysis through the use of units of comparison. First, better understanding of the sales comparison and adjustment processes can be achieved by the appraiser, the client, and reader-users of the appraisal report if the analysis is expressed in terms and units that represent actual market behavior. Second, better communication from the appraiser to the client (seller, buyer, and/or lender) results when the report and its analysis are presented in units that represent the way buyers and sellers behave on the market. The client and other reader-users of the appraisal report can also be educated to recognize the usefulness of expressing property comparisons in terms of common denominators that make the comparisons easy and direct as well as meaningful.

Finally, the use of units of comparison is a better means of handling comparisons. It expresses the comparisons in the language of informed buyers, sellers, lenders, and other market professionals, including appraisers. The typically informed purchaser in the market in question should understand (and, preferably, use) the unit of comparison that the appraiser employs. Because they are the basic building blocks applied to individual properties to formulate value estimates, units of comparison in appraisal analysis should be the units in terms of which residential properties in the market in question are actually bought, sold, rented, or built.

Uses and Limitations of Units of Comparison

Units of comparison make direct comparison of properties more readily feasible and defensible, provided that the salient characteristics of the properties being compared are judged by the appraiser (with supporting justification) to be essentially similar in terms of market reaction to them. The units of direct comparison are the total property and the gross rent multiplier.

Units of comparison can be used to adjust or account for differences in size. By reducing a property to a per unit basis, it can be compared more closely with otherwise similar residential real estate. Care must be exercised, however, not to assume that all differences in size can be adjusted or compensated for through the use of units of comparison. The differences must be relatively small; otherwise, the properties are really in different markets.

Only meaningful units of comparison that make sense in the framework of the type of property being appraised should be used. In other words, only units that reflect the thinking and behavior of market participants are appropriate. What is appropriate as a unit of comparison for residential property tends to vary somewhat from one market area to another and with the passage of time. Nevertheless, some standard units can be identified that have wide acceptability. A useful unit of comparison can be any common denominator that identifies, clarifies, and tends to represent market behavior, and therefore helps the appraiser in the analysis of property comparisons.

The use of physical units of comparison is defensible only when the appraiser can justify the assumption that there is a constant linear relationship betwen size and sales price or value. This emphasizes the importance of determining that the properties being analyzed and compared are indeed competing with one another on the same market. Area, neighborhood, and property analyses provide the basis for this determination. Competitiveness cannot be assumed or inferred from mere similarity. Units of comparison (especially physical units, such as per square foot) are used in all approaches to value estimation—cost and income capitalization as well as sales comparison.

Types of Units of Comparison

Units of comparison for residential properties generally fall into two categories: total property and physical units. For income-producing properties, there is a third category: units of use.

Direct comparison can be (and sometimes is) attempted when comparable sales properties are deemed by the appraiser to be highly competitive with the subject property and with one another. Although this rarely occurs in practice, clients (especially sellers) tend to take this approach without sufficient justification. A would-be seller might learn, for example, that a similar house in the same neighborhood sold recently for $85,000, but that it was not centrally air conditioned. Since air conditioning cost this potential seller $15,000, the seller might well reason that the property is worth at least $100,000, without taking into consideration differences in the two properties that an informed purchaser would rate and adjust for mentally (and that an appraiser would adjust for formally).

Suppose that a property contains six rooms, three bedrooms, one and a half baths, a one-car garage, and an 85-by-120-foot lot. It is 10 years old, well maintained, and essentially the same as when it was built. It is in a large subdivision of basically similar houses. The current market is active, and several sales of what appear to be comparable properties in the same neighborhood have occurred recently. In this case, a direct comparison might be attempted. The sales prices for seven comparable sales are:

$60,600	$63,500	$61,400
$63,000	$64,600	$63,000
$64,000		

By inspection, the range is $60,600 to $64,600. The median and mode are $63,000. The calculated mean is $62,871, with a standard deviation of $1,415. The 95 percent confidence interval ($\overline{X} \pm 2.447s$) is $59,408 to $66,334. The likely estimated value of the subject property would be $63,000. However, this analysis still does not suggest why the sales prices were different, what in the transactions caused the differences, and how much impact these differences have on the value of the subject property.

The gross rent multiplier is actually a unit of comparison for direct sales comparison analysis, although it is widely regarded as being the income approach for residential or amenity properties. It compares total properties directly through the ratio of sales price or value of each property to its gross unfurnished rental. It thus uses the income generated by the property as the basis for comparison and valuation. The ratio is the gross rent multiplier (monthly or annual); monthly multipliers are commonly used in the valuation of residential or amenity properties. Because of its separate significance and its approach to direct comparisons of total properties, gross rent multiplier analysis is treated in greater detail in Chapter 9.

Physical (Size) Units of Comparison

The most commonly employed units of comparison for improved residential properties (including both site and improvements together) are the following:

1. Sales price per square foot of living area.
2. Sales price per square foot of ground area covered (foundation area).
3. Sales price per cubic foot.
4. Sales price per room. (This is usually less satisfactory, because the definition or nature of a room can vary so much from one property to another.)

The Adjustment Process

Each comparable sales property must be identified and described in sufficient detail so that both the appraiser and the reader of the report adequately understand the major characteristics of the comparable properties in comparison with those of the subject property. The appraiser must then adjust the sales price of each comparable sales property for differences between it and the subject property. The final result is an indication of *adjusted sales price* for the comparable property (whether for the total property or on a unit basis). This adjusted sales price is the appraiser's estimate of what the comparable sales property would have sold for if it had possessed all of the salient characteristics of the subject property at the time of sale (including similar market conditions). This is the objective of the adjustment process.

The appraiser should consider the differences between the comparable property and the subject property for significant, pertinent characteristics only. Too detailed a listing of adjustment factors and adjustments can convey an impression of accuracy and precision that is simply not possible in a judgment art such as appraising. Each adjustment for differentials between the subject property and the comparable property should be defended and justified from evidence of the market. It is not a matter of the appraiser's opinion.

The underlying principle in terms of which adjustments are made or measured is the principle of contribution or marginal productivity. The appraiser must always answer two questions: What difference does the presence or absence of the factor being considered (if it is an attribute) make in the probable sales price or value of the property in the present local market? What difference does a varying amount of the factor (if it is a variable) make in the probable sales price or value?

In assembling a list of factors for which adjustments should be made, the appraiser should take special care to include all those elements for which deductions are made in the subject property in estimating accrued depreciation in the cost approach and in estimating rent differentials in gross rent multiplier analysis. The categories of elements of comparison should always be considered, whether they are actually used in the adjustment process or not. The grid from FNMA/FHLMC Form 1004/70, indicating the items of comparison between comparable sales properties and the subject property, is shown in figure 7–4.

Subject Property Is the Standard
(Physical and Locational Adjustments)

The objective of appraisal analysis is to estimate the value (most frequently the market value) of the subject property. Guides to that value are provided by the sales prices of comparable properties that have recently sold on the local market. The adjustment process is undertaken in order to account for differences between comparable sales properties and the subject property. The actual sales prices of the comparable properties are known. The element being sought in each adjustment process is the estimated price at which the comparable sales property would most probably have sold if it had possessed all of the salient physical and locational characteristics of the subject property.

Therefore, all physical and locational adjustments are made from the comparable sales property to the subject property. This means that if the subject property has a one-car garage and the comparable property in the question has a two-car garage, the comparable property is superior to the subject property in this respect. A downward adjustment in the sales price of the comparable property is required (based on market evidence of the difference that an extra stall in the garage would make). Such an adjustment is necessary to reach an indication of what the comparable property would have sold for if it had a one-car garage rather than a two-car garage.

Similarly, if the subject property has two full baths, whereas the comparable property has one full bath and one two-unit lavatory, the sales price of the comparable property should be adjusted upward. The amount of the adjustment should reflect the difference that this feature would have made in the sales price of the comparable property. The resulting adjustment provides an indication of what the comparable property would have sold for if it had two full baths instead of one full bath and a two-unit washroom. In the adjustment process for physical and locational adjustments, the subject property is taken as 100 percent. The comparable properties are treated as deviations from this norm.

Justification Required for Market Extraction

In estimating the amount of adjustment to make for the presence or absence of any factor or for varying quantities of any factor in the comparable sales property as compared with the subject property, the only valid measure is evidence of the market reactions of buyers to such a difference. These reactions are reflected in varying sales prices of otherwise identical properties with and without the factor in question, if such evidence is available.

The principle involved is the contribution made by the factor or element being considered. Cost is not the appropriate measure of the difference. Cost to install may or may not equal the sales price differential reflected in the market behavior of buyers. This applies to both cost new and cost to cure. Cost is not value, although it may be an appropriate measure of value in some circumstances.

Every adjustment should be justified by market evidence. Examination of the market behavior of typical buyers may reveal that a particular deficiency or superiority is not reflected in a sales price differential, even though the appraiser believes that it should be.

Types of Adjustments: Mechanics

Appraisers must identify and select the technique of adjustment that will be employed. They should utilize the same technique throughout

VALUATION SECTION

Purpose of Appraisal is to estimate Market Value as defined in Certification & Statement of Limiting Conditions (FHLMC Form 439/FNMA Form 1004B). If submitted for FNMA, the appraiser must attach (1) sketch or map showing location of subject, street names, distance from nearest intersection, and any detrimental conditions and (2) exterior building sketch of improvements showing dimensions.

COST APPROACH

Measurements	No. Stories	Sq. Ft.
×		=
×		=
×		=
×		=
×		=

Total Gross Living Area (List in Market Data Analysis below)

Comment on functional and economic obsolescence: _____

ESTIMATED REPRODUCTION COST — NEW — OF IMPROVEMENTS:

Dwelling	Sq. Ft. @ $	= $
	Sq. Ft. @ $	=
Extras		=
Special Energy Efficient Items		=
Porches, Patios, etc.		=
Garage/Car Port	Sq. Ft. @ $	=
Site Improvements (driveway, landscaping, etc.)		=
Total Estimated Cost New		= $
Less	Physical	Functional	Economic
Depreciation $	$		= $ ( )
Depreciated value of improvements		= $
ESTIMATED LAND VALUE (If leasehold, show only leasehold value)		= $
INDICATED VALUE BY COST APPROACH		= $

DATA ANALYSIS

The undersigned has recited three recent sales of properties most similar and proximate to subject and has considered these in the market analysis. The description includes a dollar adjustment, reflecting market reaction to those items of significant variation between the subject and comparable properties. If a significant item in the comparable property is superior to, or more favorable than, the subject property, a minus (−) adjustment is made, thus reducing the indicated value of subject; if a significant item in the comparable is inferior to, or less favorable than, the subject property, a plus (+) adjustment is made, thus increasing the indicated value of the subject.

ITEM	Subject Property	COMPARABLE NO. 1		COMPARABLE NO. 2		COMPARABLE NO. 3	
Address							
Proximity to Subj.							
Sales Price	$		$		$		$
Price/Living area	$		$		$		$
Data Source							
		DESCRIPTION	+(−)$ Adjustment	DESCRIPTION	+(−)$ Adjustment	DESCRIPTION	+(−)$ Adjustment
Date of Sale and Time Adjustment							
Location							
Site/View							
Design and Appeal							
Quality of Const.							
Age							
Condition							
Living Area Room Count and Total	Total : B-rms : Baths	Total : B-rms : Baths		Total : B-rms : Baths		Total : B-rms : Baths	
Gross Living Area	Sq.Ft.	Sq.Ft.		Sq.Ft.		Sq.Ft.	

MARKET

Basement & Bsmt. Finished Rooms

Functional Utility

Air Conditioning

Garage/Car Port

Porches, Patio, Pools, etc.

Special Energy Efficient Items

Other (e.g. fire-places, kitchen equip., remodeling)

Sales or Financing Concessions

Net Adj. (Total)   ☐ Plus; ☐ Minus $ ___   ☐ Plus; ☐ Minus $ ___   ☐ Plus; ☐ Minus $ ___
Indicated Value of Subject $ ___ $ ___ $ ___

Comments on Market Data

INDICATED VALUE BY MARKET DATA APPROACH ___ $ ___

INDICATED VALUE BY INCOME APPROACH (If applicable) Economic Market Rent $ ___ /Mo. x Gross Rent Multiplier ___ = $ ___

This appraisal is made ☐ "as is" ☐ subject to the repairs, alterations, or conditions listed below ☐ completion per plans and specifications.

Comments and Conditions of Appraisal: _____

Final Reconciliation: _____

Construction Warranty ☐ Yes ☐ No   Name of Warranty Program _____   Warranty Coverage Expires _____

This appraisal is based upon the above requirements, the certification, contingent and limiting conditions, and Market Value definition that are stated in

☐ FHLMC Form 439 (Rev. 10/78)/FNMA Form 1004B (Rev. 10/78) filed with client _____ 19 ___ ☐ attached.

I ESTIMATE THE MARKET VALUE, AS DEFINED, OF SUBJECT PROPERTY AS OF _____ 19 ___ to be $ ___

Appraiser(s) _____   Review Appraiser (If applicable) _____ ☐ Did ☐ Did Not Physically Inspect Property

FHLMC Form 70 Rev. 7/79   REVERSE   FNMA Form 1004 Rev. 7/79

Figure 7–4. FNMA Adjustment Grid (Valuation Section)

the adjustment process. Whichever technique is employed, it should reflect market reactions appropriately, both in direction and in size of adjustment.

Plus and Minus Dollar Adjustments. If dollar differences can be substantiated, the appraiser may add for deficiencies in the comparable property as compared to the subject property and subtract for elements in terms of which the comparable property is superior to the subject. If it can be justified, this technique is generally preferred, because the market reacts in terms of dollars. In addition, the sequence of adjustments is less significant if plus and minus amounts are employed, because each factor is assumed to have a separate and independent impact on sales price differentials.

Plus and Minus Percentage Adjustments. Adjustments for time and market conditions (financing) frequently cannot be expressed directly from the market in dollar amounts but typically can be represented by a percentage differential. Market conditions adjustments (including those for financing differentials) and time adjustments are made first and in that sequence. Then the physical and locational adjustments are made, based on the sale price of the comparable property as adjusted for market conditions and time. Since physical and locational adjustments need to be made in terms of the current local market, the base used for them should be adjusted to the current market first. To the extent that plus and minus percentage adjustments are employed, the appraiser should limit them to adjustments for market conditions and time whenever possible.

Cumulative Percentage Adjustments. If appraisers are convinced from the analysis that the factors involved in the adjustment process are causally interdependent and, hence, correlated with one another, they may use cumulative percentage adjustments. This leads to slightly different answers using the same individual adjustments. Generally, the larger the percentage adjustments are in one direction, the greater the difference is between plus and minus percentage adjustments and cumulative adjustments. Cumulative percentages are valid only if a causal interrelationship is shown to exist and this is not often the case.

The sequence of adjustments is not important with this technique, since the result is the same. A usual sequence convention, however, is terms and conditions of sale, time, location, and physical differences. If a comparable sales property has been adjusted downward 10 percent for terms and conditions of sale and upward 10 percent for the market to market adjustment (time of sale), and is judged to be 15 percent superior to the subject with respect to location and 5 percent inferior with respect to physical characteristics, the net adjustment on a plus or minus basis is minus 10 percent ($1.00 - 0.10 + 0.10 - 0.15 + 0.05 = 0.90$, or minus 0.10 net). If cumulative percentage adjustments are used, the net adjustment is minus 7.5 percent [$1.00 \div (1.10 \times 0.90 \times 1.15 \times 0.95) = 0.9246$].

If some adjustments are expressed directly as dollar amounts and others as percentages, the percentages must be converted to dollar amounts (as percentages of the sales price of the comparable property, adjusted for market conditions and time). This is shown in the sales adjustment grid in figure 7–3, where the time adjustment is a percentage and other adjustments are dollar amounts.

Net Adjustment to the Adjusted Sales Price. Whether plus and minus or cumulative adjustments are used, a net adjustment figure either in percentages or in dollar amount is derived. The net adjustment is added to or subtracted from the sales price of the comparable property to obtain an adjusted sales price of the comparable property. This is the appraiser's best estimate of what the comparable property would have sold for if it had possessed all the salient characteristics of the subject property. The adjusted sales price may be for the total property or for an appropriate unit of comparison utilized in the analysis.

Presentation of the Adjustment Process

A complete and detailed narrative presentation should describe each comparable property in sufficient detail for the reader of the report to understand the adjustments made and the direction and size of each adjustment in each comparable sales property.

Each adjustment should be justified in narrative form, based on the evidence of the market. A sales adjustment grid is a useful and commonly employed tabular device to summarize the adjustment process for each comparable sales property. An adjustment grid is not a substitute for narrative description, however, nor for justification of the adjustment.

Derivation of the Value Estimate

For each comparable sales property, the adjustment process results in an adjusted sales price, which may be for the total property or for the appropriate unit of comparison. The adjusted sales price figures for all the comparables should cluster around the point of tendency. This point is the sales price or unit sales price selected as the best indication or approximation of the market value of the subject property (total or unit), based on the direct sales comparison approach.

Unless there are many adjusted sales prices and the appraiser can accept the assumption that each comparable sale has equal significance or validity (and therefore should be given weight), an arithmetic average should not be used. Certainly, averaging for three to four observations is extremely hazardous. Greatest emphasis is placed on the adjusted sales price figures for the comparable properties that are regarded as most nearly similar to the subject property. One guide is the amount of adjustment required (provided that they are reasonable in size). Generally, the least adjusted comparable sales property is most likely to be a close comparable to the subject property. If a unit sales price figure is used, it must be multiplied by the number of units in the subject property to obtain the indicated value for the subject property. As an illustration of this process, the adjusted sales prices per square foot for the 8 comparables in figure 7–3 would be as follows (without size adjustment):

Sale Number	Adjusted Sales Price per Square Foot
1	$68.53
2	59.42
3	66.46
4	46.83
5	52.05
6	51.65
7	53.96
8	40.87

Clearly, the adjusted sales price per square foot decreases as size increases. The mean is $54.97 per square foot. The final estimate is $55.00 per square foot. These figures appear to lie between the range established by the more comparable properties (numbers 1, 4, 5, and 6), as noted in figure 7–3. Using $55 per square foot, for 1,270 square feet, would result in an estimated value of $69,850. Using the mean would yield an estimated value of $69,800. Usually, a single figure must be derived as the estimate of value. This figure must be rounded to an appropriate level; non-rounded figures give an improper impression of precision. Thus, the final value estimate for the subject property in figure 7–3 would most likely be $70,000.

Uses and Limitations of Direct Sales
Comparison Analysis

The direct sales comparison approach comes closest of the various approaches to value estimation to the thinking and behavior of the typical purchaser of a residence. To a large extent, it simulates market behavior. Generally, when adequate data of sufficient quality are available, greatest reliance will be placed by the appraiser on an estimate of value via the direct sales comparison approach. This is especially true for residential or amenity property appraisals.

Information developed through the sales comparison approach provides both a basis and a support for judgments used in the application of other approaches to residential value estimation. It establishes, for example, the basis for measuring estimated depreciation charges in the cost approach. It also establishes standards for estimating the gross rent multiplier and market rental in income valuation of residential or amenity properties.

In most jurisdictions, the courts have placed greatest reliance and emphasis on evidence from bona fide market sales of comparable properties in reaching judgments about market value and, hence, just compensation.

The direct sales comparison approach takes into account an important but frequently overlooked market element: the effect of financing terms on sales prices. Market price is the basic guide to market value in the direct sales comparison approach. It includes whatever constitutes the cost to the typically informed purchaser.

Sales comparison analysis is the most appropriate approach when there is an active market for comparable properties and when adequate quantities of reliable, verified market sales data are available. It is the most direct approach to value estimation, based on market activities as a reliable guide to values. It is simple and easy to understand in concept—perhaps deceptively so. Its very simplicity makes its use hazardous, however. Its application produces complications in the adjustment process.

It is difficult to use the direct sales comparison approach to estimate residential property value unless there are sufficient data of adequate quality to justify a market value conclusion. In the absence of market activity, or if the subject property is unique and there are no true comparisons, it may be impossible to apply this approach. It cannot be applied readily or realistically if the subject property is not the type that is actively traded on the market.

Of necessity, the estimate of value via the sales comparison approach is based on transactions that have already occurred. This approach requires an assumption, therefore, that market behavior and market forces in the past will continue to have the same relationship in the future. Generally, the recent past can be accepted as the best guide to the immediate or near-term future, but mere similarity of use or physical appearance does not make for true comparability among residential properties. In applying the direct sales comparison approach, the appraiser must look into market conditions and terms of sale as well as making physical comparisons to judge true comparability or competitiveness.

Summary

The direct sales comparison approach is based primarily on the principle of substitution—that informed purchasers would pay no more for residential property than the cost to them of obtaining comparable, competitive property with the same utility on the open market. When market data are available, the sales comparison approach is the best reflection of the way the typically informed purchaser reacts to the market.

The appraiser must develop a data program for comparative analysis and must effectively exploit the appropriate sources of information. The appraiser must identify the appropriate elements of comparison between comparable sales properties and the subject property. Where appropriate, the appraiser should identify the unit of comparison to be used in making sales comparisons. Comparable sales data are adjusted to the subject property, with the subject property as the standard in terms of which the comparable sales properties are evaluated and adjusted.

The market behavior and reactions of typical purchasers to differences among properties provide the guide to whether an adjustment is to be made, in what direction it is to be made, and how much it should be. This is an application of the principle of contribution. The appraiser must decide which technique of adjustment is appropriate to the particular case and must use it consistently throughout the adjustment process. An adjusted sales price is derived for each comparable sales property. These adjusted sales prices are reconciled to a final indication of the market value of the subject property. This figure is then rounded to an indication of market value of the subject property via the direct sales comparison approach.

Notes

1. Boyce, Byrl N., ed., *Real Estate Appraisal Terminology,* rev. ed. (Cambridge, Mass.: Ballinger [Joint publication of the American Institute of Real Estate Appraisers and Society of Real Estate Appraisers], 1981), p. 79.

2. See Ibid., p. 160.

3. Information concerning the SREA Market Data Center, Inc., may be obtained from:

> SREA Market Data Center, Inc.
> 24 West St. Joseph Street
> Caller Box #23
> Arcadia, CA 91006–0023

4. The discounting and analytical technique is explained in detail in chapter 4. The same principles are used for the analysis in this section.

Suggested Readings

American Institute of Real Estate Appraisers. *The Appraisal of Real Estate,* 8th ed. Chicago: American Institute of Real Estate Appraisers, 1983, chapters 12 and 13.

Bloom, George F., and Harrison, Henry S. *Appraising the Single Family Residence.* Chicago: American Institute of Real Estate Appraisers, 1978, chapter 13.

Boyce, Byrl N., ed. *Real Estate Appraisal Terminology,* rev. ed. Cambridge, Mass.: Ballinger Publishing Company (Joint publication of the American Institute of Real Estate Appraisers and Society of Real Estate Appraisers), 1981.

Epley, Donald R., and Boykin, James H. *Basic Income Property Appraisal.* Reading, Mass.: Addison-Wesley, 1983, chapter 4.

HUD Handbook: Single Family Underwriting Reports and Forms Data, no. 4190.1. Washington, D.C.: U.S. Department of Housing and Urban Development, 1974.

"Market Data Sales Demonstration." Arcadia, Calif.: SREA Market Data Center, 1981.

Ratcliff, Richard U. *Valuation for Real Estate Decisions.* Santa Cruz, Calif.: Democrat Press, 1972, chapters 6 and 7.

"Sales Data" (printed for individual states and regions). Arcadia, Calif.: SREA Market Data Center, updated quarterly.

Smith, Halbert C. *Real Estate Appraisal.* Columbus, Ohio: Grid, 1976, chapter 3.

Wendt, Paul F. *Real Estate Appraisal: Review and Outlook.* Athens: University of Georgia Press, 1974, chapter 5.

8

Site Valuation

Key Terms

Allocation A method of dividing the appraised value of a property between land and building. (Also sometimes called "Abstraction.")

Acre A land area measure containing 43,560 square feet.

Ad valorem tax A tax on real estate that is based on the value of the property.

Assemblage Combining two or more parcels into a single use or ownership. *and increase in value*

Direct capitalization of ground rents Conversion of ground rents into a present worth estimate through the capitalization process.

Excess land Land (in area or frontage) in excess of a standard site for the market.

Front foot A unit of land measure along the frontage of a property.

Land development method A method of valuing raw acreage that is designed or proposed for residential development.

Land residual technique A valuation technique that splits income between land and improvements and capitalizes the residual income to land into value. *↖ discounting*

Lot A distinct portion or parcel of land.

Plottage Two or more sites assembled under single ownership that have a greater utility than the aggregate utility of both sites separately considered. *increases value*

Plottage value The increment of value resulting from the greater utility of the plottage process.

Reconciliation The process of evaluating and selecting from among alternative indications of value to reach a final value estimate.

Square foot A unit of measure of land or improvements area used for information, comparison, or valuation purposes.

Improved properties are integral economic units in which site and improvements are used together and should be valued together. Residential properties typically are valued with site and improvements combined as a single entity. There are several types of situations, however, in which it is necessary or desirable to estimate the value of sites, or land suitable for development as sites, separately. The most likely situations for a residential appraiser are reviewed briefly here.

In some instances, the appraiser may be called upon to estimate the value of a vacant site or of vacant land that is suitable for development into sites. When improved property is valued via the cost approach, site must be valued independently. This provides the basis for estimating the contribution made by the improvements, which are valued in terms of depreciated reproduction cost new. Further, in several applications of the income approach to value estimation, it is necessary for site to be valued independently. This is true for example, with the building residual technique and the property residual technique when the site is the reversion.

For purposes of taxation, it is often necessary or required that the appraiser separate the value estimate between site and buildings or improvements. This is the case even though an improved property can realistically be appraised only on the assumption that the component parts (site and buildings) are used in conjunction with each other. This separation for analytical valuation purposes applies to both ad valorem property taxation and income taxation, especially capital gains.

Courts and condemnors often require that appraisers separate before values, after values, and damages between site and buildings. When this is necessary, the appraiser must value site independently and separately. It may also be necessary for site to be valued independently as a remainder value in the event buildings are destroyed. Finally, when land is leased, which is relatively rare but not unknown for residential sites, site must be valued separately in order to provide the base from which the interests of the lessor and the lessee are calculated.

Basic Rules and Conditions of Site Valuation

There is no fundamental difference between site valuation and the valuation of improved properties. The same valuation principles apply, and the requirements for site inspection and analysis are essentially the same. Many of the same methods of valuation are applicable, but not all. Particular emphasis is placed on direct sales comparison analysis, using the same techniques and procedures employed to value improved properties. These procedures need not be reviewed here in detail, but their specific application to site valuation is illustrated in this chapter. There are also some peculiarities to site valuation that require consideration and emphasis.

Site is Valued, Not Land

In the appraisal of residential property, residential sites are valued. As noted and defined earlier, a site is land that has been improved to the point that it is ready and suitable for residential use. Such improvements include grading, access, utilities, and site preparation. The one exception is raw, unimproved acreage that is suitable for improvement and development for residential sites. In such cases, the *land development method,* or cost of development method, is used.

Value is Estimated in Terms of Highest and Best Use

By convention, and logically, a site is valued as if it were vacant and available to be put to its highest and best use. This is true whether the site is actually vacant or is improved with buildings. Site is valued in terms of the use pattern to which it is suited and adaptable, which is legal (in terms of zoning and deed restrictions), which is feasible (in terms of market reactions), and which represents the highest present worth of the benefits to be derived from the ownership and/or use of the site. Market value is measured in terms of the most probable price that an informed purchaser would pay.

Valuation of site in terms of its highest and best use provides the basis for ascertaining whether the present use and development pattern really represents the highest and best use of the site. As noted in the later discussion of the cost approach and accrued depreciation, improper improvements (whether overimprovements or underimprovements) are indicated by a comparison of the existing improvement pattern with the pattern that represents highest and best use of the site.

Valuation of the site in terms of its highest and best use means that all functional obsolescence, as well as physical deterioration, is charged to the improvements. This is done in order to indicate and measure the extent to which the improvements contribute to the total value of the improved property. Such measurement is particularly significant when conversion or supersession of use becomes a reasonable alternative program of action for the owner or purchaser. This represents an application of the principle of contribution. The highest and best use of a site is subject to change over time. It must be ascertained by the appraiser in terms of current market conditions as of the date of the appraisal.

Reactions of Typical Purchaser
(Open Market Conditions)

All market value estimates are expressed in terms of reactions of the
typically informed purchaser on the market in question as of the date
of the appraisal. Once again, reference is made to the definition of
market value. Any method or technique of site value estimation must
therefore utilize current sales data on a competitive market. Site (and
land) values are primarily a reflection of open market activity, based
on the interaction of supply and demand forces. Market activity can
also be reflected through income, since even residential sites can be,
and sometimes are, leased. The observed market behavior of informed
purchasers on the market must therefore constitute the basis for any
approach to site valuation.

Specified Market Conditions

The value of a site, as well as the value of an improved property, can
and does change with the passage of time and with varying market
conditions. The appraiser must therefore specify the market conditions
and the neighborhood environment within which the value estimate is
made. Once again, this emphasizes the critical importance of specifying
the date as of which the appraisal is made and the significance of market,
area, and neighborhood analyses.

Production Cost is Not an Appropriate
Measure of Site Value

Even though improvements to undeveloped land to create sites do cost
money, and those costs can be measured, the rationale of the cost
approach does not apply to site valuation. Depreciation does not accrue
to land or sites. Therefore, the only approaches to site valuation are
direct sales comparison and, sometimes, income capitalization analysis.

Methods of Site Valuation

There really are only two approaches to site valuation: direct sales
comparison and income capitalization. There are variations on these
basic approaches, however, that lead to several other potentially available methods or procedures for the residential appraiser. The variations

on direct sales comparison analysis are emphasized here because they are typically most applicable to residential site valuation. They include direct sales comparisons; allocation (sometimes termed abstraction or distribution); and ideal neighborhood and site comparison. The application of regression analysis is also available for residential site valuation, as discussed in a later chapter. Occasionally applicable techniques of income capitalization are noted breifly here. They include direct capitalization of ground rents; the land development or cost-of-development method; and the land residual technique. No one method of site valuation is inherently preferable in all circumstances; each has an appropriate use under specified conditions.

Sales Comparison Analysis

Whenever adequate quantities of verified sales data of sufficient quality are available, sales comparison is the method to employ in site valuation. This is particularly true for residential site valuation. As noted in Chapter 7 in the consideration of direct sales comparison analysis for improved properties, the underlying presumption in this approach is that recent sales transactions of comparable sites that are competitive with the subject site on the local market are the best guide to the most probable current market behavior and reactions of informed purchasers.

The rationale, technique, application, uses, and limitations of direct sales comparison analysis have been discussed, explained, and illustrated earlier. There is no difference in the general fundamentals of valuation of improved properties and site valuation with sales comparisons. The basic points are reviewed here, with any differences or peculiarities for site valuation (especially residential site valuation) given special emphasis.

Rationale. Direct sales comparison analysis for site valuation is basically founded on the application of the principle of substitution—that an informed, prudent purchaser will pay no more for a residential site than the cost of acquiring a substitute site with the same amenities and utility.

Requirements. Several conditions must be met for direct sales comparison analysis to be applicable to residential site valuation. Initially, there must be a complete and detailed site description, based on site analysis for the subject property, and detailed data gathering for comparable site sales transactions. To meet professional reporting requirements, each of the comparable sites must be described in sufficient detail with respect to the salient elements of comparison so that a reader may visualize and understand what comparisons the appraiser made and why. Also, the comparable sites used in the analysis must be competitive with the subject property, and with one another, on the same market. If there is not an active market for sites of the type represented by the subject site, sales comparison analysis cannot be applied appropriately.

At least 8 to 10 comparable site sales transactions should be analyzed; 12 to 15 are preferable. At least 3 should be reported. All comparable site sales transaction data should be verified with a principal to the transaction or an unimpeachable, authoritative source. Sources of data are exactly the same as those for improved residential properties. Data banks associated with computer systems are especially good sources of leads, particularly when regression analysis is to be applied.

Elements of Comparison. In site valuation through direct sales comparisons, the date of sale of each comparable site identifies the market conditions in terms of which the transaction took place, in comparison with current (valuation date) market conditions. Location is a somewhat more critical consideration and influence in site valuation, since there is not the major offsetting effect of buildings. Neighborhood analysis and influence is particularly important as a factor in site valuation. Whenever possible, comparable sales transactions that do not require a location adjustment should be used. When an adjustment for location is necessary, the procedure shown in the case study at the end of this chapter can be used to good effect.

Only bona fide, arm's length, open market comparable sales transactions should be used in sales comparison analysis, if at all possible. Terms of financing should be the same as those generally available in the market in which the comparable property sold. If they are not, adjustment may be required for cash equivalency. Zoning and land use regulations are really a part of location, but they should be treated separately because they are important determinants of site value that set legal limits on the uses and use densities to which the site can be put. Since a site is valued as if it were vacant and available to be put to its highest and best use, zoning and other land use regulations or restrictions are crucial in determining just what is the highest and best use. Unless comparable sites have the same highest and best use as the subject site, they are not truly competitive or on the same market with the subject site, however similar they may otherwise appear.

Physical characteristics peculiar to site valuation include both variables and attributes. Variables may vary in quantity from site to site but can usually be reduced to a unit basis. Not all variables are applicable in every appraisal, but all should be considered for use in the analysis. Frontage (a variable) is more significant in built-up areas with relatively small lots. It can also influence the tax assessment and tax burden in some jurisdictions. Width influences the use of the site and siting of buildings, given set-back requirements. Depth also influences use in siting, relative to set-back requirements. It also may indicate whether there is excess land area relative to site area necessary and appropriate to residential use. Attributes are characteristics that the site either possesses or does not or that have appropriate quality (acceptable to the market) or not. Topography, shape of lot, drainage, soil and subsoil conditions, utilities, municipal services, as well as streets, alleys, access, sidewalks, and curbs are all attributes.

Units of Comparison. It is frequently possible and desirable to account for minor physical variations in lot size by reducing the valuation analysis to a unit basis. Units of comparison make it possible to compare directly sites that vary in size or shape. Care must be exercised in applying units of comparison, however. The appraiser should not attempt to compare noncomparable sites that are really in different markets because the differences in their size or shape affect the use to which they can be appropriately put.

The standards of acceptance in the market in which the subject site is located will influence the units selected by appraisers. They must ascertain from sales data (confirmed by buyers, sellers, and/or brokers) the appropriate unit or units in terms of which sites are bought and sold on the market in question. These units will vary from one market to another. Appraisers are not justified in applying an artificial unit simply because their experience tells them that it is generally used.

Common units of comparison in residential site valuation include front foot, square foot, lot, and acre. The *front foot* unit of comparison is frequently measured in terms of a standard depth. The effective frontage of irregularly shaped lots is calculated as either the average width of the front and rear lot lines or the width of the lot at the building line. Front foot measurements are generally applicable in built-up areas, often for relatively small lots. The *square foot* unit is frequently utilized for expensive residential sites and for irregularly shaped lots.

In extreme suburban and rural areas, where land utilization is less intensive, minor variations in lot sizes are not significant or measurable influences on value. The unit of valuation is the standard *lot,* often set by the minimum area required by local zoning regulations. The *acre* as a unit of comparison is utilized more for raw land valuation than for site valuation, except in rural areas or estate developments.

The Adjustment Process. Once adjustments have been made for market conditions and time, sales prices of comparable sites are adjusted from the comparable to the subject site. The subject site is the standard in terms of which the comparable sales sites are analyzed and evaluated. It is, in effect, 100 percent, or the base of an index. In each case, the basic question is what the comparable site would have sold for if it had been identical with the subject site in every important respect.

The possible methods of adjustment are plus and minus dollar adjustments; plus and minus percentage adjustments; and cumulative percentage adjustments. The plus and minus dollar adjustments method is preferred, and the cumulative percentage adjustments method is not considered appropriate unless there is evidence that the adjustment factors are causally interrelated. The varying effects of applying these three methods of adjustment to the same comparable site sales data are shown graphically in figure 8–1.

After adjustments have been made for market conditions and time, the sequence of adjustments for physical and locational differences makes no difference in the results. The amount and direction of adjustments are determined by and derived from the market behavior of buyers, as reflected in sales price differentials. The objective is to measure the difference that the presence or absence or variation in any element of comparison makes in sales price. The process is to compare sales transactions that are identical with respect to all salient elements of comparison, except the one being tested, and to measure the effect of differences on sales price. This procedure is graphically demonstrated in the case study at the end of this chapter, which shows how several successive adjustments can be derived for use.

Reconciliation of Adjusted Sales Prices to an Estimate of Site Value. Applying the adjustment process for all significant characteristics to each comparable sales site results in an adjusted sales price (total or unit) for each comparable site. These adjusted sales prices will fall in a range that will be relatively narrow if the comparable sales data represent sites that are truly comparable and competitive with the subject site, and if the proper adjustments have been made. The market value of the subject site (total or unit) will fall within this range.

The appraiser must then estimate the most appropriate indicated market value of the subject site, based upon the reliability of the data utilized and the defensibility of each adjustment. Generally, the comparable sales that have required the least adjustment are the ones on which the heaviest reliance will be placed. This is because they are most comparable and competitive with the subject site and therefore are the best indicators of its market value, provided that the proper adjustments have been made. Judgment, experience, and analysis are all required at this point.

Statistical averaging is possible to provide a preliminary estimate of value and a test of the reliability of that figure. It can also be used to test the reliability of estimates from alternative methods of adjustment. In figure 8–1, the sales adjustment grids show the results of cumulative percentage adjustments, plus and minus percentage adjustments, and plus and minus percentage adjustments on time-adjusted

The following grids contain sales of sites comparable to a property being appraised as of May 1, 1982. In each, the adjustment process has been altered to reflect cumulative percentge adjustments (Grid 1); plus and minus percentage and dollar adjustments (Grid 2); and plus and minus percentage adjustments on time adjusted sales price (Grid 3). In each case, the same percentage and dóllar adjustments are incorporated, although they are treated differently with respect to mechanical calculations. Therefore, they result in net adjustments and indicated sales prices that are dissimilar. The purpose of this illustration is to point out the logic of the adjustment process and the assumptions inherent in the alternative approaches available to the appraiser.

Grid 1
Cumulative Percentage Adjustments

	Sale Number				
	1	2	3	4	5
Sales price	$7,100	$8,900	$10,400	$10,600	$8,400
Date of sale	1/80	1/80	6/81	5/80	2/79
Adjustments					
Time (12%/yr.)	1.28	1.28	1.11	1.24	1.38
Location	0	0	0	0.80	0.85
Frontage	0.95	0.90	0.95	0.90	0.90
Depth	0.85	0.80	0.85	0.95	0.85
Shape	1.05	1.05	1.05	0	0
Topography	1.10	1.05	1.10	0	0
Utilities	0	0	0	0	0
Composite factor[a]	1.19	1.02	1.04	0.85	.90
Adjusted Sales Price[b]	$8,449	$9,078	$10,816	$ 9,010	$7,560
Range: $7,560–$10,816					

[a]The composite factor is calculated via multiplication. For example, in comparable sale number 1, 1.19 is the product of (1.28 × 0.95 × 0.85 × 1.05 × 1.10).

[b]The Adjusted Sales Price for each sales transaction analysis is a function of the sales price × the composite factor. For example, the Adjusted Sales Price for number 1 is $8,449 ($7,100 × 1.19).

Figure 8–1. Site Valuation: Direct Sales Comparison Approach Adjustments

Grid 2
Plus and Minus Percentage Adjustments

	Sale Number				
	1	2	3	4	5
Sales price	$7,100	$8,900	$10,400	$10,600	$8,400
Date of sale	1/80	1/80	6/81	5/80	2/79
Adjustments					
Time (12%/yr.)	+.28	+.28	+.11	+.24	+.38
	+1,988	+2,492	+1,144	+2,544	+3,192
Location	0	0	0	−.20	−.15
				−2,120	−1,260
Frontage	−.05	−.10	−.05	−.10	−.10
	−355	−890	−520	−1,060	−840
Depth	−.15	−.20	−.15	−.05	−.15
	−1,065	−1,780	−1,560	−530	−1,260
Shape	+.05	+.05	+.05	0	0
	+355	+445	+520		
Topography	+.10	+.05	+.10	0	0
	+710	+445	+1,040		
Utilities	0	0	0	0	0
Net adjustment	+.23	+.08	+.06	−.11	−.02
	+1,633	+712	+624	−1,166	−168
Adjusted Sales Price	$8,733	$9,612	$11,024	$9,434	$8,232
Range: $8,232–$11,024					

Grid 3
Plus and Minus Percentage Adjustments to Time-Adjusted Sales Price

	Sale Number				
	1	2	3	4	5
Sales price	$7,100	$8,900	$10,400	$10,600	$8,400
Date of sale	1/80	1/80	6/81	5/80	2/79
Time adjustment (12%/yr.)	+.28	+.28	+.11	+.24	+.38
	+1,988	+2,492	+1,144	2,544	3,192
Time-adjusted sales price	$9,088	$11,392	$11,544	$13,144	$11,592
Other adjustments					
Location	0	0	0	−.20	−.15
Frontage	−.05	−.10	−.05	−.10	−.10
Depth	−.15	−.20	−.15	−.05	−.15
Shape	+.05	+.05	+.05	0	0
Topography	+.10	+.05	+.10	0	0
Utilities	0	0	0	0	0
Net adjustment	−.05	−.20	−.05	−.35	−.40
	−454	−2,278	−577	−4,600	−4,637
Adjusted Sales Price	$8,634	$9,114	$10,967	$8,544	$6,955
Range: $6,955–$10,967					

Figure 8–1 *(continued)*

sales price. A simple statistical analysis of these results indicates the following:

	Cumulative Percentage Adjustment	Plus and Minus Percentage Adjustment	Time Adjusted
Mean	$8,983	$9,407	$8,843
Standard deviation	1,192	1,060	1,439
Range	3,247	2,792	4,012
Median	9,010	9,434	8,634
Visual inspection (judgment)	9,000	9,400	8,600

The final figure selected should be rounded to an appropriate level. This is the indicated market value of the subject site, either total or per unit. If value per unit is estimated, this figure must be multiplied by the number of units in the subject site to produce a value estimate for the subject site.

Presentation of the Analysis. Both for analysis purposes and for ease of understanding by the reader of the report, the appraiser should develop a grid that shows all of the adjustments for each major feature for each comparable site. This adjustment grid summarizes in tabular form all of the analysis that the appraiser has applied to the adjustment process. The grid is a useful and helpful device for presentation. It must be supplemented, however, by a written justification for every adjustment that is made. The market is the final arbiter of the direction and amount of each adjustment, and all adjustments must be supported by evidence from the market.

The uses and limitations of direct sales comparison analysis were discussed in detail in Chapter 7. The comments there regarding improved property valuation are equally applicable to site valuation. The most significant consideration is that direct sales comparison analysis is always the best method of site valuation when there are sufficient comparable sales data of required quality from an active market for sites competitive with the subject site.

Ideal Neighborhood and Site Comparison Method

A variation of the direct sales comparison approach (which uses the subject site as the base or standard in terms of which sites representing comparable sales are analyzed) is the ideal neighborhood method. This approach establishes a constant base in terms of an ideal neighborhood or site. The chief limitation with this approach is that the weights assigned to the various features of the neighborhood are essentially arbitrary. They must be carefully adapted to each individual appraisal problem. The method has very limited practical applicability.

Allocation

Allocation (sometimes also called abstraction or the distribution technique) is based on the relationship of lot value to building costs or value. In the U.S. Department of Housing and Urban Development *HUD Handbook,* it is erroneously referred to as the land residual method.[1] The allocation technique involves subtracting the value of buildings from sales figures of improved residential properties. The remainder is the indicated value of the site in each sale. This method has limited applicability as an indicator of value. The appraiser must be able to justify the division of value or sales price of improved residential properties between the site and the buildings. The method should be applied only to situations in which there is a lack of good, current sales data for vacant sites that are essentially similar to and competitive with the subject site.

It may be necessary to attempt to apply the allocation technique if the subject site is in a built-up neighborhood with no recent sales of lots. Used very carefully, it may work in a fully developed neighborhood of very similar properties. Even then, the result is often an impression rather than a supported opinion. It is not sufficiently conclusive to be effective as a single tool in the great majority of cases.

A variant of the allocation technique is the ratio of site value to total property value. In this variant, appraisers attempt to ascertain the proportion of total property value or sales price for the total property, which is typically the contribution of the site. There must be a high degree of comparability among the properties selected, and they must be in the same neighborhood and subject to the same market influences. All sales must be normal in terms of financing and conditions of sale. Based on their observations and experience, appraisers reach a conclusion regarding the typical percentage of sales price or value that is attributable to the site. The question then arises whether the subject is typical and whether it will be or is developed in a typical fashion. The key to the entire process is justification of the percentage or proportion of value attributed to the site.

Suppose, for example, that a comparable residence recently sold for $77,000. The site is highly competitive with the subject site in all respects. The building is a typical improvement and is estimated to have a depreciated present worth of $64,000, which is 83 percent of sales price; therefore, the site is presumed to be worth 17 percent of property value. The building-to-site ratio is 4.88:1. This variant of the allocation technique suffers from the same limitations as does the cost approach in the case of depreciated improvements. The problem is to estimate the value of a depreciated building separately and directly. The allocation technique fails completely if the percentages vary or if the subject property is not typical of its market.

In appraising new developments, it is sometimes possible and appropriate to assume that the new residences represent the highest and best use of the sites. If this can be done, then the cost of the building may be subtracted from the sales price of the improved property. If appropriate adjustments are made so that the building costs include an appropriate proportion of overhead and profit to the builder-developer, the remainder may be regarded as the value or the contribution of the site to the entire property. If the properties in question are highly similar to and highly competitive with the subject property, a basis for valuation of the subject site may be developed.

Suppose, for example, that a new residence on a highly competitive comparable site just sold for $79,980. The direct construction cost of the building was $47,160. Indirect costs were 12 percent, and builder's overhead and profit were 20 percent of total costs. The sales expenses were 2 percent of selling price. Total allocation to building and sales expense is figured as follows:

1. Direct and indirect building costs: $47,160 × 1.12 = $52,819.
2. Building costs plus profit and overhead: $52,819 × 1.2 = $63,383.
3. Total building plus sales expenses: $63,383 + (0.02 × $70,980) = $64,983.
4. Allocation to site: $79,980 − $64,983 = $14,997 (rounded to $15,000).

The foregoing is the variant that is referred to in the *HUD Handbook* as the land residual method.[2]

Some appraisers utilize the ratio between the *assessment* of site and buildings and apply this ratio to each comparable sale of improved property. This is even more treacherous than the other variants of the allocation technique. It involves the further assumption that the assessors have applied a consistent and realistic valuation technique to both site and buildings. Use of the tax assessment ratio is not recommended for residential site valuation.

Land Residual Technique

The land residual technique is used almost exclusively for sites of in-come-producing properties. The basic idea is that the site is assumed to be improved with a new building that represents the highest and best use of the site. The reproduction cost new of that building is then estimated. Next, the annual income necessary to cover the investment in the building (return on and of investment) is deducted from the annual net operating income forecast to be produced by the entire improved property. The remaining or residual net income is available to support the investment in the land. Capitalized at an appropriate rate, this residual income indicates the present worth or value of the site. The land residual technique is rarely applicable to the valuation of residential sites.

Direct Capitalization of Ground Rental

Residential sites are sometimes rented on long-term ground leases, as in Hawaii and Baltimore. The annual (or monthly) net rent can be capitalized directly to develop an estimate of site value. Suppose, for example, that a site is on a long-term net lease, with a ground rent of $100 per month, or $1,200 per year. If the appropriate rate for capi-talization of ground rent is 10 percent, the estimated value by direct capitalization is $1,200 ÷ 0.10 = $12,000. If the remaining term of the lease is 40, 50, or more years, there is really no need to take the reversion into account. If it is 20 years, however, then the amount of the reversion can be significant in the total present worth. Suppose, for example, that the net ground rent is $1,200 per year for 20 years, the reversion is forecast to be twice present worth, and the discount rate is 10 percent. By mortgage-equity analysis, the overall rate for capitalization purposes is 0.082540. Then the present worth (value) of the site is $1,200 ÷ 0.08254 = $14,538.

Land Development (Cost of Development) Method

In the valuation of raw acreage that is either designed or proposed for residential development, it is possible to use the land development technique. It is not appropriate for the valuation of individual sites, because it starts with an assumption that the sales price of the completed sites is known. It is useful, however, in ascertaining how much a developer would be justified in paying for raw acreage for development. Figure 8–2 shows this technique in an oversimplified form.

Formulas and Tables

Largely as a result of assessment practices and writings, site valuation is sometimes subjected to standardized formulas that are claimed to be

---

Based on study and analysis of comparable property sales, it is concluded that lots can be marketed as follows:

First year—50 lots at $6,000 each
Second year—50 lots at $6,750 each
Third year—50 lots at $7,050 each

Based on these market findings, the appraisal yields the following results, assuming a developer's discount rate of 25 percent.

Present worth of lot sales:

First year, 50 lots at $6,000 = $300,000, discounted to present worth at 25 percent for one year, or $300,000 · .8000 =	$240,000
Second year, 50 lots at $6,750 = $337,500 discounted to present worth for two years or $337,500 · .6400 =	216,000
Third year, 50 lots at $7,050 = $352,500 discounted to present worth for three years or $352,500 · .5120 =	180,480
Total Present Worth of Anticipated Lot Sales	$636,480

Less development costs (assumes all costs incurred in first year):

Street grading and paving at $500 per lot =	$ 75,000
Sanitary and storm sewers at $750 per lot =	112,500
Curb and gutters at $250 per lot =	37,500
Watermains at $300 per lot =	45,000
Other costs (legal, filing, sales brokerage, property taxes, and overhead, etc.)	$100,000
Total development costs	$370,000
Residual value of raw land	$266,480

Value per acre, $266,480 ÷ 50 = $5,329.60, rounded to $5,330 per acre

Figure 8–2. Land Development Method

generally applicable. In particular, precalculated depth tables and corner-influence tables are used to indicate the standardized adjustments made for those two factors. These tables are not sensitive, however, to local market variations or to market changes over time. Such tables and formula approaches are artificial and sterile substitutes for market and property analysis. They cannot replace analysis of current local market data. Their use should be avoided by appraisers.

Assemblage, Plottage, and Excess Land

When sites vary significantly in size, they frequently are really in different markets because they are adapted or suited for different uses. Even when zoning and deed restrictions limit the use to single-family residential development, the type of residence that is most suited to the site may vary with size. This is really an element of comparison under the direct sales comparison approach. It is mentioned separately here, however, because it often does not enter into the calculations directly. Evidence of one or more of these features may cause the site to be discarded as a comparable sale because of its significantly different utility.

Assemblage is the additional cost required to bring two or more smaller lots into common ownership for use. This cost may or may not be reflected in value, depending on the reactions of the market.[3] *Plottage* involves combining two or more sites under one ownership in order to develop one site that may have greater utility than the two sites would have separately. *Plottage value* is an increment in value resulting from the combination of two or more sites.[4] Plottage value must be ascertained from analysis of the reactions of the market to the new, larger site. The usual indicator is a higher-than-market sales price per unit of area or size. Generally, when plottage value is encountered, this indicates that the site in question has a different highest and best use from the subject site and therefore is not an appropriate comparable site for use in direct sales comparison analysis.

Plottage may be negative as well as positive. A larger-than-average site, which is so developed or so shaped that it cannot be put to a higher and more valuable use, may result in a lower unit value for the site. The area or frontage (or both) in excess of a normal, standard site for the neighborhood or market is regarded as *excess land*.[5] The appraiser must turn to the market to ascertain how much, if any, additional value results from the additional site area that is excess. In the FHA valuation system, excess land is entirely discounted in estimating the value of the site. Excess land is described, but it is not appraised, and a requirement is made that the excess land be excluded from the mortgage security.

Site Improvements (Improvements to Land)

Site improvements (landscaping, walks, driveways, walls, and the like) may be regarded as physical attributes of a site and may be included as part of the comparative adjustment process in the direct sales comparison approach. On occasion, however, the appraiser may segregate site improvements for separate treatment. Inclusion of site improvements in the adjustment analysis is preferable in most instances.

The general rule for the valuation of site improvements is to estimate their depreciated value (depreciated cost new) in place. The basic question is what contribution these site improvements make to the value of the site and the value of the total property. Site improvements valuation is usually a consideration only when properties improved with buildings are being appraised. When site improvements are included as part of the adjustment analysis in direct sales comparison analysis for site valuation, the judgment of the market provides a standard for assigning value to such improvements. Cost does not create value for site improvements any more than it does for the site itself or for buildings. The preferred method for valuation is to treat site improvements as one factor in the adjustment comparison process and to turn to the market to discover how much more an informed buyer would pay for site improvements that exist as of the date of the appraisal.

Summary

Residential sites are frequently valued separately because of the requirements of the appraisal assignment. Site rather than land is valued. Site means a parcel of land that is improved to the extent that it is ready for use as a residential site as of the date of the appraisal. A residential site is always valued as if it were vacant and available to be put to its highest and best use. It is valued in terms of its highest and best use.

Regardless of the method of site valuation employed, the viewpoint and reactions of the typically informed purchaser on the market at the time of the appraisal provide the standards for site valuation. The direct sales comparison approach is always utilized in residential site valuation unless insufficient or inadequate comparable sales data are available. If the sales comparison approach cannot be utilized, it is sometimes possible to estimate the value of a residential site by allocation. This technique must be applied with extreme care and caution, however, and it is generally not recommended. The sales comparison approach to site valuation represents an application of the principle of substitution, which is based on the premise that informed purchasers would pay no more for sites than the cost to them of acquiring equally desirable sites with the same amenities and utility as the subject site.

Detailed information must be obtained from the market on sales of comparable sites. These comparables must be sufficiently described so that direct comparisons may be made in terms of the salient, pertinent characteristics of both the comparable sites and the subject site. Comparable sales data on sites are first adjusted for terms of financing and conditions of sale and then for time. Once market conditions and time adjustments have been made, then comparable sales data on sites are compared with the subject site with respect to physical characteristics and location. All comparable sales data must be verified. Comparable sales sites should be as nearly similar to the subject site as possible.

Adjustments are made in comparable sales data to bring the comparable sites into line with the subject site. The subject site is the standard in terms of which adjustments are made. All physical and locational adjustments are made from the comparable site to the subject site. All adjustments should be derived from market evidence and justified from the behavior of informed buyers on the market. Adjustments in sales prices of the comparable sites may be made in terms of plus and minus dollar amounts or plus and minus percentages. Whichever method is selected should be used exclusively and consistently throughout the entire adjustment process.

The adjustment process results in an indication of adjusted sales price for each comparable site. The adjusted sales price for each site may be developed for the total site or on a unit basis. The adjusted sales prices of comparable sites (total or unit) are reconciled into an indication of market value (total or unit) for the subject site. If sufficient data are available, statistical analysis can be an aid in the reconciliation process. The selection of a unit of comparison or unit of analysis should be dictated by the behavior of the market.

Formulas and tables to adjust for lot depth, corner influence, or irregular shapes are too generalized and too abstract to employ in site valuation. Site improvements are best treated as physical characteristics of a site and included among the adjustment factors in the direct sales comparison approach. Sites can also be valued by some variant of income capitalization if they are producing money rental income (actual or imputed). This is not often true of residential sites. Acreage that is suitable or proposed for development into residential sites can be valued via the land development method of income capitalization.

Notes

1. *HUD Handbook: Valuation Analysis for Home Mortgage Insurance,* no. 4150.1 (Washington, D.C.: U.S. Department of Housing and Urban Development, 1972), pp. 2–23; and *HUD Handbook: The Valuation Analysis Handbook for Project Mortgage Insurance,* no. 4465.1 (Washington, D.C.: U.S. Department of Housing and Urban Development, 1972), pp. 2–4.
2. Ibid.
3. See Boyce, Byrl N., ed., *Real Estate Appraisal Terminology,* rev. ed. (Cambridge, Mass.: Ballinger [Joint publication of the American Institute of Real Estate Appraisers and Society of Real Estate Appraisers], 1981), p. 19.
4. Ibid., p. 188.
5. Ibid., p. 95.

Suggested Readings

American Institute of Real Estate Appraisers. *The Appraisal of Real Estate,* 8th ed. Chicago: American Institute of Real Estate Appraisers, 1983, chapter 8.

Bloom, George F., and Harrison, Henry S. *Appraising the Single Family Residence.* Chicago: American Institute of Real Estate Appraisers, 1978, chapter 9.

Boyce, Byrl N., ed. *Real Estate Appraisal Terminology,* rev. ed. Cambridge, Mass.: Ballinger (Joint publication of the American Institute of Real Estate Appraisers and Society of Real Estate Appraisers), 1981.

HUD Handbook: Valuation Analysis for Home Mortgage Insurance, no. 4150.1. Washington, D.C.: U.S. Department of Housing and Urban Development, 1973.

HUD Handbook: Valuation Analysis for Project Mortgage Insurance, no. 4465.1. Washington, D.C.: U.S. Department of Housing and Urban Development, 1972.

Kinnard, William N., Jr. *Income Property Valuation.* Lexington, Mass.: Lexington Books, D.C. Heath, 1971, chapter 15.
Smith, Halbert C. *Real Estate Appraisal.* Columbus, Ohio: Grid, 1976, chapter 4.

Case Study:
Site Valuation

You have recently been asked to appraise a vacant site between Avenues E and F in Dodge City. You have made a city analysis and a general neighborhood analysis. A schematic map of the neighborhood is provided to assist you in visualizing the property. The zoning is the same (commercial A-2) throughout the neighborhood shown.

One of the main things you notice in the neighborhood is that the properties west of Avenue C are relatively homogenous. Going east from Avenue C, there appears to be a definite improvement in quality and values, beginning between Avenue C and Avenue D and increasing as you move farther east.

With the following data, you are to make a thorough analysis of land values in this area. Develop supportable opinions for time, depth and location adjustments. Finally, reach an estimate of the value of the subject site (80′ × 175′) as of 1982, using the following market data:

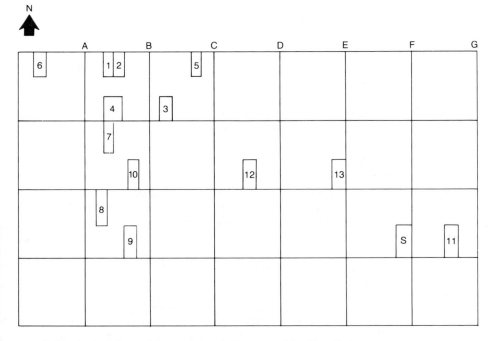

Schematic Map of Location of Comparable Site Sales

Sale Number	Year	Size	Sales Price	Sales Price per Front Foot (Rounded)
1	1979	50' × 125'	$3,380	$67.60
2	1982	60' × 125'	4,500	75.00
3	1977	75' × 125'	4,775	63.65
4	1981	100' × 125'	7,350	73.50
5	1978	55' × 125'	3,600	65.45
6	1980	65' × 125'	4,610	70.90
7	1978	50' × 150'	3,580	71.60
8	1981	55' × 175'	4,650	84.55
9	1982	60' × 175'	5,160	86.00
10	1979	65' × 150'	4,820	74.15
11	1978	75' × 175'	5,750	76.65
12	1979	70' × 150'	5,430	77.60
13	1980	75' × 150'	6,445	85.95

Time Adjustment —Sales 1 through 6 are all located west of Avenue C, have the same depth, and are similar in zoning, shape and location. There is only one major variable—time. Analysis of these sales indicated the following:

			Percentage Increase		
Year	Sale Number	Sales Price per Front Foot	Total to 1982	Over Past Year	Time Factor to 1982
1977	3	$63.65	—	—	1.18
1978	5	65.45	+ 3	+2	1.15
1979	1	67.60	+ 6	+3	1.11
1980	6	70.90	+11	+5	1.06
1981	4	73.50	+15	+4	1.03
1982	2	75.00	+18	+2	1.00

Depth Adjustment—Now that the adjustments for time have been developed, the analysis turns to other differing factors. Next an adjustment for depth is extracted from the data.

Sales 7, 8, 9, and 10 are all located west of Avenue C and are in a homogeneous area. This leaves two unknowns—depth and time. The time adjustment has been solved. By adjusting these four sales for time, the depth differential can be isolated and measured. The standard depth is 125 feet. Sale 2 indicates $75 per front foot (F.F.) at this depth currently. The time factor data are as follows:

	Sale		Time Factor to	Adjusted Sales Price to 1982		
Year	Number	Sales Price	1982	Total/F.F.	$/F.F.	Depth
1978	7	$3,580	1.15	$4,117/50'	= $82.34	150'
1981	8	4,650	1.03	$4,790/55'	= $87.09	175'
1982	9	5,160	1.00	$5,160/60'	= $86.00	175'
1979	10	4,820	1.11	$5,350/65'	= $82.30	150'

After adjusting for time, depth seems to affect sales price as follows:

Depth	Adjusted Sales Price per F.F.	Percentage Adjustment for Depth
125'	$75.00	Base
150'	$82.30	+10
175'	$86.50	+15
150 to 175'		+ 5

Location Adjustment—Now that the adjustments for time and depth have been developed, the analysis turns to indications of locational influence on value (or sales price).

Sale 11 brought $76.65 per front foot in 1978. If this is adjusted for time, then:

$$\$76.65 \times 1.15 = \$88.15/\text{F.F.}$$

If Sale 11 had been west of Avenue C, it would have brought only $86.50 per front foot, yielding the following location adjustment:

$$\$88.15 \div \$86.50 = 102\%$$

Utilizing the same logic for parcels 12 and 13, the following location adjustments are indicated:

	Sales Price per F.F.	×	Time	=	Time Adjusted Sales Price	÷	Depth	=	Percentage Adjustment for Location
Sale 12	$77.60	×	1.11	=	$86.14	÷	$82.30	=	105
Sale 13	$85.95	×	1.06	=	$91.11	÷	$82.30	=	111

It would seen from the foregoing analysis that, as you proceed eastward from Avenue C, prices appear to increase between Avenue C and Avenue D by 5%; between Avenue D and Avenue E by 11%; and then trail off to a 3% increase between Avenue F and Avenue G. In other words, there is a location advantage in being located east of Avenue C but that advantage seems to peak between Avenue D and E and then decline beyond Avenue E. The subject property would seem to fall in between the 11% location adjustment indicated by Sale 13 and the 2% location adjustment indicated by Sale 11. Due to location of the subject indicated on the schematic map, a 5% location adjustment between Avenues E and F would seem reasonable.

The adjustment for location would then be as follows:

Between Avenues	Location Adjustment
C and D	+ 5%
D and E	+11%
E and F	+ 5%
F and G	+ 2%

Application of Adjustment Factors—There are several ways to apply this analysis to estimate the value of the subject site. Probably the simplest is to start with the supported conclusion that the 1982 land with 125 feet of depth located west of Avenue C had a value of $75 per front foot (based on Sale 2). This would indicate a value for the subject property as follows:

Base 125' Lot Avenue C	+	Depth Adjustment	+	Location Adjustment	=	Value per F.F.
$75/F.F.	+	+15% +$11.25	+	+5% +$3.75	=	$90.00

Site Value = $90/F.F. × 80' = $7,200

The argument might be more conclusive, however, if each of the individual sales were adjusted to the subject, resulting in the adjustment table that follows:

Sale Number	Sales Price per F.F.	×	Time	=	Time Adjusted Sales Price	+	Depth	+	Location	=	Value F.F.
1	$67.60	×	1.11	=	$75.04		+15% +$11.26		5% +$3.75		$90.05
2	75.00	×	1.00	=	75.00		+15% +$11.25		+5% +$3.75		90.00
3	63.65	×	1.18	=	75.11		+15% +$11.27		+5% +$3.75		90.13
4	73.50	×	1.03	=	75.70		+15% +$11.36		+5% +$3.78		90.84
5	65.45	×	1.15	=	75.27		+15% +$11.29		+5% +$3.76		90.32
6	70.90	×	1.06	=	75.15		+15% +$11.27		+5% +$3.76		90.18
7	71.60	×	1.15	=	82.34		+5% +$ 4.12		+5% +$4.12		90.58
8	84.55	×	1.03	=	88.78		-0-		+5% +$4.44		93.22
9	86.00	×	1.00	=	86.00		-0-		+5% +$4.30		90.30
10	74.15	×	1.11	=	82.31		+5% +$ 4.12		+5% +$4.12		90.55

Sale Number	Sales Price per F.F.	× Time =	Time Adjusted Sales Price	+ Depth	+ Location	= Value F.F.
11	76.65	× 1.15 =	88.15	-0-	+2% +$2.64	89.91
12	77.60	× 1.11 =	86.14	+5% +$ 4.31	-0-	90.45
13	85.95	× 1.06 =	91.11	+5% +$ 4.56	-5% -$4.56	91.11

The primary point to be made here is that, if enough market data are available and if they are properly analyzed, then adjustment factors for the various differences can usually (or at least quite often) be discovered in the market with minimum reliance on the appraiser's judgment and experience. The market seldom if ever works out quite this neatly. The problem presented here was developed for discussion purposes and as an aid to the learning process.

9

Income and Value; Gross Rent Multiplier Analysis

Key Terms

Annual capitalization factor A multiplier utilized in the conversion of income into a present worth estimate.

Annual rate of capitalization The ratio that represents the relationship between future income and value.

Economic rent The surplus payment in excess of that necessary to bring a property on the market.

Gross monthly unfurnished rental A potential gross rent utilized in gross rent multiplier analysis.

Gross rent multiplier (GRM) The ratio of sales price to gross monthly unfurnished rental for single-family residential properties.

Gross rent multiplier (GRM) analysis A valuation approach that analyzes sales prices and gross rents of comparable properties and applies the results in estimating the value of the subject property.

Income capitalization The process of converting income into a capital value.

Market rent The rent that a property would most probably command on the open market.

Direct sales comparison analysis measures value in exchange, operating primarily through the principle of substitution or opportunity cost. An alternative approach to the valuation of real property is to measure value from use to the typically informed, prudent purchaser-investor, basically through the principles of substitution and marginal productivity. This is the income approach. Because residential property (improved or sites) can be and sometimes is rented, it is capable of producing income. Rental income can be the basis for estimating the value of residential property, just as it is used in value estimation for income-producing investment real estate.

Income and Value

As noted earlier, one definition or concept of value is that it is the present worth of anticipated future benefits. These future benefits may be in the form of money income or amenities. Since amenities cannot be measured directly, they are inferred from the market behavior of buyers, and especially from the prices paid by these buyers. Market behavior can be measured, which is what the appraiser does in sales comparison analysis.

When the anticipated future benefits are in the form of money income, the relationship between that money income (usually on an annual basis) and market prices of competing properties or investments can be measured. That relationship is expressed as a ratio or a rate. If the assumption can be accepted that this relationship is the same or constant for similar types of properties under similar market conditions, then the market ratio or rate can be applied to the future annual net income forecast for the subject property to produce an estimate of its present worth or value (as defined). This process is called capitalization.[1]

Any marketable property or space that can be rented is a potential candidate for capitalization of future annual income into a present worth figure. The relationship between gross income and sales price or value is called a multiplier. It is the ratio of sales price or value to periodic gross income. Technically, the application of a multiplier to periodic gross income to estimate value is not income capitalization as the term is used in real estate appraising, since that term is reserved for the capitalization of net income to a present worth or value estimate. The relationship between net income and sales price or value is either an annual rate or its reciprocal, a multiplier. Income capitalization analysis in real estate appraising is the application of the appropriate annual rate of capitalization to the annual net income forecast for the subject property. It is used to derive an estimate of present worth or value.

The typical purchaser of income-producing property is an absentee investor who is looking for the financial benefits of investment income, rather than the financial benefits and/or amenities of owner-occupancy. This is seldom the case with purchasers of residential properties, even though single-family residences are sometimes rented.

The Nature of Income Capitalization

For income-producing investment properties, the appraiser is seeking to capitalize the net income forecast to be produced by the property over the investment holding period, including the reversion receivable at the end of the forecast investment holding period, at the appropriate rate of capitalization. This rate of capitalization is frequently, but not necessarily, an overall rate, which expresses a direct relationship between net operating income and sales price or value.

Income capitalization for income-producing real estate is always based on net income. The most frequently used measure of net property income is net operating income (NOI). This is the before-tax annual net income produced from operating the property as an investment. It is derived as follows:

Potential gross rental income (PGI)—100 percent occupancy

  Less allowance for vacancy and credit loss (V and C)
  Equals rent collections
  Plus other non-rental property income
  Equals effective gross income (EGI)
  Less operating expenses (including replacement reserves) of the
    real estate as an investment

Equals net operating income (NOI)

The rate or rates of capitalization applied to forecast future net income in income capitalization are composites or weighted averages of the cash flow rates required by equity investors and mortgage lenders to induce them to commit investment funds to the property. Annual net income is divided by an annual rate of capitalization or multiplied by an annual capitalization multiplier to derive the estimate of value as defined for the subject property.

*The Relationship of Gross Rent Multiplier Analysis to
Income Capitalization*

Although it utilizes forecast future income as a basis for valuation, gross rent multiplier analysis is not income capitalization, nor is it part of the income approach to valuation. Income capitalization and the income approach deal specifically and exclusively with net income. A gross rent multiplier is really one unit of comparison in direct sales comparison analysis. It compares properties on the basis of both their capacity to generate income and the relationship of that income to sales price.

Gross income or rental generating capacity is presumably attributable to the real estate itself: its characteristics, its attractiveness and utility, its use potential, and its location. Net income, on the other hand, is partly the result of management by or for the owner-investor. A gross income multiplier (GIM) is used for income-producing real estate because such properties may generate income other than rental income. For residential properties, on the other hand, a gross rent multiplier (GRM) is calculated and used because the only income produced is rental income.

A gross income multiplier or gross rent multiplier may be calculated using either potential gross rental income (which is the rent roll at 100 percent occupancy) or effective gross rental income (which is actual or expected rent collections: potential gross minus allowance for vacancy and credit loss). Either potential gross or effective gross can be used to calculate a gross income (rent) multiplier. For income-producing investment properties effective gross is preferred by many but not all appraisers and valuation authorities. Whichever is used, it must be used consistently throughout the analysis for comparability and reliability of results.

Gross Rent Multiplier Analysis

As noted above, gross rent multipliers (GRMs) are used for residential-amenity property valuation. This is because residential-amenity properties rarely, if ever, produce other non-rental income. Gross rent multipliers are simply numbers that express the ratio between the sales price of a residential property and its *gross monthly unfurnished rental.* When residential properties are rented in any significant number in a market, the sales price and gross monthly unfurnished rental of similar properties will tend to move in the same direction, because they are subject to the same market forces and influences. Moreover, there is a strong tendency for the ratio between sales prices and gross monthly unfurnished rentals to be fairly consistent for the same type of property under the same market conditions.

Gross rent multiplier analysis is simple and direct. It can also be badly misused and underappreciated if it is not handled appropriately. A gross rent multiplier is "the relationship (ratio) between sales price (value) and monthly rental income for single-family residential properties."[2]

Gross rent multiplier analysis is:

"That approach in appraisal analysis which is based on the proposition that an informed purchaser would pay no more for a property than the cost of obtaining a return (in income or amenities) of the same amount and embodying the same risk as that involved in the subject property. This approach is applicable when sufficient numbers of comparable properties are rented at the time of sale. The gross income (rent) multiplier approach is not applicable when few or no comparable properties are rented in the competitive market. This approach also is questionable in market situations in which market rentals and sales prices do not bear a constant relationship to each other."[3]

If the appropriate gross rent multiplier for a particular type of residential property in a given market at a given time can be ascertained from sales data of comparable properties, then it can be used as a guide to the market value of the property being appraised. Value is estimated by multiplying the appropriate gross rent multiplier by the market rental of the subject property. Residential properties are typically not purchased for investment income or profit. Therefore, net income is not employed in estimating residential property value. Gross rent tends to vary with the forces of the real estate market. Net income is also subject to management and operating considerations.

Gross rent multiplier analysis is really part of direct sales comparison analysis. A gross rent multiplier is a unit of comparison for direct sales comparisons. Historically, gross rent multiplier analysis has been called the income approach for residential properties, primarily because it was deemed necessary to have three approaches in every appraisal, regardless of type of property. This rigid requirement no longer applies in appraisal thought or practice. Gross rent multiplier analysis may be separated from the adjustment process of direct sales comparison analysis, however, because it provides a direct estimate of value from market sales data, just as regression analysis does.

Process or Technique

Gross rent multiplier analysis estimates value by multiplying the gross market rental of the property being appraised by a multiplier developed from a number of actual sales transactions for comparable properties. The application of gross rent multiplier analysis requires three steps. The first two involve considerable market analysis and data gathering. The first step is to estimate the current monthly market rental of the subject property. This is followed by calculation of the appropriate gross rent multiplier from sales of comparable properties that were rented at the time of the sale. The third and final step is to multiply the market rental of the subject property by the gross rent multiplier to obtain an estimate of market value of the subject property. Symbolically, the process can be represented as:

$$\frac{SP}{GR} = GRM \qquad GRM \times MR = MV$$

where SP = Sales Price
GR = Gross Monthly Unfurnished Rent
GRM = Gross Rent Multiplier
MR = Market Rent
MV = Market Value.

Both the market rental and the gross rent multiplier applicable to a particular appraisal problem are determined by market conditions. The basis for selecting an appropriate gross rent multiplier and an appropriate market rental for the subject property is a body of market data documented with the same thoroughness and attention to detail as is required in the direct sales comparison approach. Gross rent multiplier analysis is essentially comparative sales and comparative rental analysis within the framework of given market conditions. There is no fixed multiplier over different market areas or different market conditions. Each multiplier is a function of market conditions and market data at the time of the analysis. The analysis relies on data on market activity to produce a direct indication of value.

The valuation principles involved in gross rent multiplier analysis are substitution, contribution, and anticipation. An informed investor-purchaser will pay no more for residential property than the cost of acquiring a rental income stream of the same size and with the same risks as that which the subject property can produce. The measure of value of a residential property may be the rental income that it is capable of producing *(gross monthly unfurnished rental),* discounted at the appropriate rate. For residential property valuation, the process of discounting is handled by multiplying the monthly market rental of the subject property by the gross rent multiplier. This process is a reflection of the fact that the GRM is always less then the remaining economic life (REL) of the improvements, expressed in months. The expected rental income stream that the subject property is capable of producing must be projected into the future. Thus, the value of the subject property may be measured by the present worth of the anticipated rental income. Value becomes the amount that an informed purchaser is justified in paying now for the right to this future rental income stream.

Assumptions

The applicability of gross rent multiplier analysis depends on a number of important assumptions or conditions to be met. The appraiser must recognize these and the limitations that they impose on the use of gross rent multiplier analysis. The sales prices and the gross monthly unfurnished rentals of residential properties are assumed to be subject to the same market and neighborhood influences and trends. They will both move in the same direction and in essentially the same proportion, in response to changes in these market influences. The operating expenses and cost of ownership of competitive or comparable properties are essentially similar to one another, if not identical.

Sales and rental data from the local market are assumed to be available for properties that are truly comparable and competitive with the subject property. The market rental estimated for the subject property will continue essentially unchanged into the foreseeable future. The gross rent multiplier actually reflects the amenities of owner-occupancy in relating market rental to sales price or market value. Ownership amenities are not reflected in the monthly rental. They must be reflected in the multiplier to justify the conclusion that the property being appraised would sell at the same price whether it were offered for rental or for owner-occupancy. Finally, it is assumed that no unusual external influences are at work to upset the relationship reflected in the gross rent multiplier.

The Role of Amenities

Residential real estate is basically amenity property intended for use and enjoyment by owner-occupants. A valuation technique that treats rental income as a proxy for ownership amenities and that values residential real estate in terms of tenant occupancy must be approached and used with caution. Amenities to owners and tenants tend to be different. Owners occupy homes; tenants occupy houses. The amenities to owner-occupants of residences are not readily convertible into dollars of income on the market; yet they are reflected in sales price.

Owner-occupant amenity benefits include pride of ownership, freedom of use, comfort, privacy, convenience, prestige, hedge against adversity and inflation, forced saving, safeguard against economic variance, and retirement plan. Ownership amenities tend to increase in proportion to the market value of the property. Generally, as amenities and price level increase, the gross rent multiplier also rises. The difficulty in estimating the value of amenities directly is one major reason why gross rent multiplier analysis must be used with care and caution. The assumption that the multiplier reflects the amenities to owner-occupants in relating gross monthly unfurnished rental to sales price must be borne out in the experience of the market.

Data Requirements and Sources

The data required for appropriate application of gross rent multiplier analysis, and the sources from which those data may be obtained, are essentially those noted for the direct sales comparison approach. The difference is that information about gross monthly unfurnished rentals of comparable properties is also required. Just as in the direct sales comparison approach, an adequate quantity of reliable and verified data is required for appropriate application of gross rent multiplier analysis.

Comparable sales properties must be truly comparable with the subject property. The appraiser should note enough details to ascertain that they are comparable. This involves type, area, number of rooms, functional utility, value range, and condition. The comparable sales properties should have been rented at the time of sale. Sometimes a multiplier can be calculated from rentals and sales prices of different properties, but the resulting answer is much less reliable or defensible. Comparable sales must be bona fide, arm's length transactions.

The sales price, terms of sale, conditions of sale, and rental must be verified with one or more of the participants in the transaction. At least eight to ten reliable comparable sales of rented property should be found. More would be desirable. Neighborhood and market influences on the comparable properties must be as nearly similar to those affecting the subject property as possible.

Rental data may be obtained both for comparable properties that sold recently and were rented at the time of sale and for comparable properties that are rented on the current market. True comparability between the rented properties and the subject property is required. Gross monthly unfurnished rental must be obtained. Furnished rentals should be either adjusted or eliminated from the analysis. Rentals must be verified in the same manner as sales prices.

The sources from which required data can and should be obtained are the same as those listed and explained for direct sales comparison analysis.

Estimation of Market Rental

In gross rent multiplier analysis, the task of the appraiser is to estimate the gross monthly unfurnished rental of the subject property if it were placed on the current market for rent. The appraiser uses current rentals on comparable properties as a guide to making this estimate. Market rent is "the rental income that a property would most probably command on the open market as indicated by current rentals being paid for comparable space (as of the effective date of the appraisal)."[4] The term market rent (actually, *market rental*) is preferred to *economic rent,* which has traditionally been used in appraisal analysis. *Economic rent* is a technical term in economics which means "the surplus payment in excess of that necessary to bring the property on the market (or to attract any factor of production into production)."[5] Economic rent should not be used to mean market rental.

For residential property, monthly rental is most commonly used. Unfurnished monthly rental data must be obtained. There is too much variation in furnished rentals in most markets for it to be an effective measure. The rental used is gross or contract rental, rather than net rental. Contract rental is the amount called for in a written lease or oral agreement. Potential gross rental is always used for residential properties. Effective gross income is meaningful only for income properties in which vacancy allowances must be made. Actual contract rental for the subject may or may not be the same as market rental, indicated by comparable rentals on the market. If actual current rental is a close approximation of estimated market rental, then actual current rental may be used in estimating the value of the subject property through gross rent multiplier analysis; if not, market rental must be used.

The market is the final judge of the rent that a property can command on the market as of the date of the appraisal. All data must be verified market information. Rental properties used in estimating market rental for the subject property must be as nearly comparable to the subject property as possible. In particular, rents should be current and in the same market as the subject property.

The appraiser must gather adequate descriptive information on the comparable rental properties. In the appraisal report, the salient and pertinent features of the comparable rental properties are compared with those of the subject property. This means that appraisers must go back to their description of the improvements in the subject property and carefully consider comparable rental properties in terms of this description. Imputed or estimated rentals for the comparable properties are not appropriate data for use in gross rent multiplier analysis. They should be actual rentals on the market.

Market data are required to justify rental differences based on variations of comparable rental properties from the subject property. The monthly rentals of the comparable rental properties can be reduced to some unit of comparison, provided that the comparable properties are very similar in both property and market characteristics to the subject property, and to one another. This unit of comparison need not be one that represents actual market behavior, provided it is logically defensible and produces good analytical results.

Figure 9–1 demonstrates the derivation and analysis of market rentals, gross rent multipliers, and other analytical processes.

You are appraising a single-family residential home in an area where tenant occupancy is dominant. In a search of that area, you have found thirteen recent sales that are quite similar to the subject property, and you have also been able to obtain monthly rentals associated with each sale. The data are as follows:

Sale Number	Location	Sales Price	Monthly Rental
1	101 South Eagleville	$84,000	$625
2	65 Meadowood	96,000	725
3	61 Birchwood Heights	91,500	690
4	11 Baxter	82,500	625
5	17 Willowbrook	99,000	725
6	42 Separatist	97,500	725
7	9 Lynnwood	90,000	675
8	85 Storrs Road	89,400	675
9	30 Dog Lane	85,500	625
10	27 Hillside	87,000	625[a]
11	22 Eastwood	94,500	700
12	19 Westwood	98,100	725
13	10 Fairfield	93,000	700

[a]Because of a functional deficiency (incurable) this rental is judged to be $25 below market.

The subject property is located at 30 Hunting Lodge Road and is currently renting at $675 per month, which is judged to be its market rental.

Sale Number	GRM (rounded)
1	134
2	132
3	133
4	132
5	137
6	134
7	133
8	132
9	137
10	139[a]
11	135
12	135
13	133

[a]This is the unadjusted GRM for sale number 10. Adjusting for below market rental due to the functional incurable deficiency the GRM would be 134 ($87,000 ÷ $650) which is more within the range indicated by other market comparables. Alternatively, this transaction could easily be dropped from the analysis, with no change in the final results.

The range of GRMs is 132–137 (this range incorporates the adjustment made in the GRM for sale 10). This would seem to indicate a GRM for the subject property of 135. Therefore, the indicated value of the subject property is $91,125 ($V = MR \times GRM =$ $675 × 135). This would likely be rounded to $91,000.

To demonstrate the reduction of monthly rentals of comparable rental properties to a rental per square foot per month, consider the following data:

Figure 9–1. Gross Rent Multiplier (GRM) Analysis

Sale Number	Area (sq. ft.)	Monthly Rental per Sq. Ft.
1	1,248	$0.50
2	1,464	0.50
3	1,364	0.51
4	1,250	0.50
5	1,540	0.47
6	1,464	0.50
7	1,386	0.49
8	1,354	0.50
9	1,318	0.47
10	1,318	0.47(.49)[a]
11	1,384	0.51
12	1,464	0.50
13	1,386	0.51

[a]Adjusted

Clearly, houses of this type in the current local market are renting for $0.50 per square foot per month, whether landlords and tenants realize it or not. This can be applied to the subject property (1,400 square feet) to test whether the actual rental of $675 per month is a close approximation to market rental. In this case, indicated market rental would be $700 per month ($1,400 × $0.50). The difference is $25, or 3.70 percent. Whether this is close enough to use $675 for value estimation is a matter of the appraiser's judgment. In any event, the difference is minor.

Figure 9–1 *(continued)*

Adjustments

Ideally, adjustments in comparable rentals for differences between comparable properties and the subject property should not have to be made, and should not be made. Comparable rental properties should be sufficiently similar to the subject property so that adjustments are not necessary. When there are sufficient numbers of good comparable rentals, it is preferable to omit a comparable rather than to adjust a rental. Sale number 10 in figure 9–1 is an example.

If there are too few comparable rentals to permit dropping any, however, and if comparable rental properties are not sufficiently similar to the subject property to permit direct comparison and the use of market rentals without adjustment, then adjustments for differences must be made and justified on the basis of market behavior of tenants in reaction to differences in rental properties. These differences must be those between the comparable rentals and then-prevailing market rentals.

Adjustments should be made only when the comparable rental is clearly not a market rental, and the appraiser has a good indication why. Such situations would include obvious differences between the comparable rental property and the subject property or market standards. This is demonstrated in the case of Sale 10 in figure 9–1. Another example would be when a significantly non-market rental on the property is based on an existing lease, although this is highly unlikely for a residential property.

If an adjustment in rental is to be made, it should be made without a corresponding adjustment (in direction and proportion) in sales price. After adjustments are made, an adjusted gross rental is obtained for each comparable rental property. This is the appraiser's best estimate of what the comparable rental property would have rented for in its current local market at a competitive market rate. Sale 10 in figure 9–1, for example, required an upward adjustment in monthly rental of $25.

Estimate of Indicated Market Rental
of the Subject Property

Adjusted rentals for the comparable rental properties should fall into a pattern within a relatively narrow range. The appraiser then reconciles these rentals into an indication of market rental for the subject property by selecting the rent that is most probable for the subject property, given the market data and adjustments used. Reconciliation is often assisted by reducing comparable rentals to a per-unit basis. This is especially effective in adjusting for differences in size. The results often show a clearer pattern for selection of the per unit market rental, as is demonstrated in the conversion of monthly rental to monthly rental per square foot. It will be recalled that the indicated market rental for the subject property was $.50 per square foot per month, or $700 per month.

If there is a sufficient number of comparable rentals, sample statistics can be used to provide an indication of market rental for the subject property. The comparable rental properties must be very similar to, and highly competitive with, the subject property.

For example, the mean rental for the 13 comparable properties in figure 9–1 (with Sale 10 adjusted to $650 per month) is $681.92. The mean rental for 12 properties (with Sale 10 omitted) is $684.58. The median rental is $690. All these indicators suggest that the actual current rental of $675 per month is a reasonable approximation of market rental and can be used defensibly in estimating value through gross rent multiplier analysis. Also, the mean market rental per square foot for the 12 properties (omitting Sale 10) is $.497, which clearly indicates use of a $.50 figure. The estimated market rental for the subject property is typically rounded to a level that reflects the behavior of rentals in the current local market. The market rental for subject residential properties is therefore estimated by direct market comparison with residences that are currently rented on the local market.

Estimation of Gross Rent Multipliers

Gross rent multipliers are simply numbers that express the ratio between the sales price of a residential property and the gross rental income being produced by that property at the time of sale. The appropriate gross rent multiplier for the subject property is that indicated by several comparable sales of rental properties on the current local market.

The same standards for comparable sales properties apply in gross rent multiplier analysis as are applied in the direct sales comparison approach. The sales properties must be as nearly comparable with the subject property as possible, with respect to type, area, number of rooms, functional utility, value range, condition, time of sale, market conditions, and neighborhood influence. The appraiser must know enough detail about each of the comparable sales properties to be able to demonstrate that they are effectively competitive and comparable with the subject property.

Based upon the description of the subject improvements, there should be commentary in the appraisal report on the salient features of comparability and differences between the comparable sales properties and the subject property. The same features and characteristics that are noted in the subject property and accounted for in both the direct sales comparison and cost approaches must be considered in the application of gross rent multiplier analysis.

Sales prices need not be adjusted if the comparable sales properties are effective comparables with the subject property. If adjustments are made, they should be made in rentals only. Any adjustments of both sales prices and rentals in the same direction and the same proportion will result in exactly the same gross rent multiplier as is obtained on an unadjusted basis. This is one of the major advantages of the approach: the gross rent multiplier can be estimated with unadjusted sales and rental data for comparable sales rental properties. Both sales prices and rentals are subject to precisely the same market and neighborhood influences. If the assumption that these are truly comparable properties is valid, then no adjustments are required. If the assumption is not valid, then gross rent multiplier analysis should not be used. In particular, the appraiser should avoid the occasional, erroneous practice of adjusting the sales price for time without making any corresponding adjustment in rental.

The gross rent multiplier varies by type of property, neighborhood and market influence, price level, and time. It must be recalculated for virtually every residential appraisal problem. There is no standard multiplier for a market or for a particular residence. If such a standard multiplier is employed, it may represent a wide departure from actual current local market conditions. The current local market determines the appropriate gross rent multiplier for each type of residential property, and the appraiser must utilize appropriate data from the current local market to calculate the multiplier in each residential appraisal problem.

Mechanics of Gross Rent Multiplier Estimation

The gross rent multiplier for residential properties is obtained by dividing the sales price of a residential property by its gross monthly unfurnished rental (SP ÷ GR = GRM). Rounding is not employed except in a very minor way. For example, if a residential property sold for $52,500, and rented for $405 per month at the time, the gross rent multiplier is 129.6 ($52,500 ÷ 405 = 129.6). The multiplier for this particular property should be rounded to the nearest whole number (130). Rounding is more likely and more properly applied to the multiplier selected from several sales transactions through reconcilation. Figure 9–1 shows clearly the calculation of a gross rent multiplier from sales price and monthly unfurnished rental of 13 comparable sales on the local market that were rented at the time of sale.

When several gross rent multipliers have been obtained from comparable sales of rental properties, they should fall into a pattern in a relatively narrow range around a point of tendency. This will occur if the properties are truly comparable to the subject property and to one another and if no unusual market influences or individual property influences distort the results. The appraiser then selects the gross rent multiplier indicated by this pattern as that which is applicable to properties of the type being appraised in the current local market. This is the multiplier that will be applied to the estimated market rental of the subject property to provide an estimate of value as defined.

If there are sufficient data, as in the case of figure 9–1, the appraiser can apply sample statistics to estimate the gross rent multiplier indicated for the market, and to be used in estimating the value of the subject property. A frequency distribution can be developed for visual analysis. For example, the frequency distribution for the multipliers calculated in figure 9–1 would be:

GRM	Frequency
132	3
133	3
134*	3
135	2
137	2

*Sale 10 with rent adjusted to $650.

From this distribution, it can be seen clearly that the modal values of the multiplier are 132, 133, and 134. The median is 134. The mean for all 13 gross rent multipliers with the rental in Sale 10 adjusted is 133.92. This rounds to 134. With Sale 10 dropped, the mean is the same. The indicated gross rent multiplier is therefore 134.

If too few data are available to justify the use of sample statistics, a judgmental selection is required or the whole analysis might be dropped. For example, if five comparable sales of rental properties show gross rent multipliers of 127, 129, 130, 133, and 134, the most probable indicated GRM for the type of property in question in the local market to be applied to the subject property is 130. This is the median. The mean is 130.8, or 131. The appraiser would most likely use 130. In reaching an estimate of the appropriate gross rent multiplier to select and use, analysis and judgment are required. Moreover, care must be taken not to round the GRM so much that the final results are distorted. This requires experience and good working knowledge of the market. As another example, consider the following:

Sale Number	Sales Price	Monthly Rental	GRM
1	$63,000	$480	131.3
2	67,500	510	132.4
3	67,500	495	136.4
4	61,500	450	136.7

The indicated GRM for the subject property is estimated to be 135. (As a point of information, the mean GRM is 134.2 and the median GRM is 134.4.)

Estimation of Value via Gross Rent Multiplier Analysis

Once the market rental for the subject property and the gross rent multiplier have been estimated via comparative analysis with rental properties and sales of rental properties, the estimate of market value of the subject property is obtained by multiplying the market rental by the gross rent multiplier ($V_o = MR \times GRM$). If the monthly rental estimated for the subject property is $480, for example, and the GRM indicated by comparative analysis is 140, the calculated indication of market value of the subject property is $67,200 ($480 × 140).

In figure 9–1, value estimates can be derived as follows:

$$135 \times \$675 = \$91,125$$
$$135 \times \$700 = \$94,500$$

The range is $3,375 ($94,500 − $91,125), or 3.70 percent. The best estimate of value appears to be $92,000.[6] This gives a range of −0.95 percent to +2.72 percent.

Uses and Limitations of Gross Rent Multiplier Analysis

When applied properly with reliable, verified market data on sales and rentals of truly comparable properties, gross rent multiplier analysis is a simple and direct method for estimating the market value of residential property. In a market in which residences are rented frequently enough to provide an adequate volume of data, gross rent multiplier analysis will reflect the behavior of purchasers. With appropriate data, gross rent multiplier analysis minimizes or even eliminates the necessity for direct adjustment of individual property differences, such as are required in the sales comparison approach.

The FHA recommends gross rent multiplier analysis as one important approach to value estimation. The analysis is also included in the FNMA/FHLMC Appraisal Report Form 1004/70. In some markets, gross rent multiplier analysis is widely used and understood by appraisers, buyers, sellers, and others involved in residential real estate transactions.

There are also hazards and limitations to the use of gross rent multiplier analysis. There must be a sufficient volume of reliable, verified sales data and rental data for comparable properties for gross rent multiplier analysis to be applied effectively. If there is little sales activity of rented residential properties, the analysis may not properly be used. Amenities of owner-occupancy may not be reflected in sales prices of properties that are rented when sold. If this is the case, then the gross rent multiplier is not an accurate market measure.

If the neighborhood is in transition (changing or conflicting uses, conversions, changes in social character or tenancy, or designations for rehabilitation and/or renewal), prices tend to be less responsive to change than rentals are. Tenants can move out quickly as an alternative to paying a different rent. Owners usually cannot move quickly without financial loss. In such cases, the assumption of a direct and constant relationship between sales price or value and monthly unfurnished market rental is not met.

Several other limitations and hazards might be noted. Rent controls can establish an artificial barrier to equal and proportionate movements of rentals and sales prices. Serious physical deterioration of the property is generally reflected more in sales price than in rental. An excessively unfavorable or favorable tax burden is usually reflected in sales price but not in rental. Changes in zoning or code enforcements can affect sales prices more than rentals.

Real estate markets are imperfect. Gross rentals may not readily and consistently reflect all differences among properties. The relationship between rentals and sales prices is not always a perfect reflection of the market attractiveness of the property. Operating costs or cost of occupancy may not be similar among comparable properties in a given market. As a result, gross rental may not reflect accurately the relative market attractiveness of the property. The very simplicity of the GRM approach may lead to carelessness or lack of attention to detail on the part of the appraiser. This is not a basic fault of the approach but, rather, a pitfall to be avoided.

Summary

Gross rent multiplier analysis is based on the assumption that there is a direct and constant market relationship between sales price or value and gross unfurnished rental, so that the value of the subject property can be estimated directly from its market rental and the market-derived gross rent multiplier. If this assumption is not supportable, the procedure should not be used. Gross rent multiplier analysis is really a unit of comparison in the direct sales comparison approach to value estimation. It is not a part of income capitalization, which uses net income to estimate value.

The principles of substitution, contribution, and anticipation are involved in gross rent multiplier analysis. Gross rent multiplier analysis requires a substantial quantity of reliable, verified data on market sales of truly comparable properties that sold recently in the local market and were rented at the time of sale. Data on unfurnished rentals of truly comparable properties are also required in sufficient quantity to reflect the current local market and to estimate market rental.

The gross rent multiplier is a ratio expressing the market relationship between sales price and gross monthly unfurnished rental of residential property of a particular type in a given market at a given time:

$$\frac{SP}{GR} = GRM$$

Rental value (market rental) of the subject property is obtained by comparative analysis of rentals of comparable properties in the current local market. Adjustments may be made in comparable rentals to reflect differences between the comparable rental properties and the subject property, but unadjusted figures are preferred.

The gross rent multiplier for the subject property is best obtained by comparative analysis of recent sales of competitive properties that were rented at the time of sale. Adjustments are not necessary in comparative rental property sales because the same proportionate adjustments would be made in both sales price and rental. The resulting gross rent multiplier figure is the same whether adjustments are made or not. If adjustments must be made in sales price or gross rental at comparable properties, those sales data probably should not be used in the analysis.

Sample statistics can be applied to rental and sales data to obtain the estimates of market rental and the gross rent multiplier to apply to the valuation of the subject property, provided sufficient quantities of reliable, verified data are available. The value of the subject property is estimated by multiplying its market rental by the indicated gross rent multiplier: $V_o = \text{MR} \times \text{GRM}$. The market value estimate is obtained by rounding the resulting product to an appropriate level.

Notes

1. For a more detailed definition of capitalization, see Boyce, Byrl N., ed., *Real Estate Appraisal Terminology,* rev. ed. (Cambridge, Mass.: Ballinger [Joint publication of the American Institute of Real Estate Appraisers and Society of Real Estate Appraisers], 1981), p. 40.

2. Ibid., p. 123.

3. Ibid., p. 122.

4. Ibid., p. 160.

5. Ibid., p. 87.

6. Note that this value estimate is slightly at variance with the judgment exercised by the appraiser in figure 9–1—which resulted in an estimate of $91,125.

Suggested Readings

Bloom, George F., and Harrison, Henry S. *Appraising the Single Family Residence.* Chicago: American Institute of Real Estate Appraisers, 1978, chapter 11.

Boyce, Byrl N., ed. *Real Estate Appraisal Terminology.* rev. ed. Cambridge, Mass.: Ballinger (Joint publication of the American Institute of Real Estate Appraisers and Society of Real Estate Appraisers), 1981.

The Official Guide to Appraisal Reporting. Chicago: Society of Real Estate Appraisers, 1983, pp. 19–21, 26–27 and 37–38.

HUD Handbook: Single Family Underwriting Reports and Forms Data, no. 4190.1. Washington, D.C.: U.S. Department of Housing and Urban Development, 1974.

HUD Handbook: Valuation Analysis Handbook for Project Mortgage Insurance, no. 4465.1. Washington, D.C.: U.S. Department of Housing and Urban Development, 1972.

HUD Handbook: Valuation Analysis for Home Mortgage Insurance, no. 4150.1. Washington, D.C.: U.S. Department of Housing and Urban Development, 1973.

Stebbins, H. Grady, Jr. *A Guide to Appraising Residences,* 3rd ed. Chicago: Society of Real Estate Appraisers, 1976, pp. 42–45.

Wendt, Paul F. *Real Estate Appraisal: Review and Outlook.* Athens: University of Georgia Press, 1974, chapter 7.

10 The Cost Approach: Estimating Reproduction Cost New of Improvements

Key Terms

Comparable unit method   A method of cost estimation that lumps together all components of the structure and converts the lump sum amount to a unit basis (e.g., per square foot, per cubic foot).

Cost services   Manuals that provide unit cost information for benchmark structures, structural components, equipment, and features as of a given date and for a base location.

Direct costs   Costs that are directly related to site acquisition and construction of improvements.

Indirect costs   Costs in the development of a property that are not included in a general contract for construction or for land acquisition (e.g., fees, financing costs, surveys, appraisals, overhead during construction).

Quantity survey method   A method of cost estimation that replicates the contractor's original procedure in detail.

Replacement cost   The current cost of constructing a building of equivalent utility to the one being appraised and according to current standards, design, and layout.

Reproduction cost   The current cost of constructing an exact replica of a building being appraised, incorporating all the obsolescence of the subject building.

Trade breakdown (segregated or builder's) method   A method of cost estimation that breaks the major functional parts of the structure into an installed unit cost.

Unit-in-place method   A method of cost estimation that includes materials and labor in the unit cost of component sections of the structure "in place."

In the cost approach to value estimation for residential properties, the potential purchaser is assumed to consider producing a substitute residence with the same utility as the residential property being appraised. The cost to this rational, informed purchaser (not the cost to a contractor or builder) is the measure of the value of the subject property. This approach measures value as cost of production; this is the third

249

alternative course of action potentially available to a purchaser considering acquisition of the subject property.

Cost of production to the buyer includes all direct and indirect construction costs, plus builder's overhead and profit. Strictly speaking, land does not have a cost of production because it is already in existence. A site can have a cost of production, however, reflecting the cost of preparing the land to make it suitable for residential use.

The alternative property produced for the buyer must have the same utility as the subject property. Since utility cannot be measured directly, cost of production means the cost to the buyer of producing an exact replica of the subject property, in the same location and the same condition as the subject property, as of the valuation date.

Valuation Principles of the Cost Approach

The informed, rational purchaser will pay no more for a residential property than the cost of producing a substitute property (usually a replica) with the same utility as the subject property. Rigid, strict application of the principle of substitution would make the cost approach simply one case or application in direct sales comparison analysis. This would result in true replacement cost. Because utility cannot be measured directly, however, indirect measurement through money bids and offers provides the best approximation in a market-oriented economy.

The measure of the present worth of the improvements (especially major buildings) is the amount that they add or contribute to site value in developing the value of the entire property. Moreover, deficiencies are measured by the amount their absence detracts from value. Curability is tested by the amount by which the addition or correction of an item would increase value.

Improvements on and to the site can be improper through either overimprovement or underimprovement. Thus, improvements may detract from the total value of the property because they do not represent the highest and best use of the site. Overimprovement or underimprovement will result in a charge of accrued depreciation for functional obsolescence. Since a site is valued as if it were vacant and available to be put to its highest and best use, functional obsolescence in terms of overimprovement or underimprovement is based on a comparison of the existing structure with the highest and best use of the site.

Steps in the Cost Approach

The following steps are involved in property valuation by the cost approach:

1. Estimate the value of the site as if it were vacant and available to be put to its highest and best use.
2. Estimate reproduction cost new of improvements.
3. Estimate all elements of accrued depreciation.
4. Subtract total accrued depreciation from reproduction cost new of improvements. This results in an estimate of the depreciated reproduction cost new of improvements, which is the measure of the present worth or contribution of the improvements to the total value of the property.
5. Add estimated depreciated present worth of site improvements (if not already included in step 4). This gives the total present worth of all improvements.
6. Add total present worth of all improvements to established site value.
7. Round the figure obtained in step 6 to an appropriate level. This represents an indication of value (most frequently, market value) of the subject property via the cost approach.

Mechanics of the Cost Approach

The field inspections and appraiser's observations of the neighborhood and the property being appraised provide the foundation for analysis throughout the cost approach. The appraiser applies judgment, experience, and skill in translating the findings and observations to estimates of site value, reproduction cost new, and elements of accrued depreciation. Neighborhood analysis provides insights into the valuation of site and of external influences creating locational obsolescence, if any. Site analysis provides the basis for site valuation and for estimating highest and best use of the site. Improvements analysis (buildings and site improvements) provides the basis for estimating diminished utility (accrued depreciation charges), especially for physical deterioration and functional obsolescence.

The appraiser should employ a detailed checklist when making the field inspections. The features of the neighborhood and property that will lead to charges for accrued depreciation may then be identified and later recalled for evaluation. Field notes should include pertinent comments on inharmonious or intrusive features of the neighborhood as well as on the physical appearance and observed condition of improvements. Data on recent major repairs, additions, or improvements and notation of the age and condition of short-lived components of the structure(s) and of equipment should also be included. In addition, the appraiser should note comments leading to estimation of effective age and remaining economic life of the structures(s) and of short-lived items; an estimate of general deterioration of the structures(s); an estimate of rehabilitation required (or deferred maintenance); and an estimate of functionally obsolete items, including cost to cure if curable. Finally, there must be accurate measurement and notation of quality, to provide the basis for the reproduction cost estimate.

Special Considerations in the Cost Approach

Cost is not the same as value, and cost does not create value. These points have been emphasized earlier but must be reiterated here. Under certain circumstances, however, cost may be an appropriate measure of value. All approaches to market value estimation are market-oriented and must reflect market data and market behavior of purchasers (and builders, in the case of the cost approach). Moreover, all approaches to value estimation are comparative approaches, since they involve the comparison of data and behavior related to competitive properties with those related to the subject property.

The cost approach is market-oriented. It involves market data on costs, site sales, and purchaser reaction to differences among properties in order to provide the basis for depreciation charges. It is also a comparative approach. The data and market behavior used as the standards for the subject property are provided by other similar, competitive properties.

The estimate of accrued depreciation (diminished utility)—which is discussed in greater detail in Chapter 11—depends on market data about the reactions and behavior of market participants (especially buyers) with respect to the type of observed deficiencies or superadequacies in the residence being appraised. The appraiser's judgment is also required in making adjustments for property differences and in estimating the several elements of accrued depreciation. Formula approaches are inappropriate and potentially misleading. Analytical comparisons, not mathematical formulas, are necessary to apply the cost approach properly. The appraiser must constantly turn to the market for justification for adjustments and charges.

When a site is improved with a new structure(s) that represents the highest and best use of the site, cost new tends to indicate the upper limit of value. This is based on the application of the principle of substitution. The estimate of value via the cost approach does not necessarily represent the upper limit of value. Cost new must often be discounted to reflect the waiting time required for construction to be completed.

Summation versus Separability. The cost approach is frequently referred to as the summation approach because it involves estimating the value (contribution or present worth) of site, improvements, and site improvements independently, then summing them to obtain the estimate of property value. It must be clear and definite, however, that the object of value estimation in real estate appraisal is usually the whole property, not any of its component parts. The separation is made for analytical purposes only.

Each segment is valued in terms of the existing use pattern of all the segments in conjunction with one another. All segments together contribute to property value. Their fractional values cannot be used independently. Even the site value is not consistent with the existing situation because, in fact, the site is not vacant and available to be put to its highest and best use. The value estimate is not separable. Fractional value estimates are not generally consistent with acceptable professional appraisal practice.

The value of the property in question is a direct function of the combination of the site and improvements it contains. The appraiser must exercise special care in distinguishing the separation of site and improvements for analytical purposes, and must avoid the improper conclusion that each therefore has a separate value that is independent of the other.

Relationship to Other Approaches. The cost approach requires findings from direct sales comparison analysis for the estimation of site value and for justifying many depreciation charges. It also requires findings from gross rent multiplier analysis to account for rent loss and to capitalize rent loss in measuring functional incurable obsolescence and locational obsolescence. Direct sales comparison analysis sometimes utilizes cost data in measuring adjustments. The land residual technique in income capitalization analysis utilizes an estimate of reproduction cost new of improvements.

Uses and Applications of the Cost Approach

As with the other alternative approaches to residential value estimation, the cost approach has particular applicability and usefulness under specified circumstances. Several are discussed here.

Special Purpose Properties. The cost approach is often the only avenue for estimating value of special-purpose properties. In the case of residential properties, unique or highly individualized structures for which there are no effective market comparisons can frequently be appraised only by the cost approach.

No-Market Appraisals. When no comparable sales data are available, neither the direct sales comparison approach nor gross rent multiplier analysis can be applied. This leaves only the cost approach for the appraiser. This situation may occur in temporary conditions of no market activity (at least among properties comparable to the subject property) or in very small communities in which the volume of general market activity is necessarily small.

New or Proposed Construction. When properties involving new or proposed construction that represents the highest and best use of the site are to be appraised, the cost approach can be quite effective. This situation most nearly approximates the conditions under which the basic theory or rationale of the cost approach is realized. It is applicable when the cost approach estimate requires little or no estimation of accrued depreciation, so that cost of production indicates a realistic alternative course of action available to the informed, rational potential purchaser.

Estimation of Highest and Best Use. The cost approach can be used effectively in hypothesizing improvements on a site to develop a conclusion regarding the highest and best use of the site. Although this technique is more commonly applied to proposed income-property uses, it also has applicability in selecting among alternative proposed residential developments.

Property Insurance Purposes. In estimating value for fire and casualty insurance purposes, the cost approach is the basis on which compensation for loss is usually calculated.

Limitations of the Cost Approach

The applicability and appropriateness of a cost approach estimate to value depend on accurate, defensible estimation of accrued depreciation (diminished utility). In the cost approach, accrued depreciation must be estimated by the appraiser directly. Generally, the greater the amount of accrued depreciation (diminished utility) observed in an existing residence and the more the estimate of value depends on the estimation of that accrued depreciation, the less that the value estimate via the cost approach may be reliable. This is the most significant limitation of the cost approach.

The less well maintained or the less appropriate the improvements are to the site, the less applicable or reliable the cost approach becomes.

Also, estimation of reproduction cost new frequently requires outside expert assistance and can be excessively expensive and time-consuming, particularly when the quantity survey or unit-in-place methods are employed. Further, production of a new structure on a vacant site may not reflect the thinking of the typical buyer on the local market, especially for existing residential properties.

The cost approach does not set the upper limit to value, since accrued depreciation can be overestimated as well as underestimated. Nor does cost new necessarily set the upper limit to value. With waiting time discounted, reproduction cost new tends to set the upper limit to the payment an informed buyer would make. There is growing professional sentiment that the cost approach is a poor substitute for direct sales comparison analysis, especially in the valuation of residential properties.

The Role of Estimated Cost New

When new or proposed construction represents the highest and best use of the site, cost new of the improvements may indicate the upper limit to value. This depends in part on what elements are included in cost new to the buyer. The informed buyer would pay no more than this total cost, including all the indirect cost elements, provided that waiting time is included as a cost. Waiting cost is usually measured by opportunity cost of income lost or by interest charges during the waiting period.

A cost new estimate is based on the most probable cost that would be incurred by the buyer. Normal methods and materials of construction are assumed that are typical of the current, local market in which the subject property is being appraised. Detailed cost new estimates are usually made for major structures only, especially in residential appraising. The estimate of cost new is the base or starting point for the estimation of accrued depreciation (diminished utility) in the cost approach. Thus, it must be both accurate and representative of the current, local market.

Both in practice and in concept, site and improvements are ordinarily not separable by either the market or the appraiser. Nevertheless, there are special circumstances in which separate estimates of the present worth or value of the improvements are sought in order to measure the contribution of the improvements to total property value. The very nature of the assignment may dictate such separation. In such cases, the starting point is usually an estimation of cost new.

For example, many state laws require separate valuation of site and improvements for ad valorem property tax purposes. Moreover, this practice is widespread among assessors, especially for residential properties. Cost new as of a given date is the necessary starting point for such valuations. Also, when partial takings occur in eminent domain proceedings, courts and public agencies frequently require that appraisers separate site and buildings in making their estimates of before value and after value. While this is not basically good appraisal practice or theory, the appraiser must be able to apply the required techniques. In addition, when vacant land or site is valued, it is frequently necessary to assume hypothetical new structures representing alternative legal and feasible uses of the site. Cost new is a necessary element in this type of analysis in seeking to arrive at a conclusion of the highest and best use (or most probable use) of the site. Finally, in the case of supersession of use (conversion, rehabilitation, demolition) cost new and/or cost of effecting change are important ingredients in reaching a conclusion about feasibility.

Reproduction Cost New versus Replacement Cost New

In the cost approach to residential valuation, reproduction cost new is used as the starting point for estimating accrued depreciation to, and hence present worth of, the building(s). This is because all of the functional obsolescence present in the structure must be built in first before accrued depreciation (diminshed utility) can be identified and measured properly. Thus, a replica of the present structure is hypothesized at current prices. Depreciation is charged at present prices. The result is an estimate of the present worth or contribution of the structure as of the valuation date.

At the same time, replacement cost has significance in appraisal practice. Its nature should be understood and carefully distinguished from reproduction cost. *Reproduction cost* (new) is "The cost of construction at current prices of an exact duplicate or replica using the same materials, construction standards, design, layout, and quality of workmanship, embodying all the deficiencies, superadequacies and obsolescence of the subject building"[1]

The essence of reproduction cost new, then, is that the new structure whose cost is estimated has all the functional obsolescence of the subject building; all of its locational obsolescence, if any; but none of its physical deterioration. If a residence contains 12-foot ceilings, for example, when 8-foot ceiling heights are curently acceptable, reproduction cost would include the extra expense of the higher ceilings. If a residence contains a gravity hot air heating system when the current market is demanding and obtaining forced hot air or hot water, reproduction cost still includes the expense of a gravity hot air system.

Replacement cost (new) is "The cost of construction at current prices of a building having utility equivalent to the building being appraised but built with modern materials and according to current standards, design and layout. The use of the replacement cost concept presumable eliminates all functional obsolescence, and the only depreciation to be measured is physical deterioration and economic [locational] obsolescence."[2]

The essence of replacement cost is that it represents the same utility, whereas reproduction cost requires the same physical structure. Conceptually, replacement cost would be preferable because rational purchasers or investors would replace utility rather than physical improvements if they were to start over. Rational purchasers would take advantage of changes in tastes and technology to produce structures that met modern standards. Unfortunately for this argument, utility cannot be measured directly; it must be inferred from prices and market behavior on a comparative basis. Therefore, reproduction cost tends to be used in practice and is emphasized here.

In applying replacement cost, the appraiser would assume construction of a residence with 8-foot instead of 12-foot ceilings and a forced hot air or hot water heating system instead of a gravity hot air system. Replacement cost new would presumably eliminate all functional obsolescence, and the only depreciation to be measured would be physical and locational. One difficulty with measuring physical deterioration against replacement cost new is that dissimilar items are compared, and the physical deterioration is charged against the hypothetical residence rather than against the one being appraised.

In residential appraising, reproduction cost new is used in the cost approach. The appraiser estimates accrued depreciation against a replica of the subject structure, using current prices, costs, and standards. Reproduction cost new is used as a starting point for the accrued depreciation estimate; as a basis for analysis of highest and best use of the site; as an estimation of present worth (contribution) of new or proposed construction; and as a guide to the feasibility of rehabilitation or restoration for badly deteriorated or damaged (e.g., by fire) structures.

In some cases, a reasonable alternative course of action to purchasing or retaining an existing improved property is to produce a new one, either on the same site or a different one. Replacement cost new, then, is a reasonable guide to the upper limit to which a rational purchaser or investor should go. It is also applicable in cases involving an analysis of the feasibility of restoration or rehabilitation.

Throughout the remainder of this discussion, cost new of residential improvements means reproduction cost new. Despite the aforementioned differences in concept, reproduction cost new and replacement cost new tend to be used interchangeably in practice. The FNMA/ FHLMC Form 1004/70, for example, uses reproduction cost new, whereas the Marshall and Swift cost example at the end of this chapter is labelled Replacement Cost Example. The SREA Standards of Professional Practice and Conduct and *A Guide to Appraising Residences* stipulate the use of reproduction cost new, as does the SREA's *The Official Guide to Appraisal Reporting*.[3] This variation in usage reinforces the importance of defining technical terminology and concepts in appraisal reporting so as to avoid (or at least minimize) confusion in the client's mind as well as the appraiser's.

Data Requirements and Sources

Market data, preferably confirmed or verified with principals or participants involved in sales transactions, are as essential to the development of an estimate of reproduction cost new as they are for comparable sales or comparable rental information. If defensible estimates are to be made, the appraiser must have accurate, current, local data on costs (both direct and indirect) and on unit costs of construction by type and quality of construction. Appraisers must also be aware of and exploit effectively the appropriate sources of these data.

Cost Data Requirements

Depending on the degree of detail in the estimate of cost new, the appraiser needs current, local market data on unit costs, equipment costs (installed), material prices, building trade wage rates and practices, financing costs, fees, selling expenses, builder's overhead, and profit margins. This information must represent the most probable or standard rates for the current, local market. It must also be specific enough to the particular type and quality of construction being appraised to represent an accurate depiction of cost to the typical purchaser. Varying degrees of detail in cost new estimates are shown in the Marshall and Swift Replacement Cost Example at the end of this chapter.

The cost new figure developed by the appraiser must reflect all ingredients of cost to the most probable, typical purchaser. Value as defined is seen and measured through the eyes of this typical purchaser and represents the highest price that an informed purchaser acting prudently would pay. Reproduction cost new is what the typically informed purchaser would have to pay, and would pay, to obtain the improvements under current, local market conditions.

In emphasizing that the cost figure developed by the appraiser is cost to the purchaser, cost new is divided for analytical purposes into two general categories: direct and indirect. These categories are not necessarily identified separately in the unit cost elements of many cost estimates. Rather, they represent a convenient mental checklist for the appraiser to use in assuring that all necessary and appropriate elements of cost are included in the estimate of reproduction cost new.

Direct costs

    Labor
    Materials
    Equipment
    Subcontractors' fees and charges

Indirect costs

    Contractor's or builder's overhead
    Contractor's or builder's profit
    Architect's fees
    Surveyor's fees
    Legal fees and expenses
    Permit and license fees
    Insurance premiums
    Taxes
    Financing charges
    Selling expenses: advertising, promotion, sales commissions or
      fees
    Vacancy carrying charges until first occupancy: waiting/holding
      expense

Broad general averages are not adequate for estimates of reproduction cost new. The figure represents the most probable cost for the structure being reproduced and appraised. Therefore, it must be specific to the type of property, type of construction, and market conditions as of the date of the appraisal. Costs reflect market conditions and competition on that market. Particularly when cost services are used, the appraiser must make all necessary adjustments carefully to ensure that the unit costs and the final estimate of reproduction cost new represent the best possible approximation of what a new replica of the residence being appraised would actually cost. The data must therefore be specific with respect to type of structure, type of construction, quality of construction, materials and equipment, local market conditions, and current market conditions as of the date of the appraisal.

Sources of Cost Data

The appraiser must be familiar with and exploit effectively appropriate sources of current, local cost data. The sources utilized in any given appraisal problem depend on the degree of detail required, the type of data required, and the level of accuracy required. All cost estimates should be as accurate as possible, of course, but different sources and techniques result in varying levels of detail and precision.

The appraiser must judge how significant the cost estimate and the ensuing cost approach value estimate will be to the particular appraisal problem and must seek data from sources appropriate to that need. Greater detail and greater precision require more time, effort, and expense for the appraiser and the client. The data sources utilized and the data developed from these sources should be consistent with the character of the appraisal assignment. Most important, the degree of detail in the cost new estimate is dictated by, and in turn determines, the method(s) to be used in estimating accrued depreciation.

All cost data are market data. Thus, the data sources utilized must permit a cost estimate for a replica of the subject structure under current, local market conditions. Local contractors and builders are an important and continuing source of data for the appraiser, since builders are constantly in touch with the local market. They can provide data on unit construction costs, costs of completed structures, wage rates, and materials and equipment prices (often charging a fee for such information). Contractors' records and files will provide information about specific completed structures as well as the costs of sample or model houses in subdivision developments. Cost differentials for variations from the basic model(s) can also be obtained. Appraisers can also request bids or estimates for specific structures from contractors. This bidding typically involves a fee for the contractor's time and effort. It is usually undertaken only in special cases—when the structure is highly unusual, when major reliance must be placed on the estimate of value via the cost approach, and when the nature of the appraisal problem and the fee warrant the expense.

For common types of construction and structures, it is frequently feasible to utilize benchmark or standard structure estimates as the base from which specific cost estimates are made. In such cases, the appraiser must be particularly sensitive to differences between the benchmark structure and the structure being appraised. Cost differentials must be justified carefully, and the benchmark structure should be as nearly identical to the subject residence as possible.

Adjustments must be made for variations in quality, materials, time, and market. Time and market adjustments are the most difficult to substantiate. Every effort should be made to keep benchmark data as current and as localized as possible. Adjustments are based on continuing analysis of wage rates and materials and equipment prices. These benchmark estimates may be developed from local contractors; the appraiser's own files; market surveys by FHA regional offices, appraisal society chapters, university research groups, lending institutions, or builders' associations; and cost services.

Cost estimation is a highly specialized technical skill. When the nature of the appraisal problem warrants it, the best and most accurate way to estimate reproduction cost new is to retain a cost estimator. This takes time and money, however, and should be undertaken only when it is really necessary and appropriate to the problem.

Construction cost studies are frequently made in local market areas (often on a continuing or periodic basis). They typically provide data on benchmark structures and must be adjusted for specific application to individual subject structures. The appraiser must recognize the components of cost differentials and must be prepared to substantiate the adjustments made in the benchmark estimate.

With cost surveys, time adjustments frequently must be made. This is usually accomplished through an index number adjustment (as shown in the Replacement Cost Example at the end of this chapter) to account for price and wage rate changes since the date of the survey. Local area cost studies may be available from the same sources already listed for benchmark estimates.

If they are maintained systematically, the appraiser's own files can be an important source of cost data. To be effective, the files should be cross-indexed by type of construction, quality grade of construction, and time. The basic ingredients of cost differentials should be identified, especially building perimeter (exterior walls, foundation area, and roof area), shape, number of exterior corners, number and configuration of interior partitions (size and shape of rooms), and type and quality of equipment. Data in the appraiser's files may be obtained from cost studies and surveys, previous cost estimates or contractors' bids, previous appraisals, and data on benchmark structures.

Cost services typically provide unit cost information for benchmark structures as well as segregated cost figures for structural components, equipment, and features as of a given data and for a base location. Thus, they represent average, generalized data for particular types of construction. These data must be adjusted by the appraiser for specific structural variations between the base structure and the improvement being appraised for market area and for time. Most cost services provide index number series for time and area adjustments.

Cost services typically provide information about structures with different qualities of construction and materials. They specify the base data for the cost data. They usually provide detailed information for making individual adjustments for structural variations (e.g., hot water heat in the subject structure versus forced hot air in the base structure), either on a unit or a lump sum basis.

Cost services also usually provide data on site improvements costs, both unit and lump sum, depending on which is pertinent and appropriate. Many offer detailed cost data and formulas for estimating the cost of structural units, elements, and components. These data and formulas permit the appraiser to develop cost estimates without necessarily using a benchmark structure as the starting point. Most cost services are published in manual form, with periodic (monthly, quarterly) revisions or supplements that provide information for making time and local market or regional adjustments.

Selection of a cost service is largely a matter of personal experience and preference. Appraisers should experiment with several cost services (and, indeed, have several available) and should select the one that best suits their needs and desires on the basis of results produced in test situations. Sometimes, a particular service will not provide adjustment factors for a given area, making its use in that area difficult and its accuracy possibly questionable. Many areas are served by local or regional cost services that tend to reflect local conditions well. National services may also be useful. The list at the end of this chapter includes some of the most widely used national cost services.

Cost services are relatively easy and quick references for cost estimation, especially for fairly standard structures, quality, and materials. Cost estimates may be made for times other than the present by using index number adjustments for the local market. Benchmark cost estimates can be developed for subsequent adjustment. Unit cost and lump sum estimates can be made for specific elements of construction. Good approximations of cost new that are adequate for most residential appraisal problems can be developed if care is exercised. Cost service estimates, if properly developed, are generally accepted by the FHA, the VA, the FNMA, the FHLMC, lenders, insurers, and even many courts.

Cost data are valid only in terms of the structural specifications detailed in the cost manual. The appraiser must read carefully, understand, and adhere strictly to the specifications provided for the base structure. All deviations in the subject residence must be adjusted for. This can lead to a highly complex and confusing cost estimate in some instances. Cost service data are still general averages, even when they are adjusted for time and location. The adjustment factors themselves represent averages. They may not reflect local conditions and changes adequately, especially for a particular type or element of construction. Data or adjustment factors from one cost service cannot be mixed with those of another service.

Adjustments are crucial to the application of cost service figures for estimates of cost new. If the data from any service are to be applicable to a particular residential appraisal problem, the system must allow as close comparability with the subject residence as possible. Deviations in the subject structure from the base structure in the cost manual must be clearly and carefully identified, and cost differentials stemming from them must be documented. In many instances, the formulas for adjustment are provided in the cost manual itself. Adjustments must be made for differences in structural components and content, including equipment; structure size, especially perimeter; materials; location; and time.

Cost Estimation

Reproduction cost new is almost always developed on a unit basis, with various units used. It is therefore essential that the number and type of units in the residence being appraised be recorded as accurately as possible. This depends on a thorough, detailed, accurate description of the structure, its contents, its quality, and its condition. To provide the proper setting for the estimation of cost new, the description of the improvements (buildings) must include, at least, building components, quantities, units, and condition.

The amount of detail required in itemizing structural contents and components is directly related to the nature of the appraisal problem and the type of depreciation analysis to be undertaken. It also depends on the degree of emphasis and reliance to be placed on the estimate of value via the cost approach.

In any estimate of cost new, the appraiser should avoid mindless application of mechanical formulas. Judgment and analysis are still required. This means avoiding generalized, average data and recognizing that the estimate is the most probable cost new to the purchaser of a specific structure as an improvement on a residential site. Generally, the greater the detail and accuracy required in an estimate of cost new, the greater the probability is that outside technical assistance will be required by the appraiser. When the estimate of cost new is truly critical to the success of an appraisal assignment, the appraiser should hire a professional cost estimator or architect—or at least should seek detailed bids from a knowledgeable builder. This will add to the cost and the time required for completing the appraisal assignment. When the services of a cost estimator are not essential, the amount of detail provided should follow the generally accepted standards of good professional practice, the standards of the local market, and the requirements of the client. The FNMA/FHLMC Form 1004/70, for example, clearly does not require segregated cost estimates or detailed breakdown analysis of accrued depreciation.

Methods of Cost Estimation

Several alternative methods of cost estimation are potentially at the appraiser's disposal. The choice is really limited, however, because the method employed depends on the method of estimating accrued depreciation that is to be used. The greater the emphasis on detailed, breakdown depreciation analysis, the greater the need for a more detailed breakdown method of cost estimation.

Cost estimating methods vary in time and expense required to complete them. The more demanding and detailed the estimate, the more expensive and time-consuming it usually is and the greater the reliance that must be placed on outside technicians to make the estimate. Whether appraisers hire cost estimators or not, however, they should understand and appreciate the components of each method.

The methods of cost estimation considered here are those most commonly utilized and accepted. Terminology may vary somewhat in different parts of the United States. Whatever method is employed, the appraiser must make sure of precisely which elements of cost are included. The estimate must consider all segments of both direct and indirect costs applicable in the appraisal problem at hand. Most cost estimates and cost services specify the elements included. Frequently, the appraiser will have to adjust the base figure upward by an appropriate percentage to reflect indirect cost items that are not included in the estimate from a cost estimator or from a service.

In this discussion, the methods of cost estimation are presented in decreasing order of accuracy and precision as well as decreasing order of costliness, complexity, detail, and time to complete. Whatever method is used, accurate measurement and description of improvements are essential. Every method employs unit prices to develop a total cost estimate. In addition, all methods may be converted to a cost per square foot or per cubic foot of building simply be dividing the total cost estimate by the number of square feet or cubic feet in the structure.

Quantity Survey Method. This is the most detailed, complex, costly, and time-consuming method of cost estimation. It should be attempted only by an expert. It is rarely used for residential appraising because of the time and expense involved. Following the same procedure that an informed contractor presumably would follow in developing a detailed bid for construction, the quantity survey method involves a calculation of all types of labor and materials, subcontractors' fees, and equipment required for reproduction new of the residence. Each item of cost is priced in terms of current, local prices and wages per unit (e.g., per hour, per thousand board feet, per pound). The unit figures are then multiplied by the number of units required to create the structure. Overhead, profit, and other indirect costs are added in as a lump sum or as an appropriate percentage at the end.

This method requires detailed knowledge of literally hundreds of prices and wage rates; complete familiarity with local market standards and practices (e.g., union work rules, profit margins and markups); and a thorough working knowledge of residential construction. Accurate, precise measurement and calculation of quantities are essential to the proper application of this method. Moreover, each quantity survey estimate is a customized, specific estimate for the particular structure in question.

The quantity survey method is applicable to residential appraising only when highly individual, possibly unique, structures are appraised. Because of the time involved and the degree of expertise required, it is extremely costly to the client. It is justified only when the nature of the problem and the structure warrant the expense. The degree of added precision is not usually required in residential appraising. The quantity survey method is not essential to the application of a detailed breakdown depreciation analysis, although it is certainly applicable in such a case.

Unit-in-Place Method. This method of cost estimation involves estimating the unit cost of materials or component sections of the structure installed or in place. The unit consists of both materials and the labor necessary to put them in place, per unit. The installed or in-place cost of exterior walls, for example, from the paint to the siding to the wallpaper on the interior, might be calculated at so much per square foot or per linear foot. This unit cost is then multiplied by the number of square feet or linear feet to obtain the installed cost of exterior walls in place. The same process is followed for all other component units of the structure. Lump sum additions are made for equipment and fixtures, whose cost includes expense of installation. The installed cost on either a unit or a lump sum basis typically includes contractor's overhead and profit. Other indirect costs are added at the end either as lump sums or as appropriate percentages.

The unit-in-place method is usually slightly quicker and less expensive than the quantity survey method, but it provides less detail and less precision. It is still too expensive and time-consuming to be warranted in most residential appraisals. It does develop component cost estimates that are highly compatible with detailed breakdown depreciation analysis. The level of technical expertise required for the unit-in-place method is not so high as that for the quantity survey method. Experienced appraisers can sometimes apply it themselves, often with assistance or advice from a knowledgeable contractor. It is also possible to develop a unit-in-place estimate with the use of several of the cost services, appropriately adjusted for location and time. Accurate measurement and description are essential for the successful application of the unit-in-place method.

Trade Breakdown, Segregated, or Builder's Method. This method is similar to the unit-in-place method, but in this case, the units are the major functional parts of the structure. An installed unit cost (including or excluding overhead and profit) is developed from current, local market data for each component part of the structure: excavation, foundation, frame, exterior walls, roof, roofing, interior walls (partitions), painting-decoration, floors, plumbing, heating system, electrical system, and so forth. This unit cost is then multiplied by the appropriate number of units (e.g., square feet, linear feet, outlets) to obtain the installed cost estimate for each component segment of the structure. The installed cost of fixtures, fireplaces, and equipment are added as lump sums per element. Then, appropriate indirect costs are added to obtain the final total. These indirect costs would include contractor's overhead and profit if they are not already incorporated into unit costs.

The trade breakdown method most nearly represents the thinking (if not necessarily the actions in preparing bid estimates) of most residential contractors. It can be understood readily by both appraiser and client. This method is less complex and time-consuming than either the quantity survey method or the unit-in-place method. Therefore, it is less costly. It can be applied in formal narrative reports without undue difficulty when breakdown depreciation analysis is appropriate. The trade breakdown method is most nearly compatible of all cost estimating methods with the breakdown method of estimating accrued depreciation recommended by professional appraisal organizations.

The trade breakdown, segregated, or builder's method can be applied through the use of cost services, again with appropriate time and location adjustments (as shown in the Replacement Cost Example at the end of this chapter). It can also be developed readily from contractors' bids or estimates and from cost data frequently found in the professional appraiser's own files. This method can be applied through the use of base or benchmark structures, with adjustments made for specific differences or deviations from the base in the residence being appraised. Accurate measurement and description are still required for effective application of the trade breakdown method. It is widely used and accepted by professional real estate appraisers, lenders, insurers, and clients.

most generally used by appraisers

Comparative Unit Method. This method is applied by lumping together all components of the structure on a unit basis: cost per square foot of building area; cost per square foot of foundation area; cost per cubic foot of building volume. Accurate measurement and description are also essential in this method, especially since unit variations can lead to significant differences in the final cost estimate.

The costs estimated are completed construction costs, including all installation expenses and usually builder's overhead and profit as well. Special care must be taken to be sure of exactly what is included in the unit cost figures, so that appropriate upward adjustments may be made for other indirect costs if necessary. Unit costs may be obtained by analyzing benchmark structures and then dividing by the appropriate number of units in the benchmark structure. These benchmarks may be obtained from estimates by local contractors, actual costs of residences built by local contractors, the appraiser's own files and records, or cost services.

In every instance, extreme care must be exercised in identifying all adjustments to be made from the base structure to the particular structure being appraised—for contents, quality, materials, equipment, and size. If the method is to be applied properly, the benchmark structure should be as nearly comparable to the subject structure as possible. Time and location adjustments may also be necessary, especially if past data or cost service figures are used.

The comparative unit method is the least accurate of the alternatives available to the appraiser, but it is also the easiest to apply, the least time-consuming, and the least costly. Properly applied, it will suffice in residential appraising when the recommended breakdown method of estimating accrued depreciation is not required. Incurable physical deterioration can be estimated only on a lump sum basis (straight-line, age-life) when this method is employed for cost estimation. It does not provide sufficient detail for application of breakdown depreciation analysis.

The unit employed in the analysis (square foot of living area, square foot of foundation area, cubic foot of volume) depends in large measure on the standards and requirements of the local market and of the client. Square foot analysis is generally recommended by professional appraisal groups, but cubic foot estimates are still widely and successfully used. In applying the comparative unit method, the accuracy of the results depends almost entirely in the degree of refinement with which the appraiser makes plus and minus adjustments to the unit cost of the base structure and on the degree of real comparability between the benchmark structure and the subject structure. This method is acceptable and widely used in practice.

Use of Cost Services

Cost service data may be utilized in all methods of estimating reproduction cost new except the quantity survey method. Not all cost services may be so applied, however. Care must be taken to make sure the appropriate data are available through a particular cost service before an attempt is made to use it. The appraiser must read carefully and understand fully the specifications for the base structure selected from the cost service. The basis for differences and variations between the benchmark structure and the subject structure must be clearly understood.

The appraiser must also understand fully the elements of total cost that are included in the unit costs provided by the cost service and those that are not included. Missing appropriate elements (almost always indirect costs) must be added to develop a final estimate of total cost new. The appraiser must understand and apply properly the formula or technique for adjusting for differences between the benchmark structure and the subject structure—for materials, quality of construction, structural components, time, and location (market area). To do this, the appraiser must understand the technique of index number adjustment as well as specific item adjustment.

Site Improvements

The cost new (installed) of site improvements may be estimated directly; then depreciation can be estimated in much the same manner as is done for major structures. Cost services, contractors, and/or cost estimators may be employed, depending on the importance and the complexity of the cost estimating problem. More commonly, site improvements and minor buildings are valued directly on a depreciated cost basis, as is. Minor variations in this estimate are usually not critical because of the small impact they have on total property value. When site improvements represent a significant part of total value in the cost approach, expert specialists should be retained (e.g., landscape architects or nurserymen for extensive plantings, specialists for swimming pools).

The best approach is to utilize comparable sales data of otherwise similar properties with and without the particular type of site improvement and to measure directly from the market the difference or contribution the presence or absence of the particular item makes in market price. For minor items, however, a cost new estimate via a cost service or manual (with subsequent deduction for depreciation on a straight age-life basis) will usually produce adequate and acceptable results.

Total Reproduction Cost New

Whether site improvements are excluded from or included in the reproduction cost new estimate, the final total figure is obtained by summing the products of unit costs times the number of units in the subject structure, adding lump sum amounts for specific items of equipment, and finally adding indirect costs that are not already included in the installed unit and lump sum costs. The result is the most probable reproduction cost new of the structure (and site improvements, if included) that a typical purchaser would have to pay for a new replica.

Summary

The cost approach reflects one alternative method available to a potential purchaser for acquiring a residential property with the same utility as the subject property: producing a replica of the subject property. The cost approach to residential valuation involves making an estimate of what it would cost a typically informed purchaser to produce a replica of the subject property in its present condition. Site value is estimated separately as if the site were vacant and available to be put to its highest and best use. While cost does not create value and cost is not synonymous with value, cost of production may be an appropriate measure of value under certain conditions.

The indication of value via the cost approach is obtained by summing the following factors:

1. Value of site as if vacant and available to be put to its highest and best use.
2. Estimated depreciated reproduction cost new (present worth) of improvements (buildings).
3. Estimated depreciated reproduction cost new (present worth) of site improvements.

The estimate of value via the cost approach depends heavily on the direct estimation of accrued depreciation charged against the reproduction cost new of the improvements on the site. This is the chief limitation to the applicability of the cost approach.

The cost approach is most appropriately applied to the valuation of residential properties on which the improvements are new (or nearly so) and represent the highest and best use of the site. The starting point for estimating the present worth or contribution of the structure (or improvements) on the site to the value of the total property is to estimate its reproduction cost new as of the date of the appraisal. Reproduction cost new involves estimating the cost of producing a new replica of the subject structure. Cost new is the cost to a typical purchaser. It includes both direct and indirect costs (which include contractor's profit and overhead, among many other items). Detailed improvements analysis, involving accurate description and measurement of the structure, is critical to successful estimation of reproduction cost new.

All methods of cost estimation involve some use of unit costs. The unit cost is multiplied by the number of units to derive the total cost of the particular structural component or of the entire structure. Several alternative methods of estimating reproduction cost new are available to the appraiser. In decreasing order of detail, complexity, time, and expense, they are the quantity survey method, the unit-in-place method, the trade breakdown method (contractor's method, segregated method), and the comparative unit (cubic foot or square foot) method.

The selection of the appropriate method of cost estimation in any appraisal problem depends on the method to be used for estimating accrued depreciation, the degree of reliance to be placed on the estimate of value via the cost approach, and the time and money available to make the appraisal. Cost estimates can be developed via all methods except the quantity survey method with the use of data from cost services and manuals, provided that the data are applied with care and understanding. Site improvements are commonly valued at depreciated value or contribution as is, but they may be included in the estimate of reproduction cost new.

Notes

1. Boyce, Byrl N., Ed., *Real Estate Appraisal Terminology*, rev. ed. (Cambridge, Mass.: Ballinger [Joint publication of the American Institute of Real Estate Appraisers and Society of Real Estate Appraisers], 1981), p. 205.
2. Ibid.
3. "Replacement Cost Example: One Story" (Los Angeles: Marshall and Swift, 1980); "Standards of Professional Practice and Conduct" (Chicago: Society of Real Estate Appraisers, 1979); Stebbins, H. Grady, Jr., *A Guide to Appraising Residences* (Chicago: Society of Real Estate Appraisers, 1976); and *The Official Guide to Appraisal Reporting* (Chicago: Society of Real Estate Appraisers, 1983).

Suggested Readings

American Institute of Real Estate Appraisers. *The Appraisal of Real Estate,* 8th ed. Chicago: American Institute of Real Estate Appraisers, 1983, chapters 18 and 19.
Bloom, George F., and Harrison, Henry S. *Appraising the Single Family Residence.* Chicago: American Institute of Real Estate Appraisers, 1978, chapter 12 and appendix H.
Boyce, Byrl N., ed. *Real Estate Appraisal Terminology,* rev. ed. Cambridge, Mass.: Ballinger (Joint publication of the American Institute of Real Estate Appraisers and Society of Real Estate Appraisers), 1981.
Epley, Donald R., and Boykin, James H. *Basic Income Property Appraisal.* Reading, Mass.: Addison-Wesley, 1983.
Ratcliff, Richard U. *Valuation for Real Estate Decisions.* Santa Cruz, Calif.: Democrat Press, 1972, chapter 5.
Smith, Halbert C. *Real Estate Appraisal.* Columbus, Ohio: Grid, 1976, chapter 7.
Wendt, Paul F. *Real Estate Appraisal: Review and Outlook.* Athens: University of Georgia Press, 1974, chapter 8.

Selected Cost Manuals and Services

Boeckh Building Cost Guides: Residential. Milwaukee: Boeckh Publications, Division of American Appraisal Associates, Inc., published annually.

Boeckh Building Valuation Manual, 2nd ed. Milwaukee: Boeckh Publications, Division of American Appraisal Associates, Inc., published bimonthly (looseleaf).

Dodge Building Cost Calculator & Valuation Guide. New York: McGraw-Hill Information Systems Company, published quarterly (looseleaf).

Marshall Valuation Service. Los Angeles: Marshall and Swift Publication Company, published monthly (looseleaf).

Residential Cost Handbook. Los Angeles: Marshall and Swift Publication Company, published quarterly (looseleaf).

REPLACEMENT COST EXAMPLE

ONE STORY
(WITH BASEMENT)

FAIR QUALITY

Presented by

MARSHALL and SWIFT
Publication Company

1617 BEVERLY BOULEVARD • P.O. BOX 26307 • LOS ANGELES, CALIFORNIA 90026

*Copies of this material are available, without charge, to current subscribers or
qualified instructors for free distribution to appraisal students.*

Reprinted with Permission

RCH

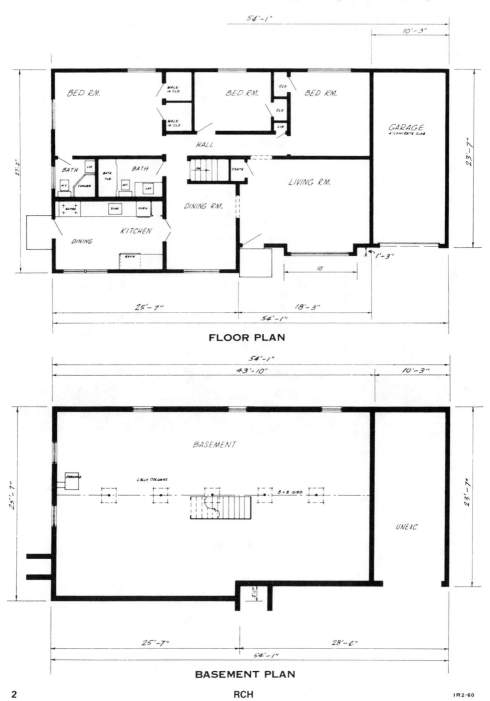

FLOOR PLAN

BASEMENT PLAN

SUBJECT RESIDENCE DESCRIPTION

BASEMENT:	Concrete walls approximately 5' below grade. No abnormal soil conditions. 4" thick concrete floor. No interior finish. 3-1/2" steel pipe columns supporting wood floor structure above. Incidental heating from the furnace.
STRUCTURAL FRAME:	All frame members are wood. Average workmanship and material.
EXTERIOR FINISH:	Painted wood shingle with sheathing.
ROOF:	235 lb. asphalt shingles over 15 lb. felt on plywood sheathing. Metal gutters and downspouts.
INTERIOR FINISH:	1/2" drywall, taped and spackled; wallpaper or paint finish throughout. Ceramic tile in baths.
SASH AND DOORS:	Sliding aluminum sash. Hollow core natural finish interior doors. Panel entry door with transom lights.
FLOORS:	Vinyl asbestos tile in kitchen, entry hall and baths. Remainder hardwood on wood subfloor.
PLUMBING:	Eight average quality fixtures and a plumbing rough-in as follows: 1 bathtub with shower over, 1 stall shower, 2 lavatories, 2 toilets, 1 kitchen sink, 1 water heater and a washer-dryer service.
CABINETS AND CLOSETS:	Kitchen cabinets are a natural finish plywood veneer. Laminated plastic countertops and splash. Hollow core slab closet doors.
HEATING:	Oil fired hot water boiler with fin type baseboard radiators, with exhaust chimney. The building is located in an extreme climate.
INSULATION:	3-1/2" batt insulation in the exterior walls. 6" batts with loose mineral wool insulation in the ceiling.
ELECTRICAL:	Average number of convenience outlets. Inexpensive fixtures in kitchen, dining room and hall.
BUILT-IN APPLIANCES:	Built-in electric oven and range, kitchen and bath exhaust fans.
ATTACHED GARAGE:	Frame, painted wood shingle, concrete floor, single sectional wood overhead door. Roof and cover conform to that of house.
GENERAL QUALITY:	Residence and garage are of fair quality throughout.

SQUARE FOOT APPRAISAL FORM
for use with the **RESIDENTIAL COST HANDBOOK**

Appraisal for _____ Property owner _____

Address _____

Appraiser _____ Date _____

TYPE	QUALITY	STYLE	EXTERIOR WALLS	GARAGE TYPE
Single Family ☒	Low	No. Stories _ONE_	Hardboard	Detached
Multiple	Fair ☒	Bi-level	Stucco	Attached ☒
Town House	Average	Split Level	Siding or Shingle ☒	Built-In
Row House	Good	1½ story - Fin.	Masonry Veneer	Subterranean
Mfg. House	Very Good	1½ story - Unf.	Common Brick	Carport
	Excellent	End Row	Face Brick or Stone	Garage Area
		Inside Row	Concrete Block	_242 SQ. FT._

FLOOR AREA
1st _1,138 SQ.FT._
2nd _____
3rd _____
Total _1,138 SQ.FT._

BASEMENT AREA
Unf. _1,084 SQ.FT._
Fin. _____

NUMBER OF MULTIPLE UNITS _____

NUMBER OF PLUMBING
Fixtures _8_   Rough-in _1_

MFG. HOUSING
Alum., Ribbed
Alum. Lap Siding
Hardboard

BALCONY AREA

PORCH AREA
(a) _14 SQ.FT._
(b) _12 SQ.FT._

1100 SQ.FT. COST: 1000 S.F. @ $24.70 + 1200 S.F. @ $23.96 ÷ 2 = $24.33

	Quan.	Cost			Extension
			+	−	
1100 SQ.FT. COST: (header row above)					
1. COMPUTE RESIDENCE BASIC COST: Floor area x selected sq. ft. cost	1,138	$24.33			$ 27,688
2. Basic residence cost adjustments Lines 3-13. Describe and indicate plus or minus			+	−	
3. Roofing _ASPHALT SHINGLE (BASE)_					
4. Flooring 1st floor _WOOD SUBFLOOR (BASE)_					
5. Flooring upper floors _70% HARDWOOD @ $2.76 = $1.93 + 30% RES.FLR. @ $.70 = $.21_	1,138	2.14	+		2,435
6. Heating-Cooling _HOT WATER BASEBOARD (EXTREME CLIMATE)_	1,138	1.54	+		1,753
7. Insulation _(EXTREME CLIMATE)_	1,138	.29	+		330
8. Interior Finish _DRYWALL (BASE)_					
9. Plumbing _8 FIXT. + 1 R.I. (6 FIXT. + 1 R.I. = BASE)_	2	370	+		740
10. Built-in appliances _RANGE AND OVEN_	1	450	+		450
11. _KITCHEN AND BATH EXHAUST_	2	70	+		140
12. Fireplace					
13. Miscellaneous					
14. SUBTOTAL ADJ. RESIDENCE COST: Line 1 plus or minus Lines 3-13					$ 33,536
15. BASEMENT, UNFINISHED _8" POURED CONCRETE WALLS_	1,084	5.67	+		6,146
16. Add for basement garage: Single ☐ Double ☐ _____					
17. Add for basement outside entrance					
18. Add for basement interior finish					
19. Porches or balconies, describe _OPEN W/STEPS @ $5.36 + ROOF @ $3.84_	14	9.20	+		129
20. _OPEN W/STEPS_	12	5.36	+		64
21. SUBTOTAL RESIDENCE COST: Total of Lines 14-20					$ 39,875
22. GARAGE OR CARPORT - sq. ft. area x selected sq. ft. cost	242	10.95	+		2,650
23. Attached garage - deduct for common wall	23.58	24.95		−	588
24. Garage roofing adjustment					
25. Garage miscellaneous					
26. SUBTOTAL GARAGE COST: Line 22 plus or minus Lines 23-25					2,062
27. SUBTOTAL OF ALL BUILDING IMPROVEMENTS: Sum of Lines 21 and 26					$ 41,937
28. Current Cost Multiplier _1.00_ x Local Multiplier _1.01_ x Line 27					$ 42,356
29. Depreciation: Age _____ Condition _____ Deduction _____ % of Line 28					
30. Depreciated cost of building improvements: Line 28 less Line 29					
31. Yard improvements cost: List, total, apply local multiplier and depreciate on reverse side					
32. Landscaping cost: List and compute on reverse side					
33. Lot or land value					
34. **TOTAL INDICATED VALUE:** Total of Lines 30-33					

4   FORM 1007　　　　　　　　　　　　RCH　　　　　　　　　　　　　1 R4-60(R)

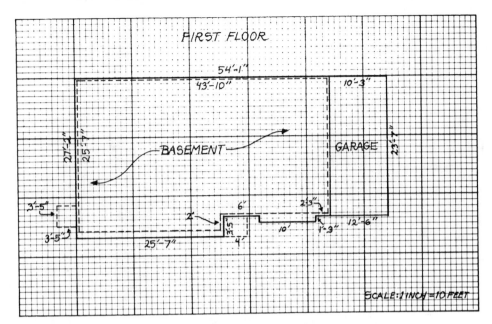

NOTES AND COMPUTATIONS

NOTE: CONVERT INCHES TO DECIMALS TO COMPUTE AREAS.

RESIDENCE:
  25.58' × 27.17' = 695 SQ. FT.
  18.25' × 23.58' = 430 " "
  10.0' × 1.25' = 13 " "
                    ‾‾‾‾‾‾‾‾‾‾‾
                    1,138 SQ. FT.

BASEMENT:
  25.58' × 25.58' = 654 SQ. FT.
  18.25' × 23.58' = 430 " "
                    ‾‾‾‾‾‾‾‾‾‾‾
                    1,084 SQ. FT.

GARAGE:
  10.25' × 23.58' = 242 SQ. FT.

PORCHES:
  4.0' × 3.42' = 14 SQ. FT.
  3.42' × 3.42 = 12 " "

BASIC DESCRIPTION

Square Foot Costs
Fair Quality

Houses of Fair Quality are frequently mass produced. Low cost production is a primary consideration. Although overall quality of materials and workmanship is below average, these homes are not substandard and will meet minimum requirements of lending institutions, mortgage insuring agencies and building codes. Architectural detail is limited by the low cost aspect. Interior finish is plain with few refinements. The exterior front elevation may have inexpensive finish materials which add to its appearance.

RESIDENCE

FOUNDATION . . . . . Continuous concrete perimeter foundation and piers.

FLOOR STRUCTURE . . Wood structure and subfloor on first and upper floors. Use Square Foot Adjustments to correct basic residence cost for concrete slab.

FLOOR COVER . . . . . Carpet, asphalt or vinyl asbestos tile. Floor cover costs are not included in basic residence cost. Use Square Foot Adjustments to add for floor cover.

EXTERIOR WALL . . . . Moderate fenestration using inexpensive sash. Front elevations may have some inexpensive trim.

ROOF . . . . Rafters or pre-fab trusses with plywood or inexpensive wood sheathing. Lightweight asphalt shingles or built-up roofing with small rock. Roof slope is usually 4 in 12 or less. Small eave. Use Square Foot Adjustments to correct basic residence cost for other types of roofing.

INTERIOR FINISH . . . Walls are taped and painted drywall. Enamel painted walls and ceilings in kitchen and baths. Inexpensive stock cabinets of paint grade wood. Small pullman or vanity in bath. Countertops of laminated plastic with low splash. Low cost hardware. Stock, hollow core doors with inexpensive hardware. Stock base and casing. Moderate wardrobe and linen closets with inexpensive doors. Use Square Foot Adjustments to correct for plaster interior.

HEATING . . . . Gas fired forced air furnace. Minimum output and ductwork. Use Square Foot Adjustments to correct for other types of heating or cooling.

ELECTRICAL . . . . . . Minimum number of outlets and inexpensive fixtures.

PLUMBING . . . . Six competitively priced white fixtures and a plumbing rough-in are included in the basic residence costs. The fixtures can include any of the following: water heater, laundry tray, stall shower, toilet, lavatory, tub with shower over, kitchen sink. Use Lump Sum Adjustments to correct basic residence cost for more or less than six plumbing fixtures and a rough-in.

INSULATION . . . . . . Wall and ceiling insulation are included in the basic residence cost. Use the Segregated Cost Section to correct the basic residence costs for no wall or ceiling insulation.

BUILT-IN APPLIANCES . None included in basic residence cost. Add from Lump Sum Adjustments.

FIREPLACE . . . . . . None included in basic residence cost. Add from Lump Sum Adjustments.

page A-7

ONE STORY

Square Foot Costs
Fair Quality

RESIDENCE COSTS (per sq. ft. of floor area)

Sq. Ft. Area	WOOD FRAME Plywood or Hardboard	Stucco	Siding or Shingle	Masonry Veneer	Sq. Ft. Area	MASONRY Common Brick	Concrete Block
800	$24.48	$25.39	$25.64	$28.21			
900	24.01	24.90	25.14	27.62	800	$28.87	$27.83
1000	23.61	24.47	24.70	27.10	900	28.25	27.26
1200	22.92	23.75	23.96	26.23	1000	27.70	26.76
1400	22.35	23.16	23.36	25.51	1200	26.79	25.91
1600	21.87	22.65	22.84	24.90	1400	26.04	25.22
1800	21.45	22.22	22.40	24.38	1600	25.40	24.63
2000	21.09	21.84	22.01	23.92	1800	24.86	24.12
2200	20.76	21.50	21.66	23.52	2000	24.38	23.68
2400	20.47	21.19	21.35	23.15	2200	23.95	23.28
					2400	23.57	22.93

SQUARE FOOT ADJUSTMENTS (Additions or deductions to the above costs)

ROOFING:
(Apply to total flr. area)
Asphalt shingle	(base)	
Built-up, small rock	(base)	
Wood shingle	+ $ .67	
Wood shake	+ .81	
Composition roll	- .27	

FLOORS:
(Apply to individual flr. area)
Wood subfloor only	(base)	
Concrete slab only	-$1.13	
Hardwood	+ 1.13	
Carpet	+ 2.76	
Resilient flr. cover	+ .70	
Ceramic tile	+ 3.86	

HEATING:
(Apply to total flr. area)
Forced air, gas	(base)	
Elec. or oil-fired	- $ .35	
Flr. or wall furnace	- .23	
Gravity furnace	- .81	
Electric, radiant	+ .43	
Basebrd or panel	+ .37	
Hot water, basebrd.	+ .48	
Warm & cooled air	+ .28	
Heat pump	+ .72	

CLIMATE
	Mild	Moderate	Extreme
		(base)	+ $ .46
	- $ .16		+ .69
			+ .55
	+ .10		+ .33
	+ .01		+ .52
	+ .14		+ .81
		.82	+ 1.54
	1.42		+ 2.31
	1.51		+ 2.53

INSULATION . . . . . . - $ .19   (base) + $ .29

PLASTER INTERIOR . . . . + $ .45

LUMP SUM ADJUSTMENTS (*) Indicates items included in base cost.

PLUMBING: (* 6 fixt. - rough-in)
Per fixture	(base)	
Plbg. fixture, rough-in	+ or - $370	
Tub enclosure	+ 130	

BUILT-IN APPLIANCES:
(For complete list, see Page B-13)
Range & oven		
Range hood and fan	+ $ 450	
Dishwasher	+ 110	
Garbage disposer	+ 370	
Exhaust fan or bath heater	+ 136	
Trash compactor	+ 320	

FIREPLACES (Other types, see Page B-13)
Single, 1 story	$ 900 to $1,250
Double, 1 story	1,300 to 1,825

ADJUSTED BASEMENT COSTS * (per sq. ft. of basement area)

Description	200	400	800	1200	1600	2000
Unf. basement, 6" conc. walls	$9.82	$7.71	$6.06	$5.17	$4.76	$4.40
Unf. basement, 8" conc. walls	10.82	8.43	6.56	5.67	5.23	4.71
Unf. basement, 10" conc. walls	11.80	9.12	7.05	6.05	5.44	5.01
Fin. cost per sq. ft. of finished area	$3.07	$2.67	$2.32	$2.14	$2.02	$1.93

*Reduce costs 7% for conc. block walls.

PORCH COSTS (per sq. ft. of porch area, including foundation. Other types, Page B-14).

Outside entrance: $480

Sq. Ft. Area	Open Slab	Open W/Steps	Add For Roof	Add For Ceiling	Sq. Ft. Area	Open Slab	Open W/Steps	Add For Roof	Add For Ceiling
25	$1.80	$5.36	$3.84	$1.20	100	$1.59	$4.51	$3.25	$1.02
50	1.69	4.92	3.53	1.11	200	1.49	4.14	2.99	.94

GARAGE COSTS (per sq. ft. of garage area)

Type	Area	Plywood or Hardboard	Stucco	Siding or Shingle	Masonry Veneer	Common Brick	Concrete Block
Detached	200	$10.28	$10.75	$10.95	$13.56	$14.14	$13.00
	400	8.32	8.70	8.87	10.52	11.03	10.15
	600	7.75	8.11	8.26	9.48	9.94	9.15
Wall cost per lin. ft.		$21.71	$24.54	$24.95	$30.02	$32.29	$28.55

ATTACHED GARAGE - Compute as detached, then deduct the above cost per linear foot of common wall. **BASEMENT GARAGE** - Add lump sum to unfinished basement cost, single $670, double $825. **OPEN CARPORT** - All sizes, $4.85 per square foot. Add garage wall cost per lin. ft. for enclosed storage or utility area. **INTERIOR FINISH** - Built-in and basement garage costs include interior finish. Add to detached and attached garage costs as follows: Ceiling, $1.07 per square foot; walls, $5.32 per linear foot.

page A-19

SEGREGATED COST APPRAISAL FORM

for use with the **RESIDENTIAL COST HANDBOOK**

1. Owner _____ Appraiser _____

2. Property Address _____

3. Quality _FAIR_____ Type _SINGLE FAMILY_____ Number of Stories _ONE_____ Date _____

	UNITS	QUALITY	QUANTITY	UNIT COST	LUMP SUM EXTENSION
4. Foundation _CONCRETE - FRAME_	Square Ft. of Floor	FAIR	1,138	$ .88	$ 1,001
5. Basement—Bulk Excavation _5 FT. DEPTH - SOFT SOIL_	Cubic Ft. of Volume	FAIR	5,420	.11	596
6. Wall _7 FT. HEIGHT - 8" UNF. WALLS_	Square Ft. of Wall	FAIR	973	3.71	3,610
7. Floor/Ceiling _CONCRETE FLOOR_	Square Ft. of Floor	FAIR	1,084	1.86	2,016
8. Stairway/Entrance _UNFIN. OPEN RISER_	Each	FAIR	1	220	220
9. Floor Structure _WOOD SUBFLOOR_	Square Ft. of Floor	FAIR	1,138	2.43	2,765
10. Floor Cover _70% HARDWOOD = $1.86 + 30% V.A.T. = $.21_	Square Ft. of Floor	FAIR	1,138	2.07	2,356
11. Exterior Wall _WD. SHGL. + SHEATHING + INSULATION_	Lineal Ft. of Wall	FAIR V. GOOD	121	49.83	6,029
12. COMMON WALL - PLAIN FINISH Gable Wall _WD. SHGL. + SHEATHING_	Square Ft. of Wall Square Ft. of Wall	FAIR FAIR	24 82	20.77 2.87	498 235
13. Ceiling _DRYWALL, PAINTED @ $.66 + INSUL. @ $.38_	Square Ft. of Floor	FAIR V. GOOD	1,138	1.04	1,184
14. Roof _ASPHALT SHINGLE @ $3.16 × 1.03 (SLOPE)_	Square Ft. of 1st Floor	FAIR	1,138	3.26	3,710
15. Roof Dormers _NONE_	Lineal Ft. Across Face				
16. Interior Construction _ONE STORY_	Square Ft. of Floor	FAIR	1,138	5.56	6,327
17. Heating & Cooling _BASEBD. HOT WATER @ $2.65 × 1.07 (OIL)_	Square Ft. of Floor	V. GOOD	1,138	2.84	3,232
18. Electrical _RESIDENCE_	Square Ft. of Floor	FAIR	1,138	1.20	1,366
19. Plumbing _8 FIXT. @ $360 EA. + 1 R.I. @ $125_	Square Ft. or Each	FAIR	1	3,005	3,005
20. Fireplace _____	Each				
21. Built-in Appliances _RANGE @ $230 + OVEN @ $390_	Each	FAIR	1	620	620
22. _EXHAUST FANS_		FAIR	2	65	130
23. Stairways _NONE_	Each				
24. Balconies _NONE_	Square Ft. of Balcony				
25. Attic Finish _NONE_	Square Ft. of Floor				
26. Porches _STEPS @ $5.22 + ROOF @ $3.11 × 1.03 (SLOPE)_	Square Ft. of Porch	FAIR	14	8.42	118
27. _STEPS @ $5.22_		FAIR	12	5.22	63
28. Garage—Foundation _FRAME_	Lineal Ft. of Wall	FAIR	44	3.76	165
29. Exterior Wall _SHGL. + SHEATHING_	Lineal Ft. of Wall	FAIR	44	27.04	1,190
30. Floor and Roof _CONC. @ $1.04 + ROOF @ $2.45 × 1.03 (SLOPE)_	Square Ft. of Floor	FAIR	242	3.56	862
31. Subtotal of Building Improvements _____					$ 41,298
32. Current Cost Multiplier _1.02_ × Local Multiplier _1.01_ × Line 31 _____					$ 42,545

33. Depreciation: Age _____ Condition _____ Deduction _____ % of Line 32 _____

34. Depreciated Cost of Building Improvements: Line 32 Less Line 33 _____

35. Yard Improvements *(from back of form)* _____

36. Lot or Land Value _____

37. **TOTAL PROPERTY VALUE** _____

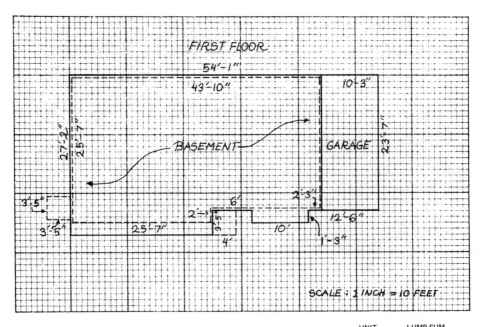

	QUANTITY	UNIT COST	LUMP SUM EXTENSION
Yard Improvements			
38. Fence			
39. Paving			
40. Landscaping			
41. Miscellaneous			
42.			
43.			
44.			
45. Total Yard Improvements			

AREAS   NOTES AND COMPUTATIONS   *PERIMETERS*

RESIDENCE: 25.58′ × 27.17′ = 695 sq.ft.   *RESIDENCE:* 144 LIN. FT.
          18.25′ × 23.58′ = 430 sq. ft.
          10.0′ × 1.25′ = 13 " " / 1,138 sq.ft.

BASEMENT: 25.58′ × 25.58′ = 654 sq.ft.   *BASEMENT:* 139 LIN. FT.
          18.25′ × 23.58′ = 430 " " / 1,084 sq ft.

GARAGE: 10.25′ × 23.58″ = 242 sq.ft.   *GARAGE:*   44 LIN. FT.
PORCHES: 4.0′ × 3.42′ = 14 sq.ft
          3.42′ × 3.42′ = 12 sq.ft.
GABLE WALLS: 3.0′ × 27.17′ = 82 sq.ft.

8   RCH   IR8-60

Segregated Costs
Foundation, Basements

FOUNDATION . . . BASEMENT

FOUNDATION . . . Apply the following costs to the floor area of all one story buildings. For multi-story buildings, increase cost 60% for each additional story above the first and apply cost to the ground floor area only, including any built-in garage area. Costs include minimal site preparation, trenching, formwork, perimeter foundation and an allowance for interior piers or foundations. Where footings are poured monolithically with a concrete slab floor, use 70% of the costs given below for the first floor. Basement walls are not a part of the foundation, but of the basement, which is computed separately. When basement walls replace part of the foundation, a lower cost classification may be considered. Always include a cost for foundation, whether there is a basement or not. Pilings or special foundations should be priced from Section C. Costs are affected mainly by the load supported. Use Low quality for light buildings and Excellent where heavy foundations are required. If the building site is not level but slopes enough so that stepped footings are required, more concrete would be needed for the foundation. In cold climates where the foundation must extend below the frost line, a higher rating should be used.

Concrete Foundations:

SQ. FT. AREA	FRAME RESIDENCES					
	LOW	FAIR	AVG.	GOOD	V. GOOD	EXCL.
600	$ .84	$ .96	$1.09	$1.42	$1.61	$1.84
1000	.77	.88	1.00	1.30	1.47	1.69
1400	.72	.83	.94	1.22	1.39	1.59
1600	.71	.81	.92	1.19	1.36	1.55
2000	.68	.78	.89	1.15	1.31	1.50
2400	.66	.75	.86	1.12	1.27	1.45
2800	.64	.73	.83	1.08	1.24	1.41
3200	.63	.72	.82	1.06	1.21	1.38

SQ. FT. AREA	MASONRY & MASONRY VENEER RESIDENCES					
	LOW	FAIR	AVG.	GOOD	V. GOOD	EXCL.
600	$1.00	$1.13	$1.28	$1.63	$1.84	$2.08
1000	.91	1.03	1.16	1.49	1.69	1.90
1400	.86	.97	1.10	1.41	1.59	1.80
1600	.84	.95	1.07	1.37	1.55	1.75
2000	.81	.92	1.04	1.32	1.50	1.69
2400	.79	.89	1.01	1.29	1.45	1.64
2800	.77	.87	.98	1.25	1.41	1.59
3200	.75	.85	.96	1.22	1.38	1.56

Note: (1) Reduce costs 4% for concrete block foundation walls.
(2) Reduce costs 10% for end row or semi-detached houses and 20's for inside row.

Wood Foundations:

Frame Residences	LOW	FAIR	AVG.	GOOD	V.GOOD	EXCL
Piers or posts on concrete footings	$ .24	.27	$ .29	$ .36	......	......
Wood blocks or sills	.18	.20	.23	......		

BASEMENTS . . . Costs are an addition to the foundation costs given above.

Excavation . . . Apply costs to total cubic feet. The following costs include machine excavation and allowance for backfill and disposal. Costs vary according to type of soil, accessibility of the site, and length of the haul for disposal. If the excavation is in soil which is easy to dig with standard equipment, if the site is such that there is ample room for the equipment to operate, and if the dirt can be wasted on the site, a Low cost rating should be used. If there are aspects that make the digging more difficult such as harder soil or longer haul for disposal - Average to Good cost should be used. If there are difficult conditions, such as very hard soil or rock, or perhaps sandy soil which requires much shoring, Excellent costs should be used. For long hauls, the additional cost over two miles radius must be added from Section C.

	LOW	FAIR	AVG.	GOOD	V.GOOD	EXCL.
Cost per Cubic Foot	$ .09	$ .11	$ .13	$ .19	$ .23	$ .28

page B-6

BASEMENT . . . FLOOR

Segregated Costs
Basements
Floor Structure

BASEMENTS (CONT'D)

Basement Walls . . . Apply cost to square foot area of basement perimeter wall. The following unfinished wall costs include structural wall, waterproofing and fenestration as applicable. Finished wall costs include an interior finish commensurate with the quality as outlined in the basic descriptions in Section A. For a more detailed build-up for interior wall finish or to add above grade exterior wall finish see Section C.

TYPE	LOW	FAIR	AVG.	GOOD	V.GOOD	EXCL.
8" conc. walls, unfinished	$3.61	$3.71	$3.80	$3.99	$4.19	$4.40
8" conc. walls, finished	3.78	4.00	4.23	4.73	5.30	5.93
Each 2" variation in thickness	.51	.53	.56	.61	.67	.74

Note: (1) Deduct 15% for concrete block basement walls. Treated wood wall costs have shown no appreciable differences from masonry walls at the same quality levels.
(2) Costs for interior partitions should be added from Section C.

Basement Floors and Interior Structural Frame . . . Apply costs to basement floor area. The following costs include concrete floor, minimum electric fixtures, outlets and floor drain as applicable and cost differences in supporting structure of residence first floor. Finished concrete floor includes a weighting of finished floor cover commensurate with the quality as outlined in the basic descriptions in Section A. For a more detailed cost of described floor coverings, use Floor Cover Table page B-8.

TYPE	LOW	FAIR	AVG.	GOOD	V.GOOD	EXCL.
Concrete, plain	$1.78	$1.86	$1.95	$2.13	$2.34	$2.56
Conc., finished floor cover	2.38	2.54	2.71	3.10	3.53	4.03

Basement Ceilings . . . Apply cost to square foot area of finished ceiling. The following costs include ceiling finish only. For more detailed costs, see Ceiling Table page B-9.

TYPE	LOW	FAIR	AVG.	GOOD	V.GOOD	EXCL.
Plaster, painted	$ .70	$ .76	$ .83	$ .97	$1.06	$1.15
Drywall, painted	.62	.66	.71	.81	.87	.93
Plywood, softwood	.77	.87	.98	1.25	1.41	1.59
Acoustic tile (furred)	.98	1.06	1.16	1.36	1.48	1.61

Basement Stairways . . . Apply cost to each stairway. The following costs include the materials and labor for typical stairway.

TYPE	LOW	FAIR	AVG.	GOOD	V.GOOD	EXCL.
Unfinished, open riser	$ 200	$ 220	$ 240	$ 280	$ 305	$ 335
Finished	325	360	400	490	540	600

Basement Outside Entrance . . . Apply cost to each entrance. Below grade entrance includes excavation, walls, stairs and door. Above grade entrance includes sliding glass door access to yard.

TYPE	LOW	FAIR	AVG.	GOOD	V.GOOD	EXCL.
Below grade	$ 490	$ 535	$ 580	$ 690	$ 750	$ 820
Above grade	350	395	445	570	640	725

Note: **Basement Garages:** When appropriate, add for mechanical ventilation from Heating and Cooling Table. For fire sprinklers add $ .90 to $1.40 per sq. ft. of floor area.

FLOOR STRUCTURE . . . Apply cost to individual floor areas. Costs include basic floor frame, joists, bridging and sheathing or concrete slab floor structure. Costs vary by the size and spacing of the joists and beams, the thickness of the sheathing or slab and amount of preparation and reinforcing.

TYPE	LOW	FAIR	AVG.	GOOD	V.GOOD	EXCL.
Concrete: slab on grade	$1.27	$1.34	$1.42	$1.59	$1.78	$1.99
Elevated flat slab and joists	3.93	4.07	4.23	4.54	4.88	5.25
Cored plank on bearing walls	2.99	3.10	3.22	3.47	3.73	4.02
Steel joists: wood sheathing	3.00	3.13	3.27	3.55	3.87	4.21
Wood: joists and sheathing	2.27	2.43	2.60	2.98	3.41	3.91
Add for vapor barrier	$ .15	$ .18	$ .21	$ .29	$ .40	$ .55
Insulation	.24	.26	.29	.35	.43	.52
Foamed conc. surfacing	.32	.35	.38	.44	.52	.61

page B-7

Segregated Costs
Floor Finishes.
Masonry Exterior Walls

FLOOR . . . EXTERIOR WALL

FLOOR COVER . . . Apply to described floor. Costs vary by quantity, coloring, pattern, amount of coving and thickness of the cover. See Section C for other types.

TYPE	LOW	FAIR	AVG.	GOOD	V.GOOD	EXCL.
Asphalt tile	$ .55	$ .60	$ .65	$ .76	$ .83	$ .90
Carpet and pad	1.15	1.37	1.65	2.30	2.75	3.30
Hardwood	2.40	2.65	2.95	3.55	3.95	4.35
Linoleum	.95	1.06	1.16	1.43	1.60	1.75
Slate	4.35	4.70	5.10	5.95	6.45	7.00
Softwood	1.50	1.65	1.80	2.15	2.35	2.55
Terrazzo (exclusive of base slab)	2.70	3.10	3.50	4.60	5.25	6.00
Tile, ceramic or quarry	3.40	3.75	4.10	4.95	5.40	5.95
Wood over concrete, Hardwood	2.55	2.85	3.20	4.05	4.60	5.15
Parquet blocks, in mastic	2.45	2.70	3.00	3.60	4.00	4.40
Vinyl asbestos tile	.65	.70	.77	.92	1.01	1.10
Vinyl or rubber sheet	1.20	1.35	1.51	1.90	2.15	2.40
Vinyl tile	1.10	1.28	1.48	2.00	2.30	2.70

EXTERIOR WALL . . . Apply costs to lineal feet of exterior wall. The following costs include exterior finish, wall structure, interior finish, sash and exterior doors. The rating choice will depend mainly on the type and quality of the openings. Costs will include terior facing and finish and the amount and quality of the interior and exterior some ornamentation on the street exposure commensurate with the quality. Major ornamentation to be added separately from Section C. For common wall area of attached dwellings use the appropriate masonry or wood frame common wall cost.
Masonry:
First story wall costs per lineal foot of perimeter (ceiling height, eight feet.)

TYPE	LOW	FAIR	AVG.	GOOD	V.GOOD	EXCL.
Adobe block	$52.34	$57.42	$62.98	$75.79	$83.14	$91.20
Common brick, 8"	$69.98	74.47	79.24	89.73	95.48	101.60
block back-up, 8"	60.41	64.23	68.29	77.21	82.09	87.28
cavity, blk. back-up, 9"-10"	65.38	70.42	75.85	87.99	94.77	102.08
Concrete block, 8"	51.70	55.27	59.09	67.54	72.21	77.20
Stone, rubble veneer, 8"	74.52	81.29	88.68	105.54	115.13	125.60
ashlar veneer, 8"	87.48	95.20	103.60	122.68	133.50	145.28
Add for face brick	$ 7.85	$ 8.51	$ 9.22	$10.83	$11.74	$12.72
Insulation	2.03	2.43	2.90	4.14	4.95	5.92
Common wall	$24.64	$27.12	$29.86	$36.17	$39.82	$43.83

Multistory wall cost adjustment . . . For each foot of additional height above first story, add to the first story exterior wall costs as follows:

TYPE	LOW	FAIR	AVG.	GOOD	V.GOOD	EXCL.
Adobe block	$5.77	$6.32	$6.93	$8.33	$9.13	$10.01
Common brick, 8"	7.72	8.21	8.73	9.86	10.49	11.15
block back-up, 8"	6.66	7.08	7.52	8.49	9.02	9.58
cavity, blk. back-up, 9"-10"	7.21	7.76	8.35	9.67	10.41	11.20
Concrete block, 8"	5.70	6.09	6.50	7.42	7.93	8.47
Stone, rubble veneer, 8"	8.22	8.96	9.76	11.60	12.64	13.78
ashlar veneer, 8"	9.64	10.48	11.40	13.48	14.66	15.94
Add for face brick	$ .87	$ .94	$1.02	$1.19	$1.29	$ 1.40
Insulation	.22	.26	.32	.45	.54	.65
Common wall	$3.08	$3.35	$3.65	$4.33	$4.71	$ 5.13

GABLE WALL . . . Cost per square foot of gable wall. The following costs include gable wall structure and exterior finish only. For gable areas with interior finish use multistory costs above. For wood frame gable area use table on page B-9.

TYPE	LOW	FAIR	AVG.	GOOD	V.GOOD	EXCL.
Adobe block	$4.39	$4.81	$5.27	$6.32	$6.92	$7.58
Common brick, 8"	5.88	6.25	6.64	7.49	7.95	8.45
block back-up, 8"	5.07	5.38	5.71	6.44	6.84	7.26
cavity, blk. back-up, 9"-10"	5.49	5.90	6.35	7.34	7.89	8.49
Concrete block, 8"	4.34	4.63	4.95	5.63	6.01	6.42
Concrete, formed	4.86	5.25	5.68	6.64	7.18	7.76
Stone, rubble veneer, 8"	6.26	6.82	7.42	8.80	9.59	10.44
ashlar veneer, 8"	7.35	7.98	8.67	10.24	11.12	12.08
Add for face brick	$ .66	$ .71	$ .77	$ .91	$ .98	$1.06
Insulation	.17	.20	.24	.35	.42	.50

page B-8

EXTERIOR WALL

Segregated Costs
Wood Frame,
Exterior Wall

EXTERIOR WALL (CONT'D)
Wood Frame:
First story wall costs per lineal foot of perimeter (ceiling height, eight feet.)

TYPE	LOW	FAIR	AVG.	GOOD	V.GOOD	EXCL.
Aluminum siding	$38.84	$42.19	$45.84	$54.09	$58.77	$63.84
Asbestos siding	36.18	38.90	41.83	48.37	52.01	55.92
Hardboard sheet, embossed	36.10	38.95	42.02	48.92	52.78	56.95
Hardboard siding, horizontal	38.46	41.56	44.90	52.42	56.64	61.20
Plywood, textured	37.39	40.45	43.69	51.06	55.20	59.67
Shingles or shakes, wood	40.43	43.65	47.12	54.92	59.29	64.01
Stucco	40.36	43.80	47.62	56.20	61.04	66.31
Wood siding	41.34	44.94	48.84	57.71	62.73	68.18
Veneer, common brick	51.19	55.71	60.62	71.80	78.13	85.03
face brick	57.89	63.17	68.93	82.07	89.55	97.72
Add for sheathing	71.14	77.38	84.17	99.58	108.31	117.81
Insulation	$ 2.74	$ 3.10	$ 3.50	$ 4.47	$ 5.01	$ 5.70
Common wall	1.44	1.68	1.95	2.64	3.08	3.58
	$19.68	$20.77	$21.91	$24.39	$25.74	$27.16

Multistory wall cost adjustment . . . For each foot of additional height above first story, add to the first story exterior wall costs as follows:

TYPE	LOW	FAIR	AVG.	GOOD	V.GOOD	EXCL.
Aluminum siding	$4.28	$4.65	$5.04	$5.94	$6.45	$7.00
Asbestos siding	3.98	4.28	4.60	5.31	5.70	6.13
Hardboard sheet, embossed	3.97	4.28	4.62	5.37	5.79	6.24
Hardboard siding, horizontal	4.23	4.57	4.93	5.76	6.21	6.71
Plywood, textured	4.12	4.45	4.81	5.61	6.06	6.54
Shingles or shakes, wood	4.45	4.80	5.18	6.03	6.51	7.02
Stucco	4.44	4.82	5.23	6.17	6.70	7.27
Wood siding	4.55	4.94	5.37	6.33	6.88	7.47
Veneer, common brick	5.64	6.13	6.67	7.88	8.57	9.32
face brick	6.37	6.95	7.57	9.01	9.82	10.71
Add for sheathing	7.83	8.51	9.25	10.93	11.89	12.92
Insulation	$ .30	$ .34	$ .38	$ .49	$ .55	$ .62
Common wall	.16	.19	.22	.29	.34	.39
	$2.46	$2.55	$2.65	$2.86	$2.97	$3.08

GABLE WALL . . . Cost per square foot of gable wall. The following costs include gable wall structure and exterior finish only. For gable areas with interior finish use multistory costs above.

TYPE	LOW	FAIR	AVG.	GOOD	V.GOOD	EXCL.
Aluminum siding	$2.39	$2.59	$2.81	$3.31	$3.59	$3.89
Asbestos siding	2.22	2.38	2.56	2.95	3.17	3.40
Hardboard sheet, embossed	2.21	2.38	2.57	2.99	3.22	3.47
Hardboard siding, horizontal	2.37	2.56	2.76	3.21	3.46	3.73
Plywood, textured	2.30	2.49	2.68	3.12	3.36	3.63
Shingles or shakes, wood	2.49	2.68	2.89	3.36	3.62	3.90
Stucco	2.48	2.69	2.92	3.43	3.72	4.04
Wood siding	2.54	2.76	2.99	3.52	3.82	4.15
Veneer, common brick	3.28	3.56	3.87	4.57	4.96	5.39
face brick	3.70	4.03	4.39	5.21	5.68	6.19
Add for sheathing	4.55	4.94	5.37	6.33	6.88	7.47
Insulation	$ .17	$ .19	$ .22	$ .28	$ .31	$ .35
	.09	.10	.12	.16	.19	.22

Note: For parapets finished on both sides, add 35% to Gable Wall cost.

MISCELLANEOUS WALLS . . . Cost per square foot of exterior wall area.

TYPE	LOW	FAIR	AVG.	GOOD	V.GOOD	EXCL.
Asbestos cement, sandwich panel	$5.03	$5.60	$6.23	$7.73	$8.60	$9.58
Board and batten, box frame	3.86	4.23	4.63	5.55	6.07	6.65
Log rustic	5.68	6.41	7.23	9.21	10.39	11.73
Deduct for lack of interior finish	$ .56	$ .65	$ .74	$ .99	$1.14	$1.31

page B-9

Segregated Costs
Ceiling, Roof

CEILING. . .ROOF

CEILING . . . Apply cost to total floor area. The following costs include finished ceiling only and do not include the supporting structure since in most cases the ceiling is attached to the structure of the floor or roof joists above. If a separate structure is necessary, its cost must be added. Ceiling cost variations are influenced by thickness, materials used, method and application, and in the case of ornamented ceilings, the type of ornamentation, the intricacy of the design, and the finish. Acoustic ceiling costs vary with the material, method of attachment, type of suspension and supporting structure.

TYPE	LOW	FAIR	AVG.	GOOD	V.GOOD	EXCL
Drywall, taped and painted	$ .62	$ .66	.71	$ .81	$ .87	$ .93
Spray-on, thin-coat w/texture	.57	.60	.64	.71	.75	.79
Paint only, exposed beam	.28	.31	.34	.41	.45	.50
Plaster on lath, acoustical	.94	1.03	1.13	1.36	1.50	1.64
Spray-on, thin-coat w/texture	.64	.67	.71	.79	.83	.88
Standard, add 10% for Keene's	.75	.83	.93	1.15	1.28	1.42
Add for metal lath	.05	.06	.07	.11	.13	.16
Plaster on masonry, acoustical	.84	.91	.99	1.16	1.26	1.36
Spray-on, thin-coat w/texture	.54	.57	.61	.68	.72	.77
Standard, add 10% for Keene's	.66	.72	.79	.94	1.03	1.12
Plastic panels, with suspension system						
excluding lighting (in electrical cost)	2.15	2.37	2.60	3.15	3.48	3.82
Plywood, hardwood	1.25	1.39	1.55	1.91	2.13	2.37
Softwood	.77	.87	.98	1.25	1.41	1.59
Tile, acoustic, fiberglass	.85	.92	1.00	1.18	1.28	1.39
Wood or cane fiber	.69	.74	.80	.92	.99	1.06
Add for insulation	$ .20	$ .23	$ .26	$ .33	$ .38	.43
Suspended ceiling system	.56	.63	.70	.88		1.10
Wood furring	.29	.32	.36	.44	.49	.55
Metal furring	.42	.48	.56	.74	.86	.98

ROOF STRUCTURE AND COVER . . . Apply costs to ground floor area. Roof structure includes joists, rafters, purlins, and sheathing or deck together with necessary bracing and ties. Roof cover includes the roofing and necessary roof flashing, gravel stops, gutters, etc. Cost variations are affected by the size and spacing of the structural members, the thickness and quality of the sheathing, and the thickness and quality of the cover. The steepness, the amount of overhang, and the complexity of the roof are also cost considerations. Very large overhangs may be computed separately.

With Ceiling Joists . . . The following costs include ceiling joists, roof frame, 1" sheathing and roofing. Adjust by roof slope multipliers on top of following page.

TYPE	LOW	FAIR	AVG.	GOOD	V.GOOD	EXCL
Asphalt shingle	$2.97	$3.16	$3.36	$3.81	$4.31	$4.88
Built-up, rock	3.07	3.27	3.48	3.95	4.47	5.07
Composition, roll	2.79	2.95	3.12	3.49	3.90	4.36
Wood shingle	3.68	3.87	4.06	4.48	4.95	5.46
Rigid asbestos shingle	3.69	3.93	4.19	4.77	5.42	6.16
Wood shakes	3.78	4.00	4.23	4.72	5.28	5.90
Clay (mission tile)	4.22	4.55	4.90	5.70	6.62	7.69
Concrete tile (lightweight)	3.67	3.93	4.21	4.82	5.52	6.33
Slate	4.79	5.09	5.41	6.12	6.92	7.82

With Exposed Beam Ceiling . . . The following costs include heavy roof frame, 2" sheathing, roofing and insulation. Adjust by roof slope multipliers on top of following page.

TYPE	LOW	FAIR	AVG.	GOOD	V.GOOD	EXCL
Asphalt shingle	$3.23	$3.46	$3.70	$4.23	$4.84	$5.54
Built-up, rock	3.32	3.55	3.80	4.34	4.97	5.68
Composition, roll	3.06	3.25	3.45	3.90	4.40	4.97
Wood shingle	3.95	4.17	4.40	4.90	5.45	6.07
Rigid asbestos shingle	3.96	4.23	4.53	5.18	5.92	6.77
Wood shakes	4.05	4.31	4.59	5.21	5.91	6.70
Clay (mission) tile	4.48	4.84	5.23	6.10	7.11	8.30
Concrete tile (lightweight)	3.78	4.08	4.40	5.12	5.96	6.94
Slate	5.05	5.39	5.75	6.54	7.44	8.46

ROOF. . .INTERIOR. . .MECHANICAL

Segregated Costs
Roof, Dormers, Interior
Construction, Heating-Cooling

ROOF (CONT'D)

Roof slope multipliers:

	Rise		Run	Multiplier	Rise		Run	Multiplier
Less than	3	in	12	1.00	6	in	12	1.12
	3	in	12	1.03	8	in	12	1.20
	4	in	12	1.06	12	in	12	1.42
	5	in	12	1.08	18	in	12	1.80

ROOF DORMERS . . . Apply costs to lineal feet, measured across face of dormer. Do not include sides. Costs are for dormer frame, exterior finish and finish. Interior finish cost for dormers is automatically computed from floor, ceiling and other segregated cost tables if dormer floor area is included in total residence floor area.

TYPE	LOW	FAIR	AVG.	GOOD	V.GOOD	EXCL.
Hip or gable roof	$43.00	$48.00	$53.75	$67.00	$84.00	$105.00
Shed roof	35.50	39.75	44.50	55.75	70.00	87.75

ROOF STRUCTURE - ALTERNATE TABLE . . . Apply costs to roof area if preceding roof structure and cover tables on page B-10 are not used. Add for appropriate roof cover from Section C.

TYPE	LOW	FAIR	AVG.	GOOD	V.GOOD	EXCL.
Concrete: precast joists and deck	$3.65	$3.81	$3.97	$4.32	$4.00	$5.11
Cored plank on bearing walls	2.91	3.03	3.16	3.43	3.72	4.04
Steel joists: wood sheathing	2.82	2.95	3.08	3.37	3.69	4.03
Wood: joists and sheathing	2.46	2.60	2.76	3.09	3.46	3.87
Exposed rafters, 2" T&G sheathing	2.72	2.84	2.96	3.22	3.51	3.82

INTERIOR CONSTRUCTION . . . Apply cost to total finished floor area. The following costs include drywall interior partitions, finish, interior doors and cabinet work commensurate with the quality. Cost variations will depend upon amount and qualities encountered. If basements have interior construction similar to the floors above, this table can be used, usually with a lower rating.

TYPE	LOW	FAIR	AVG.	GOOD	V.GOOD	EXCL.
One Story	$5.00	$5.56	$6.18	$7.64	$8.50	$9.45
Split Level	4.83	5.35	5.93	7.28	8.06	8.93
Two Story	4.65	5.13	5.65	6.88	7.58	8.36
One & One-Half Story, finished	4.70	5.19	5.73	6.98	7.71	8.51
One & One-Half Story, unfin.	5.26	5.83	6.46	7.93	8.78	9.73
Multiple Residence	5.73	6.24	6.80	8.06	8.78	9.56
Town or Row House						
One Story	5.63	6.10	6.62	7.78	8.43	9.14
Multi-Story	5.41	5.82	6.27	7.26	7.81	8.41
Cabins	3.45	3.83	4.25	5.24	5.81	6.45
Add for plaster walls	$ .47	$ .50	$ .53	$ .61	$ .65	$ .69

Note: For masonry partition walls, add 6% for residences and 10% for row houses and multiples.

HEATING AND COOLING . . . Apply costs to total floor area being heated and cooled. The basic heating units include boilers, pumps, piping and ducts, registers, operating motors and fans. Costs are primarily dependent on the climate and the type of wall and insulation which affect the capacity of the central unit. The complexity and number of outlets also affect the cost. Air conditioning costs, in addition, are dependent somewhat on prevailing humidity for atmospheric coolers. The lowest priced installations would normally be in a mild climate, while the highest priced systems would be found in the best buildings in a cold climate or a hot humid climate with respect to air conditioning. In selecting a proper cost for basement heating, it is important to remember that a minimal amount of outlets would be incidental to the overall cost of the system. Air conditioning requirements per ton for residential occupancies range from 450 to 750 square feet.

MECHANICAL . . . ELECTRICAL

Segregated Costs
Heating-Cooling,
Electrical

HEATING AND COOLING (CONT'D)

Apply costs based on climate, to total floor area being heated and cooled. Add 7% to gas heating systems if oil fired.

TYPE: HEATING ONLY	LOW	FAIR	AVG.	GOOD	V.GOOD	EXCL.
Forced air furnace, electric	$1.06	$1.28	$1.55	$1.71	$1.88	$2.27
Forced air furnace, gas	.95	1.15	1.39	1.53	1.68	2.03
Gas outlets only	.21	.24	.27	.28	.30	.34
Glass panel, electric	.86	1.04	1.26	1.39	1.53	1.86
Gravity furnace, gas	.88	1.07	1.29	1.42	1.56	1.89
Floor or wall furnace	.56	.63	.71	.75	.80	.90
Baseboard, electric	.84	1.03	1.26	1.39	1.64	1.88
Baseboard, hot water, gas	1.52	1.83	2.20	2.42	2.65	3.19
Baseboard, steam, gas	1.45	1.72	2.03	2.21	2.41	2.85
Radiators, hot water, gas	1.50	1.80	2.16	2.37	2.59	3.11
Radiators, steam, gas	1.20	1.44	1.74	1.90	2.09	2.51
Floor radiant, hot water, gas	2.18	2.58	3.04	3.31	3.60	4.25
Ceiling radiant, electric	.93	1.14	1.40	1.55	1.72	2.11
Wall heaters, electric	.43	.50	.58	.62	.67	.78

COOLING ONLY	LOW	FAIR	AVG.	GOOD	V.GOOD	EXCL.
Evaporative, w/ducts	$ .77	$ .88	$1.00	$1.07	$1.14	$1.30
Refrig. A/C, w/ducts	1.18	1.49	1.89	2.12	2.39	3.02

COMBINED HEATING & COOLING	LOW	FAIR	AVG.	GOOD	V.GOOD	EXCL.
Warm and cooled air	$1.85	$2.30	$2.87	$3.20	$3.57	$4.45
Heat pump system	1.91	2.33	2.85	3.15	3.49	4.26

VENTILATION ONLY	LOW	FAIR	AVG.	GOOD	V.GOOD	EXCL.
Blowers and ducts	$ .28	$ .33	$ .40	$ .43	$ .47	$ .56

WINDOW UNITS . . . Window type refrigerated coolers range in cost from $500 to $700 per ton capacity, including installation, depending upon size, type and local sources of supply. Evaporative coolers range in cost from $70 to $90 per thousand CFM of rated capacity. In determining ton capacity, a one horsepower motor produces approximately one ton of cooling. Add wiring allowance of $110 for 220 volt units. Small individual heat pumps cost $525 to $750 per ton of rated capacity.

UNIT HEATING . . . Suspended space heaters range in cost from $11.00 to $15.00 per thousand B.T.U. of rated capacity.

SOLAR HEATING . . . Every application must be examined for its own special design costs, locational considerations, varying capacity requirements, numerous absorption systems, the different mediums and storage facilities employed and for any conventional back up systems involved.

In general, residential systems have ranged from $3.50 a square foot for a simple corrugated steel, rock and warm air system to $10.00 and up for sophisticated systems with glass or plastic collectors, hot water storage and circulation, and the best control equipment.

ELECTRICAL . . . Apply cost to total floor area. Costs include house service, wiring and light fixtures commensurate with quality. Costs are rated according to the quality of the fixtures, number of outlets and type of wiring. The costs per square foot by occupancy represents a typical electrical cost range for each occupancy at the various quantity levels.

TYPE	LOW	FAIR	AVG.	GOOD	V.GOOD	EXCL.
Romex (non-metallic sheathing) or knob and tube	$ .93	$1.14	$1.40	$2.09	$2.56	$3.14
B.X. (steel armored cable)	1.10	1.34	1.63	2.42	2.95	3.60
Flex (flexible steel conduit)	1.29	1.57	1.90	2.80	3.40	4.12
Rigid conduit	1.52	1.85	2.25	3.34	4.07	4.95
Cost per square foot, residences	$ .95	$1.20	$1.52	$2.43	$3.06	$3.87
Multiple Residences	1.37	1.69	1.92	2.69	3.18	3.77
Town or Row Houses	.99	1.22	1.50	2.27	2.80	3.44
Unfinished Areas	$ .31	$ .37	$ .45	$ .66	$ .80	$ .97

page B-12

PLUMBING . . . BUILT-INS

Segregated Costs
Plumbing, Fireplaces,
Built-in Appliances, Stairways

PLUMBING . . . Apply costs to each plumbing fixture including water heater as one fixture. The following costs include rough plumbing, fixtures, installation and a normal amount of additional connecting pipe. The costs per square foot represent a typical plumbing cost range for each occupancy. Costs should be based mainly on the quality of fixtures if cost per fixture is used. If the cost per square foot is used, the number of fixtures and quality of fixtures must be considered.

UNIT	LOW	FAIR	AVG.	GOOD	V.GOOD	EXCL.
Cost per fixture	$ 300	$ 360	$ 430	$ 610	$ 730	$ 875
Cost, rough-in only	110	125	140	175	200	225
drains and hydrants	50	55	65	85	100	115
Cost per square foot, residences	$1.45	$1.79	$2.22	$3.39	$4.19	$5.18
Multiple Residences	1.78	2.11	2.50	3.52	4.17	4.95
Town or Row Houses	1.47	1.80	2.21	3.31	4.06	4.97

FIREPLACES . . . Apply cost to each fireplace. The following costs include complete fireplace. Double fireplaces are back-to-back or one directly above the other, using a common chimney. Residences with basements, add 40%. Steel, with flue, is the prefabricated hanging or free-standing type fireplace or stove.

TYPE	LOW	FAIR	AVG.	GOOD	V.GOOD	EXCL.
Single, one story	$ 825	$ 975	$1,125	$1,525	$1,800	$2,100
Single, two story	1,075	1,250	1,450	1,925	2,250	2,600
Double, one story	1,150	1,350	1,575	2,175	2,550	3,000
Double, two story	1,400	1,625	1,900	2,600	3,000	3,600
Steel, with flue	500	575	700	950	1,100	1,300
Add for Heatilator type	$ 150	$ 170	$ 195	$ 250	$ 280	$ 320
Raised Hearth	80	100	125	185	230	280
Log Lighter	45	55	65	85	100	120

BUILT-IN APPLIANCES . . . Apply cost to each built-in appliance. Costs include installation, extra utility outlets and cabinet work as applicable except for free-standing appliances.

APPLIANCE	LOW	FAIR	AVG.	GOOD	V.GOOD	EXCL.
Range & oven combination, gas	$ 350	$ 395	$ 445	$ 565	$ 640	$ 720
Range top, gas	180	200	225	275	305	340
Oven, gas	330	360	400	480	530	580
Add for electric appliances		30	40	50	60	70
Oven, electronic microwave	375	415	465	575	645	715
Range fan and hood	95	110	135	170	200	225
Exhaust fan		65	75	95	105	120
Refrigerator-freezer (built-in)	450	505	565	715	800	900
Dishwasher	340	370	405	485	530	580
Mixer-blender (food center)	120	125	135	150	160	170
Garbage disposer	120	135	150	185	205	230
Radio-intercom	200	225	255	325	365	415
Add per satellite	35	40	45	60	70	80
Gas incinerator	375	400	430	490	525	560
Vacuum cleaner system, 3 outlets	770	800	840	915	955	1,000
Add for extra outlets	100	105	115	130	140	150
Bathroom heater, electric	60	70	80	105	120	140
Trash compactor	300	320	345	395	420	450

FREE STANDING APPLIANCES	LOW	FAIR	AVG.	GOOD	V.GOOD	EXCL.
Refrigerator	$ 265	$ 320	$ 390	$ 575	$ 710	$ 850
Washer	250	285	325	425	480	550
Dryer, electric	150	180	225	315	380	450
Add for gas dryer	30	35	35	40	45	50

STAIRWAYS . . . Apply cost to each full flight of stairs. The following costs include stair framing, finish and railings. For partial flights, use proportionate cost.

FRAME - FINISH	LOW	FAIR	AVG.	GOOD	V.GOOD	EXCL.
Interior: Softwood	$ 500	$ 575	$ 660	$ 870	$1,000	$1,150
Hardwood	625	750	890	1,265	1,510	1,800
Disappearing attic	120	135	150	190	215	240
Metal, spiral	1,600	1,750	1,925	2,325	2,550	2,800
Exterior: Softwood	$ 325	$ 375	$ 435	$ 580	$ 670	$ 775
Wood-cement compo.	575	650	730	930	1,045	1,180
Steel pans/prefab. conc. on steel	650	745	860	1,135	1,305	1,500

page B-13

GARAGES

Segregated Costs
Attached, Detached,
Built-in

Garages for residences and multiple dwellings have a relatively low cost in relation to the living units and their construction is not usually complicated by plumbing, heating, etc. For this reason, they can easily be priced from Section A. If greater detail is needed or a garage is of extraordinary construction, has interior finish, plumbing, or built-in features, it may be priced from the Segregated components in this section and Section C.

GARAGE FOUNDATION . . . Apply costs to lineal feet of exterior wall. Do not apply to built-in garages.

TYPE	LOW	FAIR	AVG.	GOOD	V.GOOD	EXCL.
Frame-stucco or siding	$3.45	$3.76	$4.11	$4.89	$5.34	$5.83
Masonry & masonry veneer	4.09	4.45	4.85	5.75	6.26	6.82

GARAGE EXTERIOR WALL . . . Apply costs to lineal feet of all exterior wall except that which is common with residence.
Masonry:

TYPE	LOW	FAIR	AVG.	GOOD	V.GOOD	EXCL.
Adobe block	$28.79	$30.98	$33.35	$38.63	$41.57	$44.74
Common brick, 8"	38.49	40.14	41.86	45.52	47.47	49.50
block back-up, 8"	33.23	34.66	36.16	39.35	41.05	42.82
cavity, blk. back-up, 9"-10"	35.96	38.00	40.16	44.84	47.39	50.08
Concrete block, 8"	28.44	29.83	31.29	34.43	36.11	37.88
Stone, rubble veneer	40.99	43.87	46.96	53.79	57.57	61.62
ashlar veneer	48.14	51.39	54.86	62.53	66.75	71.26
Add for face brick	$ 4.32	$ 4.59	$ 4.88	$ 5.52	$ 5.87	$ 6.24

Wood Frame:

TYPE	LOW	FAIR	AVG.	GOOD	V.GOOD	EXCL.
Aluminum siding	$23.30	$24.41	$25.57	$28.06	$29.39	$30.78
Asbestos siding	21.71	22.51	23.34	25.09	26.01	26.97
Hardboard sheet, embossed	21.66	22.53	23.44	25.37	26.39	27.45
Hardboard siding, horizontal	23.08	24.04	25.05	27.19	28.32	29.50
Plywood, textured	22.44	23.39	24.38	26.48	27.60	28.77
Shingles or shakes, wood	24.26	25.25	26.29	28.48	29.65	30.86
Stucco	24.22	25.37	26.57	29.14	30.52	31.96
Wood siding	24.80	25.99	27.24	29.93	31.37	32.88
Veneer, common brick	30.17	31.11	32.07	34.10	35.16	36.25
face brick	34.73	35.78	36.86	39.12	40.30	41.52
stone	42.68	43.83	45.01	47.46	48.74	50.05
Add for sheathing	$ 1.64	$ 1.79	1.95	$ 2.31	$ 2.52	$ 2.75
Insulation	.86	.97	1.09	1.37	1.54	1.73

Garage Wall Interior Finish . . . If interior of garage wall is finished, add to above exterior wall cost from this table.

TYPE	LOW	FAIR	AVG.	GOOD	V.GOOD	EXCL.
Plaster, painted	$5.97	$6.37	$6.80	$7.73	$8.25	$8.80
Drywall, painted	4.65	5.01	5.39	6.25	6.73	7.24
Plywood, painted	5.12	5.50	5.90	6.80	7.30	7.83
Hardboard, painted	5.02	5.37	5.74	6.57	7.02	7.50

GARAGE FLOOR . . . Apply cost to floor area. If residence or apartment has a built-in garage with living area above, use the following table to determine the cost of the floor and supporting columns. Add for exterior wall, wall interior finish and ceiling finish from appropriate garage cost tables. Do not include garage foundation. Cost for foundation is included in residence foundation cost.

TYPE	LOW	FAIR	AVG.	GOOD	V.GOOD	EXCL.
Concrete floor	$ .92	$1.04	$1.17	$1.48	$1.67	$1.88
Asphalt floor	.50	.58	.66	.88	1.01	1.16
Built-in garage supporting columns	$ .31	$ .33	$ .36	$ .41	$ .44	$ .47

Segregated Costs
Balconies, Attics,
Porches

PORCHES

BALCONIES OR STAIR LANDINGS . . . Apply cost to floor area.

QUALITY	WOOD FLOOR		CEMENT COMPOSITION FLOOR	
	WOOD RAIL	ORN. IRON RAIL	WOOD RAIL	ORN. IRON RAIL
Low	$ 6.55	$ 8.45	$ 7.80	$ 9.80
Fair	7.15	9.20	8.45	10.60
Average	7.80	10.00	9.15	11.45
Good	9.25	11.85	10.80	13.40
Very Good	10.10	12.85	11.70	14.50
Excellent	11.00	14.00	12.70	15.65

Note: Add for balcony roofs and ceiling or soffit finish from porch roof tables below.

ATTICS . . . Attic finish may be priced from the appropriate Segregated components or Unit-in-Place Cost tables or from the following cost range below computed on square foot of floor area. Costs include softwood floor cover and stairway, drywall ceiling, and minimum electrical. Plumbing and partition walls are not included and may be added from Section C.

	LOW	FAIR	AVG.	GOOD	V.GOOD	EXCL.
Attic Finish	$2.55	$2.84	$3.17	$3.94	$4.39	$4.89

PORCHES . . . Apply all component costs to porch floor area.

Open Concrete Porches - Including Perimeter Foundation

QUALITY	25 SQ. FT.		100 SQ. FT.		200 SQ. FT.	
	WITH STEPS	SLAB	WITH STEPS	SLAB	WITH STEPS	SLAB
Low	$4.80	$1.62	$4.02	$1.43	$3.78	$1.35
Fair	5.22	1.75	4.32	1.53	4.06	1.45
Average	5.60	1.89	4.63	1.63	4.36	1.54
Good	6.46	2.20	5.34	1.85	5.04	1.74
Very Good	6.94	2.37	5.73	1.97	5.41	1.85
Excellent	7.45	2.56	6.15	2.10	5.81	1.97

Note: Use $1.20 per square foot for slab porches or patios without perimeter foundation.

Open Wood Porches or Decks - With Wood Steps

QUALITY	25 SQ. FT.	100 SQ. FT.	200 SQ. FT.	300 SQ. FT.
Low	$6.50	$5.45	$4.72	$4.13
Fair	7.22	6.08	5.27	4.61
Average	8.02	6.78	5.89	5.14
Good	9.90	8.43	7.36	6.41
Very Good	11.00	9.40	8.22	7.15
Excellent	12.22	10.48	9.18	7.98

Note: Increase cost 5% for each foot of height above 3 feet.

Add For Porch Roof and Posts - (No Ceiling Included)

TYPE	LOW	FAIR	AVG.	GOOD	V.GOOD	EXCL.
Asphalt shingle	$2.85	$3.11	3.35	$3.90	$4.21	$4.54
Built-up, rock	2.98	3.21	3.46	4.03	4.34	4.68
Composition, roll	2.71	2.90	3.10	3.54	3.78	4.04
Wood shingle	3.57	3.79	4.02	4.52	4.80	5.09
Rigid asbestos shingle	3.58	3.87	4.18	4.87	5.26	5.68
Wood shakes	3.67	3.92	4.19	4.79	5.12	5.47
Clay (mission) tile	4.09	4.48	4.90	5.87	6.42	7.03
Concrete tile (lightweight)	3.56	3.86	4.19	4.93	5.35	5.08
Slate	4.65	5.00	5.38	6.24	6.71	7.22

Note: For pitched roof, use residence roof slope multipliers.

Add For Porch Ceiling or Soffit Finish

TYPE	LOW	FAIR	AVG.	GOOD	V.GOOD	EXCL.
Plaster	$ .88	$ .99	$1.11	$1.41	$1.58	$1.78
Wood, painted	1.01	1.13	1.26	1.56	1.74	1.94
Hardboard, painted	.91	1.03	1.15	1.47	1.65	1.86

Segregated Costs
Basement Garages,
Carports

GARAGES ... CARPORTS

GARAGE (CONT'D)

GARAGE ROOF . . . Apply costs to ground floor.

TYPE	LOW	FAIR	AVG.	GOOD	V.GOOD	EXCL.
Asphalt shingle	$2.22	$2.45	$2.71	$3.31	$3.66	$4.04
Built-up, rock	2.30	2.61	2.81	3.44	3.88	4.20
Composition, roll	2.09	2.29	2.52	3.03	3.32	3.64
Wood shingle	2.76	3.00	3.27	3.87	4.21	4.58
Rigid asbestos shingle	2.77	3.07	3.40	4.16	4.61	5.10
Wood shakes	2.83	3.10	3.40	4.09	4.49	4.92
Clay (mission) tile	3.17	3.56	3.99	5.02	5.63	6.32
Concrete tile (lightweight)	2.75	3.06	3.40	4.22	4.69	5.22
Slate	3.59	3.96	4.37	5.33	5.88	6.49

Note: *For pitched roof, use residence roof slope multipliers on page B-11.*

Garage Ceiling . . . If garage has a finished ceiling add to above garage roof cost from this table. Costs include ceiling joist allowance.

TYPE	LOW	FAIR	AVG.	GOOD	V.GOOD	EXCL.
Plaster, painted	$1.05	$1.11	$1.17	$1.31	$1.39	$1.47
Drywall, painted	.97	1.02	1.07	1.19	1.25	1.31
Plywood, painted	1.12	1.21	1.30	1.51	1.62	1.75
Hardboard, painted	1.08	1.16	1.25	1.45	1.56	1.68

BASEMENT GARAGE . . . Add lump sum to unfinished residence basement cost. Costs include overhead door, partition wall, wall and ceiling finish, interior door and minimum electrical. All other components are included with the unfinished basement costs.

TYPE	LOW	FAIR	AVG.	GOOD	V.GOOD	EXCL.
Single	$ 605	$ 650	$ 700	$ 795	$ 860	$ 920
Double	735	790	855	995	1,070	1,155

CARPORTS . . . Apply costs to floor area of carport. The following costs include roofing, roof frame, supporting posts and bracing, painting, concrete slab, and enclosed storage commensurate with the quality.

TYPE	LOW	FAIR	AVG.	GOOD	V.GOOD	EXCL.
Aluminum, corrugated	$3.85	$4.29	$4.79	$5.96	$6.65	$7.41
Asphalt shingle	4.53	5.21	6.00	7.95	9.15	10.53
Built-up, rock	4.69	5.48	6.40	8.74	10.21	11.93
Composition, roll	4.45	5.12	5.89	7.80	8.97	10.32
Wood shingle	5.52	6.35	7.29	9.64	11.08	12.74
Rigid asbestos shingle	5.54	6.48	7.58	10.37	12.13	14.19
Wood shakes	5.66	6.52	7.52	9.99	11.51	13.27
Clay (mission) tile	6.47	7.60	8.92	12.30	14.44	16.96
Concrete tile (lightweight)	5.50	6.46	7.60	10.50	12.34	14.50
Slate	7.33	8.42	9.68	12.79	14.70	16.90
Deduct for asphalt floor	$ .43	$ .47	$ .51	$ .61	$ .66	$ .72

Note: *(1) For pitched roof, use residence roof slope multipliers.*
(2) Porch ceiling costs may be added to the above costs when appropriate.

COMPLETION OF BUILDING VALUATION

Contractor's overhead and profit, sales taxes, permit fees, interest on interim construction financing, and insurance during construction are included in the above costs. Not included are financing costs, real estate taxes, local jurisdictional hook-up fees, or brokers' commissions. See Introduction for further listing.

Depreciation suggestions are given in Section E.

Fire insurance exclusion suggestions based on percentages of the total cost are listed in Section D. The portion to be excluded may be deducted directly from the segregated cost components, or omitted, instead of using a percentage if appropriate.

Current Cost Multipliers and Local Multipliers which bring the basic costs up to date for each locality are found in the Green Supplement, Section F.

page B-16

CURRENT COST MULTIPLIERS

CURRENT COST MULTIPLIER . . . . Apply these multipliers to the costs on the following pages in the handbook to arrive at a current cost level.

PAGES	FRAME	MASONRY
SECTION A		
A-1 thru A-82 (Single Family Residences)		
A-113 thru A-130 (Apartments)	1.00	1.00
A-131 thru A-148 (Town Houses)		1.10
A-149 thru A-162 (Urban Row Houses)	1.06	1.07
SECTION B	1.03	1.04
B-1 thru B-13 (Segregated Costs)		
SECTION C	1.02	1.02
C-1 thru C-14 (Yard Improvements & Unit-in-Place)		
C-15 thru C-26 (Unit-in-Place & Mobile Homes)	1.14	1.16
	1.11	1.13

LOCAL MULTIPLIERS

LOCAL MULTIPLIERS . . . . Apply these multipliers to the costs in the handbook to arrive at a local cost level.

UNITED STATES

	FRAME	MASONRY		FRAME	MASONRY
ALABAMA					
ANNISTON	.93	.93	**CALIFORNIA (Cont'd)**		
AUBURN,OPELEIKA,PHENIX C.	.81	.83	HUNTINGTON-NEWPORT B.	1.12	1.13
BESSEMER	.93	.93	IMPERIAL CO.	1.13	1.14
BIRMINGHAM	.95	.95	LAGUNA-SAN CLEMENTE	1.16	1.17
DOTHAN	.83	.84	LAKE ARROWHEAD-BIG BEAR	1.16	1.17
FLORENCE	.91	.92	LAKE TAHOE	1.16	1.18
GADSDEN	.96	.96	LOS ANGELES	1.05	1.06
HUNTSVILLE	.93	.94	MADERA	1.12	1.12
MOBILE	.96	.97	MARIN CO.	1.16	1.17
MONTGOMERY	.84	.85	MARIPOSA CO.	1.12	1.14
TUSCALOOSA	.89	.90	MENDOCINO CO.	1.11	1.12
ALASKA			MERCED	1.04	1.06
ANCHORAGE			MODESTO	1.05	1.06
FAIRBANKS	1.47	1.51	MONO CO.	1.02	1.04
JUNEAU	1.59	1.61	NAPA CO.	1.15	1.16
KENAI PENINSULA	1.50	1.52	NEVADA CO.	1.17	1.18
KETCHIKAN	1.49	1.55	OAKLAND-ALAMEDA	1.14	1.16
KODIAK	1.53	1.60	ORANGE CO. (X/BEACHES)	1.15	1.17
SITKA	1.58	1.65	PALM SPRINGS-INDIO	1.12	1.12
	1.51	1.60	PASO ROBLES	1.10	1.10
ARIZONA			PLACER CO.	1.14	1.15
DOUGLAS			PASO ROBLES	1.10	1.11
FLAGSTAFF	1.04	1.05	REDDING	1.10	1.12
NOGALES	1.06	1.08	RIVERSIDE	1.10	1.11
PHOENIX	1.04	1.04	SACRAMENTO	1.11	1.11
PRESCOTT	1.05	1.06	SALINAS	1.11	1.12
TUCSON	1.06	1.07	SAN BERNARDINO	1.14	1.16
YUMA	1.04	1.04	SAN DIEGO	1.11	1.11
	1.01	1.02	SAN FRANCISCO	1.10	1.10
ARKANSAS			SAN JOSE	1.16	1.17
BLYTHEVILLE			SAN LUIS OBISPO	1.15	1.16
FAYETTEVILLE	.85	.87	SAN MATEO CO.	1.11	1.12
FORT SMITH	.88	.89	SANTA BARBARA	1.15	1.16
HOT SPRINGS	.88	.89	SANTA CLARA	1.15	1.16
JONESBORO	.88	.89	SANTA CRUZ	1.15	1.16
LITTLE ROCK	.86	.87	SANTA MARIA-LOMPOC	1.14	1.16
TEXARKANA	.87	.88	SANTA ROSA	1.11	1.12
WEST MEMPHIS	.88	.89	SOLANO CO.	1.14	1.16
	.87	.89	STOCKTON	1.14	1.14
CALIFORNIA			SUSANVILLE	1.07	1.09
ANTELOPE VALLEY			TULARE CO.	1.14	1.14
BAKERSFIELD	1.12	1.13	TUOLUMNE CO.	1.06	1.07
BARSTOW	1.13	1.13	VENTURA CO.	1.10	1.13
BISHOP-MAMMOTH LAKES	1.12	1.13	VICTORVILLE-HESPERIA	1.11	1.11
BLYTHE	1.18	1.18	YOLO CO.	1.13	1.14
BUTTE CO.	1.15	1.16	YUBA CITY-MARYSVILLE	1.09	1.10
CALAVERAS CO.	1.09	1.11		1.09	1.11
COALINGA	1.10	1.12	**COLORADO**		
CONTRA COSTA CO.	1.10	1.12	BOULDER		
EL DORADO CO.	1.15	1.17	COLORADO SPRINGS	1.01	1.02
EUREKA	1.12	1.13	DENVER	1.00	1.01
FRESNO	1.14	1.15	GRAND JUNCTION	1.02	1.03
HANFORD	1.06	1.07	GREELEY	1.01	1.02
	1.07	1.08	PUEBLO	.99	1.00

page F-2

11 Estimation of Accrued Depreciation (Diminished Utility)

Key Terms

Accrued depreciation (diminished utility) Total depreciation from all sources, measured as the difference between reproduction cost new of the improvements and the present worth of those improvements as of the date of the appraisal.

Age-life method A method of estimating physical incurable deterioration by applying the ratio of estimated effective age to typically anticipated economic life to current reproduction cost new of the improvements.

Curable depreciation Those items of physical deterioration and/or functional obsolescence whose cost to cure is equal to or less than the anticipated addition to utility.

Defect An existing component of a structure that is providing below-standard performance or causing above-normal occupancy expenses.

Deficiency An inadequacy in a structure or in any of its components.

Economic life The time period over which improvements are expected to contribute to the total value of the property.

Economic obsolescence Loss in value of a structure because of negative market economic, financial or industrial forces outside the site.

Engineering breakdown method A method of estimating accrued depreciation by which estimates are made for individual components separately and totally.

External obsolescence Loss in value from diminished utility of a structure because of negative influences (both economic and locational) outside the site.

Functional obsolescence Loss in value brought about by impairment of functional capacity or efficiency.

Incurable depreciation Those items of physical deterioration and/or functional obsolescence whose cost to cure is greater than the anticipated addition to utility.

Locational obsolescence Loss in value brought about by negative environmental forces outside the boundaries of the property.

Modified age-life method A modification of the age-life method whereby cost to cure all curable items is deducted from reproduction cost new before measuring incurable items.

Observed condition breakdown method A method of estimating accrued depreciation by separately estimating physical deterioration and functional and locational obsolescence and then summing the results.

Physical deterioration   A loss in value resulting from an impairment of physical condition.

Physical life   That period of time over which the structure is expected to continue as a functioning entity.

Superadequacy   An excess capacity or quality in a structure or in any of its components.

Useful life   That period of time over which the structure is expected to perform the function for which it was intended.

Accrued depreciation is defined as follows:

> "The difference between reproduction cost new or replacement cost new of the improvements and the present worth of those improvements, both measured as of the date of the appraisal. In measuring accrued depreciation, the appraiser is interested in identifying and measuring the loss in utility experienced by the subject structure in its present condition, as compared to the utility it would have as a new improvement representing the highest and best use of the site. Accrued depreciation is sometimes referred to as diminished utility."[1]

Accrued depreciation is not a loss in value experienced by the improvements, because cost is not equal to value nor does cost alone measure value. Accrued depreciation is not historical fact or loss from historical cost. The cost base from which accrued depreciation is measured is the reproduction cost new as of the date of the appraisal, not historical or actual cost. The appraiser is taking the position that an alternative course of action for the informed, rational buyer is to build a replica of the subject residence with the same utility as of the date of the appaisal. Accrued depreciation is not the same as accounting depreciation or cost recovery.

The appraiser is attempting to identify and measure the utility of the improvements and, hence, their contribution to the value of the entire property as of the date of the appraisal. As the difference between reproduction cost new and present worth as of the date of the appraisal, accrued depreciation is a measure of the loss in utility experienced by the subject structure in its present condition in comparison with the utility it would have as a new improvement that represented the highest and best use of the site.

Only man-made improvements are subject to accrued depreciation. Land does not depreciate. Land value may decrease or increase because of market forces, but this is not depreciation. Depreciation is not a marketwide phenomenon. It is related to a specific structure or improvement, considered in terms of a specific location on a specific site.

Accrued depreciation is based on the accumulated experience of the structure or improvements as of the date of the appraisal. This experience is reflected in the observed condition of the structure or improvements noted by the appraiser during his field inspection of the property.

Accrued depreciation is a direct function of the passage of time, although it is not necessarily proportionate in amount to time or age. The condition and appropriateness of the improvements depend primarily on their age and on changing standards of the market, both of which do vary with the passage of time. Accrued depreciation is held to be systematically related to the passage of time. This is the basis for age-life techniques of measuring accrued depreciation and for forecasting remaining economic life and/or market acceptance of the subject improvements.

Reasons for Measuring Accrued Depreciation

The purpose of any appraisal is to estimate value. In the application of the cost approach, the present worth (contribution) of improvements is estimated independently of site value. Typically, this requires deducting accrued depreciation from reproduction cost new of the improvements. The accrued depreciation experienced by the improvements as of the date of the appraisal must therefore be estimated in order to make this deduction.

In the cost approach, site is valued as if it were vacant and available to be put to its highest and best use. The remainder or difference between total property value and site value is the proportion of value attributable to the improvements—their contribution to total property value. Accrued depreciation must be estimated to permit the appraiser to arrive at an estimate of this contribution. The contribution of the improvements to total property value provides the appraiser and the client with a guide to the future use of the property. By indicating the total of accrued depreciation experienced by the improvements (and only by the improvement), the analysis points up the possibility of the financial hazards of a proposed supersession of use, a renovation program, or a conversion program.

The final objective of cost approach analysis is to measure the cost of producing a property with the same utility as that of the subject property as of the valuation date. Expressed in these terms, the present worth of the improvements is measured by subtracting the diminished utility (or loss in utility) of the improvements "as is" from the total utility represented by the reproduction cost new of the improvements. The resulting indication of present worth is or should be a measure of the remaining utility of the improvements as perceived by an informed, rational potential purchaser.

Since utility cannot be measured directly, it is inferred from price and cost data. The measure sought in the cost approach is the remaining utility of the improvements, indicated by market cost and price data in conjunction with the observed behavior of buyers on the local market. Accrued depreciation, therefore, is really an estimate of diminished utility. "Accrued" implies the passage of time. Actually, the comparison is one between the improvements "as is" and the reproduction cost new of those improvements (total utility) at the same instant of time— the date of the appraisal. Extreme care must be taken to differentiate this charge from the accounting concept, which is based on historical costs. While the term accrued depreciation is generally used in appraisal literature, it must be clearly understood that it refers to a measure of diminished utility of the improvements. This is then deducted from reproduction cost new to arrive at a measure of remaining utility in the improvements as perceived by the informed, rational buyer.

Utility is an economic concept. The amount of diminished utility measured by the appraiser is the loss in capacity to satisfy human desires, from all causes, experienced by the improvements in their present condition in comparison with a new structure representing the highest and best use of the site. The total is a lump sum that represents the deduction from reproduction cost new that prudent, informed purchasers would make in arriving at the price they would pay for the subject property "as is," as of the valuation date.

The measurement of accrued depreciation (diminished utility) requires the appraiser to consider carefully the several forces that cause the improvements to lose utility and, hence, value and to explain their operation fully to the client. This is essential for effective application of the cost approach to value estimation.

**Principles of Measuring Accrued Depreciation
(Diminished Utility)**

The diminished utility associated with age and condition reduces the economic life of the structure. It is deducted from the total utility represented by the reproduction cost new of the improvements. The diminished utility associated with functional and locational inutility (termed functional and locational obsolescence) is based on comparison with total utility represented by an ideal improvement constituting the highest and best use of the site. A new replica of the subject structure can exhibit either functional or locational inutility (obsolescence), or both. The lump sum deduction is obtained by estimating the component elements of diminished utility from each category of causes and then summing them.

Measurement Based on Market Behavior

Diminished utility (accrued depreciation) is appropriately measured from market facts, comparative market sales and rental data, and the observed behavior of informed buyers on the local market. Its measurement is really a problem in comparative market analysis. Charges for accrued depreciation should be justified and supported by evidence from the market. The subject property is competing with others serving the same market and should be compared with them, to the extent possible, in estimating all elements of diminished utility.

All components of accrued depreciation are considered from the viewpoint of the informed, rational buyer. The appraiser should ascertain how the market, represented by a prudent buyer and/or lender, looks at the subject improvements. How would such a buyer or lender react to them? How much should be deducted for diminished utility for each cause or source? The market provides the rationale for the prudent buyer's actions and reactions to the subject improvements. The market conditions prevailing on the date of the appraisal represent the setting in which this behavior occurs. Each element of accrued depreciation should be considered separately and individually in the context of existing market conditions.

Economic Life as the Standard for Measurement

Real estate is an asset that produces benefits (primarily amenities in the case of residential property) over a period of years. The remaining utility of residential property, or of a residential structure, at any point in time is measured by the discounted present worth of all future benefits anticipated from the ownership of the property by an informed, rational potential purchaser. The period of time over which a prudent and informed buyer anticipates receiving these benefits is the *remaining economic life* of the improvements. This is the period for discounting future benefits to present worth or remaining utility. *Economic life* of the structure is the base from which total utility is estimated. Remaining economic life is the base from which remaining utility is estimated. The difference between economic life and remaining economic life is effective age. This is the base from which diminished utility is estimated.

Physical life is the period of time over which the structure may be expected to remain in existence as a functioning entity. It is generally too long to be meaningful as a guide to the behavior of the prudent buyer. It is an engineering rather than a market concept.

Useful life is "The period of time over which the structure may reasonably be expected to perform the function for which it was designed or intended."[2] At the end of its useful life, a structure becomes valueless; it contributes nothing to the value of the total property over and above site value. Conversion or renovation (rehabilitation, modernization, remodeling) may well extend the useful life of a structure. Generally, useful life is much longer than economic life and is too long a period to influence the market behavior of prudent purchasers.

Economic life is defined as follows:

> "The period over which improvements to real estate contribute to the value of the property. This establishes the capital recovery period for improvements in the traditional residual techniques of income capitalization. It is also used in the estimation of accrued depreciation (diminished utility) in the Cost Approach to value estimation."[3]

It is therefore the period of time over which the structure may reasonably be expected to be competitive on the market in the use for which it was designed or intended. It is the period during which the structure is expected by the prudent buyer to produce a competitive net return of income or amenities. Economic life represents the significant time period to the prudent buyer. It is the period over which total utility is measured.

The component elements of a structure have no independent, residual utility or worth beyond the termination of the economic life of the entire structure. The purpose of an appraisal, after all, is to estimate property value. A property has value because it has utility and only so long as it is capable of providing utility in competition with other similar properties on the same market. Utility is a relative concept. When use must be changed through renovation or reconstruction to maintain utility, economic life has expired for the original use pattern. Thus, economic life, as the period over which total utility is absorbed, is the significant time period for the prudent purchaser and for the appraiser.

Remaining economic life is defined as follows:

> "The number of years remaining in the economic life of the structure or the structural component, as of the date of the appraisal. In part a function of the attitudes and reactions of typical buyers in the market, and in part a function of the market reactions to competitive properties on the market."[4]

Thus, it is the period of time from the date of the appraisal to the expiration of economic life, over which the remaining utility of the structure is absorbed or used up. It is the period that the prudent purchaser has in mind when buying the property. It is the period that the appraiser must ascertain in making the appraisal.

Effective age is defined as follows:

> "As applied to a structure, the age of a similar structure of equivalent utility, condition, and remaining life expectancy as distinct from chronological age; the years of age indicated by the condition and utility of the structure. If a building has better than average maintenance, its effective age may be less than actual age; if there has been inadequate maintenance, it may be greater. A 40-year-old building may have an effective age of 20 years due to rehabilitation or modernization."[5]

It is also the difference between total economic life and remaining economic life of the structure as of the valuation date. Depending on maintenance, condition and market acceptance of the improvements which directly influences remaining economic life, effective age may be greater or less than actual or chronological age. It is measured in economic terms as an indicator of diminished utility (accrued depreciation).

All elements of accrued depreciation have the effect of reducing remaining economic life or increasing effective age by causing a loss in utility. Physical conditions and forces among others, cause diminished utility. Appropriate measurement of diminished utility or accrued depreciation is in economic terms, however.

The estimate of remaining economic life is the most critical conclusion the appraiser must reach in measuring diminished utility. Confirmed and verified data on market behavior of informed buyers is necessary to justify the conclusion. The data must be current. Changing market standards and conditions, as well as physical wearing out of the improvements, work to reduce economic life. It is an observed market fact that typically informed purchasers generally tend to pay less as the age of the structure increases.

Reliability

The reliability of the estimated present worth of the improvements (estimated depreciated reproduction cost new) tends to decrease as greater reliance must be placed on large charges for accrued depreciation that reflect diminished utility. For this reason, the older and less well maintained a residence is, the less defensible will be the value indication developed through the cost approach.

Property Inspection and Observed Condition

All charges for diminished utility stemming from causes internal to the structure or property itself must be based upon the appraiser's field inspection of the property and the appraiser's own observations of conditions. The description of the improvements prepared by the appraiser both for use in the appraisal process and in the report to the client must include a commentary on all the conditions for which deductions are to be made from reproduction cost new. The field inspection is therefore an important aspect of the analysis and measurement of accrued depreciation.

The observation of conditions and the description of improvements identify the elements of rehabilitation required; the physical condition of the improvements; their functional adequacy or inadequacies; and whether they represent an appropriate improvement to the site or an overimprovement or underimprovement. The description must be in sufficient detail to permit proper deductions and charges for specific items. The reasons for the charges must be clear to the client or reader of the report as well as to the appraiser. The elements for which charges are made must cross-check with the salient characteristics of the improvements used in the adjustment processes of the direct sales comparison approach and gross rent multiplier analysis. Charges for diminished utility cannot legitimately be made in the cost approach on items that are not considered and compared in the other two, and vice versa.

Area and Neighborhood Analysis (Location Analysis)

All charges of accrued depreciation for negative locational influences on the subject improvements must be based on analysis of the external forces at work on the subject property. These forces are identified primarily in the description and analysis of the neighborhood according to observed conditions identified during the field inspection. The external forces for which accrued depreciation is charged must be specific to the subject property (or to a small group of competitive properties) in comparison with otherwise similar and competitive properties. They do not represent a general area influence on all properties used as comparisons in the same market area as the subject. Moreover, the negative influences must be strong enough to be measurable in the sales price or value of the subject, in comparison to similar properties that are not subject to these influences.

Relationship to the Direct Sales Comparison Approach and Gross Rent Multiplier Analysis

Measuring accrued depreciation requires good market information about the reactions and behavior of buyers and tenants. These reactions are indicated by sales prices and rents and by differentials in prices and rents based on varying property and structural conditions. The direct estimation of accrued depreciation is really a substitute or surrogate for the adjustment process in the direct sales comparison approach and gross rent multiplier analysis. All of these estimates require confirmed market evidence for support and justification. Evidence from the sales comparison approach is used in testing whether a particular deficiency, defect, or condition is curable. Evidence on market sales is useful for indicating the way an informed, prudent purchaser would react (in terms of sales price paid) to a given condition. Sales prices of otherwise similar properties, one with the condition or deficiency and one without, provide the best guide to the appropriate charge to be made. Such evidence is not commonly available, however. Data and findings from gross rent multiplier analysis are essential in justifying rent loss estimates attributable to specific condition, as well as in capitalizing indicated rent losses into lump sum deductions.

Alternative Methods of Measurement

There is no one way to measure accrued depreciation (diminished utility) experienced by a residential structure. The appraiser must apply a logical, consistent method that is appropriate in terms of the data available. Certain methods are more widely accepted than others. The measurement of accrued depreciation is a logical, analytical process that utilizes the best possible volume of verified market data as can be made available. The appraiser should concentrate on the logical application of basic principles rather than focusing on mechanical techniques and formulas without understanding or explaining their implications.

**Types and Causes of Accrued Depreciation
(Diminished Utility)**

Improvements may experience accrued depreciation from several basic
causes. Whatever method of measurement is employed, the appraiser
must consider each of these potential sources of diminished utility, and
must evaluate the improvements in terms of each source. All categories
of accrued depreciation represent reduction in the total utility of the
structure in relation to its reproduction cost new, in the eyes of the
informed, prudent buyer. Thus, each of the sources operates to reduce
the remaining economic life (or to increase the effective age) of the
improvements. Together, they reflect the combined impact of market
and physical forces on the present worth or contribution of the improvements to total property value.

Categories of Accrued Depreciation

There are three categories of accrued depreciation for the measurement
of diminished utility. Each is identified here in terms of the cause(s)
leading to it. Each has several sub-categories.

Physical Deterioration. Physical deterioration is "A reduction in utility
resulting from the impairment of physical condition."[6] The cause of
the reduction in utility is physical, but the effect is economic: as utility
diminishes, remaining economic life is reduced. Physical deterioration
is intrinsic to the structure. Although all aspects of physical deterioration could be measured together as the combined percentage of original economic life used up as of the date of the appraisal, it is common
and convenient to divide them into curable (also known as "deferred
maintenance") and incurable components. Incurable physical deterioration can be further subdivided appropriately into short-lived (sometimes called "deferred curable") and long-lived elements for purposes
of analysis. The short-lived items are those components of the structure
whose remaining economic lives are shorter, or are expected to be
shorter, than the remaining economic life of the entire structure. The
long-lived items are those components of the structure whose remaining
economic life is the same as that of the entire structure.

Curable physical deterioration represents what the prudent buyer
would anticipate correcting upon purchase of the property. The cost
of effecting the correction or cure would be no more than the anticipated
addition to utility and, hence, to present worth associated with the cure.
"Curable Physical Deterioration is frequently called 'deferred main-

tenance' or rehabilitation because these terms reflect the type of activity typically associated with correcting the condition."[7] Examples of curable physical deterioration include repair or replacement of a worn-out component (roof, floor tile); reconditioning (painting, wallpapering); and repair of broken items (cracked windows, floor or wall tiles). It is called curable physical deterioration because the buyer would be economically or financially justified in correcting or curing the condition.

Incurable physical deterioration is defined as:

"Physical deterioration which in terms of market conditions as of the date of the appraisal is not feasible or economically justified to correct. The cost of correcting the condition or effecting the cure is estimated to be greater than the anticipated increase in utility, and hence ultimately in value, of the property that will result from correcting or curing the condition. For the purpose of appraisal analysis, Incurable Physical Deterioration may be divided into short-lived and long-lived elements."[8]

Correction of the condition may well be technically or technologically possible, yet the condition can be incurable. There is little that cannot be corrected at a price, given current technology. However, the prudent purchaser or owner would not correct a condition unless the anticipated return in terms of increased amenities, utility, and value is greater than the cost. If market conditions change, an item that formerly was incurable can become curable. Thus, the estimate of curability is always made as of the date of the appraisal.

Many components or elements of a structure, as well as items of equipment that are valued as part of the realty, have a remaining economic life that is shorter than that of the entire structure. In the normal course of events, therefore, they will have to be replaced by a prudent owner before the structure is converted, renovated, or demolished. The informed, prudent purchaser buys in anticipation of doing just that. The short-lived items are technically incurable as of the date of the appraisal, because enough utility remains in them to render immediate replacement uneconomic. They have some remaining economic life.

Since it is not economically feasible to replace such items immediately, this condition is sometimes called "deferred curable" physical deterioration. This label indicates that they will become curable within a specific, anticipated period of time, but that that point has not yet been reached. Whatever terminology is used, the important point for the appraiser is to recognize that some items in the structure will most probably have to be replaced because of the action of physical forces before the remaining utility of the structure itself has been fully consumed. These short-lived items must be treated separately from the basic components of the structure.

Long-lived items include the basic structure or components (foundation, framing, partitions, subfloors and the like) that, in the normal course of events, have an economic life as long as that of the entire structure. Their physical lives may be indefinite, but they have no independent utility or value beyond the economic life of the structure, considered as an economic entity. Except in extreme cases of damage or unusual market circumstances, these items are not curable. They can usually be replaced or conditions of deterioration can be corrected, at substantial expense, but the impact on the utility and remaining economic life of the structure will not be enough to warrant the expenditure.

Functional Obsolescence. Functional obsolescence is the "impairment of functional capacity or efficiency. [It] reflects the loss in value brought about by such factors as over-capacity, inadequacy, and changes in the art, that affect the property item itself or its relation with other items comprising a larger property."[9] It is therefore a reduction in utility of the structure, or of one or more of its components, resulting from the decreased capacity of the structure or component to perform the function for which it is intended, in terms of market standards as of the date of the appraisal. It is labeled "functional obsolescence" because it reflects the fact that the structural component is outmoded or inefficient, judged by current market standards of performance or acceptability.

Functional obsolescence is curable "when the cost of replacing the outmoded or unacceptable component is at least offset by the anticipated increase in utility, and hence ultimately in value, resulting from the replacement."[10] Curable functional obsolescence can result from an inadequacy or defect in the structure, or in one of its components. Insufficient closet space, inadequate cabinetry in the kitchen, or a boiler of inadequate size are examples. These can all represent curable functional obsolescence if their addition or replacement is expected to add more to the value of the structure than the cost of installation or replacement. If a structural component is measurably greater in capacity or quality and more costly than a prudent purchaser or owner would include in the particular type of residence under current market standards, utility is also diminished. Cost new is excessive, and occupancy costs may be excessive as well. The prudent purchaser would replace the component with a standard one only if the cost of the replacement would be reflected in a greater increase in utility and hence in value.

Incurable functional obsolescence is "Functional obsolescence that results from structural deficiencies or superadequacies that the prudent purchaser or owner would not be justified in replacing, adding, or removing, because the cost of effecting a cure would be greater than the anticipated increase in utility resulting from the replacement, addition or removal."[11] "Deficiencies" include lacks or missing items as well as inadequacies. "Defects" are existing items performing at below-standard levels.

Functional obsolescence, both curable and incurable, is not necessarily a function of, or directly related to, age. A structual component or condition can be outmoded or unacceptable under current market conditions even in a new structure. Nevertheless, functional obsolescence is more likely to emerge with the passage of time, as tastes, standards of performance and technology change.

A residence may lack elements that are considered standard in the current market for the type of house in question. Some of its components may be inadequate in capacity or performance. The room layout may be poor by the market's standards. There may be inadequate heating or electrical systems. A second floor bath may be lacking in a two-story Cape Cod residence. While these deficiencies or defects may be technically possible to correct, they are incurable if the cost to correct them is greater than the anticipated addition to value resulting from the cure.

A residence may have a foundation that is unnecessarily thick for the region and the type of house. It may have excessively high ceilings by current standards of acceptability. The heating system may have significantly excess capacity for the size of house and climate. Such items add unnecessarily to reproduction cost new. They may also (in the case of too-high ceilings, for example) add to the cost of maintenance, upkeep and occupancy. All such items represent reductions in the utility and hence the value of the structure. If their correction is not warranted by a comparison of the cost to cure with the anticipated increase in utility and hence value from effecting the cure, they are incurable.

External Obsolescence. Physical deterioration and functional obsolescence stem from factors and characteristics within the structure itself. In addition, market forces external to the structure or the property frequently operate to influence the value of the structure (and thus the property). These external market forces are typically divided into locational obsolescence and economic obsolence.

Locational obsolescence is sometimes called environmental obsolescence. In this context, the traditional, broader term "economic obsolescence" is still widely used, but it is something of a misnomer. All elements of accrued depreciation are economic in their impact on utility and value. "Locational obsolescence" or even "environmental obsolescence" is preferred terminology to describe the condition that leads to a charge for accrued depreciation or diminished utility that results from real estate being fixed in location. Locational obsolescence is "that loss in value experienced by a structure as a result of negative environmental forces outside the boundaries of the property."[12] As noted, locational obsolescence should be distinguished and separated from *economic obsolescence,* which is discussed below.

Locational obsolescence is almost always incurable. Real estate is fixed in location. The site cannot be moved, and the structure usually cannot economically be moved. It is also rarely feasible to buy the external influence in order to eliminate it. To constitute locational obsolescence, a negative external influence must be strong enough to be measurable. It must be reflected in the differential of sales prices or terms of sale, or time on the market of otherwise similar and competitive properties. For example, a high-voltage overhead electric transmission line in proximity to a residence may not be aesthetically appealing, but it does not constitute locational obsolescence unless there is market evidence that prudent buyers pay more for otherwise similar residences that are not impacted by proximity to that power line. The same can be said about the introduction of incompatible or disruptive uses into the immediate neighborhood.

Locational obsolescence is reflected as part of diminished utility for the improvements only. Any loss in property value attributable to the negative external influence that is experienced by the site is already reflected in the estimated market value of the site. Therefore, observed and measured locational obsolescence must be allocated appropriately between site and building to avoid double counting.

Locational obsolescence is usually specific to the subject property or to a very few properties in its immediate neighborhood. A general neighborhood influence (poor reputation, bad street pattern, poor water service, high tax assessments) usually sets the standard of comparability and competitiveness for the subject property and reflected in the level of comparable property sales prices and site sales prices. Only if the reproduction cost new of improvements reflects an ideal property can general neighborhood influence be a factor in locational obsolescence.

Economic obsolescence, on the other hand, is generally market-wide. A major shift in mortgage loan interest rates, in property taxes, or in construction labor costs that increased the spread between reproduction cost new and present worth of improvements or a structure would represent economic obsolescence.

Economic obsolescence historically has been defined as:

"Impairment of desirability or useful life arising from factors external to the property, such as economic forces or environmental changes which affect supply-demand relationships in the market. Loss in the use and value of a property arising from the factors of economic obsolescence is to be distinguished from loss in value from physical deterioration and functional obsolescence, both of which are inherent in the property."[13]

The same measurement techniques and allocation requirements (between site and building value impacts) apply to economic obsolescence as apply to locational obsolescence.

Measurement of Accrued Depreciation (Diminished Utility) by Extraction

Indirect measurement of diminished utility is performed by extraction. The present worth of the improvements (remaining utility) is subtracted from their reproduction cost new (total utility). The resulting answer is an estimate of the lump sum amount of accrued depreciation (diminished utility). The present worth or contribution of the improvements, in turn, is derived by subtracting site value from total property value. Suppose, for example, that a residential property is estimated to have a defined value of $95,000 based on valuation via direct sales comparison or gross rent multiplier analysis. Site value is reliably estimated at $16,000 via direct sales comparison analysis. The present worth of the improvements (building and site) is thus $79,000. If reproduction cost new of the improvement is $89,350, then total accrued depreciation is $10,350 ($89,350 − $79,000).

Reliability

Measurement by extraction from market sales data is really the most reliable method of estimating diminished utility, provided that adequate comparable sales data are available to permit subtraction of site value from sales prices of virtually identical properties. The remainder provides the indication of present worth or contribution of the subject improvements to use in estimating accrued depreciation. This method requires adequate numbers of reliable comparable sales data, plus a defensible method for allocating sales price between site and improvements in the comparable properties and in the subject property. It also requires a reliable estimate of reproduction cost new of the subject improvements. This method is as reliable as the estimates of property value (sales price), site value, and reproduction cost new developed and used by the appraiser.

Limitations

Adequate comparable sales data are not always available in the form, quantity, and quality necessary to apply the indirect measurement method appropriately. If they are, then property value has already been estimated reliably, and the need for an estimate of accrued depreciation is questionable. If the present worth of the improvements can be estimated reliably via some other approach, there is serious question about the propriety of using this estimate in attempting to apply the cost approach. Such an attempt would involve circular reasoning. The resulting indication of value via the cost approach is not really a check against the other value approaches, because it uses the conclusion of these other approaches to develop its own. Unless the objective of the assignment is to estimate accrued depreciation or diminshed utility for its own sake, indirect measurement becomes an almost meaningless exercise in logic. Since, in most appraisal assignments, the present worth of improvements is an intermediate answer on the way to an estimate of property value, diminished utility as such is rarely the final objective.

Direct Measurement of Accrued Depreciation (Diminished Utility)

Direct estimation of accrued depreciation is much more tenuous and difficult than measurement by abstraction. It is usually necessary for the appraiser to take this approach, however, if the estimate of value via the cost approach is to serve as a reasonably independent check against the indications of value derived through the direct sales comparison approach and gross rent multiplier analysis. Generally, direct estimation of accrued depreciation (diminished utility) becomes more difficult the older the improvements are. This is because the amount of diminished utility experienced by the improvements tends to increase with age. This is partly a function of physical deterioration and partly a function of changing market standards and tastes and changing technology.

Alternative Methods Available

There is more than one way to estimate accrued depreciation directly. There are almost innumerable variations on the basic theme. Any one of several alternative methods is acceptable, provided that it is applied consistently and logically and that it reflects the manner in which an informed, prudent buyer would react to the conditions encountered in the structure.

Overall or Simple Age-Life Method. This technique is widely used, but often erroneously. It involves estimating the effective age of the improvements by deducting the remaining economic life from the total economic life.[14] Effective age is then expressed as a percentage of total economic life. This percentage is applied to the reproduction cost new of the improvements to obtain a figure representing the lump sum deduction for diminished utility.

One major defect in this approach is that is does not recognize curable elements independently (i.e., elements whose remaining economic lives are zero), nor does it recognize that short-lived items may have remaining economic lives that are shorter than that of the total structure. The age-life method does not consider functional or locational obsolescence directly, and it seriously underestimates accrued depreciation when obsolescence is present in the subject improvements in any significant amount. This method does have the advantage of simplicity, but it is a deceptive simplicity because too many elements are obscured by being lumped together.

It is possible to use this method (if the facts and conditions of the case warrant its use) when an estimate of reproduction cost new has been made on a comparative unit (square foot or cubic foot) basis. A comparative unit cost new estimate does not permit use of the observed condition breakdown method, explained later in this section.

Modified Age-Life Method. In this approach, the separability of curable items of diminished utility is recognized. The cost to cure all curable items, both physical and functional, is estimated first. The sum of these costs is then deducted from reproduction cost new of the improvements. Then, a percentage lump sum deduction covering all incurable elements is found by applying the percentage derived from dividing total economic life into effective age to the remaining reproduction cost new of improvements. This method still essentially ignores the impact of locational obsolescence or incurable functional obsolescence and understates total accrued depreciation when either or both is present. Although curable items are recognized, this approach still does not always allow for individual differences in remaining economic life among components of the structure, particularly short-lived items. It is often predicated on the presumption that one age-life ratio is applicable to the entire structure.

This approach also has the advantage of simplicity. It can be applied with care in situations in which reproduction cost new is estimated via a comparative unit (square foot or cubic foot) method, using either local figures derived by the appraiser or a national cost service. This approach presumes that utility is reduced on a straight-line basis. Age-life analysis may be acceptable when there is little or no economic obsolescence or incurable functional obsolescence, and when the structure is relatively new.

Engineering Breakdown Method. In this approach, a different straight-line percentage is applied to each of the major components of the structure. All categories of diminished utility are lumped together, however, for each component. This approach has the advantage of treating at least the major components of the structure separately. It recognizes the fact that they have different economic lives and different effective ages.

The engineering breakdown method is sometimes applied in terms of physical rather than economic life. The result is that the estimate of diminished utility is related to the capacity of the structural components to survive, rather than their capacity to perform the function for which they are intended and their marketability. Functional and locational obsolescence are not specifically considered separately in this method. If unusual elements of obsolescence are not present, however, the method may be applied satisfactorily to an economic life base. This is really a detailed age-life method. It also presumes straight-line reduction in utility. This method has little practical applicability for the professional real estate appraiser.

Observed Condition Breakdown Method. There are several variations on this basic method. Each involves considering the several elements of diminished utility separately and measuring the amount of each. The several estimates are then added to create a lump sum deduction from reproduction cost new. In practice, appraisers typically will consider and measure all curable items (physical and functional) first. Then, they will turn to an analysis of physical, functional, and locational incurable items—in that order. The reason for this procedure is that incurable items in residential structures cannot be measured properly until all curable items have been accounted for. This method requires an estimate of reproduction cost new that is at least as detailed as that provided by the trade breakdown or segregated cost method of cost estimation.

Physical deterioration is considered in three segments: curable, incurable short-lived (deferred curable), and incurable long-lived. Curable items are deducted first. In each instance, the test of curability must be applied. The cost to cure a component may exceed its reproduction cost new as part of the structure when the structure is being built. For incurable short-lived items, the actual age of each separate component is estimated as a percentage of the useful or economic life of that component on a straight-line basis. The appropriate percentage is applied to the reproduction cost new of each component to estimate the amount of diminished utility. In some instances, only a portion of the component is included as a short-lived item, because part of it has already been cured. If the floor covering in the kitchen is so worn out that it is a curable item, for example, then the reproduction cost new of the kitchen floor covering is deducted from the reproduction cost new of total floor covering or finish flooring in the rest of the house before the age-life percentage is applied. It is preferable to use actual age in estimating the percentage of economic life of a short-lived item that is used up. This is not always possible, however, since actual age may not be known or discoverable. If this is the case, the appraiser must estimate effective age and/or remaining economic life in relation to total useful or economic life. Using actual age for short-lived items, when it is available, eliminates the necessity for the appraiser to make an estimate. This assumes normal usage and condition, when actual age and effective age are essentially equal.

For incurable physical items, the ratio of effective age to remaining economic life for the individual basic structural components (whose remaining economic life is as great as that of the entire structure) is then applied as a percentage to the reproduction cost new of each component. This results in an estimate of the diminished utility for each component. The base figure to which this percentage is applied for each structural component is the reproduction cost new of that component less any curable physical deterioration charged against that component.

It is important to include a charge for incurable physical deterioration against overhead, contractor's profit, and any other indirect costs that are not specifically included in the reproduction cost new of the structural components. Overhead, profit, and other indirect costs are a part of total reproduction cost new that is also used up over the economic life of the structure. The elements of incurable physical deterioration are sometimes lumped together into the bone structure of the building. If this is done, extreme care must be taken to make sure that all the residual elements of the structure that are not included as curable or deferred curable items are included under the bone structure estimate of incurable physical deterioration.

The effective age utilized in estimating incurable physical deterioration is the effective age after curable items are cured. Effecting the cure by replacing and/or rehabilitating curable items may well reduce the effective age, thereby extending the remaining economic life of the structure. The extension of remaining economic life (or the reduction of effective age) resulting from effecting cures of curable items cannot be very great. It must be realistic in terms of what is cured, the cost to cure, and the proportion of cost to cure in relation to total reproduction cost new.

For curable functional obsolescence, the test of curability must be applied to each item in this situation. The measure of diminished utility is the cost to effect the cure. The cost to cure may exceed reproduction cost new. Since the reproduction cost new of a standard item is not included in the reproduction cost of the entire structure, the measure of a curable functional deficiency or defect is the excess of the cost to cure over the reproduction cost new of a standard item installed when the structure was built. Otherwise, a charge would be made against a nonexistent item and double counting would result. If curing a functional deficiency involves replacement (e.g., modernization), then the excess cost to cure is the cost of installing the modern fixture less the depreciated value of the existing fixture or component.

An incurable functional deficiency can be measured by the rent loss attributed to the deficiency in comparison with standard residences, multiplied by the gross income multiplier. Both the rent loss and the gross rent multiplier must be derived from gross rent multiplier analysis. Alternatively, sales comparisons may be employed to measure incurable functional obsolescence if sufficient sales data are available. A comparison of otherwise similar properties, some with the deficiency and some without it, should reveal the deduction in sales price made by prudent buyers. This comparison requires adequate, reliable market sales data, and such data are often not available. Incurable functional superadequacies may be measured by the capitalized value of the rent loss or excess cost of ownership due to the condition. The gross rent multiplier is used to capitalize the monthly rent loss or increased cost for residential properties. In this case, rent loss is based upon the added expense (e.g., extra heating costs, added taxes) attributable to the superadequacy, plus the excess reproduction cost new of the item over and above the cost that may be supported by an increase in market rental as a result of the existence of the item.

Locational obsolescence may be measured in two ways. Whichever method of measurement is employed, the appraiser must allocate total locational obsolescence between site and improvements. The locational obsolescence of the site is already reflected in its estimated market value. Locational obsolescence may be estimated directly by comparison of market sales of otherwise similar properties, some of which are subject to the negative influence and some of which are not. This requires adequate, reliable data, which are often not available.

Most commonly, locational obsolescence is measured by capitalizing the rent loss attributable to the negative locational influence. Both the rent loss and the gross rent multiplier used to estimate total locational obsolescence must be derived from gross rent multiplier analysis. In either case, the diminished utility attributable to negative locational influences must be allocated between building and site. This is most commonly done by utilizing a ratio of site value to building value among properties that are competitive with the subject property.

Economic obsolescence, if any, is similarly measured.

Inclusion of All Components

The appraiser must exercise great care to ensure that all components of the structure are included in the estimate of accrued depreciation. All components will be subject to some deterioration, and all must be considered for other factors as well. Each component should be included once and only once in the analysis; care must be taken to avoid double counting. This is why the observed condition breakdown method is recommended. It requires a detailed analysis of the components of the structure. Care must also be taken to include overhead in the total lump sum estimate of diminished utility. It is a portion of the reproduction cost new of improvements and has no value at the expiration of the economic life of the structure. This applies particularly to the estimate of incurable physical deterioration.

Test of Curability

An observed condition is curable if the cost to cure the condition is no greater than the anticipated addition to utility and, hence, present worth resulting from effecting the cure. Curability, therefore, is exclusively an economic phenomenon, not a physical one. In applying the test of curability, the appraiser should recognize that the cost to cure a condition may be greater than the cost of installation of the item to be cured had it been done during original construction. The gain is not the total utility added by correcting the condition, but the present worth of that utility.

Varying Lives of Components

The appraiser must recognize that many components of the structure have total economic lives and remaining economic lives that are shorter than the total economic life and remaining economic life of the entire structure. For this reason, the observed condition breakdown method of estimating diminished utility is recommended.

Sequence of Analysis

Most commonly, physical, functional, and locational charges for diminished utility are made in that order. This is not necessarily required, however, nor is it necessarily the most appropriate approach. Curable items should always be deducted before incurable elements are calculated and charged in residential structures, in order to avoid double counting. Some appraisers advocate charging for functional and locational obsolescence first. Then incurable physical deterioration is recognized as a residual charge. If this is done, however, the details of the technique for estimating incurable functional obsolescence and locational obsolescence must be amended to account for the fact that no incurable physical deterioration has yet been charged. Also, to avoid double counting, items fully charged under the heading of incurable functional obsolescence or external (locational and/or economic) obsolescence should not be deducted again for physical deterioration.

Amount of Required Detail

The detailed methods for estimating accrued depreciation, especially the observed condition breakdown method, are more sophisticated than the analysis that a prudent market participant would ordinarily apply. The appraiser resorts to detailed breakdown analysis, however, so that overall error is minimized. These are all estimates. The expectation is that the range and categories of error and uncertainty can be reduced if the deductions are made on an item or component basis. The amount of detail required and possible depends on the method employed in estimating reproduction cost new. Breakdown analysis is not possible when a comparison unit basis (square foot, cubic foot) is used to estimate reproduction cost new.

Market Data Base

The appraiser must be able to justify the deductions for accrued depreciation with market evidence that is both adequate and reliable. This includes the estimate of cost to cure, the estimate of remaining economic life, the estimate of total economic life, the estimate of rent loss, and the use of the gross rent multiplier. In brief, effective estimation of diminished utility, and hence of value via the cost approach, requires evidence and support from the two other alternative approaches to value estimation. When market data are so inadequate or so unreliable that neither the direct sales comparison approach nor gross rent multiplier analysis can be applied effectively, there is serious question whether the cost approach is any more reliable. The real proof of deductions for diminished utility from all causes lies in a study of comparable sales and comparable rental properties. This applies equally to the estimation of locational obsolescence.

Emphasis on Economic Life

The appraiser should use economic life and remaining economic life as the basis for the estimates of effective age and for the charges for diminished utility. Structures typically will last and will even be useful, with reasonable maintenance, for a period much longer than the market is willing to recognize or pay for. Similarly, lenders typically consider the economic life of the improvements rather than their physical life in making a judgment about how long a mortgage loan term should be. Most important, even though they may be physically sound, individual components of the structure typically have no residual utility or value independent of the remaining economic life of the entire structure. Even though it exists physically, a residential structure has value only as an economic entity.

Age-Life Charges on a Straight-Line Basis

Even though it may be demonstrated mathematically and conceptually that the rate by which utility is reduced varies during the economic life, straight-line charges on a simple age-life basis represent a reasonable approximation of the way the prudent purchaser reacts to the property as of the date of the appraisal. Moreover, the introduction of any curvilinear formula or equation simply adds to the complexity of an already complicated procedure and opens the door to further disagreement and controversy. Straight-line age-life charges can be used, provided that effective age and total economic life can be justified after all curable items are corrected.

Reliability of the Estimate of Accrued Depreciation

The estimate of accrued depreciation is precisely that—an estimate. Under given circumstances, it is equally possible that it is underestimated or overestimated, resulting in an overestimate or underestimate of property value. This realization should underscore the important fact that the estimate of value via the cost approach does not set the upper limit to value.

Only Improvements Experience Accrued Depreciation

Charges for accrued depreciation are made against the improvements only. They are deductions from the reproduction cost new of the improvements. Site as such does not depreciate. This fact is particularly important in estimating locational obsolescence. Only the portion of locational obsolescence that is allocated to the building is a deduction. Otherwise, there will be double counting and excessive charges, since the estimated market value of the site already reflects the negative locational influence.

Importance of Structural Quality and Materials

Poor structural quality, inferior construction and workmanship, and improper or inferior materials may cause a reduction in utility even though the improvements have experienced no deterioration at all. Buyers may not accept the improvements, even in brand-new structures. This emphasizes the importance of a detailed description of the improvements as well as a careful analysis of the standards applied by the typical prudent buyer in the market at the time of the appraisal.

Classifications and Terminology

It is less important for the appraiser to worry about precise terminology or about classifying a condition for which a charge should be made under the appropriate heading, than it is to recognize the condition and make an appropriate deduction. For example, long and fruitless argument can result over the issue of whether an improper improvement represents incurable functional obsolescence or locational obsolescence. The important point is to recognize the condition and to measure it appropriately in terms of standards of the market. It is important, however, to distinguish carefully between curable and incurable items. This distinction is critical for the appraiser, since the appraiser's job is to estimate the present worth of improvements in order to estimate the value of the property.

Present Worth and Value Estimation
via the Cost Approach

The estimated present worth of the improvements (structures) in the cost approach is the depreciated reproduction cost new of the improvements. This figure measures the contribution of the improvements to total property value. It is measured in the following format:

Reproduction Cost New of Improvements
    Less: Accrued Depreciation
        1. Physical Deterioration
            a. Curable Physical Deterioration (sometimes called "Deferred Maintenance")
            b. Incurable Physical Deterioration: Short-Lived Items (sometimes called "Deferred Curable")
            c. Incurable Physical Deterioration; Long-Lived Items
        2. Functional Obsolescence
            a. Curable Functional Obsolescence
                (1) Deficiencies
                (2) Defects
                (3) Superadequacies
            b. Incurable Functional Obsolescence
                (1) Deficiencies
                (2) Defects
                (3) Superadequacies
        3. External Obsolescence
            a. Locational Obsolescence
            b. Economic Obsolescence
    Equals: Present Worth or Contribution of Improvements
                (Depreciated Reproduction Cost New of Improvements)

This estimate should always be summarized in the appraisal report, using a format similar to the one above and as illustrated in the Case

Study at the end of this chapter. The ultimate objective of estimating and measuring reproduction cost new, accrued depreciation, and site value is to estimate the defined value of the subject property as of the valuation date via the cost approach. Value is estimated via the cost approach, utilizing the aforementioned steps and adding the present worth or contribution of site improvements and site value.

A value estimate via the cost approach is always a summation of the contributions of the component physical parts of the subject property. These components (site, improvements, and site improvements, including all direct costs) are separated and then summed for analytical purposes only. They must be valued and analyzed as parts of an integral economic unit. The present worth of the components has no meaning or status except in terms of the components being used in conjunction with one another in a specific use pattern.

Summary

Accrued depreciation represents the amount of diminished utility observed in the improvements as of the date of the appraisal. Diminished utility is the difference betwen the total utility represented by the reproduction cost new and the remaining utility in the improvements, both estimated as of the date of the appraisal. Accrued depreciation (diminished utility) is experienced by man-made improvements only; it is not experienced by site or land. Total utility is reflected in the economic life of the improvements. Remaining utility is reflected in the remaining economic life of the improvements. Diminished utility or accrued depreciation is therefore a measure of the reduction in economic life experienced by the improvements as of the date of the appraisal. This is the effective age. All elements of diminished utility should be measured in terms of remaining economic life.

Effective age of the improvements is the difference between total economic life, represented by reproduction cost new, and remaining economic life as of the date of the appraisal. Physical life of the structure or any of its components is an irrelevant consideration, because no component of the structure usually has residual value or utility independent of the economic life of the entire structure. Accrued depreciation is most reliably measured indirectly, by subtracting the present worth of improvements from the reproduction cost new of the improvements as of the date of the appraisal. Since present worth of the improvements is not usually known, however, direct estimation of accrued depreciation is typically required. Diminished utility or accrued depreciation is a lump sum deduction from total utility, represented by reproduction cost new as of the date of the appraisal. For purposes of analysis, accrued depreciation is broken down into several categories, based upon the causes of diminished utility.

The observed condition breakdown method of estimating accrued depreciation requires an estimate of reproduction cost new of improvements that is at least as detailed as that provided by the trade breakdown or segregated cost method of cost estimation. The components of accrued depreciation are as follows:

1. Physical Deterioration
    a. Curable Physical Deterioration (sometimes called "Deferred Maintenance")
    b. Incurable Physical Deterioration: Short-Lived Items (sometimes called "Deferred Curable")
    c. Incurable Physical Deterioration: Long-Lived Items
2. Functional Obsolence
    a. Curable Functional Obsolescence
        (1) Deficiencies
        (2) Defects
        (3) Superadequacies
    b. Incurable Functional Obsolescence
        (1) Deficiencies
        (2) Defects
        (3) Superadequacies
3. External Obsolescence
    a. Locational Obsolescence (Incurable)
    b. Economic Obsolescence (Incurable)

Direct measurement of accrued depreciation requires reliable market data at all stages for the estimate of present worth to be supportable. The estimation of accrued depreciation as a lump sum deduction from reproduction cost new, as of the date of the appraisal, is always considered from the viewpoint and standards of the informed, prudent purchaser.

The test of curability is whether the anticipated increase in utility or value resulting from the correction of the condition will at least equal the cost of effecting the cure. All deductions for accrued depreciation must be based upon observed conditions noted in the field inspection of the property and reported in the description of the improvments and the neighborhood analysis that are contained in the appraisal report.

In actual residential appraisal practice, comparative unit (square foot or cubic foot) cost new estimates and a modified age-life method of estimating accrued depreciation are commonly used. The estimated defined value of the subject property via the cost approach is found by:

1. *Subtracting* Total Estimated Accrued Depreciation from Estimated Reproduction Cost New of Improvements
2. *Adding* Depreciated Cost of Site Improvements; and
3. *Adding* Site Value.

Notes

1. Boyce, Byrl N., ed., *Real Estate Appraisal Terminology,* rev. ed. (Cambridge, Mass.: Ballinger [Joint publication of the American Institute of Real Estate Appraisers and Society of Real Estate Appraisers], 1981), p. 3.
2. Ibid., p. 250.
3. Ibid., p. 87.
4. Ibid., p. 204.
5. Ibid., pp. 87–88.
6. Ibid., p. 185.
7. Ibid.
8. Ibid.
9. Ibid., p. 114.
10. Ibid.
11. Ibid.
12. Ibid., p. 155.
13. Ibid., p. 87.
14. If the property has experienced normal (average) maintenance, then actual age and effective age may be the same.

Suggested Readings

American Institute of Real Estate Appraisers. *The Appraisal of Real Estate,* 8th ed. Chicago: American Institute of Real Estate Appraisers, 1983, chapter 20.
Bloom, George F., and Harrison, Henry S. *Appraising the Single Family Residence.* Chicago: American Institute of Real Estate Appraisers, 1978, chapter 12 and appendix H.
Boyce, Byrl N., ed. *Real Estate Appraisal Terminology,* rev. ed. Cambridge, Mass.: Ballinger (Joint publication of the American Institute of Real Estate Appraisers and Society of Real Estate Appraisers), 1981.

Corgel, John B., and Smith, Halbert C. *The Concept and Estimation of Economic Life in the Residential Appraisal Process.* Chicago: Society of Real Estate Appraisers, 1981.

Epley, Donald R., and Boykin, James H. *Basic Income Property Appraisal.* Reading, Mass.: Addison-Wesley, 1983, chapter 5.

Ratcliff, Richard U. *Valuation for Real Estate Decisions.* Santa Cruz, Calif.: Democrat Press, 1972, chapter 5.

Smith, Halbert C. *Real Estate Appraisal.* Columbus, Ohio: Grid, 1976, Chapter 7.

Wendt, Paul F. *Real Estate Appraisal: Review and Outlook.* Athens: University of Georgia Press, 1974, chapter 8.

Case Study:
Cost Approach and
Depreciation Analysis

You are appraising a 1,700 square foot single-family residence that is 12 years old. It is typical of other improvements in the neighborhood and has an estimated effective age of 12 years. Items needing rehabilitation (deferred maintenance) at the time of appraisal include exterior and interior painting with an estimated cost of $3,000, refinish flooring, estimated at $900, and replacement of shades and screens, estimated at $290.

The following short-lived items have been noted, and their respective costs new, effective ages, and normal life expectancies (useful lives) have been estimated:

Component	Reproduction Cost New ($)	Effective Actual Age (yrs.)	Useful Life (yrs)
Finish Flooring	880[a]	8	15
Roof Cover	1,660	12	20
Plumbing Fixtures	1,800	10	30
Electrical Fixtures	400	10	30
Heating Plant	5,980	10	20
Sheet Metal	600	8	15
Carpet	2,200	4	8
Kitchen Equipment	2,680	10	15

[a]Assumes that $900 curable physical deterioration is, in fact, cured. Thus, total reproduction cost new ($1,780) less cured items ($900) leaves $880.

The total estimated reproduction cost new of the house is $70,200 as indicated by the trade breakdown method (see below). After completion of the rehabilitation, it is estimated that the house will have an effective age of 10 years. Similar houses in the neighborhood are estimated to have an economic life new of 50 years.

In terms of current-day standards, the property suffers a deficiency in that it has only one bathroom. Today, similar properties are constructed with two bathrooms. The cost of adding an additional bath today is $3,200, which would be reflected in a price or value increase of $3,200. A second bath added during new construction would cost $2,000. There is also a functional defect because of crawl space and slab floor construction in lieu of a three-quarter or full basement. An analysis of similar properties with the same deficiency indicates a rent loss of $15 per month. The gross rent multiplier for the subject property of 127 has been derived from the market.

The depreciated value of site improvements is estimated at $3,600. The value of the site by the direct sales comparison approach is $16,400.

**Estimation of Reproduction Cost New
of Improvements: Trade
Breakdown Method**

I. Direct Costs (including labor, materials, equipment, and subcontractor's fees)

A.	Excavation and backfill	$ 400
B.	Iron and steel	500
C.	Footings, piers, foundations	2,800
D.	Rough-in framing	12,000
E.	Concrete flat work	1,500
F.	Exterior siding	1,000
G.	Finished millwork	6,000
H.	Lath and plaster	4,000
I.	Finished flooring	1,780
J.	Insulation	600
K.	Roofing	1,660
L.	Plumbing	6,000
M.	Electrical	2,000
N.	Heating and cooling	5,980
O.	Painting exterior and interior	3,000
P.	Sheet metal	600
Q.	Hardware	300
R.	Shades and screens	~~200~~ 290
S.	Carpeting	2,200
T.	Kitchen equipment	2,680
	Total Direct Costs	~~$55,200~~ (78.6%) 55 290

II. Indirect Costs (including profit and overhead, architect's fees, survey, legal fees, permits and licenses, insurance, taxes, financing charges, selling expenses, and holding expenses)

Total Indirect Costs $15,000 (21.4%)

III. Estimated Reproduction Cost New of Improvements $70,200

Estimate of Physical Deterioration:

Curable Physical Deterioration

Item	Cost to Cure	Reproduction Cost New
1. Painting	$3,000	$3,000
2. Flooring	900	900
3. Shades and Screens	290	290
Total Curable Physical	$4,190	$4,190

Incurable Physical Deterioration (Short-Lived)

Effective (handwritten)

Component	Reproduction Cost New	Life Expectancy	~~Actual~~ Effective Age	% Depreciation	$ Depreciation
1. Flooring	$ 880	15	8	53%	$ 466
2. Roof	1,660	20	12	60	996
3. Plumbing	1,800	30	10	33	594
4. Electrical	400	30	10	33	132
5. Heating	5,980	20	10	50	2,990
6. Sheet Metal	600	15	8	53	318
7. Carpet	2,200	8	4	50	1,100
8. Kitchen Equipment	2,680	15	10	67	1,796
	$16,200				$8,392

Total Incurable Physical Deterioration (Short-Lived) $8,392

Incurable Physical Deterioration (Long-Lived)

1. Reproduction Cost New		$70,200
2. Less Reproduction Cost New from		
(a) Physical Curable Deterioration	$ 4,190	
(b) Physical Incurable (Short-Lived)	$16,200	−20,390
3. Total Long-Lived (Remaining)		$49,810
4. Effective Age—10 years		
5. Economic Life (New)—50 years		
6. Effective Age ÷ Economic Life		× .20
Total Incurable Physical Deterioration (Long-Lived)		$ 9,962

after deficiencies are cured. (handwritten)

Estimate of Functional Obsolescence

Curable Functional Obsolescence

Deficiency (Addition)
   Addition of full bath:

Cost to add bath	$3,200
Reproduction cost new of bath (during construction)	− 2,000
Total Curable Functional Obsolescence	$1,200

Incurable Functional Obsolescence

Defect (substructure)

Rent Loss	$ 15
GRM	× 127
Total Incurable Functional	$1,905

Total Estimate of Accrued Depreciation

1. Physical Deterioration	
a. Curable	$ 4,190
b. Incurable—Short-Lived	8,392
c. Incurable—Long-Lived	9,962
Total	$22,544
2. Functional Obsolescence	
a. Curable	$ 1,200
b. Incurable	1,905
Total	$ 3,105
3. External Obsolescence	-0-
Total Accrued Depreciation	$25,649

Summation and Value Estimate by Cost Approach

Estimated Reproduction Cost New	$70,200
Estimated Accrued Depreciation	− 25,649
Estimated Reproduction Cost New less Accrued Depreciation	$44,551
Estimated Depreciated Value of Site Improvements	$ 3,600
Estimated Site Value	$16,400
Estimated Value by the Cost Approach	$64,551
Rounded	$64,550

12 Statistical Tools and Data Analysis

Key Terms

Average deviation *(A.D.)* A measure of dispersion derived by summing the absolute differences between the mean of a data set and each individual item within the data set and dividing this sum by the number of items.

Central tendency A generic term referring to summary measures of a data set around which all values in the data set tend to cluster.

Confidence interval The range around the mean (as determined by its standard error) within which one may be confident that the true population mean lies.

Descriptive statistics The characterization of a particular data set by way of measures of central tendency and dispersion.

Dispersion A measure of variability in a data set, usually from a point of central tendency.

Frequency distribution The placement of data into groups according to the frequency with which they appear in the data set.

Inferential statistics Predictions about the values of a population (universe), based upon a sample of observations from that population and related facts and calculations.

Mean $(\overline{X})$ A measure of central tendency: the calculated average.

Median *(Md)* A measure of central tendency: a positional average.

Mode *(Mo)* A measure of central tendency: the most frequent value.

Population In statistics, all of the items, people, or objects within a given area or category.

Primary data Data gathered firsthand as a result of a specific survey.

Range The difference between the largest and the smallest items in a data set.

Sample A finite number of observations drawn from a universe or population.

Sampling The act of drawing a sample from a universe or population.

Secondary data Data gathered by others and usually available in published form.

Standard deviation *(s)* A measure of dispersion, variability, or scatter in a data set that, together with the arithmetic mean, fully describes that data set.

Universe See *population*.

Statistics is the process of collecting and classifying data, analyzing and interpreting those data, and making judgments and decisions on the basis of that analysis. This is precisely what appraisers do—or should do. The only difference is that there are formal and precise rules to be followed in statistical analysis; the limitations, as well as the applications of statistical measures, are identifiable.

The decisions or conclusions drawn from statistical analysis are based upon the data themselves. The appraiser is going to the market in using statistical analysis and tools. The results or answers are single numbers that describe a set of data, called observations, and allow the appraiser to draw conclusions or inferences about the market from which the data or observations are derived.

Characteristics of Statistics

A statistic is a single number that describes a characteristic of a set of data or observations known as a sample. Basic characteristics that are typically and easily described are central tendency, dispersion, association, and reliability. *Central tendency* is a value around which the values in the data set tend to cluster or concentrate; it is a value that may be taken as representative or typical of the data set. *Dispersion* is a measure of the extent to which the actual values in the data set are clustered closely around the measure of central tendency or are widely dispersed around it. Dispersion is used to test and evaluate how representative or typical of the data set the measure of central tendency is. *Association* is a measure of how closely the values of two or more variables are associated with one another, or how closely changes in the value of one are associated with changes in the value of the other(s). Association is used for estimation or prediction of the value of one variable (known as the dependent variable), given the value of the other variables (known as the independent variables). *Reliability* is a measure of the level of confidence that is attributable to other statistical measures. It indicates the probability that a given statistic is representative of the data set or statistical population from which it is derived. Reliability can also be used to indicate the range within which the true value of a statistical measure most probably falls. Statistical reliability is not synonymous with either accuracy or validity.

Sample versus Population

A statistical *population,* or statistical *universe,* consists of all the items, people, or objects within a given area or category. For example, all people living within a given community; all the single-family residences in a given neighborhood, all the mortgages originated in a given community over a specified period of time, and all the rental housing units in a given area are populations. Data on a statistical population are obtained by taking census or enumeration. Characteristics of a population are called *parameters,* which include measures of central tendency and measures of dispersion.

A *sample* is a set of observations or data drawn from a population. It is smaller than the population and is used to represent the population as a basis for analysis. The use of samples economizes on time, effort, and money. Appraisers almost always work with samples, except when dealing with Census data on human populations. All single-family residences sold in a community over the past two years, for example, would be a sample of all single-family residences existing in that community. A survey of mortgage loans made by three banks in a community would be a sample of total mortgage lending in that community. Ten rentals of single-family residences in an area would be a sample of all single-family rentals in that area. Samples may be derived through various techniques or procedures, which will be enumerated here. Sample size is an influence on the representativeness of a sample. Generally, the larger a sample is, the more nearly it and its characteristics may be accepted as representative of the population from which it is drawn. Characteristics of samples are called *statistics*.

Descriptive versus Inferential Statistics

Descriptive statistics involve identifying the characteristics of a sample. These include measures of central tendency or averages, dispersion, association, and statistical reliability of sample data.

Inferential statistics involve estimating population characteristics (parameters) from sample characteristics (statistics). Estimating what is typical or normal or reasonable in a real estate market, for example, requires inferring from a sample what the market characteristics are— interest rates, construction costs per square foot, and number of two-bedroom, single-family rentals. Inferential statistics also includes forecasting or predicting the value of a variable for an observation that is not included within the sample. If the ratio between sales price and gross rental income, for example, is derived from a sample, that ratio (the gross rent multiplier) can be applied to the gross rental income of another property that is not in the sample to estimate its value or most probable selling price. As another example, the population of a community in 1985 can be forecast from data from 1960 through 1980.

Finally, inferential statistics can be used to test whether a particular observation is likely to have come from the same population as the sample did, given that the sample is representative of the population. An appraiser can test, for example, whether a particular residential sale is a comparable sales transaction or is competing on the same market by measuring whether it is likely that it came from the same population or market as sales transactions in the sample.

Uses and Limitations of Statistical Analysis

Statistical analysis is not a cure-all or a magic technique that solves all the appraiser's problems. Neither is it a mysterious or highly abstract mathematical process with no relation to the work of the appraiser. Rather, it is a systematic, consistent, and precise quantitative tool that can and should be used by appraisers in conjunction with other tools of analysis and evaluation. It is merely a process for obtaining meaningful and useful generalizations about sets of numbers that appraisers work with continuously.

Among its many uses, statistical analysis enables real estate appraisers and analysts to identify and measure general characteristics of data sets that are used throughout all the steps in the appraisal framework. It provides savings in time, effort, and money by enabling the appraiser to work with systematic samples of data. It also enables the appraiser to process data sets in a way that provides precise and consistent results. This makes comparisons realistic and defensible.

Statistical analysis allows the appraiser to draw conclusions and inferences about the market (population) from relatively small data sets (samples). These conclusions and inferences can relate to forecast future changes or trends as well as to current market conditions. Further, statistical analysis allows the appraiser to test the reliability of measures derived from samples as well as inferences or conclusions drawn about the market (population). By indicating the range of probable error, it provides the appraiser with an indication of the level of confidence that may be assigned to any statistical measure or conclusion. Finally, statistical analysis can be an important aid in decision-making by the appraiser, as well as for the client or employer. Since this is the reason for making an appraisal in the first place, it is a significant help in the entire appraisal process.

Statistical analysis is not without limitations. As the size of a sample decreases, for example, the reliability of statistical measures and inferences based on it decreases more than proportionately. Statistical analysis should be used with caution in dealing with very small data sets (less than 10 observations). In statistical analysis, a small data set is one with less than 30 observations.

Improper generalization arise most often when there are insufficient or inadequate data in the sample to draw a conclusion about the market (population). If the sample is not representative of the population, the inferences drawn will be improper. A sample of only three comparable sales, for example, is insufficient to indicate market or typical sales prices per square foot of living area. In addition, totally reliable and supportable statistics on rentals of two-bedroom houses in a market area cannot be used as a basis for estimating three- or four-bedroom house rentals in that market.

Bias is a tendency for certain results to be obtained. This may arise from the predilections of the appraiser or from the way in which the sample is collected. If the appraiser gathers data on residential mortgage loan terms from commercial banks only, for example, the statistical measures and the inferences drawn from them will reflect the policies and legal limitations of commercial banks, rather than of the entire market. Unemployment data that reflect only new claims for unemployment compensation may not be appropriate for analyzing the trend in area unemployment. Using only a sample of sales of rented houses may not reflect the trend in sales prices of all residences in an area.

Statistics found for one sample or one sample set may not be transferable to other samples *(improper deduction)*. The generalizations found cannot be treated as general laws. The annual rate of change in construction costs found for one type of residence for a given area over a given period of time, for example, cannot usually be applied to another type of construction or another area or another time period. In addition, while an average may be a good representation of an entire data set (sample), it cannot be used as a description of every member of either the sample or the population. Further, statistics are not valid for data sets unless the items have in common at least those characteristics that are relevant to the purpose of the study *(improper comparisons)*. Commercial and residential lot sales cannot be used together to obtain valid measures of sales price per square foot. Masonry and frame construction cannot be combined to derive valid measures of unit construction costs.

Two variables may be closely associated in value or movement, so that knowing the value of one enables the appraiser to predict reliably the value of the other. This does not mean, however, that either causes the other. Unit sales prices may vary closely with the passage of time, but the passage of time does not in itself cause unit prices to change. Neither does a change in unit prices cause time to pass.

Statistical calculations may result in very detailed, precise mathematical results. This precision or detail should not be used when it suggests a degree of accuracy that does not exist. An average sales price per square foot of living area, for example, may be calculated as $42.877542. If the original data are all expressed to the nearest half dollar, then the statistic used should be $43 per square foot. If the original data are expressed in dollars and cents to the nearest cent, then $42.88 should be used.

Oversimplification results when partial evidence or half-truths are presented, so that the conclusions are not based upon complete and thus accurate data analysis. To show that the sales price varies with the passage of time, for example, or that construction cost per unit varies with the size of the house is to present an oversimplification. Extension of historic trends is hazardous. Assuming that the past will persist in the future is invalid without careful consideration of the causes of past and probably future change. Simple *extrapolation* of past population trends, for example, without careful analysis of trends in birthrates, death rates, and net migration, can lead to widely divergent forecasts. In general, the further into the future a projection is made, the more suspect it is from a statistical standpoint.

Data Collection and Presentation

The kinds of data required to carry out the several steps of the appraisal framework are discussed elsewhere. Similarly, sources of the required data are considered in the discussions of the uses of data that appear throughout the text. The discussion here centers on those aspects of data collection and presentation that are significant for statistical analysis.

Primary versus Secondary Data

Primary data are data that are gathered firsthand by the appraiser as a result of a specific survey. Typically, the source is either a participant in the activity being surveyed or an official repository of data. Information on property sales obtained from the buyer, the seller, a participating attorney, the broker, or the lender are primary data; so is information derived from the recorded deed or mortgage. Primary data tend to be more accurate, assuming that the data source is neither misleading nor misinformed. Collecting primary data is time-consuming and expensive, however. Primary data are generally obtained from personal interviews, from mail surveys, or from consulting official records and files. Primary data are therefore verified by the data gatherer as coming from an authoritative or knowledgeable source.

Secondary data are data that have been gathered by others and are usually available in published form. Census information is secondary data; so are the sales data published by the SREA Market Data Center. Using published secondary data saves time, effort, and money. Their reliability, however, depends on the care employed by the data gatherers. The user has not veritifed the data and, indeed, may be required to do so for some purposes, such as testimony in court. One potential hazard in using secondary data is that the user may not be informed about how the data were gathered, what sampling technique (if any) was employed, and whether and how the data were rounded.

Variables versus Attributes

Characteristics of items (also called variates) about which data are gathered may be either attributes or variables. Attributes are qualitative characteristics of variates that are usually divisible into categories: yes and no—that an item either possesses the attribute or it does not. Sex, employment (or unemployment) status, new (or existing) construction, tenant (or owner) occupancy, and vacant (or occupied) status are all attributes. In addition, such characteristics as type of construction, location, race, or house orientation may also be classified as attributes, even though there can be more than two categories for these items. The important point is that they do not vary on a quantitative scale. There is little that can be done with attributes in statistical analysis beyond tabulating and calculating percentages or ratios. Attributes are sometimes converted, however, into dummy variables on an ordinal scale. Thus, the value of "yes" would be 1, and the value of "no" would be 0.

Variables are quantitative characteristics whose value can vary on an arithmetic scale, usually by size or time. Thus, sale price, lot size, number of bedrooms, population, and construction cost per square foot are all variables. Most statistical analysis is concerned with describing and drawing inferences from sets of variables.

There are two general types of variables: discrete and continuous. Discrete variables are data that have distinct values, with no intermediate values. The number of bedrooms, bathrooms, or garage stalls in houses are all discrete variables. Care must be exercised in using the results of statistical analysis with discrete variables, so that nonsense conclusions are avoided. It makes little sense, for example, to conclude that the average house in a given area has 1.287 bathrooms. Continuous variables are data that can have almost any value on a given scale. Lot size, living area, sales price, and monthly rental are continuous variables.

Samples and Sampling

A *sample* is a data set drawn from a population. Virtually all statistical analysis undertaken by appraisers deals with samples. The intent of a sample, and of sampling, is that it is representative of the population from which it was drawn and that sample characteristics can be used to infer population characteristics. Samples provide a good approximation of population characteristics. A complete census or enumeration may be impossible, but because of the ease of computation and data manipulation (including storage capacity), a sample may provide more accurate results than a census.

Major limitations and disadvantages of samples include sampling error and bias. There is always the possibility (determined by the laws of probability) that a sample will not be representative of the population from which it is drawn (sampling error), no matter how carefully or systematically the sample is taken. Construction cost estimates, for example, can be heavily weighted by distress bids from contractors without the appraiser knowing it. Bias is the incorrect estimation of population parameters from a poorly designed or executed sample. Every item in the population should have an equal opportunity or chance to be selected in the sample. In surveys, nonresponse produces bias. The analyst also may not be measuring the characteristic that were intended to be measured. Refusals by principals to verify sales or rental data can also produce bias.

Types of Samples

Probability samples are samples in which the items or observations are selected for inclusion in the sample by some chance device. Every item in the population must have a known chance (greater than zero) to be selected. Probability samples produce by far the better, more reliable statistical results. Real estate appraisers frequently must deal with nonprobability samples, however, since not every house in a given area is sold or rented, borrowed upon, occupied, or constructed during a given time period.

A simple random sample is one in which every item in the population has an equal chance to be selected. Selecting a simple random sample usually involves assigning each item in a population a number, and then choosing the sample items by using a table of random numbers. Other types of probability samples include systematic samples, in which the items in the population are arranged randomly and chosen according to a set formula; stratified samples, in which the population is arranged in strata according to some characteristic and each stratum is randomly sampled; and cluster samples, in which population data are clustered and the clusters are picked at random.

Nonprobability samples are samples in which not every item in the population has a known, nonzero chance of being included. They include quota samples and judgment samples. Most samples used in real estate appraisal are nonprobability samples. They are less representative with less reliability than probability samples. As the sample size increases, however, the accuracy and reliability of judgment samples also increases. Any judgment bias remains undiminished, however.

Data Tabulation and Presentation

Both for analytical purposes and for reporting results, it is generally necessary to arrange sample data in some systematic fashion. To illustrate these procedures, as well as to provide materials for later illustrative use, the following three data sets will be used:

Data Set 1:   A sample of ten new houses of very similar construction was taken. The construction cost per square foot of each was found to be as follows:

House Number	Cost per Square Foot ($)
1	54.63
2	53.79
3	54.33
4	54.42
5	53.94
6	54.18
7	54.45
8	54.27
9	54.30
10	54.15

Data Set 2:   A recent survey of residential mortgage loan originations reveals the following pattern of contract interest rates, together with the frequency of their occurrence:

Interest Rate (%)	Number of Loans
11.25	3
11.50	18
11.75	41
12.00	72
12.25	83
12.50	76
12.75	57
13.00	43
13.25	26
13.50	9
	428 = Σf

Date Set 3: A survey of a neighborhood indicates that there are 11 vacant residential lots with the following depths:

Lot Number	Depth (Ft.)
1	150
2	170
3	166
4	150
5	160
6	170
7	153
8	250
9	171
10	170
11	162

Data set tabulations are simply lists of data with no particular systematic pattern. The tabulations of data in Data Sets 1 and 3 illustrate this. While they do present the data, they do not convey much information for interpretation and analysis. Moreover, they are not readily susceptible to statistical analysis, except for the calculation of the arithmetic mean, as will be illustrated later.

An array is a tabulation of data in chronological sequence of observations by size or value of the variable. The data may be arrayed in ascending or descending order of value. The usual convention is to go from lowest to highest. For Data sets 1 and 3, the arrays would be:

Data Set 1: Cost per Square Foot ($)	Data Set 3: Lot Depth (Ft.)
53.79	150
53.94	150
54.15	153
54.18	160
54.27	162

Data Set 1: Cost per Square Foot ($)	Data Set 3: Lot Depth (Ft.)
54.30	166
54.33	170
54.42	170
54.45	170
54.63	171
	250

To array the data in Data Set 2 would be relatively meaningless, in part because they are already presented in order, in part because it would be extremely difficult to interpret and analyze visually such a mass of data in array format, and in part because it would be extremely time-consuming.

Frequency distributions are tabulations that list the values of the variables (X) in ascending order plus the number of times or frequency (f) that each value appears. Data Set 2 is a frequency distribution, with the interest rate as the X-value and the number of loans made at each interest rate as the frequency (f).

Data Set 3 could also be converted to a frequency distribution, as follows:

Lot Depth (X)	Number of Observations (f)
150	2
153	1
160	1
162	1
166	1
170	3
171	1
250	1

Data Set 1 or its array cannot be made into a meaningful frequency distribution on the basis of the raw data since each value occurs only once. A frequency distribution based on grouping of observations into class intervals can be derived, however. The rules for deriving the size and number of class intervals can be found in any basic statistics text. Using these rules, the frequency distribution for Data Set 1 would be as follows:

Cost per Square Foot ($)	f	Midpoint of Interval ($)
53.76–53.90	1	53.83
53.91–54.05	1	53.98
54.06–54.20	2	54.13
54.21–54.35	3	54.28
54.36–54.50	2	54.43
54.51–54.65	1	54.58

For presentation purposes and for visual analysis and interpretation, data may be presented pictorially. Although many possible forms of graphic presentation are available for use, the most common and useful are the bar chart, the histogram, the scatter diagram, the arithmetic scale graph, the semilogarithmic scale graph, and the curve (normal curve).

Measures of Central Tendency

Measures of central tendency are averages; they are summary measures of data sets. They seek to portray the most representative or typical value of the variable in a sample data set, array, or frequency distribution. They represent the single value of the variable around which all the values in the sample tend to cluster. The measures or averages considered here are the arithmetic mean, the median and the mode of samples.

The symbols used in these measures are as follows:

X: The variable whose values are included in the sample; the value of a single observation of the variable.

n: The number of observations or items in the sample.

f: The number of times or frequency that a given value of X appears in the sample.

Σ: Summation sign.

ΣX: The sum of the values of the variable in the sample.

Σf: The sum of the frequencies in the sample (also equal to n).

ΣfX: The sum of the products of the X-values and their respective frequencies.

$\overline{X}$: The arithmetic mean of a sample.

Md: The median of a sample.

Mo: The mode of a sample.

X_m: The midpoint of a class interval.

Arithmetic Mean

The arithmetic mean $(\overline{X})$ of a sample is the familiar average of common usage. In general, the arithmetic mean is calculated by summing the values of a sample data set and then dividing by the number of observations in the sample. The basic formula is: $\overline{X} = \dfrac{\Sigma X}{n}$.

Simple Arithmetic Mean (Ungrouped Data). Data Sets 1 and 3 show ungrouped data. For each data set, the arithmetic mean is found by: $\overline{X} = \dfrac{\Sigma X}{n}$. In Data Set 1, $\Sigma X = \$542.46$ and $n = 10$. Therefore, $\overline{X} = \dfrac{\$542.46}{10} = \$54.25$ per square foot. In Data Set 3, $\Sigma X = 1{,}872$ and $n = 11$. Therefore, $\overline{X} = \dfrac{1{,}872}{11} = 170.18$ feet.

Weighted Arithmetic Mean (Ungrouped Data). The formula for the weighted arithmetic mean for ungrouped data is: $\overline{X} = \dfrac{\Sigma f X}{\Sigma f}$ or $\dfrac{\Sigma f X}{n}$. Data Set 2 is a frequency distribution of ungrouped data. To find $\overline{X}$, the following tabulation would be used:

X	f	fX
11.25	3	33.75
11.50	18	207.00
11.75	41	481.75
12.00	72	864.00
12.25	83	1,016.75
12.50	76	950.00
12.75	57	726.75
13.00	43	559.00
13.25	26	344.50
13.50	9	121.50
	428	5,305.00

Thus, $\Sigma f X = 5{,}305.00$ and $\Sigma f = 428$. Then, $\overline{X} = \dfrac{5{,}305.00}{428} = 12.39\%$.

Weighted Arithmetic Mean (Grouped Data). Grouped data are those in class intervals in a frequency distribution. The grouped data from Data Set 1 illustrate this. The formula for the weighted arithmetic mean is:

$$\overline{X} = \frac{\Sigma f X_m}{\Sigma f}$$

where X_m is the midpoint of each class interval.

The arithmetic mean for the frequency distribution from Data Set 1 is calculated as follows:

X_m	f	fX_m
$53.83	1	$ 53.83
53.98	1	53.98
54.13	2	108.26
54.28	3	162.84
54.43	2	108.86
54.58	1	54.58
	10	$542.35

Thus, $\Sigma fX_m = \$542.35$ and $\Sigma f = 10$. Then, $\overline{X} = \dfrac{\$542.35}{10} = \$54.24$.

Median

The median is a positional average. It is the value of the observation at the middle of the array or frequency distribution. Half the values in the data set are at or below the median, and half are at or above the median. If the number of observations in a sample is odd, the median is the value of the middle item; if the number is even, the median is midway between the two middle items. Sample data must be arrayed or presented in a frequency distribution before the median can be found.

Median for Ungrouped Data. The formula to find the location of the median is $Md = \dfrac{n + 1}{2}$; the corresponding value is the median. For Data Set 3, the location of the median is $Md = \dfrac{11 + 1}{2} = 6$. Thus, the sixth item in the array (166 feet) is the median.

For Data Set 1, the location of the median is $Md = \dfrac{10 + 1}{2} = 5.5$. Thus, the median is midway between the fifth and sixth observations in the array. The median, then, is the arithmetic mean of the observations $54.27 and $54.30 or $54.285 (not rounded arithmetically, but realistically $54.29).

For Data Set 2, the location of the median is $Md = \dfrac{428 + 1}{2} = 214.50$. Thus the median is between items 214 and 215. Because there are several observations for each value of X, the frequencies are summed cumulatively until the 214th and 215th items are reached, as follows:

X	f	Cumulative f
11.25%	3	3
11.50%	18	21
11.75%	41	62
12.00%	72	134
12.25%	83	217

Thus, both the 214th and 215th items have a value of 12.25 percent. The median for this sample is therefore 12.25 percent.

Median for Grouped Data. The midpoints of class-interval grouped data do not necessarily represent any actual observation. It is assumed that actual values are evenly distributed within each class interval. To find the location of the median, the formula is:

$$Md = L + \frac{i(n/2 - F)}{f}$$

where L = lower limit of the median class interval
$\quad\quad i$ = size of the class interval
$\quad\quad F$ = cumulative frequency before the median interval
$\quad\quad f$ = frequency of the median interval

Using Data Set 1 arranged as a grouped-data frequency distribution, the median interval is found where the median is

$$\frac{n + 1}{2} = \frac{10 + 1}{2} = 5.5$$

Adding the cumulative frequencies reveals that the median interval is $54.21–$54.35. Then

$$L = \$54.21 \quad\quad F = 4 \quad\quad n/2 = 5$$
$$i = \quad .15 \quad\quad f = 3$$

The median is then:

$$Md = \$54.21 + \frac{.15\ (5 - 4)}{3} = \$54.26$$

Mode

The mode is also a positional average. It is the value of the variable that has the greatest frequency. When data are arrayed or organized in a frequency distribution, the modal value can be identified by visual inspection. Since it appears most often in a data set, the mode may be considered as typical of that sample. A distribution can be unimodal (one mode), bimodal (two modes), or multimodal (more than two modes). In a sample such as Data Set 1, it can be argued that there is no mode, since each value appears only once. Even if it were held to have ten modes, the mode would be useless in this case as a representative or typical value. Unlike the mean and the median, the mode in a unimodal sample is always an actual observed value.

Mode for Data not Grouped in Class Intervals. In an array or frequency distribution of data that are not grouped in class intervals, the mode can be found by visual inspection. In Data Set 3, the array indicates that there are three observations of 170 feet of depth, two of 150 feet, and one each of all the others. Clearly, Mo = 170 feet.

In Data Set 2, the frequency distribution shows that there are 83 observations at 12.25 percent. This is a greater frequency than exists for any other interest rate. Thus, Mo = 12. 25 percent.

Mode for Data Grouped in Class Intervals. While it is theoretically possible to calculate a mode for a frequency distribution grouping in class intervals, accepted practice suggests that the most useful procedure is simply to identify the modal interval. Thus, for Data Set 1 grouped in class intervals, the modal interval is $54.21 − $54.35, since it has a greater frequency than any other interval.

Uses and Limitations of Averages (Measures of Central Tendency)

Averages can be used to characterize an entire data set with a single number than can be taken as representative or typical of that data set or sample. They also observe the pattern of individual observation values, especially regarding how much they diverge from the average. Different averages have different uses and applications. The selection of the appropriate average in any given case depends on the application of the results to problem solving or decision making (the purpose of the analysis) and the character and distribution of the underlying data.

The arithmetic mean $(\overline{X})$ is well known and widely used. Its value may not coincide with any actual observed value. Its mathematical properties make it usable for subsequent statistical analysis, measures, and tests. Each value in the data set is taken into account and included in the calculation although extreme values can influence the value of the mean, especially in small samples. The position of individual values does not affect the calculation; it is not necessary to form an array or frequency distribution to calculate the mean. The mean cannot be computed for open-ended frequency distributions.

The median (*Md*) is easy to understand and to compute. It is affected by the number but not the value of extreme values. The median is useful when the mean is affected by extreme values, and it can be used for open-ended distributions or when the data can be ranked but not measured. The median is of little use for subsequent statistical measures and tests. For a median to be located, data must be arrayed or arranged in a frequency distribution. There is no particular advantage in using the median when it is very close to the mean.

The mode (*Mo*) is easy to find if it exists. Operationally, the mode may not exist or there may be more than one. The mode has no mathematical properties for further statistical measures and tests. For identification of the mode, data should be arrayed or arranged in a frequency distribution. The mode can be used for open-ended distribution; it is affected by selection of number and size of class intervals; and it is useful for highly skewed distributions, especially of discrete variables. There is no real advantage in using the mode when it is very close to the mean, except for discrete variables. Except for class-interval grouped data, the mode is always an actual observation value.

Measures of Dispersion (Variation)

An average (measure of central tendency) is a single value or number around which the values in a sample data set tend to cluster. To this extent, the average describes or represents the entire data set. An average is rarely a perfect representation of the sample data, since data tend to vary from or be dispersed around the average. The extent to which the data values differ from the average is called a measure of *dispersion*. The difference between the average and the value of a single observation is called *variation*. A measure of dispersion is a single number that describes or represents the variation of the entire data set from its average. The average around which variation is almost always measured is the mean. The three most common measures of dispersion, which are considered here, are the range, the average deviation, and the standard deviation.

The Range

The *range* is merely the difference between the highest value in the sample and the lowest value. The formula is: Range = Highest Minus Lowest. For Data Set 1, the range is $54.63 − $53.79 = $0.84. For Data Set 2, the range is 13.50 percent − 11.25 percent = 2.25 percent. For Data Set 3, the range is 250 feet − 150 feet = 100 feet. The range is a simple but relatively crude and uninformative measure of dispersion. It indicates nothing about the intervening values, their pattern, or their location. Moreover, the range can never decrease as sample size increases, as the other measures of dispersion do.

Average Deviation

The average or mean deviation is a measure of how much the actual values of the sample data deviate from the mean, on the average. It is the arithmetic mean of the absolute value differences between observed values and the mean of the sample. The absolute differences are used because the sum of the deviations from the mean, taking sign into account, is always zero.

The formula for average deviation is

$$A.D. = \frac{\Sigma |X - \overline{X}|}{n} \quad \text{or} \quad \frac{\Sigma |d|}{n} \quad \text{where } d = X - \overline{X}$$

For frequency distributions,

$$A.D. = \frac{\Sigma f |X - \overline{X}|}{\Sigma f}$$

For the sample represented by Data Set 1, the average deviation is calculated as follows (Note: $\overline{X}$ has already been calculated as $54.25):

X	$|X - \overline{X}|$
$53.79	$0.46
53.94	0.31
54.15	0.10
54.18	0.07
54.27	0.02
54.30	0.05
54.33	0.08
54.42	0.17
54.45	0.20
54.63	0.38
	$\Sigma |X - \overline{X}| = \$1.84$

Thus, $A.D. = \dfrac{\$1.84}{10} = \$0.18$. This means that, on the average the individual observation values deviated from the mean by \$0.18, or 0.33 percent (\$0.18 ÷ \$54.25). This is a very tight fit and suggests that the mean is a good descriptive representative of the sample. An average deviation can also be calculated from the median, but this measure is not widely used.

For Data Set 2, the average deviation is calculated as follows:

$$A.D. = \frac{\Sigma f|X - \overline{X}|}{\Sigma f} \qquad (\overline{X} = 12.39 \text{ percent})$$

X	$|X - \overline{X}|$	f	$f|X - \overline{X}|$
11.25	1.14	3	3.42
11.50	0.89	18	16.02
11.75	0.64	41	26.24
12.00	0.39	72	28.08
12.25	0.14	83	11.62
12.50	0.11	76	8.36
12.75	0.36	57	20.52
13.00	0.61	43	26.23
13.25	0.86	26	22.36
13.50	1.11	9	9.99
		$\Sigma f = 428$	$\Sigma f|X - \overline{X}| = 172.84$

Thus, $A.D. = \dfrac{172.84}{428} = 0.40$ percent, or 3.23 percent of $\overline{X}$. For Data Set 3, $\overline{X} = 170.18$, $n = 11$, $\Sigma|X - \overline{X}| = 161.26$. Then, $A.D. = \dfrac{161.26}{11} = 14.66$ feet or 8.61 percent of $\overline{X}$. The average deviation cannot be used in further statistical calculations. Its only mathematical properties are that, in a reasonably symmetrical series of data, approximately 57.5 percent of the items can be expected to fall within the range of $\overline{X} \pm 1\ A.D.$

Standard Deviation

As noted, the average deviation is based on variation from the mean. Since the sum of deviations from the mean is zero, absolute differences are used so that all the values are positive. Another measure of difference between the mean and individual observation values is the square of the differences. This is called *variance*. Since the differences are squared, the values are all positive. One mathematical characteristic of the mean is that the sum of the squared differences from the mean is a minimum; that is, total variance around the mean is less than the total variance is around any other value in that data set.

The standard deviation(s) is the square root of the average variance around the mean. The formula for ungrouped data is

$$s = \sqrt{\frac{\Sigma(X - \overline{X})^2}{n - 1}}$$

The formula for a frequency distribution is

$$s = \sqrt{\frac{\Sigma f(X - \overline{X})^2}{n - 1}}$$

The expression $(X - \overline{X})^2$ is the variance or squared difference from the mean. The term $(n - 1)$ is used rather than n in calculating average variance because one degree of freedom is lost when $\overline{X}$ is calculated. A data set has as many degrees of freedom as there are observations (n). Every time a statistic is calculated directly from the data, one degree of freedom is lost.

For Data Set 1, the standard deviation is calculated as follows:

$$\overline{X} = 54.25$$
$$n = 10$$

X	$(X - \overline{X})$	$(X - \overline{X})^2$
53.79	−0.46	.2116
53.94	−0.31	.0961
54.15	−0.10	.0100
54.18	−0.07	.0049
54.27	0.02	.0004
54.30	0.05	.0025
54.33	0.08	.0064
54.42	0.17	.0289
54.45	0.20	.0400
54.63	0.38	.1444
		$\Sigma(X - \overline{X})^2 = .5452$

Then,

$$s = \sqrt{\frac{.5452}{9}} = \sqrt{.0606} = .2461.$$

The standard deviation for Data Set 2 is calculated as follows:

$$\overline{X} = 12.39$$
$$n = 428$$

X	$(X - \overline{X})$	$(X - \overline{X})^2$	f	$f(X - \overline{X})^2$
11.25	−1.14	1.2996	3	3.8988
11.50	−0.89	.7921	18	14.2578
11.75	−0.64	.4096	41	16.7936
12.00	−0.39	.1521	72	10.9512
12.25	−0.14	.0196	83	1.6268
12.50	0.11	.0121	76	.9196
12.75	0.36	.1296	57	7.3872
13.00	0.61	.3721	43	16.0003
13.25	0.86	.7396	26	19.2296
13.50	1.11	1.2321	9	11.0889

$$\Sigma f(X - \overline{X})^2 = 102.1538$$

Then,

$$s = \sqrt{\frac{102.1538}{427}} = \sqrt{.2392} = .4891 \quad \text{or} \quad .49$$

Generally, as the size of the sample increases, the standard deviation decreases. This means that the mean becomes a better and more reliable representative or typical value for the sample. This is particularly important for very small samples. Based on the characteristics of the normal curve (discussed in more detail in Chapter 13), for a reasonably symmetric data set, 68 percent of the observations should fall within the range of $\overline{X} \pm 1s$; 95 percent of the observation should fall within the range $\overline{X} \pm 2s$; 99.74 percent of the observations should fall within the range of $\overline{X} \pm 3s$.

A small standard deviation means a high degree of uniformity of the data and, hence, reliability and representativeness of the mean. The obverse is true for a large standard deviation. The standard deviation is used in subsequent statistical measures and tests, including inference about population characteristics. It can also be used to test whether a given observation is likely to have come from the same population as the sample data. Moreover, the standard deviation is somewhat complicated to calculate (without a sophisticated calculator), moderately difficult to understand, and difficult to define and explain relative to other measures of dispersion.

Summary

Statistical analysis is the systematic process of gathering and arranging data; analyzing and interpreting data sets; and drawing conclusions and inferences from the analysis. Statistical analysis has particular application to the work of the appraiser because appraisers are continually drawing inferences about populations or markets from samples. Almost all the data sets that appraisers work with are samples. Appraisers frequently work with nonprobability samples, whose results are less reliable than those of probability samples. Statistical and sampling error can be decreased by increasing the size of sample used, but bias cannot. Sample size is critical to the usefulness and applicability of statistical measures. Very small samples (less than ten observations) may produce unreliable results.

Data sets typically should (or must) be organized into arrays or frequency distributions for statistical analysis, as well as for effective presentation. Two major categories of measures of descriptive statistics are measures of central tendency (averages) and measures of dispersion. Measures of central tendency are single numbers that describe sample data sets by identifying the value around which the values in the sample tend to cluster. The three averages considered here, and most commonly used, are the arithmetic mean, the median, and the mode. For reasonably symmetrical data sets, the best average to use is the mean, because it has mathematical properties that allow it to be used in further statistical analysis.

Measures of dispersion are single numbers that describe sample data sets by identifying the extent to which the data in the sample vary or deviate from a measure of central tendency, usually the mean. The three measures of dispersion considered here, and most commonly used, are the range, the average deviation, and the standard deviation. Wherever it is applicable and appropriate, the standard deviation should be used. This is because it has mathematical properties, especially in relation to the mean, that allow it to be used in further statistical analysis.

Suggested Readings

Bloom, George F., and Harrison, Henry S. *Appraising the Single Family Residence.* Chicago: American Institute of Real Estate Appraisers, 1978, pp. 436–454.

Boyce, Byrl N., Ed. *Real Estate Appraisal Terminology*, rev. ed. Cambridge, Mass.: Ballinger (Joint publication of the American Institute of Real Estate Appraisers and Society of Real Estate Appraisers), 1981.

Dilmore, Gene. *Quantitative Techniques in Real-Estate Counseling.* Lexington, Mass.: Lexington Books, D.C. Heath, 1981, chapter 1.

Elzey, Freeman F. *A First Reader in Statistics,* 2nd ed. Belmont, Calif.: Wadsworth, 1974.

Lapin, Lawrence L. *Statistics for Modern Business Decisions,* 3rd ed. New York: Harcourt Brace Jovanovich, 1982.

Spurr, William A., and Bonini, Charles P. *Statistical Analysis for Business Decisions,* rev. ed. Homewood, Ill.: Richard D. Irwin, 1973.

13

Applications of Statistical Tools

Key Terms

Coefficient of correlation (r or R) A measure of the degree of relationship between variables and the way in which they move together.

Coefficient of determination (r^2 or R^2) The proportion of total variance in the dependent variable that is explained by the independent variable(s).

Correlation analysis A statistical technique that measures the degree to which two or more variables are associated.

Multiple regression analysis Measurement of the simultaneous influence of a number of independent variables upon a dependent variable.

Normal curve A graphic representation of the normal distribution.

Normal distribution A probability distribution based on the results of large samples and large numbers of samples from the population of a continuous variable.

Regression analysis The process of describing the association in movement between the value of the dependent variable and the value(s) of the independent variable(s).

Regression coefficients (a and b) The intercept (a and b_0) and slope (b, b_1, b_2, . . .) in a regression equation.

Scatter diagram A graphic representation of the data in regression analysis.

Standard error of the estimate (s_{yx}) A measure of dispersion associated with the regression equation (line).

Standard error of the mean ($s_{\bar{x}}$) A measure of dispersion to test and indicate how well the sample mean ($\overline{X}$) estimates the population mean (μ).

Standard error of the regression coefficient (s_b) A measure of dispersion around the slope (b) of the regression line to test its statistical significance.

Statistical inference A technique for drawing inferences about the population (market) from sample data and to test how representative of the population (market) those sample data may be.

***t*-Statistic** The number of standard deviation units the observation in

345

a data set is above or below the mean for small samples with fewer than 30 degrees of freedom.

Z-Statistic   The number of standard deviation units the observation in a data set is above or below the mean for large samples with 30 or more degrees of freedom.

The quantitative tools of statistics presented and discussed in Chapter 12 have wide applicability in the work of the real estate appraiser. Their major uses are twofold: to draw inferences about the market (population) from sample data and sample statistics and to test how representative of the market those sample data and statistics are.

The emphasis on estimating market characteristics from samples should not be taken to mean that the applicability of statistical analysis and other quantitative tools is restricted to the portions of the appraisal framework labeled market and area analysis—far from it. Since appraisal analysis utilizes market data extensively and exclusively in market value estimation, it is important to be able to use figures and measures that are typical, representative, normal, or going market. Statistical analysis enables the appraiser to do just that.

Statistical Inference and Prediction

The appraiser needs to be able to infer what market characteristics are so that market value can be estimated in terms of market conditions and trends. What is market rent? What is the appropriate cost per square foot to use in estimating reproduction cost new? What are typical terms of financing? What are property tax rates and tax burdens likely to be in the foreseeable future? What is the typical size house for the submarket being considered? What is the community's population likely to be in the foreseeable future? How many households will this likely represent, and what proportion are likely to seek ownership housing? What are past and likely future trends in construction costs? The list of such questions is almost endless.

Statistical inference is one technique for deriving answers to these and similar questions. It is based on the assumption that past and current structural relationships and causal influences in the market will continue as observed and measured. It is not a substitute for the appraiser's judgment; rather, it can be an aid to making better judgments.

The Normal Curve and the Normal Distribution

The *normal curve* is a graphic representation of the normal distribution. The *normal distribution* is a probability distribution with very special characteristics. It is based on the results of large samples and large numbers of samples from a population of a continuous variable. The normal curve is the familiar bell-shaped curve. It is symmetrical; both halves have exactly the same shape. Both halves also contain the same number of observations, with the same distribution of values. The mean, median, and mode are identical in value—at the midpoint of the curve (or distribution), directly under the apex (see figure 13–1).

The distance from the mean is measured in standard deviations. The number of standard deviations a given observation value is away from the mean indicates the probability of occurrence of that observation from the population from which the sample(s) is drawn. It is particularly significant to researchers and data research programs that the distribution of the means of several samples drawn from the same population tends to be normal, even if the distributions of the samples are not. The normal distribution is also convenient to researchers because the range of probabilities has been computed and compiled into tables, simplifying work and saving time. Based on the Z-table, 68.26 percent of the observations will fall within the range of the mean plus or minus one standard deviation; 95.44 percent of the observations will fall within the range of the mean plus or minus two standard deviations; and 99.74 percent of the observations will fall within the range of the mean plus or minus three standard deviations.

The Z-Table

The Z-table (table 13–1) shows the probabilities of any observation falling a specified distance (measured in standard deviatons) from the mean. The Z-table shows half the distribution, so the numbers must be added to obtain the distance in both directions around the mean. The value of Z is the difference between the observed value and the mean, divided by the standard deviation.

$$Z = \frac{X - \overline{X}}{s}$$

Given Z, the table shows the probability of a value falling within that range $(\overline{X} \pm Z)$; the probability of a value being a specified distance from the mean, or farther; and the probability of an observation being that far away from the mean in either direction (one-tail test), or in both directions (two-tail test). Given the level of confidence (or probability level) desired, table 13–1 shows how far away an observation can be from the mean and still meet the test of acceptability. This can be for a range around the mean (called the *confidence interval*), using the two-tail test, or for one direction, using the one-tail test. Since the

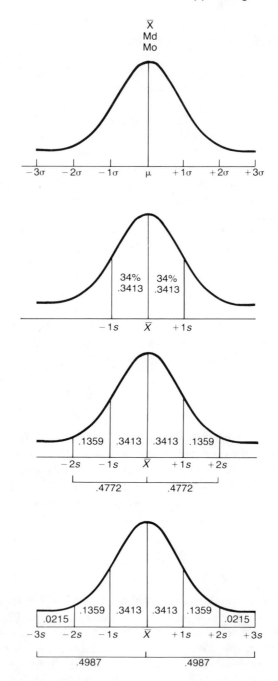

Figure 13–1. Normal Curves

Table 13–1
Z-Table: Areas under the Normal Curve

Z	.00	.01	.02	.03	.04	.05	.06	.07	.08	.09
0.0	.0000	.0040	.0080	.0120	.0160	.0199	.0239	.0279	.0319	.0359
0.1	.0398	.0438	.0478	.0517	.0057	.0596	.0636	.0675	.0714	.0753
0.2	.0793	.0832	.0871	.0910	.0948	.0987	.1026	.1064	.1103	.1141
0.3	.1179	.1217	.1255	.1293	.1331	.1368	.1406	.1443	.1480	.1517
0.4	.1554	.1591	.1628	.1664	.1700	.1736	.1772	.1808	.1844	.1879
0.5	.1915	.1950	.1985	.2019	.2054	.2088	.2123	.2157	.2190	.2224
0.6	.2257	.2291	.2324	.2357	.2389	.2422	.2454	.2486	.2517	.2549
0.7	.2580	.2611	.2642	.2673	.2704	.2734	.2764	.2794	.2823	.2852
0.8	.2881	.2910	.2939	.2967	.2995	.3023	.3051	.3078	.3106	.3133
0.9	.3159	.3186	.3212	.3238	.3264	.3289	.3315	.3340	.3365	.3389
1.0	.3413	.3438	.3461	.3485	.3508	.3531	.3554	.3577	.3599	.3621
1.1	.3643	.3665	.3686	.3708	.3729	.3749	.3770	.3790	.3810	.3830
1.2	.3849	.3869	.3888	.3907	.3925	.3944	.3962	.3980	.3997	.4015
1.3	.4032	.4049	.4066	.4082	.4099	.4115	.4131	.4147	.4162	.4177
1.4	.4192	.4207	.4222	.4236	.4251	.4265	.4279	.4292	.4306	.4319
1.5	.4332	.4345	.4357	.4370	.4382	.4394	.4406	.4418	.4429	.4441
1.6	.4452	.4463	.4474	.4484	.4495	.4505	.4515	.4525	.4535	.4545
1.7	.4554	.4564	.4573	.4582	.4591	.4599	.4608	.4616	.4625	.4633
1.8	.4641	.4649	.4656	.4664	.4671	.4678	.4686	.4693	.4699	.4706
1.9	.4713	.4719	.4726	.4732	.4738	.4744	.4750	.4756	.4761	.4767
2.0	.4772	.4778	.4783	.4788	.4793	.4798	.4803	.4808	.4812	.4817
2.1	.4821	.4826	.4830	.4834	.4838	.4842	.4846	.4850	.4854	.4857
2.2	.4861	.4864	.4868	.4871	.4875	.4878	.4881	.4884	.4887	.4890
2.3	.4893	.4896	.4898	.4901	.4904	.4906	.4909	.4911	.4913	.4916
2.4	.4918	.4920	.4922	.4925	.4927	.4929	.4931	.4932	.4934	.4936
2.5	.4938	.4940	.4941	.4943	.4945	.4946	.4948	.4949	.4951	.4952
2.6	.4953	.4955	.4956	.4957	.4959	.4960	.4961	.4962	.4963	.4964
2.7	.4965	.4966	.4967	.4968	.4969	.4970	.4971	.4972	.4973	.4974
2.8	.4974	.4975	.4976	.4977	.4977	.4978	.4979	.4979	.4980	.4981
2.9	.4981	.4982	.4982	.4983	.4984	.4984	.4985	.4985	.4986	.4986
3.0	.4987	.4987	.4987	.4988	.4988	.4989	.4989	.4989	.4990	.4990

normal distribution is symmetrical, for a given Z-value, the probability of an outcome between an observation (X) and the sample mean $(\overline{X})$ or population mean (μ) is the same whether the observation is greater or less than the mean. The Z-table is applicable for sample statistics with 30 or more degrees of freedom.

The t-Table

When sample statistics have less than 30 degrees of freedom, the t-table (table 13–2) must be used. This is because the reliability of sample statistics (especially averages) decreases markedly as sample size and

Table 13–2
***t*-Table: *t* Distribution**

Degrees of Freedom	$t_{.100}$	$t_{.050}$	$t_{.025}$	$t_{.010}$	$t_{.005}$
1	3.078	6.314	12.706	31.821	63.657
2	1.886	2.920	4.303	6.965	9.925
3	1.638	2.353	3.182	4.541	5.841
4	1.533	2.132	2.776	3.747	4.604
5	1.476	2.015	2.571	3.365	4.032
6	1.440	1.943	2.447	3.143	3.707
7	1.415	1.895	2.365	2.998	3.499
8	1.397	1.860	2.306	2.896	3.355
9	1.383	1.833	2.262	2.821	3.250
10	1.372	1.812	2.228	2.764	3.169
11	1.363	1.796	2.201	2.718	3.106
12	1.356	1.782	2.179	2.681	3.055
13	1.350	1.771	2.160	2.650	3.012
14	1.345	1.761	2.145	2.624	2.977
15	1.341	1.753	2.131	2.602	2.947
16	1.337	1.746	2.120	2.583	2.921
17	1.333	1.740	2.110	2.567	2.898
18	1.330	1.734	2.101	2.552	2.878
19	1.328	1.729	2.093	2.539	2.861
20	1.325	1.725	2.086	2.528	2.845
21	1.323	1.721	2.080	2.518	2.831
22	1.321	1.717	2.074	2.508	2.819
23	1.319	1.714	2.069	2.500	2.807
24	1.318	1.711	2.064	2.492	2.797
25	1.316	1.708	2.060	2.485	2.787
26	1.315	1.706	2.056	2.479	2.779
27	1.314	1.703	2.052	2.473	2.771
28	1.313	1.701	2.048	2.467	2.763
29	1.311	1.699	2.045	2.462	2.756
∞	1.282	1.645	1.960	2.326	2.576

number of degrees of freedom decrease. For each number of degrees of freedom (shown in the first column), the *t*-table shows the number of standard deviations away from the mean represented by different levels of significance. The level of significance is the complement of the level of confidence. The most common levels of significance used in statistical analysis are .01, .05 and .10. These correspond to the 99 percent, 95 percent, and 90 percent levels of confidence.

The *t*-values shown in the .005 column are for the 1 percent level of significance (99 percent level of confidence), using the two-tail test. The .025 column is for the 5 percent level of significance, and the .05 column is for the 10 percent level, both using the two-tail test to derive a confidence interval. For the one-tail test, the .01, .05 and .10 columns are for the 1 percent, 5 percent and 10 percent levels of significance, respectively.

It is to be noted that as sample size (and thus degrees of freedom) increases toward 30 or more, t-tables and Z-tables merge. The t-value for a 95 percent confidence interval for greater than 29 degrees of freedom, for example, is read from table 13–2 as 1.96. Likewise, for a 99 percent confidence interval, the t-value is 2.576. The corresponding Z-values may be found in table 13–1 by first looking in the body of the table for that number representing one-half of the confidence interval (i.e., .4750 for a 95 percent confidence interval and .4950 for a 99 percent confidence interval). This is because the Z-table shows half the distribution. The corresponding Z-values (from table 13–1) are 1.96 for the 95 percent confidence interval and 2.575 for the 99 percent confidence interval.

Confidence Intervals

A confidence interval is the probability or confidence level associated with a given range of Z- or t-values around the mean. Thus, the 95 percent confidence interval for 30 or more degrees of freedom is $X \pm 1.96s$. The Z-value is 1.96 when the probability is .4750, and $2 \times .4750 = .9500$. Similarly, the 99 percent confidence interval for 15 degrees of freedom is $X \pm 2.947s$. The .005 column in the t-table for 15 degrees of freedom is 2.947.

Standard Error of the Mean

A major use of a sample mean $(\overline{X})$ is to estimate the population mean (μ) to indicate what is typical or normal. The standard error of the mean $(s_{\bar{x}})$ is a measure of dispersion to test and indicate how good an estimator $\overline{X}$ is of μ. The formula is: $s_{\bar{x}} = \dfrac{s}{\sqrt{n}}$.

Obviously, the larger the sample, the smaller $s_{\bar{x}}$ becomes. Since sample means tend to be normally distributed, the Z-table can always be used to estimate the confidence interval for the sample mean as an estimator of the population mean.

Application of Statistical Inference Using
the Normal Curve

Any distribution can be precisely and unequivocally described or defined by its mean and standard deviation. Thus, all that is needed to apply the statistical inference techniques covered here are $\overline{X}$, s, and n

($n-1$ will give the degrees of freedom). To estimate population mean from sample mean, the following illustrations use Data Sets 1, 2, and 3 from Chapter 12. The required data and statistics are as follows:

Data Set	$\overline{X}$	s	n	df
1	54.25	.2461	10	9
2	12.39	0.49	428	427
3	170.18	27.69	11	10

Then, $s_{\overline{x}} = \dfrac{s}{\sqrt{n}}$

$$\text{Data Set 1: } s_{\overline{x}} = \frac{.2461}{\sqrt{10}} = \frac{.2461}{3.1623} = .0778$$

$$\text{Data Set 2: } s_{\overline{x}} = \frac{0.49}{\sqrt{428}} = \frac{0.49}{20.6882} = .0237$$

$$\text{Data Set 3: } s_{\overline{x}} = \frac{27.69}{\sqrt{11}} = \frac{27.69}{3.3166} = 8.3489$$

The 95 percent confidence interval for Data Set 1 is $\overline{X} \pm 2.262\, s_{\overline{x}}$ (t-table). This is \$54.25 $\pm$ 2.262 (.0778) or \$54.25 $\pm$ \$0.176. Thus, the appraiser can be 95 percent confident that the market average cost per square foot lies between \$54.07 and \$54.43. This is ± 0.3 percent. The 99 percent confidence interval for Data Set 1 is $\overline{X} \pm 3.250\, s_{\overline{x}}$. This is a range of \$54.25 $\pm$ \$.253, or \$54.00 to \$54.50. This is ± 0.5 percent.

For Data Set 2, the 95 percent confidence interval (Z-table) is 12.39 percent $\pm$ 1.96 (.0237), or 12.34 percent to 12.44 percent. The 99 percent confidence interval is 12.39 percent $\pm$ 2.575 $s_{\overline{x}}$. This is a range of 12.39 percent $\pm$ .06 percent, or 12.33 percent to 12.45 percent. The 95 percent range is ± 0.4 percent, while the 99 percent range is $\pm$ 0.5 percent, of $\overline{X}$.

Finally, in Data Set 3, the 95 percent confidence interval (t-table) is 170.18 $\pm$ 2.228 (8.3489). This is a range of 151.58 feet to 188.78 feet. The 99 percent confidence interval is 170.18 $\pm$ 3.169 (8.3489), or 143.72 feet to 194.64 feet. These are ranges of ± 10.9 percent and ± 15.6 percent, respectively.

Thus, it has been shown that the sample means of Data Sets 1 and 2 are good estimators of their respective population means, even though Data Set 1 is a small sample. The sample mean of Data Set 3, however, is an unreliable estimator of its population mean. This confirms the suspicion that the data are not consistent, as the tabulation of raw data in Chapter 12 showed.

Utilizing the data in Data Set 2, the following methodology is employed in estimating the probability of occurrence of a given observation. What is the probability that a residential mortgage loan will have an interest rate between 12.39 percent and 12.75 percent? First find Z.

$$Z = \frac{X - \overline{X}}{s} = \frac{12.75 - 12.39}{0.49} = \frac{0.36}{0.49} = 0.73$$

Look in Z-table for probability when $Z = 0.73$. The probability is .2673 or 26.73 percent that the interest rate will fall betwen 12.39 percent and 12.75 percent.

What is the probability that the interest rate will be between 12.25 percent and 12.75 percent? This requires finding two Z-values, since one value is less than $\overline{X}$ and the other is greater than $\overline{X}$:

$$Z = \frac{12.75 - 12.39}{0.49} = 0.73$$

$$Z = \frac{12.25 - 12.39}{0.49} = \frac{-0.14}{0.49} = -0.28 \text{ (disregard sign)}$$

The Z-table shows a probability of .2673 for $Z = 0.73$ and a probability of .1103 for $Z = 0.28$. The total probability is .2673 + .1103 = .3776, or 37.76 percent.

What is the probability that an interest rate will be no higher than 13.00%?

$$Z = \frac{13.00 - 12.39}{0.49} = \frac{0.61}{0.49} = 1.24$$

The probability that the interest rate is between 13.00 percent and 12.39 percent is .3925 (Z-table). Also, the probability that the interest rate is at least 12.39 percent is .5000. Thus, the total probability is .5000 + .3925 = .8925, or 89.25 percent.

What is the probability that the interest rate will be 11.75 percent or lower?

$$Z = \frac{11.75 - 12.39}{0.49} = \frac{-0.89}{0.49} = -1.31 \text{ (disregard sign)}$$

The probability that the interest rate will be between 11.75 percent and 12.39 percent is .4049. The probability that the interest rate will be below 12.39 percent at all is .5000. Therefore, the probability that the interest rate will be 11.75 percent or lower is .5000 − .4049 = .0951 or 9.51 percent.

What is the probability in Data Set 3 of Chapter 12 that the 250-foot lot is in the same competitive market as the others in the sample based on size considerations only; that is, what is the probability that it came from the same population?

$$\overline{X} = 170.18 \qquad s = 27.69 \qquad df = 10$$

Since df is less than 30, the t-table must be used. This is a one-tail test, since the question is whether a lot as deep as 250 feet could come from the same population. The t-value is

$$\frac{250 - 170.18}{27.69} = \frac{79.82}{27.69} = 2.88$$

For 10 degrees of freedom, the critical t-value at the .01 level of significance is 2.764. The calculated t-value is 2.88, which is larger. Therefore, there is less than a .01 probability (less than 1 chance in 100) that a lot as deep as 250 feet would come from the same population.

Regression and Correlation Analysis

The calculation of regression lines and the several measures of regression and correlation are moderately complicated and time-consuming without the availability of a programmable calculator, preprogrammed calculator, or computer. While those calculations are presented here in detail, it should be stressed that the emphasis is on the meaning and the underlying ideas of regression and correlation analysis, the measures that are produced by the analysis, and the interpretation and use of the results. As with any other mathematical or statistical tools, regression and correlation analysis are not perfect. Accordingly, a healthy respect for the limitations as well as the applications of the analysis is necessary. The most significant appraisal applications of regression and correlation analysis at present are in the valuation of sites or lots and in the valuation of single-family residences.

The objective of regression and correlation analysis is to estimate or predict the value of a variable that is the object of the analysis. The prediction is based on the value(s) of one or more other variables whose values are held to be associated with that of the unknown variable, often but not necessarily in a causal relationship. One might attempt to estimate or predict the sales price of a residence if its square foot area is known. It might well be possible to estimate the monthly rental of a residence if its square foot area, age, location, number of bedrooms, and number of garage stalls were known. Population for a community might be estimated for a given date (time being the known variable).

The underlying rationale of regression and correlation analysis is that there is an association between movement in the values of the unknown variable (called the dependent variable and given the symbol Y) and movement in the values of the known variable(s) (called the independent variables and given the symbol X). Regression analysis is the process of describing the association in movement between the value of the dependent variable (Y) and the values of the independent variables ($X_1, X_2, \ldots$). A regression equation or regression line is calculated to give the best fit to the data in the sample. The goodness of fit is measured by statistical processes. Correlation analysis is the process of measuring how much the movement in the values of the independent variables ($X_1, X_2, \ldots$) explains movements or changes in the value of the dependent variable (Y). It shows how close the association is between the movements of X and Y, and, therefore, how good a predictor of the values of Y the values of X are.

Regression Analysis

Suppose that a sample of 20 recent residential sales in an area were taken and the following data on sales price and household income were obtained:

Sale Number	Sale Price ($000)	Income ($000)
1	35	15
2	100	60
3	150	75
4	50	20
5	140	80
6	70	30
7	40	17
8	45	18
9	60	23
10	90	42
11	125	70
12	45	21
13	50	20
14	60	26
15	58	32
16	40	17
17	65	40
18	40	18
19	40	16
20	80	56

It would be possible to describe sales price by its mean and standard deviation: $69,150 and $34,758, respectively. This information would be of little or no use in estimating the value or most probable sales price of another house in the same area, especially because of the extremely large standard deviation. However, suppose that it is assumed there is a relationship or association between sales price and the income of the household purchasing the house. Assume, further, that a household with an income of $25,000 is looking for a house in this area. What price are they likely to pay?

The first step is to plot the data on a scatter diagram, as shown in figure 13–2. This shows visually whether there appears to be any association between sales price (Y) and household income (X). Assuming that there appears to be an association (sales price increases as income increases), the next step is to calculate the regression equation.

The regression equation in general form is $Y_c = a + bX$. This describes a straight line. Here, Y_c is the calculated value of Y [the

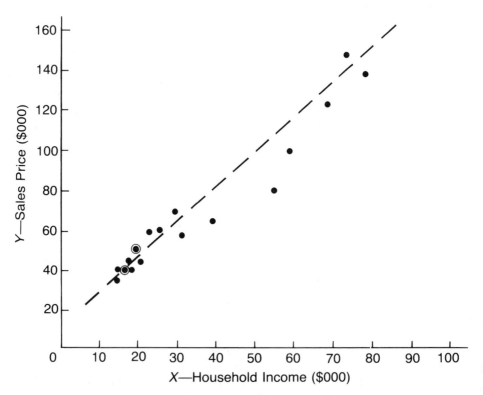

Figure 13–2. Scatter Diagram

predicted value (in this case, sales price) given the value of X]; a is the constant (the value of Y_c when $X = 0$); and b is the coefficient of X, the b coefficient. This is the amount of change in the value of Y per one-unit change in the value of X. The sign of the b-coefficient indicates the direction of the change.

Calculating the values of the regression coefficients a and b is a complicated process. It is done by the method of least squares, which minimizes the sum of the squares of the differences between the observed values of Y and the calculated values of Y_c. Squared differences are called variance. Minimum squared differences are encountered around a mean. Thus, the regression equation is, in effect, a moving mean of Y-values, given the values of X. The preliminary calculations that are necessary to develop the values of a and b, as well as measures of significance and reliability, are shown in table 13–3.

From table 13–3, $Y_c = 14.97 + 1.56X$. This translates to: $Y_c = \$14{,}970 + 1.56$ (Household Income). If $X = \$25{,}000$, then $Y_c = 14.97 + 1.56 (25.0) = 14.97 + 39.00 = 53.97$. In other words, the forecast sales price when the household income is $25,000 is $53,970.

Since the regression equation has the characteristics of a mean, it has a standard deviation associated with it. This is called the standard error of the estimate, and has the symbol s_{yx}. The standard error of the estimate is used to measure the representativeness of the regression equation in the same way that s is a test of the reliability of $\overline{X}$ in a sample. In this example, $s_{yx} = 8.77$, or $8,770.

Since the regression coefficient (b) is calculated with the characteristics of a mean, it also has an associated standard deviation. This is the standard error of the regression coefficient, which has the symbol s_b. The standard error of the regression coefficient is used to test whether b is statistically significant. That is, could this association between X and Y have occurred by chance? In this example, $s_b = 0.0931$. To test whether b is statistically significant, a t-value is calculated. This measures how many standard errors the value of b is away from zero. If there is no association in movement between X and Y, then $b = 0$. In this example,

$$t = \frac{b}{s_b} = \frac{1.56}{0.0931} = 16.76$$

As noted in Chapter 12, one degree of freedom is lost for every statistic calculated from the raw data. Here, both a and b are statistics, so two degrees of freedom are lost. The general formula for degrees of freedom is df $= n - m$, where

n = number of observations

m = number of coefficients calculated.

In this example, df = $n - m$ = 20 - 2 = 18. If there were seven X-variables, there would be one a-coefficient and seven b-coefficients for a total of eight degrees of freedom lost. Then m = 8 and df = 12.

The confidence interval around the regression line is given by the standard error of the estimate times the Z- or t-value determined by the desired level of confidence and the number of degrees of freedom. In this example, s_{yx} = \$8,770 and df = 18. With df = 18, the t-table shows that the 95 percent confidence interval is $Y_c \pm 2.101s_{yx}$. The 99 percent confidence interval is $Y_c \pm 2.878s_{yx}$. The 95 percent confidence interval, when household income is \$25,000, equals \$53,970 $\pm$ 2.101(\$8,770), or \$53,970 $\pm$ \$18,426. This is a range of \$35,544 to \$72,396. The 99 percent interval is larger. This shows that household income is a highly unreliable estimator of sales price, even though there is association in movement between the values of the two variables.

The t-test value (calculated above) is compared with the critical t-value from the t- or Z-table for the desired level of confidence. In this case, the t-test produced a value of 16.76. The t-value for the 1 percent level of significance and 18 degrees of freedom is 2.878. Since 16.76 is much larger than 2.878, it is extremely unlikely that the association in movement between sales price and household income occurred by chance. Thus, there is association between the two, even though household income is not a good, reliable predictor of sales price.

Figure 13–2, table 13–3, and the subsequent calculations deal exclusively with simple linear regression, which means that there is only one independent variable. Provided that sophisticated calculating and data storage equipment (a computer) is available, it is possible to calculate regression equations with two or more independent variables. This is called multiple regression. The same kinds of measures and tests are produced, except that there is one b-coefficient for each independent variable. The general equation for multiple linear regression is: $Y_c = a + b_1 X_1 + b_2 X_2 + \ldots b_n X_n$, where n is the number of independent variables. Multiple regression shows, measures, and tests the combined effect of all the independent variables on the value of the dependent variables. Some examples will be presented later in this chapter to illustrate the application of multiple linear regression analysis to residential site appraisal.

Correlation Analysis

Correlation measures how closely the values of X and Y are associated and how much movements in the value of X explain movements in the value of Y. Correlation can be positive, if the values move in the same direction together, or negative, if they move in opposite directions. The sum of the squared differences between observed values of Y and $\overline{Y}$ constitutes total variance. The sum of the squared differences between observed values of Y and Y_c values (calculated from the regression equation) is the unexplained variance. The sum of the squared differences between Y_c and $\overline{Y}$ is explained variance. Thus,

$$(Y_c - \overline{Y})^2 = (Y - \overline{Y})^2 - (Y - Y_c)^2.$$

The higher the percentage of total variance that is explained or accounted for by the regression equation, the higher the correlation between movements in the value of X and movements in the value of Y. This percentage of explained variance is called the *coefficient of determination* for simple linear regression and is given the symbol r^2. For multiple regression, it is called the *coefficient of multiple determination* and is given the symbol R^2.

In the example presented, $r^2 = +.94$. This means that 94 percent of the variance of sales price from its mean is explained or accounted for by household income. This is a relatively high figure, which suggests that there is high or close correlation between sales price and household income for this sample, and possibly for its market area.

*Uses and Limitations of Regression
and Correlation Analysis*

Regression analysis can show whether there is association in movement between Y (the dependent variable) and X (the independent variable(s)). It describes this relationship through the regression equation. It can show whether the relationship in movement between X and Y could have happened by chance. Regression analysis can also be used to estimate or predict the value of Y given a value of X (one or more independent variables). It can also test how reliable that estimate or prediction is.

Correlation analysis measures how much of the total variance of Y from its mean is explained or accounted for by the regression equation. Therefore, it measures how close the relationship is in value changes of X and Y. Regression and correlation analysis are reliable only for relatively large samples. Causation is neither identified nor implied. Relatively sophisticated calculating equipment is required. Regression and correlation are mechanical, mathematical processes. They are not a substitute for judgment and qualitative analysis or evaluations. The results can be no better than the data gathered and used.

Table 13–3
Regression Analysis: Data Calculation

Sale Number	Income (X)	Sales Price (Y)	X^2	XY	Y^2	$X - \overline{X}$	$Y - \overline{Y}$
1	15	35	225	525	1,225	−19.80	−34.15
2	60	100	3,600	6,000	10,000	25.20	30.85
3	75	150	5,625	11,250	22,500	40.20	80.85
4	20	50	400	1,000	2,500	−14.80	−19.15
5	80	140	6,400	11,200	19,600	45.20	70.85
6	30	70	900	2,100	4,900	− 4.80	0.85
7	17	40	289	680	1,600	−17.80	−29.15
8	18	45	324	810	2,025	−16.80	−24.15
9	23	60	529	1,380	3,600	−11.80	− 9.15
10	42	90	1,764	3,780	8,100	7.20	20.85
11	70	125	4,900	8,750	15,625	35.20	55.85
12	21	45	441	945	2,025	−13.80	−24.15
13	20	50	400	1,000	2,500	−14.80	−19.15
14	26	60	676	1,560	3,600	− 8.80	− 9.15
15	32	58	1,024	1,856	3,364	− 2.80	−11.15
16	17	40	289	680	1,600	−17.80	−29.15
17	40	65	1,600	2,600	4,225	5.20	− 4.15
18	18	40	324	720	1,600	−16.80	−29.15
19	16	40	256	640	1,600	−18.80	−29.15
20	56	80	3,136	4,480	6,400	21.20	10.85
	$\Sigma X =$ 696	$\Sigma Y =$ 1,383	$\Sigma X^2 =$ 33,102	$\Sigma XY =$ 61,956	$\Sigma Y^2 =$ 118,589	0	0

Note: $\overline{X} = 34.80$; $\overline{Y} = 69.15$; $s_x = 21.62$; $s_y = 34.76$.

Regression Coefficients

$$Y_c = a + bX$$

$$a = \frac{(\Sigma Y)(\Sigma X^2) - (\Sigma X)(\Sigma XY)}{n(\Sigma X^2) - (\Sigma X)^2}$$

$$= \frac{(1,383)(33,102) - (696)(61,956)}{(20)(33,102) - (696)^2} = \frac{2,658,690}{177,624} = 14.97$$

$$b = \frac{n(\Sigma XY) - (\Sigma X)(\Sigma Y)}{n(\Sigma X^2) - (\Sigma X)^2}$$

$$= \frac{20(61,956) - (696)(1,383)}{20(33,102) - (696)^2} = \frac{276,552}{177,624} = 1.56$$

$$Y_c = 14.97 + 1.56X$$

Standard Error of the Estimate

$$s_{yx} = \sqrt{\frac{\Sigma Y^2 - \overline{Y}\Sigma Y - b(\Sigma XY - \overline{X}\Sigma Y)}{n - m}}$$

$$= \sqrt{\frac{118,589 - (69.15)(1,383) - 1.56\,[61,956 - (34.8)(1,383)]}{18}}$$

$$= \sqrt{\frac{1,383.49}{18}} = \sqrt{76.86} = 8.77$$

Table 13–3 *(continued)*

Sale Number	$(X - \bar{X})^2$	$(X - \bar{X})(Y - \bar{Y})$	$(Y - \bar{Y})^2$	Y_c	$Y - Y_c$	$(Y - Y_c)^2$
1	392.04	676.17	1,166.22	38.37	− 3.37	11.36
2	635.04	777.42	951.72	108.57	− 8.57	73.44
3	1,616.04	3,250.17	6,536.72	131.97	18.03	325.08
4	219.04	283.42	366.72	46.17	3.83	14.67
5	2,043.04	3,202.42	5,019.72	139.77	0.23	0.05
6	23.04	− 4.08	0.72	61.77	8.23	67.73
7	316.84	518.87	849.72	41.49	− 1.49	2.22
8	282.24	405.72	583.22	43.05	1.95	3.80
9	139.24	107.97	83.72	50.85	9.15	83.72
10	51.84	150.12	434.72	80.49	9.51	90.44
11	1,239.04	1,965.92	3,119.22	124.17	0.83	0.69
12	190.44	333.27	583.22	47.73	− 2.73	7.45
13	219.04	283.42	366.72	46.17	3.83	14.67
14	77.44	80.52	83.72	55.53	4.47	19.98
15	7.84	31.22	124.32	64.89	− 6.89	47.47
16	316.84	518.87	849.72	41.49	− 1.49	2.22
17	27.04	− 21.58	17.22	77.37	− 12.37	153.02
18	282.24	489.72	849.72	43.05	− 3.05	9.30
19	353.44	548.02	849.72	39.93	0.07	0.005
20	449.44	230.02	117.72	102.33	− 22.33	498.63
	$\Sigma(X - \bar{X})^2 =$ 8,881.20	$\Sigma(X - \bar{X})$ $(Y - \bar{Y}) =$ 13,827.60	$\Sigma(Y - \bar{Y})^2 =$ 22,954.50			$\Sigma(Y - Y_c)^2 =$ 1,425.96

Standard Error of the Regression Coefficient

$$s_b = \frac{s_{yx}}{\sqrt{\Sigma X^2 - \bar{X}\Sigma X}}$$

$$= \frac{8.77}{\sqrt{33,102 - 34.8(696)}}$$

$$= \frac{8.77}{\sqrt{8,881.20}} = \frac{8.77}{94.24} = .0931$$

Correlation

Total Variance $= \Sigma(Y - \bar{Y})^2 = 22,954.50$
Unexplained Variance $= \Sigma(Y - Y_c)^2 = 1,425.96$
Explained Variance $= \Sigma(Y_c - \bar{Y})^2 = 21,528.54$

Coefficient of Determination

$$r^2 = \frac{\text{Explained Variance}}{\text{Total Variance}} = \frac{21,528.54}{22,954.50} = .9379, \quad \text{or} \quad 94\%$$

Coefficient of Correlation

$$r = \sqrt{.9379} = .9684, \quad \text{or} \quad 97\%$$

Also,

$$r = b\left(\frac{s_x}{s_y}\right) = 1.56\left(\frac{21.62}{34.76}\right) = .9703$$

Application of Regression Analysis to Site Valuation

The techniques, applications, and uses of regression analysis explained earlier are applied here to the site valuation problem presented in Chapter 8. The data employed are the same: sales prices and salient site and transaction characteristics for comparable sites.

The important consideration in evaluating regression analysis as a method of site valuation is that it enables the appraiser-analyst to estimate most probable sales price (value) directly from market data. The basic requirements are a sufficient quantity of good, reliable, verified comparable sales transaction data—and, of course, calculating equipment. Regression analysis also enables the appraiser-analyst to test the reliability of the results, especially the value estimate. It is a bit difficult to explain to an uninitiated reader, but it can be used both to supplement and to test the results of the sales adjustment process. Judgmental skill is still required of the appraiser in the selection of the independent variable(s) to use and in the interpretation of results.

In the following application, simple linear regression is applied initially in two separate regression models, utilizing square footage and front footage as independent (predictor) variables, respectively. The results of these two applications are then compared. Subsequently, two multiple regression models are presented, and the results are exhibited for perusal and discussion purposes.

Application of Simple Linear Regression Models

Simple linear regression may be used to estimate sales price or value with only one adjustment factor or element of comparison. This can be a realistic approach when all the other elements of comparison are nearly identical with those of the subject site. When several elements of comparison or adjustment factors have strong influences on sales price and value, however, as in the case of the 13 comparable site sales analyzed in Chapter 8, simple linear regression analysis is not a good value estimator.

The comparable sales in Chapter 8 were analyzed in terms of the simple linear regression between sales price and site area in square feet, and between sales price and front footage. The resulting estimating equations were:

$$Y_c = a + bX$$
$$\text{Sales Price} = \$478 + \$0.41 \text{ per Square Foot}$$
$$\text{Sales Price} = \$-52 + \$75 \text{ per Front Foot}$$

The other measures were as follows:

	Square Foot	Front Foot
r^2	.7090	.8279
Standard Error	$ 527	$ 494
Confidence Interval (95%)	±$1,160	±$1,087
Estimated Value	$6,218	$5,948

Clearly, neither of these measures is a particularly good or reliable estimator of value, especially when these results are compared with those from multiple regression analysis presented in the next section. However, these comparative measures do show that front footage is a better single estimator than square footage in this instance. This is one use of the analysis—indicating the better or best single independent variable.

Application of Multiple Linear Regression Models

The computer runs in this section, in comparison with the more traditional appraisal techniques presented in the example in Chapter 8, show the applicability of multiple regression analysis to site valuation. The appraiser-analyst identifies the significant items of comparison from site and market analysis in exactly the way it is done for the traditional adjustment process. Data on these variables are fed into a computer or calculator programmed for multiple regression analysis. The calculations are so numerous and involved that high-speed calculating equipment is essential.

Regression analysis, whether simple linear or multiple linear, provides a specific value estimate for the subject property, using the same comparable sales data employed in the sales adjustment process in Chapter 8. With the sales adjustment process, the appraiser still must reconcile the 13 adjusted sales prices to a single value estimate. Regression analysis provides tests of reliability and statistical significance for the measures produced, which the sales adjustment process cannot do. If a range of estimated value is required or desirable, both the sales adjustment process and regression analysis can provide it. The difference is that regression analysis produces a statistically defensible and measurable probability range.

Multiple Regression Analysis. In the computer run below, the 13 comparable sites analyzed via traditional appraisal methodology in Chapter 8 were processed in a multiple regression model using date of sale, square footage, and location as independent variables.

Observation	X (1) Date	X (2) Sq. Ft.	X (3) Location	Y Price
1	79.000	6250.000	1.000	3380.000
2	82.000	7500.000	1.000	4500.000
3	77.000	9375.000	1.000	4775.000
4	81.000	12500.000	1.000	7350.000
5	78.000	6875.000	1.000	3600.000
6	80.000	8125.000	1.000	4610.000
7	78.000	7500.000	1.000	3580.000
8	81.000	9625.000	1.000	4650.000
9	82.000	10500.000	1.000	5160.000
10	79.000	9750.000	1.000	4820.000
11	78.000	13125.000	2.000	5750.000
12	79.000	10500.000	4.000	5430.000
13	80.000	11250.000	5.000	6445.000

Mean of raw data:

	79.538	9451.923	1.615	4926.923

Standard deviation of raw data:

	1.613	2133.279	1.325	1137.341

Correlation Matrix:

	Date	Sq. Ft.	Location	Price
Date	1.0000	.12619	−.05097	.32095
Sq. Ft.		1.0000	.41294	.89635
Location			1.0000	.46466

.86386 = Coefficient of multiple determination (R^2)
.92718 = Multiple correlation coefficient (R)

Regression Coefficients:

$$121.90029 = b(3)$$
$$.43140 = b(2)$$
$$147.77806 = b(1)$$
$$-10909.02986 = b(0) \text{ or } a$$

The multiple regression formula for this data set would, therefore, be:

$$Y = -10909.02986 + 147.77806 \ (X_1)$$
$$+ .43140 \ (X_2) + 121.90029 \ (X_3)$$

Substituting relevant values in the equation for the subject property:

Price = −10909.02986 + 147.77806 (Subject Date of Sale)
     + .43140 (Subject Sq. Ft.) + 121.90029 (Subject Location—3)

The indicated price for subject property is $7,450. That price of $7,450 is derived from the above equation of relationships, explaining

86.386 percent of the variance in price for the sample data. This indicates a value per front foot for the subject property of $93.13.

Multiple Regression Analysis (Continued). In the foregoing analysis, both frontage and depth were incorporated in the square footage of each comparable. A second multiple regression analysis was run in which these two items were separated. The output of that analysis is as follows

	X (1)	X (2)	X (3)	X (4)	Y
Observation	Date	F.F.	Depth	Location	Price
1	79.000	50.000	125.000	1.000	3380.000
2	82.000	60.000	125.000	1.000	4500.000
3	77.000	75.000	125.000	1.000	4775.000
4	81.000	100.000	125.000	1.000	7350.000
5	78.000	55.000	125.000	1.000	3600.000
6	80.000	65.000	125.000	1.000	4610.000
7	78.000	50.000	150.000	1.000	3580.000
8	81.000	55.000	175.000	1.000	4650.000
9	82.000	60.000	175.000	1.000	5160.000
10	79.000	65.000	150.000	1.000	4820.000
11	78.000	75.000	175.000	2.000	5750.000
12	79.000	70.000	150.000	4.000	5430.000
13	80.000	75.000	150.000	5.000	6445.000

Mean of raw data:

	79.538	65.769	144.231	1.615	4926.923

Standard deviation of raw data:

	1.613	13.670	20.801	1.325	1137.341

Correlation Matrix:

	Date	F.F.	Depth	Location	Price
Date	1.0000	.07412	.16237	− .05097	.32095
F.F.		1.0000	− .12963	.27069	.90923
Depth			1.0000	.21509	.18720
Location				1.0000	.46466

.99485 = Coefficient of Multiple Determination (R^2)
.99742 = Multiple Correlation Coefficient (R)

Regression coefficients:

$$166.44759 = b(4)$$
$$12.06008 = b(3)$$
$$72.23827 = b(2)$$
$$148.73567 = b(1)$$
$$-13628.48089 = b(0) \text{ or } a$$

The multiple regression formula for this data set would, therefore, be:

$$Y = -13628.48089 + 148.73567 \ (X_1)$$
$$+ \ 72.23827 \ (X_2) + 12.06008 \ (X_3)$$
$$+ \ 166.44759 \ (X_4)$$

Substituting relevant values in the equation for the subject property:

Price = $-13628.48089 + 148.73567$ (Subject Date of Sale)
+ 72.23827 (Subject Front Feet)
+ 12.06008 (Subject Depth)
+ 166.44759 (Subject Location—3).

The indicated price for subject property is $6,957, rounded to $7,000. This price of $7,000 is derived from the above equation of relationships, explaining 99.485 percent of the variance in price for the sample data. This indicates a value per front foot for the subject property of $87.50.

Applications of Quantitative Tools to Market Analysis

The tools and measures of quantitative and statistical analysis presented here are only illustrative of the wide variety available to the real estate analyst. Measures of market delineation and definition, for example, have been consciously omitted in the interest of time and space limitations, as have many of the advanced and detailed measures of mathematics and statistics. Those covered here, however, are the most common and the most widely used. These tools and measures have applicability in market and area analysis as well as throughout the several steps in the appraisal framework. Appraisers nearly always must work with samples, and the measures presented and discussed here all emphasize the analysis and interpretation of samples.

Market Description

Typical, representative, or normal current market conditions are identified primarily through the use of averages (mean, median, and mode). Samples are almost invariably required. The reliability of the sample mean can be tested and measured by the standard deviation. The extent to which the sample mean is a good representative of the population mean is indicated by the confidence interval given by the standard error of the mean. These measures can be applied to any market variable, provided that sufficient data are included in the sample and that the sample is reasonably symmetrical.

Suppose, for example, that an appraiser wants (or needs) to estimate the age of a typical house in an area. A sample of 40 houses is taken, with the following results:

Age	Frequency
12	1
14	1
15	3
16	5
17	11
18	8
19	4
20	3
22	2
24	2

The mean is 17.75 years, whereas both the median and the mode are 17 years. The range is 12 years, the average deviation is 1.74 years, and the standard deviation is 2.41 years. The 95 percent confidence interval for the sample mean is 13.03 to 22.47 years, and the 99 percent confidence interval is 11.54 to 23.96 years. The standard error of the mean is 0.38 years. The 95 percent confidence interval for the population mean as estimated by the sample mean is 17.01 to 18.49 years. The 99 percent confidence interval is 16.77 to 18.73 years.

These measures all show that the distribution is slightly skewed to the right (upper values), but that the sample mean is a good estimator for its sample as well as for the population mean. The appraiser can confidently use 17.75 years as the typical age of houses in this area. The important point is that statistical analysis has enabled the appraiser to test the average(s) that might be used and to judge whether the average(s) can be used with confidence.

Market Growth and Change

In addition to current market conditions, market growth or change must also be estimated, measured, or predicted by the appraiser. Index numbers can be used to identify past trends in market measures, but they do not provide a basis for forecasting directly from the data. What can be done, however, is to derive the rate of change (annual or per period) indicated by the data. Both straight-line and exponential rates can be derived from the first and last figures in order to forecast into the future.

Suppose, for example, that the following population data were obtained for a community:

Year	Population	Index Number
1974	17,700	100.00
1975	18,350	103.67
1976	19,100	107.91
1977	19,700	111.30
1978	20,650	116.67
1979	21,300	120.34
1980	22,100	124.86
1981	22,600	127.68
1982	23,400	132.20

The straight-line increase per year is 712.50. The straight-line rate of increase per year is 4.03%. The exponential (compound) rate of increase per year is 3.55%.

Simple linear regression analysis can also be applied. The linear regression equation is

$$Y_c = a + bX = 17667.76 + 719.18X$$

where X is the number of years away from the base year.

The standard error of the estimate (s_{yx}) is 84.6, and the coefficient of determination (r^2) is .9982, or 99.82 percent. The 95 percent confidence interval (df = 7) is $Y_c \pm 2.365s_{yx}$. This is $Y_c \pm 200.08$. The 99 percent confidence is $Y_c \pm 3.499s_{yx}$. This is $Y_c \pm 296.02$.

These measures indicate an exceptionally high degree of correlation between population and the passage of time. The regression equation is a good estimator or predictor of population, since the standard error of the estimate is quite small. The basic confidence intervals are relatively narrow, despite the small sample size.

Applying these several measures to forecasting population for 1985 and 1988 yields the following results:

	1985	1988
Straight-Line Amount	25,538	27,675
Straight-Line Rate	25,546	27,686
Compound Rate	25,979	28,845
Regression Line	25,579	27,736

Clearly, the relationship between time and population is linear or straight-line. There is virtually no difference between the straight-line amount, the straight-line rate, and the linear regression forecasts. The reason for using the regression forecast is that its results can be tested and evaluated statistically, whereas the others cannot.

Uses and Limitations of Quantitative and Statistical Tools for Appraisers

Quantitative, mathematical, and statistical tools (and measures) deal with numbers and their relationships. The result of every appraisal analysis is a number that is derived from processing other numbers. The techniques, tools, and processes described and illustrated here enable the appraiser to approach the manipulation of data and numbers in a systematic, meaningful, and productive fashion. Different tools and techniques exist to cope with different circumstances. The choice of the appropriate measure or process to fit the nature of the problem and the data is a decision that must be made by the analyst. It is necessary to know and apply the rules of procedure so that the tools and techniques used are employed correctly.

Statistical tools, in particular, can be used to describe current market conditions and relationships as of the appraisal date. This is what is really meant when appraisers talk about using market data. Averages, especially the mean, can be used to indicate what is typical, normal, representative, or going market. The decision on which average to use depends on the nature or objective of the problem, the character of the sample data used, and whether the average is to be (or can be) used in further statistical analysis. The reliability of the mean, in particular, as representative of the sample data can be tested and evaluated by the standard deviation. The range and average deviation also help in deciding whether an average can be used legitimately to describe a sample data set. The reliability of the sample mean as an estimator of the population mean can also be tested and evaluated. This is important in drawing inferences about what is typical, representative, or normal in the market. The probability that a given observation (e.g., a comparable sale) came from the same competitive market as the sample data can be tested and evaluated. This is important in evaluating comparability of market data. It is also important in judging whether the subject property appears to be in line with the market with respect to some characteristic.

Market changes or trends can be identified for forecasting or prediction purposes. Since value is the present worth of anticipated future benefits, the appraiser is necessarily future-oriented. Index numbers, ratios, and rates (especially rates of change) can be used to measure market changes over time and to forecast or predict future values and quantities. Regression analysis, where applicable, can be applied to forecasting or prediction by using time as one independent variable.

Regression analysis has the advantage of allowing the appraiser-analyst to test the statistical reliability and significance of the measurs produced.

Quantitative and statistical tools cannot produce results that are any better than the data that are employed in the analysis. Statistical analysis based on nonprobability samples, especially small samples, produces unreliable results. The tests of reliability are not necessarily valid or meaningful in such situations. Sample size is critical to good statistical results. The extremely small samples traditionally used in appraising cannot produce reliable measures. This is true whether or not statistical analysis is used.

Statistical and quantitative tools are mechanical mathematical devices. They are not a substitute for judgment. Indeed, more judgment is required when statistical analysis is employed, because the selection of data, sample size, sampling technique, and tools of analysis are critical to good, useful results. Statistical analysis has the major advantage of indicating to the appraiser-analyst what the reliability and significance of market measures are. There is no way of judging how reliable, significant, or meaningful nonstatistical measures are. Quantitative and statistical analyses (especially the latter) are responsive to the appraiser's fundamental precept: go to the market. In this approach, the data are utilized with minimum intrusion of the appraiser's own biases and predilections into the analysis.

Summary

Statistical inference allows the analyst to estimate or infer population characteristics from sample characteristics. This is especially true of the mean, using the standard error of the mean ($s_{\bar{x}}$). The normal curve (or normal distribution) and its associated Z-table and t-table enable the appraiser-analyst to make two important types of judgments: (1) the probability or likelihood that a given value or observation will occur within the same population or market and (2) the confidence interval within which the value of a variable will most probably occur. The confidence interval, based on the Z-table and the t-table, shows how reliable a statistical measure (especially a mean) is.

Statistical inference permits the appraiser-analyst to estimate the value of an observation or item that is not included in the sample, but is assumed to be in the same population because it has similar characteristics to those in the sample. Reliability, confidence interval, and significance tests all emphasize the critical importance of sample size or, more properly, the number of degrees of freedom in a sample. Since one degree of freedom is lost every time a statistic is calculated from the sample data directly (df $= n - m$), it is important to have sufficiently large samples so that df is at or near 30.

Index numbers, rates, and ratios all show relationships between variables. They can be used for estimation or prediction so long as the assumption that the same structural (or causative) relationship prevails is supportable.

Regression analysis allows for estimation of the value of the dependent variable (Y) given the values of the independent variable(s), or X-values. Both linear and curvilinear relationships can be measured with regression analysis. The value of the dependent variable is estimated or predicted in simple linear regression by $Y_c = a + bX$. The value of the dependent variable is estimated or predicted in multiple linear regression by $Y_c = a + b_1 X_1 + b_2 X_2 + \cdots b_n X_n$. Statistical reliability in regression analysis is tested and measured through the confidence intervals provided by s_{yx} for the regression equation, and by s_b for each regression coefficient. The statistical significance (non-randomness) of the association between movements in the values of X and Y is tested and measured through the t-test for regression coefficients. The closeness of association between movements in the values of X and Y is measured by the coefficient of determination (r^2 or R^2). This is called correlation analysis, which meausres and indicates the percentage of total variance in Y explained or accounted for by the regression equation.

Quantitative tools and statistical analysis can be applied to both market description and market forecasting. Quantitative and statistical analyses are not substitutes for the appraiser's judgment. Rather, they are aids to better decisions and judgments. Statistical and quantitative tools are limited in their usefulness by their applicability to the problem at hand and by the availability and quality of sample data in sufficient quantity.

Suggested Readings

Bloom, George F., and Harrison, Henry S. *Appraising the Single Family Residence.* Chicago: American Institute of Real Estate Appraisers, 1978, pp. 436–454.

Boyce, Byrl N., ed. *Real Estate Appraisal Terminology,* rev. ed. Cambridge, Mass.: Ballinger (Joint publication of the American Institute of Real Estate Appraisers and Society of Real Estate Appraisers), 1981.

Chiswick, Barry R., and Chiswick, Stephen J. *Statistics and Econo-*

metrics: A Problem-Solving Text. Baltimore: University Park Press, 1975.

Dilmore, Gene. *Quantitative Techniques in Real-Estate Counseling.* Lexington, Mass.: Lexington Books, D.C. Heath, 1981, chapters 1 and 5.

Elzey, Freeman F. *A First Reader in Statistics,* 2nd ed. Belmont, Calif.: Wadsworth, 1974.

Lapin, Lawrence L. *Statistics of Modern Business Decisions,* 3rd ed. New York: Harcourt Brace Jovanovich, 1982.

Morton, T. Gregory. "Regression Analysis Appraisal Models: Selected Topics and Issues" (Real Estate Report No. 19). Storrs: Center for Real Estate and Urban Economic Studies, The University of Connecticut, 1976.

Spurr, William A., and Bonini, Charles P. *Statistical Analysis for Business Decisions,* rev. ed. Homewood, Ill.: Richard D. Irwin, 1973.

14 Reconciliation and Final Value Estimate

Key Terms

Indications of value   The bottom-line results based upon application of different valuation approaches or procedures—typically, the direct sales comparison approach, gross rent multiplier analysis, and the cost approach.

Range of indicated value   Generally, the upper and lower indications of value from the different approaches used in the appraisal.

Reconciliation   The process by which the appraiser evaluates, chooses, and selects from among alternative conclusions to reach a single answer (final value estimate).

Single (final) value estimate   The appraiser's opinion resulting from the application of appraisal analysis, including the process of reconciliation, to the appraisal problem.

The ultimate objective of any residential appraisal is to estimate the defined value of specified rights in described residential real estate as of a given date. Indeed, the estimation of value is the objective of any appraisal. The value most commonly sought for residential real estate is market value. The residential appraiser will likely have more than one indicator of value, based on the application of different valuation approaches or procedures. These will typically include value indications from the direct sales comparison approach, gross rent multiplier analysis, and the cost approach—and possibly regression analysis as well. Regression analysis is regarded as a different approach by some, although it is simply a variant form of direct sales comparison analysis. In any event, slightly different estimates of value most probably will emerge from using the several different procedures; sometimes, the differences will not be so slight.

The task still confronting the appraiser is to reconcile these several differing estimates of value (however slight or great the differences) into a single, final estimate of property value as of the valuation date. Most appraisal assignments require a single value estimate for the client's use. Typically, buyers, sellers, lenders, insurers, taxing authorities, condemners, and the courts all want to know the value of the property. This is especially true for residential appraisals. It may well prove to be helpful and useful to indicate, in addition, the most probable range within which market value will likely fall. This can be particularly helpful in selling or buying decisions; it is especially useful in reporting investment value for investment decisions. The use of a range for residential properties is considered later.

In the process of selecting the final single estimate of value from among the alternative and frequently varying value indications developed in the analysis, the appraiser must go through two distinct, important procedures. First, there must be a review of all the previous work and analysis; the data, logic, and techniques must be checked and verified. Second, the appraiser must apply logic and judgment through the procedure termed reconciliation to arrive at the final estimate of value. In this process, several important considerations must be kept in mind, as well as several pitfalls avoided. These are the subject of the discussion here.

Review of the Different Approaches or Procedures

It is both appropriate and necessary to review the appraiser's work and analysis before attempting to reconcile the findings and reach the final value conclusion(s). Review is not reconciliation. It is a preparation of the findings and indications of value for reconciliation.

Multiple Indications of Value

As already noted, application of two or more of the alternative approaches to value estimation to any appraisal problem will usually result in preliminary indications of value that are somewhat at variance. Ideally, of course, if all necessary data were available and if the techniques of analysis were applied properly, the value indications from the several approaches would be the same. This rarely occurs in practice, however. All required data are not always available, judgmental decisions are not always perfect, and real estate markets are imperfect.

When the answers do vary, the appraiser should seek to understand why. If there is wide variance among the answers or if one of the indications appears out of line (but not only under these circumstances), the appraiser must review all the work to discover if any revisions are necessary. Logic, applications of technique, and calculations can be altered if review shows them to be improper or inadequate. Data cannot be revised by the appraiser. Even if they are inadequate, they represent the facts of the marketplace that have been developed in the analysis.

Review and adjustment need not necessarily narrow the range of variation. It is just as likely that the range will be widened as a result of the review.

What to Review

Initially, the appraiser should check mechanics: techniques, calculations, and adjustments. Errors might have been made; if they are found, they must be corrected. Next, the appraiser must check logic and analysis: the thinking and steps that have gone into the value estimation in each approach employed. There is a considerable amount of decision making, judgment, and choosing throughout the framework of appraisal analysis. The appraiser should review each of these factors for appropriateness and for the assumptions, estimates, and conclusions made at each step.

In addition, the appraiser must check applicability: the relationship of the underlying principles of each approach or procedure to the nature of the appraisal problem and of the property being appraised. Finally, the appraiser must check the reliability and adequacy of data and data sources. All data should have been verified. Nothing can be done to alter the data, but an evaluation of their adequacy can influence the emphasis placed on the value estimate(s) from each approach, using different data, in the reconciliation process. The sources should also be reliable and dependable.

Consistency of Items and Findings

At several points throughout the appraisal framework or process, findings and judgments emerge that are based on previous data or analysis. Internal consistency is essential if the value indications derived from the several approaches and procedures employed are to be compatible and reconcilable with one another. Examples of the kinds of checks for internal consistency that the appraiser should apply are included in the following list. The appraiser's answer to each question should be yes; otherwise, a reevaluation of that part of the analysis is required.

1. Do the patterns of sales prices and unit prices developed for direct sales comparison analysis and gross rent multiplier analysis reinforce and complement each other?
2. Are the same dimensions, sizes, and areas used in the direct sales comparison approach and the cost approach?

3. Are the salient property features used in the adjustment process in direct sales comparison all based on the property characteristics identified in the field inspection and reported in the property description?

4. Is the adjustment for time or date of sale (if any) used in the direct sales comparison approach compatible with the trends in sales prices indicated in the market area and neighborhood analysis?

5. Are the same sales transactions data used in regression analysis as are employed in direct sales comparison and/or gross rent multiplier analysis?

6. Are the major elements for which sales price adjustments are made in direct sales comparison analysis used as the independent variables in regression analysis?

7. Are the elements for which adjustments are made in the direct sales comparison approach the same as, and compatible with, those for which charges for accrued depreciation are made in the cost approach? In particular, are the adjustments for age and condition compatible with the charges for physical deterioration?

8. Is every item of condition, functional inutility, or negative locational influence that is identified in the neighborhood analysis or property description included as a sales adjustment factor and/or an element of accrued depreciation?

9. Are the adjustments in comparable rentals (if any) compatible with adjustments made in the direct sales comparison approach and/or with accrued depreciation charges made in the cost approach?

10. Are all items or conditions for which charges for accrued depreciation are made described fully and adequately in the property description, and is the basis for all accrued depreciation charges fully supported and justified in the description of the improvements?

11. Are the charges for locational obsolescence (if any) compatible with the market environment identified in the neighborhood analysis and property description?

12. Is any charge for incurable functional obsolescence for underimprovements or overimprovements clearly related to the highest and best use of the site?

13. Is the highest and best use assigned to the site demonstrably legal and physically possible from information contained in the site analysis, and does it have clear market acceptability from evidence provided in the area and neighborhood analysis?

14. Is the highest and best use assigned to the improved property compatible with the existing structure(s)?

15. Is the process of rounding value estimates consistent among the several valuation approaches employed?

16. Is the remaining economic life for income-producing investment properties used in physical residual techniques of income capitalization the same as the remaining economic life used in the cost approach?
17. Is the market rental for income-producing investment properties estimated for potential gross income in income capitalization the same as that used in gross rent multiplier analysis?

Review of Direct Sales Comparison Approach

1. Check the volume, adequacy, and reliability of market sales data. Make sure all are verified. Make sure sufficient numbers of sales data are available to justify the analysis.
2. Check the market data basis for adjustments between comparable sales properties and the subject property.
3. Check the adequacy of descriptions of comparable sales properties, especially as a basis for adjustments on salient features of the subject property.
4. Check the comparability of comparable sales properties to the subject property.
5. Check the selection and applicability of units of comparison
6. Check the terms of sale and conditions of sale of comparable sales properties.
7. Check arithmetic in the adjustments, the direction of adjustments, and the consistency of the size of adjustments among comparable sales properties.
8. Check the consistency and arithmetic accuracy of the use of units of comparison.
9. Check the accuracy of measurements and of area and unit calculations.
10. Check the reconciliation of adjusted sales prices of comparable sales properties to an indication of value.

Review of Gross Rent Multiplier Analysis

1. Check the volume, adequacy, and reliability of comparable sales and comparable rental data. Make sure all data are verified. Make sure sufficient numbers of sales and rental data are available to justify use of the analysis.
2. Check the market data basis for adjustments between comparable rental properties and the subject property.

3. Check the adequacy of descriptions of comparable sales and comparable rental properties as a basis for adjustments on salient features of the subject property.
4. Check the comparability of comparable sales and comparable rental properties to the subject property.
5. Check the appropriateness and reconciliation of market rent selection from indications of comparable rental properties.
6. Check the appropriateness of gross rent multiplier reconciliation and selection from data on comparable sales of rented properties.
7. Check calculations and arithmetic—the gross rent multiplier for each comparable sale of rented property and the indicated gross rent multiplier times market rent used to obtain an indication of value for the subject property.
8. Check the consistency and arithmetic accuracy of the use of units of comparison.

Review of Cost Approach

1. Check the property description and field observations for indications of contents, quality, and condition of the subject property. Check the accuracy of measurements and of size and area calculations.
2. Check the comparability of comparable sales sites to the subject site.
3. Check market data for adequacy and reliability in making adjustments from comparable site sales to estimate site value.
4. Check the selection and use of units of comparison in estimating site value.
5. Check the appropriateness of reconciliation and selection of estimated site value.
6. Check the appropriateness of unit cost selection.
7. Check the completeness of coverage of cost new elements.
8. Check arithmetic and calculations in the estimate of reproduction cost new.
9. Check the appropriateness of the method of estimating reproduction cost new.
10. Check the market data basis for accrued depreciation charges.
11. Check the description and observational basis of the types and amounts of accured depreciation charged.
12. Check the relationship and consistency of depreciation charges to measures employed in the direct sales comparison approach (ad-

justments) and in gross rent multiplier analysis (rent loss estimate, gross rent multiplier).

13. Check arithmetic in subtracting accrued depreciation charges from reproduction cost new.
14. Check for double counting and/or omissions in making accrued depreciation charges.
15. Check the market data basis for assigning present worth to site improvements.
16. Check arithmetic in summing the site value estimate, the estimate of the present worth of structure(s), and the estimate of present worth of site improvements into an indication of total property value.

Review of Regression Analysis

The appraisal applications of regression analysis are basically a supplement to value estimation via direct sales comparison analysis. The technique differs enough from the sales adjustment process, however, to warrant separate consideration in the review process:

1. Check the volume, adequacy, and reliability of market sales (and rents if applicable) data. Make sure all data are verified. Make sure sufficient numbers of sales data are available to justify the use of the analysis.
2. Check to see that pertinent property characteristics and influences on value are included as independent variables.
3. Make sure that values for all independent variables are included in all comparable sales transactions used in the analysis.
4. Check the tests to make sure that the relationship between the dependent variable (sales price) and the independent variables (property, transaction, and market characteristics) is in fact linear.
5. Check the decimal values of the calculated coefficients for the estimating regression equation to make sure that the resulting dollar values are accurately represented.
6. Make sure that the proper coefficients are applied to their related independent variables.
7. Test the statistical significance of the calculated coefficients, dropping the independent variables whose coefficients are found to be nonsignificant.
8. Check the interpretation of the calculated results: the coefficient of determination (R^2 or r^2); the standard error of the estimate (s_{yx});

the *t* test for significance of regression coefficients; and the regression coefficients themselves (*a* and *b*).

9. Make sure that the values of each of the independent variables for the subject property are measured accurately.
10. Check the accuracy of the calculation of estimated value (most probable sales price) for the subject property from the estimating regression equation.

Reconciliation

The appraiser is seeking value as defined in the appraisal problem. It should represent the best, most probable estimate—given the facts, assumptions, and market conditions in terms of which the appraisal is made. For residential properties, the objective of the appraisal is nearly always to estimate market value. The appraiser must consider the application of all alternative approaches, whether or not they are actually applied in the particular case. The appraiser's experience and judgment, the nature of the property and of the appraisal problem, and the availability and adequacy of market data combine to determine which approaches shall actually be applied.

Where possible and defensible, all approaches (and variations on them) except income capitalization should be used in estimating residential property value. Frequently, complete reliance cannot be placed on any one approach, no matter how logical its application might appear in the abstract. Even when the greatest reliance is expected to be placed on the indication of value derived from application of one approach (most frequently, the direct sales comparison approach in residential appraising), and even when this fact is well known in advance, estimating value via other approaches can serve as a check on the appraiser's thinking and work.

The problem is to work two or more indications of value derived via alternative approaches into one value estimate for the property or into a completely defensible, most probable range within which the value will be found. This process is known as reconciliation.

Reconciliation Defined

Reconciliation is "The process by which the appraiser evaluates, chooses and selects from among two or more alternative conclusions or indications to reach a single answer (final value estimate)."[1] The term *reconciliation* is preferred to the traditional and still widely used term, *correlation,* to describe this process. Correlation is a long-established process of statistical analysis. Conflict in terminology should be avoided wherever possible. Therefore, *reconciliation* is used because it describes accurately and precisely what the appraiser does: reconciling several value indications with one another and their underlying rationales to derive a single value estimate.

Final reconciliation is the application of the process of evaluating alternative conclusions and selecting from the indications of value derived from each of the approaches utilized in the appraisal problem to arrive at a final estimate of value. Appraisers weigh the relative significance, applicability, and defensibility of the indication of value derived from each approach; they place most weight and reliance on the one which, in their professional judgment, best approximates the value being sought in the appraisal. Appraisers reconcile the facts, trends, and observations developed in the analysis and review the conclusions and their probable validity and reliability.[2] The essence of final reconciliation is to develop one defensible, rational conclusion that approximates the one value (as defined in the appraisal) whose existence is known but whose quantity is being sought.

Reconciliation is, in fact, an examination of conscience by which appraisers evaluate their own analysis. As both a thought process and a procedure, reconciliation is employed throughout the entire appraisal framework and throughout the several steps of each of the approaches to value estimation. Wherever several indicators of any value (rental, unit cost, sales price) are resolved into a single indicator, reconciliation takes place, consciously or unconsciously, every time the appraiser makes a selection or choice from among several alternatives anywhere in the appraisal analysis. It is not restricted to the section of the appraisal report entitled reconciliation, nor is it restricted to final reconciliation to a final estimate of value—although final reconciliation is by far the most significant application of the process. The purpose of this discussion is to bring the process to the conscious level as much as possible and to make its application as logical and defensible as possible.

What Reconciliation Is Not

Correction of past errors in thinking and technique is actually part of the review process that precedes reconciliation. It prepares the materials and conclusions developed in the appraisal framwork for reconciliation into a final value estimate. Review is related to reconciliation because it includes the necessity to reconsider the various choices and selections that were made throughout the appraisal framework and in each of the major approaches.

Reconciliation requires the application of careful judgment and analysis. No mathematical or mechanical formula can substitute for this. Averaging is a type of formula with particular pitfalls, because it is so simple and easy to apply. The appraiser's task is to apply qualitative judgment, rather than simply quantitative mechanics. It has been demonstrated that sample statistics can be used to estimate the most probable value from a set of data when sufficient quantities of market data or observations are available. Both the arithmetic mean (simple or weighted) and the median can be employed successfully; they can be tested for reliability or representativeness by standard deviation, for the mean, and average deviation, for the median. Taking sample statistics, however, in itself is not reconciliation.

If a sufficient number of data or observations is not available, sample averages are so unreliable (and possibly unrepresentative as well) that they should not be used. This limitation is particularly applicable to final reconciliation, where there usually are no more than three indications of value (observations) from different valuation approaches. This means that when an average is taken, there are only two degrees of freedom left. The 95 percent confidence interval around a mean, with only two degrees of freedom, is $X \pm 4.303s$. The 99 percent confidence interval is $X \pm 9.925s$. Thus, even if the three value indications are very close, the mean is a highly unreliable value estimator with so few observations.

Suppose, for example, that a residential property has been valued at $91,600 via the direct sales comparison approach, $92,800 via gross rent multiplier analysis, and $88,700 via the cost approach. This is a spread of only 4.6 percent from lowest to highest, which is a fairly narrow range. The mean is $91,033 and the standard deviation is $2,108. The 95 percent confidence interval is $81,962 to $100,104; the 99 percent confidence interval is $70,111 to $111,955. Both these intervals are well outside the range of the three value indications.

While the objective of final reconciliation is to arrive at a single estimate of value that is convincing and defensible, it does not follow that the range of value indicated by the conclusions of the three approaches will necessarily be narrowed. Indeed, it was pointed out in the discussion of the review process that the range may well be widened as a result of that review. The indications of value from each of the approaches applied in the particular appraisal problem are not changed through the reconciliation process. These indications are simply the information used by the appraiser in making the final judgment of the most probable, convincing, and defensible estimate of value in view of the data and analysis available. The final estimate of value is most likely to be within the indicated range, however.

Characteristics of the Reconciliation Process

There are two constraints on the appraiser in applying judgment to the selection of a final value estimate: the availability and reliability of verified market data and the appropriateness of the particular approach to the appraisal problem. Data must be available in sufficient quantity and must be adequate in quality (reliability) to warrant basing a final judgment on them. They must come from reliable sources and must be verified. The particular approach to value estimation must be appropriate to the appraisal problem, the character of the property, and the value being sought in the appraisal with respect to underlying principles, logic, consistency, and defensibility. Appraisers examine the data, the processing of the data, and their reasoning to select the best approximation to the type of value being sought, based on the applicability of the underlying theory to the problem at hand and the availability and reliability of required data. The most appropriate approach (usually the direct sales comparison approach in residential appraisals), for example, may not be supported by sufficient quantity or reliability of data to warrant placing greatest emphasis or reliance on it.

The data are analyzed and tested to estimate the probable accuracy of the indication of value derived from each of the approaches employed. After analyzing both the data and the appropriateness of each approach to the problem at hand, the appraiser may minimize or even ignore the indication of value developed in one or more of the approaches used. The appraiser relies most heavily (but not necessarily exclusively) on the indication of value that represents the best combination of applicability or appropriateness to the problem, supported by adequate, reliable data. The appraiser must approach the entire appraisal framework and the final reconciliation process from the point of view of the typically informed, rational purchaser in the market in question. The analysis that produces the selection of a final value estimate should lead to a conclusion that best reflects the attitudes, responses, and behavior of such a purchaser.

Relationship to the Objective of the Appraisal

The appraiser is seeking a final value estimate that most closely approximates the value being sought, as defined in the appraisal problem. It should be the best, most probable value figure obtainable under current market circumstances. Therefore, the appraiser must conduct the analysis throughout the appraisal, and especially in the final reconciliation process, with the nature and characteristics of that value constantly in mind.

The definition of value establishes the criteria for judgment and selection by the appraiser. In the vast majority of residential appraisals, market value is the value being sought. This means that the final value estimate must be consistent with the reactions and behavior of an informed, rational purchaser operating on the open market in competition with other informed, rational buyers. The appraiser must recognize that the portion of the total bundle of rights of ownership being appraised will markedly affect the value estimate. The final value estimate must be consistent with the rights to be appraised, which are identified in the definition of the appraisal problem.

Especially when market value is to be estimated, but in other cases as well, the valuation date establishes the market conditions in terms of which value is estimated. The appraiser must ensure that the final value estimate is consistent with the market conditions in force as of the date of the appraisal and used as the basis of the analysis. The limiting and contingent conditions and assumptions in terms of which the appraisal is made are identified in the definition of the problem. The final value estimate derived through the final reconciliation process must indicate the impact of these limitations and assumptions.

Under normal market conditions, the greatest emphasis in residential appraisals will be placed on the indication of value developed via the direct sales comparison approach. This approach most nearly reflects the thinking and behavior of the typically informed and rational purchaser through whose eyes the appraiser views the property, the market, and the appraisal problem. Whenever there are variations among the indications of value from different approaches, the greatest emphasis will be placed on the conclusion from the direct sales comparison approach. Adequate and reliable market data must be available in sufficient quantity, however, to permit effective sales comparisons and to justify adjustments for variations among comparable properties. Further, the subject property must not be substantially differentiated from competitive properties in a normally active market. This most nearly approximates the requirements of the definition of market value.

Pitfalls and Hazards in the Reconciliation Process

Several common, but erroneous, impressions about the applicability of the several approaches to value estimation should be carefully avoided by the appraiser throughout the appraisal analysis, but especially in the final reconciliation process. These misimpressions include the following:

1. *The cost approach sets the upper limit to value.* This oft-quoted, highly erroneous view must be dispelled in the appraiser's mind.

There is absolutely no requirement that depreciation must always be underestimated. When improvements represent the highest and best use of the site, the cost new tends to set the upper limit, provided that there is no discount for waiting until construction is completed. Cost itself does not set the upper lmit, and the estimate of value via the cost approach most certainly does not.

2. *The direct sales comparison approach is the only appropriate approach for appraising residential properties.* Data may be inadequate; the market may be inactive; highly unusual market conditions may prevail; the analysis may be inappropriately applied. If the appraiser has an acceptable volume of highly reliable market data, if application of the techniques of direct sales comparison analysis is proper and mechanically correct, and if adjustments are made with full market justification, then the indication of value via the direct sales comparison approach is most probably the best indication of value (especially market value). In the absence of these conditions, however, other approaches are not only appropriate but necessary for estimating residential property value.

3. *Gross rent multiplier analysis is not applicable to residential property appraisal, because residences are typically not income-producing properties.* In the rare situation in which the local residential market is literally a no-rent market, it may not be possible to apply gross rent multiplier analysis. This does not mean, however, that it is inapplicable to residential properties in general. Moreover, close investigation of most market areas will usually reveal enough cases of rentals to warrant consideration of GRM analysis.

4. *The final value estimate is developed by averaging.* This misconception was discussed earlier, but it is so widespread (if practice is any guide to belief) that it is emphasized again as a pitfall to avoid.

5. *Reconciliation consists of a brief summary of the appraisal framework and the steps involved in applying the three approaches.* As noted earlier, such activity constitutes the review that precedes final correlation. Mere recitation without careful exercise of judgment does not help the client, and it does not support the appraiser's final conclusion.

The Final Value Estimate

The final value estimate is the appraiser's opinion or conclusion resulting from the application of the framework of appraisal analysis, including final reconciliation, to the appraisal problem. It stems from the evaluation of each of the indications of value developed in each approach to value estimation utilized in the appraisal. It is the value that most nearly represents what the typically informed, rational purchaser would pay for a residential property (the subject property) if it were available for sale on the open market as of the date of the appraisal, given all the data (and only those data) utilized by the appraiser in the analysis.

The final value estimate is the conclusion that the appraiser truly believes to be logical, reasonable, convincing, and defensible—consistent with the appraiser's best professional efforts at approximating and measuring the value sought, as defined in the appraisal problem. Market value is most frequently sought in residential appraisals; therefore, the final estimate of value for a residential property is typically market value.

A final value estimate is an opinion. It is an opinion based on the appraiser's knowledge, analysis, professional judgment, and experience. That experience must be supported and justified by market facts and by logical and convincing analysis.

A final value estimate is valid only under carefully stipulated assumptions and conditions as of the date of the appraisal (which, in turn, reflects specified market conditions). It cannot be transferred over time or space. It is specific to a particular appraisal problem.

Single Value Estimate versus Range of Indicated Value

As noted earlier, most residential appraisal assignments require that the appraisers develop a single estimate of market value. In addition, however, it is sometimes useful and helpful to the client to provide an indication of the range within which market value most probably falls. As a broad generalization, residential appraisers should always provide a point estimate of market value; they may add the indicated range as an aid to the client. The point estimate of market value is a judgmental figure based on the appraiser's evaluation of the reliability and defensibility of the several indications of value produced from the different approaches used in the appraisal analysis. It is analogous to a weighted average, with qualitative weights assigned to each indication of value.

The final value estimate may be the same as one of the actual value indications—the one best supported by good, reliable market data and most applicable to the appraisal problem. Suppose, for example, that the value indications for a residential property were $87,000 from direct sales comparison analysis, $90,200 from gross rent multiplier analysis, $85,700 from regression analysis, and $87,800 from the cost approach. In this case, if the data used were plentiful and were judged to be reliable, the appraiser might well choose $87,000 as the final value estimate.

The final value estimate may differ from all the indications of value produced by the different approaches used in the analysis. The appraiser might well select $88,000 as the final value estimate for the aforementioned property, for example, on the grounds that the several indications of value tend to cluster slightly above the figure produced by direct sales comparison analysis. This would be acceptable if the appraiser had confidence in the data used in the other approaches.

The *range of indicated value* is generally provided by the upper and lower indications of value from the different approaches used in the appraisal. It is not a statistical interval. The range for the aforementioned property, for example, would be $85,700 to $90,200 or, more likely, $86,000 to $90,000. This is −1.1 percent and +3.4 percent from $87,000, and ±2.3 percent from $88,000.

Rounding

The final value estimate is precisely that—an estimate. As such, it must be appropriately rounded to eliminate any implication or unwarranted claim of precision or excessive accuracy. Rounding brings the estimate to a reasonable degree of accuracy that is consistent with the standards of the local market, the price level or range within which the value estimate falls, and the type of property involved. Thus, in the foregoing example, $87,000 or $88,000 would be more likely as a final value estimate than $87,400, $87,600, or $87,800.

Curable Depreciation

Curable accrued depreciation represents an expenditure that an informed, prudent purchaser would make upon acquisition of the property. Thus, that purchaser would deduct the amount of curable accrued depreciation (measured by the cost to cure) from the purchase price that would otherwise be paid to acquire the subject property.

Curable depreciation includes "Those items of physical deterioration and functional obsolescence which are economically feasible to cure and hence are customarily repaired or replaced by a prudent property owner."[3] Significant in most residential appraisals is curable physical deterioration or deferred maintenance. The purchaser (and appraiser) can usually identify what needs to be done and approximately how much it will cost, including new exterior painting, refinishing floors, repairing broken equipment, and the like. Outmoded fixtures and equipment (curable functional obsolescence) are similarly treated by the typical informed purchaser (and appraiser).

Elements of curable depreciation are usually incorporated in the condition of the subject property as an element of comparison in the sales adjustment process in direct sales comparison analysis; in the adjustment process to derive market rental in gross rent multiplier analysis; and in regression analysis. If the amount of curable accrued depreciation in the subject property is not reflected in either the comparable sales properties or the sales adjustment process, then this amount should be deducted from the indication of value produced by direct sales comparison analysis before a final estimate of value is reached.

Similarly, if the amount of curable accrued depreciation in the subject property is not reflected in either comparable rentals or the rental adjustment process, then this amount should be deducted from the indication of value produced by gross rent multiplier analysis before a final estimate of value is reached. Moreover, if the amount of curable accrued depreciation in the subject property is not reflected in an independent variable for condition, then this amount should be deducted from the indication of value produced by regression analysis before a final estimate of value is reached.

Frequently, the amount of curable accrued depreciation is such a small figure that this adjustment is insignificant and therefore unnecessary. A general rule of thumb would be to omit the adjustment if curable accrued depreciation is less than 0.5 percent of estimated property value. As an example, consider the following indications of value:

Direct sales comparison approach	$77,300
Gross rent multiplier analysis	75,600
Regression analysis	79,050
Cost approach	76,600

Suppose that items of curable accrued depreciation total $1,600. These are not reflected in any indication of value except that from the cost approach. A deduction of $1,600 from each of the other indications of value is made before final reconciliation takes place. The adjusted indications of value then become the following:

Direct sales comparison approach	$75,700
Gross rent multiplier analysis	74,000
Regression analysis	77,450
Cost approach	76,600

The final estimate of value would then be $76,000, instead of $77,000 (or more) without the adjustment.

Summary

Reconciliation is a process of logical analysis whereby a basis for selection among alternative results or conclusions is developed. While it is applied throughout the entire appraisal framework, it is especially important in selecting a final value estimate from among two or more indications of value obtained through alternative approaches to value estimation. Prior to the final reconciliation of value indicators into a final estimate of value, the appraiser should review all data, analyses, and calculations in all the approaches used. In the review process, particular care should be taken to check for internal consistency and compatibility of data, analyses, and findings among the several approaches to value estimation employed.

Mechanical processes (especially, but not only, averaging) are not a valid substitute for reasoned judgment in the final reconciliation of two or more indications of value into a final value estimate. The final value estimate represents the appraiser's reasoned professional opinion of the value of the subject property, consistent with the definition of value being sought, the quantity and quality of available data, the applicability of the underlying theory of the several approaches to value estimation to the problem at hand, and the assumptions and limiting conditions in terms of which the appraisal is made. The final value estimate should be rounded appropriately to emphasize the fact that it is an estimate.

When they are not included in the indications of value produced by the other approaches to value, charges for curable accrued depreciation reflected in the cost approach should be deducted from the other indications of value before the final reconciliation to a final value estimate is made.

Notes

1. Boyce, Byrl, N., ed., *Real Estate Appraisal Terminology*, rev. ed. (Cambridge, Mass.: Ballinger Publishing Company [Joint publication of the American Institute of Real Estate Appraisers and Society of Real Estate Appraisers], 1981), p. 202.

2. See Ibid., p. 103.
3. Ibid., p. 68.

Suggested Readings

American Institute of Real Estate Appraisers. *The Appraisal of Real Estate,* 8th ed. Chicago: American Institute of Real Estate Appraisers, 1983, chapter 21.

Bloom, George F., and Harrison, Henry S. *Appraising the Single Family Residence.* Chicago: American Institute of Real Estate Appraisers, 1978, chapter 15.

Boyce, Byrl N., ed. *Real Estate Appraisal Terminology,* rev. ed. Cambridge, Mass.: Ballinger (Joint publication of the American Institute of Real Estate Appraisers and Society of Real Estate Appraisers), 1981.

Epley, Donald R., and Boykin, James H. *Basic Income Property Appraisal.* Reading, Mass.: Addison-Wesley, 1983, chapter 17.

The Official Guide to Appraisal Reporting. Chicago: Society of Real Estate Appraisers, 1983, pp. 4–6, 27–28 and 38–39.

Ratcliff, Richard U. *Valuation for Real Estate Decisions.* Santa Cruz, Calif.: Democrat Press, 1972, chapters 4, 6, and 7.

Smith, Halbert C. *Real Estate Appraisal.* Columbus, Ohio: Grid, 1976, chapter 10.

Stebbins, H. Grady, Jr. *A Guide to Appraising Residences,* 3rd ed. Chicago: Society of Real Estate Appraisers, 1976, pp. 65–68.

Wendt, Paul F. *Real Estate Appraisal: Review and Outlook.* Athens: University of Georgia Press, 1974, chapter 10.

15 Appraisal Reporting; Professional Ethics and Standards of Practice

Key Terms

Appraisal report The culmination of appraisers' efforts and skills, presenting all their assumptions, data, analysis, findings, and conclusions.

Demonstration report A requirement for applicants for admission to membership and designation in professional appraisal societies and institutes as evidence of the applicant's ability to present an appraisal report in a professional, convincing manner.

Form report Standardized forms upon which most of the information is provided by checking appropriate boxes or filling in blanks.

Letter of opinion A statement of a range within which a final opinion would most probably fall if an appraisal were made.

Letter report A brief summary, in letter form, of the results of an appraisal, containing the final value conclusion and other information pertinent to the assignment.

Narrative report A full written report explaining to the reader (client) what was done, how it was done, and why by presenting the facts, analysis, and findings of the appraiser in a natural and logical sequence.

The appraiser's work is not completed when a final estimate of value is reached, no matter how defensible or supportable or convincing that final value estimate may be. An appraisal assignment is undertaken because a client or employer has a decision to make or a problem to solve and because a supportable estimate of the value of some interest in real estate will be helpful in making that decision or solving that problem. The final step in the appraisal framework is to communicate the appraiser's findings and conclusions effectively and convincingly to the user of the information.

Communication involves transmitting or reporting facts, information, and ideas from one person to another. There must be a clear and unequivocal transfer of information in terms that both parties understand and accept. There should be no room for misunderstanding or misinterpretation by either party. Communication is intended to transfer information—to inform by transmitting facts, data, assumptions,

391

definitions, and conclusions. Communication is also a means for answering a question or responding to a directive. It can force action (or inaction) and can offer alternatives or choices. It can help identify a problem and can report a solution (or no solution) to the problem. Finally, it can (and an appraisal report should) convince the reader or listener on a matter. Appraisal reporting is an important form of communication.

The findings of the appraiser are reported to the client, employer, or others. Whatever form that report may take, a complete analysis of market data and property characteristics must underlie the report. The field notes, working papers, and other pertinent documents should be retained in the appraiser's files for future reference. The entire appraisal framework should be applied in every appraisal assignment, regardless of the form and manner of reporting the appraiser's findings and conclusions.

An appraisal assignment typically requires that an appraisal report be prepared and presented to the client or employer. It sometimes happens, however, that a client will specifically request an oral report only. In this event, the appraiser should still prepare a draft appraisal report containing all the required components of any appraisal report and should retain it on file. One exception to this general rule may occur when the appraiser is asked to make a preliminary study or survey to identify the range within which the estimate of value is most likely to fall, and to help the client or employer decide whether to proceed with a formal appraisal. In this instance, a true appraisal is not made and no formal conclusion or estimate of value is developed.

Appraisal Reports

The appraisal report is the culmination of the appraiser's efforts and skills. It is a presentation of all the appraiser's assumptions, data, analyses, findings, and conclusions. It is the document that is transmitted to the client when the appraisal assignment is completed. If it is prepared and presented properly and well, the appraisal report should lead an intelligent but basically uninformed reader step by step through the logical processes followed by the appraiser. The reader should arrive inevitably at the same conclusion as the appraiser.

Frequently (as in mortgage loan decisions or court proceedings in eminent domain), the appraisal report must stand alone on its own merits. The appraiser is not always available to justify, explain, or expand upon statements contained in the report. Therefore, whatever type of report is prepared, it must be complete in all significant respects.

Completeness does not mean padding or superfluous materials, however. To be complete and convincing, the report should indicate what the appraiser did and how and why it was done. The report should show clearly the appraiser's assumptions, the data employed, the steps in the analysis, and the conclusions.

The appraiser must always remember why and for whom the appraisal report is being prepared. Within limits, the appraiser's presentation can and should be adjusted to take into account the probable readers of the report. This refers to the manner of the presentation and the degree of detail, not the content.

Types of Appraisal Reports

Appraisal reports will vary in type and length, depending on the nature of the assignment and the client's or employer's wishes. Whatever form the appraisal report takes, however, the process the appraiser employs should be exactly the same. A brief letter or short-form report requires the same data, the same analysis, the same care, and the same substantiation as does a full narrative report or even a demonstration report. The appraisal report is simply the evidence to the client of the appraiser's work and conclusions; the thought processes that underlie it must always be complete. In brief, all that varies from one type of report to another is the amount of information and background material that is transmitted to the client.

Letter Report. Sometimes the appraiser's report to the client is in letter form, briefly summarizing the results of the appraisal. It contains the appraiser's final value conclusion and may include other information pertinent to the assignment. The letter report must be supported by as much information and analysis as is contained in the complete appraisal (typically handwritten) retained in the appraiser's files. The use of letter reports is discouraged in professional appraisal practice, primarily because it is too easy to omit a critical or required component. Such use is permitted, however, when the client requests or requires it.

Letter of Opinion. A letter of opinion, based on a preliminary study, is a statement of a range within which a final opinion would most probably fall if an appraisal were made. A letter of opinion is to be distinguished from a letter report. Serious problems may arise if the letter of opinion is subsequently used as an appraisal report to obtain mortgage financing. Since an appraisal has not been made, the letter of opinion is not an appraisal report, and that fact must be clearly stated in the letter. It is acknowledged, however, that there is some need for this service and that the professional real estate appraiser is the best qualified person to perform it. Before accepting such an assignment, the appraiser should be certain that the client has a legitimate need for a letter of opinion.

Form Report. Many clients and employers require form reports, especially for volume work. These usually are standardized two-page or four-page forms on which most of the information is provided by checking appropriate boxes or filling in blanks. While they provide standardization and ease of comparison, form reports frequently do not permit the appraiser to express the findings or analysis adequately. The appraiser should add narrative commentary if there is insufficient space in the form to express precisely what needs to be communicated. Appraisers should remember that any deficiency in the report is their responsibility, not that of the form, the client, or the printer.

Form reports are widely used in residential appraising, particularly when the appraisal is undertaken at the request of a mortgage lender or mortgage insurer. There is no general standardization of appraisal report forms, and many clients (and appraisers) have their own custom-designed forms. The approved FNMA/FHLMC forms, however, enjoy particularly widespread acceptance and use.

Narrative Report. Even in simple residential appraisal reporting, the narrative report is best suited to permit the appraiser to explain to the reader what was done, how it was done, and why. Every professional appraiser should be thoroughly familiar with the techniques and requirements of narrative report writing. Narrative reports can run from a few pages to hundreds of pages, with or without detailed exhibits. The one pitfall to avoid in the development and presentation of a narrative report is the tendency to overdo and write too long a report. From experience, judgment, and the client's wishes, the appraiser must decide how much is enough to do the job fully and convincingly.

In this connection, a one-page summary of salient facts and conclusions is particularly useful for the client or the reader, especially when it is placed at the beginning of the report. This permits the client to absorb the essence of the appraiser's findings, with the full report that follows serving to explain and substantiate them. It is important that the narrative appraisal follow a natural and logical sequence in presenting the facts, analyses, and findings of the appraiser. A good and useful rule is to work from the general to the specific, from background materials to data pertaining to the property being appraised.

Applicants for admission to membership (and professional designation) in the Society of Real Estate Appraisers (SREA) and other professional appraisal societies and institutes are required to submit demonstration narrative appraisal reports as evidence of their ability to present an appraisal report in a professional, convincing manner. The requirements for such a demonstration report typically exceed what is necessary and good in normal professional practice, because the report is a demonstration of the applicant's ability to deal with all aspects of report preparation. It is intended as an example of the applicant's best effort.

Elements of Appraisal Reports

An appraisal report may have a variety of ingredients. Some are essential in any report; some are required under specific circumstances (e.g., by a client or to satisfy SREA admission requirements); and some are highly desirable when time and circumstances permit. In deciding what information should or should not be included in any appraisal report, the appraiser can apply several tests. The following list of questions provides a guide to the appraiser in resolving the issues:

1. *Is it required* by the client (or the professional society)?
2. *Is it necessary* for understanding by the reader or for processing into the final value estimate?
3. *Will it help* the reader in understanding the presentation or the appraiser in developing the final value estimate?
4. *Is it useful* in the development of the appraiser's argument or the reader's understanding?
5. *Is it feasible* in terms of the fee and the time limitations imposed on the assignment? This should be a consideration before the assignment is undertaken and the fee set. Once agreement is reached, professional appraisers are obligated to exert their best efforts regardless of the attractiveness of the financial or time arrangements to which they have agreed.
6. *Is it well done?* Does it really convince the reader, as well as being necessary and useful?
7. *Is it well presented and well expressed?* Can it be followed easily by the intelligent lay reader?
8. *Is it inevitable* in the nature of the appraisal framework?

Perhaps the most important question of all is: so what? What does the inclusion of the particular item add to the development of the appraiser's argument and to the reader's understanding? The appraiser should ask this question about every item of doubt; the alert reader certainly will ask it of the appraiser, whether the appraiser happens to be present or not.

In deciding what should be included in the narrative appraisal report, a careful distinction must be made between the ideal report that is postulated for demonstration purposes for admission to a professional appraisal society and a report that represents desirable, good professional practice. While the ideal always exists as a target toward which to strive, that which is good and desirable is always acceptable in practice. No report is ever perfect; convincing acceptability is the best one can expect.

Essentials of Appraisal Reports. Regardless of the form of the report, any report prepared by a professional appraiser should contain the following as a minimum:

1. *Identification of the property:* a clear and unequivocal statement including both a legal description and at least a brief physical description, plus an indication of the property rights being appraised.
2. *Statement of purpose or objective of the appraisal:* indication of the value to be estimated, preferably defined from an authoritative source.
3. *Indication of the date as of which the value estimate is made.*
4. *The data and reasoning:* analysis supporting the value conclusion. The omission of any of the three usual approaches to value should be explained and supported.
5. *Indication of the value estimate:* final conclusion and recommendation, if any.
6. *Statement of assumptions and special or limiting conditions.*
7. *Certification by the appraiser:* Specific elements to be included are listed in the SREA "Standards of Professional Practice and Conduct" in the appendix.
8. *Signature of the appraiser.*

Even a letter appraisal must contain these elements as a minimum if it is to perform its function for the client. They represent minimally acceptable professional practice.

Elements of Narrative Appraisal Reports. In addition to the foregoing essential elements required of any appraisal report, whatever its form, a narrative appraisal report will normally include the following:

1. *Letter of transmittal:* This is another way of summarizing the report.

It should contain all the essentials already enumerated and should be addressed to the client. It should also indicate that an appraisal report in narrative form is being transmitted with it.

2. *Table of contents:* This is particularly useful in long reports, so that the reader may find specific sections without undue search.

3. *Summary of salient facts and conclusions:* Especially in longer, more detailed reports, this is a useful aid to the client or reader. It summarizes succinctly, at the outset, the basic points that the client is seeking.

4. *Area and neighborhood analysis:* In a narrative report, the appraiser should share with the reader the findings and conclusions about the external market influences at work on the value of the subject property. The presentation should be analytical and should be related to the valuation problem at hand. It should not be a mere itemization of facts and figures, nor a glowing recitation of the features of the area that are not pertinent to estimating the value of the subject property.

5. *Site and improvements analysis:* This involves showing the appraiser's findings from inspection of site and building, including an indication of both positive and negative features that influence value. This discussion should set out succinctly the basis for the adjustments and/or deductions made by the appraiser in applying the several alternative analytical approaches to value estimation.

6. *Conclusion of highest and best use:* The appraiser should define highest and best use for the reader and should indicate the conclusions for the subject property, supporting those conclusions with evidence from market, neighborhood, and property analyses. A discussion of the impact of zoning restrictions and other land use (or property use) regulations is usually in order here.

7. *Application of value estimation methods:* One or more of the alternative approaches to value estimation should be discussed and described in enough detail for the reader to understand the basis for the appraiser's conclusions as well as the handling of the data employed. Commentary on the availability and probable validity of data for each of the approaches employed will assist the reader in following the appraiser's analysis and conclusions. Whenever one or more of the basic alternative approaches to value estimation is not utilized by the appraiser in the analysis (and, hence, not presented in the report), there should be a brief explanation of the inapplicability of the approach or of the lack of suitable data for applying the approach in the present situation.

8. *Reconciliation and final value estimate:* The appraiser should indicate carefully the reasons for selecting the final value estimate

chosen from among the alternative indications developed in each of the approaches utilized in the appraisal. The reader should be convinced by the logic and the manner of presentation that the figure selected is the most appropriate one under the circumstances.

9. *Exhibits:* To assist the reader in following the presentation, as well as to visualize the physical environment of the subject property, the appraiser should include exhibits that are carefully and accurately prepared and are presented in a professional and comprehensible fashion. These exhibits would normally include the following

    a. *Photographs:* These should provide several views of the subject property and of comparable sales and rental properties, as well as of the immediate neighborhood of the subject property. They should be dated.

    b. *Area and neighborhood maps:* These will help the reader understand the relationship of the subject property to public facilities, centers of employment and trade, streets and transportation facilities, and comparable sales and rental properties. Zoning can also be noted on the maps to illustrate the pattern of permitted land uses in the vicinity of the subject property.

    c. *Plot plan and floor plan:* Drawn carefully and accurately to scale, these plans can help the reader understand the written description of the subject property and visualize both positive and negative features of the property discussed in the report.

    d. *Tables and graphs:* Compilations of data utilized in the body of the report can best be presented among the exhibits (frequently called appendices or addenda), so that the data are available for the interested reader without interrupting the flow of the narrative by including them in body of the report.

Frequently, the appraiser will provide more than the client requests or thinks is necessary. One of the functions (among many) of a professional narrative appraisal report is to educate the client to the character of a truly professional report. Appraisers have an obligation to their clients, their profession, and themselves to provide professional reports whenever narrative reporting is requested or appropriate.

Demonstration Narrative Appraisal Reports

Much of what is recommended for any narrative appraisal report is required when applicants submit a demonstration narrative appraisal report in support of a request for admission to a professional appraisal society. The Society of Real Estate Appraisers, for example, has specific requirements regarding the content and general physical character of a demonstration narrative report that go far beyond the suggested items discussed here.

The purpose of the demonstration appraisal report (as opposed to the purpose of the appraisal itself) is for applicants to indicate, through an example of their best possible work, that they fully understand the basic residential appraisal methods and techniques and to show how the applicants would apply them in narrative report form. The layout, organization, typing, grammar, spelling, and general appearance of the demonstration report must be highly professional. Form and organization are not a substitute, however, for content. The demonstration report remains basically a test of the applicant's ability to apply, in practice, the methods and techniques of residential appraising in a valid and convincing fashion.

Specifically, a property used in a demonstration narrative residential report for SREA must have the following characteristics:

1. It must be a residential property with no more than four units.
2. It must suffer from incurable physical deterioration and either functional obsolescence or economic obsolescence.
3. It must be a property in which the applicant has no interest.
4. It must not be a property that was used as part of classroom work in any appraisal course.
5. It must neither be in nor be subject to litigation in the courts.

Form and Manner of Presentation of
Appraisal Reports

For any narrative appraisal report (and especially for demonstration narrative appraisal reports), the form, appearance, and manner of presentation are important ingredients in giving the proper impression of professional effort. The appraisal report is the image of the appraiser. Form is no substitute for content, but it is a significant consideration. The following elements are significant:

1. *Sequence:* The order in which materials are presented in the report is not ordinarily stipulated. A logical sequence, however, from the general to the particular and from background to the specifics of the subject property, adds greatly to the impact of the report on the reader.

2. *Vocabulary:* Appraisals are rarely written for other appraisers. The lay reader should be able to follow the appraiser's argument without a glossary or dictionary. Highly technical terminology should be minimized and should be defined where used. The terms used should be employed consistently and should be consistent with accepted professional appraisal practice. *Real Estate Appraisal Terminology* is an excellent source for all terms and definitions.[1]

3. *Objectivity:* The manner of presentation should clearly underscore the appraiser's professional detachment from, or lack of personal interest in, the results of the analysis.

4. *Logical development:* The appraiser's analysis and presentation should flow logically and convincingly to the final value estimate.

5. *Style:* The written report should read easily and flow well. Aside from avoiding excessive technical jargon, the report should be well organized to lead the reader through the appraiser's thought processes to the conclusion. Direct and simple prose is preferred to flowery phraseology and the intrusion of excessive verbiage.

6. *Appearance:* The report should be neat and clean. It should show care in the preparation of exhibits. It should be carefully proofread and should have no obvious spelling or grammatical errors.

Professionalism and Ethics

The appraiser must aspire to professional status if appraisal work is to achieve the acceptance and recognition that it really requires. One important ingredient (if not the most important ingredient) in realizing professional status is a pattern of truly professional behavior. Professional appraisal groups have established standards of practice and professional conduct or codes of ethics to guide the appraiser in this quest. In addition, professional appraisal groups provide educational programs and assist in the development and advancement of appraisal theory and research in their efforts to bring appraising to the status of a true profession.

The basic ingredients of professional behavior are a high level of technical competence and unimpeachable integrity. Achieving and maintaining these elements are the responsibility of the individual appraiser, but professional appraisal organizations can help individual members by providing guidelines for behavior as well as facilities for self-development and self-improvement. In this discussion, the rules and guidelines established by the SREA are used as the frame of reference.

Professional Behavior

In the appraisal profession, with almost exclusive reliance placed on the opinions or judgments of appraisers, the hallmarks of professional behavior are technical competence, objectivity, and unquestioned honesty or integrity. Technical competence is achieved and maintained through continuing education and training. This includes both general background fields, such as economics, urban land economics, finance, and mathematics, and specific appraisal subjects. Continuing education is necessary both to expand appraisers' horizons and to keep them current with new developments in theory and practice. Formal courses, seminars and clinics, and professional publications are the vehicles provided by professional appraisal organizations. Constant development of the body of appraisal knowledge is required. Professional appraisers have a responsibility to contribute to this development by sharing their thinking and experience with others in the field through program appearances and publication of journal articles. Continuing research into both theory and applied techniques is also required. Support of academic efforts in this area is the responsibility of both individual appraisers and their professional organizations. Background education makes it possible to make new experiences more meaningful; expanded experience uncovers issues requiring further research and/or study. Appraisers should strive constantly to enhance their abilities by undertaking new and different assignments.

Appraisers must constantly avoid involvement (financial or personal) with any appraisal assignments. Opinions become suspect unless the appraisers retain detachment (objectivity) from the properties themselves and are involved only with valuation and the appraisal process. Because they provide a personal service, appraisers' reputations are critical to their success and effectiveness. Rigid adherence to standards of professional practice and professional conduct is necessary if one's reputation as an objective, competent appraiser is not to be undermined.

Ethics involve consideration for and concern about the impact of one's actions and behavior on others. The three groups of others about whom the professional appraiser must be concerned are other professional appraisers, especially members of professional appraisal organizations (and the organizations themselves); clients and employers; and the general public (including the courts).

The SREA, along with other professional appraisal organizations, has a code of ethics to which all members must subscribe. The code deals specifically with member relations with the three groups of others just listed. Claims of violations of the code of ethics (or of the "Standards of Professional Practice and Conduct") are investigated and adjudicated in accordance with the association's disciplinary rules and procedures.

It is essential that a profession and professional associations police the behavior of their membership. The alternative (or occasionally a supplement) is state licensing. While licensing does establish minimum standards of competence or training before a licensee can practice the discipline, licensing alone rarely can set and enforce standards of ethical behavior that result in public trust. Licensing can and does establish and enforce standards of legal (or illegal) behavior, but licensed professions have public trust and recognition as professions by virtue of the standards set by the profession itself—either in conjunction with or in addition to licensing standards.

SREA Standards of Professional Practice

For appraiser-members the SREA has two categories of regulated behavior: standards of valuation practice and standards of reporting practice.

Standards of Valuation Practice. Every appraisal assignment must result in a written appraisal that follows the steps of the appraisal framework. Appraisers cannot sum fractional parts of a property so that the reported value exceeds the value that would be derived if the property were valued as a whole. Estimates of value are always made as of a given date. The appraiser's value conclusion must not be predicated on the assumed completion of public improvements unless the appraiser clearly defines the conditions, extent, and effects of such an assumption. Even then, the assumption must be based on sound valuation principles and market probabilities.

Standards of Reporting Practice. Every appraisal report should contain seven specified components. It is unethical to omit any component without good cause and without noting the reason in the report. The contents of the appraiser's certification in every appraisal report are specified. A written copy of every appraisal report should be retained on file.

An appraisal report on a part of a whole property may be issued only when it is clearly stated that it is an appraisal of a fractional interest and as such can be used only in a manner consistent with such limitation. Reports must reflect the appraiser's own work and conclusions. The appraiser may not issue a separate report when another appraiser assigned to appraise the same property has had a role in the development of the conclusion of value.

Appraisers must keep their findings confidential. All appraisal work is performed for a client's exclusive use. Appraisers may not reveal in any way the substance of any appraisal unless (1) the client has given formal, prior approval; (2) the appraisers are required to do so through due process of law, such as in giving testimony in court proceedings; and/or (3) they are required to do so in compliance with the rules and regulations of the Society of Real Estate Appraisers.

SREA Standards of Professional Conduct

Member appraisers must always conduct themselves in a manner that reflects credit on themselves and the profession. They should not demean the work or character of other appraisers. However, members do have a responsibility to report unethical or unprofessional conduct on the part of others in the organization. Members must not claim competence they do not have or accept assignments that they are not qualified by experience or training to handle. It is appropriate to associate with others so qualified, however, provided that full credit is given to those associates and that the client's consent is obtained.

Appraisers must seek business in a dignified and professional manner, relying primarily on their reputation, training, and experience for employment. Specifically, the member appraiser must not actively solicit business through advertising or other overt means, engage in competitive bidding with other appraisers solely in terms of price, or attempt to supplant another appraiser who has already been given an assignment. Fees must be based on time, effort, and professional reputation: they may never be contingent on the finding of a predetermined value or on the amount of value or damages estimated.

Once appraisers accept an assignment, they should put forth their best effort and do the best possible job, regardless of the fee. The time to worry about monetary and time constraints is before agreement is reached with the client, not after. Member-appraisers must maintain their objectivity at all times in making appraisals and must under no circumstances become advocates of any opinion other than their own unbiased and objective value conclusion.

Summary

The appraisal report is evidence of the quality of the appraiser's work, analyses, and findings. The report should be as complete and comprehensive as is necessary to fulfill the assignment. The appraisal report should be a clear, concise, logical presentation of what the appraiser did and of how and why it was done. It should lead the reader through the analysis logically and inevitably to the value conclusion.

The form and content of an appraisal report may vary with the requirements of the particular assignment, but all appraisal reports must contain certain necessary elements. The process of data collection, analysis, and development of conclusions followed by the appraiser in carrying out an appraisal assignment should be the same, regardless of the form or size of the written report. A demonstration narrative appraisal report should be recognized by the applicant as an examination and should represent the best possible work of which the applicant is capable.

Appraisers must recognize that a good reputation is their most valuable professional asset. Appraisers must pursue and maintain a reputation for high technical competence, complete objectivity, and unimpeachable integrity in their work. Professional appraisers must adhere to the guidelines for conduct and practice established by the standards, code of ethics, and bylaws of their professional organizations.

Note

1. Boyce, Byrl N., ed., *Real Estate Appraisal Terminology,* rev. ed. (Cambridge, Mass.: Ballinger [Joint publication of the American Institute of Real Estate Appraisers and Society of Real Estate Appraisers], 1981).

Suggested Readings

American Institute of Real Estate Appraisers. *The Appraisal of Real Estate,* 8th ed. Chicago: American Institute of Real Estate Appraisers, 1983, chapter 22 and appendix A.

Bloom, George F., and Harrison, Henry S. *Appraising the Single Family Residence.* Chicago: American Institute of Real Estate Appraisers, 1978, chapters 3 and 15 and appendices A, B, and K.

Boyce, Byrl N., ed. *Real Estate Appraisal Terminology,* rev. ed. Cambridge, Mass.: Ballinger (Joint publication of the American Institute of Real Estate Appraisers and Society of Real Estate Appraisers), 1981.

Communicating the Appraisal: A Guide to Report Writing. Chicago: American Institute of Real Estate Appraisers, 1982.

The Official Guide to Appraisal Reporting. Chicago: Society of Real Estate Appraisers, 1983, passim.

Kahn, Sanders A., and Case, Frederick E. *Real Estate Appraisal and Investment,* 2nd ed. New York: Ronald Press, 1977, chapter 14.

Smith, Halbert C. *Real Estate Appraisal.* Columbus, Ohio: Grid, 1976, chapter 10.

"Standards of Professional Practice and Conduct." Chicago: Society of Real Estate Appraisers, 1979.

Stebbins, H. Grady, Jr. *A Guide to Appraising Residences,* 3rd ed. Chicago: Society of Real Estate Appraisers, 1976, pp. 69–96.

16 Alternatives to Single-Family Detached Residences

Key Terms

Condominium Fee ownership of individual units in a multifamily setting and a share of undivided interest in the common areas of the development.

Cooperative Stock ownership in an apartment owned by a corporation for which the stockholder is issued a long-term proprietary lease.

Financial dependency A proportional sharing among shareholder-owners of expenses of the corporation that owns a cooperative.

Manufactured housing Factory-produced housing built on a foundation or chassis for transport to its occupancy site.

Mobile home A factory-produced transportable dwelling unit built on a chassis and containing plumbing, heating, and electrical systems for connection at its occupancy site, with or without a permanent foundation.

Moburbia A suburban mobile home community.

Modular home A factory-produced transportable building unit (for residential, commercial, educational, or industrial purposes) to be used by itself or incorporated into a modular structure at a building site.

Planned unit development (PUD) Clustering buildings or placing them on smaller than typical lots in order to create large, open, park-like areas within a development without substantially changing the overall density typical of conventional development and zoning.

Proprietary lease The lease issued to shareholder-owners in a cooperative.

Shareholder-owner The holder of stock and a proprietary lease in a cooperative apartment corporation.

Since at least 1960, alternative forms of housing with special characteristics, usually in multifamily settings, have brought about substantial changes in select housing markets in the United States. The most significant change is the availability of effective competitive alternatives to the single-family detached residence. The single-family detached residence is the traditional form of housing known in most markets and is the form to which examples and applications in this text have been directed thus far.

The emphasis in this chapter is on alternative forms of housing; however, the appraisal principles and methodology discussed throughout this text for single-family detached residences are also applicable to these alternative forms of housing. In appraising these alternative forms, the concern is still for the valuation of rights in the property. Four types of alternative forms of housing have been selected for discussion: condominiums, cooperatives, planned unit developments (PUDs), and mobile homes or manufactured housing. Each form is considered separately, and a short discussion of comparisons and contrasts follows the presentation of the first three alternative forms.

Condominiums

A *condominium* is defined as "A form of fee ownership of whole units or separate portions of multi-unit buildings by statute which provides the mechanics and facilities for formal filing and recording of a divided interest in real property, where the division is vertical as well as horizontal."[1] The definition can be stated more succintly as "Fee ownership of units in a multi-unit property and joint ownership of the common areas."[2]

Condominium has become an accepted and frequently used term, but some confusion remains about what it actually means. Specifically, the condominium is a creation of state legislation. It represents a form of ownership of a dwelling unit located in a multifamily development, as well as a proportion of the land and other assets of the development.

This legal structure provides the owner of a condominium unit two distinct ownership interests. The first ownership interest is the fee simple in the apartment or townhouse unit in the real estate development. The unit is privately owned; it can be independently and exclusively used or leased by the condominium buyer, mortgaged, and subsequently sold without reference to other unit owners in the development. The second portion of the condominium owner's interest is a percentage of the common areas, such as land, walks, drives, elevators, corridors, open space, and any other amenities associated with the development. The latter would include such facilities for common use of unit owners as swimming pools, golf courses, tennis courts, playgrounds, and the like. All unit owners share an undivided interest in the common areas of a development but cannot lay claim to a specific portion of those common areas.

Residential condominiums exist in many forms. Most commonly, individual units serve as the primary homes of their owner-occupants. Many such condominiums are in high- or mid-rise structures. Another popular use of condominium ownership is found in the second-home or resort market. Such units typically serve as vacation homes for their owners and are most frequently found in warm-climate resort areas and ski areas. Resort condominium units are often occupied by their owners for only a few weeks each year. During the remaining time, the owners rent their units to other vacationers. This form of condominium ownership is very much like the time-sharing arrangements that are also prevalent in resort areas. A further extension of the time-sharing arrangement has been the creation of the "condhotel," whereby hotel rooms are sold to seasonal occupants. Under the sales contract, the owner occupies the room for a specified period of time during each calendar year and agrees to sublet it for the remaining time, at resort rates, through the management of the facility.

As with other forms of housing, including single-family detached houses, condominium developments vary widely in form, in price level, and in size. They are designed to appeal to wide-ranging market segments. However, a single thread of appeal appears at all levels of condominium development and in all market segments. That thread is the desire for a multifamily living environment with the benefits of both individual homeownership and group management. It must be remembered that the condominium is a creation of state legislation and is not necessarily identifiable as a particular type of building or housing structure. The condominium represents a specific form of ownership; for this form of ownership to be maintained, the individual unit must be located in a multifamily setting.

Valuation of Condominium Units

As with single-family detached residential appraisals, the appraisal of a condominium unit may utilize all three approaches to value. The sales comparison approach often provides the most logical and defensible approach to value for individual condominium units. If an active rental market for condominium units exists, gross rent multiplier analysis may be applied. Application of the cost approach to individual condominium units may be questioned, since the condominium unit cannot be reproduced separately from the development. It would be inappropriate, however, to reject the cost approach out of hand.

The FNMA/FHLMC Form 1073/465 for the appraisal of individual condominium or PUD units is shown in figure 16–1. The front page of this specialized appraisal report form is essentially the same as that of

APPRAISAL REPORT — INDIVIDUAL ☐ CONDOMINIUM OR ☐ PUD UNIT

To be completed by Lender

Borrower _____ Census Tract _____ Map Reference _____
Unit No. _____ Project Name/Phase No. _____ File No. _____
Address _____
City _____ County _____ State _____ Zip Code _____
Actual Real Estate Taxes $ _____ (yr.) Sales Price $ _____ Property Rights Appraised ☐ Fee ☐ Leasehold
Loan Charges to be Paid by Seller $ _____ Other Sales Concessions _____
Lender/Client _____ Lender's Address _____
Occupant _____ Appraiser _____

☐ FNMA 1073A required ☐ FHLMC 465 Addendum A required ☐ FHLMC 465 Addendum B required

Instructions to Appraiser _____

NEIGHBORHOOD

Location	☐ Urban	☐ Suburban	☐ Rural
Built Up	☐ Over 75%	☐ 25% to 75%	☐ Under 25%
Growth Rate ☐ Fully Developed	☐ Rapid	☐ Steady	☐ Slow
Property Values	☐ Increasing	☐ Stable	☐ Declining
Demand/Supply	☐ Shortage	☐ In Balance	☐ Oversupply
Marketing Time	☐ Under 3 Mos.	☐ 4–6 Mos.	☐ Over 6 Mos.

Present Land Use ____% 1 Family ____% 2–4 Family ____% Apts. ____% Condo ____% Commercial ____% Industrial ____% Vacant
Change in Present Land Use ☐ Not Likely ☐ Likely* ☐ Taking Place*
*From _____ To _____

Predominant Occupancy ☐ Owner ☐ Tenant ☐ % Vacant
Condominium: Price Range $ _____ to $ _____ Predominant $ _____ Age _____ yrs. to _____ yrs. Predominant _____ yrs.
Single Family: Price Range $ _____ to $ _____ Predominant $ _____ Age _____ yrs. to _____ yrs. Predominant _____ yrs.

Describe potential for additional Condo/PUD units in nearby area _____

NEIGHBORHOOD RATING	Good	Avg.	Fair	Poor
Adequacy of Shopping	☐	☐	☐	☐
Employment Opportunities . . .	☐	☐	☐	☐
Recreational Facilities	☐	☐	☐	☐
Adequacy of Utilities	☐	☐	☐	☐
Property Compatibility	☐	☐	☐	☐
Protection from Detrimental Cond.	☐	☐	☐	☐
Police and Fire Protection	☐	☐	☐	☐
General Appearance of Properties .	☐	☐	☐	☐
Appeal to Market	☐	☐	☐	☐

	Distance	Access or Convenience
Public Transportation		
Employment Centers		
Neighborhood Shopping		
Grammar Schools		
Freeway Access		

Note: FHLMC/FNMA do not consider race or the racial composition of the neighborhood to be reliable appraisal factors.

Describe those factors, favorable or unfavorable, affecting marketability (e.g. public parks, schools, noise, view, mkt. area population size & financial ability) _____

SITE

Lot Dimensions (if PUD) _____ = _____ Sq. Ft. ☐ Corner Lot Project Density When Completed as Planned _____ Units/Acre
Zoning Classification _____ Present Improvements ☐ do ☐ do not conform to zoning regulations.
Highest and Best Use: ☐ Present Use ☐ Other (describe) _____

	Public	Other (specify)
Elec.	☐	☐
Gas	☐	☐
Water	☐	☐
San.Sewer	☐	☐
	☐ Underground Elec. & Tel.	

OFF-SITE IMPROVEMENTS	Public	Private
Street Access:	☐	☐
Surface:		
Maintenance:	☐	☐
	☐ Storm Sewer	☐ Curb/Gutter
	☐ Sidewalk	☐ Street Lights

Project Ingress/Egress (adequacy)	
Topo	
Size/Shape	
View Amenity	
Drainage/Flood Conditions	

Is property located in a HUD Identified Special Flood Hazard Area? ☐ No ☐ Yes

COMMENTS (including any easements, encroachments or adverse conditions) _____

PROJECT IMPROVEMENTS

TYPE
☐ Existing ☐ Approx. Year Built 19___ ☐ Converted (19___) Original Use ___
☐ Condo ☐ PUD
☐ Proposed ☐ Under Construction

PROJECT
☐ Elevator ☐ Walk-up No. of Stories ___
☐ Row or Town House ☐ Other (specify) ___
☐ Primary Residence ☐ Second Home or Recreational

If Completed: No. Phases ___ No. Units ___ No. Sold ___
If Incomplete: Planned No. Phases ___ No. Units ___ No. Sold ___
Units in Subject Phase: Total ___ Completed ___ Sold ___ Rented ___
Approx. No. Units for Sale: Subject Project ___ Subject Phase ___
Exterior Wall ___ Roof Covering ___ Security Features ___
Elevator: No. ___ Adequacy & Condition ___ Soundproofing: Vertical ___ Horizontal ___
Parking: Total No. Spaces ___ Ratio ___ Spaces/Unit ___ Type ___ No. Spaces for Guest Parking ___

Describe common elements or recreational facilities ___
Are any common elements, rec. facilities or parking leased to Owners Assoc.? ___ If yes, attach addendum describing rental, terms and options.

PROJECT RATING — Good Avg. Fair Poor
Location . . . . ☐☐☐☐
General Appearance . . . . ☐☐☐☐
Amenities & Recreational Facilities . . . ☐☐☐☐
Density (units per acre) . . . . ☐☐☐☐
Unit Mix . . . . ☐☐☐☐
Quality of Constr. (mat'l. & finish) . . . ☐☐☐☐
Condition of Exterior . . . . ☐☐☐☐
Condition of Interior . . . . ☐☐☐☐
Appeal to Market . . . . ☐☐☐☐

SUBJECT UNIT

☐ Existing ☐ Proposed ☐ Under Constr. Floor No. ___ Unit Livable Area ___
Parking for Unit: No. ___ Type ___ ☐ Assigned ☐ Owned ☐ Basement ☐ % Finished
Convenience to Unit ___

Room List	Foyer	Liv	Din	Kit	Bdrm	Bath	Fam	Rec	Lndry	Other
Basement										
1st Level										
2nd Level										

Floors: ☐ Hardwood ☐ Carpet over ___
Int. Walls: ☐ Drywall ☐ Plaster
Trim/Finish: ☐ Good ☐ Average ☐ Fair ☐ Poor
Bath Floor: ☐ Ceramic ☐ Wainscot: ☐ Ceramic
Windows (type): ___ ☐ Storm Sash ☐ Screens ☐ Combo
Kitchen Equip.: ☐ Refrig. ☐ Range/Oven ☐ Fan/Hood ☐ Washer ☐ Dryer
☐ Intercom ☐ Disposal ☐ Dishwasher ☐ Microwave ☐ Compactor
HEAT: Type ___ Fuel ___ Cond. ___
AIR COND.: ☐ Central ☐ Other ☐ Adequate ☐ Inadequate

UNIT RATING — Good Avg. Fair Poor
Condition of Improvements . . . . . ☐☐☐☐
Room Sizes and Layout . . . . ☐☐☐☐
Adequacy of Closets and Storage . . ☐☐☐☐
Kit. Equip., Cabinets & Workspace . ☐☐☐☐
Plumbing—Adequacy and Condition . ☐☐☐☐
Electrical—Adequacy and Condition . ☐☐☐☐
Adequacy of Soundproofing . . . . . ☐☐☐☐
Adequacy of Insulation. . . . . ☐☐☐☐
Location within Project or View . . . ☐☐☐☐
Overall Livability . . . . ☐☐☐☐
Appeal and Marketability . . . . . . ☐☐☐☐
Est. Effective Age . . . . ___ to ___ yrs.
Est. Remaining Economic Life . . . . ___ to ___ yrs.

☐ Earth Sheltered Housing Design ☐ Solar Design/Landscape ☐ Solar Space Heat/Air Cond. ☐ Solar Hot Water
☐ Flue Damper ☐ Elec./Mech., Gas Furn. Ignition ☐ Auto. Setback Thermostat ☐ Dble./Triple Glazed Windows ☐ Caulk/Weatherstrip
INSULATION (state R-Factor if known) ☐ Walls ___ ☐ Ceiling ___ ☐ Floor ___ ☐ Roof/Attic ☐ Water Heater
If rehab proposed, do plans and specs provide for adequate energy conservation? If no, attach description of modification needed.
ENERGY EFFICIENCY APPEARS: ☐ High ☐ Adequate ☐ Low   Energy Audit ☐ Yes (attach, if available) ☐ No

COMMENTS (special features, functional or physical inadequacies, modernization or repairs needed, etc.) ___

FHLMC Form 465 9/80   ATTACH DESCRIPTIVE PHOTOGRAPHS OF SUBJECT PROPERTY AND STREET SCENE   FNMA Form 1073 9/80

Figure 16–1. FNMA/FHLMC Appraisal Report Form 1073/465: Condominium or PUD Unit

BUDGET ANALYSIS

Unit Charge $ _____ /Mo. x 12 = $ _____ /yr. ($ _____ /Sq. Ft./year of livable area). Ground Rent (if any) $ _____ /yr.

Utilities included in unit charge: ☐ None ☐ Heat ☐ Air Cond. ☐ Electricity ☐ Gas ☐ Water ☐ Sewer

Note any fees, other than regular Condo/PUD charges, for use of facilities _____

To properly maintain the project and provide the services anticipated, the budget appears: ☐ High ☐ Adequate ☐ Inadequate

Compared to other competitive projects of similar quality and design subject unit charge appears: ☐ High ☐ Reasonable ☐ Low

Management Group: ☐ Owners Association ☐ Developer ☐ Management Agent (identify) _____

Quality of Management and its enforcement of Rules and Regulations appears: ☐ Superior ☐ Good ☐ Adequate ☐ Inadequate

Special or unusual characteristics in the Condo/PUD Documents or otherwise known to the appraiser, that would affect marketability (if none, so state) _____

Comments _____

COST APPROACH

NOTE: FHLMC does not require the cost approach in the appraisal of condominium or PUD units.

Cost Approach (to be used only for detached, semi-detached, and town house units)

Reproduction Cost New _____ Sq. Ft. @ $ _____ per Sq. Ft. = ... $ _____

Less Depreciation: Physical $ _____ Functional $ _____ Economic $ _____ (_____)

Depreciated Value of Improvements: . . . . $ _____

Add Land Value (if leasehold, show only leasehold value—attach calculations) . . . . $ _____

Pro-rata Share of Value of Amenities . . . . $ _____

Total Indicated Value: ☐ FEE SIMPLE ☐ LEASEHOLD . . . . $ _____

Comments regarding estimate of depreciation and value of land and amenity package _____

ANALYSIS

The appraiser, whenever possible, should analyze two comparable sales from within the subject project. However, when appraising a unit in a new or newly converted project, at least two comparables should be selected from outside the subject project. In the following analysis, the comparable should always be adjusted to the subject unit and not vice versa. If a significant feature of the comparable is superior to the subject unit, a minus (−) adjustment should be made to the comparable; if such a feature of the comparable is inferior to the subject, a plus (+) adjustment should be made to the comparable.

LIST ONLY THOSE ITEMS THAT REQUIRE ADJUSTMENT

ITEM	Subject Property	COMPARABLE NO. 1		COMPARABLE NO. 2		COMPARABLE NO. 3	
		DESCRIPTION	+(−)$ Adjustment	DESCRIPTION	+(−)$ Adjustment	DESCRIPTION	+(−)$ Adjustment
Address-Unit No. Project Name							
Proximity to Subj.							
Sales Price	$		$		$		$
Price/Living Area	$		$		$		$
Data Source							
Date of Sale and Time Adjustment							
Location							
Site/View							
Design and Appeal							
Quality of Constr.							
Age							
Condition							
Living Area, Room Count and Total	Total / B.rms / Baths	Total / B.rms / Baths		Total / B.rms / Baths		Total / B.rms / Baths	

MARKET DATA

	Sq. ft.	Sq. ft.	Sq. ft.	Sq. ft.
Gross Living Area				
Basement & Bsmt. Finished Rooms				
Functional Utility				
Air Conditioning				
Storage				
Parking Facilities				
Common Elements and Recreation Facilities				
Mo. Assessment				
Leasehold/Fee				
Special Energy Efficient Items				
Other (e.g. fireplaces, kitchen equip., remodeling)				
Sales or Financing Concessions				
Net Adj. (total)	☐Plus ☐Minus $	☐Plus ☐Minus $	☐Plus ☐Minus $	☐Plus ☐Minus $
Indicated Value of Subject	$	$	$	$

Comments on Market Data Analysis _____

INDICATED VALUE BY MARKET DATA APPROACH .... $ _____

INDICATED VALUE BY INCOME APPROACH (if applicable) Economic Market Rent $ _____ /Mo. x Gross Rent Multiplier _____ = $ _____

This appraisal is made ☐ "as is". ☐ subject to the repairs, alterations, or conditions listed below. ☐ subject to completion per plans and specifications.

Comments and Conditions of Appraisal _____

Final Reconciliation _____

Construction Warranty ☐ Yes ☐ No   Name of Warranty Program _____ Warranty Coverage Expires _____, 19 ___

This appraisal is based upon the above requirements, the certification, contingent and limiting conditions, and Market Value definition that are stated in

☐ FHLMC Form 439 (Rev. 10/78)/FNMA Form 1004B (Rev. 10/78) filed with client , 19 ___ ☐ attached

I ESTIMATE THE MARKET VALUE, AS DEFINED, OF SUBJECT PROPERTY AS OF _____, 19 ___ to be $ _____

Appraiser(s) _____   Review Appraiser (if applicable) _____

Date Report Signed _____, 19 ___   ☐ Did ☐ Did Not Physically Inspect Property

FHLMC Form 465 9/80   REVERSE   FNMA Form 1073 9/80

Figure 16.1 (*continued*)

FNMA/FHLMC Form 1004/70, which has been illustrated and discussed earlier in this text. Minor differences appear mostly on the bottom half of the front page. The project improvement section on Form 1073/465, for example, replaces the improvements section on Form 1004/70. In addition, the room list and the interior finish and equipment section on the residential appraisal report form are incorporated into the subject unit section on the condominium form. Finally, the property rating section on Form 1004/70 has been replaced by the unit rating section on Form 1073/465, although each covers substantially the same features.

On the reverse side of these two appraisal report forms (the valuation section) some significant differences are noted. First, the budget analysis section on Form 1073/465 is unique to the condominium/PUD appraisal. Second, the cost approach on the condominium form has been telescoped and does not require the same level of analysis as is necessary in the residential appraisal report form. In addition, Form 1073/465 specifies that the cost approach in the appraisal of condominium or PUD units is not required by FHLMC.

The differences in the market data analysis sections of the two forms are also noteworthy. Two items of comparison in Form 1004/70 in the section on market data analysis (garage/carport and porches, patio, pools, etc.) have been expanded in the condominium form to include storage, parking facilities, common elements and recreation facilities, monthly assessment, and leasehold/fee (a reference to the interest being valued, which already has been analyzed in the cost approach section).

Figure 16–2 shows the project analysis form (Addendum A) and the analysis of annual income and expenses—operating budget form (Addendum B). Either or both of these forms may have to be submitted under specific guidelines that are outlined in the instructions section of Addendum A.

Cooperatives

A *cooperative* is defined as:

> A form of ownership whereby the owner of stock in a cooperative apartment or housing corporation pays a proportionate share of the interest and real estate taxes paid by the corporation. This proportionate share is based on the proportion of the total stock owned, and the interest that is deductible can relate to any debt incurred by the corporation to acquire, construct, alter, rehabilitate or maintain the building or land. The cooperative must be bona fide, i.e., stock ownership must give the stockholder the right to live in an apartment or

house on the property owned or leased by the corporation though the stockholder need not actually be required to live there.[3]

A further definition of a cooperative apartment is as follows: "An apartment owned by a corporation, either for or not for profit, or by a trust, in which each owner purchases stock to the extent of the value of the apartment, title being evidenced by a proprietary lease."[4] The cooperative, therefore, is a form of ownership that is similar in many ways to the condominium.

In a typical cooperative arrangement, a corporation is formed to purchase the real estate. The corporation will be the mortgagor on any loan on the property. In most cases, a mortgagee will not lend the total purchase price of the real estate to the cooperative corporation. In order to raise the capital necessary to cover the difference between the loan amount and the purchase price, stock is sold to the prospective tenants. As a result, the equity value is spread over the various units in the development to establish a purchase price, reflected in a certain number of stock shares for each unit. Once the prospective tenant has bought the requisite number of shares for the unit, the corporation issues the tenant a long-term lease on the unit, called a *proprietary lease*. The lease gives the holder rights equivalent in economic benefit to outright ownership in exchange for rent paid to the corporation. The rent, paid monthly, is credited toward the corporation's blanket mortgage loan on the building. Assessments for repairs to common areas or individual units are also shared proportionally by shareholder-owners. The purchaser also has an interest in the common elements associated with the leased unit.

The cooperative operates with a board of directors who represents all shareholder-owners. Incorporated into the proprietary lease are rules concerning behavior, occupancy, payments, and leasing. It is the board's responsibility to establish and enforce these rules. The board also screens and approves prospective tenant-owners.

The cooperative is a unique form of housing, but not a new one. It dates back to the post-World War I era but has changed in format in recent years to accommodate the changing needs in the market. A major housing shortage in post-World War I Europe brought about the development of cooperatives on that continent. Today, European cooperatives are intended mainly to provide housing for low- and middle-income people. The luxury cooperative is an American creation. In Europe, luxury apartments are usually condominiums.

Much of the cooperative housing in the United States was developed during the 1940s and 1950s. It was most popular in large urban centers, such as New York City, San Francisco, and Miami. Today, the major

PROJECT ANALYSIS ☐ CONDOMINIUM OR ☐ PUD — ADDENDUM A TO FHLMC FORM 465 9/80

INSTRUCTIONS

The following outlines the appraisal documentation required on each Condominium or PUD Unit loan submitted to FHLMC. The Individual Unit Appraisal Report and Project Analysis must be signed by an appraiser approved by the Seller/Servicer submitting the loan to FHLMC. It is preferred, but not required, that each of these forms be signed by the same appraiser. FHLMC does not require the cost approach in the appraisal of an individual condominium or PUD unit, however, if the lender or appraiser desires, the Cost Approach Section may be completed.

APPRAISAL REPORT INDIVIDUAL CONDOMINIUM OR PUD UNIT (FHLMC Form 465/FNMA Form 1073)

This must be submitted with each individual loan and the date of the estimate of Market Value must be within ninety (90) days of the date of closing of the mortgage.

PROJECT ANALYSIS (FHLMC Form 465 ADDENDUM A)

PART I: This must be submitted if less than 70% of the individual units in the project or section/phase have been sold. To establish this 70% requirement, a sale under an option to purchase contract cannot be counted, and multiple sales to one owner must be counted as one sale. A section/phase is one established by the Condo/PUD documents and is of sufficient size to contain an adequate number of units to support any common elements or recreational facilities, which are included in the sale price or appraised value of an individual unit. Subject section/phase may be combined with other completed, sold and occupied section(s)/phase(s) to meet this requirement, provided all are under a common Owners Association.

PART II: This must be submitted if the project is in the process of conversion or the conversion process has been completed less than two years.

ANALYSIS OF ANNUAL INCOME & EXPENSES—OPERATING BUDGET (FHLMC Form 465 ADDENDUM B/FNMA Form 1073A, Page 1)

This must be submitted ONLY if the project or section/phase has not been operated and managed by the Owners Association for at least two years. The upper portion is to be completed in detail by the Developer, Owners Association or Management Agent. The completion of the lower portion is the responsibility of the Seller/Servicer. It can be prepared by a staff member of the Seller/Servicer, a property manager or an approved appraiser, provided the person who signs is qualified, in the opinion of the Seller/Servicer, to make the required analysis.

To facilitate the submission, the Seller/Servicer may submit a clearly reproduced signed copy of Addendum A and/or Addendum B, if required, provided each is dated within 12 months of the date of the estimate of Market Value of the Individual Unit. If reproduced copies of the Addendum A and/or Addendum B are furnished the Appraiser, and submitted to FHLMC, the Appraiser who signs the Individual Condominium or PUD Unit Appraisal Report should note in the following Comments Section any significant changes or variances which are observed when making the inspection.

COMMENTS SECTION

Date _____ 19 ____   Signature(s) _____

PROJECT ANALYSIS

Part I must be completed if less than 70% of the individual units in the project or section/phase have been sold. To establish this 70% requirement, a sale under an option to purchase contract cannot be counted, and multiple sales to one owner must be counted as one sale. Part II must be completed if the project is in the process of conversion or the conversion process has been completed less than two years.

Project Name _____

Address or Location _____

City _____ State _____ Zip _____ Phase No. _____

If the project is not completed, discuss the proposed overall development or conversion plan and stage of completion including the number of sections, units and recreational facilities per section and the estimated completion date of each section

Describe the common elements and recreational facilities, and comment on their adequacy, quality and condition

Are the recreational facilities available for use by individuals other than unit owners and guests? If yes, comment as to effect on marketability

Describe and comment on the adequacy of the following:

Storage space _____

Laundry facilities _____

Trash removal _____

Parking facilities _____

Soundproofing material _____

PART I

FHLMC Form 465 ADDENDUM A 9/80

Figure 16–2. FNMA/FHLMC Form 1073/465 Addenda: Condominium or PUD Unit (Addendums A and B)

PROJECT ANALYSIS

Individual Unit Room Count			Livable Area Sq. Ft.	Price Range	Price Per Sq. Ft.	Monthly Assoc. Dues	Number of Units		
Total	Bedrooms	Baths					Planned	Sold	Completed
				$　　　to $	$　　　to $				
			TOTAL						

Discuss sales performance to date (per phase/section, if applicable) _____

Estimated absorption time, after completion, for _____ unsold units, at existing prices, in subject project/phase is _____ months.
Comment on any unit type(s) on which sales appear to be slow _____

Discuss project density as it compares to others in the area from a standpoint of marketability _____

State the approximate number of units currently for sale by developer in prior phases. If more than one prior phase, list for each phase _____

Discuss any rental or sales concessions being offered (if none known, so state) _____

If the developer(s) plans to retain any unsold units for rental, discuss number, voting rights and comparability of unit charges _____

Describe nearby competition including sale prices, rate of sales, sellout time, etc. _____

Describe potential for additional Condo/PUD units in nearby area, considering land availability, zoning, utilities, apartments subject to conversions, etc. _____

PART I CONTINUED

General comments including any probable changes in the economic base or neighborhood which would either favorably or unfavorably affect Condo/PUD sales

Date _____ 19 _____   Appraiser(s) Signature: _____

THIS SECTION MUST BE COMPLETED IF THE PROPERTY IS IN THE PROCESS OF CONVERSION OR RECENTLY CONVERTED

Itemize major alterations, modernization and repairs _____

Describe any incomplete items including estimated completion date _____

Has the Appraiser reviewed engineering reports on the structural integrity of the buildings and the condition of the major physical components and systems of the project? _____ If yes, describe any unfavorable conditions indicated _____

How many of the units were sold to tenants? _____ Percentage of sales price discount to tenants: _____ %
Describe other sales concessions to tenants _____

Estimated absorption time for _____ unsold units is _____ months. How many of the unsold units are rented? _____
General Comments _____

Date _____ 19 _____   Appraiser(s) Signature: _____

(REVERSE)

FHLMC Form 465, ADDENDUM A 9/80

PART II

Figure 16.2 *(continued)*

ANALYSIS OF ANNUAL INCOME AND EXPENSES — OPERATING BUDGET

For FNMA submissions complete both pages of this form. For FHLMC submissions complete this side only. Note: If developer control has terminated and the Home Owners Association has been controlled by Unit Owners for two or more years, FHLMC does not require this form.

Project Name _____

Address or Location _____ City _____ State _____ Zip _____

STATEMENT OF ANNUAL PROJECT OPERATING BUDGET AND RESERVES FOR THE YEAR 19 _____

COMPLETE ONLY THOSE ITEMS WHICH ARE PAID BY OWNERS ASSOCIATION WHICH INCLUDES SUBJECT UNIT.

Budget below is for: ☐ Entire project   ☐ Phase No. _____

ADMINISTRATIVE EXPENSES

Office expenses, supplies, equipment rental, etc. .... $_____

Telephone ....

Office salaries (itemize) ....

Management fee (name of management firm) _____

Legal and audit ....

OPERATING EXPENSES

Fuel ....

Utilities (Gas $_____ Electricity $_____ Water & Sewer $_____)

Trash & Garbage Removal ....

Exterminating ....

Supplies ....

REPAIRS AND MAINTENANCE

Decorating (exterior and interior) ....

Cleaning expenses and supplies ....

Snow removal ....

Building maintenance and repairs ....

Elevator maintenance and repairs ....

Heating and air conditioning maintenance and repairs ....

Pool maintenance and repairs ....

Parking area maintenance and repairs ....

Private street maintenance and repairs ....

Gardening and yard maintenance and repairs including shrub replacement ....

Other (specify) ....

Salaries (itemize including employee benefits and payroll taxes) ....

FIXED EXPENSES

Real estate taxes (if PUD) ....

Other (Taxes $_____ Assessments $_____ Regime Fees $_____)

Licenses ....

SERVICER, OWNERS ASSOCIATION OR MANAGEMENT AGENT

Insurance premiums
Ground rent
Recreational or other facilities rental

TOTAL EXPENSES

REPLACEMENT RESERVES List Each Item	Yrs. of Estimated Remaining Life	Expected Replacement Cost	Average Yearly Cost
		$	$

TOTAL REPLACEMENT RESERVES . . . . $
TOTAL ANNUAL EXPENSES AND REPLACEMENT RESERVES $

Project Annual Income from: Condo/PUD charges $ _____ Other $ _____ Total $ _____

Itemize other income _____

If the income is less than the budget, discuss deficit _____

Actual funds now held: for payment of operating expenses $ _____ in Replacement Reserve fund $ _____

No. of Unit Owners over 30 days delinquent in Association charges _____ in Special Assessment charges _____

Explain any indebtedness or leases on the common area or parking, utilities or other facilities (if none, so state) _____

Certified Correct: Organization _____

Date _____ By _____ Title _____

I certify that I have analyzed the above Statement of Operating Budget and Reserves. In my opinion, except as stated below, the items as set forth in this Budget appear sufficient to maintain the project, including replacement of major items, in a manner adequate to protect its marketability.

Comments on Budget and Reserves _____

Date _____ 19 ___ Organization _____

By _____ Title _____

TO BE COMPLETED BY SELLER/

Seller/Servicer's Use Only.

FHLMC Form 465 ADDENDUM B 9/80

FNMA Form 1073A 9/80
1 of 2

Figure 16.2 (continued)

Required for FNMA - FHLMC does not require this page.

STATEMENT OF ANNUAL PROJECT INCOME AND EXPENSES FOR THE YEAR 19___

COMPLETE ONLY THOSE ITEMS WHICH WERE RECEIVED OR PAID BY THE OWNERS ASSOCIATION WHICH INCLUDES SUBJECT UNIT.

GROSS ANNUAL INCOME:

Condo/PUD charges: $ _____ per mo. X _____ units X 12 = _____ $ _____

Other Income (itemized): _____

TOTAL INCOME FROM ALL SOURCES $ _____

ADMINISTRATIVE EXPENSES

Office expenses, supplies, equipment rental, etc. . . . . $ _____

Telephone . . . .

Office salaries (itemized)

Management fee (name of management firm) _____

Legal and audit . . . .

OPERATING EXPENSES

Fuel . . . .

Utilities (Gas $ _____ Electricity $ _____ Water & Sewer $ _____)

Trash & Garbage Removal . . . .

Exterminating . . . .

Supplies . . . .

REPAIRS AND MAINTENANCE

Decorating (exterior and interior) . . . .

Cleaning expenses and supplies . . . .

Snow removal . . . .

Building maintenance and repairs . . . .

Elevator maintenance and repairs . . . .

Heating and air conditioning maintenance and repairs . .

Pool maintenance and repairs . . . .

Parking area maintenance and repairs . . . .

Private street maintenance and repairs . . . .

Gardening and yard maintenance and repairs including shrub replacement

Replacement expenses (itemize) _____

Other (specify) _____

OWNERS ASSOCIATION OR MANAGEMENT AGENT

TO BE COMPLETED BY SELLER/SERVICER,

Salaries (itemize including employee benefits and payroll taxes)

FIXED EXPENSES

Real estate taxes (if PUD)

Other taxes or assessments

Licenses

Insurance premiums

Ground rent

Recreational or other facilities rental

TOTAL EXPENSES $

TOTAL ANNUAL NET SURPLUS (deficit) $

Discuss disposition of surplus or, (deficit), method of funding:

Does inspection of project indicate that funds spent during preceding year for maintenance and repairs were sufficient to maintain project in a manner likely to be acceptable to the market? If answer is no, explain:

Above statement of income and expenses is certified to be correct:

Organization

By   Title   Date

FNMA Form 1073A 9/80
2 of 2

Figure 16.2 *(continued)*

market for cooperatives, which are on the decline since the advent of condominiums, is still the New York City area. Major metropolitan centers that are characterized by a high density of population are still attractive for cooperative housing. In 1975, a HUD condominium-cooperative study revealed some facts that substantiate this point. At that time, 36 percent of cooperative units were high-rise structures of more than three stories.[5] Seventy-five percent of the cooperative units had two or fewer bedrooms, virtually all were primary residences, and all had very few, if any, of the amenities that are usually associated with the condominium.[6]

The Proprietary Lease

The proprietary leaseholder is not liable for the default of others if the premises and lease are abandoned prior to the expiration of the lease. This is a major change from the situation during the 1930s, when many proprietary leaseholders faced personal bankruptcy because they abandoned their cooperative apartments to avoid unbearable assessments caused by the default of other tenants.[7] The proprietary lease for the conventional cooperative is generally negotiated for terms of from 20 to 50 years, with the right of automatic renewal given to the cooperator (lessee).[8] This term protects the owner-shareholder from the rent increases generally associated with annual leases in rental housing.

Proprietary leases may have many provisions. The following 12 terms are common to most proprietary leases, however:

1. There is a stipulation about who may occupy the apartment, including a prohibition against permanent guests.
2. Voting the stock will probably depend on not being in default on any payments. The vote is usually proportionate to the number of shares owned.
3. The lease and stock are inseparable. One must retain the stock to retain the lease, and vice versa.
4. The number of shares allocated to the apartment being leased will be stated to determine the price and assessment.
5. Carrying charges and direct payments are defined precisely. Examples are painting, gas, and electricity.
6. Both resale and subleasing will usually require the approval of the board of directors.
7. If stock is sold at a profit to a new tenant, the seller may not be eligible to keep the excess if this is so stated in the lease.
8. Management services are stipulated. These are important to assure smooth operations.
9. An apartment which has been leased to a new tenant will have

to be vacated by the promised delivery date. Carrying charges are specified if this condition is not met.

10. Books and records of the cooperative will usually be available for review during business hours. The books are required to be accurate and up-to-date.

11. The corporation's obligations to its stockholders should be stated. Some of the common stipulations are providing for quiet enjoyment; requiring all tenants to maintain homeowners' insurance; rendering yearly financial information to shareholders for tax purposes; and allowing the stockholder to know the warrantees of the sponsor.

12. An enumeration of all mortgage loans may be available to all shareholders. This is rarely done, but when it is, a simple list of each tenant's share of the debt outstanding is provided.[9]

The policies of cooperative housing are controlled and determined by its member-owners. The proprietary lease is the main vehicle through which those policies are made known to all.

Valuation of Cooperative Units

As with the valuation of condominium units, potentially all approaches to value can be applied to the valuation of cooperative apartments. The same reservations also appear in the application of the cost approach because of the allocation problem. Again, the most logical and defensible approach is sales comparison. There may also be some comparability between the sale of condominium units and the value of cooperative stock in some markets.

Finally, in valuing a cooperative unit, the mortgage debt obligation may require adjustment, particularly if any comparables are from a different cooperative corporation. Such an adjustment may be required to account for any premium paid for the stock in recognition of a favorable financing package.

Planned Unit Developments (PUDs)

A *planned unit development* (PUD) is defined as:

A type of land development which may be at variance with traditional zoning and lot layout. May be residential, commercial or industrial. Buildings are clustered and/or set on smaller lots than usual. Result is a development with an overall density the same or slightly greater than is typical of conventional developments and zoning, but containing large open park-like areas with buildings concentrated in a few

areas. Individual properties are owned in fee with either joint ownership of the open areas or, if local law requires, with open areas
deeded to the city.[10]

Planned unit developments are usually restricted (by zoning and
setback regulations, subdivision laws, and construction considerations)
to developments in which the units are situated in single-family structures or townhouses. In this respect, they create neighborhoods in which
the members of the neighborhood own a portion of the common amenities. Therefore, if one is creating or converting a project in which the
units are stacked on top of each other, the PUD alternative is generally
not feasible. As a result, most PUDs are conceived, designed, and built
specifically as PUDs. Although PUD housing can be in fee simple or
condominium ownership, few rental properties are converted to PUDs.
The majority of rental property conversions are to the condominium
form of ownership.

Valuation of Planned Unit Developments (PUDs)

As noted earlier in figure 16–1, FNMA/FHLMC Form 1073/465 is
applicable to either individual condominium or PUD units. As a result,
the comments in the previous discussion of valuation of condominium
units apply equally to the valuation of PUD units.

**Comparisons and Contrasts: Condominiums,
Cooperatives, and Planned Unit Developments (PUDs)**

Condominiums and PUDs have recently gained in popularity at the
expense of cooperatives. Some characteristics that distinguish these
alternative forms of housing and that may, in part, account for the
advantages of one form over the other are financial dependency, flexibility of resale, and design flexibility.

Financial dependency is the main distinguishing characteristic of
the cooperative. In the cooperative, all expenses are shared, including
the monthly mortgage debt payment that is assessed to the corporation
that owns the cooperative. The corporation divides these expenses
proportionally among all share-owners as their monthly rent and expense fees. This qualifies as a financial dependency. One shareholder's
default on the monthly mortgage payment could mean default of the
blanket mortgage loan on the building.

Condominiums and PUDs offer the opportunity to obtain debt
financing that is almost identical to the financing of single-family de-

tached residences. Each individual unit must be financed separately by its owner. If that owner defaults, no other owner in the complex is affected. Only maintenance fees for the common areas and amenities are shared.

Because of financial dependency, resale is a more difficult process with the cooperative. Each prospective shareholder-owner is scrutinized by the cooperative board, and individual financial stability is essential. (Approval by the cooperative board is usually required.) Since new owners are held by the terms of the original mortgage loan, they have to produce a significant sum of cash at the outset. This sum becomes greater as the loan is paid down. In the past, a cooperative corporation's stock and a proprietary lease were not considered sufficient collateral for mortgage loans, and personal notes were the only alternative. This can be a major deficiency in the cooperative form of ownership; however, some lending institutions are beginning to consider a share in a cooperative on the same basis as ownership of a condominium unit or single-family residence when financing is being arranged.[11]

A condominium, on the other hand, is more salable. Resale effects on neighboring units is slight because of the individual financing of each unit. Thus, the initial cash outlay is less and a new mortgage loan can usually be obtained. Each owner can also refinance the mortgage loan for needed cash.

Restrictions may be placed on the amount of interior design work permitted in a coopertive because of the financial dependency among unit shareholders. If an owner defaults, the other members would be responsible for re-leasing the unit. During the time the apartment is vacant, the other shareholders would be assessed a proportionate percentage of the fees that relate to the vacant apartment. In the condominium, owners have full flexibility of interior design or decorating, with no effect on other owners.

These distinguishing characteristics make the condominium or PUD unit appear to be a more attractive alternative in most cases. In some markets, however, the cooperative form of housing ownership has become widely accepted. Correcting the deficiency in financing arrangements and providing a screening device for potential shareholder-owners in the rules of the cooperative board, among other controls, may provide cooperatives with an advantage in those markets.

Mobile Homes and Manufactured Housing

A *mobile home* is defined in *Real Estate Appraisal Terminology* as "A house trailer; a complete livable dwelling unit equipped with wheels so that it may be towed from place to place by a truck or automobile, depending on its size and the highway regulations of the states through which it will travel."[12] A more contemporary definition of a mobile home is "A structure, transportable in one or more sections, which exceeds eight body feet in width or 32 body feet in length, built on a permanent chassis and designed to be used as a dwelling with or without a permanent foundation when connected to the required utilities, and includes the plumbing, heating, air conditioning and electrical systems contained therein."[13] The latter definition is broad enough to include a broad range of housing alternatives under the general category of manufactured housing.

mobile home & are synonous

After suffering substantial losses and bankruptcies in the 1974–1975 recession, the mobile home industry has survived and currently dominates the shelter market for housing in the under-$35,000 price range. This dominance in this market segment has been brought about by the substantial price increases resulting from inflationary pressures on conventionally built housing and the savings made possible through the production of housing in a factory. The gap between prices for conventionally produced housing and manufactured housing widened so much in the late 1970s that the percentage of mobile homes in the under-$35,000 price range increased from 62 percent in 1976 to 93 percent in 1979.[14]

Recent changes in the perception of mobile homes by market participants and intermediaries might be best exemplified by the definition of the term *moburbia:*

> A suburban mobile home community (rental, condo, or PUD form of rentership or ownership) offering all of the amenities and luxuries found in most good quality housing developments, such as swimming pools, club houses, tennis and golf courses, and other recreational facilities. Moburbia contrasts sharply with mobile home parks built some 20 years ago when most parks of any size were usually located in the suburban area because that was the only place they could be built. Moburbias are usually situated in convenient locations, as proximity to shopping centers, schools and transportation are major concerns in planning suburban communities.[15]

In his assessment of the future for the traditional mobile home industry, Taylor offers the following:

> 1.   Single Site Occupancy—About 52 percent of mobile homes are currently placed on individually owned property in rural or small town locations. Simultaneously, restrictive zoning currently prohibits the placement of mobile homes within many communities. As the need for economical housing continues to grow and the manufactured home

more closely resembles a site-built home in appearance and financing terms, it is expected that local demands will bring about a change in zoning and planning attitude which will be more favorable to both the mobile and modular home.

2.   Mobile Home Communities—The traditional mobile home park with its inclusion of amenities for the use of tenants has, in fact, been a pioneering effort in what planners now call planned unit development. As the manufactured home continues to acquire increasing importance in the nation's housing market, different types of land development will become more popular with both developers and consumers. Historically, it has been common for the homeowner to purchase his home and then rent space and facilities from the development.

But the greater use of the PUD, as well as the condominiums and the subdivision approach, suggests that the purchase of the land, as well as the home, will become more widely practiced, and the common areas (streets and recreational facilities) will be turned over to a homeowner's association by the developer upon project completion.

3.   Urban Housing—The capability exists for fixed site town houses, row houses, duplexes and even high-rise buildings to be built from manufactured units or modules. While this has been done to some degree, the full potential of the production economics and speed possible with modular construction will not be realized until building codes and union restrictions are modified to recognize its practicality and inevitability.[16]

Valuation of Mobile Homes

As with the alternative forms of housing discussed earlier, the same valuation principles and methodology apply to mobile homes as apply to single-family detached residences. In the appraisal of mobile homes, special attention should be given to neighborhood analysis (particularly if the unit is part of a self-contained community), highest and best use (particularly in rental communities), and site analysis (also particularly in rental communities). For cost estimation, several different sources and methods are available to the appraiser; the materials published by Marshall and Swift on manufactured housing are especially recommended.[17]

Figure 16–3 provides an example of a form report for a mobile home appraisal. There are notable similarities between data requirements on this form report and those discussed earlier for single-family detached residential, condominium, and PUD units. Although it does not appear on the form, gross rent multiplier analysis does apply in situations when a rental market exists. The appraiser is cautioned,

MOBILEHOME APPRAISAL REPORT

Mobilehome Park Name_____

Address_____

City _____ State_____ Zip_____

AREA TRENDS

Predominate: SRF ☐   Income ☐   Commercial ☐
                Mobile Home Park ☐   Other ☐

Trend Improving: Fast ☐   Moderate ☐   Slow ☐
                    Stable ☐   Static ☐   Declining ☐

Vacancy Area_____%   Area_____% builtup

Vacancy Mobilehome Park _____%

Total spaces in park _____ Total vacant spaces _____

Year park constructed _____ Quality_____

Recreational facilities available _____

W
I
D
T
H

I
N

F
E
E
T

Length in feet

Foundation: ☐ Piers   ☐ Steel I Beam   ☐ 2x6   ☐ 2x4

Exterior: ☐ Aluminum ☐ Simulated Wood Siding ☐ Wood
Siding ☐ Window Shutters ☐ Simulated Veneer ☐ Alum
Roof w/paint ☐Alum Roof w/gravel ☐ **2x2 Exterior Stud**
☐ **2x4 Exterior Stud Walls**   ☐ **2x3 Exterior Stud Walls**

Remarks: _____

_____

MARKETABILITY	Good	Average	Fair	Poor
Location to: Schools				
Shopping				
Transportation				
Employment				

All utilities are in except: Paving ☐   Curb & Gutters ☐
              Electricity ☐   Sewer ☐   Sidewalk ☐
                                Gas ☐   Water ☐

Topography: ☐ Level   ☐Hillside (above) (below) street level

Remarks concerning site — park, etc.: _____

Interior: ☐ 2x3 Interior Stud Walls ☐ 1x3 Interior Stud Walls
☐ Paneling ☐ Wall Paper ☐ Other_____

Heat: ☐ Forced Air   ☐ Gas Wall   ☐ **Electric Wall**
                                    or Baseboard Heat

Quality Classification: ☐ Conventional ☐ Modern ☐ Rustic
              ☐ Low   ☐ Fair   ☐ Average   ☐ Good   ☐ Very Good

CALCULATIONS:

Mobile home _____ sq. ft. @ $_____ = $_____

Total Extras $_____

Covered carport (excluding concrete)

_____x _____ = _____ sq. ft. @ $_____ = $_____

Covered porch (excluding concrete or floor)

_____x _____ = _____ sq. ft. @ $_____ = $_____

Enclosed patio (excluding concrete or floor)

_____x _____ = _____ sq. ft. @ $_____ = $_____

Utility sheds — Total sq. ft. _____ @ $_____ = $_____

Total Replacement Cost $_____

DEPRECIATION:

Physical Deterioration _____%

Functional Obsolescence _____%

Locational Diminished Utility _____%

Locational Increased Utility _____%

Total ± _____%

Total depreciation ± _____% $_____

Depreciated value of mobilehome or
COST APPROACH VALUE $_____

Remarks: _____

_____

MOBILEHOME DESCRIPTION AND ANALYSIS

ROOM DESCRIPTION

Rms		Floors	Walls	Extras			
	LR			Fireplace	$	Insul	$
	DR			Ex Bath		Air Cond	
	BK			Shwr & Dr		Dshwshr	
	Kit			Tub Encl		Decorate	
	FmRm			Pul Lav		Other	
	Bath			G Disp			
	Util			Ex Fan			
	Bdrm			R&O			
				Hood		Tot Exts	$

Manufacture _____ Model _____

Serial No. _____ Size _____ x _____

Appearance: ☐ Excellent ☐ Good ☐ Average ☐ Fair ☐ Poor

Condition: ☐ Excellent ☐ Good ☐ Average ☐ Fair ☐ Poor

Rooms: Total _____ Bedrooms _____ Baths _____

Fam Rm _____ Den _____ Utility _____

Source: Taylor, Gerald C., *Introduction to Mobile Home/Manufactured Housing Appraising,* 3rd rev. (Chicago: Society of Real Estate Appraisers, 1983). Reprinted with permission.

Figure 16–3. Mobile Home Appraisal Report Form

MOBILE HOME
MARKET DATA ANALYSIS

Subject	Comp #1	Comp #2	Comp #3
Park Name	Park Name	Park Name	Park Name
Address	Address	Address	Address
Size	Size	Size	Size
Rooms	Rooms	Rooms	Rooms
Age	Age	Age	Age
Condition	Condition	Condition	Condition
Quality	Quality	Quality	Quality
Lot Size	Lot Size	Lot Size	Lot Size
Date	Date	Date	Date
Terms	Terms	Terms	Terms
Sale Price	Sale Price	Sale Price	Sale Price
Included Extras	Included Extras	Included Extras	Included Extras
Per Sq. Ft.	Per Sq. Ft.	Per Sq. Ft.	Per Sq. Ft.

Comments _____

MARKET ADJUSTMENTS

	Comp #1 (+)	(—)		Comp #2 (+)	(—)		Comp #3 (+)	(—)
Location			Location			Location		
Size			Size			Size		
Age			Age			Age		
Condition			Condition			Condition		
Quality			Quality			Quality		
Time			Time			Time		
Terms			Terms			Terms		
Extras			Extras			Extras		
Misc.			Misc.			Misc.		
Totals			Totals			Totals		
Net Adjustment	$		Net Adjustment	$		Net Adjustment	$	
Ind. Value	$		Ind. Value	$		Ind. Value	$	

Indicated value by
THE MARKET APPROACH $_____

CORRELATION OF VALUE INDICATORS

COST APPROACH TO VALUE $_____

MARKET DATA APPROACH TO VALUE $_____

Date AS OF   19

Correlated Estimated Value $_____

Appraiser_____ Class_____

Review Appraiser _____

Remarks: _____
_____
_____
_____

Figure 16.3 *(continued)*

however, to distinguish between rents for furnished or unfurnished mobile homes and to verify who pays for utilities. The form emphasizes the cost and sales comparison approaches.

Summary

The major emphasis throughout this text has been on valuation of the most traditional form of residential property—detached single-family housing. In this chapter, discussion has centered on other forms: condominiums; cooperatives; planned unit developments (PUDs); and manufactured housing. Although there are some exceptions, these alternative forms of housing offer individual unit ownership in a multifamily setting, with common areas and, in some instances, shared amenities.

Each of the alternative forms of housing has its own peculiar characteristics. Although each form is considered first in the context of serving as a primary home for its occupants, other uses are recognized, such as vacation homes and investment vehicles. The flexibility and ubiquity of the condominium form of ownership, particularly in resort areas, lends itself most readily to ownership based on different motivations.

All alternative forms of housing may be appraised by traditional appraisal methodology, although sales comparison analysis often provides the most logical and defensible approach. The unique characteristics of each alternative form of housing may require special considerations, however, in the application of traditional appraisal methodology. Specialized appraisal report forms are often utilized in the valuation of these alternative forms of housing.

Notes

1. Boyce, Byrl N., Ed., *Real Estate Appraisal Terminology,* rev. ed. (Cambridge, Mass.: Ballinger [Joint publication of the American Institute of Real Estate Appraisers and Society of Real Estate Appraisers], 1981), p. 56.

2. Ibid.

3. Ibid., p. 61.

4. Ibid.

5. *HUD Condominium Cooperative Study,* vol. 1 (Washington, D.C.: U.S. Government Printing Office, July 1975), p. III-30.

6. Ibid.

7. Clurman, David, and Hebard, Edna L., *Condominiums and Cooperatives* (New York: Wiley-Interscience, 1970), p. 167.

8. Ibid., p. 182.

9. Ibid., pp. 182–186.

10. Boyce, *Terminology*, pp. 186–187.

11. Downs, James C., Jr. *Principles of Real Estate Management,* 12th ed. (Chicago: Institute of Real Estate Management of the National Association of Realtors, 1980), p. 223.

12. Boyce, *Terminology*, p. 166.

13. Taylor, Gerald C., *Introduction to Mobile Home/Manufactured Housing Appraising,* 3rd revision. (Chicago: Society of Real Estate Appraisers, 1983), p. 1-2.

14. Ibid., p. 1-9.

15. Ibid., p. 1-2.

16. Ibid., pp. 1-7, 1-8.

17. *Residential Cost Handbook (Manufactured Housing)* (Los Angeles: Marshall and Swift, 1981), pp. A-93–A-108.

Suggested Readings

Boyce, Byrl N., ed., *Real Estate Appraisal Terminology,* rev. ed. Cambridge, Mass.: Ballinger (Joint publication of the American Institute of Real Estate Appraisers and Society of Real Estate Appraisers), 1981.

Clurman, David, and Hebard, Edna L. *Condominiums and Cooperatives.* New York: Wiley-Interscience, 1970.

Downs, James C., Jr. *Principles of Real Estate Management.* 12th ed. Chicago: Institute of Real Estate Management of the National Association of Realtors, 1980.

Dombal, Robert W. "Appraising Condominiums: Suggested Data Analysis Techniques" (an Educational Memorandum). Chicago: American Institute of Real Estate Appraisers of the National Association of Realtors, 1976.

Dombal, Robert W. *Residential Condominium: A Guide to Analysis and Appraisal.* Chicago: American Institute of Real Estate Appraisers of the National Association of Realtors, 1976.

Expense Analysis: Condominiums, Cooperatives, and Planned Unit Developments. Chicago: Institute of Real Estate Management of the National Association of Realtors, published annually.

HUD Condominium Cooperative Study (3 vols.). Washington, D.C.: U.S. Government Printing Office, July 1975.

O'Mara, W. Paul, et al. *Residential Development Handbook.* Washington, D.C.: Urban Land Institute, 1978.

Taylor, Gerald C. *Introduction to Mobile Home/Manufactured Housing Appraising,* 3rd revision. Chicago: Society of Real Estate Appraisers, 1983.

17

Introduction to Income Capitalization

Key Terms

Annuity A series of income payments that are collectible at equal periodic intervals.

Capital recovery The recapture of invested capital over some finite timeframe, through periodic cash flow and/or reversionary interests.

Capitalization A process whereby income is converted to a lump sum capital value.

Cash throw-off to equity (CTO) Residual income to the equity investor after the payment of debt service (also termed before-tax cash flow to equity). *NOT—ADS equals CTO*

Debt service coverage ratio (DSCR) The ratio of net operating income (NOI) to annual debt service (ADS).

Discounted cash flow model A valuation methodology that isolates differences in the timing and amount of cash flows and discounts the cash flows to a present value estimate.

Effective gross income (EGI) In income producing property, potential gross income less vacancy and credit loss plus other (e.g., service) income.

Leased fee An encumbered fee in that the right of use and occupancy has been leased to others.

Leasehold A lessee's right to use and enjoy real estate for a stated period of time and under certain conditions set forth in the lease.

Net operating income (NOI) Annual income remaining after deducting operating expenses (fixed and variable expenses, including repairs and replacements) from effective gross income (EGI).

Ordinary annuity A series of income payments of equal amount that are collectible at equal periodic intervals, at the end of each period.

Ratio model A valuation methodology that capitalizes income to the total property or to any of the components of the total property at an appropriate rate of capitalization to derive total property value or the value of one of its components.

Rent collections Potential gross income less vacancy and credit loss.

Residual An amount, quantity, or remainder left over at the end of a specified time, and applicable to both periodic cash flows and reversions.

Residual techniques   Techniques within the income approach used to value physical, legal, and financial components of the total property.

Reversion   Rights in real estate which are available to or revert to the fee owner at the end of some specified timeframe (e.g., investment holding period, lease term, economic life of improvements).

Income capitalization is the process of converting a stream or series of income payments into a lump sum capital value.[1] It is applied to the valuation of real estate on the premise that value is the present worth of anticipated or forecast future benefits. Present worth is obtained by discounting (i.e., the form of capitalization applied to calculate the present worth of a future income stream).

The future benefits forecast for a property in income capitalization analysis are money income. Amenities cannot be capitalized directly because they have no directly measurable dollar equivalent. In addition, income capitalization differs from gross rent multiplier or gross income multiplier analysis in that the income capitalized or discounted is net income produced by the property. The typical purchaser or owner is presumed to be an investor seeking money income; however, rental income can be imputed to owner-occupied properties that can also be rented, so that income capitalization analysis can be applied.

As noted previously, there are three alternative ways of approaching an appraisal or valuation problem. Sales comparison and cost analysis are applicable to all types of properties, including both amenity and income-producing real estate. Income capitalization, on the other hand, is generally applicable only to investment real estate expected or capable of producing money income (rental properties). In such cases, net operating income can be capitalized to a present worth or value figure as a supplement or alternative to the other two approaches.

There are several distinguishing characteristics of income-producing properties for appraisal purposes. Money income is the basis for valuation. Valuation is undertaken from the viewpoint of the typical, informed investor. The market is stratified in terms of investor demand. This means that it is incumbent upon the appraiser to identify which properties represent competitive, comparable investments. Income is produced because potential users are willing to pay rent for space, so emphasis must be placed upon use analysis. This ties in with the definition of market value. It further emphasizes the importance of evaluating functional utility in terms of anticipated use or user. Leasing, financing, and the impact of income taxes on buyer-investor decisions must also be taken into account—whether directly or by inference from market behavior.

The valuation principles illustrated throughout the text for amenity properties are equally applicable in income capitalization analysis. Supply and demand applies to the availability and need for rental space for different types of users. Highest and best use analysis involves consideration of the many possible alternatives. The selected alternative is the one that produces the highest present worth relative to the amount of the investment. Substitution is applicable to the selection of typical rentals, vacancy ratios, operating expenses, mortgage financing terms, and rates of capitalization.

Contribution is especially important in income capitalization because the capitalized value of any component of the forecast income stream measures the contribution to total property value made by the property component producing that portion of the income stream. This is particularly significant in residual analysis. Anticipation is also important, because income capitalization always involves estimating the present worth of forecast future income streams. Change emphasizes the importance of good analytical market and income forecasting, rather than mechanical extensions of past trends. Conformity and variable proportions are important in estimating highest and best use, especially since many income properties can have several uses or users.

Rationale of Income Capitalization

There are basically two categories of valuation models which represent different, alternative frameworks for capitalizing income to a present worth or value estimate. Both models represent a mechanical procedure and not appraising per se. In effect, the models represent the processing of numbers to derive a numer, whereas appraising (valuation) involves judgment about what numbers to use and how. The two categories of valuation models are ratio models (direct capitalization, multiplier models) and discounted cash flow models (discounting, yield models).

The general *ratio model* is $V = \dfrac{NOI}{R}$. The general characteristics of the model include the fact that it may be used to value either the total property or any of the components of that property. In the general model for total property valuation, R is a ratio of annual net income to value (i.e., a rate). The reciprocal of that rate may be used as a multiplier. For other components of total property value, the rate also represents a ratio of the income allocable to the component divided by the value of the component. In the ratio model, the rate is called a capitalization rate. This is true regardless of whether total property value or one component's value is being estimated. That capitalization rate includes both a return on and a return of invested capital. This return on and of capital invested is typically expressed on an annual basis over some apparent or implied remaining economic life.

In ratio models, time is included only implicitly. First-year income, current-year income, or stabilized income is used in the model. There is no specific reversion estimated or forecast. A special case of the ratio model is capitalization in perpetuity. Implicitly, the property or interest being valued in the perpetuity model can be resold at any time in the future for its current value or for what was actually paid for it. In other words, the reversion in the perpetuity model is equal to the original investment or value.

The general *discounted cash flow model* is

$$V = \sum_{t=1}^{n} \frac{CF_t}{(1 + y)^t}$$

The cash flow (*CF*) noted in the numerator of this model is typically separated into annual cash flow (income) and reversion. In other words, the model might be restated more simply as follows:

$$V = PW \text{ Cash Flows} + PW \text{ Reversion}$$

In the model, *y* represents a yield rate and can be applied to the valuation of the total property [discount rate (Y_o)] or any of the components of total property value. For example, in debt valuation, *y* becomes an interest rate (Y_m), and in equity valuation, *y* becomes an equity yield rate (Y_e).

In discounted cash flow models, time is specifically and explicitly incorporated into the calculation. The duration of cash flows or the income projection period is related to some very specific, finite time frame (e.g., the investor's holding period, the remaining term of a lease, the remaining term of a loan or note, or the remaining economic life of improvements.) The timing of cash flows and whether payments are in arrears or in advance are also specified in the discounted cash flow model. Income forecasts are explicitly required in this model, which recognizes that all components affecting operating income can vary. Reversions are separately and explicitly estimated, although not necessarily in actual dollar amount.

As is probably already clear from the foregoing statements, the pattern of income and forecasts of the future are of much greater significance in discounted cash flow models than in ratio models. All models, however, require an estimate of first-year income; that is, all require estimation of first-year market rental, effective gross income, net operating income, annual debt service, and cash throw-off to equity. Obviously, other deductions and outflows must also be estimated for both models in the first year. Both equity investor and mortgage lender are investors. Each pays out a lump sum of capital funds in expectation of profit over time. All investors have two prime objectives: maintaining capital intact and receiving a return on capital investment. Maintaining capital intact has the first priority. This means getting back the entire amount of the investor's original investment. Capital recovery or some provision for capital recovery is essential in the investor's calculus and needs to be accommodated prior to earning a return on investment. Capital recovery represents return of investment.

Full capital recovery must be accomplished at the end of some specified investment holding period. It may be received in periodic payments over the holding period, as a lump sum at the end of the period through resale of the asset, or as some combination of the two. If the entire original investment is not expected to be recovered through resale, then there will be capital loss. That capital loss must be recovered from periodic income payments over the investment holding period, because without full capital recovery there can be no true return on investment.

After an investment offers the prospect of return of capital, then the investor is also seeking a gain or profit. This can be receivable periodically, in a lump sum, or as a combination of the two. This is return on investment. While other objectives may enter into the investor's calculus, return of and return on investment are paramount in income-property valuation.

Income Estimating and Forecasting

The starting point in income capitalization is to estimate what income is to be capitalized. By convention, based on the realities of market behavior, annual income forecasts and estimates are made, with income receivable at the end of the year. It is possible to adjust for differences in timing of income flows, but the annual, end-of-year convention is used in all the examples throughout the remainder of this chapter. Income estimation starts with the current year, commencing as of the date of the appraisal. Basically, it seeks to answer three questions:

1. How much annual income is estimated to be received? (This is the quantity of income forecasst.)
2. What is the risk associated with the income estimate or forecast,

and what is the likelihood that this amount will actually be received at the expected times? (This is the quality of income forecast.)
3.   Over what time period is the estimated income expected to be received? (This is the duration of income forecast.)

Income Produced by Investment Real Estate

Net operating income (NOI) is the annual income flow utilized in analyzing investment real estate. It is effective gross income (EGI) less annualized operating expenses. Net operating income is available to cover required return on investment plus required annual capital recovery of investment. Alternatively, net operating income is available to cover annual debt service (ADS) plus required return on equity investment plus required annual share of forecast capital loss from resale in mortgage-equity analysis. Net operating income, therefore, contains return on investment plus annual proration of any required capital recovery. Capital recovery is the amount of investment in improvements in physical residual analysis. It is the amount of forecast capital loss on resale in mortgage-equity or leased-fee/leasehold analysis. If capital gain is forecast on resale, no deduction from net operating income for capital recovery is required.

A net operating income stream can have the characteristics of a level annuity, a decreasing annuity, an increasing annuity, or a variable annuity. Any income stream can be treated as a series of individual reversions. This is the general case (i.e., the case of the variable annuity). Level-annuity and straight-line (declining annuity) capitalization are merely shortcut methods for dealing with special cases. The character of the forecast income stream determines which method of capital recovery is applicable. Gross income, vacancy, and operating expenses are being forecast; net operating income represents the residual of these individual forecasts.

In addition to the periodic income stream, a reversion or lump sum at the end of an income projection period must be forecast. In physical residuals, the income projection period is often the remaining economic life of the improvements. Traditionally, the amount of reversion at that point in time was presumed to be the present worth (value) of the site as of the date of the appraisal. The reversion is the proceeds of resale/conversion/refinancing for the entire property when the income projection period is less than the remaining economic life of improvements. This applies in mortgage-equity analysis and in leased-fee/leasehold valuation.

Identification of Income Characteristics

The income characteristics are derived from the analysis of the most probable income stream: market data for market value estimation and property, lease contract, and investor data for investment value estimation. The amount of income must be forecast for each year of the income projection period. That income is net operating income. It equals potential gross income (PGI) less allowance for vacancy and credit loss, (V & C), less operating expenses (OE) for each applicable year of the income projection period (n). As for timing of the income stream, payments at the end of the year are normally assumed and used. Conversion to beginning-of-year payments is readily accomplished, however. It also matters whether payments start immediately or are deferred to a later date. These factors are usually based on lease terms.

Typically, annual payments are used. Adjustments can be made for monthly, quarterly, and so on, payments, but the figures are then typically converted to annual flows for further analysis. The longer the time period, the greater the present worth of a given net operating income stream. The further into the future the income is receivable, (i.e., the longer deferred), the lower the present worth of that individual segment of the income stream.

Income streams may be either changing or level. The latter type is easiest to treat and usually results from a long-term net lease. Changing income streams may be either declining, increasing, or uneven (variable). The latter type is the most common, and the income can be treated as a series of individual reversions. Indeed, any income stream can be valued as a series of individual reversions. Increasing and decreasing annuities are simply specialized forms of the variable annuity and generally are both limited and limiting with respect to assumptions about rates or amounts of change. Step-up or step-down leases are perhaps the best examples of increasing or declining annuities; however, their use is no longer as widespread as it was prior to indexing (e.g., the Consumer Price Index). Since the use of an index often allows income to change more frequently and is generally uncontrollable within the specific terms of the lease, the treatment of these forms of annuity is more properly and logically accomplished as a variable annuity.

Uncertainty or risk is usually reflected in the discount rate and/or equity yield rate employed; the greater the risk, the higher the rate and, hence, the lower the present worth or value. Risk or uncertainty always exists, because the income stream is projected or forecast into the future. Risk or uncertainty may also be treated within the income stream itself. If it is, however, there should be no concomitant rate adjustment, as that would reflect double counting.

Estimation of Annual Income

The first step in the income capitalization process is to estimate annual future income flow. This is an annualized cash flow forecast. If it is expected to be variable, it must be estimated for each year of the income projection period. The first income flow that is forecast is that of potential gross income (PGI). This reflects the market-based rent roll at 100 percent occupancy and is always expressed on an annual basis. As part of a continuing example, assume that an apartment property has 20 units with market rental of $400 per month each. Therefore, PGI is $96,000 (20 × $400 × 12). While the example utilizes rent per dwelling unit per month as the unit of comparison, it might also have employed a per room or per square foot of living area basis and been annualized. Other examples of units of comparison are: office buildings—per square foot of net rentable area per month or per year; industrial buildings—per square foot of building area per year or per month; hospitals and nursing homes—per bed per month or per year; and retail space—per square foot of selling area or gross leasable area per year or per month.

Market data and standards from competitive properties provide the basis for the estimate of allowance for vacancy and credit loss (V & C) which serves as a deduction from potential gross income. Vacancy is not the only basis for credit (income) loss; nonpayment or slow payment of rent produces similar results. Experience of the subject property and published studies or surveys may also be used to make this estimate. Note that normal good management, neither excessively good nor bad, is assumed. The deduction of an allowance for vacancy and credit loss, often as a percentage, from potential gross income provides an estimate of the actual collections. If a V & C of 5 percent is assumed for the continuing example, that would mean a reduction of $4,800 from PGI, or estimated rent collections of $91,200. Other income, such as concessions or nonrental income, is added to the net rent roll to obtain effective gross income (EGI). Other income will tend to vary with occupancy and is usually estimated per occupied unit. Concessions such as laundry machines, equipment rental, and sale of utilities are examples of other income. For the continuing example, other (concession) income is assumed to be $100 per occupied unit per year or an amount of $1,900. Added to the net rent roll this provides an estimate of EGI of $93,100 annually. This represents forecast annual cash receipts. The format is as follows:

Potential Gross Income (PGI)	$96,000
($400/month, 20 units, 12 months)	
Less Vacancy & Credit Loss (V & C—5%)	4,800
Equals Rent Collections	$91,200
Plus Other Income ($100/unit, 19 units)[a]	1,900
Equals Effective Gross Income (EGI)	$93,100

[a]Although there are 20 units, only 19 units are considered occupied because of the 5% V & C allowance.

The next step in the process is to derive net operating income (NOI) from effective gross income. To accomplish this, the appraiser must deduct stabilized annual operating expenses. Operating expenses are the expenditures that the owner-investor must make by law, by custom, or by contract to protect continued generation of gross income by the property. These expenses are based on a three- to five-year experience of the subject property, plus market standards. What the owner-investor actually will pay and what the tenant(s) will pay depend on market custom or contract lease terms. Once again, normal good management is assumed. A management fee is always deducted, even when the owner manages the property in order to identify the NOI the property produces solely as an investment.

Operating expenses are generally divided into four basic categories: fixed expenses that tend not to vary with occupancy (e.g., property taxes, insurance); variable expenses that tend to vary with occupancy (e.g., utilities, management fees, heating and cooling); repairs and maintenance; and replacements that consists of items in the structure and equipment with shorter economic or useful lives than the building. For the continuing example, consider the following level of operating expenses:

Fixed expenses:	
Taxes	$13,200
Insurance	1,800
Total fixed expenses	$15,000
Variable expenses:	
Management (4% of effective gross)	$ 3,724
Electricity (common areas only)	500
Sewer and water	380
Heating	9,120
Miscellaneous (supplies, etc.)	500
Total variable expenses	$14,224
Repairs and maintenance (including maintenance personnel)	$15,870
Replacements (annual average)	$ 2,100
Total Operating Expenses	$47,194

It should be noted that several items have been excluded from expenses because they do not represent expenditures necessary to maintain the property's ability to generate the forecast gross income. Some of these items are business and income taxes, depreciation, debt service, business expenses, and capital outlays. It should also be noted that a ratio of operating expenses (OE) to effective gross income (EGI) can be calculated and compared with competitive properties in the market as a test of normal good management. In this case, the operating expense ratio $\left(\dfrac{OE}{EGI}\right)$ is equal to \$47,194 ÷ \$93,100, or 50.69 percent.

For much of appraisal analysis, net operating income (NOI) represents the bottom-line estimate. Net operating income is typical or normal forecast annual cash flow. It differs from accounting or income tax concepts of net income. Net operating income is effective gross income less operating expenses. For the continuing example, NOI is \$45,906 (\$93,100 − \$47,194).

An additional periodic cash flow (cash throw-off to equity) may be of interest to the appraiser in subsequent appraisal analysis. Cash throw-off (CTO) is a before-tax cash flow to the equity position and is the difference between NOI and annual debt service (ADS). For the continuing example, assume that lenders are willing to lend on a debt service coverage ratio (DSCR) of 1.2 and on the following terms: 12 percent, 20-year maturity, fully amortized with monthly payments. Dividing the NOI by the debt service coverage ratio (DSCR) indicates the amount of annual debt service this property income can support. In this instance, that amount is \$38,255 (\$45,906 ÷ 1.2). The difference between net operating income and this amount of ADS provides an estimate of first-year cash throw-off to equity in the amount of \$7,651. The principal amount on the mortgage may be determined by capitalizing the annual debt service (ADS) at the mortgage constant (R_m), which is obtainable from the terms of the mortgage and is .132132 (.011011 × 12). Thus, the principal amount on the mortgage is \$38,255 ÷ .132132 = \$289,521. The balance outstanding on the mortgage at the end of the fifth year (the income projection period) is \$265,616 (\$3,187.92 ÷ .012002). This information will prove useful later in the chapter when the income flow is analyzed for valuation purposes. For now, a summary of cash flow forecasts appears in table 17–1, with comments on assumptions that have been made or results that have been obtained from the assumptions made.

The final portion of the forecasting puzzle is to estimate the reversion. Reversion amount is not readily estimated in many cases; if full amortization of the improvements over the remaining economic life is assumed, then the reversion is the site value. Often, for sake of

Table 17–1
Cash Flow Projections

	Year 1	Year 2	Year 3	Year 4	Year 5
Potential Gross Income (PGI)	$96,000	$98,880	$101,846	$104,901	$108,048
Less Vacancy and Credit (Income) Loss (V & C—5%)	4,800	4,944	5,092	5,245	5,402
Equals Rent Collections	91,200	93,936	96,754	99,656	102,646
Plus Other Income	1,900	1,900	1,900	1,900	1,900
Equals Effective Gross Income (EGI)	93,100	95,836	98,654	101,556	104,546
Minus Operating Expenses (OE)	47,194	49,554	52,032	54,634	57,366
Equals Net Operating Income (NOI)	45,906	46,282	46,622	46,922	47,180
Minus Annual Debt Service (ADS)	38,255	38,255	38,255	38,255	38,255
Equals Cash Throw-off to Equity (CTO)	$ 7,651	$ 8,027	$ 8,367	$ 8,667	$ 8,925

Note: The projections here assume that potential gross income increases by 3 percent per year; since vacancy and income loss remains a constant percentage and other income is stable, the 3 percent growth carries through to rent collections. The rate of increase for effective gross income is 2.94 percent. Operating expenses are assumed to increase at a 5 percent annual rate. Net operating income, which represents the residual of the cash flow analysis and assumptions, increases at an average rate of 0.69 percent annually. Note that this latter figure represents a calculation after the fact, (i.e., a calculated rate of growth rather than a forecast rate). Since annual debt service is presumed constant, cash throw-off to equity is shown to increase at a calculated average compound rate of 3.93 percent.

simplicity, the forecast reversion under such circumstances is the site value as of the valuation date. In other words, the presumption is that there is no possibility of capital gain treatment. This form of forecasting is often used in physical residual techniques. However, these assumptions are very unrealistic. It should also be noted that the remaining economic life of the improvements must be the same as that used in the cost analysis. Changed site value can also be included, however.

More typical of the estimation of a reversion would be the inclusion of forecast capital loss or capital gain on resale: if not in the total property, then certainly in the equity position. Such a forecasting technique is used in discounted cash flow analysis, property residual and mortgage-equity techniques, and leased-fee valuation. In any case, the income projection period is less than the remaining economic life of the improvements. The forecast itself may be a relative measure (e.g., a percentage of present worth) or a specified dollar amount. For the former, if resale proceeds five years hence are projected at 90 percent of present worth, then a capital loss is projected and would have to be recovered from periodic income. On the other hand, if resale proceeds five years hence are projected at 115 percent of present worth, then a capital gain is being forecast, which will enhance the return on equity investment.

As noted, the other alternative is to forecast the dollar amount of resale price of the total property or property component that is being analyzed. The logic of this position is more than a bit suspect, since the presumed objective of the appraisal is to estimate value (however defined) today. Forecasting the resale price or value of an asset at some time in the future when the ultimate object of the analysis is to estimate value today is an extremely difficult, if not impossible, task. Obviously, a projection of expected change in value or price is much more reasonable to ask of the appraiser in forecasting the reversion.

Rates of Return

In its simplest form, a rate is a ratio expressed as a percentage on an annual basis. There is much confusion and variety in the use of rate terminology in appraising. The basic objective of technical terminology is to be descriptive of the phenomenon it identifies and to be unequivocal and unique in the sense that a term should not be confused with or a duplicate of another. It is necessary for the appraiser to distinguish among rates carefully and use the terms properly. As used in appraisal-investment analysis, the following terms apply:[2]

Nominal rate: The contract rate on a mortgage or the apparent rate on an investment. The annual payment of interest or income divided by the original amount of a loan or investment.

Effective rate: The actual rate paid on a loan or produced by an investment. Actual annual payments divided by actual investment or loan outstanding. A discounted mortgage, for example, provides a different effective rate from the nominal rate of interest.

Rate of interest (Y_m): The rate on borrowed money; the loan or borrowing rate. Often this is referred to as the mortgage interest rate.

Discount rate (Y_o): The rate of return on a real estate investment; the annual percentage rate that reflects the competitive rate of return on an investment. This is the rate that reflects the compensation necessary to attract an investor or lender to give up liquidity, to wait or defer consumption, and to assume the risks of investing. Sometimes this rate is referred to as the risk rate in appraisal analysis.

Capital recovery rate: This is a capital recapture rate or the annual return of invested capital, expressed as an annual rate. Often, it is applied in appraisal analysis only to improvements or wasting assets with a finite economic life although its applicability is much broader than that (i.e., the capital investment regardless of whether it is land or improvements). The capital recapture rate is also synonymous with the amortization rate which expresses the investor's desire or expectation to recover an investment over a specified period of time. This is especially utilized in mortgage lending and represents the rate at which principal is repaid over the nominal term of the loan.

Capitalization rate (R): The sum of a discount rate and a capital recovery rate. It is applied to any income stream with a finite term over which the invested principal is to be returned to the investor or lender. In income property appraising, the capitalization rate is applied to the income attributable to the improvements in physical residual techniques and to the income produced for the equity investment in either mortgage equity or discounted cash flow analysis.

Mortgage constant (R_m): The total annual payments of principal and interest (annual debt service) on a level-payment amortized mortgage, expressed as a percentage of the initial principal amount of the loan. Analogous to a capitalization rate on a mortgage loan.

Equity yield rate (Y_e): Internal rate of return to the equity position. It is that rate of discount at which the present worth of the total income forecast to be received on the equity investment is equal to the cost of that investment. As indicated in the term itself, it represents a yield to the equity position.

Equity dividend rate (R_e): This is the annual cash throw-off to the equity investment (before-tax cash flow) divided by the original amount of the equity investment. The equity dividend rate is a cash flow rate or capitalization rate, as opposed to a yield rate.

Overall rate (R_o): The forecast annual net operating income divided by value or sales price. This is the direct ratio between forecast annual net operating income and value or sales price.

Overall rates and discount rates are discussed in greater detail in the following sections. These rates, or some form thereof, are the rates that are applicable to the basic models presented at the beginning of this chapter.

Overall Rates

An overall rate combines in one rate or factor/multiplier the required rate of return on investment positions plus an annual rate of recovery of invested capital. In physical residual techniques of capitalization, the overall rate includes return on and of investment in the site at the discount rate, return on investment in the improvements at the discount rate, and return of investment in the improvements at the capital recovery rate. In mortgage-equity analysis, the overall rate includes return on the equity investment at the equity yield rate, return on and of the loan investment via the mortgage constant, an annual rate of return representing build-up on debt via the sinking fund factor at the equity yield rate, and an annual return of forecast capital loss (or gain) via the sinking fund factor at the equity yield rate. In discounted cash flow models, the mortgage-equity format essentially applies; it represents a mechanical process that is built into compound interest/compound discount tables.

For direct capitalization, the overall rate must represent what informed, prudent, and rational investors are requiring and obtaining for similar, competitive property investments in the current market. Here, similar refers to similarity with respect to risk and duration of income or investment return. Comparability of sales terms of the competitive properties used to derive overall rates is essential. Most important, the character (timing, duration, variability) of forecast effective gross income and net operating income for competitive properties must be very similar to those forecast for the subject property.

The overall rate is a weighted average of component investment claims on the net operating income produced by an income property. The claims may be physical (site, improvements); legal (leased fee, leasehold); or investment-financial (mortgage, equity). The rates required to cover each component claim are weighted by the proportion of total property investment each represents.

Gross income multipliers and gross rent multipliers are based on gross income receipts (either potential gross or effective gross). Technically, they are not part of income capitalization, which utilizes net income. Gross income multipliers and/or gross rent multipliers can be used effectively, however, as a starting point to estimate or derive both the overall rate and the discount rate.

Discount Rates

A discount rate is a rate of return required to be earned on total property investment to meet investment requirements or expectations of mortgage lender(s) and/or equity investor(s). It is the weighted average of the mortgage interest rate and the equity yield rate, weighted by the proportions of total investment represented by mortgage(s) and equity. It is, therefore, a weighted average cost of capital. The discount rate includes compensation for time preference, liquidity preference, management, and risk. Time preference refers to giving up consumption or alternative use of money. Liquidity preference refers to giving up ready conversion to cash at face or par value. Management refers to the cost of handling the investment; risk refers to the probability of lower income, loss of principal, purchasing power loss, interest rate variation, and/or the nonfulfillment of forecasts.

While possible, it is extremely difficult to derive discount rates from direct market comparisons. The chief reason for this is that it is difficult to obtain data on net operating income less capital recovery for truly comparable sales properties. If all the conditions for comparability are met for a sufficient number of comparable sales properties, then a discount rate can be derived via what is really sales comparison analysis. Alternatively, it may be derived through some form of statistical technique. Such methodology is little used, however, since the same data can produce an estimate of the overall rate, which can be used, in turn, to estimate value directly. As a result, discount rates are derived (as noted earlier) through simple weighted-average band of investment or mortgage-equity analysis. Discount rates may also be abstracted from the gross income multiplier.

Capital Recovery and Capitalization Rates

The basic objective of any investor is to maintain the invested capital intact and to get it back at the end of the income projection period or investment holding period. If it is not forecast to be fully returned as the reversion on resale, then there is a forecast capital loss that must be recovered periodically as a part of net operating income. The emphasis is on recovery of capital invested regardless of the component of the property in which the capital is presumed to be invested, as in physical residual techniques. Two other items of concern are important in providing for capital recovery: the time period for capital recovery, or the income projection period; and the timing of capital recovery, or the number and length of periods over which capital is to be recovered. There are three basic methods of providing for capital recovery. In each case, annual capital recovery payments reduce the remaining investment available to produce income in the subsequent year.

Straight-Line Capital Recovery. Under straight-line capital recovery, the appraiser simply divides 100 percent of the capital loss to be recovered by the number of years in the capital recovery period to obtain a straight-line capital recovery rate. This represents equal annual capital recovery amounts over the capital recovery period. The implications and assumptions of straight-line capital recovery are very limiting. Net operating income is assumed to be declining annually at a specified rate. Either no reinvestment is assumed or reinvestment is assumed to occur at a zero compound interest rate. Capital recovery payments are the largest under straight-line capital recovery, so the amount of net operating income available as return on investment is the lowest. Straight-line capital recovery is widely used, easily calculated, and readily explained and understood, but it has major limitations. Net operating income rarely follows the assumed declining pattern; in fact, the use of straight-line capital recovery in the capitalization process tends to produce low value estimates relative to other forms of capital recovery.

Sinking Fund Capital Recovery. Sinking fund capital recovery presumes equal annual payments are reinvested in a sinking fund to accumulate at a safe rate or a reinvestment rate lower than the discount rate. The portion of net operating income left for return on property investment is greater than under straight-line recovery, but less (in the earlier years at least) than under level-annuity capital recovery assumptions. Forecast capital loss is recoverable in a lump sum at the end of the income projection period. The implications of sinking fund capital recovery include the assumption that capital recovery payments from net operating income cannot be reinvested at the discount rate but, rather, are reinvested at the safe rate (or at least a lower rate) to ensure liquidity. Further, full capital recovery at the end of the income projection period is presumed to be acceptable to the investor. Also, net operating income is presumed to be a level annuity, but a larger proportion must be allocated to capital recovery deposits than under level-annuity capital recovery. Sinking fund capital recovery seldom represents what actually happens in practice. Value can be influenced by varying interpretations and applications of the safe rate. The sinking fund capitalization method results in an intermediate value estimate. It is also complex and not easily understood.

Level-Annuity Capital Recovery. Under level-annuity capital recovery, small but increasing annual payments are made that total the full amount of forecast capital recovery over the income projection period. The rate is the equivalent of equal annual deposits in a sinking fund to accumulate at the discount rate to the end of the income projection period. The application of level-annuity capital recovery requires that net operating income is a level annuity. Further, capital recovery payments are reinvested and discounted at the discount rate; capital recovery is receivable annually with reinvestment at the instigation of the owner-investor. Level-annuity capital recovery is a shortcut method of treating the net operating income stream as a series of individual reversions when net operating income is forecast to be constant or level. Level-annuity capital recovery and capitalization are applicable to long-term leases and with tenants who have good credit ratings. The method is therefore applicable to net leases and is also applicable when contract rent is below market rent. It tends to represent much investor thinking and behavior. Nevertheless, it is complex and more involved than straight-line capital recovery or straight-line capitalization, and is not fully understood by many investors and practitioners.

Capitalization Rates

The capitalization rate is equal to the discount rate plus the appropriate capital recovery rate, both of which are identified from market evidence for the type of property involved. Both capitalization rates and their reciprocal capitalization factors (or multipliers) can be calculated directly. Level-annuity capitalization rates and capitalization factors can be obtained directly from published compound interest/compound discount tables. A capitalization rate or capitalization factor is applied to net income attributable to that portion of the total investment on which recovery of the investment is required by the investor out of annual income or cash flow over the capital recovery period. It therefore represents both the return on investment and a return of the amount of investment involved. The applicability and limitations of capitalization rates and factors are subject to the same conditions that apply to alternative methods of capital recovery. The applicability of any given method depends on the character of the forecast net operating income.

Techniques of Property Valuation
with Income Capitalization

As indicated at the beginning of this chapter, there are two basic categories of valuation models: ratio models and discounted cash flow models. Ratio models generally deal with direct capitalization via the overall rate, which may be applied either to property, and thus to net operating income, or to any number of property components, so long as an appropriately defined rate is included for capitalization of the income allocable to each component. Discounted cash flow models, on the other hand, require a forecast of cash flows to the total property or to property components over some specified investment holding period. Discounted cash flow models are also applicable within a wide range of capitalization techniques in valuation analysis.

Income properties can be divided into analytical components for valuation purposes. The present worth of any one component may be estimated independently, and the income required to cover that investment amount at the indicated discount rate is deducted from net operating income. The remaining or residual income is then capitalized to derive the present worth of the unknown portion. The present worths of the two components are then added to produce the estimated value of the property. Net operating income itself is a residual. Whichever property or investment component is selected and used, the residual is determined by the character of the property, the nature of the problem, and the availability of the data. The appraiser does not really have a choice; it is the market that determines the technique to be used.

Technique selection depends upon which technique most nearly approximates the thinking and behavior of investor-purchasers in the local market for the type of property being appraised as of the valuation date. For example, in physical residual techniques, site and improve-

three techniques of income capitalization {land, building, site}

ments are the components for analytical purposes. In building residual analysis, site value is estimated independently, as if vacant and available to be put to its highest and best use. Income required to cover the investment in the site is derived through the application of a discount rate (possibly adjusted for capital recovery) to site investments. Residual income available to cover the investment in improvements is discounted at the appropriate capitalization rate to obtain the present worth or contribution of the improvements to total property value.

In the land residual technique, cost new of improvements, either actual or hypothetical, is estimated in terms of highest and best use of the site. The income required to cover investment in improvements (cost) is derived by application of an appropriate capitalization rate. The residual income available to cover the investment in the site is capitalized at the discount rate (possibly adjusted for capital recovery) to obtain the present worth or contribution of the site. In property residual analysis, net operating income is capitalized at the appropriate capitalization rate to estimate a present worth of the income stream. Since this calculation results in recovery of the entire property investment through net operating income, the present worth of the reversion must be added back. The reversion is discounted at the present worth of one factor (based on the discount rate) to obtain its present worth.

For the physical residual techniques, the income projection period is typically the remaining economic life of the improvements. This must be the same as that used in cost analysis. Typically, site is the reversion; its value may or may not be assumed to be constant. If present worth of the site is the amount of the reversion, its applicability is limited when such assumptions do not represent investor-purchaser thinking and market behavior. Obviously, physical residual techniques are not applicable when the required data are not available. They are most helpful, however, in highest and best use analysis.

Residual analysis involving the legal components (leased fee/leasehold) is applicable when there is a long-term lease on the property. Leased-fee value is estimated via the property residual technique except that the amount of the reversion is not usually restricted to the present worth of the site. The leasehold represents the residual. Leasehold value is significant primarily when contract rent is less than market rental. Lease renewal options and percentage leases make residual analysis very difficult to apply. The income projection period is the remaining term of the lease. For reasons mentioned earlier, forecasting the reversion amount in dollar terms can be difficult and questionable.

In mortgage-equity analysis, the present worth or principal amount of the mortgage or mortgagee's interest can be estimated directly. This can be accomplished through debt service coverage ratio analysis or can simply represent a given amount or ratio in any appraisal problem. Equity, therefore, is the residual. Cash throw-off to equity is the residual income after deducting annual debt service on the mortgage from net operating income. The net cash reversion is available to the equity position after deducting the outstanding balance of the loan from forecast proceeds of resale at the end of the income projection period. The present worth of the equity position is the sum of the present worth of cash throw-off to equity discounted at the capitalization rate (ITAO), based upon the equity yield rate, plus the present worth of the net cash reversion also discounted (PW1—reversion factor) at the equity yield rate.

Under the mortgage-equity concept, the income projection period is the investment holding period. The analysis is complicated, however, because mortgage amortization and concurrent equity buildup are realistically included. It is also difficult to apply the mortgage-equity concept unless net operating income is forecast as a level annuity. This is easily resolved, however, with the application of a discounted cash flow model. The mortgage-equity model, or a variation of it, in the discounted cash flow context tends to reflect investor-purchaser thinking and market behavior. It is difficult to explain, however, and not easily understood. Further, the forecast reversion or proceeds of resale can be questionable if an attempt is made to forecast in dollars as opposed to a percentage of present value.

Applications of Income Capitalization

As noted earlier, the original principal amount on the mortgage can be determined by capitalizing annual debt service (ADS) at the mortgage constant (R_m). Annual debt service was calculated at \$38,255 (NOI ÷ DSCR or \$45,906 ÷ 1.2) and the mortgage constant at .132132. Therefore, the mortgage amount under these terms and conditions is equal to \$289,521 (\$38,255 ÷ .132132). Balance outstanding (b) at the end of year 5 (the projected holding period) is a function of the monthly mortgage payment (\$3,187.92) capitalized at the ITAO for the remaining term of 15 years (.012002) or \$265,616 (\$3,187.92 ÷ .012002). With the information available, elements of both basic categories of valuation models (ratio and discounted cash flow) will be utilized in the analysis of this property.

First, a discounted cash flow equity residual model will be employed to determine property value (V_o) under some very specific assumptions. Then, a discount rate (Y_o) and overall rate (R_o) will be extracted from the value estimate derived from the discounted cash flow model. Reversion assumptions will then be revised to accommodate forecast levels of capital gain and loss to identify their impact on value. To employ the model, two additional items must be estimated and forecast: equity yield requirements (Y_e) and property reversion (PR). The estimate of Y_e is 15 percent and the property reversion five years hence is forecast to be equal to the present worth of the property (V_o). Summarizing the models and inputs (assumptions) thus far:

$$\text{Value of the Total Property } (V_o) =$$
$$\text{Value of the Mortgage } (V_m) + \text{Value of the Equity } (V_e)$$

or

$$V_o = V_m + V_e$$
$$V_m = \$289,521 \text{ (calculated earlier)}$$
$$Y_e = 15\% \text{ (given)}$$
$$PR = 1.0\ V_o \text{ (no change forecast)}$$
$$V_e = \text{PW CTO} + \text{PW ER @ } Y_e$$
$$\text{PW ER} = (V_o - b) \text{ @ } Y_e$$

PW CTO is as follows:

Year	CTO	PW Factor @ 15%	PW CTO
1	$7,651	.869565	6,653
2	8,027	.756144	6,070
3	8,367	.657516	5,501
4	8,667	.571753	4,955
5	8,925	.497177	4,437

The sum of discounted cash flows to equity is $27,616. Note that the present value (reversion) factor for five years at 15 percent is .497177, which can be substituted in the foregoing formula for the calculation of the equity reversion (ER). Substituting in the basic models provides the following:

$$V_m = \$289,521$$
$$V_e = \$27,616 + .497177 (V_o - \$265,616)$$
$$V_o = \$289,521 + [\$27,616 + .497177 (V_o - \$265,616)]$$
$$V_o = \$317,137 + [.497177\ V_o - \$132,058]$$
$$V_o = .497177\ V_o + \$185,079$$
$$.502823\ V_o = \$185,079$$
$$V_o = \$368,080, \text{ say } \$368,000$$

Therefore:

$$V_o = \$368,000$$
$$V_m = \underline{289,521}$$
$$V_e = \$78,479$$

Analysis of the foregoing calculations indicates a loan-to-value ratio of 78.7 percent ($289,521 ÷ $368,000) and its complement (equity-to-value ratio) of 21.3 percent. The implied overall rate (R_o) is 12.47 percent ($45,906 ÷ $368,000). The discount rate is a bit more difficult to derive and the following chart might prove helpful in the calculation:

n	$\$$	
0	− 368,000	
1	45,906	
2	46,282	
3	46,622	
4	47,922	
5	47,180	+ 368,000

The discount rate (Y_o) in this instance is the rate that discounts all cash flows such that they equal the original investment or present worth estimate (V_o). The discount rate can be bracketed fairly easily in this case between the overall rate (R_o) of 12.47 percent and the average rate of return (ARR) of 12.73 percent [$46,582.40 (average income) ÷ $368,000]. $(Y_o = 12.60$ percent by financial calculator.)

If a 10 percent capital loss in total property value were projected, logic and intuition would suggest that, other things being equal, value (V_o) would be adversely affected; R_o would increase; and Y_o would decrease. The change in the expanded model above would be reflected only in the equity reversion; that is,

$$ER = (.9\ V_o - b)$$

and

$$V_o = \$289,521 + \$27,616 + .497177\ (.9\ V_o - \$265,616)$$
$$V_o = \$317,137 + .447459\ V_o - \$132,058$$
$$V_o - .447459\ V_o = \$185,079$$
$$.552541\ V_o = \$185,079$$
$$V_o = \$334,960, \text{ say } \$335,000$$

The loan-to-value ratio in this case is 86+ percent, and the equity-to-value ratio is slightly below 14 percent. R_o has increased to 13.70 percent and Y_o (with a property reversion of $301,500) has decreased to 12.32 percent. The brackets for the latter are R_o of 13.70 percent and an average rate of return of 11.91 percent ($39,882.40 ÷ $335,000).

With a 10 percent capital gain projected, the following values, rates, and ratios are derived:

$$
\begin{aligned}
V_o &= \$408,500 \\
V_m &= \$289,521, \text{ or } 71\% \\
V_e &= \$118,979, \text{ or } 29\% \\
PR &= \$449,350 \ (1.1 \ V_o) \\
R_o &= 11.24\% \\
Y_o &= 12.93\% \\
\text{ARR} &= 13.40\% \quad (\$54,752.40 ÷ \$408,500)
\end{aligned}
$$

Summary

Income capitalization is an alternative to direct sales comparison and cost analysis as a means of estimating value for income-producing real estate. The result of income capitalization is the present worth of anticipated future benefits (forecast future income), which can be market value or investment value, depending upon underlying assumptions and which data are available and compiled. The process of discounting future net incomes is used to capitalize to a present worth estimate.

Net operating income to the property and the forecast reversion are the components of future income discounted to a present worth estimate. The quantity, quality, duration, and timing of future income forecasts to be received influence both the rate of discount to be used and the present worth or value of the property. Investors expect to receive return of their original investment (capital recovery) and return or profit on the investment (rate of return, yield rate). If the reversion is not expected to provide for full recovery of capital, then a portion of net operating income must be allocated to capital recovery each year.

Net operating income equals effective gross income minus operating expenses. Direct capitalization of net operating income with an overall rate is the simplest and best method to use, if it can be supported with market data. An overall rate is the weighted average of a discount and a capital recovery rate. The discount rate is a weighted average of mortgage debt service requirements and equity yield expectations. Thus, terms of financing influence value at least through the determination of the discount rate. Residual techniques of value estimation are used when direct capitalization or discounted cash flow analysis is not feasible or supportable. For analytical purposes, income-producing real estate can be divided between site and improvements (physical); leased fee and leasehold (legal); or mortgage and equity (financial/investment). The method of providing for capital recovery depends on the character of the net operating income stream forecast.

Notes

1. For a definition of *capitalization*, see Boyce, Byrl N., ed., *Real Estate Appraisal Terminology*, rev. ed. (Cambridge, Mass.: Ballinger [Joint publication of the American Institute of Real Estate Appraisers and Society of Real Estate Appraisers], 1981), p. 40.
2. Ibid., pp. 39, 41, 80, 88, 92, 93, 169, 174, 179, and 200.

Suggested Readings

American Institute of Real Estate Appraisers. *The Appraisal of Real Estate,* 8th ed. Chicago: American Institute of Real Estate Appraisers, 1983, chapters 14–17.

Boyce, Byrl N., Ed. *Real Estate Appraisal Terminology*, rev. ed. Cambridge, Mass.: Ballinger (Joint publication of the American Institute of Real Estate Appraisers and Society of Real Estate Appraisers), 1981.

Epley, Donald R., and Boykin, James H. *Basic Income Property Appraisal.* Reading, Mass.: Addison-Wesley, 1983, chapters 7, 8, and 11–15.

Kahn, Sanders A., and Case, Frederick E. *Real Estate Appraisal and Investment,* 2nd ed. New York: Ronald Press, 1977, chapters 8–11.

Kinnard, William N., Jr. *Income Property Valuation.* Lexington, Mass.: Lexington Books, D.C. Heath, 1971.

Kinnard, William N., Jr., and Boyce, Byrl N. *Principles of Income Property Appraising,* rev. ed. Chicago: Society of Real Estate Appraisers, 1981, Sessions 1–11.

Messner, Stephen D., et al. *Marketing Investment Real Estate: Finance, Taxation, Techniques,* 2nd ed. Chicago: Realtors National Marketing Institute of the National Association of Realtors, 1982, chapter 3.

Ratcliff, Richard U. *Valuation for Real Estate Decisions.* Santa Cruz, Calif.: Democrat Press, 1972, chapter 9.

Smith, Halbert C. *Real Estate Appraisal.* Columbus, Ohio: Grid, 1976, chapters 5 and 6.

Wendt, Paul F. *Real Estate Appraisal: Review and Outlook.* Athens: University of Georgia Press, 1974, chapter 6.

Appendix A
Arithmetic and
Algebra Review

The end result of every appraisal assignment is a number: the estimated value of the property being appraised. This is true regardless of the type of value being estimated, the type of real estate involved, or the property interest being appraised. That number, or value estimate, is the result of processing, analyzing, and manipulating other numbers throughout all the steps in the appraisal framework.

Numbers and figures are required and needed in market and area analysis, in property description and analysis, and in the application of each of the alternative approaches to value estimation. In order to carry out these analyses effectively, the appraiser must be familiar with the basic rules and procedures of arithmetic and algebra.

This appendix contains a review of the basic rules and procedures of arithmetic and algebra as they apply to the work of the real estate appraiser. The important point to keep in mind is that these tools and procedures have practical application. They are used in examples and illustrations, as well as in problems, throughout this text and in appraisal practice.

The numbers that represent values of market and property characteristics are called *data*. The square foot area of a house, the population of a community, the reproduction cost new of a structure, the monthly rental on a residential property—these and countless other numbers relating to real estate markets and properties are all data.

Data are the basic building blocks of quantitative analysis. It is therefore necessary to understand how data are assembled and organized so that they can be used in arithmetic and algebraic as well as statistical analyses (see Chapter 12).

Symbols and Notations

Because mathematics is a language, some vocabulary is needed as part of this review. Not all of the symbols and notations listed here will be used directly in the review that follows, but most of them will be useful elsewhere in this text and beyond.

Symbol or Notation	Meaning
$+$	Add; positive sign
$-$	Subtract; negative sign
$\pm$	Plus or minus sign
$a \cdot b$, ab, $a \times b$, $a(b)$	a multiplied by b
$a \div b$, a/b	a divided by b
a^2	a squared: the value of a multiplied by a
a^n	a raised to the nth power: a multiplied by a $n-1$ times
$\sqrt{a}$	Square root of a: the number multiplied by itself that equals a
$\sqrt[n]{a}$	nth root of a: the number multiplied by itself $n-1$ times that equals a
parentheses ( ), brackets [ ], braces { }	Grouping symbols that indicate that quantities or symbols within are a single unit
a_i	a subscript i; i identifies a specific value of variable a, such as a_1, a_2, a_3
Σ	Capital sigma; summation sign ("sum of")
$\sum_{i=1}^{n} a_i$	Sum of all a's beginning with a_1 through a_n
$=$	Equals
$\neq$	Not equal
$<$	Less than (e.g., $1 < 2$)
$>$	Greater than (e.g., $2 > 1$)
$\leq$	Less than or equal to
$\geq$	Greater than or equal to
$\lvert a \rvert$	Absolute value of a; the value of expressions without regard to sign

Definitions, Properties, and Operations with Numbers

Mathematics deals either with numbers (arithmetic) or with symbols that represent numbers (algebra). Although there are many different types of numbers—such as natural numbers, real numbers, complex numbers, imaginary numbers—the discussion here will focus on those numbers, and their properties, that are of direct relevance to appraisers.

Integers. Integers are the most basic *whole numbers.* They may be positive or negative and are expressed as

$$\ldots -10, -9, \ldots, -1, 0, +1, \ldots, +9, +10, \ldots$$

Thus, numbers such as 0.224, ½, $\sqrt{3}$ are *not* integers.

Natural Numbers. Natural numbers are simply the positive integers (*not* including zero) used for counting:

$$1, 2, 3, 4, 5, 6, 7, 8, 9, \ldots$$

Thus, numbers such as -5, 0.224, $\sqrt{3}$, 0 are *not* natural numbers.

Properties of Zero. Zero is a number; indeed, it is an integer. The integer zero has some unique properties, which should be noted:

$x + 0 = x$

$x - 0 = x$

$x \cdot 0 = 0$

$0 \div x = 0$

$x \div 0 =$ an impossible manipulation with basic algebra

If $x \cdot y = 0$, then either x or y or both equal 0.

Factors. A factor is a natural number that, when divided into another natural number, yields a natural number as quotient; for example, 2 is a factor of 18 because $2 \cdot 9 = 18$. In addition,

$1 \cdot 18 = 18$

$3 \cdot 6 = 18$

$6 \cdot 3 = 18$

$9 \cdot 2 = 18$

$18 \cdot 1 = 18$

Thus, 1, 2, 3, 6, 9 and 18 are *all* factors of 18.

Prime Numbers. Any natural numbers whose *only* factor is 1 are called prime numbers, or primes. Thus, 2, 3, 5, 7, 11, 13, 17, 19, 23, 29, 31, 37 are primes. The most direct way to test whether or not a number is prime is to attempt to divide it by successively larger primes until the square of the last prime tested is larger than the number being tested. For example, to test whether 43 is a prime, attempt to divide it as follows:

$43 \div 2 \neq$ a natural number

$43 \div 3 \neq$ a natural number

$43 \div 5 \neq$ a natural number

$43 \div 7 \neq$ a natural number

$7^2 = 49$, and $49 > 43$; thus, 43 is a prime.

Properties of Natural Numbers. A basic theorem of arithmetic states that any natural number a can be expressed as the product of prime factors. This process of reducing natural numbers into prime factors is called *prime factorization.* For example:

$70 = 2 \cdot 35$

$70 = 2 \cdot 5 \cdot 7$ (note that order is not critical)

or

$24 = 2 \cdot 12$

$24 = 2 \cdot 3 \cdot 4$

$24 = 2 \cdot 3 \cdot 2 \cdot 2$

In each case, an attempt was made to divide the number by a prime. As soon as a prime was discovered, the remaining nonprime factors were tested until *all* factors were prime.

Operations with Numbers. Numbers can be manipulated or processed to produce other numbers. The result (the other numbers) are essentially answers to questions, such as: What is the result of adding 7 and 9? What is the result of dividing 72 by 18?

There are four basic operations with numbers in arithmetic: addition, subtraction, multiplication, and division.

Addition. When two or more numbers are added together, the result is called a *sum.* The order of the numbers does not affect the result. Both positive and negative numbers can be added in the same sequence, although adding a negative number is the same as subtracting that number. Thus,

$$2 + 8 + 9 + 3 = 22$$
$$9 + 8 + 3 + 2 = 22$$
$$8 + (-2) + 7 + (-4) = 9$$
$$7 + 8 + (-4) + (-2) = 9$$

Subtraction. When one number is subtracted from another, the result is called a *difference.* The order of the numbers does affect the result. Negative numbers may be subtracted, but the result is the same as adding that number. Thus,

$$9 - 6 \quad = 3, \quad \text{but} \quad 6 - 9 = -3$$
$$17 - (-4) = 21, \quad 17 + 4 \quad = 21$$

Multiplication. When one number (the *multiplicand*) is multiplied by another (the *multiplier*), the result is called a *product.* A series can be multiplied in successive operations. The sequence of the numbers does not affect the result. Negative numbers can be multiplied. The product will be negative when an odd number of negative numbers is involved; the product will be positive when an even number of negative numbers is involved. Thus,

$$6 \cdot 7 \cdot 5 = 210, \quad 5 \cdot 6 \cdot 7 = 210$$
$$5 \cdot (-3) \cdot 2 = -30, \quad 5 \cdot (-3) \cdot (-2) = 30$$

A multiplier is sometimes called a *coefficient.* Thus, since $5 \cdot 7 = 35$, 5 may be said to be a coefficient of 7.

When each of a series of different numbers (multiplicands) is multiplied by the same number (multiplier or coefficient), that coefficient is called a *constant.* The symbol for a constant is k.

Division. When one number (the *dividend*) is divided by another (the *divisor*), the result is called a *quotient.* The divisor is always divided into the dividend. In fractions (discussed later), the *numerator* is the dividend, and the *denominator* is the divisor; thus the value of a fraction is always found by dividing the denominator into the numerator. A series of numbers can be divided successively. The sequence of the numbers (identity of the dividend) does affect the result. Negative numbers can be used in division. The quotient will be negative when an odd number of negative numbers is involved; the quotient will be positive when an even number of negative numbers is involved. Thus,

$$27 \div 3 = 9, \quad \text{but} \quad 3 \div 27 = \frac{3}{27} = \frac{1}{9}$$
$$72 \div 3 \div 2 = 12, \quad 72 \div 2 \div 3 = 12$$
$$18 \div (-6) = -3, \quad (-18) \div (-6) = 3$$

Priority of Operations. It is possible to carry out different operations successively with a series or sequence of numbers. If there are no grouping symbols or symbols of inclusion, then all multiplication and division operations are carried out *before* any addition or subtraction occurs. The sequence of multiplication/division or addition/subtraction operations does not affect the final result. Thus,

$$6 \cdot 5 \div 3 = 10, \quad 6 \div 3 \cdot 5 = 10$$
$$6 \cdot 5 + 4 = 34, \quad \text{but} \quad 6 + 5 \cdot 4 = 26$$

However,

$$6 \cdot (5 + 4) = 54, \quad \text{and} \quad (6 + 5) \cdot 4 = 44$$

Signs. The concept of *absolute value* is required to manipulate signs of numbers and symbols. The absolute value of a number or symbol is simply the value of that number or symbol without regard to sign. Thus,

$$|x| = x, \quad |5| = 5$$
$$|-x| = x, \quad |-5| = 5, \quad \left|-\frac{1}{2}\right| = \frac{1}{2}$$

When *adding* and *subtracting* numbers, follow these rules:

1. Adding numbers with the *same* sign:

$$(+5) + (+7) + (+2) + (+1) = +15$$
$$(-5) + (-7) + (-2) + (-1) = -15$$

(Note: Simply add | | and use *common sign* for total.)

2. Adding numbers with *different* signs:

$$(+5) + (-7) = -2$$

Note: Find the difference in | | and use the sign of the *largest* for the answer. For several numbers, add + and − numbers separately, then apply this rule.

3. Subtracting numbers with *different* signs:

$$(+5) - (+7) = -2$$
$$(+5) - (-7) = 12$$

Note: Change the signs of numbers being subtracted, and use the addition rule.)

When *multiplying* and *dividing* numbers, follow these rules:

1. Multiplying and/or dividing numbers with the *same* sign:

$$2 \cdot 5 = 10, \qquad (-2) \cdot (-5) = 10$$
$$10 \div 5 = 2, \qquad (-10) \div (-5) = 2$$

Note: With like signs, the product or quotient is *positive.*

2. Multiplying and/or dividing numbers with *different* signs:

$$2(-5) = -10 \qquad -2(5) = -10$$
$$10 \div (-5) = -2 \qquad -10 \div -5 = -2$$

Note: With different signs, the product or quotient is *negative.* When there are more than two numbers, the product or quotient of an even number of negative numbers is *positive;* when there is an odd number of negative numbers, the product or quotient is *negative.*

Grouping Symbols (Symbols of Inclusion). In arithmetic operations, parentheses ( ), brackets [ ], or braces { } are used as grouping symbols to indicate that the numbers or values within the symbols are to be treated as a single value in the manipulations required by the operational signs. Grouping symbols or symbols of inclusion override the rule for priority or sequence of operations noted earlier. In other words, they indicate when addition and/or subtraction are to occur before multiplication and/or division.

The operations indicated within the parentheses, brackets, or braces are always performed first. Then the single value indicated by the grouping symbols is processed further in the expression.

When one or more sets of grouping symbols are included within other grouping symbols, the rule is to perform the operations required within the innermost set of grouping symbols first, then to work outward successively. Work from inside to outside the successive sets of grouping symbols. Thus,

$$6 + (5 + 4) = 6 + 9 = 15$$
$$(6 + 5) + 4 = 11 + 4 = 15$$
$$6 \cdot 5 + 4 \div 4 - 3 = 30 + 1 - 3 = 28$$

but

$$6 \cdot (5 + 4) \div (4 - 3) = 6 \cdot 9 \div 1 = 54$$

and

$$6 \cdot [(5 + 4) \div (4 - 3)] = 6 \cdot (9 \div 1)$$
$$= 6 \cdot 9 = 54$$

Fractions (Rational Numbers)

A rational number may be defined as division of two integers so long as the denominator is not equal to zero. Examples of rational numbers (fractions) are

$$\frac{231}{456}, \quad \frac{-5}{-6}, \quad \frac{0}{5}, \quad \frac{15}{9}$$

A variety of operations may be conducted with fractions. They may be added, subtracted, multiplied, or divided. The operations and rules for whole numbers also apply to fractions, with the following variations:

$$\frac{a}{b} = \frac{c}{d}, \quad \text{if} \quad a \cdot d = b \cdot c$$

$$\frac{4}{8} = \frac{7}{14}, \quad \text{since} \quad 4 \cdot 14 = 56 \quad \text{and} \quad 8 \cdot 7 = 56$$

Reducing fractions to lowest terms is done as follows:

$$\frac{70}{110} = \frac{2 \cdot 5 \cdot 7}{2 \cdot 5 \cdot 11} = \frac{\not2 \cdot \not5 \cdot 7}{\not2 \cdot \not5 \cdot 11} = \frac{7}{11}$$

$$\frac{2}{10} = \frac{2 \cdot 1}{2 \cdot 5} = \frac{\not2 \cdot 1}{\not2 \cdot 5} = \frac{1}{5}$$

Note: Express the numerator and the denominator as the product of prime factors and eliminate the common factors. Remember that only *prime factors* common to the numerator and denominator can be removed from the fraction. Thus,

$$\frac{13 + 2}{7 + 2} \neq \frac{13}{7}, \quad \text{but} \quad \frac{13 + 2}{7 + 2} = \frac{15}{9}$$

$$\frac{15}{9} = \frac{3 \cdot 5}{3 \cdot 3} = \frac{\not3 \cdot 5}{\not3 \cdot 3} = \frac{5}{3}$$

The basic operations with rational numbers (fractions) are as follows:

1. The *sum* of two fractions:

$$\frac{a}{b} + \frac{c}{d} = \frac{ad + bc}{bd}$$

Thus,

$$\frac{3}{4} + \frac{7}{8} = \frac{3(8) + 4(7)}{4 \cdot 8} = \frac{52}{32} = \frac{13}{8}$$

Note: This process simply converts each fraction to the same or least common denominator. Thus,

$$\frac{3}{4} = \frac{6}{8} \quad \text{and} \quad \frac{6}{8} + \frac{7}{8} = \frac{13}{8}$$

2. The *sign* of a fraction:

$$\frac{a}{-b} = -\frac{a}{b} = \frac{-a}{b} \quad \text{or} \quad \frac{-3}{4} = \frac{3}{-4} = -\frac{3}{4}$$

Note: This relates to the rule of dividing numbers with unlike signs.

3. The *difference* between two fractions:

$$\frac{a}{b} - \frac{c}{d} = \frac{a}{b} + \frac{-c}{d}$$

or, using the addition rule,

$$\frac{a}{b} - \frac{c}{d} = \frac{a \cdot d - b \cdot c}{b \cdot d}$$

Thus,

$$\frac{3}{4} - \frac{7}{8} = \frac{3}{4} + \frac{-7}{8} = \frac{3 \cdot 8 - 7 \cdot 4}{4 \cdot 8} = \frac{-4}{32} = \frac{-1}{8}$$

$$\frac{3}{4} = \frac{6}{8} \quad \text{and} \quad \frac{6}{8} - \frac{7}{8} = \frac{-1}{8} \quad \text{or} \quad -\frac{1}{8} \quad \text{or} \quad \frac{1}{-8}$$

4. The *product* of two fractions:

$$\frac{a}{b} \cdot \frac{c}{d} = \frac{a \cdot c}{b \cdot d}$$

Thus,

$$\frac{3}{5} \cdot \frac{7}{6} = \frac{21}{30} = \frac{3 \cdot 7}{3 \cdot 2 \cdot 5} = \frac{7}{10}$$

5. The *quotient* of two fractions:

$$\frac{a}{b} \div \frac{c}{d} = \frac{a}{b} \cdot \frac{d}{c} = \frac{ad}{bc}$$

Thus,

$$\frac{3}{5} \div \frac{7}{6} = \frac{3 \cdot 6}{5 \cdot 7} = \frac{18}{35}$$

Note: Dividing by a fraction is the same as multiplying by its reciprocal.

Decimals. Fractions may be expressed as *decimal numbers* simply by dividing the numerator by the denominator:

$$\frac{4}{5} = .8, \qquad \frac{3}{4} = .75$$

In essence, any terminating decimal (a fraction in which the division process terminates with no remainder) may be thought of as a fraction in which the denominator is some power of 10. That power of 10 is determined by the number of digits to the right of the decimal point. Thus,

$$1.8 = 1 + \frac{8}{10} = \frac{18}{10} = \frac{2 \cdot 3 \cdot 3}{2 \cdot 5} = \frac{9}{5}$$

$$1.81 = 1 + \frac{81}{100}, \qquad 1.8145 = 1 + \frac{8,145}{10,000}$$

Decimals can be added, subtracted, multiplied, and/or divided in the same way that integers can. Some further rules also apply, however:

1. In *addition* or *subtraction* of decimal figures, the sum or difference will contain as many decimal places (digits to the right of the decimal point) as the number in the addition or subtraction with the largest number of decimal places. Thus, $3.627 + 1.86742 + 2.1942 - 5.93 = 1.75862$.
2. When decimal figures are *multiplied,* the product contains as many decimal places as the *sum* of the decimal places in the multiplicand and the multiplier(s). Thus, $3.627 \times 2.1942 = 7.9583634$ (3 decimal places + 4 decimal places = 7 decimal places).
3. In *division* of decimal figures, the decimal point in both the dividend (numerator) and the divisor (denominator) are moved enough places to the right to make the divisor a whole number (integer). Then division is carried out in accordance with the basic rules outlined earlier. Thus, $1.6437 \div 1.012$ is translated to $1643.7 \div 1012$; then $1643.7 \div 1012 = 1.624209486\ldots$, rounded to 1.624.

Rounding and Significant Digits. The quotient can contain an indefinite number of decimal places, and the actual answer frequently will be an approximation. The number of decimal places in the quotient actually used will usually be determined in accordance with the rules of rounding and significant digits. These rules state that the number of significant digits in any decimal solution should not exceed the number of decimal places (or digits for integers) in the least accurate or most rounded figure used in the operation. For example:

$$\frac{1.6437}{1.012} = 1.62409486\ldots$$

However, the quotient would be expressed as 1.624, since the most rounded number in the division is 1.012 (the divisor).

Ratios, Percentages, Rates, Index Numbers, Complements, and Reciprocals

A *ratio* is the result of dividing one number into another. A ratio may be expressed as an integer, a fraction, or a decimal figure. Thus, a ratio is simply a quotient, although in words it is expressed as the numerical relationship of the numerator to the denominator. It is therefore a comparison of two numbers by division. Thus:

The ratio of 56 to 14 is $56 \div 14 = 4$, or 4.0.

The ratio of 14 to 56 is $14 \div 56 = 0.25$, or ¼.

The ratio of 9 to 5 is $9 \div 5 = 1.8$, or $^{18}/_{10} = \frac{9}{5}$.

A *percentage* is a ratio (usually decimal) of two numbers multiplied by 100 or expressed on a base of 100. The numerator is expressed as a percentage *of* the denominator. Thus,

$$15 \div 75 = .2 \times 100 = 20\%$$
$$151.52 \div 10,000 = .015152 \times 100 = 1.5152\%$$

As noted, ratios include fractions, percentages (expressed on a base of 100), and rates. They are a convenient and useful device for expressing relationships. Ratios can also be used for comparative purposes. It is relatively meaningless to say, for example, that unemployment is 15,750 in one labor market area and 28,625 in another unless the labor force (base) in each is also known. To say, however, that unemployment is 6.3 percent in market A and 8.2 percent in market B gives a basis for comparison and judgment.

The gross rent multiplier (GRM) used in appraisal analysis is a ratio:

$$GRM = \frac{\text{sales price}}{\text{gross rent}}$$

Construction cost per square foot is also a ratio: of total construction cost to total square foot area. (It is also a mean; a mean is a ratio.)

Calculating a ratio is extremely simple and direct. The only real problem is in the selection of the numerator and the base. The base is the standard in terms of which the numerator is compared. In comparing a part with the whole, the whole is usually the base. In comparing like items over time, the prior or first time period is usually the base. In comparing a cause and effect or in comparing an independent event with one that is at least partly dependent on it, the independent or causal event is usually the base.

A *rate* is a percentage ratio expressed in terms of some time period ("per period"). Thus, whereas 8.55 percent is a percentage, 8.55 percent per year is an annual rate.

1. *Simple rates (straight-line rates):* Linear regression equations show simple rates of change in the dependent variable per unit change in the independent variable. If the change in index numbers (see later discussion) of cost per square foot from 1960 to 1984 (83.8, or 83.8 percent) is divided by the number of years between 1960 and 1984 (24), the result in the simple or straight-line rate of change per year is

$$\frac{83.8}{24} = 3.49\% \text{ per year}$$

The same result is obtained if the dollar costs per square foot are used:

$$\frac{16.08 - 8.75}{24} = \frac{7.33}{24} = \$0.31 \text{ per year}$$

$$\frac{0.31}{8.75} = 3.54\%.$$

The difference is the result of rounding.

A simple or straight-line rate of change per period or per unit means that the same *amount* of change is experienced per period or per unit. The rate of change is always expressed as a percentage of the base. A straight line (on an arithmetic scale) means a constant amount of change per period or per unit.

2. *Compound Rates:* When each item or value is expressed as a percentage of the immediately preceding item (rather than of the base), a constant rate of change results in continually changing amounts of

change. This is called an *exponential* or *logarithmic curve.* An exponential curve on a semilogarithmic graph is a straight line.

The basic compound interest formula is $S = (1 + i)^n$, which is called an exponential expression. The exponent is n—the number of times a number is counted in multiplying by itself. Thus, $5^4 = 5 \times 5 \times 5 \times 5 = 625$, and $(1.08)^6 = 1.08 \times 1.08 \times 1.08 \times 1.08 \times 1.08 \times 1.08 = 1.586874$.

Example: Suppose it is concluded that market prices in a given market area have been increasing 7.5 percent per year. On a straight-line basis, the increase over four years would be $.075 \times 4 = .30$, or 30 percent. On a compound or exponential basis, the increase over four years would be $1.075 \times 1.075 \times 1.075 \times 1.075 = 1.3355$, or 33.55 percent.

Index numbers are series of ratios that are all related to a base value of 100. The individual numbers (ratios) in the series are all expressed in terms of the base value (actually, as percentages without the percentage sign). They show the relative change from one observation to another relative to the base (often over time). Suppose, for example, that local construction costs per square foot over several years are as follows:

Year	Cost per Square Foot ($)
1960	8.75
1965	8.93
1970	9.38
1975	9.80
1980	11.12
1982	13.34
1984 (est.)	16.08

If 1960 is taken as the base period, then $8.75 = 100$. The series of index numbers then becomes:

Year	Calculation	Index Number
1960	8.75/8.75	100.0
1965	8.93/8.75	102.1
1970	9.38/8.75	107.2
1975	9.80/8.75	112.0
1980	11.80/8.75	134.9
1982	13.34/8.75	152.5
1984	16.08/8.75	183.8

To find the percentage change from 1980 to 1984, make the 1980 index number the base and the 1984 index number the numerator:

$$\frac{183.8}{134.9} = 136.2 - 100 = 36.2\% \text{ change}$$

The *complement* of a fraction or decimal of percentage figure less than one is the difference between one and the fraction, decimal or percentage. Thus:

The complement of ⅝ is 1 − ⅝ = ⅜.

The complement of 0.625 is 1 − 0.625 = 0.375.

The complement of 62.5% is 100 percent − 62.5 percent = 37.5 percent.

The *reciprocal* of a number is one divided by that number. Thus:

The reciprocal of 5 is 1 ÷ 5 = ⅕, or 0.2.

The reciprocal of 6.25 is 1 ÷ 6.25 = 0.16, or ⁴/₂₅.

The reciprocal of ⅝ is 1 ÷ ⅝ = ⁸/₈ ÷ ⅝ = ⁶⁴/₄₀ = ⁸/₅.

Algebra Review

Arithmetic is concerned with the manipulation (addition, subtraction, multiplication, and division) of numbers; algebra is concerned with the same type of manipulations, but with symbols. Certain rules govern the manner in which these symbols are manipulated. Most readers are familiar with the operations that are presented here; however, many may not be aware of the simple basic rules that apply to such operations. By learning the rules, one can justify each operation to be performed with symbols (or numbers) and can be confident that the solution to a problem is correct.

Commutative Laws

The commutative law of *addition* states:

$$x + y = y + x$$

That is, the sum of two or more numbers is the same no matter what the order of their addition. Thus,

$$5 + 6 + 7 = 7 + 6 + 5 = 18$$

The commutative law of *multiplication* utilizes the same concept:

$$x \cdot y = y \cdot x$$

Thus,

$$5 \cdot 6 \cdot 7 = 7 \cdot 6 \cdot 5 = 210$$

Associative Laws

The associative law of addition and multiplication simply adds the concept of grouping symbols (discussed earlier).

$$\text{Addition: } x + (y + z) = (x + y) + z$$
$$\text{Multiplication: } x \cdot (y \cdot z) = (x \cdot y) \cdot z$$

Distributive Law

The distributive law is illustrated as follows:

$$x \cdot (y + z) = xy + xz$$

Thus,

$$6 \cdot (5 + 4) = 6 \cdot 5 + 6 \cdot 4 = 30 + 24 = 54$$

Note: In general, symbols enclosed with grouping symbols should be treated as a single unit.

As an example, simplify the following:

$$(6 + 7x) + 3x$$

The solution is

$$\text{Associative law: } 6 + (7x + 3x)$$
$$\text{Distributive law: } 6 + (7 + 3)x, \qquad 6 + 10x$$

Operations with Equalities (Equations)

An equation is a mathematical expression that relates one group of quantities (numbers or symbols) to another group, usually by an equality sign ($=$). The assertion that two expressions are equal is important to the solution of problems. Individual quantities are made up of constants (usually numbers), coefficients (multipliers), and variables. Variables are usually unknowns and are represented by symbols, such as letters of the alphabet. The following list summarizes the basic operations with equalities:

1. *Reflexive:* $x = x$
2. *Symmetric:* If $x = y$, then $y = x$
3. *Transitive:* If $x = y$ and $y = z$, then $x = z$. For example,

$$y = 4x - 5(-x + 4) = 4x + 5x - 20$$
$$y = 4z - 5(-z + 4) = 9z - 20$$

Therefore, $9x = 9z$ and $x = z$

4. *Arithmetic axiom:* Both sides of an equation will remain equal if equal amounts are added to, subtracted from, multiplied by, or divided into both sides of the equation, as follows:

$$2x + 5 = 7, \quad 2x + 10 = 12 \quad \text{(adding 5)}$$
$$2x + 5 = 7, \quad 2x = 2 \quad \text{(subtracting 5)}$$
$$2x + 5 = 7, \quad 5(2x + 5) = 35 \quad \text{(multiplying by 5)}$$
$$2x + 5 = 7, \quad \frac{2x + 5}{5} = \frac{7}{5} \quad \text{(dividing by 5)}$$

5. *Transposition:* Any term may be transposed from one side of the equation to the other without destroying the equality, provided that the sign of the transposed term is changed. Thus, if $8x - 4 = 20$, then $8x = 20 + 4$. In this case, the effect has been the same as adding $+4$ to both sides of the equation.
6. *Solving equations:* When an equation contains only one unknown value (symbol), the rules of operations presented thus far may be used to solve (i.e., determine a value for) the equation. For example:

Given: $7x - 4x + 4 = -5x + 20.$

Step 1: Move unknown value (x) to one side of the equation:

$$7x - 4x + 4 = -5x + 20$$
$$3x + 4 = -5x + 20 \quad \text{(collect like terms)}$$
$$\underline{+5x = +5x} \qquad \text{(add } 5x \text{ to each side)}$$
$$8x + 4 = 20$$

Step 2:

$$8x + 4 = 20$$
$$\underline{-4 = -4} \quad \text{(subtract 4 from each side)}$$
$$8x \quad = 16 \quad \text{(divide each side by 8)}$$
$$x \quad = 2$$

Appendix B
Installments to Amortize One (Monthly ITAO) and Mortgage Constants (R_m)

1–30, 35 and 40 Years
5%–20% in ½% Increments

Monthly ITAO
and
Mortgage Constants (R_m)

	Interest Rate			
	5.00%		5.50%	
Year	ITAO	R_m	ITAO	R_m
1	0.085607	1.027284	0.085837	1.030044
2	0.043871	0.526452	0.044096	0.529152
3	0.029971	0.359652	0.030196	0.362352
4	0.023029	0.276348	0.023256	0.279072
5	0.018871	0.226452	0.019101	0.229212
6	0.016105	0.193260	0.016338	0.196056
7	0.014134	0.169608	0.014370	0.172440
8	0.012660	0.151920	0.012899	0.154788
9	0.011517	0.138204	0.011760	0.141120
10	0.010607	0.127284	0.010853	0.130236
11	0.009864	0.118368	0.010114	0.121368
12	0.009249	0.110988	0.009502	0.114024
13	0.008731	0.104772	0.008987	0.107844
14	0.008289	0.099468	0.008548	0.102576
15	0.007908	0.094896	0.008171	0.098052
16	0.007577	0.090924	0.007843	0.094116
17	0.007287	0.087444	0.007556	0.090672
18	0.007030	0.084360	0.007303	0.087636
19	0.006803	0.081636	0.007079	0.084948
20	0.006600	0.079200	0.006879	0.082548
21	0.006417	0.077004	0.006700	0.080400
22	0.006253	0.075036	0.006538	0.078456
23	0.006104	0.073248	0.006393	0.076716
24	0.005969	0.071628	0.006261	0.075132
25	0.005846	0.070152	0.006141	0.073692
26	0.005733	0.068796	0.006031	0.072372
27	0.005630	0.067560	0.005931	0.071172
28	0.005536	0.066432	0.005840	0.070080
29	0.005449	0.065388	0.005755	0.069060
30	0.005368	0.064416	0.005678	0.068136
35	0.005047	0.060564	0.005370	0.064440
40	0.004822	0.057864	0.005158	0.061896

Monthly ITAO
and
Mortgage Constants (R_m)

| | Interest Rate | | | |
| | 6.00% | | 6.50% | |
Year	ITAO	R_m	ITAO	R_m
1	0.086066	1.032792	0.086296	1.035552
2	0.044321	0.531852	0.044546	0.534552
3	0.030422	0.365064	0.030649	0.367788
4	0.023485	0.281820	0.023715	0.284580
5	0.019333	0.231996	0.019566	0.234792
6	0.016573	0.198876	0.016810	0.201720
7	0.014609	0.175308	0.014849	0.178188
8	0.013141	0.157692	0.013386	0.160632
9	0.012006	0.144072	0.012255	0.147060
10	0.011102	0.133224	0.011355	0.136260
11	0.010367	0.124404	0.010624	0.127488
12	0.009759	0.117108	0.010019	0.120228
13	0.009247	0.110964	0.009512	0.114144
14	0.008812	0.105744	0.009081	0.108972
15	0.008439	0.101268	0.008711	0.104532
16	0.008114	0.097368	0.008391	0.100692
17	0.007831	0.093972	0.008111	0.097332
18	0.007582	0.090984	0.007866	0.094392
19	0.007361	0.088332	0.007649	0.091788
20	0.007164	0.085968	0.007456	0.089472
21	0.006989	0.083868	0.007284	0.087408
22	0.006831	0.081972	0.007129	0.085548
23	0.006688	0.080256	0.006991	0.083892
24	0.006560	0.078720	0.006865	0.082380
25	0.006443	0.077316	0.006752	0.081024
26	0.006337	0.076044	0.006649	0.079788
27	0.006240	0.074880	0.006556	0.078672
28	0.006151	0.073812	0.006470	0.077640
29	0.006070	0.072840	0.006392	0.076704
30	0.005996	0.071952	0.006321	0.075852
35	0.005702	0.068424	0.006042	0.072504
40	0.005502	0.066024	0.005855	0.070260

Monthly ITAO
and
Mortgage Constants (R_m)

Year	Interest Rate			
	7.00%		7.50%	
	ITAO	R_m	ITAO	R_m
1	0.086527	1.038324	0.086757	1.041084
2	0.044773	0.537276	0.045000	0.540000
3	0.030877	0.370524	0.031106	0.373272
4	0.023946	0.287352	0.024179	0.290148
5	0.019801	0.237612	0.020038	0.240456
6	0.017049	0.204588	0.017290	0.207480
7	0.015093	0.181116	0.015338	0.184056
8	0.013634	0.163608	0.013884	0.166608
9	0.012506	0.150072	0.012761	0.153132
10	0.011611	0.139332	0.011870	0.142440
11	0.010884	0.130608	0.011148	0.133776
12	0.010284	0.123408	0.010552	0.126624
13	0.009781	0.117372	0.010054	0.120648
14	0.009354	0.112248	0.009631	0.115572
15	0.008988	0.107856	0.009270	0.111240
16	0.008672	0.104064	0.008958	0.107496
17	0.008397	0.100764	0.008687	0.104244
18	0.008155	0.097860	0.008450	0.101400
19	0.007942	0.095304	0.008241	0.098892
20	0.007753	0.093036	0.008056	0.096672
21	0.007585	0.091020	0.007892	0.094704
22	0.007434	0.089208	0.007745	0.092940
23	0.007299	0.087588	0.007614	0.091368
24	0.007178	0.086136	0.007496	0.089952
25	0.007068	0.084816	0.007390	0.088680
26	0.006968	0.083616	0.007294	0.087528
27	0.006878	0.082536	0.007207	0.086484
28	0.006796	0.081552	0.007129	0.085548
29	0.006721	0.080652	0.007057	0.084684
30	0.006653	0.079836	0.006992	0.083904
35	0.006389	0.076668	0.006742	0.080904
40	0.006214	0.074568	0.006581	0.078972

Monthly ITAO
and
Mortgage Constants (R_m)

Year	Interest Rate			
	8.00%		8.50%	
	ITAO	R_m	ITAO	R_m
1	0.086988	1.043856	0.087220	1.046640
2	0.045227	0.542724	0.045456	0.545472
3	0.031336	0.376032	0.031568	0.378816
4	0.024413	0.292956	0.024648	0.295776
5	0.020276	0.243312	0.020517	0.246204
6	0.017533	0.210396	0.017778	0.213336
7	0.015586	0.187032	0.015836	0.190032
8	0.014137	0.169644	0.014392	0.172704
9	0.013019	0.156228	0.013279	0.159348
10	0.012133	0.145596	0.012399	0.148788
11	0.011415	0.136980	0.011686	0.140232
12	0.010825	0.129900	0.011101	0.133212
13	0.010331	0.123972	0.010612	0.127344
14	0.009913	0.118956	0.010199	0.122388
15	0.009557	0.114684	0.009847	0.118164
16	0.009249	0.110988	0.009545	0.114540
17	0.008983	0.107796	0.009283	0.111396
18	0.008750	0.105000	0.009055	0.108660
19	0.008545	0.102540	0.008854	0.106248
20	0.008364	0.100368	0.008678	0.104136
21	0.008204	0.098448	0.008522	0.102264
22	0.008062	0.096744	0.008384	0.100608
23	0.007935	0.095220	0.008261	0.099132
24	0.007821	0.093852	0.008151	0.097812
25	0.007718	0.092616	0.008052	0.096624
26	0.007626	0.091512	0.007964	0.095568
27	0.007543	0.090516	0.007884	0.094608
28	0.007468	0.089616	0.007812	0.093744
29	0.007399	0.088788	0.007748	0.092976
30	0.007338	0.088056	0.007689	0.092268
35	0.007103	0.085236	0.007469	0.089628
40	0.006953	0.083436	0.007331	0.087972

Monthly ITAO
and
Mortgage Constants (R_m)

	Interest Rate			
	9.00%		9.50%	
Year	ITAO	R_m	ITAO	R_m
1	0.087451	1.049412	0.087684	1.052208
2	0.045685	0.548220	0.045914	0.550968
3	0.031800	0.381600	0.032033	0.384396
4	0.024885	0.298620	0.025123	0.301476
5	0.020758	0.249096	0.021002	0.252024
6	0.018026	0.216312	0.018275	0.219300
7	0.016089	0.193068	0.016344	0.196128
8	0.014650	0.175800	0.014911	0.178932
9	0.013543	0.162516	0.013809	0.165708
10	0.012668	0.152016	0.012940	0.155280
11	0.011961	0.143532	0.012239	0.146868
12	0.011380	0.136560	0.011664	0.139968
13	0.010897	0.130764	0.011186	0.134232
14	0.010489	0.125868	0.010784	0.129408
15	0.010143	0.121716	0.010442	0.125304
16	0.009845	0.118140	0.010150	0.121800
17	0.009588	0.115056	0.009898	0.118776
18	0.009364	0.112368	0.009679	0.116148
19	0.009169	0.110028	0.009488	0.113856
20	0.008997	0.107964	0.009321	0.111852
21	0.008846	0.106152	0.009174	0.110088
22	0.008712	0.104544	0.009045	0.108540
23	0.008593	0.103116	0.008930	0.107160
24	0.008487	0.101844	0.008828	0.105936
25	0.008392	0.100704	0.008737	0.104844
26	0.008307	0.099684	0.008656	0.103872
27	0.008231	0.098772	0.008584	0.103008
28	0.008163	0.097956	0.008519	0.102228
29	0.008102	0.097224	0.008461	0.101532
30	0.008046	0.096552	0.008409	0.100908
35	0.007840	0.094080	0.008216	0.098592
40	0.007714	0.092568	0.008101	0.097212

Monthly ITAO
and
Mortgage Constants (R_m)

| | Interest Rate | | | |
| | 10.00% | | 10.50% | |
Year	ITAO	R_m	ITAO	R_m
1	0.087916	1.054992	0.088149	1.057788
2	0.046145	0.553740	0.046376	0.556512
3	0.032267	0.387204	0.032502	0.390024
4	0.025363	0.304356	0.025603	0.307236
5	0.021247	0.254964	0.021494	0.257928
6	0.018526	0.222312	0.018779	0.225348
7	0.016601	0.199212	0.016861	0.202332
8	0.015174	0.182088	0.015440	0.185280
9	0.014079	0.168948	0.014351	0.172212
10	0.013215	0.158580	0.013493	0.161916
11	0.012520	0.150240	0.012804	0.153648
12	0.011951	0.143412	0.012241	0.146892
13	0.011478	0.137736	0.011775	0.141300
14	0.011082	0.132984	0.011384	0.136608
15	0.010746	0.128952	0.011054	0.132648
16	0.010459	0.125508	0.010772	0.129264
17	0.010212	0.122544	0.010531	0.126372
18	0.009998	0.119976	0.010322	0.123864
19	0.009813	0.117756	0.010141	0.121692
20	0.009650	0.115800	0.009984	0.119808
21	0.009508	0.114096	0.009846	0.118152
22	0.009382	0.112584	0.009725	0.116700
23	0.009272	0.111264	0.009619	0.115428
24	0.009174	0.110088	0.009525	0.114300
25	0.009087	0.109044	0.009442	0.113304
26	0.009010	0.108120	0.009368	0.112416
27	0.008941	0.107292	0.009303	0.111636
28	0.008880	0.106560	0.009245	0.110940
29	0.008825	0.105900	0.009193	0.110316
30	0.008776	0.105312	0.009147	0.109764
35	0.008597	0.103164	0.008981	0.107772
40	0.008491	0.101892	0.008886	0.106632

Monthly ITAO
and
Mortgage Constants (R_m)

Year	Interest Rate 11.00% ITAO	R_m	Interest Rate 11.50% ITAO	R_m
1	0.088382	1.060584	0.088615	1.063380
2	0.046608	0.559296	0.046840	0.562080
3	0.032739	0.392868	0.032976	0.395712
4	0.025846	0.310152	0.026089	0.313068
5	0.021742	0.260904	0.021993	0.263916
6	0.019034	0.228408	0.019291	0.231492
7	0.017122	0.205464	0.017386	0.208632
8	0.015708	0.188496	0.015979	0.191748
9	0.014626	0.175512	0.014904	0.178848
10	0.013775	0.165300	0.014060	0.168720
11	0.013092	0.157104	0.013384	0.160608
12	0.012536	0.150432	0.012833	0.153996
13	0.012075	0.144900	0.012379	0.148548
14	0.011691	0.140292	0.012001	0.144012
15	0.011366	0.136392	0.011682	0.140184
16	0.011090	0.133080	0.011412	0.136944
17	0.010854	0.130248	0.011181	0.134172
18	0.010650	0.127800	0.010983	0.131796
19	0.010475	0.125700	0.010812	0.129744
20	0.010322	0.123864	0.010664	0.127968
21	0.010189	0.122268	0.010536	0.126432
22	0.010072	0.120864	0.010424	0.125088
23	0.009970	0.119640	0.010326	0.123912
24	0.009880	0.118560	0.010240	0.122880
25	0.009801	0.117612	0.010165	0.121980
26	0.009731	0.116772	0.010098	0.121176
27	0.009670	0.116040	0.010040	0.120480
28	0.009615	0.115380	0.009989	0.119868
29	0.009566	0.114792	0.009943	0.119316
30	0.009523	0.114276	0.009903	0.118836
35	0.009370	0.112440	0.009783	0.117396
40	0.009283	0.111396	0.009683	0.116196

Monthly ITAO
and
Mortgage Constants (R_m)

| | Interest Rate | | | |
| | 12.00% | | 12.50% | |
Year	ITAO	R_m	ITAO	R_m
1	0.088849	1.066188	0.089083	1.068996
2	0.047073	0.564876	0.047307	0.567684
3	0.033214	0.398568	0.033454	0.401448
4	0.026334	0.316008	0.026580	0.318960
5	0.022244	0.266928	0.022498	0.269976
6	0.019550	0.234600	0.019811	0.237732
7	0.017653	0.211836	0.017921	0.215052
8	0.016253	0.195036	0.016529	0.198348
9	0.015184	0.182208	0.015468	0.185616
10	0.014347	0.172164	0.014638	0.175656
11	0.013678	0.164136	0.013975	0.167700
12	0.013134	0.157608	0.013439	0.161268
13	0.012687	0.152244	0.012998	0.155976
14	0.012314	0.147768	0.012632	0.151584
15	0.012002	0.144024	0.012325	0.147900
16	0.011737	0.140844	0.012067	0.144804
17	0.011512	0.138144	0.011847	0.142164
18	0.011320	0.135840	0.011660	0.139920
19	0.011154	0.133848	0.011500	0.138000
20	0.011011	0.132132	0.011361	0.136332
21	0.010887	0.130644	0.011242	0.134904
22	0.010779	0.129348	0.011139	0.133668
23	0.010686	0.128232	0.011049	0.132588
24	0.010604	0.127248	0.010971	0.131652
25	0.010532	0.126384	0.010904	0.130848
26	0.010470	0.125640	0.010844	0.130128
27	0.010414	0.124968	0.010792	0.129504
28	0.010366	0.124392	0.010747	0.128964
29	0.010324	0.123888	0.010707	0.128484
30	0.010286	0.123432	0.010673	0.128076
35	0.010155	0.121860	0.010553	0.126636
40	0.010085	0.121020	0.010489	0.125868

Monthly ITAO
and
Mortgage Constants (R_m)

	Interest Rate			
	13.00%		13.50%	
Year	ITAO ×12 ≤	R_m	ITAO	R_m
1	0.089317	1.071804	0.089552	1.074624
2	0.047542	0.570504	0.047777	0.573324
3	0.033694	0.404328	0.033935	0.407220
4	0.026827	0.321924	0.027076	0.324912
5	0.022753	0.273036	0.023010	0.276120
6	0.020074	0.240888	0.020339	0.244068
7	0.018192	0.218304	0.018465	0.221580
8	0.016807	0.201684	0.017088	0.205056
9	0.015754	0.189048	0.016042	0.192504
10	0.014931	0.179172	0.015227	0.182724
11	0.014276	0.171312	0.014580	0.174960
12	0.013746	0.164952	0.014057	0.168684
13	0.013312	0.159744	0.013630	0.163560
14	0.012953	0.155436	0.013277	0.159324
15	0.012652	0.151824	0.012983	0.155796
16	0.012400	0.148800	0.012737	0.152844
17	0.012186	0.146232	0.012529	0.150348
18	0.012004	0.144048	0.012352	0.148224
19	0.011849	0.142188	0.012202	0.146424
20	0.011716	0.140592	0.012074	0.144888
21	0.011601	0.139212	0.011964	0.143568
22	0.011502	0.138024	0.011869	0.142428
23	0.011417	0.137004	0.011788	0.141456
24	0.011343	0.136116	0.011717	0.140604
25	0.011278	0.135336	0.011656	0.139872
26	0.011222	0.134664	0.011604	0.139248
27	0.011174	0.134088	0.011558	0.138696
28	0.011131	0.133572	0.011518	0.138216
29	0.011094	0.133128	0.011484	0.137808
30	0.011062	0.132744	0.011454	0.137448
35	0.010952	0.131424	0.011353	0.136236
40	0.010895	0.130740	0.011303	0.135636

Monthly ITAO
and
Mortgage Constants (R_m)

	Interest Rate			
	14.00%		14.50%	
Year	ITAO	R_m	ITAO	R_m
1	0.089787	1.077444	0.090023	1.080276
2	0.048013	0.576156	0.048249	0.578988
3	0.034178	0.410136	0.034421	0.413052
4	0.027326	0.327912	0.027578	0.330936
5	0.023268	0.279216	0.023528	0.282336
6	0.020606	0.247272	0.020874	0.250488
7	0.018740	0.224880	0.019017	0.228204
8	0.017372	0.208464	0.017657	0.211884
9	0.016334	0.196008	0.016628	0.199536
10	0.015527	0.186324	0.015829	0.189948
11	0.014887	0.178644	0.015196	0.182352
12	0.014371	0.172452	0.014688	0.176256
13	0.013951	0.167412	0.014275	0.171300
14	0.013605	0.163260	0.013936	0.167232
15	0.013317	0.159804	0.013655	0.163860
16	0.013077	0.156924	0.013421	0.161052
17	0.012875	0.154500	0.013224	0.158688
18	0.012704	0.152448	0.013059	0.156708
19	0.012559	0.150708	0.012919	0.155028
20	0.012435	0.149220	0.012800	0.153600
21	0.012330	0.147960	0.012699	0.152388
22	0.012239	0.146868	0.012613	0.151356
23	0.012162	0.145944	0.012539	0.150468
24	0.012095	0.145140	0.012476	0.149712
25	0.012038	0.144456	0.012422	0.149064
26	0.011988	0.143856	0.012375	0.148500
27	0.011945	0.143340	0.012335	0.148020
28	0.011908	0.142896	0.012301	0.147612
29	0.011876	0.142512	0.012271	0.147252
30	0.011849	0.142188	0.012246	0.146952
35	0.011757	0.141084	0.012162	0.145944
40	0.011711	0.140532	0.012121	0.145452

Monthly ITAO
and
Mortgage Constants (R_m)

| | Interest Rate | | | |
| | 15.00% | | 15.50% | |
Year	ITAO	R_m	ITAO	R_m
1	0.090258	1.083096	0.090494	1.085928
2	0.048487	0.581844	0.048725	0.584700
3	0.034665	0.415980	0.034911	0.418932
4	0.027831	0.333972	0.028085	0.337020
5	0.023790	0.285480	0.024053	0.288636
6	0.021145	0.253740	0.021417	0.257004
7	0.019297	0.231564	0.019578	0.234936
8	0.017945	0.215340	0.018236	0.218832
9	0.016924	0.203088	0.017224	0.206688
10	0.016133	0.193596	0.016441	0.197292
11	0.015509	0.186108	0.015825	0.189900
12	0.015009	0.180108	0.015332	0.183984
13	0.014603	0.175236	0.014933	0.179196
14	0.014270	0.171240	0.014608	0.175296
15	0.013996	0.167952	0.014340	0.172080
16	0.013768	0.165216	0.014118	0.169416
17	0.013577	0.162924	0.013933	0.167196
18	0.013417	0.161004	0.013778	0.165336
19	0.013282	0.159384	0.013648	0.163776
20	0.013168	0.158016	0.013539	0.162468
21	0.013071	0.156852	0.013446	0.161352
22	0.012989	0.155868	0.013368	0.160416
23	0.012919	0.155028	0.013302	0.159624
24	0.012859	0.154308	0.013245	0.158940
25	0.012808	0.153696	0.013197	0.158364
26	0.012765	0.153180	0.013157	0.157884
27	0.012727	0.152724	0.013122	0.157464
28	0.012695	0.152340	0.013092	0.157104
29	0.012668	0.152016	0.013067	0.156804
30	0.012644	0.151728	0.013045	0.156540
35	0.012568	0.150816	0.012976	0.155712
40	0.012532	0.150384	0.012944	0.155328

Monthly ITAO
and
Mortgage Constants (R_m)

Year	Interest Rate 16.00%		Interest Rate 16.50%	
	ITAO	R_m	ITAO	R_m
1	0.090731	1.088772	0.090968	1.091616
2	0.048963	0.587556	0.049202	0.590424
3	0.035157	0.421884	0.035404	0.424848
4	0.028340	0.340080	0.028597	0.343164
5	0.024318	0.291816	0.024585	0.295020
6	0.021692	0.260304	0.021968	0.263616
7	0.019862	0.238344	0.020148	0.241776
8	0.018529	0.222348	0.018824	0.225888
9	0.017525	0.210300	0.017829	0.213948
10	0.016751	0.201012	0.017064	0.204768
11	0.016143	0.193716	0.016464	0.197568
12	0.015658	0.187896	0.015987	0.191844
13	0.015267	0.183204	0.015604	0.187248
14	0.014948	0.179376	0.015292	0.183504
15	0.014687	0.176244	0.015037	0.180444
16	0.014471	0.173652	0.014827	0.177924
17	0.014292	0.171504	0.014654	0.175848
18	0.014142	0.169704	0.014510	0.174120
19	0.014017	0.168204	0.014389	0.172668
20	0.013913	0.166956	0.014289	0.171486
21	0.013824	0.165888	0.014205	0.170460
22	0.013750	0.165000	0.014134	0.169608
23	0.013687	0.164244	0.014075	0.168900
24	0.013634	0.163608	0.014025	0.168300
25	0.013589	0.163068	0.013982	0.167784
26	0.013551	0.162612	0.013947	0.167364
27	0.013518	0.162216	0.013917	0.167004
28	0.013491	0.161892	0.013891	0.166692
29	0.013467	0.161604	0.013870	0.166440
30	0.013448	0.161376	0.013851	0.166212
35	0.013385	0.160620	0.013795	0.165540
40	0.013356	0.160272	0.013770	0.165240

Monthly ITAO
and
Mortgage Constants (R_m)

Year	Interest Rate			
	17.00%		17.50%	
	ITAO	R_m	ITAO	R_m
1	0.091205	1.094460	0.091442	1.097304
2	0.049442	0.593304	0.049683	0.596196
3	0.035653	0.427836	0.035902	0.430824
4	0.028855	0.346260	0.029114	0.349368
5	0.024853	0.298236	0.025122	0.301464
6	0.022246	0.266952	0.022526	0.270312
7	0.020436	0.245232	0.020726	0.248712
8	0.019121	0.229452	0.019421	0.233052
9	0.018136	0.217632	0.018445	0.221340
10	0.017380	0.208560	0.017698	0.212376
11	0.016788	0.201456	0.017115	0.205380
12	0.016319	0.195828	0.016654	0.199848
13	0.015943	0.191316	0.016285	0.195420
14	0.015638	0.187656	0.015988	0.191856
15	0.015390	0.184680	0.015746	0.188952
16	0.015186	0.182232	0.015548	0.186576
17	0.015018	0.180216	0.015386	0.184632
18	0.014879	0.178548	0.015252	0.183024
19	0.014764	0.177168	0.015141	0.181692
20	0.014668	0.176016	0.015049	0.180588
21	0.014588	0.175056	0.014973	0.179676
22	0.014521	0.174252	0.014910	0.178920
23	0.014465	0.173580	0.014857	0.178284
24	0.014418	0.173016	0.014812	0.177744
25	0.014378	0.172536	0.014775	0.177300
26	0.014345	0.172140	0.014744	0.176928
27	0.014317	0.171804	0.014718	0.176616
28	0.014293	0.171516	0.014697	0.176364
29	0.014273	0.171276	0.014679	0.176148
30	0.014257	0.171084	0.014663	0.175956
35	0.014205	0.170460	0.014617	0.175404
40	0.014183	0.170196	0.014597	0.175164

Monthly ITAO
and
Mortgage Constants (R_m)

Year	Interest Rate			
	18.00%		18.50%	
	ITAO	R_m	ITAO	R_m
1	0.091680	1.100160	0.091918	1.103016
2	0.049924	0.599088	0.050166	0.601992
3	0.036152	0.433824	0.036404	0.436858
4	0.029375	0.352500	0.029637	0.355644
5	0.025393	0.304716	0.025666	0.307992
6	0.022808	0.273696	0.023091	0.277092
7	0.021018	0.252216	0.021312	0.255744
8	0.019723	0.236676	0.020027	0.240324
9	0.018757	0.225084	0.019071	0.228852
10	0.018019	0.216228	0.018342	0.220104
11	0.017444	0.209328	0.017776	0.213312
12	0.016991	0.203892	0.017331	0.207972
13	0.016630	0.199560	0.016978	0.203736
14	0.016340	0.196080	0.016694	0.200328
15	0.016104	0.193248	0.016465	0.197580
16	0.015913	0.190956	0.016280	0.195360
17	0.015756	0.189072	0.016128	0.193536
18	0.015627	0.187524	0.016004	0.192048
19	0.015521	0.186252	0.015903	0.190836
20	0.015433	0.185196	0.015819	0.189828
21	0.015361	0.184332	0.015750	0.189000
22	0.015300	0.183600	0.015693	0.188316
23	0.015250	0.183000	0.015646	0.187752
24	0.015209	0.182508	0.015607	0.187284
25	0.015174	0.182088	0.015575	0.186900
26	0.015146	0.181752	0.015548	0.186576
27	0.015122	0.181464	0.015526	0.186312
28	0.015101	0.181212	0.015507	0.186084
29	0.015085	0.181020	0.015492	0.185904
30	0.015071	0.180852	0.015479	0.185748
35	0.015029	0.180348	0.015442	0.185304
40	0.015012	0.180144	0.015427	0.185124

Monthly ITAO
and
Mortgage Constants (R_m)

| | Interest Rate | | | |
| | 19.00% | | 19.50% | |
Year	ITAO	R_m	ITAO	R_m
1	0.092157	1.105884	0.092395	1.108740
2	0.050409	0.604908	0.050652	0.607824
3	0.036656	0.439872	0.036909	0.442908
4	0.029900	0.358800	0.030165	0.361980
5	0.025941	0.311292	0.026216	0.314592
6	0.023377	0.280524	0.023664	0.283968
7	0.021608	0.259296	0.021906	0.262872
8	0.020334	0.244008	0.020642	0.247704
9	0.019387	0.232644	0.019706	0.236472
10	0.018667	0.224004	0.018995	0.227940
11	0.018110	0.217320	0.018447	0.221364
12	0.017674	0.212088	0.018019	0.216228
13	0.017328	0.207936	0.017680	0.212160
14	0.017051	0.204612	0.017411	0.208932
15	0.016829	0.201948	0.017195	0.206340
16	0.016649	0.199788	0.017021	0.204252
17	0.016503	0.198036	0.016880	0.202560
18	0.016384	0.196608	0.016766	0.201192
19	0.016287	0.195444	0.016673	0.200076
20	0.016207	0.194484	0.016597	0.199164
21	0.016141	0.193692	0.016535	0.198420
22	0.016088	0.193056	0.016484	0.197808
23	0.016043	0.192516	0.016442	0.197304
24	0.016007	0.192084	0.016408	0.196896
25	0.015977	0.191724	0.016380	0.196560
26	0.015952	0.191424	0.016357	0.196284
27	0.015931	0.191172	0.016338	0.196056
28	0.015915	0.190980	0.016323	0.195876
29	0.015901	0.190812	0.016310	0.195720
30	0.015889	0.190668	0.016299	0.195588
35	0.015855	0.190260	0.016269	0.195228
40	0.015842	0.190104	0.016257	0.195084

Monthly ITAO
and
Mortgage Constants (R_m)

	Interest Rate, 20.00%	
Year	ITAO	R_m
1	0.092635	1.111620
2	0.050896	0.610752
3	0.037164	0.445968
4	0.030430	0.365160
5	0.026494	0.317928
6	0.023953	0.287436
7	0.022206	0.266472
8	0.020953	0.251436
9	0.020027	0.240324
10	0.019326	0.231912
11	0.018786	0.225432
12	0.018366	0.220392
13	0.018035	0.216420
14	0.017773	0.213276
15	0.017563	0.210756
16	0.017395	0.208740
17	0.017259	0.207108
18	0.017149	0.205788
19	0.017060	0.204720
20	0.016988	0.203856
21	0.016929	0.203148
22	0.016882	0.202584
23	0.016843	0.202116
24	0.016811	0.201732
25	0.016785	0.201420
26	0.016763	0.201156
27	0.016746	0.200952
28	0.016731	0.200772
29	0.016720	0.200640
30	0.016710	0.200520
35	0.016683	0.200196
40	0.016673	0.200076

Appendix C
Appraisal Report Forms

RESIDENTIAL APPRAISAL REPORT

File No. _____

To be completed by Lender

| Borrower _____ | Census Tract _____ | Map Reference _____ |

Property Address _____

| City _____ | County _____ | State _____ | Zip Code _____ |

Legal Description _____

| Sale Price $ _____ | Date of Sale _____ | Loan Term _____ yrs | Property Rights Appraised ☐ Fee ☐ Leasehold ☐ DeMinimis PUD |

Actual Real Estate Taxes $ _____ (yr) Loan charges to be paid by seller $ _____ Other sales concessions _____

Lender/Client _____ Address _____

Occupant _____ Appraiser _____ Instructions to Appraiser _____

NEIGHBORHOOD

Location	☐ Urban	☐ Suburban	☐ Rural
Built Up	☐ Over 75%	☐ 25% to 75%	☐ Under 25%
Growth Rate	☐ Fully Dev.	☐ Rapid	☐ Steady	☐ Slow
Property Values	☐ Increasing	☐ Stable	☐ Declining
Demand/Supply	☐ Shortage	☐ In Balance	☐ Over Supply
Marketing Time	☐ Under 3 Mos.	☐ 4–6 Mos.	☐ Over 6 Mos.

Present Land Use ____% 1 Family ____% 2–4 Family ____% Apts. ____% Condo ____% Commercial

____% Industrial ____% Vacant ____%

Change in Present Land Use ☐ Not Likely ☐ Likely (*) ☐ Taking Place (*)

(*) From _____ To _____

Predominant Occupancy	☐ Owner	☐ Tenant	____% Vacant
Single Family Price Range	$ _____ to $ _____	Predominant Value $ _____
Single Family Age	_____ yrs to _____ yrs	Predominant Age _____ yrs

Employment Stability ☐☐☐☐
Convenience to Employment ☐☐☐☐
Convenience to Shopping ☐☐☐☐
Convenience to Schools ☐☐☐☐
Adequacy of Public Transportation ☐☐☐☐
Recreational Facilities ☐☐☐☐
Adequacy of Utilities ☐☐☐☐
Property Compatibility ☐☐☐☐
Protection from Detrimental Conditions ☐☐☐☐
Police and Fire Protection ☐☐☐☐
General Appearance of Properties ☐☐☐☐
Appeal to Market ☐☐☐☐

(rating columns: Good Avg Fair Poor)

Note: FHLMC/FNMA do not consider race or the racial composition of the neighborhood to be reliable appraisal factors.

Comments including those factors, favorable or unfavorable, affecting marketability (e.g. public parks, schools, view, noise) _____

SITE

Dimensions _____ = _____ Sq. Ft. or Acres ☐ Corner Lot

Zoning classification _____ Present improvements ☐ do ☐ do not conform to zoning regulations

Highest and best use: ☐ Present use ☐ Other (Describe) _____

	Public	Other (Describe)	OFF SITE IMPROVEMENTS	Topo _____
Elec.	☐		Street Access: ☐ Public ☐ Private	Size _____
Gas	☐		Surface _____	Shape _____
Water	☐		Maintenance: ☐ Public ☐ Private	View _____
San.Sewer	☐		☐ Storm Sewer ☐ Curb/Gutter	Drainage _____
	☐ Underground Elect. & Tel.	☐ Sidewalk ☐ Street Lights	Is the property located in a HUD Identified Special Flood Hazard Area? ☐ No ☐ Yes

Comments (favorable or unfavorable including any apparent adverse easements, encroachments or other adverse conditions) _____

IMPROVEMENTS

☐ Existing ☐ Proposed ☐ Under Constr. | No. Units _____ | Type (det, duplex, semi/det, etc.) | Design (rambler, split level, etc.) | Exterior Walls
Yrs. Age: Actual _____ Effective _____ to _____ | No. Stories _____

Roof Material | Gutters & Downspouts ☐ None | Window (Type): | | Insulation ☐ None ☐ Floor
| | ☐ Storm Sash ☐ Screens ☐ Combination | | ☐ Ceiling ☐ Roof ☐ Walls

☐ Manufactured Housing | % Basement | ☐ Floor Drain | ☐ Finished Ceiling
Foundation Walls | ☐ Outside Entrance | ☐ Sump Pump | ☐ Finished Walls
| ☐ Concrete Floor | _____ % Finished | ☐ Finished Floor
☐ Slab on Grade ☐ Crawl Space | Evidence of: ☐ Dampness ☐ Termites ☐ Settlement
Comments

BSMT

ROOM LIST

Room List	Foyer	Living	Dining	Kitchen	Den	Family Rm.	Rec. Rm.	Bedrooms	No. Baths	Laundry	Other
Basement											
1st Level											
2nd Level											

Finished area above grade contains a total of _____ rooms _____ bedrooms _____ baths. Gross Living Area _____ sq. ft. Bsmt. Area _____ sq. ft.

INTERIOR FINISH & EQUIPMENT

Kitchen Equipment: ☐ Refrigerator ☐ Range/Oven ☐ Disposal ☐ Dishwasher ☐ Fan/Hood ☐ Compactor ☐ Washer ☐ Dryer

HEAT: Type _____ Fuel _____ Cond. _____ | AIR COND: ☐ Central ☐ Other ☐ Adequate ☐ Inadequate

		Good	Avg.	Fair	Poor
Floors	☐ Hardwood	☐ Carpet Over _____			
Walls	☐ Drywall	☐ Plaster			
Trim/Finish	☐ Good	☐ Average	☐ Fair	☐ Poor	
Bath Floor	☐ Ceramic				
Bath Wainscot	☐ Ceramic				

Special Features (including energy efficient items)

PROPERTY RATING

	Good	Avg	Fair	Poor
Quality of Construction (Materials & Finish)	☐	☐	☐	☐
Condition of Improvements	☐	☐	☐	☐
Room sizes and layout	☐	☐	☐	☐
Closets and Storage	☐	☐	☐	☐
Insulation—adequacy	☐	☐	☐	☐
Plumbing—adequacy and condition	☐	☐	☐	☐
Electrical—adequacy and condition	☐	☐	☐	☐
Kitchen Cabinets—adequacy and condition	☐	☐	☐	☐
Compatibility to Neighborhood	☐	☐	☐	☐
Overall Livability	☐	☐	☐	☐
Appeal and Marketability	☐	☐	☐	☐

Yrs Est Remaining Economic Life _____ to _____ Explain if less than Loan Term _____

ATTIC: ☐ Yes ☐ No ☐ Stairway ☐ Drop-stair ☐ Scuttle ☐ Floored
Finished (Describe) _____ ☐ Heated

CAR STORAGE: ☐ Garage ☐ Built-in ☐ Attached ☐ Detached ☐ Car Port
No. Cars _____ ☐ Adequate ☐ Inadequate Condition _____

FIREPLACES, PATIOS, POOL, FENCES, etc. (describe) _____

COMMENTS (including functional or physical inadequacies, repairs needed, modernization, etc.) _____

ATTACH DESCRIPTIVE PHOTOGRAPHS OF SUBJECT PROPERTY AND STREET SCENE

FNMA Form 1004 Rev. 7/

VALUATION SECTION

Purpose of Appraisal is to estimate Market Value as defined in Certification & Statement of Limiting Conditions (FHLMC Form 439/FNMA Form 1004B). If submitted for FNMA, the appraiser must attach (1) sketch or map showing location of subject, street names, distance from nearest intersection, and any detrimental conditions and (2) exterior building sketch of improvements showing dimensions.

COST APPROACH

Measurements	No. Stories	Sq. Ft.
x	=	
x	=	
x	=	
x	=	
x	=	

Total Gross Living Area (List in Market Data Analysis below) _____

Comment on functional and economic obsolescence: _____

ESTIMATED REPRODUCTION COST — NEW — OF IMPROVEMENTS:

Dwelling	Sq. Ft. @ $	= $
	Sq. Ft. @ $	=
Extras		=
		=
Special Energy Efficient Items		=
Porches, Patios, etc.		=
Garage/Car Port	Sq. Ft. @ $	= $
Site Improvements (driveway, landscaping, etc.)		= $
Total Estimated Cost New		= $

Less | Physical | Functional | Economic
Depreciation $ _____ | $ _____ | $ _____ = $ _____

Depreciated value of improvements . . . . = $ _____

ESTIMATED LAND VALUE . . . . = $ _____
(If leasehold, show only leasehold value)

INDICATED VALUE BY COST APPROACH . . . . . . = $ _____

ANALYSIS

The undersigned has recited three recent sales of properties most similar and proximate to subject and has considered these in the market analysis. The description includes a dollar adjustment, reflecting market reaction to those items of significant variation between the subject and comparable properties. If a significant item in the comparable property is superior to, or more favorable than, the subject property, a minus (-) adjustment is made, thus reducing the indicated value of subject; if a significant item in the comparable is inferior to, or less favorable than, the subject property, a plus (+) adjustment is made, thus increasing the indicated value of the subject.

ITEM	Subject Property	COMPARABLE NO. 1		COMPARABLE NO. 2		COMPARABLE NO. 3	
		DESCRIPTION	+(—)$ Adjustment	DESCRIPTION	+(—)$ Adjustment	DESCRIPTION	+(—)$ Adjustment
Address							
Proximity to Subj.							
Sales Price	$	$		$		$	
Price/Living area	$	$		$		$	
Data Source							
Date of Sale and Time Adjustment							
Location							
Site/View							
Design and Appeal							
Quality of Const.							
Age							
Condition							
Living Area Room	Total : B-rms : Baths	Total : B-rms : Baths		Total : B-rms : Baths		Total : B-rms : Baths	

MARKET DATA

| | | Sq.Ft. | | Sq.Ft. | | Sq.Ft. | | Sq.Ft. |

Count and Total Gross Living Area

Basement & Bsmt. Finished Rooms

Functional Utility

Air Conditioning

Garage/Car Port

Porches, Patio, Pools, etc.

Special Energy Efficient Items

Other (e.g. fireplaces, kitchen equip., remodeling)

Sales or Financing Concessions

Net Adj. (Total) □ Plus; □ Minus $ | □ Plus; □ Minus $ | □ Plus; □ Minus $

Indicated Value of Subject $ | $ | $

Comments on Market Data

INDICATED VALUE BY MARKET DATA APPROACH $

INDICATED VALUE BY INCOME APPROACH (If applicable) Economic Market Rent $ _____ /Mo. x Gross Rent Multiplier _____ = $ _____

This appraisal is made □ "as is" □ subject to the repairs, alterations, or conditions listed below □ completion per plans and specifications.

Comments and Conditions of Appraisal:

Final Reconciliation:

Construction Warranty □ Yes □ No Name of Warranty Program _____ Warranty Coverage Expires _____

This appraisal is based upon the above requirements, the certification, contingent and limiting conditions, and Market Value definition that are stated in

□ FHLMC Form 439 (Rev. 10/78)/FNMA Form 1004B (Rev. 10/78) filed with client □ attached.

I ESTIMATE THE MARKET VALUE, AS DEFINED, OF SUBJECT PROPERTY AS OF _____ 19 _____ to be $ _____

Appraiser(s) _____ Review Appraiser (If applicable) _____ □ Did □ Did Not Physically Inspect Property

FHLMC Form 70 Rev. 7/79   REVERSE   FNMA Form 1004 Rev. 7/79

Borrower / Client			
Property Address			
City	County	State	Zip Code
Lender			

BUILDING SKETCH

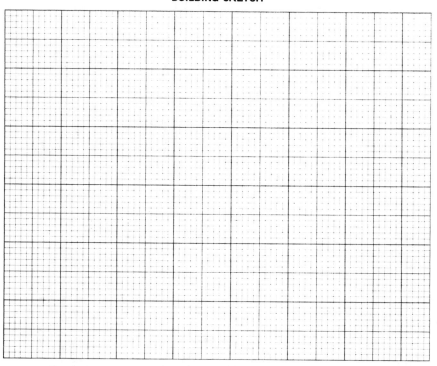

LOCATION MAP [*SUBJECT PROPERTY]

north

OVER FOR PHOTO ATTACHMENTS

FW-70A/1004A

DEFINITION OF MARKET VALUE: The highest price in terms of money which a property will bring in a competitive and open market under all conditions requisite to a fair sale, the buyer and seller, each acting prudently, knowledgeably and assuming the price is not affected by undue stimulus. Implicit in this definition is the consummation of a sale as of a specified date and the passing of title from seller to buyer under conditions whereby: (1) buyer and seller are typically motivated; (2) both parties are well informed or well advised, and each acting in what he considers his own best interest; (3) a reasonable time is allowed for exposure in the open market; (4) payment is made in cash or its equivalent; (5) financing, if any, is on terms generally available in the community at the specified date and typical for the property type in its locale; (6) the price represents a normal consideration for the property sold unaffected by special financing amounts and/or terms, services, fees, costs, or credits incurred in the transaction. ("Real Estate Appraisal Terminology," published 1975.)

CERTIFICATION AND STATEMENT OF LIMITING CONDITIONS

CERTIFICATION: The Appraiser certifies and agrees that:

1. The Appraiser has no present or contemplated future interest in the property appraised; and neither the employment to make the appraisal, nor the compensation for it, is contingent upon the appraised value of the property.

2. The Appraiser has no personal interest in or bias with respect to the subject matter of the appraisal report or the participants to the sale. The "Estimate of Market Value" in the appraisal report is not based in whole or in part upon the race, color, or national origin of the prospective owners or occupants of the property appraised, or upon the race, color or national origin of the present owners or occupants of the properties in the vicinity of the property appraised.

3. The Appraiser has personally inspected the property, both inside and out, and has made an exterior inspection of all comparable sales listed in the report. To the best of the Appraiser's knowledge and belief, all statements and information in this report are true and correct, and the Appraiser has not knowingly withheld any significant information.

4. All contingent and limiting conditions are contained herein (imposed by the terms of the assignment or by the undersigned affecting the analyses, opinions, and conclusions contained in the report).

5. This appraisal report has been made in conformity with and is subject to the requirements of the Code of Professional Ethics and Standards of Professional Conduct of the appraisal organizations with which the Appraiser is affiliated.

6. All conclusions and opinions concerning the real estate that are set forth in the appraisal report were prepared by the Appraiser whose signature appears on the appraisal report, unless indicated as "Review Appraiser." No change of any item in the appraisal report shall be made by anyone other than the Appraiser, and the Appraiser shall have no responsibility for any such unauthorized change.

CONTINGENT AND LIMITING CONDITIONS: The certification of the Appraiser appearing in the appraisal report is subject to the following conditions and to such other specific and limiting conditions as are set forth by the Appraiser in the report.

1. The Appraiser assumes no responsibility for matters of a legal nature affecting the property appraised or the title thereto, nor does the Appraiser render any opinion as to the title, which is assumed to be good and marketable. The property is appraised as though under responsible ownership.

2. Any sketch in the report may show approximate dimensions and is included to assist the reader in visualizing the property. The Appraiser has made no survey of the property.

3. The Appraiser is not required to give testimony or appear in court because of having made the appraisal with reference to the property in question, unless arrangements have been previously made therefor.

4. Any distribution of the valuation in the report between land and improvements applies only under the existing program of utilization. The separate valuations for land and building must not be used in conjunction with any other appraisal and are invalid if so used.

5. The Appraiser assumes that there are no hidden or unapparent conditions of the property, subsoil, or structures, which would render it more or less valuable. The Appraiser assumes no responsibility for such conditions, or for engineering which might be required to discover such factors.

6. Information, estimates, and opinions furnished to the Appraiser, and contained in the report, were obtained from sources considered reliable and believed to be true and correct. However, no responsibility for accuracy of such items furnished the Appraiser can be assumed by the Appraiser.

7. Disclosure of the contents of the appraisal report is governed by the Bylaws and Regulations of the professional appraisal organizations with which the Appraiser is affiliated.

8. Neither all, nor any part of the content of the report, or copy thereof (including conclusions as to the property value, the identity of the Appraiser, professional designations, reference to any professional appraisal organizations, or the firm with which the Appraiser is connected), shall be used for any purposes by anyone but the client specified in the report, the borrower if appraisal fee paid by same, the mortgagee or its successors and assigns, mortgage insurers, consultants, professional appraisal organizations, any state or federally approved financial institution, any department, agency, or instrumentality of the United States or any state or the District of Columbia, without the previous written consent of the Appraiser; nor shall it be conveyed by anyone to the public through advertising, public relations, news, sales, or other media, without the written consent and approval of the Appraiser.

9. On all appraisals, subject to satisfactory completion, repairs, or alterations, the appraisal report and value conclusion are contingent upon completion of the improvements in a workmanlike manner.

Date: . . . .   Appraiser(s) . . . .

Index

About the Authors

Byrl N. Boyce is Professor of Finance and Real Estate and Director of the Center for Real Estate and Urban Economic Studies at the University of Connecticut. He holds the SREA and CRE professional real estate designations as well as the FCA from the American Institute of Corporate Asset Management. He is the compiler and editor of *Real Estate Appraisal Terminology* and a co-author of *Industrial Real Estate*. He lectures and consults widely on the topics of Real Property Valuation and Investments. He received both a B.S. and an M.B.A. degree from Indiana University and a Ph.D. from the Pennsylvania State University. Dr. Boyce is a past president of the American Real Estate and Urban Economics Association and is a Director of Heritage Savings and Loan, Manchester, Connecticut.

William N. Kinnard, Jr., is Professor Emeritus of Finance and Real Estate within the Center for Real Estate and Urban Economic Studies at the University of Connecticut. He holds the SREA, MAI, CRE, and ASA professional real estate designations as well as the FCA from the American Institute of Corporate Asset Management. He is the author of *Income Property Valuation* and a co-author of *Industrial Real Estate*. He lectures and consults widely on Real Property Valuation and Investments. He received a B.A. with honors in Economics from Swarthmore College, an M.B.A. in Finance from the University of Pennsylvania (Wharton School), and a Ph.D. in Finance and Economics from the University of Pennsylvania. Dr. Kinnard is President of the Real Estate Counseling Group of Connecticut and is a Principal in the Real Estate Counseling Group of America.

Gross Rental 25000   Mgt #1 Mgt #2

expenses 10,000

net income 15,000

	Mgt #1	Mgt #2
investment value	$100,000	$100,000
net income	15,000	15,000
mgt loan	50,000	75,000
13%@ 20yrs.	7,030	10,545
equity	50,000	25,000
equity to net income	7,970	4455
equity yield	15.9%	17.8%

15000 15000

10545 7030

4455   7970

← equity to net income

Example of leverage

loan to value ratio

1st mgt. $(.70)(.140592) = .098414$

Rm tables
13% @ 20 years

Equity $\left(\dfrac{.30}{1.00}\right)(.12) = .0360$ ↙ new loan

$$\begin{array}{r} .098414 \\ .0360 \\ \hline \end{array}$$

basic rate $= .134414$

$= 13.44\%$

net income $= \$10,000$

$\dfrac{I}{rate} = value$

$\dfrac{10,000}{13.44\%} = \$74,405$